*Journal of Women's History*

Guide to Periodical Literature

# *Journal of Women's History*
# Guide to Periodical Literature

COMPILED BY

## Gayle V. Fischer

FOREWORD BY

## Christie Farnham

INTRODUCTION BY

## Joan Hoff

INDIANA UNIVERSITY PRESS

*Bloomington and Indianapolis*

The paper used in this publication meets the minimum requirements of
American National Standard for Information Sciences--Permanence of Paper
for Printed Library Materials, ANSI Z39.48-1984.


Manufactured in the United States of America

**Library of Congress Cataloging-in-Publication Data**

Fischer, Gayle V.
    Journal of women's history guide to periodical literature / compiled
by Gayle V. Fischer ; foreword by Christie Farnham ; introduction by
Joan Hoff.
        p.    cm.
    Includes bibliographical references.
    ISBN 0-253-32219-7. -- ISBN 0-253-20720-7  (pbk.)
    1. Women--History--Periodicals--Indexes.   I. Journal of women's
history.   II. Title.   III. Title: Guide to periodical literature.
Z7962. F57    1992
[HQ1101]
016.3054' 05--dc20                                                91-28470


1 2 3 4 5   96 95 94 93 92

# CONTENTS

CONTENTS

# FOREWORD

Christie Farnham

In the spring of 1987, more than twelve years after I began doing research in women's history and at least fourteen years after the founding of the field, the realization came to me that there were no journals devoted exclusively to women's history. True, there were high-quality feminist periodicals, such as *Signs*, which published women's history along with works in other disciplines, but there was not one single journal dealing solely with women's history. This omission struck me as exceedingly strange, not only because the past decade had seen a proliferation of new journals addressed to all sorts of scholarly subjects and periods but also because the sheer quantity of research done in women's history had long since led its practitioners to refer to it as an "explosion." Indeed, it was astonishing to me that such an essential means of promoting a field and preserving its achievements for future generations could have been neglected. Someone should certainly have founded such a journal, I believed.

Why someone else? On further reflection it seemed to me that if I saw a need, I bore some obligation to see that it was met. It was also obvious that Indiana University, where I was then a faculty member, was an ideal place to found such a periodical, since it was already home to three history journals (*American Historical Review, Journal of American History,* and *History of Education Quarterly*). So I decided to take the initiative by inviting Joan Hoff, then Executive Secretary of the Organization of American Historians, to join me.

In June 1987, we set about creating a board of nationally recognized scholars and foreign advisers; establishing a working relationship with Indiana University, which supplies a portion of our operating funds in return for the training of graduate students; and contracting with Indiana University Press for publication. Joan Catapano, Acquisitions Editor, was of inestimable value in our getting started. Having put all the pieces together, we incorporated on October 17, 1988, and published our inaugural issue in spring 1989. Such a time-consuming and costly venture as a journal could not have succeeded in its initial phases without the generous assistance of the William Bingham Foundation of Cleveland.

This reference guide grew out of our early efforts to fulfill commonly held expectations that a journal should review books in the field. Since we had neither the lead time nor the initial funds to institute a conventional book review section in our first issues, and since women's history is highly interdisciplinary, with articles appearing in widely scattered publications, we decided that it would be a valuable service to the profession to substitute bibliographies on selected topics for regular book reviews until we were in a better position to address that section of the journal.

Emilye Crosby, our first graduate assistant, had the thankless task of setting up a system for organizing and computerizing the bibliographical information which she collected. Michael Rigoli of the Organization of American Historians provided much helpful advice and access to data. Crosby was succeeded by Gayle V. Fischer, who, under Joan's and my supervision, compiled the bulk of the entries in this *Guide*.

## Women in the History Profession

The approximately fifty-five hundred individual entries which the *Guide* contains attest to the fact that women's history is the fastest-growing field in the profession. This is the result of its birth in the transforming vision of women's liberation, the vastness of the subject matter awaiting investigation (the history of at least half of the world's population), the rise of social history with its methodological advances in writing history "from the bottom up," and, most important, the prior existence of women already trained as historians.

Women had been members of the organized historical profession from its inception in the 1880s, holding token positions on its committees; but with few exceptions they were excluded from the real bases of the profession's power and prestige, i.e., positions on the faculty of the nation's major educational institutions and editorship of the foremost historical journals. The *Journal of American History* (formerly the *Mississippi Valley Historical Review*), for example, had no women editors in the early seventies, fewer than 2 percent of its book reviews were contributed by women, and in some years not a single article was authored by a woman. Unlike the *American Sociological Review*, where editors serve limited terms and the journal passes among institutions at regular intervals, history periodicals are linked to individual universities, and editors serve as long as they want. As a consequence, a small number of individuals and schools have a large influence on the shaping of the field. The situation at the ten highest-ranking graduate departments in the nation's major research universities was also dismal. For the 1968-69 academic year there were no women full professors and only four at the associate and assistant levels. Berkeley, Cornell, Harvard, Princeton, Stanford, and Wisconsin had no women; Chicago had one out of a faculty of fifty-seven, Columbia two out of seventy-two, Michigan two out of forty-four, and Yale two out of seventy-three.[1] The bias against women in the profession was clear.

In the 1920s and 1930s, women received 15 percent of all the Ph.D.'s awarded in the nation. Those percentages declined, not because of any fall in absolute numbers, but because the number of men attending graduate school increased sharply in the fifties and sixties. Women were 13 percent of the 1930-59 Ph.D. cohort, dropping to 10.4 percent in the 1960-69 cohort.[2]

During this period, academic positions throughout the humanities were seldom advertised but instead were filled through "old boy" networks. Women often depended upon letters of reference, which might contain gratuitous sexist characterizations like the following: "While she probably doesn't have the stamina for independent, scholarly work, she loves big parties and mixes well." Or, "If she has any faults, they are those that usually accompany the ambitious woman of her age." Prejudice against women's intellectual abilities was pervasive. Numerous studies showed that the same professional record was given a lower evaluation when it was attributed to a woman rather than to a man, no matter what the sex of the evaluator.[3]

The feminist movement of the sixties had a profound effect upon the younger women in the historical profession, and they began to organize to oppose gender discrimination. In 1969, women's history was not yet a recognized field of scholarship, and many students were actively discouraged from doing research in this area. Only 10.4 percent of history Ph.D.'s were women, and there were no women officers in either of the two major historical associations (the American Historical Association, which covers all fields and periods, and the Organization of American Historians, which addresses itself primarily to Americanists). At the 1969 meetings of the American Historical Association, Berenice Carroll initiated the founding of the Coordinating Committee of Women in the Historical Profession to end discrimination against women in the profession. By 1975 its additional objective of furthering instruction and research in women's history was recognized by the affiliation of the Conference Group on Women's History with the AHA. Membership, however, remains largely joint. The CCWHP/CGWH, along with permanent committees in the AHA and OAH on the status of women in the profession which were created as the result of lobbying efforts, have proved to be highly effective instruments of change.[4]

In 1970 the then ad hoc AHA Committee on the Status of Women presented its findings. Known as the "Rose Report," after the committee chair, Willie Lee Rose, the report formed the agenda for the succeeding twenty years, and the statistics it presented on women in the profession have served as a base line for evaluating women's status.

The Rose Report disclosed that not only was there gender bias, but the position of women was in some respects actually deteriorating. For example, 16 percent of full professors in history departments at coeducational colleges were women in 1959-60, but by 1968-69 only one remained, and she retired the following year. This example highlights the fact that women not only suffered from discrimination but frequently found such bias reinforced by changes in society. These women full professors were undoubtedly part of the generation of women Ph.D.'s trained in the twenties and thirties whose retirements were met by a sharp increase in the number of men who, benefiting from the GI bill following World War II, were now in graduate school. The result was a plentiful supply of males in a market where men were preferred.

The feminist movement arrived too late for women to benefit substantially from the enormous growth in higher education which took place between 1957 and 1967. Unfortunately, this expansion was to be short-lived, and academia was caught unaware of the changes which the seventies would bring--inflation, recession, cutbacks in government funding, salary erosion, and lower enrollments. Until 1970-71 faculty salaries had kept pace with those of other workers; afterwards, deterioration was more severe than in any other professional group. In addition, departments faced declining history enrollments, with B.A.'s dropping from 44,000 to 21,000 in the period from 1972 to 1979.[5]

Although partially reflecting the drop in the number of men entering the discipline as a consequence of the lure of better-paying positions elsewhere, the percentage of history doctorates awarded to women rose from 10.4 percent (1960-69) to 15.8 percent (1970-74) to 26 percent (1975-80). In addition, women were included within the goals of affirmative action. Thus, by the early seventies women historians were knocking on the door of the profession, demanding their rights, only to see that door almost closed in their faces as a result of what came to be known as the "job-hiring crisis." History departments were slow to adjust their production of Ph.D.'s to the severely contracting market. At the 1971 AHA convention, 2,300 graduate students sought positions among the 155 advertised there. Even by 1976-77 there were more than two people in the market for every Ph.D. granted that year.[6]

Under these conditions, women's entry into the profession increased the feminization of the part-time and temporary segment of the market. Even those women fortunate enough to have tenure-track positions faced the "revolving door" phenomenon, as retrenchment forced a rise in publication standards. Many women moved into public history, where women had traditionally found jobs before the field had a name. They also led in establishing organizations for the unaffiliated scholar, such as the Institute for Research in History. The difficulties of these years are summed up in statistics for academically employed women. In the cohort which was thirty-six to forty-five years old in 1987, 19 percent of the women, compared to 13.1 percent of the men, still held non-tenure-track positions.[7]

Despite all of these difficulties, women historians have made significant gains in the past twenty years. The area of greatest success has been the history organizations themselves. There are several reasons for this: the skill of women's lobbying efforts and the high quality of their leadership; the visibility of these organizations within education, which places significant pressures on them for gender equity; and the fact that advances here are less threatening to male academic culture than improvements in women's status in individual departments.

By 1991, the twenty-year lobbying effort had given the AHA one woman president and the OAH four (one of whom is an African American). Gains were made in other organizations as well. Women also served as presidents of the American Studies Association and the Southern Historical Association during this period. The percentage of women who were elected officials of the AHA increased from zero in 1969 to 38 percent in 1977 to 46 percent in 1990, when they represented but 25 percent of the membership.[8] Such success out of proportion to their percentage of the membership is frequently credited to "preferential treatment," even though a majority of women won in the 1980s when they ran against men.

Opening up the historical organizations has led to two consequences of special significance: it has increased the visibility of women and women's history in the profession, and it has opened the hiring process to all, by substituting a national listing of positions for the "old boy" system whereby mentors sought to locate jobs for their students through personal contacts. Not only is advertising more equitable for women, but it has benefited minorities and those men not privileged by the former elitist system.

Progress on other fronts has been uneven, however. In 1990 the AHA

Committee on Women Historians published a follow-up to the "Rose Report,"[9] assessing women's position in the profession twenty years later. It found a salutary increase in the visibility of women in the profession. Further, entry-level salaries had reached the same level as men's by 1987, and women's share of Ph.D.'s had risen to 38 percent by 1988. Yet major problems remain.

Despite initiatives to address the poor representation of racial and ethnic groups in the profession, their proportion of new Ph.D.'s had actually declined; and those who were offered academic positions often found themselves isolated and bereft of an accepting, collegial environment. College enrollments of minorities had also declined, reflecting cutbacks in student aid which led to fewer students in the pipeline. The absolute number of doctorates awarded to minority women from 1975 to 1988 was discouragingly small: Native Americans, 8; Hispanics, 41; Asian Americans, 42; and African Americans, 101. For purposes of comparison, it is useful to note that of the total number of Ph.D.'s awarded to academically employed historians between 1946 and 1988, 12,500 went to men and 2,500 to women.[10]

Women historians continued to experience significant inequities. The longer they remained in the profession, the further they fell behind men in rank and salary. Figures for history were more extreme than those for the rest of the humanities. Women Ph.D.'s in four-year colleges and universities earned only 80.6 percent of men's salaries in 1987. The part-time segment of the market remained "feminized," with women accounting for twice as many non-tenure-track positions and fifteen times as many adjunct positions as men. These positions characteristically carried few or no health and pension benefits. The number of women at the top of the profession continued to increase, but slowly, and was even declining in women's colleges. In the ten top-ranked research universities listed above, the percentage of women had improved but little--to 12 percent of the faculty.[11]

Although not all women historians are historians of women, the overwhelming majority of historians of women are women. Almost from its inception, women's history has been history from a feminist perspective, even though within that perspective a range of positions are held. The field, whose beginning was marked by the First Berkshire Conference on the History of Women in 1973, attended by only five hundred people, has reached early maturity. The first generation of historians of women were self-taught, but by 1990 their students had become mature scholars who were already revising earlier interpretations and questioning explanatory frameworks. The rigorous and innovative quality of scholarship in the field led to over two hundred history departments listing a specialist in women's history by 1988, and over fifty institutions offering doctoral training by that date. The field has grown to international importance. In 1990 the first conference of the International Federation for Research in Women's History was held in Madrid. This organization is composed of representatives of twenty-three nations.

The linkage of feminism, women's history, and women historians proved to be a strong combination for advancing the status of women in the historical profession. Feminism provided a framework for understanding and articulating the position of women in the profession as well as the focus and the energy for organizing a militant assault upon sexism in the academy. Feminism, in its emphasis upon equality, spoke to universalistic norms in both the profession and the nation, thereby forming a bridge to male academic culture which led to sympathetic support by many men.

If feminism provided the framework, women's history provided the vehicle for the project of improving women's status in the profession. Because women constitute half or more of the world's population, no field of history is unrelated to their concerns. Because both feminism and women's history are, at root, critiques of power and domination, their ideas reverberate throughout the field. Women historians, whatever their specialty, found not only that women's history had something to say, but that probably a lacuna existed on women which needed filling. Thus, women's history provided research topics to all subfields and, additionally, opportunities to revise and reconfigure them. The field of women's history itself has provided new positions which are generally filled by women.

And, finally, women historians themselves have been the primary engine behind advances in their professional status. This is not to deny that many men have provided support. Nevertheless, one cannot imagine the enhancement of women's professional status without their own considerable efforts. The resistance with which they have been and continue to be met is clear in the statistics presented above. In the final analysis, no group relinquishes its privileges without a challenge.

## Notes

1. OAH Committee on the Status of Women, Report for 1985; AHA's 1970 report of the Committee on the Status of Women (known as the "Rose Report").

2. Virginia Sapiro, *Women in American Society: An Introduction to Women's Studies* (Palo Alto: Mayfield, 1986), Table 4-1, p. 114; *American Historical Association Guidelines on Hiring Women Historians in Academia*, 3rd edition.

3. N. J. Hoffman, "Sexism in Letters of Recommendation: A Case for Consciousness-Raising," Modern Language Association *Newsletter* (September 1972):5-6; cited in Joan Abramson, *The Invisible Woman: Discrimination in the Academic Profession* (San Francisco: Jossey-Bass, 1976), p. 79; For examples of studies of discrimination in professional record evaluation, see L. S. Videll, "Empirical Verification of Sex Discrimination in Hiring Practices in Psychology," *American Psychologist* 25 (1970); Philip Goldberg, "Are Women Prejudiced against Women," *Transaction* (April 1968).

4. The Coordinating Committee of Women in the Historical Profession was initially cochaired by Carroll and Gerda Lerner. Their custom of dividing responsibilities led to the creation of the Conference Group on Women's History, which became an autonomous affiliate of the AHA in 1975. However, the membership is largely joint and composed of individuals, although CCWHP/CGWH acts as an umbrella organization for fifteen regional associations as well. See review of Hilda Smith, Nupur Chaudhuri, and Gerda Lerner, *A History of the Coordinating Committee of Women in the Historical*

*Profession--Conference Group on Women's History, Journal of Women's History* 2 (Winter 1991):145.

5. Joan Hoff-Wilson, "Is the History Profession an 'Endangered Species'?" *The Public Historian* (Winter 1980):19.

6. Lawrence Stone, "The AHA and the Job Market for Graduate Students," *AHA Newsletter* 10 (March 1972):22-27; "Placement Survey," *AHA Newsletter* 16 (March 1978):2.

7. *Guidelines on Hiring Women Historians.*

8. *Newsletter of the Coordinating Committee on Women in the Historical Profession* 20 (September 1989):5; "Rose Report"; Joan M. Jensen, "Committee on Women Historians, 1970-1990: A Twenty-Year Report," AHA *Perspectives* (March 1990):8, 9.

9. Jensen, "Committee on Women Historians," pp. 8, 9.

10. *Guidelines on Hiring Women; Humanities Doctorates in the United States: 1989 Profile* (Washington, D.C.: National Academy Press, 1991), p. 31.

11. *Guidelines on Hiring Women Historians*; Jensen, "Committee on Women Historians," pp. 8, 9.

# INTRODUCTION:
## An Overview of Women's History in the United States

Joan Hoff

> Equal education, for which women have clamored . . . has meant the
> extension to women of men's education in their own history and
> judgments of themselves. . . . It is basically a sex-education--
> masculine in design and spirit. . . .[1]

The *Journal Of Women's History*, pursuing its goal of serving as the journal of record for the field of women's history in the United States and abroad, is proud to present this compilation of periodical literature from 1980 to 1990 prepared by Gayle V. Fischer. Since the 1970s, women's history in the United States has been strongly rooted in the politics of women's liberation--acknowledging the need to find a collective past for the purpose of contributing to a praxis whose goal is women's autonomy and self-realization. Nowhere is this more evident than in the articles published during the last decade.

The zeal to uncover power relationships in the interest of equality and social justice has seldom been denied by historians of women until most recently, as will be noted below. In fact, methodologies developed in women's history demythologize the writing of objective history, demonstrating that "objectivity" is an impossibility and that "objective" history often amounts to nothing more or less than male history, a realization achieved by historian Mary Ritter Beard over fifty years ago, as is reflected in the introductory quotation.

Women's history also refuses to be neatly labeled in a disciplinary box. Drawing on multidisciplinary theories and methodologies, women's history has adopted a variety of strategies for achieving its goals. The globalization of the world economy, together with the media revolution of the last thirty years, which provides instant access to what is going on all over the world, portends the reinforcement of this interdisciplinary perspective in the 1990s--as does the increased influence of Third World women upon the conceptualization of women's history. Because of its interdisciplinary nature and the continued reluctance of mainstream historical journals in the United States and other nations to devote any more than 10 percent of their articles to women's history, it has proven difficult to keep track of the latest scholarship. Much of this material has been published in obscure journals, state historical periodicals, or publications which only occasionally carry historical articles.

This ten-year bibliography of periodical literature from the 1980s has been compiled to facilitate the work of scholars, teachers, and general readers in women's history. It is the hope of the editors and staff of the *Journal of Women's History* that this compilation will assist readers in keeping up with the latest scholarship and will assess those areas in which more research needs to be done, because we are assuming that periodical literature of the 1980s anticipates the subject matter of monographic publications in the field of women's history during the 1990s. A list of the serial publications from which this bibliographic reference has been prepared can be found at the end of the volume. There are forty subject entries, divided into subcategories, totaling over 5,500 individual articles that have been extensively cross-listed in order to facilitate the use of this reference work. A statistical analysis indicates that the two most researched areas in the field of women's history are *work* (including *economics* and *professions*), which accounts for 14 percent of all the entries, and *religion*, constituting 8 percent. Twenty-three percent of all entries are about countries other than the United States, and while they also reflect the dominance of economic and religious topics, some of the following generalizations about other categories apply more to American scholarship on women than to that in other countries.

One might ask why so many of the articles are about the work women do outside the home, since the middle-class, two-income family is largely a post-World War II development in most countries. Even though most of the authors of these articles are middle-class, many of them began writing about working-class families in the nineteenth and early twentieth centuries, when wives commonly supplemented their husbands' income in both urban and rural settings. In fact, there has been only one ten-year period in all of U.S. history when the average husband's family wage was sufficient to support his wife and children--the postwar baby and economic boom decade of the 1950s. While the sufficiency of the male family wage varies from country to country, working women have been common in all time periods, especially in agriculture, industry, and domestic service. In addition to an abundance of primary material about working women, the disproportionately large number of articles on women's work also reflects the influence of socialist historians, who have played a prominent role among both women scholars and women activists, especially in the United States, England, and France since 1945. Moreover, one early way to legitimize women's history since the 1960s has been to connect it with an already established subfield, in this instance labor history.

Another question that might be asked concerns the surprisingly high percentage of entries on *material and popular culture*--7 percent, equal to the percentage of articles on *politics*. This proportion is higher among historians of women in the United States than among those in other countries. This is probably due to American Studies tradition which has, since the 1960s, encouraged historians to look at how people lived privately, rather than simply at what they thought and accomplished publicly. Because of the mentalité school of historiography in France, one also finds a higher percentage of articles about the living conditions of average women in that country than of those in most other nations. Six percent of the articles in this collection are about women and *art* and women within the *family*. Five percent are about the *theoretical* aspects of writing and researching women's history in the United States and other nations. Based on titles of articles, this bibliography conveys the strong impression that a higher percentage of theoretical articles are published by historians of women outside the United States.

A number of topics each constitute 4 percent of the total entries. They are *marriage and divorce, biographies, military and war, social reform and community organizing, education,* and *African-American* women. Three percent of the articles can be found in the areas of *law and crime, ethnicity, sexuality,* and *feminism.* Only 2 percent are devoted respectively to the topics of *lifestages and lifestyles, suffrage* (including *anti-suffrage*--a topic of little interest outside the United States and England), and *birth control.* One percent of the articles are about *southern women in the United States, agriculture, health, prostitution,* and *violence.* Less than 1 percent of all the entries cover such topics as *utopias, pornography,* and *sports.*

Readers may want to use this statistical breakdown to draw a number of conclusions about their own future research and geographical area of concentration. Clearly, the small proportion of entries related to matters of *sexuality* (including *lesbianism*), *lifestages and lifestyles, birth control* (including *abortion, fertility, infanticide,* and *reproductive rights and options*), and *pornography* and *violence* against women, totaling only 6 percent of all articles, probably does not reflect the importance of these issues to contemporary women as found in public policy discussions at local, state, and national levels. Just as obviously, these articles reflect a diversity with respect to race, class, and gender that belies recent claims that women's history in the 1980s continued to focus primarily on white, middle-class women, as it had in the 1970s.

The following essay is based on monographic publications (with selective references to the periodical literature in this compilation) and is aimed at those interested in a review of trends in the field of women's history during the twentieth century in the United States, but especially since the Second World War.

## Patriarchal History

The kind of history many of us were taught from primary school through college is so familiar that we scarcely think of it as having a name. A shorthand term for that nameless though ubiquitous type of history is "patriarchal," where the standards of power, prestige, and traditional periodization abound. Such criteria have eliminated most women from historical consideration or have resulted in the peripheral inclusion of only the "exceptional" among them.

Throughout the ages, the writers of patriarchal history have emphasized the exercise of public power as the most important aspect of human life. One of the recurrent activities in the public sphere has been abrupt or violent changes in relationships between individuals and nations and between humans and their environments. It is not only politics and wars that represent these values of power and prestige and that determine traditional textbook periodization; so too does the emphasis in patriarchal history on dramatic confrontations between powerful individuals rather than on the evolution of social relations.

Consequently, one of the most common features of patriarchal history is the search for heroic or charismatic figures. This search has been reinforced in the

United States by the rise of the cult of hero worship since the 1920s because of technological advancements in mass communication, but it is also not uncommon among historians of other countries. Thus, conservative historians of the present traditionally write about conservative leaders of the past. Radical historians look for radical models as subjects of their research. Labor historians focus on class differences, while gay historians search for examples of homosexuality. Minority or ethnic historians search for prominent representatives of their respective races or ethnic backgrounds. This attempt to find historical figures representing particular political, class, sexual, racial, or ethnic preferences became particularly evident in works published during the 1970s.

To the degree, therefore, that historians of women simply emphasize finding heroines from the American past, they are continuing to write in a patriarchal mold. Even if they write about women who are less well known, they often resurrect them using traditional values of power and prestige. The same is true of historians who specialize in the study of minority or ethnic leaders. Since women and other subordinate groups simply have not produced many individuals who meet traditional patriarchal criteria, one soon runs out of these kinds of heroes. While some of these compensatory or remedial efforts are necessary to overcome the historical invisibility of these groups, such history contains serious limitations. For one, patriarchal history has placed far too much emphasis on atypical individuals whose public careers have little in common with the private lives of "average" women. This emphasis when continued by historians of women also raises the political question about whether concentrating primarily on "notable" or exceptional women can contribute to the empowerment of all women. Thus, much compensatory or remedial history perpetuates the patriarchal tradition of according more importance to the public than to the private sphere of human existence and usually consists of narratives about women's experiences that parallel those of men using standard political, socioeconomic, and cultural terminology and periodization. It is an attempt not so much to "rewrite history," as Virginia Woolf advocated in 1929, by accumulating a "mass of information" about women's daily lives, as it is to imitate conventional history.[2]

Compensatory or remedial history constituted a first step toward achieving historical visibility for powerless groups who were traditionally relegated to the invisible confines of the private sphere. Nonetheless, early compensatory history was seriously flawed because it often only substituted women for men. Even when prominent women emerged in the United States, the documentation of their lives and achievements was usually left to white males who imposed their own values on them. First, they wrote about women prescriptively, assigning them status and societal value according to prevailing mainstream standards; that is, they took female "outsiders," assigned them mainstream characteristics, and thus made "acceptable" models out of the private and public lives of women ranging from Deborah Sampson Gannett to Eleanor Roosevelt. Second, in deciding that only certain records about these exceptional women should be preserved, they allowed much documentation to suffer destruction or deterioration.

The relationship between the public male and private spheres has profoundly affected how historians write about female sexuality, especially homosocial and/or homoerotic bonding.[3] The conventional tendency has been to trivialize love relationships between women in comparison to the heterosexual home as a haven from the heartless world, or to stress how love relationships between women supported them in their public and private activities. Neither approach, however, has yet legitimized the single woman as a sexual being for whom no theoretical and historical heterosexual or homosexual apologia need be made. The staff of the *Journal of Women's History* believes that the theoretical and historical study of female friendships and sexuality is so important that it warrants its own subheading in this bibliography.

Often, interpretative battles over historical manifestations of female sexuality and friendship have been fought in book reviews. For example, there was a flood of reviews attempting to explain away the obviously intense relationship between Lorena Hickok and Eleanor Roosevelt when it was exposed, but ironically denied, in Doris Faber's book.[4] Patriarchal historians assiduously ignored Roosevelt's relationship with Hickok, disregarding over 3,000 letters they wrote each other in the 1930s and 1940s. Moreover, Roosevelt's post-1945 papers remain unprocessed and unindexed. They are still crammed into their original White House file boxes at the FDR Presidential Library in Hyde Park, even though her career assumed international dimensions through her work at the United Nations. In the minds of many historians and librarians, Roosevelt symbolically "died" when her husband did in 1945. The deficiencies of patriarchal history become most painfully evident when so prominent a person as Roosevelt can have not only her private life sanitized but also her important contributions to domestic politics and to international affairs systematically undervalued.[5] In Roosevelt's case this neglect was due not so much to the difficulty posed by her close relationships with women as to the fact that most wives of presidents of the United States have been ignored as research topics by both patriarchal *and* feminist historians. There are only a little over thirty citations on First Ladies in this collection of articles.

Female sexuality and friendship continue to pose theoretical difficulties for historians, especially biographers. The best theoretical study of female friendship is Janice Raymond's book *Passion for Friends: Toward a Philosophy of Female Affection*.[6] As Gerda Lerner has noted, there appears to be an inability or reluctance among biographers of women to analyze their subjects' public and private lives from a holistic perspective. She indicates that the reluctance to deal with the sexual preferences of women has the tendency to produce "homophobic judgements."[7] At the very least, homosocial as well as homoerotic relations between women should be subjected to the same set of historical standards currently used to analyze and describe heterosexual ones, rather than ignored or exaggerated. Several biographies about Hilda Doolittle, known to her literary friends as H.D., constitute another striking example of this dispute over how to characterize women's homosocial and/or homoerotic relations. Two books about Doolittle, in particular, contain otherwise inexplicable discrepancies regarding her sexual orientation.[8]

Patriarchal historians have also typically destroyed or ignored sources about women. In 1848, for example, the year of the Seneca Falls Conference, Charles

Francis Adams edited the letters of his famous grandmother, Abigail Adams. In the process, he systematically destroyed most of the letters written to her by women unrelated to the family--women whom he deemed unimportant. Consequently, what remains of her correspondence is primarily with women of Mercy Otis Warren's prominence, but not with numerous less "significant" women who wrote to her expressing their ideas and concerns about life during the Revolution.[9]

Another example of distortion involves the flamboyant Deborah Sampson Gannett. Familiar to many because she fought as an enlisted soldier in the War for Independence, Gannett collaborated with an editor friend, Herman Mann. In 1797 he published an account of her revolutionary activities with a title that encapsulates the classic patriarchal view of Gannett's life: *The Female Review of Memoirs of an American Young Lady Whose Life and Character Are Peculiarly Distinguished-- Being a Continental Soldier for Nearly Three Years in the Late American War during Which Time She Performed the Duties of Every Department into Which She Was Called with Punctual Exactness, Fidelity and Honor, and Preserved Her Chastity Inviolate by the Most Artful Concealment of Her Sex.*[10] Because Gannett's original manuscript was lost, all that remains is Mann's verbose account, which turns a rather rough, competent colonial woman into a genteel lady whose chastity is intact. In 1916 another patriarchal historian, John Adams Vinton, decided to reprint Mann's book with his own introduction and annotations. Although Vinton corrected the worst exaggerations and stereotypes of the first account, it remains a highly idealized and unreal portrait of Gannett. Sadly, we shall never know how she perceived herself, only how two men perceived her according to the prevailing male standards of their day.[11]

Despite the renaissance in women's history all over the world during the decades of the 1970s and 1980s, we still find similar treatment accorded to prominent women and their papers. Many are still made to fit into a mainstream mold, especially in matters involving their sexuality, and often papers involving their intimate relations are sanitized or suppressed. Seldom are the private or public lives of even those women who best fit the patriarchal prerequisites of power and prestige accorded accurate personal renditions and adequate recognition in monographs or textbooks.

Patriarchal neglect was even more blatant where "average" women were concerned. Their collective socioeconomic contributions, cultural networks, and private intrapsychic existence are now the subject of extensive historical research. Originally, sources for the history of women and minorities remained inadequate because they consisted primarily of documents collected and preserved using patriarchal standards. As of the late 1980s, the problems with source collection for the writing of women's history are, to a degree, the reverse of those in the past. Although the two volumes of *Women's History Sources: A Guide to Archives and Manuscript Collections in the United States* (1979) indicate that approximately two-thirds of the collections consist of personal papers, this basic reference lists few private documents describing those personal family activities involving sexuality, pregnancy, and child-rearing techniques of eighteenth-, nineteenth-, and early twentieth-century American women.[12]

Most of what we do know about female sexuality, fertility, and birthing patterns in these periods comes from demographic data and other aggregate statistics culled largely from courthouse and church records. Today, in contrast, we have an abundance of published testimonies, as well as official government figures, about the sexuality, pregnancies, and child-bearing habits of women since the Second World War. Yet our female ancestors in those earlier centuries may have left proportionately more diaries and letters than contemporary women in the last half of the twentieth century. Our records in this century will remain incomplete for the "average" woman, but for different reasons. The contemporary woman is now less likely to write her friends; rather, she will telephone or visit them. So we may have less intimate documentation about homosocial bonding among today's typical women than we do for eighteenth- and nineteenth-century women.

If this is correct, then archivists and historians should encourage women who are not the "notables" of our age to deposit their personal papers. Most contemporary notables will make provisions for their papers without being asked. Another valuable aspect of preserving the reflections of average contemporary women is that they may be less self-conscious and more truthful than those of prominent women who, like prominent men, often write letters or keep diaries with their future publication in mind. This subtle but significant change from diary-as-a-private-record to diary-as-a-public-record will probably alter the value of diaries and letters for research purposes in the future.

We now have a particular type of qualitative material (largely intrapersonal) about eighteenth- and nineteenth-century women, but little quantitative documentation. For most of this century we have an abundance of quantitative information, but fewer inter- and intrapersonal documents. Advances in electronic preservation have made legal and quantitative data rather than qualitative material easy to acquire and store. As a result, in the next century it may become more, rather than less, difficult to write biographies of both well-known and "average" women that integrate their public and private lives.

Despite the persistence of patriarchal history, dramatic changes have taken place during the last quarter-century in the writing of U.S. women and in the profession of history itself. Many of those currently writing women's history have led the way in making curricular and textbook changes, and in the training and placing of students and the hiring and promoting of faculty.[13] Hence, the new history about women in the United States has often been the focus of shifting ideological battles inside the profession. Analyzing the state of the art in any discipline, especially one such as history that has recently developed challenging subfields, is often a mask for talking about political and interpretive divisions created by new research. Thus, women's history has simultaneously threatened traditional patriarchal history and traditional departmental politics when it came to hiring, promotion, and tenure decisions since the early 1970s. Most important, as it has matured, women's history (and women's studies in general) has begun to challenge not only the criteria of power, prestige, and standard periodization, but also the basic theoretical foundations of patriarchal history with poststructural gender analysis.

Ironically, what we have come to call women's history is a misnomer, because the subject is really the history of gender, which is "the cultural definition of behavior appropriate to both sexes."[14] Because the new social history did not contain gender analysis when it emerged in the late 1960s, the subfield of women's history was misnamed. In fact, because the new social history of the 1960s in the United States was so intertwined with the political and cultural movements of that decade, male bias dominated the methodology and narratives to the point that it "obscur[ed] rather than uncover[ed] the actual historical experiences of women."[15] At best, early social historians knew that social and cultural anthropologists used a structural functionalist approach to distinguish gendered roles in society, without recognizing that the anthropologists usually trivialized or devalued women's activities by using a male standard of power and prestige. Thus, social historians repeated the mistake of anthropologists when they studied the family by ignoring women as individuals and underestimating their collective contributions to history.[16]

Although gender is at the heart of all socialized behavior and perceived differences between the sexes, twenty years ago the meaning of *gender* was at best only vaguely perceived among historians, in male-biased anthropological terms at best, and in grammatical terms at worst, denoting words that were masculine, feminine, or neuter and hence requiring agreement with or selection of appropriately "gendered" modifiers. Likewise in the early years of the Second Women's Movement, the words *woman*, *women*, and *sex* became common usage in historical writings, while *feminism* and *feminist* did not because they were considered too confrontational and subversive even within supposedly liberated intellectual circles during the early development of the new social history. At the height of the Second Women's Movement in the United States in the 1970s, however, the term *feminism* gained widespread usage, replacing the derogatory *Women's Lib* in popular and scholarly literature.

Beginning in the late 1970s, some self-conscious feminists among social historians insisted on distinguishing between the meanings of *sex* and *gender*, usually following the sex/gender theories of feminist anthropologist Gayle Rubin. She argued in 1975 that women's seemingly universal oppression originated not simply in economic conditions, as Marx and Engels had written, or in their reproductive capacities, as cultural feminists insisted, but in a set of social relations based on gender stereotypes that may differ from culture to culture, but which perpetuate a largely male-dominated sexual hierarchy.

The idea that men and women are more different from one another than either is from anything else must come from somewhere other than nature. Furthermore, although there is an average difference between males and females on a variety of traits, the range of variation of those traits shows considerable overlap. . . . The idea that men and women are two mutually exclusive categories must arise out of something other than a nonexistent "natural" opposition. Far from being an expression of natural differences, exclusive gender identity is the suppression of natural similarities. It requires repression: in men, of whatever is the local version of "feminine" traits; in women, of the local definition of "masculine" traits. The division of the sexes has the effect of repressing some of the personality traits of virtually everyone, men and women.[17]

Thus, *sex* as purely a biological term, referring to women's physical reproductive capabilities, increasingly became separated from socially conditioned gender characteristics in the minds of many feminists in the Second Women's Movement and in the discipline of history by the late 1970s. For example, the first edition of a nationally published list of readings and course outlines in women's history used largely in the 1970s did not carry the word *gender* in any of the titles; however, in the 1987 edition, gender appeared "as an organizing principle in one out of nine" entries, and it dominated papers given at the Eighth Berkshire Conference on the History of Women in 1990.[18]

In the 1980s there was a tendency in history classes and in the articles in this bibliography to substitute the word *gender* for *feminist* or *women* for a variety of reasons. First, since *gender* clearly includes the study of men as well as women, it was considered more inclusive; and second, it is more politically acceptable on most campuses in the face of the conservative backlash than, at least, the term *feminist*. Thus, the use of *gender* has become problematic because it has become politicized: at either extreme of the political spectrum, the term can be used to essentialize women or to depoliticize gender, as noted below. To confuse matters further, many government and institutional forms in the United States have incorrectly substituted *gender* for *sex*. Surely the census bureau does not want to know how each individual in the United States was socialized. It simply wants to know each individual's biological sex.

## Stages of Development in U.S. Women's History

Misnomer or not, in this century U.S. women's history has passed through three discernible stages of development that diverge from traditional patriarchal history: (1) the *remedial stage*; (2) the *prefeminist stage*; and (3) the *feminist stage*. A fourth, *postfeminist stage* under the influence of poststructuralism is now emerging that is theoretically most sophisticated and intriguing, but carries with it some disturbing political overtones for the Second Women's Movement. The first stage occurred in the late nineteenth and early twentieth centuries, when historians attempted to make up for the previously deficient historical treatment of women by producing remedial histories of "exceptional" women. Some of these early histories were written by professional women historians who were activists, and some by amateur historians who had participated in the campaign for suffrage, or the First Women's Movement, at the end of the last century.[19] The suffragists-turned-historians were laudatory about the feminine qualities of their subjects, while using victim or slave images to describe the general conditions of women in society. Subsequently, professional and amateur historians alike adopted the dichotomous view of women as both superior and subordinate that histories had propagated since the beginning of recorded history and that has led to women's veneration but not their empowerment.

By portraying women as exploited and exceptional, the remedialists created an interpretative problem: they needed to explain how certain women overcame discrimination and excelled while others were defeated by it. This problem has not been completely resolved in contemporary works on individual women in all areas of the world, especially those who have successfully challenged the societal limitations placed upon their own personal and public lives, as many of the articles in the biography sections of this bibliography indicate. In addition to their simplistic and often contradictory biographical portraits of such women, these early twentieth-century amateur historians also wrote descriptive institutional histories of women's organizations and studies of literature prescribing women's domestic and social roles but did not speculate about the relationships or interconnectedness among socioeconomic or legal statuses of women to the larger society. Stressing the differences between the private sphere of women and the public sphere of men, these historians unwittingly reinstated patriarchal notions about the family and femininity among the first and second generations of suffrage leaders.

Largely descriptive and ancedotal, whether written by women (with the exception of works by Alice Morse Earle)[20] or men, this compensatory or remedial approach to women's history flourished from the first decade of the twentieth century until the 1940s in the works of such professional historians as Edith Abbott, Mary Ritter Beard, Mary Sumner Benson, Elisabeth Anthony Dexter, Abbie Graham, Richard Morris, and Julia Cherry Spruill.[21] In the 1950s and 1960s it could still be found in the writings of Mildred Adams, Catherine Cleverdon, Olivia E. Coolidge, Emily Taft Douglas, Eleanor Flexnor, Roger Fulford, and Alan P. Grimes--all of whom made a commitment to suffrage as a patriarchal standard of excellence for their female subjects and also made suffrage synonymous with feminism. Other historians concentrated on "exceptional" women or on specific groups of working women, such as those in the South or in the early factory system.[22] Except in the writings of Mary Ritter Beard, man was the "measure of excellence." Beard remains one of the few historians of women to have broken with their traditional academic training and institutional affiliation.

The second stage of development in U.S. women's history can be considered prefeminist. These histories contain some of the same remedial and contradictory features of the earlier conventional works, especially the concentration on "notables," because these early historians of women were still trained in the traditional patriarchal mode of the 1950s and 1960s. However, the second-stage historians did begin to look at political events and movements other than suffrage and to ask new questions of old data from a female--but not necessarily a feminist--point of view. (I am dating the emergence of modern feminism in the late 1960s to the formation of the Second Women's Movement.) By and large, however, these historians continued to research the lives of "exceptional" rather than ordinary women and to write political or institutional histories.

As they progressed, however, this generation of historians became more critical of their female subjects, especially the suffragists and the women who participated in the Progressive Movement. Their negativism attested to the influence of Richard Hofstadter, who dealt harshly with most reform periods in U.S. history. Ironically, Hofstadter's "status anxiety" and "status decline" explanations for reform activity did not take into consideration the gendered humanitarian motivations of female as opposed to male Progressives.[23] Nonetheless, his ideas were often uncritically applied to both sexes by women and men historians during this period.

Twenty years ago the profession generally accepted a women's history that found fault with individual women and women's organizations because it dovetailed with the history being written in other fields. Criticism of early U.S. reform movements increased as the civil rights and antiwar movements began to influence the politics of younger historians. By the beginning of the 1970s, women's history reflected the left-of-center concerns of many historians while it retained traditional periodization, e.g., the American Revolution, the age of Jackson, the Civil War and Reconstruction, and the origins of the First and Second World Wars.

The best-known among the prefeminist historians are Carl Degler, David M. Kennedy, Aileen S. Kraditor, Christopher Lasch, Gerda Lerner, William O'Neill, David Potter, Robert Riegel, Anne Firor Scott, Andrew Sinclair, Page Smith, and Barbara Welter.[24] Writing in the late 1960s and early 1970s, they depicted women's early attempts to achieve equality and influence American society, and the shallowness of the separate-sphere ideology of the suffragists. In particular, some of these historians condemned the suffragists for allowing race and class interests to narrow their assessment of women's problems and to limit their demands to the right to vote. Others judged those women draped in the "cult of true womanhood" harshly by the standards of their own time, reserving their praise for only the very first generation of suffragists led by Susan B. Anthony and Elizabeth Cady Stanton, who met the increasingly radical political standards of the Vietnam and Watergate eras. The deficiencies of this anachronistic historical interpretation were not seriously questioned until the development of the new social history directly challenged both traditional patriarchal and prefeminist histories by featuring the concerns of ordinary rather than exceptional people; by elevating rather than condemning the private sphere occupied by women in contrast to the public one of men; and by attending to how women of the past *perceived* themselves and positively bonded with each other within the much-debated domestic circle rather than to the pejorative contemporary review of domesticity that Betty Friedan's *Feminine Mystique* had prompted among many second-stage historians.[25]

The new social history of the late 1960s produced the third, or modern feminist, phase in American women's history. In keeping with their left-of-center politics and their involvement in the Second Women's Movement, the men and women who wrote the new social history deliberately added a feminist agenda to their research programs. Most of these historians had received traditional graduate training, and thus initially used the conventional sources of their predecessors, but they freed themselves from these sources by employing new methodologies that questioned the older data.[26]

Many of the questions they asked came directly or indirectly from the political agendas of the civil rights, antiwar, and Second Women's movements. For example, how did the black family remain intact in the face of slavery? How did blacks, women, and immigrant groups develop distinctive family and kinship patterns that were largely ignored or undetected by the dominant power structure? Did such networks serve as a defense against psychic and other forms of exploitation? How were formal or informal rituals transmitted intergenerationally? Do women and men experience the major events of history similarly? How did the socialization of children differ among different class and racial groupings? What is the significance of homosocial bonding among women? How much conscious sense of community and collective action can be found among the powerless? Do gender behavior patterns cut across class and time, or are they historically variable, that is, determined by particular socioeconomic and cultural periods? What contributions have women and minorities made during times of war, depression, or other national dislocations? What is the political and cultural significance of iconographic representations of women, especially in times of national trauma? Why do periods of conservative backlash inevitably follow wars, and what gendered implications do they contain? Do subcultural organizations have different functions and modes of operation than those run by white males? Have changes in the legal status of U.S. women since the colonial period reflected more about the evolution of the country's political economy than about "progress" in women's rights? And finally, is there a "timeless" definition of feminism that can be applied to all of American or any other national history?

Most of these questions cannot be answered by traditional historical approaches to research. Conscious feminist historians all over the world have begun to use innovative methods involving oral history, ethnography, sociology, ethnology, semiotics, family reconstitution, collective biographical sketches (prosopography), and various forms of statistical and computerized demographic analysis, such as multiple regression analysis, and other microhistory techniques. Most recently, they have begun to answer such questions with poststructural perspectives borrowed from literature, philosophy, and film criticism. These innovations led first to the reconstruction of the aggregate history of female and other subcultural groups from incomplete and hence largely ignored data, and now to the deconstruction of the concept of gender itself. Once believed inadequate for historical analysis, such sources as obscure legal, church, census, and other demographic records, as well as folklore, films, female literature, transcripts of interviews, music, and evidence of informal community and interest-group networks, have all yielded new and valuable historical information on women. Although 23 percent of the articles in this bibliography are about countries other than the United States, they are not varied enough to determine whether a similar pattern of development can be found elsewhere. Clearly, these avant-garde American historians were borrowing advanced methodology in a variety of disciplines from other countries, especially France and England. The 1986 International Conference on Women's History in Amsterdam demonstrated both the intellectual borrowing that had taken place in the last two decades, and the remaining differences in national historiographies of women.[27]

Since it was influenced by the new social history *and* the Second Women's Movement, the third stage of U.S. women's history was not initially taken seriously by the predominantly white male historical establishment. Such men viewed such historical research as either marginal or too ideological and present-minded. In addition, they devalued the subject matter--e.g., female culture, female networks, sexuality, female socialization, and women's life cycle within the family--and therefore often discounted feminist contributions to research as being unscientific or "nonobjective" and hence less deserving of recognition for promotion or tenure. Until this third stage in the writing of U.S. women's history emerged, even historians of the family largely ignored women because they did not employ gender analysis.[28] And if one takes seriously the arrogant "ten commandments" for the writing of women's history that family historian Lawrence Stone proclaimed in the April 11, 1985, issue of the *New York Review of Books*, there are many establishment historians who still think that women should be written about only "in relation to men and children."[29]

In summary, third-stage women's history went beyond the male-defined interests and values of the early new social history by establishing gender as a fundamental category of analysis. Feminist historians--too numerous to mention by name here, and including many who conduct research on women in all areas of the world, not simply those in the United States--have begun to show the importance of women struggling to reconcile their roles in the public and private spheres. They have also begun to restore women in positive ways to the subfields of economic, urban, religious, and family history, in which they had been ignored (or removed altogether) by traditional patriarchal historians and considered only negatively or marginally by the second-stage prefeminist historians. Most important, some of these modern feminist historians took up the task of writing about class, racial, sexual, and other significant differences among women.

At first, the most striking aspect of this latest stage in U.S. women's history appeared to be the intersection of women's common experience over time with an improved understanding of the specific experiences of women in particular historical periods. Often centering on the life cycle of women, feminist historians have tried to reflect the totality of women's public and private lives. Three thematic areas of emphasis have emerged from their research. They can be summed up in the terms *family, functionalism*, and *feminism*. Initially, feminist historians successfully placed women as a gender category into family history. If anything, women's gendered roles within the family have been analyzed more extensively by these third-stage historians than any other aspect of female life. Second, such historians have exposed the traditional way in which women were accorded "functionalist treatment"--that is, the prescriptive view that female existence is largely circumscribed by roles within the patriarchal family structure.[30] Instead, they have redefined functionalism to mean the work of women inside and outside the home in relation to the predominant sexist and racist market and political economy. Third, they have attempted to trace the origins and development of several distinct types of historical feminism. Historical interpretations employing all three themes increasingly rely on some form of poststructural gender analysis.

*Trends in Third-Stage Feminist Scholarship*

Until the mid-1970s, most published works on U.S. women reflected a stable and homogeneous society--not one based on diverse and often dissatisfied marginal groups--except for those discussing certain working-class women located primarily in the eastern corridor.[31] Thus, despite the more sophisticated methodology, the new social history approach, and the left-of-center backgrounds of these third-stage scholars, great emphasis continued to be placed on the private activities of women within the larger constructs of the family, religion, community, and female networks inside and outside the home. Because they concentrated on the similarities among women across class, race, and ethnic lines to a much greater degree than their liberal or radical colleagues in other parts of the world, the initial scholarship by third-stage historians in the United States suspiciously resembled the 1950s consensus scholarship, which the liberal and radical historians of women's history had originally repudiated. The bulk of the earliest historical writings of third-stage feminists paint a rather positive, homogeneous picture of U.S. women. To summarize, U.S. history looks more humane, more progressive, and more concerned about social justice when women are integrated into it. Yet at the same time, these writings also promoted the ideas of American exceptionalism, patriotism, and unending progress based on traditional middle-class, liberal notions about political and legal individualism. (It is not clear from the entries in this bibliography whether the same generalizations hold true with regard to the historical writings about women in other parts of the world where the influence of socialism in intellectual and political circles has been much greater since World War II than in the United States. This has meant that class, race, and comparative analysis appears consistently stronger in the writings of non-U.S. historians of women.)

How did this happen? These first histories by third-stage feminist historians were largely the result of the relatively easy access to, and abundance of, sources on white, northeastern, middle- and working-class women. Thus, despite its methodological and often theoretical sophistication drawn from postwar European and English intellectual developments, the new social history in the United States did not initially consist of comparative, cross-national studies or concentrate on class diversity that existed among American women of the past and present. It was also insufficiently attentive to regionalism (until the last half of the 1980s, for example, western women in the United States remained the orphans of women's history), to racial or ethnic diversity, and to conflict between different socioeconomic classes of women, while placing too much stress on women as depositories of sexuality, on motherhood, and on their fulfillment primarily in a heterosexual family setting rather than on their contributions to other aspects of private life and to public life outside the workforce. Women's lives in nonnuclear families--either alone as single mothers, with other single or never-married women, or in lesbian relationships--was also largely ignored until the mid-1970s. Until then many of the new social history theories seldom progressed beyond traditional economic analytical categories or simplistic cultural notions about the "eternal feminine."

Nonetheless, the enormous outpouring of scholarship that has taken place in the field of U.S. women's history in the last twenty years not only has become more diverse in content, as this collection of articles from the 1980s clearly indicates, but it has also contributed to the acceptance of such research in women's history by tenure committees and the integration of material on women into survey and other classes. Much remains to be done, however. Although feminist scholarship has dramatically altered two subfields within the discipline of history--the new social history and the new legal history--women continue to be studied and taught primarily as a separate group rather than integrated into all historical fields.

Although the discipline of history (and the humanities in general) is far from being transformed by the new social history with its emphasis on women and minorities, both have already come under attack from neoconservatives. Recent critics ranging from such politicos as President George Bush and William Bennett, former head of the Department of Education and former U.S. drug "czar," to intellectuals of some stature such as Allan Bloom, Gertrude Himmelfarb, and Theodore Hamerow, and most recently to lightweight thinkers such as Dinesh D'Souza and Camille Paglia, fear that this new scholarship, in particular, has already undermined the patriarchal underpinnings of conventional history and of Western culture itself.[32]

The attack on the diversity and pluralism in American academe (called "political correctness") by such neoconservatives reached a fever pitch in the United States in the late 1980s and early 1990s. Criticism of "political correctness" has taken on the added legitimacy of "patriotic correctness" in the wake of the Gulf War. The critics of "political correctness" offer a variety of contradictory depictions of intellectual life at American institutions of higher education because they have wrapped themselves in the mantle of the "privilege" (rather than "right") of free speech, patriotism, and praise for great white Western scholarship. Thus, according to Bennett, universities in the United States are dominated by "a herd of independent minds" all moving in the same direction and by a "balkanized" view of society that has no respect for the marketplace or ideas and breeds ethnic and racial violence because of the supposed overemphasis on multiculturalism, diversity, and deconstructionism. The fact that most liberal/radical professors from the 1960s would not know how to deconstruct a binary opposition if their livelihood depended on it, and that it is the conservative groups on most American campuses who are actively organizing and dominating the intellectual and political discourse in the early 1990s, simply is lost is this "hysteria over 'political correctness'" now raging in the United States. So the ultimate irony of the neoconservative position is that it has coopted the long-standing liberal one in the United States that the price for entry into mainstream American society is assimilation based on white, male standards.

There is still another irony associated with the putative threat that the new social history and multifaceted humanities programs, advocating the right of the average person to be heard and understood, represent to American neoconservatives in the last decade of the twentieth century. The new social history in particular initially produced some of the most unreadable books and articles, hence limiting its influence. The same is equally, if not more, true of recent scholarship based on semiotics and deconstruction. Without intelligibly written women's history, the better utilization of sources counts for little in educating women (and the general public) about our past, present, and future. Currently, modern feminist historians are attempting to develop an analytical narrative style of historical writing that can be readily understood despite the complexity of the methodology or theoretical construct employed.[33]

Such analytical narration must explain female intentionality and intersubjectivity in other than the psychological terminology of deviance or exclusionary terms about the politics of differences, and portray women not only in groups but also as important individuals who are *inside* rather than *outside* the history of their particular time periods. The best analytical narrative, therefore, recovers women's intentionality (female agency within patriarchal structures) so as to restore the premise of women's subjectivity (allowing the female subject to interpret her own actions and interactions so as to be "realized as subject both to herself and in history").[34] If the intentionality and intersubjectivity of women were analyzed and they were restored to their historical and individual agency, figures such as Pocahontas, Anne Hutchinson, Elizabeth Freeman, Abigail Adams, Maria Stewart, Susan B. Anthony, Harriet Tubman, Mary McLeod Bethune, Eleanor Roosevelt, and Fannie Lou Hamer would become integral to U.S. history classes instead of the oddities they remain. Successfully employed, analytical narratives would rescue the study of "notable" or exceptional women from the suspect categories of compensatory, "classist," or liberal individualist history. Unfortunately, the standard type of biographical article by historians making up the 4 percent of the periodical literature for the decade of the 1980s was not particularly sophisticated from a methodological or analytic point of view.
Whether this resistance to analytical narration in historical biography will continue during the 1990s remains to be seen.

Other trends in this third stage of historiography about women have been revealed by previous surveys of articles and books written in the United States and abroad. For example, after reviewing U.S. and European periodical and monographic literature, in addition to Ph.D. dissertations, from 1975 to 1980, Hilda L. Smith found a disturbing concentration on "women's role in the family, the various stages in their life cycles (usually biologically determined), and their relationships among themselves rather than those with public institutions in general or men in particular (except in the family)." Smith saw the same trend continuing in periodical literature from 1982 to 1986 and concluded that women's history is in danger of becoming "merely a branch of social history," to the neglect of women's intellectual, political, or other individual achievements.[35] The relatively large number of articles published in the 1980s on women and politics (7 percent) in the United States and other nations would seem to indicate that this particular trend did not continue unabated.

Other historians have suggested that women's history, in part because of its current methodological sophistication and growing number of practitioners and publications, is well on its way to becoming an *alternative to*, rather than merely a subfield of, the discipline. While this remains to be seen, the periodical literature of the past decade clearly indicates that *women's history is the fastest-growing historical subfield in the United States.*

Historians, influenced by the politics of reform movements of the 1960s in the United States, began to apply more positive (and more complicated) interpretations and generalizations in studying women's private and public lives, compared to the standard views of U.S. women that prevailed under patriarchal history twenty years ago. Generally speaking, the result by the first half of the 1970s was a historiography that stressed the commonality of subordinate and oppressive female experiences across class and race lines. The best examples of this type of women's history did this *without* minimizing the differences between classes of women and women of color. As the new history matured, it also began to stress how women were distinguished from men by socialized gender characteristics in almost every aspect of their private and public existence.[36] Gender analysis, in other words, became a major contribution of women's history to all other historical subfields, including social, economic, political, and intellectual history *before* the younger generation of poststructuralist historians of women "discovered" it at the end of the 1980s. By that time women's history was already explaining common gender experiences and identities among American women without ignoring obvious class and race diversity. During that same decade, feminist activists in the U.S. had also succeeded in projecting some modicum of common female identity for political purposes, and in asserting themselves in various walks of public and private life.

At this crucial juncture, poststructural analysis and deconstructionist methodology entered the American academic world and began to assert just the opposite by denying commonalities among women of the past and present and by questioning whether there will be any distinctive female identity in the future. Some poststructural (gender) historians, for example, "acknowledge, celebrate and support the instigation of all differences that divide and constitute both men and women" to the point that they no longer identify their work as being *about women.*

In this sense, deconstruction represents an attack on radical political feminism in the United States, as well as on the feminist historical interpretations of the last twenty years that stressed the common personal and/or public experiences of women. For deconstructionists, material experiences became abstract representations drawn from textual analysis; personal identities and agency became subjects constructed exclusively by nonmaterial discourses; and flesh-and-blood women became social constructs--with no "natural" or physiological context except as a set of symbolic meanings constructing sexual difference. Feminist politics, according to the poststructuralists, no longer could be used to alleviate conditions of oppression because "identity is not an objectively determined sense of self defined by needs" any more than "politics is . . . the collective coming to consciousness of similarly situated individual subjects."[37]

If experience could not be based on relatively unchanging socioeconomic categories or on the diversity and variability of common gender *identities*, then there could be no materially based history from which contemporary feminist activists could draw sustenance and advice for opposing and criticizing the remaining areas of oppression experienced by women in the United States and other countries. Thus, instead of remaining simply another useful methodological innovation for studying women's history and making that history more relevant to radical political feminism, poststructuralism has become a potentially politically paralyzing and intellectually irrelevant exercise for endlessly analyzing myriad representations of cultural forms and discourses.

Under the influence of poststructuralism, women's history in the late 1980s became more and more removed from the political and legal arena in which the battle for rights of women and minorities was being waged. In the process such history has inadvertently contributed to the rationalization of the violent and abusive portrayals of women now so common in various forms of popular culture in the United States, because poststructural theories lead to a totally relativistic view of the world in which there are no centers of power, and no societal harms that cannot be deconstructed on paper. Reality, according to poststructuralists, consists of only decentered, genderless individuals whose very real and objective material problems and experiential contact with oppression can be reduced to linguistic exercises through deconstructing binary oppositions.

Yet difference and dominance go hand in hand in the sense that both continue to be defined in America and other societies by male criteria. Simply because gender differences can be variously interpreted by researchers so that they are found to be "historically and culturally specific," and because they are social rather than biological, does not mean that they are also benign, neutral, or noncategorical.[38] To the contrary, their very historical and cultural diversity often masks their oppressive commonality--namely, that gender is, in fact, about the power of men over women. Simone de Beauvoir captured the historical significance of this enduring patriarchal form of female oppression when she proclaimed in 1949: "Throughout history [women] have always been subordinated to men, and hence their dependency is not the result of a historical event or a social change--it was not something that occurred."[39]

Since deconstruction can also lead to an antiessentialist particularism and political paralysis, it should be viewed primarily as a methodological tool for historical research--nothing more and nothing less. Even with this caveat, some women of color are justifiably concerned that a "race for theory" now exists among academic humanists in the United States, based largely on French poststructural hypotheses that radical feminists and feminists of color have come to consider dangerous.[40] Their concern about deconstruction is twofold: first, they suspect that deconstruction may become the hegemonic practice in elite academic circles, thereby displacing the collective understanding of racism that women of color have struggled to obtain by using African or rationalist modes of analysis; and second, they suspect that feminists who use deconstructionist techniques may be unintentionally racist because deconstruction prompts them to suggest that race, like gender, is a discursively constructed binarism. Gerda Lerner and Linda Gordon have both suggested much more constructive approaches.

For example, Lerner has reconceptualized a "holistic" history--one that would understand "interrelated aspects of the system of patriarchal dominance" rather than continuing "to regard class, race and gender dominance as separate, though intersecting and overlapping systems."[41] Linda Gordon has described this as tension between writing history with the "mythic power" to inspire moral and political action and writing accurate history which, even if it cannot contain the absolute truth in the way "grand" patriarchal history purported to, will at least point out the "objective lies" from the past about women's public and private lives. "There may be no objective canon of historiography," according to Gordon, "but there are degrees of accuracy; there are better and worse pieces of history. The challenge is precisely to maintain this tension between accuracy and [the] mythic power [of history]." To the degree that historians of women exclusively emphasize one or the other, their writings will not serve the cause of political and legal reform on behalf of women in the United States and abroad. In particular, Gordon has noted that she fears the current emphasis among historians of women on "'difference' is becoming a substitute, an accommodating affable, and even lazy substitute, for opposition."[42]

Nonetheless, it is becoming increasingly common among poststructural and socialist feminists to deny both categories of "woman" and "women" because they represent a false or fictive "universalization of sex class that does not focus on specificity and only recognizes the homogeneity of women." This criticism is almost as simplistic as were the early patriarchal views of women. While it is desirable to avoid imposing a "false sense of commonality" on different groups of women in specific time periods, it is equally desirable to recognize that women are perceived in all societies as "an always-already constituted group" because of the specific prevailing "discourse of engendered sex 'difference,'" which presumes that sex and gender are the same thing. Rather than deny any "specific unity" among women, therefore, we should try to identify it historically along with a description of their *relevant* subjective and objective differences. In other words, as Zillah Eisenstein has noted, "the tension between diversity and unity" must become the focus--not one extreme or the other.[43]

In summary, under the influence of the Second Women's Movement, historians of women first began challenging patriarchal stereotypes of women in the early 1970s and then interpreted a set of common female experiences to explain how women sought to coordinate their private lives with their public ones. This synthesis is now being challenged by poststructural histories, some of which focus so much on the existence of multiple "masculinities" that they are "implicitly denying the existence of patriarchy" and espousing theories about the predominance of differences among women in which "the voice of gender risks being lost entirely." In other words, deconstructionist techniques that focus increasingly on "male sensitivity and male persecution" downplay male privilege and, hence, not only depoliticize the use of the word *gender*, but also seem to deny that feminism can or should be a coherent philosophy or ideology in the writing of women's history.[44]

A 1990 exchange between Linda Gordon and Joan Wallach Scott encapsulated the debate over the meaning of feminism between poststructural and other theoreticians of women's history in the United States. In summary, their disagreement centered on whether linguistic/psychoanalytical analysis as practiced by deconstructionists is the best way to practice feminist history. This approach privileges the "text"--that the social construction of reality (which appears in these "texts"--which can be more than just written words) is the only reality. Epistemology and linguistics, then, are the keys to analyzing power relationships. A man beats his wife: What constitutes "reality" in this situation--is there anything separate from the interpretation/construction of that event? For those who subscribe to deconstruction, the answer is no. The question for those who do not subscribe to deconstruction is whether or not this framework addresses fully the consequences of such power relationships.

Gordon charged that such analysis dismissed the "reality" which is separate from constructions. Since linguistic analysis cannot take place without words, this emphasis eliminates the possibility of including marginalized groups which did/do not produce written texts running counter to the feminist commitment to social change and inclusive analysis. By highlighting the text alone, Gordon argues that a crucial aspect of power relationships is ignored, an aspect that has "real" consequences in the world, and particularly for women. This leads to the kind of pluralism that whitewashes power differentials and makes gender equal to "difference in itself."

For her part, Scott attacked what she perceived as Gordon's failure to sufficiently probe the texts which formed the basis of her book *Heroes of Their Own Lives: The Politics and History of Family Violence*, primarily by remaining wedded to the theory of social control. This theory, according to Scott, leaves Gordon in the land of dualism and simple oppositions and an overly simple notion of agency of women who decided to take advantage of the services of their child-saving agencies in Boston from the 1880s through the 1960s. Scott argued that Gordon did not analyze the texts produced by the social workers; after all, the social workers, not the clients, produced the texts, making them dubious sources for information about the clients' experiences. And there is no reality separate from the social construction of experience, no "'real family oppressions' experienced outside the labels."[45]

Both Gordon and Scott end up charging that the other is claiming superiority for her own theoretical approach (and by implication for her "own" brand of feminism). Nonetheless, their debate over each other's work underscores the vitality of theory for women's history, as do the 5 percent of theoretical articles in this compilation.

Unfortunately, a less sophisticated and constructive debate has been initiated by younger poststructural historians for whom feminism, and even the future of women's history, has little relevance. These poststructural historians claim that women's history has lost its identity and go so far as to predict that women's history is about to "dissolve." Apparently, their deliberate depoliticization of power through representations of women's history as totally diffuse and decentered has created their own private identity crisis and sense of lack of agency that they now attribute to the subfield of women's history as a whole. Women's history will "dissolve" only when it has nothing to offer contemporary feminism. Therefore, in addition to its apoliticalness, if not actually neoconservativism, the other possible danger poststructuralism constitutes for women's history circles is that it is destabilizing this subfield by insisting on its demise. These arguments by postfeminists are not unlike those by neoconservatives who have tried to undermine all of post-World War II revisionist history with theories about posthistory or the death of history now that the Cold War is over.[46]

Obviously, women's history in the United States (and other countries) is alive and well, despite the extremes to which some want to carry postfeminist and poststructural arguments as the world enters a post-Cold War era and the twenty-first century.

# Notes

I want to thank Christie Farnham, Gayle Fischer, and Georg'ann Cattelona for reading earlier versions of this essay.

1. Ann Lane, ed., *Mary Ritter Beard: A Source Book* (Boston: Northeastern University Press, 1988; reprint of 1977 Schocken Books edition), pp. 204-205, citing Beard's 56-page syllabus published by the American Association of University Women in 1934, entitled "A Changing Political Economy as It Affects Women."

2. The terms *resurrection*, *contribution*, *compensatory*, and *her-story* have all been used to describe what this essay refers to as remedial history. See Mari Jo Buhle, Ann G. Gordon, and Nancy Schrom, "Women in American Society: An Historical Contribution," *Radical America* 5, no. 4 (July-August 1971): 3-66; Berenice A. Carroll, ed., *Liberating Women's History: Theoretical and Critical Essays* (Urbana: University of Illinois Press, 1976), pp. 75-92; Linda Gordon et al., "Historical Phallacies: Sexism in American Historical Writing," ibid., pp. 55-74; and Joan Wallach Scott, "Women in History: The Modern Period," *Past and Present* 101 (November 1983): 141-157 (Virginia Woolf quotation at 141). In this essay Scott uses the term *conventional history* to refer to patriarchal history. For a discussion of the economic, cultural, and political significance of the doctrine of separate spheres, see Barbara Welter, "The Cult of True Womanhood: 1820-1860," *American Quarterly* 18 (Summer 1966): 151-174; Linda K. Kerber and Jane De Hart Mathews, eds., *Women's America: Refocusing the Past* (New York: Oxford University Press, 1982), pp. 3-22; Anne Firor Scott, "On Seeing and Not Seeing: A Case of Historical Invisibility," *Journal of American History* 71 (June 1984): 7-21; and Linda Kerber, "Separate Spheres, Female Worlds, Woman's Place: The Rhetoric of Women's History," *Journal of American History* 75 (June 1988): 9-39.

3. Carroll Smith-Rosenberg, "The Female World of Love and Ritual: Relations between Women in Nineteenth Century America," *Signs* 1 (Autumn 1975): 1-29. With this article Smith-Rosenberg set in motion a debate over women's erotic lives with each other that is still in progress, despite all attempts to downplay the importance of women's socially constructed and distinctive culture within what

remains the reality of a private female sphere. See Kerber, "Separate Spheres,"
pp. 14-17, 37-39.

4. Doris Faber, *The Life of Lorena Hickok: E.R.'s Friend* (New York: William
Morrow, 1980). *Washington Post*, October 23, 1979, p. C1; *New York Times
Book Review*, February 17, 1980, pp. 3, 25. One of the most even-handed reviews
of this controversial book was by Christopher Lehmann-Haupt in *Books of the
Times* 3, no. 3 (March 1980): 117-119. Historians Joseph P. Lash and Arthur M.
Schlesinger, Jr., have consistently contributed to this misleadingly mainstream
view of Eleanor Roosevelt. Ironically, both Lash and Schlesinger belatedly and
misleadingly tried to employ the theories of Smith-Rosenberg about nonphysical,
homosocial bonding among nineteenth-century women to explain Roosevelt's
extraordinarily close and affectionate relationships with other women. See
*Washington Post* citation in this footnote and Lasch, *Eleanor Roosevelt and Her
Friends* (New York: Doubleday, 1982), pp. xii, xiii, 30, 143-291; reviewed, *New
York Times Book Review*, June 13, 1982, pp. 11, 25, 28. For criticisms of Lasch's
and Schlesinger's self-appointed roles as guardians of Eleanor Roosevelt's
reputation and image by other scholars, see *Los Angeles Times*, May 8, 1984, and
the collection of revisionist essays about Eleanor Roosevelt edited by Joan
Hoff-Wilson and Marjorie Lightman, *Without Precedent: The Life and Career of
Eleanor Roosevelt* (Bloomington: Indiana University Press, 1984).

5. Fortunately, Blanche Wiesen Cook's forthcoming biography *The Many Lives
of Eleanor Roosevelt* should do much to correct this neglect and misrepresentation.

6. Janice G. Raymond, *Passion for Friends: Toward a Philosophy of Female
Affection* (Boston: Beacon, 1986).

7. Gerda Lerner, "Where Biographers Fear to Tread," *Women's Review of
Books*, September 1987, p. 12.

8. Susan Stanford Friedman, *Psyche Reborn: The Emergence of H.D.*
(Bloomington: Indiana University Press, 1982); and Janice S. Robinson, *The Life
and Work of an American Poet* (New York: Houghton Mifflin, 1982). It was not
surprising to find Friedman's book, which stressed Hilda Doolittle's emotionally
intense relationships with women, reviewed or summarized in women's
publications, and Robinson's work, which emphasized her relationships with men,
given attention by mainstream publications such as the *New York Times*. See *Ms.*,
February 1982, pp. 65-66, 79; and *New York Times Book Review*, February 14,
1982, pp. 3, 26.

9. For documentation on Charles Adams's destruction of his grandmother's
papers, see L. H. Butterfield, ed., *Adams Family Correspondence* (Cambridge:
Harvard University Press, 1963), vol. 1, p. xxvii, fn. 13. Mary Beth Norton was
one of the first U.S. historians to call attention to the neglect or destruction of
women's papers when she recounted the extraordinary life of Sarah Haggar
Wheaton Osborn (1714-1796), who apparently "wrote more than fifty volumes of
diaries and commentaries, each ranging from 100 to 300 pages in length," of
which only one slim published volume remains. See "'My Resting Reaping
Times': Sarah Osborn's Defense of Her 'Unfeminine' Activities," *Signs* 2, no. 2
(Winter 1976): 515-529.

10. Herman Mann, *The Female Review of Memoirs of an American Young Lady Whose Life and Character Are Peculiarly Distinguished--Being a Continental Soldier for Nearly Three Years in the Late American War during Which Time She Performed the Duties of Every Department into Which She Was Called with Punctual Exactness, Fidelity and Honor, and Preserved Her Chastity Inviolate by the Most Artful Concealment of Her Sex* (Dedham, Mass.: printed by Nathaniel and Benjamin Heaton for the author, 1797).

11. Herman Mann, *The Female Review: Life of Deborah Sampson, the Female Soldier in the War of the Revolution*, with an introduction and notes by John Adams Vinton (Boston: J. K. Wiggin and W. P. Lunt, 1866).

12. Andrea Hinding, ed., *Women's History Sources Survey* (New York: R. R. Bowker, 1979), 2 vols.; idem, paper delivered at 1984 Society of American Archivists annual meeting.

13. This was at the 1988 NEH Conference on Graduate Training in U.S. Women's History at Wingspread, attended by 70 scholars representing 60 public and private institutions.

14. Elizabeth H. Pleck, "Women's History: Gender as a Category," in James B. Gardner and George Rollie Adams, eds., *Ordinary People and Everyday Life* (Nashville: American Association for State and Local History, 1983), p. 54.

15. The new social history directly challenged traditional patriarchal history by concerning itself with the affairs of ordinary people, and private rather than public matters, conceptualizing such historical phenomena as family relationships, fertility, and sexuality in terms of micro interpersonal power and macro social processes. But initially the new social history in the form of family history ignored women as a separate social category. For example, early scholarship in family history most frequently dealt with categories such as 'household,' 'single parents,' 'children,' 'adolescents,' and 'the aged,' without recognizing that each of these is fundamentally divided by sex. "The result [was] history that either ignore[d] women or [gave] the false impression that female and male experiences with the primary institution of the family were the same." See Nancy F. Cott and Elizabeth H. Pleck, *A Heritage of Her Own: Toward a New Social History of American History* (New York: Simon and Schuster, 1979), pp. 16, 17 (quotation). See also Ellen Ross, "Women and Family," *Feminist Studies* 5 (1979): 182 (quotation).

16. Ellen Carol DuBois et al., *Feminist Scholarship: Kindling in the Groves of Academe* (Urbana: University of Illinois Press, 1985), pp. 20-24.

17. Gayle Rubin, "The Traffic in Women," in *Toward an Anthropology of Women*, ed. Rayna Rapp Reiter (New York: Monthly Review Press, 1975), pp. 157-210, quote from pp. 179-180. Also see Virginia Sapiro, *Women in American Society: An Introduction to Women's Studies* (Palo Alto, Calif.: Mayfield Publishing Company, 1986), pp. 78-82, passim; and *Hunter College Women's Studies Collective, Women's Realities, Women's Choices: An Introduction to Women's Studies* (New York: Oxford University Press, 1983), pp. 173-180, passim.

18. Annette K. Baxter and Louise L. Stevenson, eds., *Women's History: Selected Reading Lists and Course Outlines from American Colleges and*

*Universities* (New York: Marcus Wiener, 1987), p. 3 (quotation). A continuation of this trend was reflected in the syllabi exchanged at the 1988 Conference on Graduate Training in U.S. Women's History. See note 13 above.

19. For example, eleven of the twenty-two women historians who were listed in the first edition of *Notable American Women* were also active participants in the First Women's Movement. See Kathryn Kish Sklar, "American Female Historians in Context, 1770-1930," *Feminist Studies* 3 (1975): 173. Classic examples of activists as amateur historians are Elizabeth Cady Stanton, Mathilda J. Gage, and Susan B. Anthony, eds., *The History of Woman Suffrage*, 6 vols. (Rochester, N.Y.: Charles Mann, 1886); and Carrie Chapman Catt, *Woman Suffrage and Politics: The Inner Story of the Suffrage Movement* (New York: Scribners, 1926).

20. Alice Morse Earle, *Home Life in Colonial Days* (New York: Macmillan, 1898); idem, *Colonial Dames and Good Wives* (New York: Frederick Unger, 1962; reprint of original 1895 edition). Before Earle, the typical anecdotal descriptions of women could be found in Alexander Garden, *Anecdotes of the American Revolution* (Charleston, S.C.: A. E. Miller, 1828), and Elizabeth F. Ellet, *The Women of the American Revolution*, 3 vols. (New York: Charles Scribner, 1853-54).

21. Edith Abbott, *Women in Industry; A Study in American Economic History* (New York: Appleton, 1910); Mary Ritter Beard, *Woman's Work in Municipalities* (New York: National Municipal League Series, 1915); idem, *On Understanding Women* (New York: Longman's, Greene, 1931); idem, *America through Women's Eyes* (New York: Macmillan, 1933); idem and Martha Bensley Bruere, eds., *Laughing Their Way: Women's Humor in America* (New York: Macmillan, 1934); idem, *Woman as Force in History: A Study in Traditions and Realities* (New York: Macmillan, 1946); Mary Sumner Benson, *Women in Eighteenth-Century America: A Study of Opinion and Social Usage* (New York: Columbia University Press, 1935); Elisabeth Williams (Anthony) Dexter, *Colonial Women of Affairs: A Study of Women in Business and the Professions in American before 1776* (Boston: Houghton Mifflin, 1924); idem, *Career Women of America, 1776-1840* (New York: Houghton Mifflin, 1950); Abbie Graham, *Ladies in Revolt* (New York: Woman's Press, 1934); Richard Morris, *Studies in the History of American Law with Special Reference to the Seventeenth and Eighteenth Centuries* (New York: Columbia University Press, 1930), pp. 126-200; Julia Cherry Spruill, *Women's Life and Work in the Southern Colonies* (Chapel Hill: University of North Carolina Press, 1928).

22. Mildred Adams, *The Right to Be People* (Philadelphia: Lippincott, 1967); Catherine Lyle Cleverdon, *The Woman Suffrage Movement in Canada* (Toronto: University of Toronto Press, 1950); Olivia E. Coolidge, *Edith Wharton, 1862-1937* (New York: Scribner, 1964); idem, *Women's Rights: The Suffrage Movement in America, 1848-1920* (New York: Dutton, 1966); Emily Taft Douglas, *Remember the Ladies: The Story of Great Women Who Helped Shape America* (New York: Putman, 1966); idem, *Margaret Sanger: Pioneer of the Future* (New York: Holt, Rinehart and Winston, 1969); Eleanor Flexner, *Century of Struggle: The Woman's Rights Movement in the United States* (New York:

Atheneum, 1968); idem, *Mary Wollstonecraft: A Biography* (New York: Coward, McCann and Geoghegan, 1972); Roger Fulford, *Votes for Women: The Story of a Struggle* (London: Faber and Faber, 1957); Alan Pendleton Grimes, *The Puritan Ethic and Woman Suffrage* (New York: Oxford University Press, 1967).

23. Anne Scott, *Making the Invisible Woman Visible* (Urbana: University of Illinois Press, 1984), p. 152; Carol Bacchi, "First Wave Feminism: History's Judgment," unpublished paper, 1980, p. 6.

24. Carl Degler, *At Odds: Women and the Family in America from the Revolution to the Present* (New York: Oxford University Press, 1980); idem, "What Ought to Be and What Was: Women's Sexuality in the Nineteenth Century," *American Historical Review* 79 (December 1974): 1479-90; idem, *Is There a History of Women?* (Oxford: Clarendon Press, 1974); David M. Kennedy, *Birth Control in America: The Career of Margaret Sanger* (New Haven, Conn.: Yale University Press, 1970); Aileen S. Kraditor, *The Ideas of the Woman Suffrage Movement, 1890-1920* (New York: Columbia University Press, 1965); idem, ed., *Up from the Pedestal: Selected Writings in the History of American Feminism* (Chicago: Quadrangle Books, 1968); Christopher Lasch, *The New Radicalism in America, 1889-1963* (New York: Knopf, 1965); idem, ed., *The Social Thought of Jane Addams* (Indianapolis: Bobbs-Merrill, 1965); idem, *Haven in a Heartless World: The Family Besieged* (New York: Basic Books, 1977); William L. O'Neill, *Everyone Was Brave: The Rise and Fall of Feminism in America* (Chicago: Quadrangle Press, 1969); idem, ed., *The Woman Movement: Feminism in the United States and England* (Chicago: Quadrangle Press, 1971); David Morris Potter, *History and American Society: Essays of David M. Potter*, ed. Don E. Fehrenbacher (New York: Oxford University Press, 1973); Robert Edgar Riegel, *American Feminists* (Lawrence: University of Kansas Press, 1963); Anne Firor Scott, *The Southern Lady: From Pedestal to Politics, 1830-1930* (Chicago: University of Chicago Press, 1970); idem, ed., *What Is Happening to American Women* (Atlanta: Southern Newspaper Publishers Association Foundation, 1970); idem, *Women in American Life: Selected Readings* (Boston: Houghton-Mifflin, 1970); idem, *The American Woman: Who Was She?* (Englewood Cliffs, N.J.: Prentice Hall, 1971); idem and Andrew M. Scott, *One Half the People: The Fight for Woman Suffrage* (Philadelphia: Lippincott, 1975); idem, *Women and Men: Changing Roles, Relationships, and Perceptions--Report of a Workshop*, ed. Libby A. Caster and Anne F. Scott with Wendy Martyna (Palo Alto, Calif.: Aspen Institute for Humanistic Studies, 1977); idem, *Making the Invisible Woman Visible*; Andrew Sinclair, *The Better Half: The Emancipation of the American Woman* (New York: Harper and Row, 1965); Page Smith, *Daughters of the Promised Land* (Boston: Little, Brown, 1970); and Welter, "The Cult of True Womanhood."

25. Kerber, "Separate Spheres," pp. 11-14.

26. Two of the few second-stage historians to make the shift to third-stage methodology and interpretations were Anne Firor Scott and Gerda Lerner. For example, in her collection of essays *Making the Invisible Woman Visible* (1984), Scott recounts the transition she made from prefeminist to feminist historical

writing. The essays and lectures in her book contribute not only to our understanding of one woman's personal and professional odyssey but also to the general field of white women's history during a time when the new social history collided so productively with the study of the "other half" of the American population. In particular, Anne Scott has demonstrated in her own life and work that "the historian who calls attention to something hitherto overlooked . . . teaches others to have a broader vision of the past." Her unending (and highly successful) campaign to make white southern women not only visible but also integrated and important components of U.S. history laid solid groundwork for others who would follow. She did not, however, account for race or class differences among southern women, as she herself admitted in 1984. See Scott, "On Seeing and Not Seeing," p. 7. Scott has recently extended her research to include African American women. See "Most Invisible of All: Black Women's Voluntary Associations," *Journal of Southern History* 56 (February 1990): 3-22.

Even more impressive is the first volume of Lerner's work *Women and History: The Creation of Patriarchy* (New York: Oxford University Press, 1986), because she does not ignore class or race. Picking up where Simone de Beauvoir left off, this is an ambitious theoretical and multidisciplinary effort in which Lerner argues that male dominance over women is the product of historical development and, therefore, is not "natural" or immutable. Just as particular historical processes created patriarchy, so too particular historical events can end it. Lerner also argues that the first forms of slavery were based on gender, not class. Lerner not only has transcended the limitations of the second-stage, prefeminist historians, but has also overcome the limitations of Marxist theory that influenced her early work. Writing in her forthcoming second volume of *Women and History* about a "holistic history" of women and men that would illuminate "how the patriarchal system organizes and secures the cooperation of women without which it cannot exist," Lerner is attempting to reconceptualize history through understanding of the "interrelated aspects of the system of patriarchal dominance" rather than continuing "to regard class, race and gender dominance as separate, though intersecting and overlapping systems." See Lerner, "Placing Women in History: A Theoretical Framework," unpublished 1988 paper.

27. Arina Angerman et al., eds., *Current Issues in Women's History* (London: Routledge, 1989), pp. 1-20.

28. Cott and Pleck, *A Heritage of Her Own*, p. 17. See also notes 15 and 16 above.

29. *New York Review of Books*, April 11, 1985, p. 21. For a rejoinder to Stone's remarks, see Joan Scott, letter to editor, *New York Review of Books*, May 30, 1985, pp. 52-53.

30. Susan Moller Okin, *Women in Western Political Thought* (Princeton, N.J.: Princeton University Press, 1979), pp. 10-11; Judith A. Baer, *The Chains of Protection: The Judicial Response to Women's Labor Legislation* (Westport, Conn.: Greenwood Press, 1978), pp. 168-169, 180-181, 216-217; Jo Freeman, "Women and Public Policy: An Overview," in Ellen Boneparth, ed., *Women, Power and Policy* (Elinsford, N.Y.: Pergamon Press, 1982), pp. 49, 62-65.

31. For an exaggerated summary of these early characteristics of third-stage feminist history, which does not recognize the diversity that began to appear by the 1970s, see Nancy A. Hewitt, "Beyond the Search for Sisterhood: American Women's History in the 1980s," *Social History* 10, no. 3 (1986): 299-321; and Louise M. Newman, "Critical Theory and the History of Women: What's at Stake in Deconstructing Women's History," *Journal Of Women's History* 2, no. 3 (Winter 1991): 58-68.

32. Allan David Bloom, *The Closing of the American Mind: How Higher Education Has Failed Democracy and Impoverished the Souls of Today's Students* (New York: Simon and Schuster, 1987); Gertrude Himmelfarb, *The New History and the Old* (Cambridge: Belknap Press of Harvard University Press, 1987); and Theodore S. Hamerow, *Reflections on History and Historians* (Madison: University of Wisconsin Press, 1987); idem, "Decline of the Historical Profession," *OAH Newsletter* (November 1987); Dinesh D'Souza, *Illiberal Education: The Politics of Race and Sex on Campus* (New York: Free Press/Macmillan, 1991); and Camille Paglia, "Ninnies, Pedants, Tyrants and Other Academics," *New York Times Book Review*, May 5, 1991, pp. 1, 29. For a critique of this conservative school of historical thought and of the conservative attack on what it perceives to be liberal or radical political correctness in higher education, see Carl N. Degler, "Is the New Social History Threatening Clio?" *OAH Newsletter* 16, no. 3 (August 1988): 4-5; Linda Kerber, American Studies Association Keynote Address, October 1988; and Michael Kinsley, "Hysteria over Political Correctness," *New York Times*, May 3, 1991, p. A25.

33. One of the best examples of feminist analytical narrative can be found in Kathleen Barry, *Susan B. Anthony: A Biography of a Singular Feminist* (New York: New York University Press, 1988).

34. Kathleen Barry, "The New Historical Syntheses: Woman's Biography," *Journal of Women's History* 1, no. 3 (Winter 1990): 75-76.

35. Hilda L. Smith, "Female Bonds and the Family: Recent Directions in Women's History," in Paula Treichler, Cheris Kramarae, and Beth Stafford, eds., *For Alma Mater: Theory and Practice in Feminist Scholarship* (Urbana: University of Illinois Press, 1985), pp. 272-291; idem, "Female Bonds and the Family: Continuing Doubts," unpublished paper, portions of which appeared in the Organization of American Historians *Newsletter*, February 1987, pp. 13-14 (quotations are on p. 13). Joan W. Scott also noted a similar trend in "Women in History: The Modern Period," pp. 151-153.

36. Lisa Vogel, "Telling Tales: Historians of Our Own Lives," *Journal Of Women's History* 2, no. 3 (Winter 1991): 89-101. Vogel denies the "triumphalist" interpretation of the poststructural historians of women who insist that the feminist stage of women's history in the 1970s suffered from terminal "methodological and theoretical errors." Instead, she describes this early women's history as grounded in the politics of the Second Women's Movement and, therefore, concludes that its practitioners "did not essentialize women and ignore difference. They did not produce a feminism that exalted women's sphere and culture. And they did not operate within a stolidly simpleminded epistemology" (p. 92). Clare Dalton,

"Where We Stand: Observations on the Situation of Feminist Legal Thought," *Berkeley Women's Law Journal* 3 (1987-1988): 9.

37. Joan Scott, *Gender and the Politics of History* (New York: Columbia University Press, 1988), pp. 2, 11.

38. Jeffrey Weeks, "Questions of Identity," in *The Cultural Construction of Sexuality*, ed. Pat Caplan (London: Tavistock, 1987), p. 31. See also Kathleen Barry, "Deconstructing Deconstruction (or, Whatever Happened to Feminist Studies?), *Ms.: The World of Women* (January/February 1991): 83-85. Barry notes that the politics of differences almost always result in the exclusion rather than inclusion of marginal groups by making them the "other."

39. Simone de Beauvoir, *The Second Sex* (New York: Bantam, 1961), p. xviii. For standard rationalizations about the harshness and hopelessness of de Beauvoir's assumptions, see Mary Daly, *Pure Lust: Elemental Feminist Philosophy* (Boston: Beacon, 1984), pp. 137-138.

40. Barbara Christian, "The Race for Theory," *Feminist Studies* 14, no. 1 (Spring 1988): 67-79. This issue of *Feminist Studies* addresses the problems that occur when United States feminists adapt French deconstructionist thought for academic and political purposes, as does "Learning about Women: Gender, Politics, and Power," a special issue of *Daedalus* 116, no. 4 (Fall 1987): 1-210. For a discussion of the Afro-feminist analytical model and Third World historiographer's perspectives, see *Women in Africa and the African Diaspora*, ed. Rosalyn Terborg-Penn, Sharon Harley, and Andrea Benton Rushing (Washington, D.C.: Howard University Press, 1988); Gloria I. Joseph and Jill Lewis, *Common Differences: Conflicts in Black and White Feminist Perspectives* (1981; Boston: South End Press, 1986); Chandra Talpade Mohanty, "Under Western Eyes: Feminist Scholarship and Colonial Discourses," *Boundary 2: A Journal of Post Modern Literature and Culture* 12-13 (1984): 333-359; and Maxine Molyneux, "Mobilization without Emancipation? Women's Interests, the State, and Revolution in Nicaragua," *Feminist Studies* 11 (Summer 1985): 227-254.

41. Gerda Lerner, "Placing Women in History: A Theoretical Framework," unpublished 1988 paper. Hegemonic and racist implications of deconstruction are discussed in Kathleen Barry, "Biography and the Search for Women's Subjectivity," *Women's Studies International Forum* (November 1989). Mary Poovey criticizes the ahistorical and apolitical strains of deconstruction in "Feminism and Deconstruction," *Feminist Studies* 141 (Spring 1988): 60-63.

42. Gordon, "What's New in Women's History," in Teresa de Lauretis, ed., *Feminist Studies/Critical Studies* (Bloomington: Indiana University Press, 1986), pp. 21-22, 25.

43. Zillah R. Eisenstein, *The Female Body and the Law* (Berkeley: University of California Press, 1988), pp. 3, 39-40.

44. Joan Wallach Scott, "Gender: A Useful Category of Historical Analysis," *American Historical Review* 91, no. 5 (December 1986): 1053-1075; idem, "Deconstructing Equality-versus-Difference," ibid., p. 36 (first quotation); idem, "Rewriting History," in Margaret Randolph Higonnet et al., eds., *Behind the Lines: Gender and the Two World Wars* (New Haven, Conn.: Yale University

Press, 1987), p. 22 (second quotation); Lois Banner, "A Reply to 'Culture et Pouvoir' from the Perspective of United States Women's History," *Journal Of Women's History* 1, no. 1 (Spring 1989): 104 (third and fifth quotations); Myra Dinnerstein, "Questions for the Nineties," *Women's Review of Books*, February 1989, p. 13; and Dalton, "Where We Stand," p. 11 (fourth and sixth quotations).

45. Book Reviews, *Signs* 15 (Summer 1990): 848-860 (quotation at 851, 858).

46. See "Theories about the End of Everything," introduction to the *Journal of Women's History* 1, no. 3 (Winter 1990), for reference to the end-of-history theory proclaimed by Francis Fukuyama, U.S. State Department policy planner, on the eve of the collapse of communism in Central and Eastern Europe. For other predictions about the end of women's history, see the summary of a session of the Eighth Berkshire Conference on the History of Women, where a handful of historians expressed concern about the future of women's history, in the *Chronicle of Higher Education*, July 5, 1990. This point of view was strongly challenged in a subsequent letter to the editor from Gerda Lerner and Kathryn Kish Sklar.

# AFRICA

Abiodun, Rowland. "Women in Yoruba Religious Images." *African Languages and Cultures* 2, no. 1 (1989): 1-18.

Afonja, Simi. "Changing Modes of Production and the Sexual Division of Labor among the Yoruba." *Signs* 7, no. 2 (1981): 299-313.

Alpers, Edward A. "'Ordinary Household Chores': Ritual and Power in a 19th-Century Swahili Women's Spirit Possession Cult." *International Journal of African Historical Studies* 17, no. 4 (1984): 677-702.

-----. "The Somali Community at Aden in the Nineteenth Century." *Northeast Africa Studies* 8, no. 2/3 (1986): 143-186.

-----. "State, Merchant Capital, and Gender Relations in Southern Mozambique to the End of the Nineteenth Century." *African Economic History* 13 (1984): 23-55.

Ault, James M., Jr. "Making 'Modern' Marriage 'Traditional.'" *Theory and Society* 12 (March 1983): 181-210.

Barber, Karin. "Oriki, Women and the Proliferation and Merging of Orisa." *Africa* 60, no. 3 (1990): 313-337.

Barthel, Diane L. "The Rise of Female Professional Elite: The Case of Senegal." *African Studies Review* 13, no. 3 (1975): 1-17.

-----. "Women's Educational Experience under Colonialism: Toward a Diachronic Model." *Signs* 7, no. 1 (1985): 137-154.

Berger, Iris. "Gender and Working-Class History: South Africa in Comparative Perspective." *Journal of Women's History* 1 (Fall 1989): 117-133.

-----. "Gender, Race, and Political Empowerment: South African Canning Workers, 1940-1960." *Gender & Society* 4 (September 1990): 398-420.

Biebuyck, Daniel P. "Lega Dress as Cultural Artifact." *African Arts* 15 (May 1982): 59-65, 92.

Blakeley, Brian L. "Women and Imperialism: The Colonial Office and Female Emigration to South Africa, 1901-1910." *Albion* 13 (Summer 1981): 131-149.

Bozzoli, Belinda. "Marxism, Feminism and South African Studies." *Journal of South African Studies* 9, no. 2 (1983): 139-171.

Brett-Smith, Sarah C. "Symbolic Blood: Cloths for Excised Women." *RES* 3 (Spring 1982): 15-31.

Brown, Barbara B. "Facing the 'Black Peril': The Politics of Population Control in South Africa." *Journal of South African Studies* 13 (April 1987): 256-273.

-----. "The Impact of Male Labour Migration on Women in Botswana." *African Affairs* no. 328 (1983): 367-388.

Brown, Jean Lucas. "Miji Kenda Grave and Memorial Sculptures." *African Arts* 13 (August 1980): 36-69, 99.

Bujra, Janet. "Women 'Entrepreneurs' of Early Nairobi." *Canadian Journal of African Studies* 9, no. 2 (1975): 213-234.

Burt, Eugene C. "Eroticism in Baluyia Body Arts." *African Arts* 15 (February 1982): 68-69, 88.

Burton, John W. "Nilotic Women: A Diachronic Perspective." *Journal of Modern African Studies* 20, no. 3 (1982): 467-491.

Caplan, Patricia. "Gender, Ideology and Modes of Production on the Coast of East Africa." *Paideuma* 28 (1982): 29-43.

Chauncey, George, Jr. "The Locus of Reproduction: Women's Labour in the Zambian Copperbelt, 1927-1953." *Journal of South African Studies* 7 (April 1981): 135-164.

Ciancanelli, Penelope. "Exchange, Reproduction and Sex Subordination Among the Kikuyu of East Africa." *Review of African Political Economy* 12 (Summer 1980): 25-36.

Clark, Carolyn M. "Land and Food, Women and Power, in Nineteenth Century Kikuyu." *Africa* 50, no. 4 (1980): 357-369.

Cowan, Nicole. "Women in Eritrea: An Eye-Witness Account." *Review of African Political Economy* 27/28 (1983): 143-152.

Curtin, Patricia Romero. "Laboratory for the Oral History of Slavery: The Island of Lamu on the Kenya Coast." *American Historical Review* 88 (October 1983): 858-882.

Dennis, Carolyne. "Women in African Labour History." *Journal of Asian and African Studies* 23 (January/April 1988): 125-140.

Deshen, Shlomo. "Women in the Jewish Family in Pre-Colonial Morocco." *Anthropological Quarterly* 56, no. 3 (1983): 134-144.

Dinan, Claudine. "Pragmatists or Feminists? The Professional Single Women of Accra, Ghana." *Cahiers d'Etudes Africaines* 65, no. 8 (1977): 155-176.

Duquette, Danielle Gallois. "Women Power and Initiation in the Bisagos Islands." *African Arts* 12 (May 1979): 31-35.

Eicher, Joanne, Tonye Victor Erekosima, and Carl Liedholm. "Cut and Drawn: Textile Work from Nigeria." *Craft International* 2 (Summer 1982): 16-19.

Ekejiuba, Felicia. "Omu Okwei, The Merchant Queen of Ossomari: A Biographical Sketch." *Journal of the Historical Society of Nigeria* 3, no. 4 (1967): 633-646.

Entwisle, Barbara, and Catherine M. Coles. "Demographic Surveys and Nigerian Women." *Signs* 15 (Winter 1990): 259-284.

Foss, Susan Moore. "She Who Sits as King." *African Arts* 12 (February 1979): 44-50.

Gaitskell, Deborah. "'Christian Compounds for Girls': Church Hostels for African Women in Johannesburg, 1907-1970." *Journal of South African Studies* 6

(October 1979): 44-69.

-----. "Housewives, Maids or Mothers: Some Contradictions of Domesticity for Christian Women in Johannesburg, 1903-39." *Journal of African History* 24, no. 2 (1983): 241-256.

-----, Judy Kimble, Moira Maconachie, and Elaine Unterhalter. "Class, Race and Gender: Domestic Workers in South Africa." *Review of African Political Economy* 27/28 (1983): 86-108.

Gay, Judith. "'Mummies and Babies' and Friends and Lovers in Lesotho." *Journal of Homosexuality* 11, no. 3/4 (1985): 97-116.

Geiger, Susan. "Women in Nationalist Struggle: TANU Activists in Dar es Salaam." *International Journal of African Historical Studies* 20, no. 1 (1987): 1-26.

Gunner, Elizabeth. "Songs of Innocence and Experience: Women as Composers and Performers of *Izibongo*, Zulu Praise Poetry." *Research in African Literatures* 10 (Fall 1979): 239-267.

Hansen, Karen Tranberg. "Body Politics: Sexuality, Gender, and Domestic Service in Zambia." *Journal of Women's History* 2 (Spring 1990): 120-142.

-----. "Negotiating Sex and Gender in Urban Zambia." *Journal of South African Studies* 10 (April 1984): 219-238.

Hetherington, Penelope. "Generational Change and Class Formation in Kenya: The Kamore Family." *Australian Journal of Politics and History* 36, no. 1 (1990): 51-61.

Hoffer, Carol P. "Mende and Sherbro Women in High Office." *Canadian Journal of African Studies* 4, no. 2 (1972): 151-164.

Hunt, Nancy Rose. "Domesticity and Colonialism in Belgian Africa: Usumbura's *Foyer Social*, 1946-1960." *Signs* 15 (Spring 1990): 447-474.

-----. "'Single Ladies on the Congo': Protestant Missionary Tensions and Voices." *Women's Studies International Forum* 13, no. 4 (1990): 395-404.

Isaacman, Allen, and Barbara Isaacman. "The Role of Women in the Liberation of Mozambique." *Ufahamu* 13, no. 2/3 (1984): 128-185.

Jacobs, Sylvia M. "African-American Women Missionaries and European Imperialism in Southern Africa, 1880-1920." *Women's Studies International Forum* 13, no. 4 (1990): 381-394.

-----. "'Say Africa When You Pray': The Activities of Early Black Baptist Women Missionaries Among Liberian Women and Children." *Sage* 3 (Fall 1986): 16-21.

Johnson, Judith M., Susan L. Thompson, and Gerald J. Perry. "Juju-Soup: The Witch Herbalist's Solution for Infertility." *African Studies Review* 33 (April 1990): 55-64.

Johnson, Marion. "Cloth as Money: The Cloth Strip Currencies of Africa." *Textile History* 11 (1980): 193-202.

Jules-Rosette, Bennetta. "Changing Aspects of Women's Initiation in Southern Africa." *Canadian Journal of African Studies* 13, no. 3 (1980): 389-405.

Kimble, J., and E. Unterhalter. "We Opened the Road for You, You Must Go

Forward: ANC Women's Struggles 1912-1982." *Feminist Review* 12 (1982): 11-36.

Kinsley, David. "Devotion as an Alternative to Marriage in the Lives of Some Hindu Women Devotees." *Journal of Asian and African Studies* 15 (January/April 1980): 83-93.

Kinsman, Margaret. "'Beasts of Burden': The Subordination of Southern Tswana Women, ca. 1800-1840." *Journal of South African Studies* 10 (October 1983): 39-54.

Klumpp, Donna Rey. "An Historical Overview of Maasai Dress." *Dress* 7 (1981): 95-102.

Kruks, Sonia, and Ben Wisner. "The State, the Party, and the Female Peasantry in Mozambique." *Journal of South African Studies* 11, no. 1 (1984): 106-127.

Levinsohn, Rhoda. "Rural Kwazulu Beadwork." *Ornament* 4 (September 1980): 38-41.

-----, and Morris Levinsohn. "Symbolic Significance of Traditional Zulu Beadwork." *Black Art* 3, no. 4 (1979): 29-35.

Levy, Susan E. "Dux Femina Facti: An African Queen's Cosmopolis." *Botswana Review* 1 (Summer 1989): 45-50.

Mack, John. "Bakuba Embroidery Patterns: A Commentary on Their Social and Political Implications." *Textile History* 11 (1980): 163-174.

Mandala, Elias. "Capitalism, Kinship, and Gender in the Lower Tchiri (Shire) Valley of Malawi, 1860-1960: An Alternative Theoretical Framework." *African Economic History* 13 (1984): 137-169.

Mann, Kristin. "The Dangers of Dependence: Christian Marriages Among Elite Women in Lagos Colony, 1880-1915." *Journal of African History* 24, no. 1 (1983): 37-56.

Mbilinyi, Marjorie. "The 'New Woman' and Traditional Norms in Tanzania." *Journal of Modern African Studies* 10, no. 1 (1972): 57-72.

-----. "Wife, Slave and Subject of the King: The Oppression of Women in Shambala Kingdom." *Tanzania Notes and Records* 88/89 (1982): 1-13.

-----. "'Women in Development' Ideology: The Promotion of Competition and Exploitation." *The African Review* 2, no. 1 (1984): 14-33.

Morrow, Sean. "'No Girl Leaves the School Unmarried': Mabel Shaw and the Education of Girls at Mbereshi, Northern Rhodesia, 1915-1940." *International Journal of African Historical Studies* 19, no. 4 (1986): 601-635.

Mueller, Martha. "Women and Men, Power and Powerlessness in Lesotho." *Signs* 3 (Autumn 1977): 154-166.

Murray, Jocelyn. "The Church Missionary Society and the 'Female Circumcision' Issue in Kenya 1929-1932." *Journal of Religion in Africa* [Netherlands] 8, no. 2 (1976): 92-104.

Murray-Hudson, Anne. "SWAPO: Solidarity with Our Sisters." *Review of African Political Economy* 27/28 (1983): 120-125.

Neaher, Nancy C. "Igbo Carved Doors." *African Arts* 15 (November 1981): 49-55.

O'Barr, Jean. "Pare Women: A Case of Political Involvement." *Rural Africana*

29 (1975/76): 121-134.

Ogunbiyi, I. A. "The Position of Muslim Women as Stated by Uthman B. Fudi." *Odu: A Journal of West Africa Studies* no. 11 (1969): 165-184.

Okhamafe, E. Imafedia. "African-Style Feminism in Contemporary African Literature." *Africa Today* 37, no. 1 (1990): 73-75.

Pearce, R. D. "Violet Bourdillon: Colonial Governor's Wife." *African Affairs* 82, no. 327 (1983): 267-277.

Peires, J. B. "'Soft' Believers and 'Hard' Unbelievers in Xhosa Cattle-Killing." *Journal of African History* 27, no. 3 (1986): 443-461.

Pellow, Deborah. "Sexuality in Africa." *Trends in History* 4, no. 4 (1990).

Pennell, C. R. "Women and Colonialism in Morocco: The Rif 1916-1926." *Journal of African History* 28, no. 1 (1987): 107-118.

Peters, Pauline. "Gender, Development Cycles and Historical Process: A Critique of Recent Research on Women in Botswana." *Journal of South African Studies* 10 (October 1983): 100-122.

Phillipson, D. W. "Iron Age History and Archaeology in Zambia." *Journal of African History* 15, no. 1 (1974): 1-25.

Picton, John. "Women's Weaving: The Manufacture and Use of Textiles Among the Igbirra People of Nigeria." *Textile History* 11 (1980): 63-88.

Ramphele, Mamphela. "The Dynamics of Gender Politics in the Hostels of Cape Town: Another Legacy of the South African Migrant Labour System." *Journal of South African Studies* 15 (April 1989): 393-414.

Ravenhill, Philip L. "The Interpretation of Symbolism in Wan Female Initiation." *Africa* [London] 48, no. 1 (1978): 66-78.

Reagon, Bernice Johnson. "African Diaspora Women: The Making of Cultural Workers." *Feminist Studies* 12 (Spring 1986): 77-90.

Robertson, Claire. "Changing Perspectives in Studies of African Women, 1976-1985." *Feminist Studies* 13 (Spring 1987): 87-136.

-----. "The Death of Makola and Other Tragedies: Male Strategies Against a Female-Dominated System." *Canadian Journal of African Studies* 17, no. 3 (1983): 469-495.

-----. "Invisible Workers: African Women and the Problem of the Self-Employed in Labour History." *Journal of Asian and African Studies* 23 (January-April 1988): 180-198.

-----. "Never Underestimate the Power of Women: The Transforming Vision of African Women's History." *Women's Studies International Forum* 11, no. 5 (1988): 439-454.

Roberts, Richard. "Women's Work and Women's Property: Household Social Relations in the Maraka Textile Industry of the Nineteenth Century." *Comparative Studies in Society and History* [Great Britain] 26, no. 2 (1984): 48-69.

Rogers, Susan G. "Anti-Colonial Protest in Africa: A Female Strategy Reconsidered." *Heresies* 3, no. 9 (1980): 22-25.

-----. "Efforts Toward Women's Development in Tanzania: Gender Rhetoric vs. Gender Realities." *Women and Politics* 2, no. 4 (1982): 23-41.

Schmidt, E. "Farmers, Hunters, and Gold-Washers: A Reevaluation of Women's Roles in Precolonial and Colonial Zimbabwe." *African Economic History* no. 17 (1988): 45-80.

Seidman, Gay W. "Women in Zimbabwe: Postindependence Struggles." *Feminist Studies* 10 (Fall 1984): 419-440.

Shostak, Marjorie. "What the Wind Won't Take Away: The Oral History of an African Foraging Woman." *International Journal of Oral History* 8 (November 1987): 171-181.

Sibisi, Harriet. "How Women Cope with Migrant Labor in South Africa." *Signs* 3 (Autumn 1977): 167-177.

Simkins, Charles, and Elizabeth van Heyningen. "Fertility, Morality, and Migration in the Cape Colony, 1891-1904." *The International Journal of African Historical Studies* 22, no. 1 (1989): 79-112.

Smith, Fred T. "Frafra Dress." *African Arts* 15 (May 1982): 36-42, 92.

Smith, Fred T., and Joanne B. Eicher. "The Systematic Study of African Dress and Textiles." *African Arts* 15 (May 1982): 28.

Spencer, Leon P. "Indian Christians in Colonial Kenya: The Problem in Ministry." *Indian Church History Review* 16 (June 1982): 37-50.

Stichter, Sharon. "Women and the Labor Force in Kenya 1895-1964." *Rural Africana* 29 (1975/76): 45-67.

Strobel, Margaret. "African Women: Review Essay." *Signs* 8 (Autumn 1982): 109-131.

Tibenderana, Peter K. "The Beginnings of Girls' Education in the Native Administration Schools in Northern Nigeria, 1930-1945." *Journal of African History* 26, no. 1 (1985): 93-109.

United Nations Economic Commission for Africa. "Women and National Development in African Countries: Some Profound Contradictions." *African Studies Review* 18, no. 3 (1975): 47-70.

Urdang, Stephanie. "The Last Transition? Women and Development in Mozambique." *Review of African Political Economy* 27/28 (1983): 8-32.

Vaughan, Megan. "Household Units and Historical Process in Southern Malawi." *Review of African Political Economy* 34 (December 1985): 35-45.

Verdon, Michel. "Divorce in Abutia." *Africa* 52, no. 4 (1982): 48-66.

Vidal, Claudine. "Guerre des sexes à Abijan: Masculin, Feminin, CFA." *Cahiers d'Etudes Africaines* 8, no. 1 (1977): 121-153.

Weis, Lois. "Women and Education in Ghana: Some Problems of Assessing the Change." *International Journal of Women's Studies* 3, no. 5 (1980): 431-453.

Wells, Julia. "Why Women Rebel: A Comparative Study of South African Women's Resistance in Bloemfontein (1913) and Johannesburg (1958)." *Journal of South African Studies* 10 (October 1983): 55-70.

White, E. Frances. "Africa on My Mind: Gender, Counter Discourse and African-American Nationalism." *Journal of Women's History* 2 (Spring 1990): 73-97.

White, Luise. "Prostitution, Identity and Class Consciousness in Nairobi During World War II." *Signs* 11 (Winter 1986): 255-273.

-----. "Separating the Men from the Boys: Constructions of Gender, Sexuality, and Terrorism in Central Kenya, 1939-1959." *International Journal of African Historical Studies* 23, no. 1 (1990): 1-26.

Wipper, Audrey. "African Women, Fashion and Scapegoating." *Canadian Journal of African Studies* 6, no. 2 (1972): 329-349.

-----. "Equal Rights for Women in Kenya?" *Journal of Modern African Studies* 9, no. 3 (1971): 429-442.

-----. "The Maendeleo ya Wanawake Movement in the Colonial Period." *Rural Africana* 29 (1975/76): 195-214.

-----. "The Maendeleo ya Yanawake Organization: The Co-optation of Leadership." *African Studies Review* 18 (December 1975): 99-120.

Wright, Marcia. "Technology, Marriage and Women's Work in the History of Maize Growers in Mazabuka, Zambia: A Reconnaissance." *Journal of South African Studies* 10 (October 1983): 71-85.

# AFRICAN-AMERICAN WOMEN

## Freed Women

Berthoff, Rowland. "Conventional Mentality: Free Blacks, Women, and Business Corporations as Unequal Persons, 1820-1870." *Journal of American History* 76 (December 1989): 753-784.

Blackburn, George, and Sherman L. Richards. "The Mother-Headed Family Among Free Negroes in Charleston, South Carolina, 1850-1860." *Phylon* 42 (March 1981): 11-25.

Bynum, Victoria. "On the Lowest Rung: Court Control over Poor White and Free Black Women." *Southern Exposure* 12 (November/December 1984): 40-44.

Horton, James Oliver. "Freedom's Yoke: Gender Conventions Among Antebellum Free Blacks." *Feminist Studies* 12 (Spring 1986): 51-76.

Lapsansky, Emma Jones. "Friends, Wives, and Strivings: Networks and Community Values Among Nineteenth-Century Philadelphia Afroamerican Elites." *Pennsylvania Magazine of History and Biography* 108 (January 1984): 3-24.

Lawson, Ellen N., and Marlene Morrell. "Antebellum Black Coeds at Oberlin College." *Oberlin Alumni* 60 (Winter 1980): 8-11.

Lebsock, Suzanne. "Free Black Women and the Question of Matriarchy: Petersburg, Virginia, 1784-1820." *Feminist Studies* 8 (Summer 1982): 271-292.

Mabee, Carleton. "Sojourner Truth Fights Dependence on Government: Moves Freed Slaves Off Welfare in Washington to Jobs in Upstate New York." *Afro-Americans in New York Life and History* 14 (January 1990): 7-26.

Oden, Gloria C. "The Journal of Charlotte L. Forten: The Salem-Philadelphia Years, 1854-1862, Reexamined." *Essex Institute Historical Collections* 199 (April 1983): 119-136.

Rapport, Sara. "The Freedman's Bureau as a Legal Agent for Black Men and

Women in Georgia: 1865-1868." *Georgia Historical Quarterly* 73 (Winter 1989): 26-53.

Schafer, Judith K. "'Open and Notorious Concubinage': The Emancipation of Slave Mistresses by Will and the Supreme Court in Antebellum Louisiana." *Louisiana History* 28 (Spring 1987): 165-182.

Schweninger, Loren. "Property-Owning Free African-American Women in the South, 1800-70." *Journal of Women's History* 1 (Winter 1990): 13-44.

## Late Nineteenth Century

Baldwin, Lewis V. "Black Women and African Union Methodism, 1813-1983." *Methodist History* (July 1983): 225-237.

Bigham, Darrel E. "The Black Family in Evansville and Vanderburgh County, Indiana, in 1880." *Indiana Magazine of History* 75 (June 1979): 117-146.

Birchman, Sandra. "The Mitchell House." *History News* (February 1984): 12-15.

Brooks, Evelyn. "Religion, Politics, and Gender: The Leadership of Nannie Helen Burroughs." *Journal of Religious Thought* 44 (Winter/Spring 1988): 7-22.

Butler, Anne M. "Still in Chains: Black Women in Western Prisons, 1865-1910." *Western Historical Quarterly* 20 (February 1989): 19-35.

Cunningham, Constance A. "The Sin of Omission: Black Women in Nineteenth Century American History." *Journal of Social and Behavioral Sciences* 33 (Winter 1987): 35-46.

deGraaf, Lawrence B. "Race, Sex, and Region: Black Women in the American West, 1850-1920." *Pacific Historical Review* 49 (May 1980): 285-313.

Dorsey, Carolyn A. "Despite Poor Health: Olivia Davidson Washington's Story." *Sage* 11 (Fall 1985): 69-71.

-----. "The Pre-Hampton Years of Olivia A. Davidson." *Hampton Review* 14 (Fall 1988): 44-52.

Hayden, Dolores. "Biddy Mason's Los Angeles, 1856-1891." *California History* 68 (Fall 1989): 86-99.

Jacobs, Sylvia M. "African-American Women Missionaries and European Imperialism in Southern Africa, 1880-1920." *Women's Studies International Forum* 13, no. 4 (1990): 381-394.

Jehlen, Myra. "The Ties That Bind: Race and Sex in *Pudd'nhead Wilson*." *American Literary History* 2 (Spring 1990): 39-55.

Jenkins, Maude T. "She Issued the Call: Josephine St. Pierre Ruffin, 1842-1924." *Sage* 5 (Fall 1988): 74-76.

Johnson, Whittington B. "A Black Teacher and Her School in Reconstruction Darien: The Correspondence of Hettie E. Sabattie and J. Murray Hoag." *Georgia Historical Quarterly* 75 (Spring 1991): 90-105.

Jones, Beverly W. "Mary Church Terrell and the National Association of Colored Women, 1896-1901." *Journal of Negro History* 67 (Spring 1982): 20-33.

Lawson, Ellen N. "Sarah Woodson Early: 19th Century Black Nationalist 'Sister.'" *Umoja* 5 (Summer 1981): 15-26.

Leashore, Bogart R. "Black Female Workers: Live-in Domestics in Detroit,

Michigan, 1860-1880." *Phylon* 45 (June 1984): 111-120.

Moses, Wilson Jeremiah. "Domestic Feminism, Conservativism, Sex Roles, and Black Women's Clubs, 1893-1896." *Journal of Social and Behavioral Sciences* 24 (Fall 1987): 166-177.

Reiff, Janice L., Michael R. Dahlin, and Daniel Scott Smith. "Rural Push and Urban Pull: Work and Family Experiences of Older Black Women in Southern Cities, 1880-1900." *Journal of Social History* 16 (Summer 1983): 39-48.

Riley, Glenda. "American Daughters: Black Women in the West." *Montana* 38 (Spring 1988): 14-27.

Robinson, Henry S. "Julia Mason Layton 1859-1926." *Negro History Bulletin* 45 (January/March 1982): 18-20.

Rutledge, Essie. "Black/White Relations in the Women's Movement." *Minority Voices* 6 (Fall 1989): 53-62.

Seraile, William. "Susan McKinney Steward: New York State's First African-American Woman Physician." *Afro-Americans in New York Life and History* 9 (July 1985): 27-44.

Smith, Daniel Scott, Michel Dahlin, and Mark Friedberger. "The Family Structure of the Older Black Population in the American South in 1880-1900." *Sociology and Social Research* 63, no. 3 (1979): 544-565.

Taylor, Quintard. "The Emergence of Black Communities in the Pacific Northwest, 1864-1910." *Journal of Negro History* 64 (Fall 1979): 342-354.

Wade-Gayles, Gloria. "Black Women Journalists in the South, 1880-1905: An Approach to the Study of Black Women's History." *Callaloo* 9 (February/October 1981): 138-152.

## Other

Beckett, Joyce O. "Working Women: An Historical Review of Racial Differences." *Black Sociologist* 9 (Spring/Summer 1982): 5-27.

Bennett, Neil G., David E. Bloom, and Patricia H. Craig. "The Divergence of Black and White Marriage Patterns." *American Journal of Sociology* 95 (November 1989): 692-722.

Collier-Thomas, Bettye. "The Impact of Black Women in Education: An Historical Overview." *Journal of Negro Education* 51 (Summer 1982): 173-180.

Frost, Peter. "Fair Women, Dark Men: The Forgotten Roots of Colour Prejudice." *History of European Ideas* 12, no. 5 (1990): 669-680.

Gaston, Paul M. "Irony in Utopia: The Discovery of Nancy Lewis." *Virginia Quarterly Review* 60 (Summer 1984): 473-487.

George, Carol V. R. "In the Beginning: Mother Bethel and A. M. E. Church." *American Vision* 1, no. 6 (1986): 43-46.

Goldsmith, Peter. "A Woman's Place Is in the Church: Black Pentecostalism on the Georgia Coast." *Journal of Religious Thought* 46 (Winter 1989/Spring 1990): 53-69.

Goldstein, Paul. "Julia Peterkin's Scarlet Sister Mary: A Forgotten Novel of Female Primitivism." *Southern Studies* 22 (Summer 1983): 138-145.

Guy-Sheftall, Beverly. "Black Women and Higher Education: Spelman and Bennett Colleges Revisited." *Journal of Negro Education* (Summer 1982): 278-287.

Hanchett, Catherine M. "'What Sort of People and Families...': The Edmondson Sisters." *Afro-Americans in New York Life and History* 6 (July 1982): 21-38.

Harpole, Patricia C., ed. "The Black Community in Territorial St. Anthony: A Memoir by Emily O. Goodridge Grey." *Minnesota History* 49 (Summer 1984): 42-53.

Hine, Darlene Clark. "Opportunity and Fulfillment: Sex, Race, and Class in Health Care Education." *Sage* 2 (Fall 1985): 14-19.

Howard-Vital, Michelle R. "African-American Women in Higher Education: Struggling to Gain Identity." *Journal of Black Studies* 20 (December 1989): 180-191.

Jacobs, Sylvia M. "'Say Africa When You Pray': The Activities of Early Black Baptist Women Missionaries Among Liberian Women and Children." *Sage* 3 (Fall 1986): 16-21.

Kutinski, Vera. "Unseasonal Flowers: Nature and History in Placido and Jean Toomer." *Yale Journal of Criticism* 3 (Spring 1990): 153-180.

Lantz, Herman, and Lewellyn Hendrix. "Black Fertility and the Black Family in the Nineteenth Century: A Re-Examination of the Past." *Journal of Family History* 3 (Fall 1978): 251-261.

Matthews, Mark D. "'Our Women and What They Think': Amy Jacques Garvey and the *Negro World*." *Black Scholar* 10, no. 8/9 (1979): 2-13.

McDowell, Deborah E. "The Neglected Dimension of Jessie Redmon Fauset." *Afro-Americans in New York Life and History* 5 (July 1981): 33-49.

Oden, Gloria. "The Black Putnams of Charlotte Forten's Journal." *Essex Institute Historical Collections* 126 (October 1990): 237-253.

Patton, June O. "Moonlight and Magnolias in Southern Education: The Black Mammy Memorial Institute." *Journal of Negro History* (Spring 1980): 149-155.

Perkins, Carol O. "The Pragmatic Idealism of Mary McLeod Bethune." *Sage* 5 (Fall 1988): 30-36.

Perkins, Linda M. "Heed Life's Demands: The Educational Philosophy of Fanny Jackson Coppin." *Journal of Negro Education* 51 (Summer 1982): 181-190.

Pinderhughes, Dianne M. "Black Women and National Educational Policy." *Journal of Negro Education* (Summer 1982): 301-308.

Rector, Theresa A. "Black Nuns as Educators." *Journal of Negro Education* (Summer 1982): 238-253.

Russell-Wood, A. J. R. "The Black Family in the Americas." *Societas* 8 (Winter 1978): 1-38.

Sloan, Patricia E. "Early Black Nursing Schools and Responses of Black Nurses to their Educational Programs." *Western Journal of Black Studies* 9 (Fall 1985): 158-172.

Smith, Carol Hobson. "Black Female Achievers in Academe." *Journal of Negro Education* (Summer 1982): 318-341.

Smith, Sandra N., and Earle H. West. "Charlotte Hawkins Brown." *Journal of*

*Negro Education* 51 (Summer 1982): 191-208.

Smock, Pamela J. "Remarriage Patterns of Black and White Women: Reassessing the Role of Educational Attainment." *Demography* 27 (August 1990): 467-474.

Stehno, Sandra M. "Public Responsibility for Dependent Black Children: The Advocacy of Edith Abbott and Sophonisha Breckenridge." *Social Service Review* 62, no. 3 (1988): 485-503.

## Slavery

Axelson, Diana E. "Women as Victims of Medical Experimentation: J. Marion Sims' Surgery on Slave Women, 1845-1850." *Sage* 2 (Fall 1985): 10-13.

Berlin, Ira, Steven F. Miller, and Leslie S. Rowland. "Afro-American Families in the Transition from Slavery to Freedom." *Radical History Review* 42 (1988): 89-121.

Braxton, Joanne M. "Harriet Jacobs' *Incidents in the Life of a Slave Girl*: The Re-definition of the Slave Girl Narrative." *Massachusetts Review* 27 (Summer 1986): 379-387.

Brown, Steven E. "Sexuality and the Slave Community." *Phylon* 42 (Spring 1981): 1-10.

Burnham, Dorothy. "The Life of the Afro-American Woman in Slavery." *International Journal of Women's Studies* 1 (July/August 1978): 363-377.

Campbell, John. "Work, Pregnancy, and Infant Mortality Among Southern Slaves." *Journal of Interdisciplinary History* 14 (Spring 1984): 793-812.

Campbell, Randolph B., and Donald K. Pickens, eds. " 'My Dear Husband': A Texas Slave's Love Letter, 1862." *Journal of Negro History* 65 (Fall 1980): 361-364.

Clinton, Catherine. "Fanny Kemble's Journal: A Woman Confronts Slavery on a Georgia Plantation." *Frontiers* 9, no. 3 (1987): 74-79.

Cody, Cheryll Ann. "Naming, Kinship, and Estate Dispersal: Notes on Slave Family Life on a South Carolina Plantation, 1786 to 1833." *William and Mary Quarterly* 39 (January 1982): 192-211.

Cook, Charles Orson, and James M. Poteet. " 'Dem Was Black Times, Sure 'Nough': The Slave Narratives of Lydia Jefferson and Stephen Williams." *Louisiana History* 20 (Summer 1979): 281-292.

Ellison, Mary. "Resistance to Oppression: Black Women's Response to Slavery in the United States." *Slavery and Abolition* (May 1983): 56-63.

Foley, William E. "Slave Freedom Suits Before Dred Scott: The Case of Marie Jean Scypion's Descendants." *Missouri Historical Review* 79 (October 1984): 1-23.

Getman, Karen A. "Sexual Control in the Slaveholding South: The Implementation and Maintenance of a Racial Caste System." *Harvard Women's Law Journal* 7 (Spring 1984): 115-152.

Goodson, Martia G. "Medical-Botanical Contributions of African Slave Women to American Medicine." *Western Journal of Black Studies* 11 (1987): 198-203.

-----. "The Slave Narrative Collection: A Tool for Reconstructing Afro-American

Women's History." *Western Journal of Black Studies* 3 (Summer 1979): 116-122.

Gundersen, Joan R. "The Double Bonds of Race and Sex: Black and White Women in a Colonial Virginia Parish." *Journal of Southern History* 52 (August 1986): 351-372.

Harper, C. W. "Black Aristocrats: Domestic Servants on the Antebellum Plantation." *Phylon* 46 (June 1985): 123-35.

Henke, Suzette. "*Incidents in the Life of a Slave Girl*: Autobiography as Reconstruction." *Feminist Issues* 6 (Fall 1986): 33-39.

Hine, Darlene Clark. "Female Slave Resistance: The Economics of Sex." *Western Journal of Black Studies* 3 (Summer 1979): 123-127.

Jennings, Thelma. "'Us Colored Women Had to Go Through a Plenty': Sexual Exploitation of African-American Slave Women." *Journal of Women's History* 1 (Winter 1990): 45-74.

Johnson, Michael P. "Smothered Slave Infants: Were Slave Mothers at Fault?" *Journal of Southern History* 47 (November 1981): 493-520.

Jones, Jacqueline. "'My Mother Was Much of a Woman': Black Women, Work, and the Family under Slavery." *Feminist Studies* 8 (Summer 1982): 235-270.

Klein, Herbert S., and Stanley L. Engerman. "Fertility Differentials Between Slaves in the United States and the British West Indies: A Note on Lactation Practices and Their Possible Implications." *William and Mary Quarterly* 35 (April 1978): 357-374.

Krebs, Sylvia H. "Life without 'My Folks': Letters to Former Slaves." *Atlanta History Journal* 29 (Summer 1985): 47-50.

Lerner, Gerda. "Women and Slavery." *Slavery and Abolition* 4 (December 1983): 173-198.

Littlefield, Daniel C. "Plantations, Paternalism, and Profitability: Factors Affecting African Demography in the Old British Empire." *Journal of Southern History* 47 (May 1981): 167-182.

Mabee, Carleton. "Sojourner Truth, Bold Prophet: Why Did She Never Learn to Read?" *New York History* 69, no. 1 (1988): 55-77.

Malone, Ann Patton. "Searching for the Family and Household Structure of Rural Louisiana Slaves, 1810-1864." *Louisiana History* 28 (Fall 1987): 357-380.

Mann, Susan A. "Slavery, Sharecropping, and Sexual Inequality." *Signs* 14 (Summer 1989): 774-778.

Moody, Joycelyn K. "Ripping Away the Veil of Slavery: Literacy, Communal Love, and Self-Esteem in Three Slave Women's Narratives." *Black American Literature Forum* 24 (Winter 1990): 633-648.

Mullin, Michael. "Women, and the Comparative Study of American Negro Slavery." *Slavery and Abolition* 6 (May 1985): 25-40.

Painter, Nell Irvin. "Sojourner Truth in Life and Memory: Writing the Biography of an American Exotic." *Gender & History* 2 (Spring 1990): 3-16.

Pugh, Evelyn L. "Women and Slavery: Julia Gardiner Tyler and the Duchess of Sutherland." *Virginia Magazine of History and Biography* 88 (April 1980): 186-202.

Sealander, Judith A. "Antebellum Black Press Images of Women." *Western Journal of Black Studies* 6 (Fall 1982): 159-165.

Sears, Richard. "Working Like a Slave: Views of Slavery and the Status of Women in Antebellum Kentucky." *The Register of the Kentucky Historical Society* 87 (Winter 1989): 1-19.

Seraile, William. "Henrietta Vinton Davis and the Garvey Movement." *Afro-Americans in New York Life and History* 7 (July 1983): 7-24.

Shammas, Carole. "Black Women's Work and the Evolution of Plantation Society in Virginia." *Labor History* 26 (Winter 1985): 5-28.

Shea, Deborah, ed. "Spreading Terror and Devastation Wherever They Have Been: A Norfolk Woman's Account of the Southampton Slave Insurrection." *Virginia Magazine of History and Biography* 95 (January 1987): 65-74.

Sherman, Sarah Way. "Moral Experience in Harriet Jacobs's *Incidents In The Life Of a Slave Girl.*" *NWSA Journal* 2 (Spring 1990): 167-185.

Soderlund, Jean R. "Black Women in Colonial Pennsylvania." *Pennsylvania Magazine of History and Biography* 107 (January 1983): 49-68.

Sumler-Lewis, Janice. "The Forten-Purvis Women of Philadelphia and the American Anti-Slavery Crusade." *Journal of Negro History* 66 (Winter 1981/1982): 281-288.

Tandberg, Gerilyn G., and Sally Graham Durand. "Dress-up Clothes for Field Slaves of Ante-Bellum Louisiana and Mississippi." *Costume* 15 (1981): 40-48.

-----. "Field Hand Clothing in Louisiana and Mississippi During the Ante-Bellum Period." *Dress* 6 (1980): 89-103.

Thompson, Priscilla. "Harriet Tubman, Thomas Garrett and the Underground Railroad." *Delaware History* 22 (Spring/Summer 1986): 1-21.

Trussell, James and Richard Steckel. "The Age of Slaves at Menarche and Their First Birth." *Journal of Interdisciplinary History* 8 (Winter 1978): 477-505.

Wertz, Dorothy C. "Women and Slavery: A Cross-Cultural Perspective." *International Journal of Women's Studies* 7 (September/October 1984): 372-384.

White, Deborah G. "Female Slaves: Sex Roles and Status in the Antebellum Plantation South." *Journal of Family History* 8 (Fall 1983): 248-261.

-----. "The Lives of Slave Women." *Southern Exposure* 12 (November/December 1984): 32-39.

Wood, Betty. "Some Aspects of Female Resistance to Chattel Slavery in Low Country Georgia, 1763-1815." *Historical Journal* [Great Britain] 30, no. 3 (1987): 603-622.

## Theory, Issues, and Historiography

Allen, Walter R. "The Social and Economic Statuses of Black Women in the United States." *Phylon* (March 1981): 26-40.

Aptheker, Bettina. "Black Women: Love, Labor, Sorrow, Struggle." *Science & Society* 51 (Winter 1987/88): 478-485.

Biola, Heather. "The Black Washerwoman in Southern Tradition." *Tennessee*

*Folklore Society Bulletin* 45, no. 1 (1979): 17-27.

Bontemps, Arna Alexander, and Jacqueline Fonvielle-Bontemps. "African-American Women Artists: An Historical Perspective." *Sage* 4, no. 1 (1987): 17-24.

Bracey, John H., Jr. "Afro-American Women: A Brief Guide to Writings from Historical and Feminist Perspectives." *Contributions in Black Studies* 8 (1986/1987): 106-110.

Bystydzienski, Jill. "Minority Women of North America: A Comparison of French-Canadian and Afro-American Women." *American Review of Canadian Studies* 15 (Winter 1985): 465-480.

Campbell, Karlyn Kohrs. "Style and Content in the Rhetoric of Early Afro-American Feminists." *Quarterly Journal of Speech* 72 (November 1986): 434-445.

Carpenter, Delores C. "Black Women in Religious Institutions: A Historical Summary from Slavery to the 1960s." *Journal of Religious Thought* 46 (Winter 1989/Spring 1990): 7-27.

Chitty, Arthur Ben. "Women and Black Education: Three Profiles." *Historical Magazine of the Protestant Episcopal Church* 52 (June 1983): 153-165.

Christensen, Lawrence O. "The Popular Images of Blacks vs. the Birthrights." *Missouri History Review* 81 (October 1986): 37-52.

Cole, Johnetta. "Militant Black Women in Early U.S. History." *Black Scholar* (April 1978): 38-44.

Coleman, Willi. "Black Women and Segregated Public Transportation: Ninety Years of Resistance." *Truth* 8, no. 2 (1986): 3-10.

Deck, Alice A. "Autoethnography: Zora Neale Hurston, Noni Jabavu, and Cross-Disciplinary Discourse." *Black American Literature Forum* 24 (Summer 1990): 237-256.

Dill, Bonnie Thornton. "The Dialectics of Black Womanhood." *Signs* 4 (Spring 1979): 543-555.

Geschwender, James A., and Rita Carroll-Seguin. "Exploding the Myth of African-American Progress." *Signs* 15 (Winter 1990): 285-299.

Gomez, Jewelle. "Black Women Heroes: Here's Reality, Where's the Fiction?" *Black Scholar* 17 (March/April 1986): 8-13.

Harris, William G. "Research on the Black Family: Mainstream and Dissenting Perspectives." *Journal of Ethnic Studies* 6 (Winter 1979): 45-64.

Helmbold, Lois Rita. "Writing the History of Black and White Working Class Women." *Women's Studies* 17, no. 1/2 (1989): 37-48.

Henry, Linda J. "Promoting Consciousness: The Early Archives Committee of the National Council of Negro Women." *Signs* 7 (Autumn 1981): 251-259.

Higginbotham, Elizabeth, and Sarah Watts. "The New Scholarship on Afro-American Women." *Women's Studies Quarterly* 16 (Spring/Summer 1988): 12-21.

Higginbotham, Evelyn Brooks. "Beyond the Sound of Silence: Afro-American Women's History." *Gender & History* 1 (Spring 1989): 50-67.

Hine, Darlene Clark. "An Angle of Vision: Black Women and the United States

Constitution, 1787-1987." *OAH Magazine of History* 3 (Winter 1988): 7-14.

-----. "The Ethel Johns Report: Black Women in the Nursing Profession, 1925." *Journal of Negro History* 67 (Fall 1982): 212-228.

-----. "To Be Gifted, Female, and Black." *Southwest Review* 67 (Autumn 1982): 357-369.

Hine, Darlene Clark, Patrick Kay Bidelman, and Bridgie Alexis Ford. "The Invisible Woman." *History News* (February 1984): 6-11.

Hoefel, Roseanne L. "'Broken' Silence, Un-Broken Spirits: Fragmentation in the Fiction of Black Women Writers." *Feminisms* 2 (Autumn 1989): 2-6.

King, Deborah K. "Multiple Jeopardy, Multiple Consciousness: The Context of a Black Feminist Ideology." *Signs* 14 (Autumn 1988): 42-72.

Lewis, David Levering. "Of Auguste Comte, Mary Berry, and John Blassingame: 'Long Memory, the Black Experience in America.'" *Southern Atlantic Quarterly* (Autumn 1983): 437-444.

Lupton, Mary Jane. "Singing the Black Mother: Maya Angelou and Autobiographical Continuity." *Black American Literature Forum* 24 (Summer 1990): 257-276.

Marable, Manning. "Groundings with My Sisters: Patriarchy and the Exploitation of Black Women." *Journal of Ethnic Studies* 11 (Summer 1983): 1-40.

Mason, Mary G. "Travel as Metaphor and Reality in Afro-American Women's Autobiography." *Black American Literature Forum* 24 (Summer 1990): 337-356.

Moore, Shelley. "An Historical Look at Male-Female Relationships in the Black Community." *Crisis* 93, no. 10 (1986): 20-23, 31.

Olwig, Karen Fog. "Women, 'Matrifocality' and Systems of Exchange: An Ethnohistorical Study of the Afro-American Family on St. John, West Indies." *Ethnohistory* 28 (Winter 1981): 59-81.

Omolade, Barbara. "The Unbroken Circle: A Historical and Contemporary Study of Black Single Mothers and Their Families." *Wisconsin Women's Law Journal* 3 (1987): 239-274.

Overton, Betty J. "Black Women Preachers: A Literary Overview." *Southern Quarterly* 23 (Spring 1985): 157-166.

Palmer, Phyllis Marynick. "White Women/Black Women: The Dualism of Female Identity in the United States." *Feminist Studies* 9 (Spring 1983): 151-170.

Patterson, Tiffany R. "Toward a Black Feminist Analysis: Recent Works by Black Women Scholars." *Women Organizing* no. 11 (Summer 1983): 33-36.

Reagon, Bernice Johnson. "My Black Mothers and Sisters, or on Beginning a Cultural Autobiography." *Feminist Studies* 8 (Spring 1982): 81-96.

Smith, Eleanor. "African American Women and the Extended Family: A Sociohistorical Review." *Western Journal of Black Studies* 13 (Winter 1989): 179-184.

-----. "Black American Women and Work: A Historical Review--1619-1920." *Women's Studies* 8, no. 4 (1985): 343-350.

-----. "Historical Relationships Between Black and White Women." *Western Journal of Black Studies* 4 (Winter 1980): 251-255.

Smith, Eleanor, and Paul M. Smith, Jr. "The Black Female Single-Parent Family Condition." *Journal of Black Studies* 17 (September 1986): 125-134.

Snitgen, Jeanne. "History, Identity and the Constitution of the Female Subject: Maryse Conde's 'Tituba.'" *Black Women's Writing* (1989): 55-76.

Snodgrass, J. William. "Black Women and Journalism: 1800-1950." *Western Journal of Black Studies* 6 (Fall 1982): 150-158.

Sterling, Dorothy. "To Build a Free Society: Nineteenth Century Black Women." *Southern Exposure* 12 (March/April 1984): 24-30.

Stevenson, Rosemary. "Black Women in the United States: A Bibliography of Recent Works." *Black Scholar* 16 (March/April 1985): 546-568.

Terborg-Penn, Rosalyn. "Teaching the History of Black Women: A Bibliographic Essay." *History Teacher* 13, no. 2 (1980): 245-250.

Thornbrough, Emma Lou. "The History of Black Women in Indiana: Part I." *Black History News and Notes* 13 (May 1983): 1, 4-8.

-----. "The History of Black Women in Indiana: Part II." *Black History News and Notes* 14 (August 1983): 4-7.

Wald, Priscilla. "Becoming 'Colored': The Self-Authorized Language of Difference in Zora Neale Hurston." *American Literary History* 2 (Spring 1990): 79-100.

White, E. Frances. "Africa on My Mind: Gender, Counter Discourse and African-American Nationalism." *Journal of Women's History* 2 (Spring 1990): 73-97.

Wilkerson, Margaret B. "Excavating Our History: The Importance of Biographies of Women of Color." *Black American Literature Forum* 24 (Spring 1990): 73-84.

Wilkinson, Doris Y. "The Doll Exhibit: A Psycho-Cultural Analysis of Black Female Role Stereotypes." *Journal of Popular Culture* 21, no. 2 (1987): 19-29.

Williams, Delores S. "The Color of Feminism: Or Speaking the Black Woman's Tongue." *Journal of Religious Thought* 43 (Spring-Summer 1986): 42-58.

## Twentieth Century

Aldridge, Delores. "African-American Women in the Economic Marketplace: A Continuing Struggle." *Journal of Black Studies* 20 (December 1989): 129-154.

Anderson, Karen T. "Last Hired, First Fired: Black Women Workers During World War II." *Journal of American History* 69 (June 1982): 86-97.

Anderson, Kathie Ryckman. "Eva Bell Thompson: A North Dakota Daughter." *North Dakota History* 49 (Fall 1982): 11-18.

Arnez, Nancy L. "Selected Black Female Superintendents of Public School Systems." *Journal of Negro Education* (Summer 1982): 309-317.

Aschenbrenner, Joyce, and Carolyn H. Carr. "The Dance Technique of Katherin Dunn as a Community Rite de passage." *Western Journal of Black Studies* 13 (Fall 1989): 139-143.

Austin, Gayle. "Alice Childress: Black Woman Playwright as Feminist Critic." *Southern Quarterly* 25 (Spring 1987): 53-62.

Beard, Linda Susan. "Daughters of Clio and Calliope: Afro-American Women Writers as Reclamation and Revisionist Herstorians." *Psychohistory Review* 17 (Spring 1989): 301-343.

Beeth, Howard. "Houston & History, Past and Present: A Look at Black Houston in the 1920s." *Southern Studies* 25 (Summer 1986): 172-186.

Berry, Mary Frances. "Twentieth-Century Black Women in Education." *Journal of Negro Education* (Summer 1982): 288-300.

Bogle, Kathryn Hall. "Document: Kathryn Hall Bogle's 'An American Negro Speaks of Color.'" *Oregon Historical Quarterly* 89, no. 1 (1988): 70-81.

Bogle, Kathryn Hall, and Rick Harmon, interviewer. "Interview: Kathryn Hall Bogle on the Writing of 'An American Negro Speaks of Color.'" *Oregon Historical Quarterly* 89, no. 1 (1988): 82-91.

Brady, Marilyn Dell. "Kansas Federation of Colored Women's Clubs, 1900-1930." *Kansas History* 9 (Spring 1986): 19-30.

-----. "Organizing Afro-American Girls' Clubs in Kansas in the 1920's." *Frontiers* 9, no. 2 (1987): 69-72.

Breen, William J. "Black Women and the Great War: Mobilization and Reform in the South." *Journal of Southern History* 44 (August 1978): 421-440.

Campanaro, Giorgio G. "A Case for Billie Holiday." *Ufahamu* 16, no. 2 (1988): 38-44.

Catlin, Robert A. "Organizational Effectiveness and Black Political Participation: The Case of Katie Hall." *Phylon* 46 (September 1985): 179-192.

Crawford, Vicki. "Grassroots Activists in the Mississippi Civil Rights Movement." *Sage* 5 (Fall 1988): 24-29.

Dickson, Lynda F. "Toward a Broader Angle of Vision in Uncovering Women's History: Black Women's Clubs Revisited." *Frontiers* 9, no. 2 (1987): 62-68.

Dill, Bonnie Thornton. "Race, Class, and Gender: Prospects for and All-Inclusive Sisterhood (1900-40)." *Feminist Studies* 9 (Spring 1983): 131-150.

Enloe, Cynthia and Harold Jordan. "Black Women in the Military." *Minerva: Quarterly Report on Women and the Military* 3 (Winter 1985): 108-116.

Fabre, Genevieve. "Genealogical Archaeology: Black Women Writers in the 1980s and the Search for Legacy." *Revue française d'études américaines* no. 30 (1986): 461-467.

Ferguson, Earline Rae. "The Woman's Improvement Club of Indianapolis: Black Women Pioneers in Tuberculosis Work, 1903-1938." *Indiana Magazine of History* 84, no. 3 (1988): 237-261.

Fry, Gladys-Marie. "Harriet Powers: Portrait of a Black Quilter." *Sage* 4, no. 1 (1987): 11-16.

Gilkes, Cheryl Townsend. "Successful Rebellious Professionals: The Black Woman's Professional Identity and Community Commitment." *Psychology of Women Quarterly* 6 (1982): 289-311.

Guzman, Jessie P. "The Social Contributions of the Negro Woman since 1940." *Negro History Bulletin* 11 (January 1984): 86-94.

Haiken, Elizabeth. "'The Lord Helps Those Who Help Themselves': Black Laundresses in Little Rock, Arkansas, 1917-1921." *Arkansas Historical*

*Quarterly* 49 (Spring 1990): 20-50.

Harley, Sharon. "Beyond the Classroom: The Organizational Lives of Black Female Educators in the District of Columbia, 1890-1930." *Journal of Negro Education* (Summer 1982): 254-265.

-----. "For the Good of Family and Race: Gender, Work and Domestic Roles in the Black Community, 1880-1930." *Signs* 15 (Winter 1990): 336-349.

Hawks, Joanne V. "A Challenge to Racism and Sexism: Black Women in Southern Legislatures, 1965-1986." *Sage* 5 (Fall 1988): 20-23.

Helmbold, Lois Rita. "Beyond the Family Economy: Black and White Working Class Women During the Great Depression." *Feminist Studies* 13 (Fall 1987): 629-656.

-----. "Downward Occupational Mobility During the Great Depression: Urban Black and White Working Class Women." *Labor History* 29, no. 2 (1988): 135-172.

Hine, Darlene Clark. "The Call That Never Came: Black Women Nurses and World War I, an Historical Note." *Indiana Military History Journal* 15 (January 1983): 23-27.

-----. "From Hospital to College: Black Nurse Leaders and the Rise of Collegiate Nursing Schools." *Journal of Negro Education* 51 (Summer 1982): 222-237.

Jones, Beverly W. "Race, Sex, and Class: Black Female Tobacco Workers in Durham, North Carolina, 1920-1940, and the Development of Female Consciousness." *Feminist Studies* 10 (Fall 1984): 441-452.

Jones, Jacqueline. "Fact and Fiction in Alice Walker's *The Color Purple*." *Georgia Historical Quarterly* 72 (Winter 1988): 653-669.

Jones, Phyllis. "Ragtime: Feminist, Socialist and Black Perspectives on the Self-Made Man." *Journal of American Culture* 2 (Spring 1979): 17-28.

Kremer, Gary R., and Linda Rea Gibbens. "The Missouri Home for Negro Girls: The 1930s." *American Studies* (Fall 1983): 77-93.

Lang, William L. "The Nearly Forgotten Blacks of Last Chance Gulch, 1900-1912." *Pacific Northwest Quarterly* 70 (April 1979): 50-57.

Loveland, Anne C., ed. "'But We Are Not at all Distant in Sympathy!'--Letters of Dorothy Canfield Fisher and Lillian Smith." *Vermont History* 52 (Winter 1984): 17-32.

-----. "Lillian Smith and the Problem of Segregation in the Roosevelt Era." *Southern Studies* 22 (Spring 1983): 32-34.

Moore, Brenda L. "Black, Female and in Uniform: An African-American Woman in the United States Army 1973-1979." *Minerva: Quarterly Report on Women and the Military* 8 (Summer 1990): 62-66.

Neverdon-Morton, Cynthia. "Self-Help Programs as Educative Activities of Black Women in the South, 1895-1925: Focus on Four Key Areas." *Journal of Negro Education* 51 (Summer 1982): 207-221.

Newman, Debra L. "The Propaganda and the Truth: Black Women and World War II." *Minerva: Quarterly Report on Women and the Military* 4 (Winter 1986): 72-92.

Quester, Aline O., and William H. Green. "The Labor Market Experience of

Black and White Wives in the Sixties and Seventies." *Social Science Quarterly* 66 (December 1985): 854-866.

Saunders, Deloris M. "Changes in the Status of Women During the Quarter Century (1955-1980)." *Negro Educational Review* 32 (January 1981): 56-77.

Scott, Anne Firor. "Most Invisible of All: Black Women's Voluntary Associations." *Journal of Southern History* 56 (February 1990): 3-22.

Sosna, Morton. "Race and Gender in the South: The Case of Georgia's Lillian Smith." *Georgia History Quarterly* 71 (Fall 1987): 427-437.

Stetson, Erlene. "Black Feminism in Indiana, 1893-1933." *Phylon* 44 (December 1983): 292-298.

Thompson, Delores, and Lyle Koehler. "Educated Pioneers: Black Woman at the University of Cincinnati, 1897-1940." *Queen City Heritage* 43 (Winter 1985): 21-28.

Trescott, Jacqueline. "Daisy Bates: Before and after Little Rock." *Crisis* 88 (1981): 232-235.

Tucker, Susan. "A Complex Bond: Southern Black Domestic Workers and Their White Employers." *Frontiers* 9, no. 3 (1987): 6-13.

Weber, Shirley N. "Black Power in the 1960s: A Study of Its Impact on Women's Liberation." *Journal of Black Studies* 11 (June 1981).

Williams-Burns, Winona. "Jane Ellen McAllister (b. 1899): Pioneer for Excellence in Teacher Education." *Journal of Negro Education* (Summer 1982): 342-357.

# AGRICULTURE

## Agricultural Workers

Agarwal, Bina. "Women, Poverty and Agricultural Growth in India." *Journal of Peasant Studies* 13 (July 1986): 165-220.

Ankarloo, Bengt. "Agriculture and Women's Work: Directions of Change in the West, 1700-1900." *Journal of Family History* 4 (Summer 1979): 111-120.

Atchi Reddy, M. "Female Agricultural Labourers of Nellore, 1881-1981." *Indian Economic and Social History Review* [Delhi] 20 (March 1983): 67-79.

Bell, J. H., and U. S. Pandey. "The Exclusion of Women from Australian Post-Secondary Agricultural Education and Training 1880-1969." *Australian Journal of Politics and History* 36, no. 2 (1990): 205-216.

Caldwell, Ellen M. "Ellen Glasgow and the Southern Agrarians." *American Literature* 56 (May 1984): 203-213.

Campbell, John. "Work, Pregnancy, and Infant Mortality Among Southern Slaves." *Journal of Interdisciplinary History* 14 (Spring 1984): 793-812.

Cohen, Marjorie Griffin. "The Decline of Women in Canadian Dairying." *Histoire sociale/Social History* 17 (November 1984): 307-334.

Curtin, Patricia Romero. "Laboratory for the Oral History of Slavery: The Island of Lamu on the Kenya Coast." *American Historical Review* 88 (October 1983): 858-882.

Flora, Cornelia Butler, and Jan L. Flora. "Structure of Agriculture and Women's Culture in the Great Plains." *Great Plains Quarterly* 8 (Fall 1988): 195-205.

Frader, Laura L. "Women's Work and Family Labor in the Vineyards of Lower Languedoc: Coursan 1860-1913." *Western Society for French History* 7 (November 1979): 97-98.

Fredericks, Anne. "The Creation of 'Women Work' in Agriculture: The Women's Land Army During World War I." *Insurgent Sociologist* 12 (Summer 1984): 33-40.

Goodwin, Katherine G. "'A Woman's Curiosity': Martha Gaffney and Cotton Planting on the Texas Frontier." *East Texas History Journal* 24, no. 2 (1986): 4-17.

Gundersen, Rae C. "Mary Elizabeth Lease: Voice of the Populists." *Heritage of the Great Plains* 13 (Fall 1980): 3-10.

Hein, Ruth D. "A Town Girl Becomes a Farm Helper." *Palimpsest* 71 (Summer 1990): 94-96.

Holmes, William F. "Ellen Dortch and the Farmer's Alliance." *Georgia Historical Quarterly* 69 (Summer 1985): 149-172.

Jensen, Joan M. "Buttermaking and Economic Development in Mid-Atlantic America from 1750 to 1850." *Signs* 13 (Summer 1988): 813-829.

-----. "Canning Comes to New Mexico: Women and the Agricultural Extension Service, 1914-1919." *New Mexico Historical Review* 57 (October 1982): 361-386.

-----. "Crossing Ethnic Barriers in the Southwest: Women's Agricultural Extension Education, 1914-1940." *Agricultural History* 60 (Spring 1986): 169-181.

Jones, Jacqueline. "'My Mother Was Much of a Woman': Black Women, Work, and the Family under Slavery." *Feminist Studies* 8 (Summer 1982): 235-270.

Kechnie, Margaret. "The United Farm Workers of Ontario: Developing a Political Consciousness." *Ontario History* 77 (December 1985): 267-280.

Landale, Nancy. "Agricultural Opportunity and Marriage: The United States at the Turn of the Century." *Demography* 26 (May 1989): 203-218.

Marti, Donald B. "Sisters of the Grange: Rural Feminism in the Late Nineteenth Century." *Agricultural History* 58 (July 1984): 247-261.

-----. "Woman's Work in the Grange: Mary Ann Mayo of Michigan 1882-1903." *Agricultural History* 56 (April 1982): 439-452.

Maskiell, Michelle. "Gender, Kinship and Rural Work in Colonial Punjab." *Journal of Women's History* 2 (Spring 1990): 35-72.

Mercier, Laurie K. "Women's Economic Role in Montana Agriculture: 'You Had to Make Every Minute Count.'" *Montana* 38 (Autumn 1988): 50-61.

Omvedt, Gail. "Women and Rural Revolt in India." *Journal of Peasant Studies* 5 (April 1978): 370-403.

Peires, J. B. "'Soft' Believers and 'Hard' Unbelievers in Xhosa Cattle-Killing." *Journal of African History* 27, no. 3 (1986): 443-461.

Quataert, Jean H. "The Politics of Rural Industrialization: Class, Gender, and Collective Protest in the Saxon Oberlausitz of the Late Nineteenth Century."

*Central European History* 20 (June 1987): 91-124.

Reddy, M. Atchi. "Female Agricultural Labourers of Nellore, 1881-1981." *Indian Economic and Social History Review* 20, no. 1 (1983): 67-80.

Roberts, Michael. "Sickles and Scythes: Women's Work and Men's Work at Harvest Time." *History Workshop* 7 (Spring 1979): 3-29.

Rose, Margaret. "'From the Fields to the Picket Line: Huelga Women and the Boycott,' 1965-1975." *Labor History* 31 (Summer 1990): 271-293.

Russell, Scott C., and Mark B. McDonald. "The Economic Contributions of Women in a Rural Western Navajo Community." *American Indian Quarterly* 6 (Fall/Winter 1982): 262-282.

Sayer, Karen. "'Utterly Shameless Women': Images of Women Field Workers." *Labour History Review* 55 (Spring 1990): 11-12.

Sears, Richard. "Working Like a Slave: Views of Slavery and the Status of Women in Antebellum Kentucky." *The Register of the Kentucky Historical Society* 87 (Winter 1989): 1-19.

Snell, K. D. M. "Agricultural Seasonal Unemployment, the Standard of Living, and Women's Work in the South and East, 1690-1860." *Economic History Review* 34 (August 1981): 407-437.

Strong-Boag, Veronica. "Pulling in Double Harness or Hauling a Double Load: Women, Work, and Feminism on the Canadian Prairie." *Journal of Canadian Studies* 21 (Fall 1986): 32-52.

Tutino, John. "Family Economies in Agrarian Mexico, 1750-1910." *Journal of Family History* 10 (Fall 1985): 258-271.

Weber, Devra Anne. "*Raiz Fuerte*: Oral History and Mexicana Farmworkers." *Oral History Review* 17 (Fall 1989): 47-62.

Wright, Marcia. "Technology, Marriage and Women's Work in the History of Maize Growers in Mazabuka, Zambia: A Reconnaissance." *Journal of South African Studies* 10 (October 1983): 71-85.

## Farms and Farmers

Adams, Jane H. "The Decoupling of Farm and Household: Differential Consequences of Capitalist Development on Southern Illinois and Third World Family Farms." *Comparative Studies in Society and History* [Great Britain] 30, no. 3 (1988): 453-482.

Atkins, Annette. "Women on the Farming Frontier: The View from Fiction." *Midwest Review* 3 (Spring 1981): 1-10.

Bauer, Arnold J. "Millers and Grinders: Technology and Household Economy in Meso-America." *Agricultural History* 64 (Winter 1990): 1-17.

Bourke, Joanna. "Dairywomen and Affectionate Wives: Women in the Irish Dairy Industry, 1890-1914." *Agricultural History Review* 38, no. 2 (1990): 149-164.

Brady, Marilyn Dell. "Populism and Feminism in a Newspaper by and for Women of the Kansas Farmers' Alliance, 1891-1894." *Kansas History* 7 (Winter 1984/85): 280-290.

Bryant, James. "More Than Hard Work and Good Butter." *Michigan History* 65

(July/August 1981): 32-38.

Buffalohead, Priscilla K. "Farmers, Warriors, Traders: A Fresh Look at Ojibway Women." *Minnesota History* 48 (Summer 1983): 236-244.

Collins, D. Cheryl. "Women at Work in Manhattan, Kansas, 1890-1910." *Journal of the West* 21 (April 1982): 33-40.

Eagan, Shirley C. "'Women's Work, Never Done': West Virginia Farm Women, 1880s-1920s." *West Virginia History* 49 (1990): 21-35.

Fink, Deborah. "'Mom, It's a Losing Proposition': The Decline of Women's Subsistence Production on Iowa Farms." *North Dakota Quarterly* 52 (Winter 1984): 26-33.

Fink, Deborah, and Dorothy Schweider. "Iowa Farm Women in the 1930s: A Reassessment." *Annals of Iowa* 49 (Winter 1989): 570-590.

Friedberger, Mark. "The Farm Family and the Inheritance Process: Evidence from the Corn Belt, 1870-1950." *Agricultural History* 57 (January 1983): 1-13.

Hurtado, Albert L. "'Hardly a Farm House--A Kitchen Without Them': Indian and White Households on the California Borderland Frontier in 1860." *Western Historical Quarterly* 13 (July 1982): 245-270.

Jensen, Joan M. "'I've Worked, I'm Not Afraid of Work': Farm Women in New Mexico, 1920-1940." *New Mexico Historical Review* 61, no. 1 (January 1986): 27-52.

-----. "'You May Depend She Does Not Eat Much Idle Bread': Mid-Atlantic Farm Women and Their Historians." *Agricultural History* 61 (Winter 1987): 29-46.

Lacey, Barbara E. "The World of Hannah Heaton: The Autobiography of an Eighteenth-Century Connecticut Farm Woman." *William and Mary Quarterly* 45 (April 1988): 280-304.

Lovin, Clifford R. "Farm Women in the Third Reich." *Agricultural History* 60 (Summer 1986): 105-123.

Matelic, Candace Tangorra. "Living History Farms." *Museum News* 58 (March/April 1980): 36-45.

Meusburger, Joanne. "Farm Girl." *Palimpsest* 68 (Winter 1987): 146-159.

Pearson, Jessica. "Note on Female Farmers." *Rural Sociology* 44 (Spring 1979): 189-200.

Rathge, Richard W. "Women's Contribution to the Family Farm." *Great Plains Quarterly* 9 (Winter 1989): 36-47.

Riley, Glenda. "Farm Women's Role in the Agricultural Development of South Dakota." *South Dakota History* 13 (Spring/Summer 1983): 83-121.

Schweider, Dorothy. "Education and Change in the Lives of Iowa Farm Women, 1900-1940." *Agricultural History* 60 (Spring 1986): 200-215.

-----. "South Dakota Farm Women and the Great Depression." *Journal of the West* 24 (October 1985): 6-18.

Snyder, Robert E. "Marion Post and the Farm Security Administration in Florida." *Florida Historical Quarterly* 65 (April 1987): 457-479.

Starr, Karen. "Fighting for a Future: Farm Women of the Nonpartisan League." *Minnesota History* 48 (Summer 1983): 255-262.

Sturgis, Cynthia. "'How're You Gonna Keep 'Em down on the Farm?': Rural

Women and Urban Model in Utah." *Agricultural History* 60 (Spring 1986): 182-199.

Tyler, Pamela. "The Ideal Woman as Seen by a Progressive Farmer in the 1930s." *Southern Studies* 20 (Fall 1981): 278-296.

Webb, Anne B. "Forgotten Persephones: Women Farmers on the Frontier." *Minnesota History* 50 (Winter 1986): 134-148.

Wold, Frances M., comp. and ed. "The Letters of Effie Hanson, 1917-1923: Farm Life in Troubled Times." *North Dakota History* 48 (Winter 1981): 20-43.

## Rural Life

Abbott, John. "Accomplishing 'A Man's Task': Rural Women Teachers, Male Culture, and the School Inspectorate in Turn-of-the-Century Ontario." *Ontario History* 78 (December 1986): 313-330.

Abeele, Cynthia Comacchio. "'The Mothers of the Land Must Suffer': Child and Maternal Welfare in Rural and Outpost Ontario, 1918-1940." *Ontario History* 80 (September 1988): 183-205.

Arrington, Leonard J. "Rural Life Among Nineteenth-Century Mormons: The Woman's Experience." *Agricultural History* 58 (July 1984): 239-246.

Bauman, Paula M. "Single Women Homesteaders in Wyoming, 1880-1930." *Annals of Wyoming* 58 (Spring 1986): 39-49.

Becker, Marshall J. "Hannah Freeman: An Eighteenth-Century Lenape Living and Working Among Colonial Farmers." *Pennsylvania Magazine of History and Biography* 94 (April 1990): 249-270.

Beecher, Maureen Ursenbach. "Women's Work on the Mormon Frontier." *Utah Historical Quarterly* 49 (Summer 1981): 276-290.

Borish, Linda J. "Farm Females, Fitness, and the Ideology of Physical Health in Antebellum New England." *Agricultural History* 64 (Summer 1990): 17-30.

Bourke, Joanna. "'The Health Caravan': Domestic Education and Female Labor in Rural Ireland, 1890-1914." *Eire-Ireland* 24 (Winter 1989): 7-20.

Brookes, Alan A., and Catharine A. Wilson. "'Working Away' from the Farm: The Young Women of North Huron, 1910-1930." *Ontario History* 77 (December 1985): 281-300.

Dryden, Jean E., and Sandra L. Myres. "The Letters of Barbara Alice Slater: Homesteading on the Canadian Prairies, 1909-1918." *Montana* 37 (Winter 1987): 14-33.

Faragher, John Mack. "History from the Inside-Out: Writing the History of Women in Rural America." *American Quarterly* 33 (Winter 1981): 537-557.

Farnsworth, Beatrice. "The Litigious Daughter-in-law: Family Relations in Rural Russia in the Second Half of the Nineteenth Century." *Slavic Review* 45 (Spring 1986): 49-64.

Fink, Deborah. "Ann Oleson: Rural Family and Community in Iowa, 1880-1920." *Annals of Iowa* 48 (Summer/Fall 1987): 251-263.

-----. "Rural Women and Family in Iowa." *International Journal of Women's*

*Studies* 7 (January/February 1984): 57-69.

Hagler, D. Harland. "The Ideal Woman in the Antebellum South: Lady or Farmwife?" *Journal of Southern History* 46 (August 1980): 405-418.

Hall, John A. "Disillusioned with Paradise: A Southern Woman's Impression of the Rural North in 1862." *Southern Studies* 25 (Summer 1986): 204-207.

Hansen, Botil K. "Rural Women in Late Nineteenth-Century Denmark." *Journal of Peasant Studies* 9 (January 1982): 225-240.

Harris, Katherine. "Sex Roles and Work Patterns Among Homesteading Families in Northeastern Colorado, 1873-1920." *Frontiers* 7, no. 3 (1984): 43-49.

Hinde, P. R. A. "Household Structure, Marriage and the Institution of Service in Nineteenth Century Rural England." *Local Population Studies* no. 35 (Autumn 1985): 43-51.

Janiewski, Dolores. "Women and the Making of a Rural Proletariat in the Bright Tobacco Belt, 1880-1930." *Insurgent Sociologist* 10 (Summer 1980): 16-26.

Jensen, Katharine. "Oral Histories of Rural Western American Women: Can They Contribute to Quantitative Studies?" *International Journal of Oral History* 5 (November 1984): 159-167.

Jones, David C. "'From Babies to Buttonholes': Women's Work at Agricultural Fairs." *Alberta History* 29 (Autumn 1981): 26-32.

Jones, Lu Ann. "'Mama Learned Us to Work': An Oral History of Virgie St. John Redmond." *Oral History Review* 17 (Fall 1989): 63-90.

Judd, Ellen R. "'Men Are More Able': Rural Chinese Women's Conceptions of Gender and Agency." *Pacific Affairs* 63 (Spring 1990): 40-62.

Leiber, Justin, James Pickering, and Flora Bronson White, eds. "'Mother by the Tens': Flora Adelaide Holcomb Bronson's Account of Her Life as an Illinois Schoolteacher, Poet, and Farm Wife, 1851-1927." *Journal of the Illinois State Historical Society* 76 (Winter 1983): 283-307.

Lindgren, H. Elaine. "Ethnic Women Homesteading on the Plains of North Dakota." *Great Plains Quarterly* 9 (Summer 1989): 157-173.

Lucas, Catherine. "Postmen and Postwomen in Rural Areas." *Costume* 13 (1979): 52-53.

Malone, Ann Patton. "Searching for the Family and Household Structure of Rural Louisiana Slaves, 1810-1864." *Louisiana History* 28 (Fall 1987): 357-380.

Marling, Karal Ann. "'She Brought Forth Butter in a Lordly Dish': The Origins of Minnesota Butter Sculpture." *Minnesota History* 50 (Summer 1987): 218-228.

Neil, Catherine. "Recollections of a Sheep Herder's Bride, Part One." *Alberta History* 35 (Spring 1987): 18-24.

-----. "Recollections of a Sheep Herder's Bride, Part Two." *Alberta History* 35 (Summer 1987): 20-28.

-----. "Recollections of a Sheep Herder's Bride, Part Three." *Alberta History* 35 (Autumn 1987): 22-29.

-----. "Recollections of a Sheep Herder's Bride, Part Four." *Alberta History* 36 (Winter 1988): 19-26.

Osterud, Nancy Grey, and Lu Ann Jones. "'If I Must Say So Myself': Oral Histories of Rural Women." *Oral History Review* 17 (Fall 1989): 1-24.

Rife, Gladys Talcott. "Personal Perspectives on the 1950s: Iowa's Rural Women Newspaper Columnists." *Annals of Iowa* 49 (Spring 1989): 661-682.

Riley, Glenda. "In or out of the Historical Kitchen? Interpretations of Minnesota Rural Women." *Minnesota History* 52 (Summer 1990): 61-71.

-----, ed. "Proving Up: The Memoir of 'Girl Homesteader' Martha Stoecher Norby." *South Dakota History* 16 (Spring 1986): 1-17.

Robin, Jean. "Prenuptial Pregnancy in a Rural Area of Devonshire in the Mid-Nineteenth Century: Colyton, 1851-1881." *Continuity and Change* 1, no. 1 (1986): 113-124.

Schweider, Dorothy, and Deborah Fink. "Plains Women: Rural Life in the 1930s." *Great Plains Quarterly* 8 (Spring 1988): 79-88.

Smart, Mildred B. "Bidding on a New Life: The Sale Farm Venture of Millie and Love Smart." *Michigan History* 72, no. 1 (1988): 20-23.

Sturgis, Cynthia. "'How're You Gonna Keep 'Em down on the Farm?': Rural Women and Urban Model in Utah." *Agricultural History* 60, no. 2 (Spring 1986): 182-199.

Towne, Ruth Warner. "Marie Turner Harvey and the Rural Life Movement." *Missouri Historical Review* 84 (July 1990): 384-403.

Travis, Carol. "Rural Connecticut in 1840: The Pastor's Wife's Manuscript." *Manuscripts* 36 (Summer 1984): 197-202.

Webb, Anne B. "Minnesota Women Homesteaders: 1863-1889." *Journal of Social History* 23, no.1 (1989): 115-136.

# ART

## Crafts

Arpad, Susan S. "'Pretty Much to Suit Ourselves': Midwestern Women Naming Experience through Domestic Arts." *Hayes Historical Journal* 4 (Fall 1984): 15-27.

Babcock, Barbara A. "At Home, No Womens Are Storytellers: Potteries, Stories, and Politics in Cochiti Pueblo." *Journal of the Southwest* 30 (Autumn 1988): 356-389.

Banes, Ruth A. "Doris Ulmann and Her Mountain Folk." *Journal of American Culture* 8 (Spring 1985): 29-42.

Banks, Anne. "Jessie Donaldson Schultz and Blackfeet Crafts." *Montana* 33 (Autumn 1983): 18-35.

Benhamou, Reed. "The Verdigris Industry in Eighteenth-Century Languedoc: Women's Work, Women's Art." *French Historical Studies* 16 (Spring 1990): 560-575.

Berge, Carol. "Dark Radiance: The Ancient Art of Maria Martinez, Legendary Matriarch of the Master Potters of San Ildefonso." *Art & Antiques*

(September 1988): 104-107, 134.

Brackman, Barbara. "Quilts on the Kansas Frontier." *Kansas History* 13 (Spring 1990): 13-22.

Brandimarte, Cynthia A. "Somebody's Aunt and Nobody's Mother: The American China Painter and Her Work, 1870-1920." *Winterthur Portfolio* 23 (Winter 1988): 203-224.

Buckley, Cheryl. "Women Designers in the English Pottery Industry, 1919-1939." *Woman's Art Journal* 5 (Fall 1984/Winter 1985): 11-15.

Callen, Anthea. "Sexual Division of Labor in the Arts and Crafts Movement." *Woman's Art Journal* 5 (Fall 1984/Winter 1985): 1-6.

Chinn, Jennie A. "'Some Ladies Make Quilts, But They Aren't Quilt Makers': Aesthetic Principles in Quilt Making." *Kansas History* 13 (Spring 1990): 32-44.

Connolly, Loris, and Agatha Huepenbecker. "Home Weaving in Southeast Iowa, 1833-1870." *Annals of Iowa* 48 (Summer/Fall 1985): 3-31.

Cunningham, Patricia A. "Northwest Ohio Coverlet Weavers: An Update." *Northwest Ohio Quarterly* 58 (Winter 1986): 20-24.

-----. "The Woven Record: Nineteenth-Century Coverlets and Textile Industries in Northwest Ohio." *Northwest Ohio Quarterly* 56 (Spring 1984): 43-76.

Davis, Gayle R. "Women in the Quilt Culture: An Analysis of Social Boundaries and Role Satisfaction." *Kansas History* 13 (Spring 1990): 5-12.

Davis, Natalie Zemon. "Women in the Crafts in Sixteenth-Century Lyon." *Feminist Studies* 8 (Spring 1982): 47-80.

Dewhurst, C. Kurt, Betty MacDowell, and Marsha MacDowell. "A Stitch or Sketch in Time: Michigan's Women Folk Artists." *Michigan History* 66 (July/August 1982): 8-13.

Durham, Carolyn A. "The Subversive Stitch: Female Craft, Culture and Ecriture." *Women's Studies* 17, no. 3/4 (1990): 341-360.

Eicher, Joanne, Tonye Victor Erekosima, and Carl Liedholm. "Cut and Drawn: Textile Work from Nigeria." *Craft International* 2 (Summer 1982): 16-19.

Fry, Gladys-Marie. "Harriet Powers: Portrait of a Black Quilter." *Sage* 4, no. 1 (1987): 11-16.

Hammond, Harmony. "Historias: Women Tinsmiths of New Mexico." *Heresies* 6, no. 4 (1989): 38-48.

Hedges, Elaine. "The 19th Century Diarist and Her Quilts." *Feminist Studies* 8 (Summer 1982): 293-299.

Hofter, Daryl M. "Toward a Social History of Needlework Artists." *Woman's Art Journal* 2 (Fall 1981/Winter 1982): 25-29.

Hood, Adrienne. "Early Canadian Quilts: Marriage of Art and Utility." *Rotunda* 17, no. 3 (1984-85): 28-35.

Levinsohn, Rhoda. "Rural Kwazulu Beadwork." *Ornament* 4 (September 1980): 38-41.

Madden, Mary W. "The Kansas Quilt Project: Piecing Together Our Past." *Kansas History* 13 (Spring 1990): 2-4.

Norwood, Vera L. "'Thank You For My Bones': Connections Between Contemporary Women Artists and the Traditional Arts of Their Foremothers."

*New Mexico Historical Review* 58 (January 1983): 57-80.

Omari, Mikelle Smith. "Creativity in Adversity: Afro-Bahian Women, Power, and Art." *International Review of African American Arts* 9, no. 1 (1990): 34-41.

Picton, John. "Women's Weaving: The Manufacture and Use of Textiles Among the Igbirra People of Nigeria." *Textile History* 11 (1980): 63-88.

Rowen, Mary Margaret. "Group Quilting in Kansas." *Kansas History* 13 (Spring 1990): 23-31.

Salmond, Wendy. "The Solomenko Embroidery Workshops." *The Journal of Decorative and Propaganda Arts* no. 5 (Summer 1987): 126-143.

Wolf, Toni Lesser. "Women Jewelers of the British Arts and Crafts Movement." *The Journal of Decorative and Propaganda Arts* 14 (Fall 1989): 28-45.

## Visual Fine Arts

Anglesa, Martyn, and John Preston. "'A Philosophical Landscape': Susanna Drury and the Giant's Causeway." *Art History* 3 (September 1980): 252-273.

Baird, Nancy D. "Enid Yandell: Kentucky Sculptor." *Filson Club History Quarterly* 62 (January 1988): 5-31.

Berlo, Janet Catherine. "Inuit Women and Graphic Arts: Female Creativity and Its Cultural Context." *Canadian Journal of Native Studies* 9, no. 2 (1989): 293-316.

Boime, Albert. "The Case of Rosa Bonheur: Why Should a Woman Want to Be More Like a Man?" *Art History* 4 (December 1981): 384-409.

Bonfante, Larissa. "Nudity as Costume in Classical Art." *American Journal of Archaeology* 93 (October 1989): 543-570.

Bontemps, Arna Alexander, and Jacqueline Fonvielle-Bontemps. "African-American Women Artists: An Historical Perspective." *Sage* 4, no. 1 (1987): 17-24.

Burke, Mary Alice Heekin. "Elizabeth Nourse: Cincinnati's Most Famous Woman Artist." *Queen City Heritage* 41 (Winter 1983): 65-72.

Bush, Corlann Gee. "The Way We Weren't': Images of Women and Men in Cowboy Art." *Frontiers* 7, no.3 (1984): 73-78.

Cameron, Vivian P. "Two 18th-Century French Art Critics." *Woman's Art Journal* 5 (Spring/Summer 1984): 8-11.

Casteras, Susan P. "Virgin Vows: The Early Victorian Artists' Portrayal of Nuns and Novices." *Victorian Studies* 24 (Winter 1981): 157-184.

Chavda, Jadgish J. "The Narrative Paintings of India's Jitwarpuri Women." *Woman's Art Journal* 11 (Spring/Summer 1990): 26-28.

Cooney, Bob, and Sayre Cooney Dodgson. "Fanny Cory Cooney: Montana Mother and Artist." *Montana* 30 (July 1980): 2-17.

Cuba, Stanley L. "Eve Drewelowe: Boulder Artist." *Colorado Heritage* (Summer 1990): 32-44.

Duvert, Elizabeth. "O'Keefe's Place." *Journal of the Southwest* 30 (Spring 1988): 1-11.

Feigenbaum-Knox, Rena. "Aesthetics and Ethics: A Study of Sexuality in Denis

Diderot's Art Criticism." *Western Society for French History* 9 (October 1981): 226-237.

Gallati, Barbara. "The Paintings of Sarah Poxton Ball Dodson (1847-1906)." *The American Art Journal* 15 (Winter 1983): 67-82.

Golden, Catherine. "Beatrix Potter: Naturalist Artist." *Woman's Art Journal* 11 (Spring/Summer 1990): 9-15.

Gordon, Jean. "Early American Women Artists and the Context in Which They Worked." *American Quarterly* 30 (Spring 1978): 54-69.

Graham, Julie. "American Women Artists' Groups: 1867-1930." *Woman's Art Journal* 1 (Spring/Summer 1981): 7-12.

Hanners, John. "A Tale of Two Artists: Anna Mary Howitt's Portrait of John Banvard." *Minnesota History* 50 (Spring 1987): 204-208.

Harris, Ann Sutherland. "Entering the Mainstream: Women Sculptors of the 20th Century, Part Two: Louise Bourgeois and Eva Hesse." *Gallerie: Women's Art* 2 (Winter 1989): 4-9.

Havice, Christine. "The Artist in Her Own Words." *Woman's Art Journal* 2 (Fall 1981/Winter 1982): 1-7.

Higonnet, Anne. "Writing the Gender of the Image: Art Criticism in Late Nineteenth-Century France." *Genders* no. 6 (November 1989): 60-73.

Holcomb, Adele M. "Anna Jameson: The First Professional English Art Historian." *Art History* 6 (June 1983): 171-187.

Hoppin, Martha J. "Women Artists in Boston, 1870-1900: The Pupils of William Morris Hunt." *American Art Journal* 13 (Winter 1981): 17-46.

Humey, Jean McCahon. "The Life and Art of Anna Mary Robertson Moses." *Woman's Art Journal* 1 (Fall 1980/Winter 1981): 7-12.

Hyland, Douglas K. S. "Agnes Ernst Meyer, Patron of American Modernism." *The American Art Journal* 12 (Winter 1980): 64-81.

Ingelman, Ingrid. "Women Artists in Sweden: A Two-Front Struggle." *Woman's Art Journal* 5 (Spring/Summer 1984): 1-7.

Kamerling, Bruce. "Painting Ladies: Some Early San Diego Women Artists." *Journal of San Diego History* 32, no. 3 (1986): 146-191.

Keny, James M. "A Dilemma of Riches: The Art of James and Edna Hopkins." *Timeline* 7 (February/March 1990): 18-31.

Kiesel, Margaret Matlock. "Iowans in the Arts: Ruth Suckow in the Twenties." *Annals of Iowa* 45 (Spring 1980): 259-287.

King, Richard. "Eleanor Dickinson: Religion and the Southern Artist." *Woman's Art Journal* 3 (Spring/Summer 1982): 1-5.

Kirschenbaum, Blossom S. "Nancy Elizabeth Prophet, Sculptor." *Sage* 4, no. 1 (1987): 45-52.

Kren, Margo. "Philomene Bennett: A Kansas City Artist." *Kansas Quarterly* 14 (Fall 1982): 20-33.

Langer, Cassandra L. "Beyond the Myth: The Unacknowledged Georgia O'Keefe." *Kansas Quarterly* 19, no. 4 (1987): 11-23.

Leader, Bernice Kramer. "Antifeminism in the Paintings of the Boston School." *Arts Magazine* 56, no. 5 (1982): 112-119.

Matthews, John M. "The Influence of the Texas Panhandle on Georgia O'Keefe." *Panhandle-Plains History Review* 57 (1984): 107-136.

Murray, Anne H. "Eleanor Norcross: Artist, Collector and Social Reformer." *Woman's Art Journal* 2 (Fall 1981/Winter 1982): 14-19.

Nead, Lynda. "The Female Nude: Pornography, Art and Sexuality." *Signs* 15 (Winter 1990): 323-335.

Nine, L. K. "'With a Mythical Beast/Stuck in My Breast': Kay Closson--The Artist as Woman." *Heritage of the Great Plains* 13 (Summer 1980): 43-56.

Norwood, Vera L. "'Thank You for My Bones': Connections Between Contemporary Women Artists and the Traditional Arts of Their Foremothers." *New Mexico Historical Review* 58 (January 1983): 57-80.

Noun, Louise Rosenfield. "Harriet Ketcham, Resolute Artist." *Palimpsest* 67 (May/June 1986): 70-79.

-----. "Making Her Mark: Nellie Verne Walker, Sculptor." *Palimpsest* 68 (Winter 1987): 160-173.

Nunn, Pamela Gerrish. "Ruskin's Patronage of Women Artists." *Woman's Art Journal* 2 (Fall 1981/Winter 1982): 8-13.

Pentland, Heather. "Sarah Worthington King Peter and the Cincinnati Ladies' Academy of Fine Arts." *Cincinnati Historical Society Bulletin* 39 (Spring 1981): 6-16.

Rubinstein, Charlotte Streifer. "The Early Career of Frances Flora Bond Palmer (1812-1876)." *The American Art Journal* 17 (Autumn 1985): 71-88.

-----. "The First American Women Artists." *Woman's Art Journal* 3 (Spring/Summer 1982): 6-10.

Russell, Margarita. "The Women Painters in Houbraken's *Groote Schouburgh*." *Woman's Art Journal* 2 (Spring/Summer 1981): 7-11.

Sheppard, Alice. "Suffrage Art and Feminism." *Hypatia* 5 (Summer 1990): 122-134.

-----. "There Were Ladies Present: American Women Cartoonists and Comic Artists in the Early Twentieth Century." *Journal of American Culture* 7 (Fall 1984): 38-48.

Sherwood, Dolly. "Harriet Hosmer's Sojourn in St. Louis." *Gateway Heritage* 5 (Winter 1984/85): 42-48.

Speiss, Lincoln Bunce. "St. Louis Women Artists in the Mid-19th Century." *Gateway Heritage* 3 (Spring 1983): 10-23.

Stoller, Marianne L. "The Hispanic Women Artists of New Mexico: Present and Past." *El Palacio* 92 (Summer/Fall 1986): 21-25.

Sydie, Rosalind A. "Humanism, Patronage and the Question of Women's Artistic Genius in the Italian Renaissance." *Journal of Historical Sociology* 2 (September 1989): 175-205.

-----. "Women Painters in Britain, 1768-1848." *Atlantis* 5 (April 1980): 144-175.

Taylor, Hilary. "'If a Young Painter Be Not Fierce and Arrogant God . . . Help Him': Some Women Art Students at the Slade, c. 1895-9." *Art History* 9 (June 1986): 232-244.

## Film, Television, Photography

Baker, Tracey. "Nineteenth-Century Minnesota Women Photographers." *Journal of the West* 28 (January 1989): 15-23.

Bonney, Claire. "The Nude Photograph: Some Female Perspectives." *Woman's Art Journal* 6 (Fall 1985/Winter 1986): 9-14.

-----. "Ella Hartt, Pioneer Photographer." *Alberta History* 27 (Winter 1979): 17-24.

Moenster, Kathleen. "Jessie Beals: Official Photographer of the 1904 World's Fair." *Gateway Heritage* 3 (Autumn 1982): 22-29.

Morrow, Delores J. "Female Photographers on the Frontier: Montana's Lady Photographic Artists, 1866-1900." *Montana* 32 (Summer 1982): 76-84.

Norwood, Vera. "The Photographer and the Naturalist: Laura Gilpin and Mary Austin in the Southwest." *Journal of American Culture* 5 (Summer 1982): 1-28.

Palmquist, Peter E. "Photographers in Petticoats." *Journal of the West* 21 (April 1982): 58-64.

Sochen, June. "Mildred Pierce and Women in Film." *American Quarterly* 30 (Spring 1978): 3-20.

Williams, Amie. "Dancing with Absences: The Impossible Presence of Third World Women in Film." *Ufahamu* 17 (Fall 1989): 44-56.

## General

Bernhard, Mary Elizabeth Kromer. "Portrait of a Family: Emily Dickinson's Norcross Connection." *New England Quarterly* 60 (September 1987): 363-381.

Brandimarte, Cynthia Ann. "Fannie Hurst:  A Missouri Girl Makes Good." *Missouri History Review* 81 (April 1987): 275-295.

Brumm, Ursula. "Recognizing a Female Aesthetic." *Early American Literature* 20 (Winter 1985/86): 271-277.

Buckley, Cheryl. "Made in Patriarchy: Towards a Feminist Analysis of Women and Design." *Design Issues* 3 (Fall 1986): 3-14.

Daily, Marla. "The Lone Woman of San Nicolas Island: A New Hypothesis on Her Origin." *California History* 68 (Spring/Summer 1989): 36-42.

Export, Valie. "Aspects of Feminist Actionism." *New German Critique* no. 47 (Spring/Summer 1989): 69-92.

Hallwas, John E. "The Achievement of Virginia S. Eifert." *Journal of the Illinois State Historical Society* 71 ((May 1978): 82-106.

Jones, Amelia.  "'Post-Feminism'--A  Remasculinization  of  Culture?" *M/E/A/N/I/N/G* no. 7 (May 1990): 29-40.

Kashdin, Gladys S. "Women Artists and the Institution of Feminism in America." *Proceedings of the Southeastern American Studies Association* (1979).

Kumin, Maxine. "'Stamping a Tiny Foot Against God': Some American Women Poets Writing between the Two Wars." *Quarterly Journal of the Library of Congress* 39 (Winter 1982).

MacPhail, Elizabeth C. "Lydia Knapp Horton: A 'Liberated' Woman in Early San

Diego." *Journal of San Diego History* 27 (Winter 1981): 17-42.

Main, Elaine Carol. "'Miss Paul' Hits the Glittering Chautauqua Trail." *Palimpsest* 66 (July/August 1985): 129-142.

McEwin, Florence. "An Aesthetic and Historical Background of American Women Artists since 1900." *Kansas Quarterly* 19, no. 4 (1987): 51-57.

Morris, Linda A. "Frances Miriam Whitaker: Social Satire in the Age of Gentility." *Women's Studies* 15 (1988): 99-116.

Moses, Claire G. "Comment on Session: Women and the Arts in Eighteenth-Century France." *Western Society for French History* 11 (November 1983): 139.

Robins, Corinne. "Why We Need 'Bad Girls' Rather Than 'Good' Ones!" *M/E/A/N/I/N/G* no. 8 (November 1990): 43-48.

## Literature

Alexander, Ruth Ann. "South Dakota Women Writers and the Blooming of the Pioneer Heroine, 1922-1939." *South Dakota History* 14 (Winter 1984): 281-307.

-----. "South Dakota Women Writers and the Emergence of the Pioneer Heroine." *South Dakota History* 13 (Fall 1983): 177-205.

Anderson, R. F. "'Things Wisely Ordered': John Blackwood, George Eliot, and the Publication of *Romola*." *Publishing History* no. 11 (1982): 5-40.

Anderson, William T. "Laura Ingalls Wilder and Rose Wilder Lane: The Continuing Collaboration." *South Dakota History* 16 (Summer 1986): 89-143.

-----. "The Literary Apprenticeship of Laura Ingalls Wilder." *South Dakota History* 13 (Winter 1983): 285-331.

Arend, Angelika. "Humor and Irony in Annette Von Droste-Hulshoff's 'Heidebilder' Cycle." *German Quarterly* 63 (Winter 1990): 50-58.

Armstrong, Isobel, and Alan Sinfield. "'This Drastic Split in the Functions of a Whole Woman': *An Uncollected Article by Sylvia Plath*. 'Cambridge Letter,' *Isis*, May 1956." *Literature and History* 1 (Spring 1990): 75-79.

Arnston, Laurie. "Civil War Fictional Propaganda: Mary Anne Cruse's *Cameron Hall*." *Southern Historian* 9 (Spring 1989): 66-77.

Atkinson, Colin B., and Jo Atkinson. "Maria Edgeworth, *Belinda*, and Women's Rights." *Eire-Ireland* 19 (Winter 1984): 94-118.

Avery, Gilliam. "'Remarkable and Winning': 100 Years of American Heroines." *Lion and the Unicorn* 13 (June 1989): 7-20.

Babcock, Barbara A. "At Home, No Womens Are Storytellers: Potteries, Stories, and Politics in Cochiti Pueblo." *Journal of the Southwest* 30 (Autumn 1988): 356-389.

Bailey, Jennifer. "The Dangers of Femininity in Willa Cather's Fiction." *Journal of American Studies* 16 (December 1982): 391-406.

Bancroft, Caroline. "Two Women Writers: Caroline Bancroft Recalls Her Days with Mari Sandoz." *Colorado Heritage* no. 1 (1982): 103-111.

Barash, Carol. "The Character of Difference: The Creole Woman as Cultural

Mediator in Narratives about Jamaica." *Eighteenth-Century Studies* 23 (Summer 1990): 407-423.

Barker-Nunn, Jeanne. "Telling the Mother's Story: History and Connection in the Autobiographies of Maxine Hong Kingston and Kim Chernin." *Women's Studies* 14, no. 1 (1987): 55-63.

Baym, Nina. "Reinventing Lydia Sigourney." *American Literature* 62 (September 1990): 385-404.

Bell, Millicent. "Female Regional Writing: An American Tradition." *Revue française d'études américaines* no. 30 (1986): 469-488.

Bender, Eileen. "Pioneer or Gadgeteer: Bergsonian Metaphor in the Work of Willa Cather." *Midwest Quarterly* 28 (Autumn 1986): 130-140.

Bennett, Gillian. "'And I Turned round to Her and Said . . . ': A Preliminary Analysis of Shape and Structure in Women's Storytelling." *Folklore* 100, no. 2 (1989): 167-183.

Bennett, Mildred R. "The Childhood Worlds of Willa Cather." *Great Plains Quarterly* 2 (Fall 1982): 204-209.

Bixler, Phyllis. "The Oral-Formulaic Training of a Popular Fiction Writer: Frances Hodgson Burnett." *Journal of Popular Culture* 15 (Spring 1982): 42-52.

Blodgett, Harriet. "A Woman Writer's Diary: Virginia Woolf Revisited." *Prose Studies: History, Theory, Criticism* 12 (May 1989): 57-71.

Bodenheimer, Rosemarie. "Ambition and Its Audiences: George Eliot's Performing Figures." *Victorian Studies* 34 (Autumn 1990): 7-34.

Boewe, Mary. "Back to the Cabbage Patch: The Character of Mrs. Wiggs." *Filson Club History Quarterly* 59 (April 1985): 179-204.

-----. "Young Mrs. Wiggs Meets the Old Connecticut Yankee." *Filson Club History Quarterly* 56 (January 1982): 5-13.

Bond, Adrienne. "From Addie Budress to Pearl Tull: The Secularization of the South." *Southern Quarterly* 24 (Spring 1986): 64-73.

Bonner, Thomas, Jr. "Christianity and Catholicism in the Fiction of Kate Chopin." *Southern Quarterly* 20 (Winter 1982): 118-125.

Bratton, Mary Jo Jackson. "'Marion Harland': A Literary Woman of the Old Dominion." *Virginia Cavalcade* 35 (Winter 1986): 136-143.

Bremer, Sidney H. "Lost Continuities: Alternative Urban Visions in Chicago Novels, 1890-1915." *Soundings: An Interdisciplinary Journal* 64 (Spring 1981): 29-51.

Brewer, Betty Webb. "'She Was Part of It': Emily Lawless (1845-1913)." *Eire-Ireland* 18 (Winter 1983): 119-131.

Brown, Gillian. "Getting in the Kitchen with Dinah: Domestic Politics in Uncle Tom's Cabin." *American Quarterly* 36 (Fall 1984): 503-523.

Brown, Laura. "Reading Race and Gender: Jonathan Swift." *Eighteenth-Century Studies* 23 (Summer 1990): 424-443.

Cahalan, James M. "Forging a Tradition: Emily Lawless and the Irish Literary Canon." *Colby Quarterly* 27 (March 1991): 27-39.

Caldwell, Ellen M. "Ellen Glasgow and the Southern Agrarians." *American*

*Literature* 56 (May 1984): 203-213.

Carr, Virginia Spencer. "Carson McCullers: Novelist Turned Playwright." *Southern Quarterly* 25 (Spring 1987): 37-51.

Chambers-Schiller, Lee. "'Woman Is Born to Love': The Maiden Aunt as Maternal Figure in Antebellum Literature." *Frontiers* 10 (1988): 34-43.

Clayton, Cherry. "Olive Schreiner and Katherine Mansfield: Artistic Transformations of the Outcast Figure by Two Colonial Women Writers in Exile." *English Studies in Africa* 32, no. 2 (1989): 109-120.

Conrad, Mary T. "Remembering Caroline." *Queen City Heritage* 48 (Fall 1990): 17-22.

Cooke, Miriam. "Telling Their Lives: A Hundred Years of Arab Women's Writings." *World Literature Today* 60 (1986): 212-216.

-----. "Women Write War: The Feminization of Lebanese Society in the War Literature of Emily Nasrallah." *British Society for Middle Eastern Studies Bulletin* 14 (1988): 52-67.

Curry, George. "Charles Dickens and Annie Fields." *Huntington Library Quarterly* 51, no. 1 (1988): 1-71.

Cutter, Martha J. "Mary E. Wilkins Freeman's Two New England Nuns." *Colby Quarterly* 26 (December 1990): 213-225.

Dallimore, Jonathon. "Shakespeare, Cultural Materialism, Feminism and Marxist Humanism." *New Literary History* 21 (Spring 1990): 471-494.

Danielson, Linda L. "Storyteller: Grandmother's Spider's Web." *Journal of the Southwest* 30 (Autumn 1988): 325-355.

Davidson, Cathy N. "Female Authorship and Authority: The Case of Sukey Vickery." *Early American Literature* 21 (Spring 1986): 4-28.

Davidson, Mary V. "'Defying the Stars and Challenging the Moon': The Early Correspondence of Evelyn Scott and Jean Stafford." *Southern Quarterly* 28 (Summer 1990): 25-34.

Davies, Brian. "George Eliot and Christianity." *Downside Review* 100 (January 1982): 47-61.

Desmond, John F. "Flannery O'Conner and the History behind the History." *Modern Age* 27 (Summer-Fall 1983): 290-296.

Di Biase, Linda Popp. "Forgotten Woman of The Arroyo: Olive Percival." *Southern California Quarterly* 66 (Fall 1984): 207-220.

Donovan, Josephine. "Women and the Rise of the Novel: A Feminist-Marxist Theory." *Signs* 16 (Spring 1991): 441-462.

Drake, Robert. "The Lady Frum Somewhere: Flannery O'Connor Then and Now." *Modern Age* 29 (Summer 1985): 212-223.

Elfenbein, Andrew. "Cowper's *Task* and the Anxieties of Femininity." *Eighteenth-Century Life* 13 (November 1989): 1-17.

Ensor, Allison R. "What Is the Place of Mary Noailles Murfree Today?" *Tennessee Historical Quarterly* 47 (Winter 1988): 198-205.

Ezell, Margaret J. M. "The Myth of Judith Shakespeare: Creating the Canon of Women's Literature." *New Literary History* 21 (Spring 1990): 579-592.

Fabre, Genevieve. "Genealogical Archaeology: Black Women Writers in the 1980s

and the Search for Legacy." *Revue française d'études américaines* no. 30
(1986): 461-467.

Feldman, Yael S. "Gender In/Difference in Contemporary Hebrew Fictional
Autobiographies." *Biography* 11 (Summer 1988): 189-209.

Fitzpatrick, Marjorie A. "Antonine Maillet: The Search for a Narrative Voice."
*Journal of Popular Culture* 15 (Winter 1981): 4-13.

Fleishman, Avrom. "'To Return to St. Ives': Woolf's Autobiographical Writings."
*ELH* 48 (Fall 1981): 606-618.

Foley, Barbara. "Women and the Left in the 1930s." *American Literary History*
2 (Spring 1990): 150-169.

Fox-Genovese, Elizabeth. "Between Individualism and Fragmentation: American
Culture and the New Literary Studies of Race and Gender." *American
Quarterly* 42 (March 1990): 7-34.

-----. "Myth and History: Discourse of Origins in Zora Neal Hurston and Maya
Angelou." *Black American Literature Forum* 24 (Summer 1990): 221-236.

Freibert, Lucy M. "World Views in Utopian Novels by Women." *Journal of
Popular Culture* 17 (Summer 1983): 49-60.

Furman, Necah Stewart. "Western Author Caroline Lockhart and Her Perspectives
on Wyoming." *Montana* 36 (Winter 1986): 50-59.

Gartenberg, Patricia, and Nena T. Whittemore. "A Checklist of English Women
in Print, 1475-1640." *Bulletin of Bibliography and Magazine Notes* 34, no. 1
(1977): 1-13.

Gaston, Kay Baker. "The Mac Gowan Girls." *California History* 59 (Summer
1980): 116-125.

Gillespie, Joanna Bowen. "1795: Martha Laurens Ramsay's 'Dark Night of the
Soul.'" *William and Mary Quarterly* 48 (January 1991): 68-92.

Givner, Joan. "Katherine Anne Porter (1892-1980): Queen of Texas Letters?"
*Texas Liberator* 45 (Winter 1984): 119-123.

Gladney, Margaret Rose. "A Chain Reaction of Dreams: Lillian Smith and Laurel
Falls Camp." *Journal of American Culture* 5 (Fall 1982): 50-55.

-----. "The Liberating Institution: Lillian Smith and the Laurel Falls Camp."
*Proceedings of the Southeastern American Studies Association* (1979).

-----. "Lillian Smith's Hope for Southern Women." *Southern Studies* 22 (Fall
1983): 274-284.

Goldstein, Paul. "Julia Peterkin's Scarlet Sister Mary: A Forgotten Novel of
Female Primitivism." *Southern Studies* 22 (Summer 1983): 138-145.

Gordon, Jean, and Joan McArthur. "Living Patterns in Antebellum Rural America
as Depicted by Nineteenth-Century Women Writers." *Winterthur Portfolio* 19
(Summer/Autumn 1984): 177-192.

Gould, Karen. "The Censored Word and the Body Politic: Reconsidering the
Fiction of Marie-Clair Blais." *Journal of Popular Culture* 15 (Winter 1981):
14-27.

Graulich, Melody. "Violence Against Women in Literature of the Western
Family." *Frontiers* 7, no. 3 (1984): 14-20.

Gray, Francine du Plessix. "The Russian Heroine: Gender, Sexuality and

Freedom." *Michigan Quarterly Review* 28, no. 4 (1989): 699-718.

Green, Mary Jean. "The 'Literary Feminists' and the Fight for Women's Writing in Quebec." *Journal of Canadian Studies/Revue d'etudes canadiennes* 21 (Spring 1986): 128-143.

-----, Paula Gilbert Lewis, and Karen Gould. "Inscriptions of the Feminine: A Century of Women Writing in Quebec." *American Review of Canadian Studies* 15 (Winter 1985): 361-388.

Grieder, Joesphine. "Kingdoms of Women in French Fictions of the 1780s." *Eighteenth-Century Studies* 23 (Winter 1989-90): 140-156.

Grieve, Patricia E. "Mothers and Daughters in Fifteenth-Century Spanish Sentimental Romances: Implications for *Celestina.*" *Bulletin of Hispanic Studies* 67 (October 1990): 345-356.

Gross, Robert A. "Lonesome in Eden: Dickinson, Thoreau and the Problem of Community in Nineteenth Century New England." *Canadian Review of American Studies* 14 (Spring 1983): 1-18.

Gumina, Deanna Paoli. "The Apprenticeship of Kathleen Norris." *California History* 66 (March 1987): 40-48.

Haim, Sylvia G. "The Situation of Arab Women in the Mirror of Literature." *Middle Eastern Studies* 17, no. 4 (1981): 510-530.

Halttunen, Karen. "The Domestic Drama of Louisa May Alcott." *Feminist Studies* 10 (Summer 1984): 233-254.

Hamand, Wendy F. "'No Voice From England': Mrs. Stowe, Mr. Lincoln, and the British in the Civil War." *New England Quarterly* 61 (1988): 3-24.

Harvey, Clodagh Brennan. "Some Irish Women Storytellers and Reflections on the Role of Women in the Storytelling Tradition." *Western Folklore* 48 (April 1989): 109-128.

Haythornthwaite, J. A. "The Wages of Success: 'Miss Marjoribanks,' Margaret Oliphant and the House of Blackwood." *Publishing History* no. 15 (1984): 91-105.

Herndl, Diane Price. "The Writing Cure: Charlotte Perkins Gilman, Anna O., and 'Hysterical' Writing." *NWSA Journal* 1 (Autumn 1988): 52-74.

Hiuld, Melissa. "The Texas Women's Literary Tradition: Passing It On." *Texas Liberator* 45 (Winter 1984): 115-118.

Hoefel, Roseanne L. "'Broken' Silence, Un-Broken Spirits: Fragmentation in the Fiction of Black Women Writers." *Feminisms* 2 (Autumn 1989): 2-6.

Howard, Judith A. and Carolyn Allen. "The Gendered Context of Reading." *Gender & Society* 4 (December 1990): 534-552.

Howell, Elmo. "Kate Chopin and the Creole Country." *Louisiana History* 20 (Spring 1979): 209-219.

Irvine, Lorna. "Surfacing, Surviving, Surpassing: Canada's Women Writers." *Journal of Popular Culture* 15 (Winter 1981): 70-79.

Jehlen, Myra. "The Ties That Bind: Race and Sex in *Pudd'nhead Wilson.*" *American Literary History* 2 (Spring 1990): 39-55.

Jones, Anne Goodwyn. "Gender and the Great War: The Case of Faulkner and Porter." *Women's Studies* 13, no. 1/2 (1986): 134-48.

Jones, Chris. "Helen Maria Williams and Radical Sensibility." *Prose Studies: History, Theory, Criticism* 12 (May 1989): 3-24.

Jones, Jacqueline. "Fact and Fiction in Alice Walker's *The Color Purple.*" *Georgia Historical Quarterly* 72 (Winter 1988): 653-669.

Kandiyoti, Deniz. "Slave Girls, Temptresses, and Comrades: Images of Women in the Turkish Novel." *Feminist Issues* 8, no. 1 (1988): 35-50.

Kaplan, Amy. "Edith Wharton's Profession of Authorship." *ELH* 53 (Summer 1986): 433-457.

Kaplan, Carla. "Women's Writing and Feminist Strategy." *American Literary History* 2 (Summer 1990): 339-357.

Kastan, David Scott. "Shakespeare and 'The Way of Womenkind.'" *Daedalus* 111 (Summer 1982): 115-130.

Keller, Lynn, and Cristanne Miller. "Emily Dickinson, Elizabeth Bishop, and the Rewards of Indirection." *New England Quarterly* 57 (December 1984): 533-553.

Kissel, Susan S. "Conservative Cincinnati and Its Outspoken Women Writers." *Queen City Heritage* 44 (Spring 1986): 20-29.

Kowaleski-Wallace, Beth. "Milton's Daughters: The Education of Eighteenth-Century Women Writers." *Feminist Studies* 12 (Summer 1986): 275-294.

Kubek, Elizabeth Bennett. "London as Text: Eighteenth-Century Women Writers and Reading the City." *Women's Studies* 17, no. 3/4 (1990): 303-340.

Kucich, John. "Passionate Reserve and Reserved Passion in the Works of Charlotte Bronte." *ELH* 52 (Winter 1985): 913-938.

Kutinski, Vera. "Unseasonal Flowers: Nature and History in Placido and Jean Toomer." *Yale Journal of Criticism* 3 (Spring 1990): 153-180.

Landry, Donna, and Gerald MacLean. "Of Forceps, Patents and Paternity: *Tristram Shandy.*" *Eighteenth-Century Studies* 23 (Summer 1990): 522-541.

Larsen, Anne R. "Legitimizing the Daughter's Writing: Catherine des Roches' Proverbial Good Wife." *Sixteenth Century Journal* 21 (Winter 1990): 559-574.

Lazreq, Marina. "Feminism and Difference: The Perils of Writing as a Woman on Women in Algeria." *Feminist Studies* 14 (Spring 1988): 81-107.

Loveland, Anne C., ed. "'But We Are Not At All Distant in Sympathy!'--Letters of Dorothy Canfield Fisher and Lillian Smith." *Vermont History* 52 (Winter 1984): 17-32.

Makowsky, Veronica. "Caroline Gordon on Women Writing: A Contradiction in Terms?" *Southern Quarterly* 28 (Spring 1990): 43-52.

Marsh, John R. "Margaret Mitchell and the Wide, Wide World." *Atlanta History Journal* 29 (Winter 1985/86): 37-46.

McKinley, Blaine. "Free Love and Domesticity: Lizzie M. Holmes, *Hagar Lyndon* (1893), and the Anarchist-Feminist Imagination." *Journal of American Culture* 13 (Spring 1990): 55-62.

Michaelson, Patricia Howell. "Women in the Reading Circle." *Eighteenth-Century Life* 13 (November 1989): 59-69.

Miecznikowski, Cynthia J. "The Parodic Mode and the Patriarchial Imperative:

Reading the Female Reader(s) in Tabitha Tenney's *Female Quixotism.*" *Early American Literature* 25, no. 1 (1990): 34-45.

Miller, Elise. "The Feminization of American Realist Theory." *American Literary Realism* 23 (Fall 1990): 20-41.

Miller, John E. "Freedom and Control in Laura Ingalls Wilder's De Smet." *Great Plains Quarterly* 9 (Winter 1989): 27-35.

Miyake, Lynn K. "Women's Voice in Japanese Literature: Expanding the Feminine." *Women's Studies* 17, no. 1/2 (1989): 87-101.

Moran, Patricia. "Unholy Meanings: Maternity, Creativity, and Orality in Katherine Mansfield." *Feminist Studies* 17 (Spring 1991): 105-126.

Morey, Ann-Janine. "The Reverend Idol and Other Parsonage Secrets: Women Write Romances about Ministers, 1880-1950." *Journal of Feminist Studies in Religion* 6 (Spring 1990): 87-104.

Mulhern, Chieko Irie. "Japanese Harlequin Romances as Transcultural Women's Fiction." *Journal of Asian Studies* 48 (February 1989): 50-71.

Mumm, S. D. "Writing for Their Lives: Woman Applicants to the Royal Literary Fund, 1840-1880." *Publishing History* 27 (1990): 27-48.

Murphy, Maureen. "Lady Gregory: 'The Book of the People.'" *Colby Quarterly* 27 (March 1991): 40-47.

Myerson, Joel, and Daniel Shealy. "Editing Louisa May Alcott's Journals." *Manuscripts* 62 (Winter 1990): 19-33.

-----. "Three Contemporary Accounts of Louisa May Alcott, with Glimpses of Other Concord Notables." *New England Quarterly* 59 (March 1986): 109-122.

Newton, Sarah Emily. "Wise and Foolish Virgins: 'Usable Fiction' and the Early American Conduct Tradition." *Early American Literature* 25, no. 2 (1990): 139-167.

Nooger, D. "Anna Katharine Green and Her Daughters." *Dark Lantern* 2 (1985): 1-7.

Nugent, Georgia. "This Sex Which Is Not One: De-Constructing Ovid's Hermaphrodite." *Differences* 2 (Spring 1990): 160-185.

O'Rourke, James. "'Nothing More Unnatural': Mary Shelley's Revision of Rousseau." *ELH* 56 (Fall 1989): 543-570.

Pachmuss, Temira. "Women Writers in Russian Decadence." *Journal of Contemporary History* 17 (January 1982): 111-136.

Palmer, Pamela Lynn. "Dorothy Scarborough and Karle Wilson Baker: A Literary Friendship." *Southwestern History Quarterly* 91 (July 1987): 19-32.

-----. "Karle Wilson Baker and the East Texas Experience." *East Texas Historical Journal* 24, no. 2 (1986): 46-58.

Poulos, S. M. "Rashid Jahan of 'Angare': Her Life and Work." *Indian Literature* 120/30 (1987): 108-118.

Pratt, Norma Fain. "Culture and Radical Politics: Yiddish Women Writers, 1890-1940." *American Jewish History* 70, no. 1 (1980): 68-90.

Quimby, George I. "The Wife of Portsmouth's Tale, 1813-1818: An Apology to Miss Jane Barnes." *Pacific Northwest Quarterly* 71 (July 1980): 127-130.

Rabine, Leslie W. "Textual Practice/Social Practice: Flora Tristan and the

Problem of the Woman Activist-Writer." *Western Society for French History* 11 (November 1983): 272.

Rasporich, Beverly. "Retelling Vera Lysenko: A Feminist and Ethnic Writer." *Canadian Ethnic Studies/Etudes Ethniques Au Canada* 21, no. 2 (1989): 38-52.

Ray, Rajat K. "Man, Woman and the Novel: The Rise of a New Consciousness in Bengal, 1858-1947." *Indian Economic and Social History Review* [Delhi] 16, no.1 (1979): 1-31.

Redman-Rengstorf, Susan. "The Queen City Through the Eyes of Caroline Williams." *Queen City Heritage* 48 (Fall 1990): 3-16.

Requardt, Cynthia Horsburgh. "Women's Deeds in Women's Words: Manuscripts in the Maryland Historical Society." *Maryland History Magazine* (Summer 1978): 186-204.

Ricketts, Linda. "Women Writers in American Literary History." *American Studies in Scandinavia* 12, no. 1/2 (1980).

Rodenberger, Lou. "Texas Women Writers and Their Work: No Longer 'Lady Business.'" *Texas Liberator* 45 (Winter 1984): 124-128.

Rosenfelt, Deborah. "From the Thirties: Tillie Olsen and the Radical Tradition." *Feminist Studies* 7 (Fall 1981): 371-406.

Rosowski, Susan J. "Willa Cather's Lost Lady: Art versus the Closing Frontier." *Great Plains Quarterly* 2 (Fall 1982):

Ross, Danforth. "Caroline Gordon, Uncle Rob and My Mother." *Southern Quarterly* 28 (Spring 1990): 9-22.

Ross, Marlon. "Naturalizing Gender: Woman's Place in Wordsworth's Ideological Landscape." *ELH* 53 (Summer 1986): 391-410.

Rostenberg, Leona, and Madeleine B. Stern. "Five Letters That Changed an Image: Louisa Alcott Unmasked." *Manuscripts* 37 (Winter 1985): 5-22.

Rustomji-Kerns, Roshni. "Expatriates, Immigrants and Literature: Three South Asian Women Writers." *Massachusetts Review* 29 (Winter 1988/89): 655-665.

Safanda, Elizabeth M., and Molly L. Mead. "The Ladies of French Street in Breckenridge." *Colorado Magazine* 56 (Winter/Spring 1979): 19-34.

Sandler, Stephanie. "Embodied Words: Gender in Cvetaeva's Reading of Pushkin." *Slavic & East European Review* 34 (Summer 1990): 139-157.

Scafuro, Adele. "Discourse of Sexual Violation in Mythic Accounts and Dramatic Versions of 'The Girl's Tragedy.'" *Differences* 2 (Spring 1990): 126-159.

Schoen, Carol. "Anzia Yezierska: New Light on the 'Sweatshop Cinderella'." *Melus* 7 (1980): 3-11.

Schroeder, Natalie. "Regina Maria Roche and the Early Nineteenth Century Irish Novel." *Eire-Ireland* 19 (Summer 1984): 116-130.

----. "Selected Letters of Evelyn Scott." *Southern Quarterly* 28 (Summer 1990): 63-76.

Scura, Dorthy McInnis. "The Southern Lady in the Early Novels of Ellen Glasgow." *Mississippi Quarterly* 31 (Winter 1977-78): 17-32.

Sedgwick, Eve K. "Across Gender, Across Sexuality: Willa Cather and Others." *South Atlantic Quarterly* 87 (Winter 1989): 53-72.

Shillingsburg, Miriam J. "Atlanta's Hard-Boiled Novelist." *Atlanta History*

*Journal* 25 (Winter 1981): 67-79.

Shumaker, Conrad. "'Too Terribly Good to Be Printed': Charlotte Gilman's 'The Yellow Wallpaper'." *American Literature* 57 (December 1985): 588-599.

Skaggs, Merrill Maguire. "Willa Cather's Experimental Southern Novel." *Mississippi Quarterly* 35 (Winter 1981-82): 3-14.

Sloan, Barry. "Mrs. Hall's Ireland." *Eire-Ireland* 19 (Fall 1984): 18-30.

Snitgen, Jeanne. "History, Identity and the Constitution of the Female Subject: Maryse Conde's 'Tituba.'" *Black Women's Writing* (1989): 55-76.

Sobek-Herrera, Maria. "The Discourse of Love and *Despecho*: Representations of Women in the Chicano *Decima*." *Aztlan: International Journal of Chicano Studies Research* 18 (Spring 1987): 69-82.

Southwick, Helen C. "Willa Cather's Early Career: Origins of a Legend." *Western Pennsylvania Historical Magazine* 65 (April 1982): 85-98.

Sparks, Isabel. "Three Women Writers of Northeast Kansas (Brown and Doniphan Counties, 1856-1910)." *Heritage of the Great Plains* 16 (Summer 1983): 27-39.

Stepenoff, Bonnie. "Freedom and Regret: The Dilemma of Kate Chopin." *Missouri Historical Review* 81 (July 1987): 447-466.

-----. "Kate Chopin in 'Out-at-the-Elbows' St. Louis." *Gateway Heritage* 11 (Summer 1990): 62-67.

Stineback, David. "The Case of Willa Cather." *Canadian Review of American Studies* 15 (Winter 1984): 385-395.

Sussman, Charlotte. "'I Wonder Whether Poor Miss Sally Godfrey be Living or Dead': The Married Woman and the Rise of the Novel." *Diacritics* 20 (Spring 1990): 88-102.

Sutherland, Daniel E. "The Rise and Fall of Esther B. Cheesborough: The Battles of a Literary Lady." *South Carolina Historical Magazine* 84 (January 1983): 22-34.

Thompson, Evelyn Wings. "Southern Baptist Women as Writers and Editors." *Baptist History and Heritage* 22 (July 1987): 50-58.

Toth, Emily. "Fatherless and Dispossessed: Grace Metalious as a French-Canadian Writer." *Journal of Popular Culture* 15 (Winter 1981): 28-38.

-----. "Kate Chopin and Literary Convention: 'Desirée's Baby." *Southern Studies* 20 (Summer 1981): 201-208.

Wald, Priscilla. "Becoming 'Colored': The Self-Authorized Language of Difference in Zora Neale Hurston." *American Literary History* 2 (Spring 1990): 79-100.

Walker, William. "Locke Minding Women: Literary History, Gender and the Essay." *Eighteenth-Century Studies* 23 (Spring 1990): 245-268.

Wall, Wendy. "Isabella Whitney and the Female Legacy." *ELH* 58 (Spring 1991): 35-62.

Wallace, James D. "Hawthorne and the Scribbling Women Reconsidered." *American Literature* 62 (June 1990): 201-222.

Whitlock, Gillian. "'Everything Is out of Place': Radclyffe Hall and the Lesbian Literary Tradition." *Feminist Studies* 13 (Fall 1987): 555-582.

Williams, Susan S. "Widening the World: Susan Warner, Her Readers, and the

Assumption of Authorship." *American Quarterly* 42 (December 1990): 565-586.

Woodress, James. "The Uses of Biography: The Case of Willa Cather." *Great Plains Quarterly* 2 (Fall 1982): 195-203.

Woodward, C. Vann. "Mary Chestnut in Search of Her Genre." *Yale Review* (Winter 1984): 199-209.

Yellin, Jean Fagan. "The 'Feminization' of Rebecca Harding Davis." *American Literary History* 2 (Summer 1990): 203-219.

Young, Philip. "Small World: Emerson, Longfellow, and Melville's Secret Sister." *New England Quarterly* 60 (September 1987): 382-402.

Zionkowski, Linda. "Strategies of Containment: Stephen Duck, Ann Yearsley, and the Problems of Polite Culture." *Eighteenth-Century Life* 13 (November 1989): 91-108.

# Music

Bacon, Margaret Hope. "Lucy McKim Garrison: Pioneer in Folk Music." *Pennsylvania History* 54 (January 1987): 1-16.

Banes, Ruth A. "Mythology in Music: The Ballad of Loretta Lynn." *Canadian Review of American Studies* 16 (Fall 1985): 283-300.

Bayles, Carmen Barker. "Alma Swensson and the Lindsborg, Kansas Messiah Chorus." *Heritage of the Great Plains* 13 (Summer 1980): 27-42.

Campanaro, Giorgio G. "A Case for Billie Holiday." *Ufahamu* 16, no. 2 (1988): 38-44.

Carby, Hazel V. "It Jus Be's Dat Way Sometime: The Sexual Politics of Women's Blues." *Radical America* 20, no. 4 (1986): 9-24.

Dees, Janis White. "Anna Schoen-René: Minnesota Musical Pioneer." *Minnesota History* 48 (Winter 1983): 332-338.

Gil, Carlos B. "Lydia Mendoza: Houstonian and First Lady of Mexican American Song." *Houston Review* (Summer 1981): 250-260.

Haasbrock, J. "Cecilia Wessels (1895-1970)--The 'Voice' of South Africa." *South African Journal of Cultural History* 4 (July 1990): 139-154.

Hambrick, Keith S. "The Swedish Nightingale in New Orleans: Jenny Lind's Visit of 1851." *Louisiana History* 22 (Fall 1981): 387-418.

Holditch, W. Kenneth. "The Singing Heart: A Study of the Life and Work of Pearl Rivers." *Southern Quarterly* 20 (Winter 1982): 87-117.

Johnson, Ruth, and Elna Peterson. "The Swedish Women's Chorus of Seattle." *Swedish-American Historical Quarterly* 34 (1983): 294-305.

Levy, A. H. "Double-Bars and Double-Standards: Female Composers in America, 1880-1920." *International Journal of Women's Studies* 6 (March/April 1983): 162-175.

Pendle, Karin. "Cincinnati's Musical Heritage: Three Women Who Succeeded." *Queen City Heritage* 41 (Winter 1983): 41-55.

Schrems, Suzanne H. "Radicalism and Song." *Chronicles of Oklahoma* 62 (Summer 1984): 190-206.

Shipe, Bess Paterson. "Eliza Eichelberger Ridgely, the 'Lady with a Harp'." *Maryland Historical Magazine* 77 (Fall 1982): 230-237.

Tucker, Frank H. "A Song Inspired: Katharine Lee Bates and 'America the Beautiful.'" *Colorado Heritage* no. 3 (1989): 32-42.

## Poetry

Alkalay-Gut, Karen. "Poetry by Women in America: Esthetics in Evolution." *Canadian Review of American Studies* 14 (Fall 1983): 239-258.

Ambrose, Jane P. "Amy Lowell and the Music of Her Poetry." *New England Quarterly* 62 (March 1989): 45-62.

Annas, Pamela J. "The Self in the World: The Social Context of Sylvia Plath's Late Poems." *Women's Studies* 7, no. 1/2 (1980): 171-183.

Beecher, Maureen Ursenbach. "Inadvertent Disclosure? Autobiography in the Poetry of Eliza R. Snow." *Dialogue* 23 (Spring 1990): 94-107.

Bernhard, Mary Elizabeth Kromer. "Portrait of A Family: Emily Dickinson's Norcross Connection." *New England Quarterly* 60 (September 1987): 363-381.

Bixler, Miriam E. "Martha Keller, Poet." *Journal of the Lancaster County Historical Society* 88, no. 1 (1984): 32-41.

Bringle, Mary L. "Gentle Heroism: Women Poets of the French Resistance." *Anima* 8 (Fall 1981): 13-25.

Burbick, Joan. "Emily Dickinson and the Economics of Desire." *American Literature* 58 (October 1986): 361-378.

Catarella, Teresa. "Feminine Historicizing in the *Romancero Novelesco*." *Bulletin of Hispanic Studies* 67 (October 1990): 331-344.

Christ, Carol. "The Feminine Subject in Victorian Poetry." *ELH* 54 (Summer 1987): 385-402.

Edwards, Margaret. "Frances Frost, 1905-1959: Sketch of a Vermont Poet." *Vermont History* 56, no. 2 (1988): 102-111.

Erkkila, Betsy. "Emily Dickinson on Her Own Terms." *Wilson Quarterly* 9 (Spring 1985): 98-111.

Farr, Judith. "Tampering with Poetic Genius: The Early Editing of Emily Dickinson." *Humanities* 11 (March/April 1990): 30-35.

Gunner, Elizabeth. "Songs of Innocence and Experience: Women as Composers and Performers of *Izibongo*, Zulu Praise Poetry." *Research in African Literatures* 10 (Fall 1979): 239-267.

Heitty, Abd al-Kareem al-. "The Collection and Criticism of the Early Arab Singers and Poetesses." *Al-Masaq* 2 (1989): 43-47.

Hughes, Gertrude R. "Making It *Really* New: Hilda Doolittle, Gwendolyn Brooks, and the Feminist Potential of Modern Poetry." *American Quarterly* 42 (September 1990): 375-401.

Kumin, Maxine. "'Stamping a Tiny Foot Against God': Some American Women Poets Writing Between the Two Wars." *Quarterly Journal of the Library of Congress* 39 (Winter 1982).

Leiber, Justin, James Pickering, and Flora Bronson White, eds. "'Mother by the

Tens': Flora Adelaide Holcomb Bronson's Account of Her Life as an Illinois Schoolteacher, Poet, and Farm Wife, 1851-1927." *Journal of the Illinois State Historical Society* 76 (Winter 1983): 283-307.

McCurry, Jacqueline. "'Our Lady, Dispossessed': Female Ulster Poets and Sexual Politics." *Colby Quarterly* 27 (March 1991): 4-8.

Mermin, Dorothy. "The Female Poet and the Embarrassed Reader: Elizabeth Barrett." *ELH* 48 (Summer 1981): 351-367.

-----. "Women Becoming Poets: Katherine Philips, Aphra Behn, Anne Finch." *ELH* 57 (Summer 1990): 335-356.

Middlebrook, Diane Wood. "Housewife into Poet: The Apprenticeship of Anne Sexton." *New England Quarterly* 56 (December 1983): 483-503.

Myers, Lana Wirt. "Mary Williams Ward: 'The Champion Poet of Kansas.'" *Heritage of the Great Plains* 13 (Summer 1980): 3-26.

Nichols, J. M. "The Concept of Woman in Medieval Arabic Poetry." *Maghreb Review* 6 (1981): 85-88.

Shahham, Abdullah al-. "A Portrait of the Israeli Woman as the Beloved: The Woman-Soldier in the Poetry of Mahmud Darwish after the 1967 War." *British Society for Middle Eastern Studies Bulletin* 15 (1988): 28-49.

Slotten, Martha C. "Elizabeth Graeme Ferguson: A Poet in 'The Athens of North America.'" *Pennsylvania Magazine of History and Biography* 108 (July 1984): 259-288.

Spears, Woodridge. "A Poet from the Clay Family of Kentucky, Susan Clay Sawitzky." *Filson Club History Quarterly* 57 (April 1983): 175-187.

Sutton-Ramspeck, Beth. "The Personal is Poetical: Feminist Criticism and Mary Ward's Reading of the Brontes." *Victorian Studies* 34 (Autumn 1990): 55-76.

Weinburger, Stephen. "Women, Property and Poetry in Eleventh Century Provence." *Western Society for French History* 8 (October 1980): 24-33.

## Theatre

Aschenbrenner, Joyce, and Carolyn H. Carr. "The Dance Technique of Katherin Dunn as a Community Rite de passage." *Western Journal of Black Studies* 13 (Fall 1989): 139-143.

Austin, Gayle. "Alice Childress: Black Woman Playwright as Feminist Critic." *Southern Quarterly* 25 (Spring 1987): 53-62.

Barnes, Noreen C., and Laurie J. Wolf. "Actresses of All Work: Nineteenth-Century Sources on Women in Nineteenth Century American Theatre." *Performing Arts Resources* 12 (1987): 98-134.

Barranger, Milly S. "Southern Playwrights: A Perspective on Women Writers." *Southern Quarterly* 25 (Spring 1987): 5-9.

Bassnett, S. "Struggling with the Past: Women's Theatre in Search of a History." *New Theatre Quarterly* 5 (May 1989): 107-112.

Birdwell, Christine. "The Passionate Purity That Led to Domesticity: Heroines of Repertoire Comedy-Drama." *Journal of American Culture* 10 (Summer 1987): 49-54.

Blair, Karen J. "Pagentry for Women's Rights: The Career of Hazel Mackaye, 1913-1923." *Theatre Survey* 31 (May 1990): 23-46.

Blair, Rhonda. "A History of the Women and Theatre Program." *Women & Performance* 4, no. 8 (1989): 5-13.

Branyan, Helen Baird. "Susie of American Tent Repertoire Theatre." *Journal of Popular Culture* 22 (Spring 1989): 141-147.

Brown, Janet, and Pamela Loy. "Cinderella and Slippery Jack: Sex Roles and Social Mobility Themes in Early Musical Comedy." *International Journal of Women's Studies* 4 (November/December 1981): 507-516.

Broyles-Gonzalez, Yolanda. "The Living Legacy of Chicana Performers: Preserving History through Oral Testimony." *Frontiers* 11, no. 1 (1990): 46-52.

Carr, Virginia Spencer. "Carson McCullers: Novelist Turned Playwright." *Southern Quarterly* 25 (Spring 1987): 37-51.

Carroll, Kathleen L. "The Americanization of Beatrice: Nineteenth-Century Style." *Theatre Survey* 31 (May 1990): 67-84.

Cofran, John. "The Identity of Adah Isaacs Menken: A Theatrical Mystery Solved." *Theatre Survey* 31 (May 1990): 47-54.

Cumming, Valerie. "Ellen Terry: An Aesthetic Actress and Her Costumes." *Costume* 21 (1987): 67-74.

Davis, Tracy C. "Does the Theatre Make for Good?: Actresses' Purity and Temptation in the Victorian Era." *Queen's Quarterly* 93 (Spring 1986): 33-49.

Day, Moira, and Marilyn Potts. "Elizabeth Sterling Haynes: Initiator of Alberta Theatre." *Theatre History in Canada* 8 (Spring 1987): 8-35.

DeMetz, Kaye. "Theatrical Dancing in Nineteenth Century New Orleans." *Louisiana History* 21 (Winter 1980): 23-42.

Dolan, Jill. "'What, No Beans?': Images of Women and Sexuality in Burlesque Comedy." *Journal of Popular Culture* 18 (Winter 1984): 37-48.

Hiatt, Richard G. "Lady Troupers Along the Oregon Trail." *Dutch Quarterly Review of Anglo-American Letters* 19, no. 2 (1989): 113-123.

Holditch, W. Kenneth. "Another Part of the Country: Lillian Hellman as Southern Playwright." *Southern Quarterly* 25 (Spring 1987): 11-35.

Holliday, Polly. "I Remember Alice Childress." *Southern Quarterly* 25 (Spring 1987): 63-65.

Hopkins, Counce. "Pauline Cushman: Actress in the Theatre of War." *American History Illustrated* 19, no. 9 (1985): 20-21.

Johnston, Patricia Condon. "Nelle Palmer of Stillwater: Entertainer and Innkeeper." *Minnesota History* 48 (Spring 1983): 207-212.

Kaplan, Joel H. "Mrs. Ebbsmith's Bible Burning: Page versus Stage." *Theatre Notebook* 44, no. 3 (1990): 99-101.

Keller, Betty C. "The Chastely Voluptuous Weblings." *The Beaver* 66 (April/May 1986): 13-18.

Kelly Katherine E. "The Queen's Two Bodies: Shakespeare's Boy Actress in Breeches." *Theatre Journal* 42 (March 1990): 81-93.

Koontz, Carole L. "A Real Trouper." *Timeline* 3 (February/March 1986): 50-53.

Lawrence, R. "Lillie Langtry in Canada and the USA, 1882-1917." *Theatre History in Canada* 10 (Spring 1989): 30-42.

Lojek, Helen. "Difference *Without* Indifference: The Drama of Frank McGuinness and Anne Devlin." *Eire-Ireland* 25 (Summer 1990): 56-68.

Mann, David D. "Checklist of Female Dramatists, 1660-1823." *Restoration and 18th Century Theatre Research* 5 (Summer 1990): 30-62.

Maschio, Geraldine. "Female Impersonation on the American Stage, 1860-1927: A Selected Bibliography of Performed Materials, and a Review of the Literature." *Performing Arts Resources* 12 (1987): 156-170.

Maus, Katharine Eisaman. "Horns of Dilemma: Jealousy, Gender, and Spectatorship in English Renaissance Drama." *ELH* 54 (Fall 1987): 561-584.

Moss, Jane. "Fillial (Im)Pieties: Mothers and Daughters in Quebec Women's Theatre." *The American Review of Canadian Studies* 19 (Summer 1989): 177-186.

Niazi, S. "Women in the Arabic Shadow Theatre." *Azure* 5 (1980): 20-22.

Patraka, Vivian M. "Split Britches in *Split Britches*: Performing History, Vaudeville, and the Everyday." *Women & Performance* 4, no. 8 (1989): 58-67.

Pieroth, Doris Hinson. "The Only Show in Town: Ellen Whitmore Mohrbacher's Savoy Theatre." *Chronicles of Oklahoma* 60 (Autumn 1982): 260-279.

Podlecki, Anthony J. "Could Women Attend the Theatre in Ancient Athens?" *Ancient World* 21 (Spring 1990): 27-43.

Pusey, William W., III. "The Beautiful Jersey Lily: English Actress Lillie Langtry Tours Virginia." *Virginia Cavalcade* 34 (Winter 1985): 108-117.

Raphael, Marc Lee. "From Marjorie to Tevya: The Image of the Jews in American Popular Literature, Theatre and Comedy, 1955-1965." *American Jewish History* 74 (September 1984): 66-72.

Rostenberg, Leona. "'Don't Go on the Stage': Advice from Paris." *Manuscripts* 40, no. 1 (1988): 35-40.

Schiff, Ellen. "What Kind of Way Is That for Nice Jewish Girls to Act?: Images of Jewish Women in Modern American Drama." *American Jewish History* 70 (September 1980): 106-118.

Schneider, Rebecca. "Narrative History, Female Subjectivity, and the Theatre of Linda Mussman Cross Way Cross: Going Forward by Going Back." *Women & Performance* 4, no. 1 (1988/89): 64-82.

Scobie, Ingrid Winthur. "Helen Gahagan Douglas: Broadway Star as California Politician." *California History* 66 (December 1987): 242-261.

Shaw, John. "Louisville's Own Mary Anderson Plays Rosalind at Stratford-on-Avon." *Filson Club History Quarterly* 55 (July 1981): 284-289.

Shortt, Mary. "Touring Theatrical Families in Canada West: The Hills and the Herons." *Ontario History* 74 (March 1982): 3-25.

-----. "Victorian Temptations." *The Beaver* 68 (December 1988/January 1989): 4-13.

Sigl, Patricia. "Prince Hoare's *Artist* and Anti-Theatrical Polemics in the Early 1800s: Mrs. Inchbald's Contribution." *Theatre Notebook* 44, no. 2 (1990): 62-73.

Tingley, Donald F. "Ellen Van Volkenburg, Maurice Brown, and the Chicago Little Theatre." *Illinois Historical Journal* 80 (Autumn 1987): 130-146.

# ASIA

## East (China, Japan, Korea)

Andors, Phyllis. "Women and Work in Shenzhen." *Bulletin of Concerned Asian Scholars* 20 (July/September 1988): 22-42.

-----. "Women Liberation in China: A Continuing Struggle." *China Notes* 23 (Spring/Summer 1984): 287-293.

Atsumi, Reiko. "Dilemmas and Accommodations of Married Japanese Women in White Collar Employment." *Bulletin of Concerned Asian Scholars* 20 (July/September 1988): 54-63.

Bak, Sung-Yun. "Women's Speech in Korean and English." *Korean Studies* 7 (1983): 61-77.

Barr, Allan. "Disarming Intruders: Alien Women in Liaozhai Zhiyi." *Harvard Journal of Asiatic Studies* 49 (December 1989): 501-518.

Barrett, Richard E. "Seasonality in Vital Processes in a Traditional Chinese Population: Births, Deaths, and Marriages in Colonial Taiwan, 1906-1942." *Modern China* 16 (April 1990): 190-225.

Bartman, William J. "Korean War Brides, Prostitutes and Yellow Slavery." *Minerva: Quarterly Report on Women and the Military* 7 (Summer 1989): 16-25.

Beahan, Charlotte L. "In the Public Eye: Women in Early Twentieth Century China." *Historical Reflections/Reflexions Historiques* 8 (Fall 1981): 215-238.

-----. "The Women's Movement and Nationalism in the Chinese Women's Press, 1902-1911." *Modern China* 1 (October 1975): 379-416.

Beesley, David. "From Chinese to Chinese American: Chinese Women & Families in a Sierra Nevada County." *California History* 67 (September 1988): 168-179. Beichman, Janine. "Yosano Akiko: The Early Years." *Japan Quarterly* 37 (January/March 1990): 37-54.

Bradshaw, Sister Sue. "Catholic Sisters in China: An Effort to Raise the Status of Women." *Historical Reflections/Reflexions Historiques* 8 (Fall 1981): 201-214.

-----. "Religious Women in China: Understanding of Indigenization." *Catholic Historical Review* 68 (January 1982): 28-45.

Cahill, Suzanne. "Performers and Female Taoist Adepts: Hsi Wang Mu as the Patron Diety of Women in Medieval China." *Journal of the American Oriental Society* 106 (1986): 155-168.

Carlitz, Katherine N. "Family, Society, and Tradition in Jin ping mei." *Modern China* 10 (October 1984): 387-414.

Chabot, Jeanette Toudin. "Takamure Itsue: The First Historian of Japanese Women." *Women's Studies* 8, no. 4 (1985): 287-290.

Chacon, Ramon D. "The Beginning of Racial Segregation: The Chinese in West Fresno and Chinatown's Role as Red Light District, 1870s-1920s." *Southern*

*California Quarterly* 70 (Winter 1988): 371-398.

Chai, Alice Yun. "Freed from the Elders but Locked into Labor: Korean Immigrant Women in Hawaii." *Women's Studies* 13, no. 3 (1987): 223-234.

Cherpak, Evelen M. "Remembering Days in Old China: A Navy Bride Recalls Life on the Asiatic Station in the 1920s." *American Neptune* 44 (Summer 1984): 179-185.

Cho, Haejong. "Neither Dominance: A Study of a Female Divers' Village in Korea." *Korea Journal* 19, no. 6 (1979): 23-34.

Chung, Priscilla Ching. "Power and Prestige: Palace Women in the Northern Sung (960-1126)." *Historical Reflections/Reflexions Historiques* 8 (Fall 1981): 99-112.

Chung, Sue Fawn. "The Much Maligned Empress Dowager: A Revisionist Study of the Empress Dowager Tz'u-hsi (1835-1908)." *Modern Asian Studies* 13, no. 2 (1979): 177-196.

Clarke, Elizabeth J. "The Origins of Women's Higher Education in Japan." *Japan Christian Quarterly* 46 (Winter 1980): 26-33.

Cornell, Laurel L. "Peasant Women and Divorce in Preindustrial Japan." *Signs* 15 (Summer 1990): 710-732.

Deuchler, Martina. "Neo-Confucianism: The Impulse for Action in Early Yi Korea." *Journal of Korean Studies* 2 (1980): 71-112.

Diamond, Norma. "Collectivization, Kinship, and the Status of Women in Rural China." *Bulletin of Concerned Asian Scholars* 7 (January/March 1975): 25-32.

Drucker, Alison R. "The Influence of Western Women on the Anti-Footbinding Movement 1840-1911." *Historical Reflections/Reflexions Historiques* 8 (Fall 1981): 179-200.

Ebrey, Patricia. "Conceptions of the Family in the Sung Dynasty." *Journal of Asian Studies* 43 (February 1984): 219-246.

-----. "Women in the Kinship System of the Southern Song Upper Class." *Historical Reflections/Reflexions Historiques* 8 (Fall 1981): 113-128.

-----. "The Women in Liu Kezhuang's Family." *Modern China* 10 (October 1984): 415-440.

Edwards, Walter. "The Commercialized Wedding as Ritual: A Window on Social Values." *Journal of Japanese Studies* 13 (Winter 1987): 51-78.

Elvin, Mark. "Female Virture and the State in China." *Past and Present* no. 104 (August 1984): 111-152.

Feeney, Griffith, and Hamano Kiyoshi. "Rice Price Fluctuations and Fertility in Late Tokugawa Japan." *Journal of Japanese Studies* 16 (Winter 1990): 1-30.

Feuerwerker, Yi-tsi. "Ting Ling's 'When I Was in Sha Chuan (Cloud Village).'" *Signs* 2 (August 1976): 255-279.

Fujita, Kuniko. "Women Workers, State Policy, and the International Division of Labor: The Case of Silicon Island in Japan." *Bulletin of Concerned Asian Scholars* 20 (July/September 1988): 42-54.

Furth, Charlotte. "Androgynous Males and Deficient Females: Biology and Gender Boundaries in Sixteenth and Seventeenth Century China." *Late Imperial China* 9 (December 1988): 1-31.

-----. "Concepts of Pregnancy, Childbirth and Infancy in Ch'ing Dynasty China." *Journal of Asian Studies* 46 (February 1987): 7-37.

Gates, Hill. "The Commodization of Chinese Women." *Signs* 14 (Summer 1989): 799-833.

Gipoulon, Catherine. "The Emergence of Women in Politics in China, 1898-1927." *Chinese Studies in History* 23 (Winter 1989/90): 46-67.

Graham, Masako Nakagawa. "The Consort and the Warrior: *Yokihi Monogatari.*" *Monumenta Nipponica* 451 (Spring 1990): 1-26.

Guisso, Richard W. "Thunder over the Lake: The Five Classics and the Perception of Woman in Early China." *Historical Reflections/Reflexions Historiques* 8 (Fall 1981): 47-62.

Harper, Donald. "The Sexual Arts of Ancient China as Described in a Manuscript of the Second Century B.C." *Harvard Journal of Asiatic Studies* 47, no. 2 (1987): 539-594.

Harrington, Ann M. "Women and Higher Education in the Japanese Empire (1895-1945)." *Journal of Asian History* 21, no. 2 (1987): 169-186.

Haruko, Wakita. "Marriage and Property in Premodern Japan from the Perspective of Women's History." *Journal of Japanese Studies* 10 (Winter 1984): 73-100.

Havens, Thomas R. H. "Women and War in Japan, 1937-1945." *American Historical Review* 80, no. 4 (1975): 913-934.

Holmgren, Jennifer. "The Harem in Northern Wei Politics--398-498 A.D.: A Study of T'o-pa Attitudes Towards the Institution of Empress, Empress-Dowager, and Regency Governments in the Chinese Dynastic System During Early Northern Wei." *Journal of the Economic and Social History of the Orient* 26 (February 1983): 71-96.

-----. "Marriage and Political Power in Sixth Century China: A Study of the Kao Family of Northern Ch'i, c. 520-550." *Journal of Asian History* 16, no. 1 (1982): 1-50.

-----. "Observations on Marriage and Inheritance Practices in Early Mongol and Yuan Society, with Particular Reference to the Leviate." *Journal of Asian History* 20, no. 2 (1986): 127-192.

-----. "Wei-shu Records on the Bestowal of Imperial Princesses During the Norther Wei Dynasty." *Papers on Far Eastern History* no. 27 (March 1983): 21-98.

-----. "Widow Chastity in the Northern Dynasties: The Lieh-nu Biographies in the Wei-shu." *Papers on Far Eastern History* no. 23 (March 1981): 165-186.

Honig, Emily. "Burning Incense, Pledging Sisterhood: Communities of Women Workers in the Shanghai Cotton Mills, 1919-1949." *Signs* 10 (Summer 1985): 700-714.

-----. "The Contract Labor System and Women Workers: Pre-Liberation Cotton Mills of Shanghai." *Modern China* 9 (October 1983): 421-454.

Huntley, Martha. "Presbyterian Women's Work and Rights in the Korean Mission." *American Presbyterians* 65 (Spring 1987): 37-48.

Irwin, Lee. "Divinity and Salvation: The Great Goddesses of China." *Asian*

*Folklore Studies* 49, no. 1 (1990): 53-68.

Jackal, Patricia Stranahan. "Changes in Policy for Yanan Women, 1935-1947." *Modern China* 7 (January 1981): 83-112.

Judd, Ellen R. "'Men Are More Able': Rural Chinese Women's Conceptions of Gender and Agency." *Pacific Affairs* 63 (Spring 1990): 40-62.

-----. "*Niangji*: Chinese Women and Their Natal Families." *Journal of Asian Studies* 48 (August 1989): 525-544.

Kendall, Laurel. "A Noisy and Bothersome New Custom: Delivering a Gift Box to a Korean Bride." *Journal of Ritual Studies* 3 (Summer 1989): 185-202.

Kidder, J. Edward. "Problems of Cremation in Early Japan: The Role of Empress Jito." *Humanities, Christianity and Culture* 13 (March 1979): 191-201.

Kim, Doo-hun. "Confucian Influences on Korean Society." *Korea Journal* 3, no. 9 (1963): 17-21.

Kim, Ok-Hy. "Women in the History of Catholicism in Korea." *Korea Journal* 24 (August 1984): 28-40.

Kuninobu, Junko Wada. "The Development of Feminism in Modern Japan." *Feminist Issues* 4 (Fall 1984): 3-22.

Lavely, William and Ronald Freedman. "The Origins of the Chinese Fertility Decline." *Demography* 27 (August 1990): 357-368.

Lee, Bernice J. "Female Infanticide in China." *Historical Reflections/Reflexions Historiques* 8 (Fall 1981): 163-178.

Lee, James, and Robert Y. Eng. "Population and Family History in Eighteenth Century Manchuria: Preliminary Results from Daoyi 1774-1798." *Late Imperial China* 5 (June 1984): 1-55.

Lee, James, and Jon Gjerde. "Comparative Household Morphology of Stem, Joint and Nuclear Household Systems: Norway, China, and the United States." *Continuity and Change* 1, no. 1 (1986): 89-112.

Li, Peter S. "Immigration Laws and Family Patterns: Some Demographic Changes Among Chinese Families in Canada, 1885-1971." *Canadian Ethnic Studies/Etudes Ethniques Au Canada* 12, no. 1 (1980): 58-73.

Li, Yu-ning. "Historical Roots of Changes in Women's Status in Modern China." *Asian Culture Quarterly* [Taipei] 10 (Spring 1982): 14-25.

Lidoff, Joan. "Autobiography in a Different Voice: Maxine Hong Kingston's *The Woman Warrior*." *Auto/Biography Studies* 3 (Fall 1987): 29-35.

Lim, Shirley Geok-lin. "Japanese American Women's Life Stories: Maternality in Monica Sone's *Nisei Daughter* and Joy Kogawa's *Obasan*." *Feminist Studies* 16 (Summer 1990): 289-312.

Loftus, Ronald. "Japanese Women in History and Society." *Journal of Ethnic Studies* 8 (Fall 1980): 109-122.

Mackie, Vera. "Motherhood and Pacificism in Japan, 1900-1937." *Hecate* 14 (Winter 1989): 28-49.

Mann, Susan. "Widows in the Kinship, Class, and Community Structures of Qing Dynasty China." *Journal of Asian Studies* 46 (February 1987): 37-57.

Mariko, Fujita. "'It's All Mother's Fault': Childcare and Socialization of Working Mothers in Japan." *Journal of Japanese Studies* 15 (Winter 1989): 67-92.

Matsumoto, Valerie. "Japanese American Women During World War II." *Frontiers* 8, no. 1 (1984): 6-14.

McCullough, William H. "Japanese Marriage Institutions in Heian Period." *Harvard Journal of Asiatic Studies* 27 (1967): 103-167.

McMahon, Keith. "A Case for Confucian Sexuality: The Eighteenth-Century Novel, *Yesou Puyan*." *Late Imperial China* 9 (December 1988): 32-55.

Miyake, Lynn K. "Women's Voice in Japanese Literature: Expanding the Feminine." *Women's Studies* 17, no. 1/2 (1989): 87-101.

Miyamoto, Ken. "Ito Noe and the Bluestockings." *Japan Interpreter* 10, no. 2 (1975).

Mosk, Carl. "Fertility and Occupation: Mining Districts in Prewar Japan." *Social Science History* 5 (Summer 1981): 293-316.

-----. "Nuptiality in Meiji Japan." *Journal of Social History* 13 (Spring 1980): 474-489.

Mulhern, Chieko Irie. "Japanese Harlequin Romances as Transcultural Women's Fiction." *Journal of Asian Studies* 48 (February 1989): 50-71.

Murray, Dian. "One Woman's Rise to Power: Cheng I's Wife and Pirates." *Historical Reflections/Reflexions Historiques* 8 (Fall 1981): 147-162.

Ng, Vivian. "Ideology and Sexuality: Rape Laws in Qing China." *Journal of Asian Studies* 46 (February 1987): 57-71.

Nienling, Liu. "The Vanguards of the Women's Liberation Movement--LuYin, Bingxin, and Ding Ling." *Chinese Studies in History* 23 (Winter 1989/90): 22-45.

Nomura, Gail M. "Tsugiki, A Grafting: A History of a Japanese Pioneer Woman in Washington State." *Women's Studies* 14, no. 1 (1987): 15-37.

Oh, Bonnie B. "From Three Obediences to Patriotism and Nationalism: Women's Status in Korea up to 1945." *Korea Journal* [Seoul] 22 (July 1982): 37-55.

Pan, Ku, and Trans. Burton Watson. "Two Imperial Ladies of Han." *Renditions: A Chinese-English Magazine* no. 1 (Autumn 1973): 7-14.

Papageorge, Linda Madson. "Feminism and Methodist Missionary Activity in China: The Experience of Atlanta's Laura Haygood, 1884-1900." *West Georgia College Studies in the Social Sciences* 22 (June 1983): 71-77.

Paper, Jordon. "The Persistence of Female Deities in Patriarchial China." *Journal of Feminist Studies in Religion* 6 (Spring 1990): 25-40.

Park, Jihang. "Trailblazers in a Traditional World: Korea's First Women College Graduates, 1910-45." *Social Science History* 14 (Winter 1990): 533-558.

Pascoe, Peggy. "Gender Systems in Conflict: The Marriages of Mission-Educated Chinese American Women, 1874-1939." *Journal of Social History* 22 (Summer 1989): 631-652.

Peffer, George Anthony. "Forbidden Families: Emigration Experiences of Chinese Women under the Page Law, 1875-1882." *Journal of American Ethnic History* 6 (Fall 1986): 28-46.

Prazniak, Roxann. "Weavers and Sorceresses of Chuansha: The Social Origins of Political Activism Among Rural Chinese Women." *Modern China* 12 (April 1986): 202-229.

Ritsuko, Yoshida. "Getting Married the Corporate Way." *Japan Quarterly* 37 (April/June 1990): 171-175.

Robertson, Jennifer. "Gender-Bending in Paradise: Doing 'Female' and 'Male' in Japan." *Genders* no. 5 (July 1989): 50-69.

Roden, Donald. "From Old Miss to New Professional: A Portrait of Women Educators under the American Occupation of Japan 1945-1952." *History of Education Quarterly* 23 (Winter 1983): 469-489.

Ropp, Paul S. "The Seeds of Change: Reflections on the Condition of Women in the Early and Mid-Ch'ing." *Signs* 2 (August 1976): 5-23.

Rosholt, Malcolm. "The Shoe Box Letters from China, 1913-1967." *Wisconsin Magazine of History* 73 (Winter 1989/90): 111-133.

Shapcott, Jennifer. "The Red Chrysanthemum: Yamakawa Kikue and the Socialist Women's Movement in Pre-War Japan." *Papers on Far Eastern History* no. 35 (March 1987): 1-30.

Shover, Michele. "Chico Women: Nemesis of a Rural Town's Anti-Chinese Campaigns, 1876-1888." *California History* 67 (December 1988): 228-243.

-----. "The Methodist Women and Molly White: A Chico Morality Tale." *Californians* 7 (September/October 1989): 26-31.

Smith, Robert J. "Gender Inequality in Contemporary Japan." *Journal of Japanese Studies* 13 (Winter 1987): 1-26.

-----. "Japanese Village Women: Suye-mura 1935-1936." *Journal of Japanese Studies* 7 (Summer 1981): 259-284.

-----. "Making Village Women into 'Good Wives and Wise Mothers' in Prewar Japan." *Journal of Family History* 8 (Spring 1983): 70-84.

Soon, Man Rhim. "The Status of Women in China: Yesterday and Today." *Asian Studies* [Quezon City] 20 (1982): 1-44.

Soulliere, E. "The Imperial Marriages of the Ming Dynasty." *Papers on Far Eastern History* no. 37 (March 1988): 15-42.

Steele, Valerie. "Fashion in China." *Dress* 9 (1983): 8-15.

Stranaban, Patricia. "Labor Heroines of Yan'an." *Modern China* 9 (April 1983): 228-252.

Su, Tsung. "New Women versus Old Mores: A Study of Women Characters in Ba Jin's Torrents Trilogy." *Chinese Studies in History* 23 (Spring 1990): 54-67.

Sung, Marina H. "The Chinese Lieh-nu Tradition." *Historical Reflections/Reflexions Historiques* 8 (Fall 1981): 63-74.

Sunoo, Sonia S. "Korean Women Pioneers of the Pacific Northwest." *Oregon Historical Quarterly* 79 (Spring 1978): 51-64.

Takedo, Kiyoko. "Ichikawa Fusae: Pioneer for Women's Rights in Japan." *Japan Quarterly* 31 (October/December 1984): 410-415.

Tien, H. Yuan. "Abortion in China: Incidence and Implications." *Modern China* 13 (October 1987): 441-468.

Tiesheng, Rong. "The Women's Movement in China Before and After the 1911 Revolution." *Chinese Studies in History* 16 (Spring/Summer 1983): 159-200.

Tsai, Kathryn A. "The Chinese Buddhist Monastic Order for Women: The First

Two Centuries." *Historical Reflections/Reflexions Historiques* 8 (Fall 1981): 1-20.

Tsurumi, E. Patricia. "Female Textile Workers and the Failure of Early Trade Unionism in Japan." *History Workshop* 18 (Autumn 1984): 3-27.

-----. "Japan's Early Female Emperors." *Reflections* 8 (Spring 1981).

-----. "Serving in Japan's Industrial Army: Female Textile Workers, 1868-1930." *Canadian Journal of History* 20 (August 1988): 155-176.

Tucker, Sara W. "Opportunities for Women: The Development of Professional Women's Medicine in Canton, China, 1879-1901." *Women's Studies International Forum* 13, no. 4 (1990): 357-368.

Wakita, Haruko. "Marriage and Property in Premodern Japan from the Perspective of Women's History." *Journal of Japanese Studies* 10 (Winter 1984): 73-99.

Walthall, Anne. "The Family Ideology of the Rural Entrepreneurs in Nineteenth Century Japan." *Journal of Social History* 23 (Spring 1990): 463-484.

Waltner, Ann. "Widows and Remarriage in Ming and Early Qing China." *Historical Reflections/Reflexions Historiques* 8 (Fall 1981): 129-146.

Walton, Linda. "Kinship, Marriage, and Status in Song China: A Study of the Lou Lineage of Ningbo, c. 1050-1250." *Journal of Asian History* 18, no. 1 (1984): 1-34.

Wan, Ning. "Desire and Desperation: An Analysis of the Female Characters in Cao's Yu's Play *The Thunderstorm*." *Chinese Studies in History* 20 (Winter 1986/87): 75-90.

Wang, Yeujin. "Mixing Memory and Desire: *Red Sorghum*: A Chinese Version of Masculinity and Femininity." *Public Culture* 2 (Fall 1989): 31-53.

Widmer, Ellen. "The Epistolary World of Female Talent in Seventeenth-Century China." *Late Imperial China* 10 (December 1989): 1-43.

Woon, Yuen-fong. "From Mao to Deng: Life Satisfaction Among Rural Women in an Emigrant Community in South China." *Australian Journal of Chinese Affairs* 25 (January 1991): 139-170.

Wu, Yenna. "The Inversion of Marital Hierarchy: Shrewish Wives and Henpecked Husbands in Seventeenth Century Chinese Literature." *Harvard Journal of Asiatic Studies* 48, no. 2 (1988): 363-382.

Xiao, Zhou. "Virginity and Premarital Sex in Contemporary China." *Feminist Studies* 15 (Summer 1989): 279-289.

Yamashita, Akiko. "Faith and the Sense of Human Rights Among Christians in the Meiji Period." *Japanese Religions* 12 (December 1982): 1-16.

Yang, Eun Sik. "Korean Women of America: From Subordination to Partnership, 1903-1930." *Amerasia* 11 (Fall/Winter 1984): 1-28.

Yee, May. "Chinese Canadian Women: Our Common Struggle." *Canadian Ethnic Studies/Etudes Ethniques Au Canada* 19, no. 3 (1987): 174-184.

Yoon, Hyungsook. "Gender and Personhood and the Domestic Cycle in Korean Society (I)." *Korea Journal* [Seoul] 30 (March 1990): 4-15.

-----. "Gender and Personhood and the Domestic Cycle in Korean Society (II)."

*Korea Journal* [Seoul] 30 (April 1990): 39-47.

Yoshida, Ritsuko. "Getting Married the Corporate Way." *Japan Quarterly* 37 (April/June 1990): 171-176.

Yu-ning, Li. "Sun Yat-sen and Women's Transformation." *Chinese Studies in History* 21 (Summer 1988): 58-78.

Zarrow, Peter. "He Zhen and Anarcho-Feminism in China." *Journal of Asian Studies* 47 (November 1988): 796-813.

## General

Allen, Catherine B. "Ruth Pettigrew: Taking the Gospel to the Orient." *Baptist History and Heritage* 23 (January 1988): 13-22.

Ames, Roger T. "Taoism and the Androgynous Ideal." *Historical Reflections/Reflexions Historiques* 8 (Fall 1989): 21-46.

Hart, George L., III. "Women and the Sacred in Ancient Tamilnadu." *Journal of Asian Studies* 32 (February 1973): 233-250.

Hirschman, Charles, and Philip Guest. "Multilevel Models of Fertility Determination in Four Southeast Asian Countries: 1970 and 1980." *Demography* 27 (August 1990): 397-412.

Hoyt, Fredrick B. "'When a Field Was Found Too Difficult for a Man, a Woman Should Be Sent': Adele M. Fielde in Asia, 1865-1890." *The Historian* 44 (May 1982): 314-334.

Kahn, Harold. "The Politics of Filiality." *Journal of Asian Studies* 26 (February 1967): 197-202.

Ling, S. "The Mountain Movers, Asian-American Women's Movement in Los Angeles." *Amerasia Journal* 15 (Spring 1989): 51-68.

Rustomji-Kerns, Roshni. "Expatriates, Immigrants and Literature: Three South Asian Women Writers." *Massachusetts Review* 29 (Winter 1988/89): 655-665.

Warren, William. "The Queen Who Came to Dinner." *Asia* 5 (March/April 1983): 38-43.

## South (Bangladesh, India, etc.)

Aftab, Tahera. "Reform Societies and Women's Education in Northern India in the Later 19th Century." *Journal of the Pakistan Historical Society* 35 (1987): 121-135.

Agarwal, Bina. "Women, Poverty and Agricultural Growth in India." *Journal of Peasant Studies* 13 (July 1986): 165-220.

Atchi Reddy, M. "Female Agricultural Labourers of Nellore, 1881-1981." *Indian Economic and Social History Review* [Delhi] 20 (March 1983): 67-79.

Bhargava, Ashok. "Indian Economy During Mrs. Gandhi's Regime." *Journal of Asian and African Studies* 22 (July/October 1987): 193-216.

Bhushan, Madhu. "Vimochana: Women's Struggles, Nonviolent Militancy and Direct Action in the Indian Context." *Women's Studies International Forum* 12, no. 1 (1989): 25-33.

Calman, Leslie J. "Women and Movement Politics in India." *Asian Survey* 29 (October 1989): 940-958.

Carroll, Lucy. "The Muslim Family Laws Ordinance, 1961: Provisions and Procedures--A Reference Paper for Current Research." *Contributions to Indian Sociology* 13, no. 1 (1979): 117-143.

-----. "Nizam-i-Islam: Processes and Conflicts in Pakistan's Programme of Islamisation, with Special Reference to the Position of Women." *Journal of Commonwealth and Comparative Politics* 20 (March 1982): 57-95.

-----. "Talaq-i-Tafwid and Stipulations in Muslim Marriage Contract: Important Means of Protecting the Position of the South Asian Muslim Wife." *Modern Asian Studies* 16, no. 2 (1982): 277-309.

Chakravarti, Uma, and Kumkum Roy. "In Search of Our Past: A Review of the Limitations and Possibilities of the Historiography of Women in Early India." *Economic and Political Weekly* 23 (April 30, 1988): WS-2--WS-10.

Chavda, Jagdish J. "The Narrative Paintings of India's Jitwarpuri Women." *Woman's Art Journal* 11 (Spring/Summer 1990): 26-28.

Dutt, Ashok K., Allen G. Noble, and Satish K. Davgun. "Socio-Economic Factors Affecting Marriage Distance in Two Sikh Villages of Punjab." *Journal of Cultural Geography* 2 (Fall/Winter 1981): 13-26.

Eaton, Richard Maxwell. "Sufi Folk Literature and the Expansion of Indian Islam." *History of Religions* 14 (November 1974): 117-127.

Engels, Dagmar. "The Age of Consent Act of 1891: Colonial Ideology in Bengal." *South Asia Research* 3 (November 1983): 107-134.

-----. "History and Sexuality in India: Discursive Trends." *Trends in History* 4 (1990).

-----. "The Limits of Gender Ideology: Bengali Women, the Colonial State, and the Private Sphere, 1890-1930." *Women's Studies International Forum* 12, no. 4 (1989): 425-438.

Everett, Jana Matson. "The Upsurge of Women's Activism in India." *Frontiers* 7, no. 2 (1983): 18-26.

Forbes, Geraldine H. "'Awakenings' and 'Golden Ages': Writings on Indian Women." *Views and Reviews* 2 (Spring 1976): 61-74.

-----. "Caged Tigers: 'First Wave' Feminists in India." *Women's Studies International Forum* 5, no. 6 (1982): 525-536.

-----. "In Pursuit of Justice: Women Organisations and Legal Reforms." *Samya Shakti* 1, no. 2 (1984): 33-54.

-----. "In Search of the 'Pure Heathen': Missionary Women in Nineteenth Century India." *Economic and Political Weekly* 21 (April 26,1986): WS-2--WS-8.

-----. "Women and Modernity: The Issue of Child Marriage in India." *Women's Studies International Quarterly* 2, no. 4 (1979): 407-419.

Habibuddin, S. M. "A Comparative Appraisal of the Role of Indian Feminists in the Peace Movement Between Two World Wars." *Quarterly Review of Historical Studies* [Calcutta] 23 (April-June 1983): 44-53.

Hale, Sylvia. "The Status of Women in India." *Pacific Affairs* 62 (Autumn 1989): 364-381.

Huttenback, Robert A. "The Perpetuation of Two Stereotypes--Racism and Sexism in the Imperial Adventure Story." *Bengal Past and Present* 101, Parts 1 and 2 (1984): 49-60.

Jain, K. B. "The Dowry Prohibition (Amendment) Act, 1984--A Brief Historical and Comparative Study." *Islamic and Comparative Law Quarterly* 6 (1986): 181-190.

Jayaweera, Swarna. "European Women Educators under the British Colonial Administration in Sri Lanka." *Women's Studies International Forum* 13, no. 4 (1990): 323-332.

Kapur, Ashok. "Indian Security and Defense Policies under Indira Gandhi." *Journal of Asian and African Studies* 22 (July/October 1987): 175-192.

Katzenstein, Mary Fainsod. "Organizing Against Violence: Strategies of the Indian Women's Movement." *Pacific Affairs* 62 (Spring 1989): 53-71.

Kelly, John D. "Fear of Culture: British Regulation of Indian Marriage in Post-Indenture Fiji." *Ethnohistory* 36 (Autumn 1989): 392-410.

Krishnaraj, Maithreyi. "The Status of Women in Science in India." *Journal of Higher Education* 5 (Spring 1980): 381-393.

Kumar, Radha. "Family and Factory: Women Workers in the Bombay Cotton Textile Industry, 1919-1939." *Indian Economic and Social History Review* 20 (March 1983): 81-110.

Leslie, I. Julia. "Suttee or Sati: Victim or Victor?" *Bulletin: Center for the Study of World Religions, Harvard University* 14, no. 2 (1987/88): 5-23.

Malik, Yogendra K. "Indira Gandhi: Personality, Political Power and Party Politics." *Journal of Asian and African Studies* 22 (July/October 1987): 141-155.

Malik, Yogendra K., and Dhirendra K. Vajpeyi. "India: The Years of Indira Gandhi." *Journal of Asian and African Studies* 22 (July/October 1987): 135-140.

Mani, Lata. "Production of an Official Discourse on Sati In Early Nineteenth Century Bengal." *Economic and Political Weekly* 21 (April 26, 1986): WS-32--WS-40.

Maskiell, Michelle. "Gender, Kinship and Rural Work in Colonial Punjab." *Journal of Women's History* 2 (Spring 1990): 35-72.

Mazumdar, Vina. "Comment on Suttee." *Signs* 4 (Winter 1978): 269-273.

Minault, Gail. "Making Invisible Women Visible: Studying the History of Muslim Women in South Asia." *South Asia* 9 (June 1986): 1-14.

-----. "Sayyid Mumtaz Ali and 'Huquq un Niswan': An Advocate of Women's Rights in Islam in the Late Nineteenth Century." *Modern Asian Studies* 24, no. 1 (1990): 147-192.

Ming, Hanneke. "Barracks-Concubinage in the Indies, 1887-1920." *Indonesia* no. 35 (April 1983): 65-93.

Mortimer, Joanne Stafford. "Annie Besant and India, 1913-1917." *Journal of Contemporary History* 18 (January 1983): 61-78.

O'Hanlon, Rosalind. "Cultures of Rule, Communities of Resistance: Gender,

Discourse and Tradition in Recent South Asian Historiographies." *Social Analysis* no. 25 (September 1989): 94-114.

Oldenburg, Veena Talwar. "Lifestyle as Resistance: The Case of the Courtesans of Lucknow, India." *Feminist Studies* 16 (Summer 1990): 259-288.

Omvedt, Gail. "Women and Rural Revolt in India." *Journal of Peasant Studies* 5 (April 1978): 370-403.

Pandey, S. M. "Mirabai and Her Contribuitons to the Bhakti Movement." *History of Religions* 5 (Summer 1965): 54-73.

Panhivar, M. H. "7000 Years of Women's Slavery." *Sindhological Studies* [Hyderabad, Pakistan] (Summer 1984): 33-55.

Papanek, Hanna. "False Specialization and the Purdah of Scholarship--A Review Article." *Journal of Asian Studies* 44 (November 1984): 127-148.

-----. "Purdah: Separate Worlds and Symbolic Shelter." *Comparative Studies in Society and History* [Great Britain] 15 (June 1973): 289-325.

Patel, Sujata. "Construction and Reconstruction of Women in Gandhi." *Economic and Political Weekly* 23 (February 20, 1988): 377-387.

Paxton, Nancy L. "Feminism under the Raj: Complicity and Resistance in the Writings of Flora Annie Steel and Annie Besant." *Women's Studies International Forum* 13, no. 4 (1990): 333-346.

Pearson, Gail. "Reserved Seats--Women and the Vote in Bombay." *Indian Economic and Social History Review* [Delhi] 20, no. 1 (1983): 47-66.

Rajan, Rajeswari Sunder. "The Subject of Sati: Pain and Death in the Contemporary Discourse on Sati." *Yale Journal of Criticism* 3 (Spring 1990): 1-28.

Ramaswamy, V. "Aspects of Women and Work in Early South India." *Indian Economic and Social History Review* 26 (January/March 1989): 81-100.

Ramusack, Barbara N. "Cultural Missionaries, Maternal Imperialists, Feminist Allies: British Women Activists in India, 1865-1945." *Women's Studies International Forum* 13, no. 4 (1990): 309-322.

-----. "Embattled Advocates: The Debate over Birth Control in India, 1920-1940." *Journal of Women's History* 1 (Fall 1989): 34-64.

Rao, R. V., and R. Chandrasekhara. "Mrs. Indira Gandhi and India's Constitutional Structures: An Era of Erosion." *Journal of Asian and African Studies* 22 (July/October 1987): 156-174.

Ray, Rajat K. "Man, Woman and the Novel: The Rise of a New Consciousness in Bengal, 1858-1947." *Indian Economic and Social History Review* [Delhi] 16, no. 1 (1979): 1-31.

Razzaque, Abdur, Nural Alam, Lokky Wai, and Andrew Foster. "Sustained Effects of the 1974-75 Faminine on Infant and Child Mortality in a Rural Area of Bangladesh." *Population Studies* 44 (March 1990): 145-154.

Reddy, M. Atchi. "Female Agricultural Labourers of Nellore, 1881-1981." *Indian Economic and Social History Review* 20, no. 1 (1983): 67-80.

Reddy, P. H. "Changing Age at Marriage in a South Indian Village." *Journal of Asian and African Studies* 25 (July-October 1990): 219-228.

Richter, William L. "Mrs. Gandhi's Neighborhood: Indian Foreign Policy toward Neighboring Countries." *Journal of Asian and African Studies* 22 (July/October 1987): 249-264.

Sheth, Surabhiben. "The Mythical Reality of Indian Women." *Lokayan Bulletin* [New Delhi] 5/6 (1987): 11-32.

Southard, Barbara. "Bengal Women's Education League: Pressure Group and Professional Association." *Modern Asian Studies* 18, no. 1 (1984): 55-88.

Stein, Dorothy K. "Women to Burn: Suttee as a Normative Institution." *Signs* 4 (Winter 1978): 253-268.

Wadley, Susan S. "Women and the Hindu Tradition." *Signs* 3 (Autumn 1977): 113-125.

Yang, Anand A. "Whose Sati? Widow Burning in Early 19th-Century India." *Journal of Women's History* 1 (Fall 1989): 8-33.

## Southeast (Burma, Vietnam, etc.)

Abdurachman, Paramita R. "'Niachile pokaraga': A Sad Story of a Moluccan Queen." *Modern Asian Studies* 22, no. 3 (1988): 571-592.

Gallen, Rita S. "Women, Family and the Political Economy of Taiwan." *Journal of Peasant Studies* 12 (October 1984): 76-92.

Kinsley, David. "Devotion as an Alternative to Marriage in the Lives of Some Hindu Women Devotees." *Journal of Asian and African Studies* 15 (January/April 1980): 83-93.

Kumar, Ann. "Javanese Court Society and Politics in the Late Eighteenth Century: The Record of a Lady Soldier." *Indonesia* 29 (April 1980): 1-49.

-----. "Political Developments: The Courts and the Company, 1784-1791." *Indonesia* 30 (October 1980): 67-111.

Lal, Brij V. "Veil of Dishonour: Sexual Jealousy and Suicide on Fiji Plantations." *Journal of Pacific History* 20 (July 1985): 135-155.

Lawson, Jacqueline E. "'She's a Pretty Woman . . . for a Gook': The Misogyny of the Vietnam War." *Journal of American Culture* 12 (Fall 1989): 55-66.

Lubin, Nancy. "Women in Soviet Central Asia: Progress and Contradictions." *Soviet Studies* 33, no. 2 (1981): 182-203.

Manderson, Lenore. "Going Through the Motions: Aspects of the Activities of the Pergerakan *Kawm Ibu Umno* Malaysia, 1949-71." *International Journal of Women's Studies* 2 (January/February 1979): 1-26.

Muecke, M. A., and W. Srisuphan. "Born Female: The Development of Nursing in Thailand." *Social Science Medicine* 29 (1989): 643-652.

Rasid, Gadis. "Kartini--The Tragedy of a Letter-Writing Javanese Princess." *Hemisphere* [Australia] 28 (November/December 1983): 162-167.

Reid, Anthony. "Female Roles in Pre-Colonial Southeast Asia." *Modern Asian Studies* 22, no. 3 (1988): 629-645.

Schoeffel, Penelope. "Rank, Gender and Politics in Anciet Samoa: The Genealogy of Salamasina *O Le Tafaifa*." *Journal of Pacific History* 22 (October 1987): 174-194.

Stoler, Ann. "Class Structure and Female Autonomy in Rural Java." *Signs* 3 (Autumn 1977): 74-89.

Ta, Van Tai. "The Status of Women in Traditional Vietnam: A Comparison of the Code of the Le Dynasty (1428-1788) with the Chinese Codes." *Journal of Asian History* 15, no. 2 (1981): 97-145.

Taylor, Jean Gelman. "Educate the Javanese!" *Indonesia* 17 (May 1974): 83-98.

-----. "Raden Ajeng Kartini." *Signs* 1 (Spring 1976): 639-661.

Thomas, Nicholas. "Unstable Categories: Tapu and Gender in the Marquesas." *Journal of Pacific History* 22 (July 1987): 123-138.

Williams, Walter L. "Women and Work in the Third World: Indonesian Women's Oral Histories." *Journal of Women's History* 2 (Spring 1990): 183-195.

Yen-lin, Ku. "The Feminist Movement in Taiwan, 1972-87." *Bulletin of Concerned Asian Scholars* 21 (January/March 1989): 12-23.

# AUSTRALIA/NEW ZEALAND

Beck, Wendy, and Lesley Head. "Women in Australian Prehistory." *Australian Feminist Studies* no. 11 (Autumn 1990): 29-48.

Bell, J. H., and U. S. Pandey. "The Exclusion of Women from Australian Post-Secondary Agricultural Education and Training 1880-1969." *Australian Journal of Politics and History* 36, no. 2 (1990): 205-216.

Blackmore, Jill. "Schooling for Work: Gender Differentiation in Commercial Education in Victoria 1935-1960." *History of Education Review* [Australia] 16, no. 1 (1987).

Brooks, Raymond. "The Melbourne Tailoresses' Strike 1882-1883: An Assessment." *Labour History* 44 (May 1983): 27-38.

Conway, Jill. "Gender in Australia." *Daedalus* 114 (Winter 1985): 343-368.

Crawford, S. "An Emancipation of Sports: Recreational and Sporting Opportunities for Women in Nineteenth Century Colonial New Zealand." *Canadian Journal of the History of Sport* 16, no. 1 (1985): 38-56.

Daniels, Kay. "Women in Australia: An Annotated Guide to Records." *History Workshop* 7 (Spring 1979): 187-192.

Godden, Judith. "Sectarianism and Purity Within Woman's Sphere: Sydney Refuges During the Late Nineteenth Century." *Journal of Religious History* 14 (June 1987): 291-306.

Gothard, Janice. "'Radically Unsound and Mischievous': Female Migration to Tasmania, 1856-1863." *Australian Historical Studies* 23 (October 1989): 386-404.

Inglis, Ken. "Men, Women, and War Memorials: Anzac Australia." *Daedalus* 116 (Fall 1987): 35-60.

Jackson, Hugh. "Fertility Decline in New South Wales: The Mackellar Royal Commission Reconsidered." *Australian Historical Studies* 23 (April 1989): 260-273.

Johnson, Penelope. "Gender, Class and Work: The Council of Action for Equal Pay and the Equal Pay Campaign in Australia During World War II." *Labour*

*History* 50 (May 1986): 132-146.

Kennedy, Sally. "Useful and Expendable: Women Teachers in Western Australia in the 1920s and 1930s." *Labour History* 44 (May 1983): 18-26.

Lake, Marilyn. "Female Desires: The Meaning of World War II." *Australian Historical Studies* 24 (October 1990): 267-284.

Levesque, Andree. "Prescribers and Rebels: Attitudes to European Women's Sexuality in New Zealand 1860-1916." *Women's Studies International Forum* 4, no. 2 (1981): 133-144.

Lewis, Milton. "The Problem of Infant Feeding: The Austrailian Experience from the Mid-Nineteenth Century to the 1920s." *Journal of the History of Medicine and Allied Sciences* 35 (April 1980): 174-186.

Macintyre, Martha. "Recent Australian Feminist History." *History Workshop* 5 (Spring 1978): 98-110.

Mackinnon, Alison, and Carol Bacchi. "Sex, Resistance, and Power: Sex Reform in South Australia, c. 1905." *Australian Historical Studies* 23 (April 1988): 60-71.

Magarey, Susan. "Labour History's New Sub-title: Social History in Australia in 1981." *Social History* 8 (May 1983): 211-228.

Mathews, Jill. "Education for Femininity: Domestic Arts Education in South Australia." *Labour History* 45 (November 1983): 30-53.

-----. "'A Female of All Things': Women and the Bicentenary." *Australian Historical Studies* 23 (October 1988): 90-102.

McGrath, Ann. "The White Man's Looking Glass: Aboriginal-Colonial Gender Relations at Port Jackson." *Australian Historical Studies* 24 (October 1990): 189-206.

Molloy, Maureen. "'No Inclination to Mix With Strangers': Marriage Patterns Among Highland Scot Migrants to Cape Breton and New Zealand, 1800-1916." *Journal of Family History* 11 (July 1986): 221-243.

Montgomerie, Deborah. "Men's Jobs and Women's Work: The New Zealand Women's Land Service in World War II." *Agricultural History* 63 (Summer 1989): 1-14.

Reekie, Gail. "Industrial Action by Women Workers in Western Australia During World War II." *Labour History* 49 (November 1985): 75-82.

Reiss, Mary-Ann. "Rosa Mayreder: Pioneer of Austrian Feminism." *International Journal of Women's Studies* 7 (May/June 1984): 207-216.

Ryan, Edna. "Proving a Dispute: Laundry Workers in Sydney in 1906." *Labour History* 40 (May 1981): 98-106.

Sells, Anne. "Marriage, Motherhood, and the Mother's Union: Images in Australia, 1896-1904." *St. Mark's Review* no. 129 (March 1987): 43-50.

Shlomowitz, Ralph, and John McDonald. "Babies at Risk on Immigrant Voyages to Australia in the Nineteenth Century." *Economic History Review* 44 (February 1991): 86-101.

Smart, Judith. "Feminists, Food and the Fair Price: The Cost of Living Demonstrations in Melbourne, August-September 1917." *Labour History* 50 (May 1986): 113-131.

Strathern, Marilyn. "Between a Melanesianist and a Deconstructive Feminist." *Australian Feminist Studies* no. 10 (Summer 1989): 49-70.

Tennant, Margaret. "'Magdalens and Moral Imbeciles': Women's Homes in Nineteenth-Century New Zealand." *Women's Studies* 9, no. 5/6 (1986): 491-502.

Theobald, Marjorie R. "The PLC Mystique: Reflections on the Reform of Female Education in Nineteenth Century Australia." *Australian Historical Studies* 23 (April 1989): 241-259.

Thomas, Julian. "Amy Johnson's Truimph, Australia 1930." *Australian Historical Studies* 23 (April 1988): 72-84.

Tyrell, Ian. "International Aspects of the Women's Temperance Movement in Australia: The Influence of the American WCTU, 1882-1914." *Journal of Religious History* [Australia] 12 (June 1983): 284-304.

van Krieken, Robert. "Towards 'Good and Useful Men and Women': The State and Childhood in Sydney, 1840-1890." *Australian Historical Studies* 23 (October 1989): 405-425.

White, Kate. "May Holman: 'Australian Labor's Pioneer Woman Parliamentarian'." *Labour History* 41 (November 1981): 110-117.

Williamson, Noeline. "The Employment of Female Teachers in the Small Bush Schools of New South Wales, 1880-1890: A Case of Stay Bushed or Stay Home." *Labour History* 43 (November 1982): 1-12.

Wimhurst, Kerry. "Control and Resistance: Reformatory School Girls in Late Nineteenth Century South Australia." *Journal of Social History* 18 (Winter 1984): 273-287.

Windschuttle, Elizabeth. "Discipline, Domestic Training and Social Control: The Female School of Industry, Sydney, 1826-1847." *Labour History* 39 (November 1980): 1-14.

# BIOGRAPHY

## Autobiographies

Arana, R. Victoria. "Examining the Acquisitions of Cross-Cultural Knowledge: Women Anthropologists as Autobiographers." *Auto/Biography Studies* 4 (Fall 1988): 28-36.

Balanoff, Elizabeth. "The Gary School Crisis of the 1950s: A Personal Memoir." *Indiana Magazine of History* 83 (March 1987): 65-73.

Barker-Nunn, Jeanne. "Telling the Mother's Story: History and Connection in the Autobiographies of Maxine Hong Kingston and Kim Chernin." *Women's Studies* 14, no. 1 (1987): 55-63.

Beecher, Maureen Ursenbach. "Inadvertent Disclosure? Autobiography in the Poetry of Eliza R. Snow." *Dialogue* 23 (Spring 1990): 94-107.

Bringhurst, Newell G. "Fawn M. Brodie--Her Biographies as Autobiography." *Pacific Historical Review* 59 (May 1990): 203-230.

Bunkers, Suzanne L. "Subjectivity and Self-Reflexivity in the Study of Women's

Diaries as Autobiography." *Auto/Biography Studies* 5 (Fall 1990): 114-124.

Deck, Alice A. "Autoethnography: Zora Neale Hurston, Noni Jabavu, and Cross-Disciplinary Discourse." *Black American Literature Forum* 24 (Summer 1990): 237-256.

Drucker, Sally Ann. "'It Doesn't Say So in Mother's Prayerbook': Autobiographies in English by Immigrant Jewish Women." *American Jewish History* 79 (Autumn 1989): 55-71.

DuBois, Ellen, ed. "Spanning Two Centuries: The Autobiography of Nora Stanton Barney." *History Workshop* 22 (Autumn 1986): 131-152.

Fleishman, Avrom. "'To Return to St. Ives': Woolf's Autobiographical Writings." *ELH* 48 (Fall 1981): 606-618.

Gunn, Janet Varner. "The Autobiographical Occupation: Alice James's Diary and the Decoration of Space." *Auto/Biography Studies* 4 (Fall 1988): 37-45.

Harpole, Patricia C., ed. "The Black Community in Territorial St. Anthony: A Memoir by Emily O. Goodridge Grey." *Minnesota History* 49 (Summer 1984): 42-53.

Higgins, Anthony, ed. "Mary Wilson Thompson Memoir (Part One)." *Delaware History* 18 (Spring/Summer 1978): 43-62.

-----. "Mary Wilson Thompson Memoir (Part Two)." *Delaware History* 18 (Fall/Winter 1978): 126-151.

-----. "Mary Wilson Thompson Memoir (Part Three)." *Delaware History* 18 (Fall/Winter 1979): 194-217.

Jellison, Katherine. "'Sunshine and Rain in Iowa': Using Women's Autobiography as a Historical Source." *Annals of Iowa* 49 (Winter 1989): 591-599.

Lacey, Barbara E. "The World of Hannah Heaton: The Autobiography of an Eighteenth-Century Connecticut Farm Woman." *William and Mary Quarterly* 45 (April 1988): 280-304.

Lazzell, Ruleen. "Life on a Homestead: Memories of Minnie A. Crisp." *New Mexico Historical Review* 54 (January 1979): 59-63.

Lensink, Judy Nolte. "Expanding the Boundaries of Criticism: The Diary as Female Autobiography." *Women's Studies* 14, no. 1 (1987): 39-53.

Ling, Amy. "Revealation and Mask: Autobiographies of the Eaton Sisters." *Auto/Biography Studies* 3 (Summer 1987): 46-52.

Lupton, Mary Jane. "Singing the Black Mother: Maya Angelou and Autobiographical Continuity." *Black American Literature Forum* 24 (Summer 1990): 257-276.

Mason, Mary G. "Travel as Metaphor and Reality in Afro-American Women's Autobiography." *Black American Literature Forum* 24 (Summer 1990): 337-356.

Mayall, David. "Rescued from the Shadows of Exile: Nellie Driver, Autobiography and the British Union of Fascists." *Immigrants & Minorities* 8 (March 1989): 19-39.

Motz, Marilyn F. "Visual Autobiography: Photograph Albums of Turn-of-the-Century Midwestern Women." *American Quarterly* 41 (March 1989): 63-92.

O'Connor, June. "Dorothy Day as Autobiographer." *Religion* 20 (July 1990): 275-296.

Pratt, Linda Ray. "Lady Gregory's Memories of Robert Gregory." *Eire-Ireland* 24 (Winter 1989): 54-74.

Reagon, Bernice Johnson. "My Black Mothers and Sisters, or on Beginning a Cultural Autobiography." *Feminist Studies* 8 (Spring 1982): 81-96.

Roodenburg, Herman W. "The Autobiography of Isabella DeMoerloose: Sex, Childrearing and Popular Belief in Seventeenth Century Holland." *Journal of Social History* 18 (Summer 1985): 517-540.

Sandburg, Helga. "Eyeing the World with All Delight: Helga Sandburg Looks Back at Her Family." *Illinois Historical Journal* 81 (Summer 1988): 82-94.

Tuerk, Richard. "Assimilation in Jewish-American Autobiography: Mary Antin and Ludwig Lewisohn." *Auto/Biography Studies* 3 (Summer 1987): 26-33.

Wagner, Kathrin. "'Dichter' and 'Dichtung': Susan Baron and the 'Truth' of Autobiography." *English Studies in Africa* 32, no. 1 (1989): 1-12.

## Individual and Collective Biographies

Abel, Marjorie Ruzich. "Profiles of Nineteenth Century Women." *Historical Journal of Massachusetts* 14 (January 1986): 43-52.

Agosin, Marjorie. "Teresa Wilms Montt: A Forgotten Legend." *Women's Studies International Forum* 13, no. 3 (1990): 195-200.

Alenius, Marianne. "Charlotta Dorothea Biehl: A Scandinavian Woman of Letters and her European Background." *Culture & History* no. 8 (1990): 21-36.

Andrews-Koryta, Stepanka. "Dr. Olga Stastny, Her Service to Nebraska and the World." *Nebraska History* 68 (Spring 1987): 20-27.

Babcock, Barbara Allen. "Reconstructing the Person: The Case of Clara Shortridge Foltz." *Biography* 12 (Winter 1989): 5-16.

Baeyer, Edwinna Von. "The Horticultural Odyssey of Isabella Preson." *Canadian Horticultural History* 1, no. 3 (1987): 125-175.

Blackley, F. D. "Isabella of France, Queen of England 1308-1358 and the Late Medieval Cult of the Dead." *Canadian Journal of History* 15 (April 1980): 23-48.

Blakey, George T. "Esther Griffin White: An Awakener of Hoosier Potential." *Indiana Magazine of History* 86 (September 1990): 281-310.

Bosch, Mineke. "A Woman's Life in a Soapbox." *History Workshop* 24 (Autumn 1987): 166-170.

Bringhurst, Newell G. "Applause, Attack, and Ambivalence--Varied Responses to Fawn M. Brodie's *No Man Knows My History.*" *Utah Historical Quarterly* 57 (Winter 1989): 46-63.

-----. "Fawn Brodie and Her Quest for Independence." *Dialogue* 22 (Summer 1989): 79-96.

Buren, Jane Van. "Louisa May Alcott: A Study in Persona and Idealization." *Psychohistory Review* 9 (Summer 1981): 282-299.

Capper, Charles. "Margaret Fuller as Cultural Reformer: The Conversation in

Boston." *American Quarterly* 39, no. 4 (1987): 509-528.

Carlson, A. Cheree. "Limitations on the Comic Frame: Some Witty American Women of the Nineteenth Century." *Quarterly Journal of Speech* 74, no. 3 (1988): 310-322.

Cartwright, Alison S. "Jessie P. Slaton: A Renaissance Woman." *Michigan History* 73 (September/October 1989): 20-23.

Cederstrom, Eleanor R. "'Remember the Ladies.'" *Essex Institute Historical Collection* 119 (July 1983): 145-164.

Chapco, Ellen J. "Women at Court in Seventeenth-Century France: Madame de La Fayette and the Concept of Honne tête." *Western Society for French History* 11 (November 1983): 122-129.

Cohen, Alfred. "Mary Cary's 'The Glorious Excellence' Discovered." *The British Studies Monitor* 10 (Summer 1980): 4-7.

Cohen, Sheldon S. "Hannah Levy and the General: An Historical Enigma." *Mid-America* 68 (January 1986): 5-14.

Cole, Terrence. "The History of a History: The Making of Jeanette Paddock Nichol's *Alaska*." *Pacific Northwest Quarterly* 77 (October 1986): 130-138.

Coryell, Janet L. "Anna Ella Carroll and the Historians." *Civil War History* 35 (June 1989): 120-137.

Cowden, Gerald Steffens. "Spared by Lightning: The Story of Lucy (Harrison) Randolph Necks." *Virginia Magazine of History and Biography* 89 (July 1981): 294-307.

Crane, Elaine F. "The World of Elizabeth Drinker." *Pennsylvania Magazine of History and Biography* 107 (January 1983): 3-28.

Crawford, Rachael B. "The First Lady of the Wolcott House." *Northwest Ohio Quarterly* 50 (Summer 1978): 92-99.

Crowley, Terry. "Madonnas Before Magdalenes: Adelaide Hoodless and the Making of the Canadian Gibson Girl." *Canadian Historical Review* 67 (December 1986): 520-547.

Daughenbaugh, Leonard. "On Top of Her World--Anna Mills' Ascent of Mount Whitney." *California History* 64 (Winter 1985): 42-51.

Davis, Archibald Kimbrough. "The Lady from Boston." *Proceedings of the Massachusetts Historical Society* 91 (1979): 67-85.

Davis, Curtis Carroll. "Helping to Hold the Fort, Elizabeth Zane at Wheeling, 1782: A Case Study in Renown." *West Virginia History* 44 (Spring 1983): 212-225.

-----. "The Tribulations of Mrs. Turner: An Episode after Guilford Court House." *Maryland Historical Magazine* 76 (December 1981): 376-379.

DeHamer, Nancy. "Dakota Resources: The Rose Wilder Lane Papers at the Herbert Hoover Presidential Library." *South Dakota History* 14 (Winter 1984): 335-346.

DeSantis, Vincent P. "Belva Ann Lockwood." *Timeline* 4 (December 1987/January 1988): 42-49.

Duncan, Bobby. "Jane Y. McCallum (1878-1957): Proof That 'All Texans Are Not Males.'" *Texas Liberator* 45 (Winter 1984): 134-138.

Duran, Jane. "Anne Viscountess Conway: A Seventeenth Century Rationalist." *Hypatia* 4 (Spring 1989): 64-79.

Eckhardt, Celia. "Fanny Wright: Rebel & Communitarian Reformer." *Communal Societies* 4 (Fall 1984): 183-196.

Euvich, Amanda. "Women, Brokerage, and Aristocratic Service: The Case of Marguerite de Selne." *Western Society for French History* 15 (November 1987): 48.

Follet, Joyce Clark. "Margaret Fuller in Europe, 1846-1850." *History Today* 29 (August 1979): 506-515.

Frankforter, A. Daniel. "Hroswitha of Gandersheim and the Destiny of Women." *The Historian* 41 (February 1979): 295-314.

Fry, Amelia R. "The Two Searches for Alice Paul." *Frontiers* 7, no. 1 (1983): 21-24.

Fryer, Mary Beacock. "A Note: Mrs. Simcoe from Neglected Sources." *Ontario History* 82 (December 1990): 305-316.

Gates, Susa Young. "From Impulsive Girl to Patient Wife: Lucy Bigelow Young." *Utah Historical Quarterly* 45 (Summer 1977): 270-288.

Gelfant, Blanche H. "American Women." *Canadian Review of American Studies* 17 (Fall 1986): 355-359.

Gelles, Edith B. "The Abigail Industry." *William and Mary Quarterly* 45, no. 4 (1988): 656-683.

Ghorayeb, Rose. "Mary Ziadeh." *Signs* 5 (Winter 1979): 375-382.

Gilbert, Gail R., comp. "Margaret Morris Bridwell (1906-73): A Bibliography." *Filson Club History Quarterly* 57 (July 1983): 305-314.

Giltrow, Janet. "Painful Experience in a Distant Land: Mrs. Moodie in Canada and Mrs. Trollope in America." *Mosaic* 14 (Spring 1981): 131-144.

Greene, David L. "New Light on Mary Rowlandson." *Early American Literature* 20 (Spring 1985): 24-38.

Grube, Alberta Fabris, and Jacques Portes, eds. "An English Lady Looks at America: Frances Trollope's Domestic Manners of the Americans." *Europe and America: Criss-Crossing Perspectives, 1788-1848* (1987): 105-128.

Hamner, Ada I. Foster. "Ada Irene Foster Hamner, 1887-1986: The Way It Was . . . Memories from the Turn of the Century." Jane Leslie Newberry, ed. *North Louisiana Historical Association Journal* 19, no. 1 (1988): 18-24.

Handen, Ella. "In the Shadow of Liberty: Cornelia Bradford and Whittier House Settlement, 1724-40." *New Jersey History* 100 (Fall/Winter 1982): 49-70.

Harrell, George T. "Lady Osler." *Bulletin of the History of Medicine* 53 (Spring 1979): 81-99.

Hayes, Edmund M. "Mercy Otis Warren versus Lord Chesterfield, 1779." *William and Mary Quarterly* 40 (October 1983): 616-621.

Hilgar, Marie-France. "Anne de Beaujeu, Unofficial Regent, 1483-1492." *Western Society for French History* 11 (November 1983): 53.

Hlus, Carolyn. "Margaret Fuller: Transcendentalist: A Re-assessment." *Canadian Review of American Studies* 16 (Spring 1985): 1-14.

Hodgkin, Katharine. "The Diary of Lady Anne Clifford: A Study of Class and

Gender in the Seventeenth Century." *History Workshop* 19 (Spring 1985): 148-161.

Hook, Judith. "St. Catherine of Siena." *History Today* 30 (July 1980): 28-32.

House, Katherine L. "Abraham and Rebecca Sharp: Ordeal at the Salt River Settlement, Autumn 1786." *Filson Club History Quarterly* 61, no. 4 (1987): 478-482.

Hughes, Billy. "In Defence of Ellen Wilkinson." *History Workshop* 7 (Spring 1979): 161-169.

Humphrey, John. "The Three Daughters of Agrippina Minor." *American Journal of Ancient History* 4, no. 2 (1979): 125-143.

Hyde, Mrytle Stevens. "The English Ancestry of Elizabeth Aldous, Wife of Henry Brock of Dedham, Massachusetts." *New England Historical and Genealogical Register* 144 (April 1990): 124-137.

Jones, Michael, and Malcolm Underwood. "Lady Margaret Beaufort." *History Today* 35 (August 1985): 23-30.

Keohane, Nannerl O. "'But for Her Sex...': The Domestication of Sophie." *Revue de l'Université d'Ottawa* 49, no. 3/4 (1980): 390-400.

Kestner, Joseph. "Edward Burne-Jones and Nineteenth-Century Fear of Women." *Biography* 7 (Spring 1984): 95-122.

Kier, Kathleen E. "The Revival That Failed: Elizabeth Shaw Melville and the Stedmans: 1891-1894." *Women's Studies* 7, no. 3 (1980): 75-84.

Kornfeld, Eve. "Women in Post-Revolutionary American Culture: Susanna Haswell Rowson's American Career, 1792-1824." *Journal of American Culture* 6 (Winter 1983): 56-62.

Kreidberg, Marjorie. "An Unembarrassed Patriot: Lucy Wilder Morris." *Minnesota History* 47 (Summer 1981): 214-226.

Kunzle, David. "Marie Duval and Ally Sloper." *History Workshop* 21 (Spring 1986): 133-140.

Lackow, Manya Prozanskaya. "In the Russian *Gymnasia*." *Lilith* 15 (Winter 1990): 15-20.

Lambert, Elizabeth. "Dr. Johnson and Mrs. Thrale: The Significance of a Thraliana Entry." *Eighteenth-Century Life* 5 (Winter 1978): 26-29.

Lilly, Paul R. "What Happened in Hinton." *American Heritage* 39 (July/August 1988).

Lockwood, Allison. "Delia Bacon: The Lady Who Didn't Dig Shakespeare." *American History Illustrated* 19, no. 6 (1984): 40-46.

Marks, Arthur S. "Angelica Kauffmann and Some Americans on the Grand Tour." *The American Art Journal* 12 (Spring 1980): 4-24.

Marshall, Megan. "Three Sisters Who Showed the Way." *American Heritage* 38 (September/October 1987): 58-66.

Martin, Ged. "Queen Victoria and Canada." *The American Review of Canadian Studies* 13 (Autumn 1983): 215-234.

Maxwell, Margaret F. "Cordelia Adams Crawford of the Tonto Basin." *Journal of Arizona History* 26 (Winter 1985): 415-428.

McCrimmon, Barbara S. "Victoria Claflin Woodhull Martin." *Manuscripts* 42

(Summer 1990): 229-231.

McSherry, James. "The Invisible Lady: Sir John A. MacDonald's First Wife." *Canadian Bulletin of Medical History/Bulletin canadien d'histoire de la medicine* 1 (Summer 1984): 91-98.

Meadows, Karen. "Sisters in Spirit: Florence Dibell Bartlett, Mary Cabot Wheelwright, and Amelia Elizabeth White." *El Palacio* 92 (Summer/Fall 1986): 7-11.

Miller, Danny L. "Harriette Simpson and Harold Arnow in Cincinnati: 1934-1939." *Queen City Heritage* 47 (Summer 1989): 41-48.

Morris, Jenny. "The Gertrude Tuckwell Collection." *History Workshop* 5 (Spring 1978): 155-162.

Mortimer, Joanne Stafford. "Annie Besant and India, 1913-1917." *Journal of Contemporary History* 18 (January 1983): 61-78.

Noun, Louise. "Amelia Bloomer, A Biography: Part I, The Lily of Seneca Falls." *Annals of Iowa* 47 (Winter 1985): 575-617.

-----. "Making Her Mark: Nellie Verne Walker, Sculptor." *Palimpsest* 68 (Winter 1987): 160-173.

Opheim, Teresa, ed. "The Woman's World: Carrie Lane Chapman in the Mason City *Republican*." *Palimpsest* 62 (September/October 1981): 130-139.

Painter, Nell Irvin. "Sojourner Truth in Life and Memory: Writing the Biography of an American Exotic." *Gender & History* 2 (Spring 1990): 3-16.

Plested, Dolores. "Amazing Minnie: A Nineteenth-Century Woman of Today." *Colorado Heritage* no. 1 (1984): 18-27.

Preston, Julia Antoinette Losee. "Washtub Over the Sun." *Palimpsest* 68 (Spring 1987): 2-11.

Radbill, Kenneth A. "The Ordeal of Elizabeth Drinker." *Pennsylvania History* 47 (April 1980): 147-172.

Ransom, Diane. "'The Saskatoon Lily': A Biography of Ethel Catherwood." *Saskatchewan History* 41 (Autumn 1988): 81-98.

Reinfeld, Barbara K. "Charlotte Garrique Masaryk, 1850-1923." *Czechoslovak and Central European Journal* 8 (Summer/Winter 1989): 90-103.

Richards, Clifford. "Fort Wayne Women." *Old Fort News* 45, no. 3 (1982): 4-12.

Riley, Glenda. "From Ireland to Illinois: The Life of Helen Rose Hall." *Illinois Historical Journal* 81 (Autumn 1988): 162-180.

Roberts, Audrey. "Caroline M. Kirkland: Additions to the Canon." *Bulletin of Research in the Humanities* 86, no. 3 (1983/85): 338-346.

Roberts, Virginia Culin. "Horseback to Mount Baldy: A Ranchwoman's Holiday, 1913." *Journal of Arizona History* 21 (Spring 1980): 25-42.

-----. "The Woman Was Too Tough." *Journal of Arizona History* 26 (Winter 1985): 395-414.

Rosenfelt, Deborah. "From the Thirties: Tillie Olsen and the Radical Tradition." *Feminist Studies* 7 (Fall 1981): 371-406.

Rubenstein, David. "Ellen Wilkinson Re-considered." *History Workshop* 7 (Spring 1979): 161-169.

Rudd, Hynda. "The Unsinkable Anna Marks." *Western States Jewish Historical*

*Quarterly* 10 (April 1978): 234-237.

Santha, K. S. "The Exploitation of the Begums of Awadh by the East India Company: A Case History of Malika-i-Jaban, a Secondary Wife of Muhammad Ali Shah." *Quarterly Review of Historical Studies* 20, no. 2/3 (1980/81): 19-25.

Sapper, Neil. "Aboard the Wrong Ship in the Right Books: Doris Miller and Historical Accuracy." *East Texas History Journal* (Spring 1980): 3-11.

Schriber, Mary Suzanne. "Julia Ward Howe and the Travel Book." *New England Quarterly* 62 (June 1989): 264-279.

Serene, Frank H. "Paesano: The Struggle to Survive in Ambridge." *Pennsylvania Heritage* 6 (Fall 1980).

Shinn, Thelma J. "Harriet Prescott Spoffard: A Reconsideration." *Turn-of-the-Century Woman* 1, no. 1 (1984): 36-45.

Silberstein, Iola O. "Diversity on Converging Pathways: Mary H. Doherty and Helen G. Lotspeich." *Queen City Heritage* 41 (Winter 1983): 3-23.

Simmel, Marianne L. "A Tribute to Eugenia Hanfmann, 1905-1983." *Journal of History of the Behavioral Sciences* 22 (October 1986): 348-356.

Smith, Bonnie G. "Seeing Mary Beard." *Feminist Studies* 10 (Fall 1984): 399-416.

St. Mark, J. J. "Matilda and William Tone in New York and Washington, D. C. after 1798." *Eire-Ireland* 22 (Winter 1987): 4-10.

Stafford, Pauline. "The King's Wife in Wessex 800-1066." *Past and Present*, no. 91 (May 1981): 3-27.

Stein, Dorothy K. "Lady Lovelace's Notes: Technical Text and Cultural Context." *Victorian Studies* 28 (Autumn 1984): 33-68.

Stern, Madeleine B. "Notable Women of 19th Century America." *Manuscripts* 34 (Summer 1982).

Stewart, Elizabeth Redington. "My Darling Red Bird." *Oregon Historical Quarterly* 80 (Summer 1979): 117-133.

Stineman, Esther Lanigan. "Mary Austin Rediscovered." *Journal of the Southwest* 30 (Winter 1988): 545-551.

Street, Douglas. "La Flesche Sisters Write to St. Nicholas Magazine." *Nebraska History* 62 (Winter 1981): 515-523.

Strumingher, Laura S. "The Legacy of Flora Tristan." *International Journal of Women's Studies* 7 (May/June 1984): 232-247.

Talbott, Edna. "Mary Beck and the Female Mind." *Register of the Kentucky Historical Society* (Winter 1979): 15-24.

Tanner, Helen Hornbeck. "Erminie Wheeler-Voegelin (1903-1988), Founder of the American Society for Ethnohistory." *Ethnohistory* 38 (Winter 1991): 58-72.

Teague, Michael. "Theodore Roosevelt and Alice Hathaway Lee: A New Perspective." *Harvard Library Bulletin* 33 (Summer 1985): 225-238.

Thomas, Chantal. "Heroism in the Feminine: The Examples of Charlotte Corday and Madame Roland." *Eighteenth Century* [Lubbock] Special Issue: The French Revolution 1789-1989 (1989): 67-82.

Thomas, Julian. "Amy Johnson's Truimph, Australia 1930." *Australian Historical Studies* 23 (April 1988): 72-84.

Tingley, Donald F. "Margaret Flint: The Historian's Librarian." *Illinois Historical*

*Journal* 77 (Winter 1984): 249-254.

Walker, Ronald W. "Rachel R. Grant: The Continuing Legacy of the Feminine Ideal." *Dialogue* 15 (Autumn 1982): 105-121.

Warnicke, Retha M. "The Fall of Anne Boleyn: A Reassessment." *History* 70 (February 1985): 1-15.

Wirmark, Margareta. "Christina: Pandora or Eve." *Scandinavian Studies* 62 (Winter 1990): 116-122.

Withers, Josephine. "Eleanor Antin: Allegory of the Soul." *Feminist Studies* 12 (Spring 1986): 117-128.

Wright, Helena. "Sarah G. Bagley: A Biographical Note." *Labor History* 20 (Summer 1979): 398-413.

Zapoleon, Marguerite Wykoff. "Cincinnati Citizens: Elizabeth Campbell (1862-1962)." *Queen City Heritage* 43 (Winter 1985): 3-20.

Zedler, Beatrice H. "The Three Princesses." *Hypatia* 4 (Spring 1989): 28-63.

## Journals and Diaries

Abrahamson, Laura Alate Iversen. "Herding Cows and Waiting Tables: The Diary of Laura Alate Iversen Abrahamson." *South Dakota History* 20 (Spring 1990): 17-50.

Andreadis, A. Harriette. "True Womanhood Revisited: Women's Private Writing in Nineteenth Century Texas." *Journal of the Southwest* 31 (Summer 1989): 179-204.

Baldwin, Hélene L. "'Down Street' in Cumberland: The Diaries of Two Nineteenth-Century Ladies." *Maryland Historical Magazine* 77 (Fall 1982): 222-229.

Begos, Jane. "A Selected Bibliography of German Women's Diaries." *Women's Studies Quarterly* 17, no. 3 & 4 (1989): 95-98.

Blauvelt, Martha Tomhave. "Women, Words, and Men: Excerpts from the Diary of Mary Guion." *Journal of Women's History* 2 (Fall 1990): 177-184.

Blodgett, Harriet. "A Woman Writer's Diary: Virginia Woolf Revisited." *Prose Studies: History, Theory, Criticism* 12 (May 1989): 57-71.

Boera, A. Richard, ed. "The Edith Kermit Roosevelt Diaries." *Theodore Roosevelt Association Journal* 12 (Spring/Summer 1986): 2-11.

Bohem, Hilda. "Nellie Suydam of Glendora: Diary of an Ordinary Woman." *Southern California Quarterly* 66 (Winter 1984): 335-344.

Bunkers, Suzanne. "Reading and Interpreting Unpublished Diaries by Nineteenth Century Women." *Auto/Biography Studies* 2 (Summer 1986): 15-18.

Caine, Barbara. "Beatrice Webb and Her Diary." *Victorian Studies* 27 (Autumn 1983): 81-90.

Cruikshank, Margaret Andrews. "A Lady's Trip to Yellowstone 1883: 'Earth Could Not Furnish Another Such Sight.'" Lee H. Whittlesey, ed. *Montana* 39 (Winter 1989): 2-15.

Culley, Margo. "'I Look at Me': Self as Subject in the Diaries of American Women." *Women's Studies Quarterly* 17, no. 3 &4 (1989): 15-22.

Dahlback, Kerstin. "Christina: Strindberg's Letters and Diary." *Scandinavian Studies* 62 (Winter 1990): 108-115.

Davidoff, Leonore. "Class and Gender in Victorian England: The Diaries of Arthur J. Munby and Hannah Cullwick." *Feminist Studies* 5 (Spring 1979): 87-141.

Dawkins, Heather. "The Diaries and Photographs of Hannah Cullwick." *Art History* 10 (June 1987): 154-187.

Dix, Fae Decker, ed. "The Josephine Diaries: Glimpses of the Life of Josephine Streeper Chase, 1881-94." *Utah Historical Quarterly* 46 (Spring 1978): 167-183.

Doneson, Judith E. "American History of Anne Frank's Diary." *Holocaust and Genocide Studies* [Great Britain] 2, no. 1 (1987): 149-160.

Dowell, Cheryl Wexell. "Dear Diary, 1886-1890: Clara Lindbeck Writes from Bishop Hall." *Illinois Historical Journal* 82 (Winter 1989): 231-238.

Fries, Kena. "Diary of Kena Fries." Jean Yothers, and Paul W. Wehr, eds., trans. by Margareta Miller. *Florida Historical Quarterly* 62 (January 1984): 339-352.

Gillikin, Jo. "A Masterpiece in Modesty: The Diary of Anne Rogers Minor, 1942-1946." *Connecticut Historical Society Bulletin* 49 (Spring 1984).

Heinzelman, Kurt. "'Household Laws': Dorothy Wordsworth's *Grasmere Journal*." *Auto/Biography Studies* 2 (Winer 1986-1987): 21-26.

Hobler, James A., ed. "The Civil War Diary of Louisa Brown Pearl." *Tennessee History Quarterly* (Fall 1979): 308-321.

Hoffman, Leonore. "The Diaries of Gwendolyn Bennett." *Women's Studies Quarterly* 17, no. 3 &4 (1989): 66-73.

Huff, Cynthia. "From Faceless Chronicler to Self-Creator: The Diary of Louisa Galton, 1830-1896." *Biography* 10 (Spring 1987): 95-106.

-----. "Private Domains: Queen Victoria and Women's Diaries." *Auto/Biography Studies* 4 (Fall 1988): 46-52.

-----. "'That Profoundly Female, and Feminist Genre': The Diary as Feminist Practice." *Women's Studies Quarterly* 17, no. 3 & 4 (1989): 6-14.

Kamel, Rosa. "Interrupted Lives, Inner Resources: The Diaries of Hannah Senesh and Etty Hillesum." *Women's Studies Quarterly* 17, no. 3 & 4 (1989): 45-58.

Lensink, Judy Nolte. "Expanding the Boundaries of Criticism: The Diary as Female Autobiography." *Women's Studies* 14, no. 1 (1987): 39-53.

-----, Christine M. Kirkham, and Karen Pauba Witzke. "'My Only Confidant'--The Life and Diary of Emily Hawley Gillespie." *Annals of Iowa* 45 (Spring 1980): 288-312.

Lewis, Jane. "Re-reading Beatrice Webb's Diary." *History Workshop* 16 (Autumn 1983): 143-146.

McNinch, Marjorie, ed. "Elizabeth Gilpin's Journal of 1830." *Delaware History* 20 (Fall/Winter 1983): 223-255.

Myerson, Joel, and Daniel Shealy. "Editing Louisa May Alcott's Journals." *Manuscripts* 62 (Winter 1990): 19-33.

Paullin, Ellen Payne, ed. "Etta's Journal, January 2, 1874-July 25, 1875." *Kansas*

*History* 3 (Autumn 1980): 201-219.

-----. "Etta's Journal, January 2, 1874-July 25, 1875 (Second Installment)." *Kansas History* 3 (Winter 1980): 255-278.

Riley, Glenda, and Carol Benning. "The 1836-1845 Diary of Sarah Browne Armstrong Adamson of Fayette County, Ohio." *Old Northwest* 10 (Fall 1984): 285-306.

Rusinowa, Izabella. "European Utopians in America: The Diary of Kalikst Wolski." *Quaderno* 1 (1988).

Sanders, James, ed. "Times Hard but Grit Good: Lydia Moxley's 1877 Diary." *Annals of Iowa* 47 (Winter 1984): 270-290.

Scott, Joan Wallach. "New Documents on the Lives of French Women: The Journal of Caroline B., 1864-1868." *Signs* 12 (Spring 1987): 568-572.

Stephens, Lester D., ed. "A Righteous Aim: Emma Lelonte Furman's (b. 1847) 1918 Diary." *Georgia History Quarterly* 62 (Fall 1978): 213-224.

Stewart, Imogen. "Betsy Sheridan's Journal." *Costume* 22 (1988): 39-43.

Uhltenburg, Joy. "Excerpts from the Diary of Elizabeth Oakes Smith." *Signs* 9 (Spring 1984): 534-548.

Woodcock, John. "The Therapeutic Journals of Joanna Field and Etty Hillesum." *Auto/Biography Studies* 5 (Summer 1989): 15-25.

## Letters

Alford, Terry. "'. . . Hoping to Hear From You Soon': The Begging Correspondence of Alexander T. Stewart." *Manuscripts* 40 (Spring 1988): 89-100.

Anderson, George M. "An Early Commuter: The Letters of James and Mary Anderson." *Maryland Historical Magazine* 75 (Fall 1980): 217-232.

Azadovskij, Konstantin. "The 'Letter' in the Writings of Marina Tsvetaeva." *Culture & History* no. 8 (1990): 61-68.

Biemer, Linda, ed. "Business Letters of Alida Schuyler Livingston, 1680-1726." *New York History* 63 (April 1982): 183-207.

Bjørn, Claus. "Edification and Information: Letter-Writing in Denmark around 1800. The Case of the Reventlow Family." *Culture & History* no. 8 (1990): 37-50.

Blum, Dilys E. "Englishwomen's Dress in Eighteenth-Century India: The Margaret Fowke Correspondence (1776-1786)." *Costume* 17 (1983): 47-58.

Buecker, Thomas R., ed. "Letters from a Post Surgeon's Wife." *Annals of Wyoming* 53 (Fall 1981): 44-63.

Cowden, Gerald Steffens, ed. "'My dear Mr. W': Mary Lincoln Writes to Alexander Williamson." *Journal of the Illinois State Historical Society* 76 (Spring 1983): 71-74.

Dahlback, Kerstin. "Christina: Strindberg's Letters and Diary." *Scandinavian Studies* 62 (Winter 1990): 108-115.

Derounian, Kathryn Zabelle. "'A Dear Dear Friend': Six Letters from Debor Norris to Sally Wister, 1778-1779." *Pennsylvania Magazine of History and*

*Biography* 108 (October 1984): 487-516.

Dryden, Jean E., and Sandra L. Myres. "The Letters of Barbara Alice Slater: Homesteading on the Canadian Prairies, 1909-1918." *Montana* 37 (Winter 1987): 14-33.

Dublin, Thomas, ed. "The Letters of Mary Paul, 1845-1849." *Vermont History* 48, no. 2 (1980): 77-88.

Evans, William R. "Robert Frost and Helen Thomas: Five Revealing Letters." *Dartmouth College Library Bulletin* 30 (November 1989): 2-10.

Freeman, Olga, ed. "Almira Raymond Letters 1840-1880." *Oregon Historical Quarterly* 85 (Fall 1984): 291-303.

Friedman, Alice T. "Portrait of a Marriage:   The Willoughby Letters of 1585-1586." *Signs* 11 (Spring 1986): 529-541.

Fuller, Rosalie Trail. "A Holdrege High School Teacher, 1900-1905: The Letters of Sadie B. Smith." *Nebraska History* 60 (Fall 1979): 372-400.

Gelles, Edith B. "A Virtuous Affair: The Correspondence Between Abigail Adams and James Lovell." *American Quarterly* 39 (Summer 1987): 252-269.

George, Joseph, Jr., ed. "'A True Childe of Sorrow':  Two Letters of Mary E. Surratt (1823-65)." *Maryland History Magazine* 80 (Winter 1985): 402-405.

Hileman, Sharon. "Autobiographical Narrative in the Letters of Jane Carlyle." *Auto/Biography Studies* 4 (Winter 1988): 107-117.

Hollis, Florence Davenport.  "The Home Front in Americus During the Great War:  The 1918 Correspondence of Florence Davenport Hollis [1849-1954]." Elizabeth Champion, ed. *Journal of Southwest Georgia History* 5 (Fall 1987): 38-63.

Holder, Ray, ed. "My Dear Husband:  Letters of a Plantation Mistress:  Martha Dubose Winans to William Winans, 1834-44." *Journal of Mississippi History* 49 (November 1987): 301-324.

Kammen, Carol, ed. "The Letters of Calista Hall." *New York History* 63 (April 1982): 209-234.

Langley, Harold D. "A Naval Dependent in Washington, 1837-1842: Letters of Marian Coote Speiden." *Records of the Columbia Historical Society of Washington, D.C.* 50 (1980).

Lawrence, Jenny. "Miriam Berry Whitcher Speaks Her Mind: Letters Home, 1846-1852." *New York Historical Society Quarterly* 63 (January 1979): 24-53.

Leider, Emily. "'Your Picture Hangs in My Salon,' The Letters of Gertrude Atherton to Ambrose Bierce." *California History* 60 (Winter 1981/82): 332-349.

Mason, Tim. "Comrade and Lover: Rosa Luxemburg's Letters to Leo Jogiches." *History Workshop* 13 (Spring 1982): 94-109.

Onion, Margaret Kent, ed. "Love Letters in the Year of Seneca Falls." *Vermont History* 47 (Summer 1979): 214-223.

Peterson, John M., ed. "Letters of Edward and Sarah Fitch, Lawrence, Kansas, 1855-1863, Part I." *Kansas History* 12 (Spring 1989): 48-70.

Rasid, Gadis. "Kartini--The Tragedy of a Letter-Writing Javanese Princess." *Hemisphere* [Australia] 28 (November/December 1983): 162-167.

Rosholt, Malcolm. "The Shoe Box Letters from China, 1913-1967." *Wisconsin Magazine of History* 73 (Winter 1989/90): 111-133.

Ross, Frances Mitchell, ed. "'A Tie Between Us That Time Cannot Sever': Latta Family Letters, 1855-1872." *Arkansas Historical Quarterly* 40 (Spring 1981): 31-78.

Tessman, Norm, ed. "The Personal Journal and Arizona Letters of Margaret Hunt McCormick." *Journal of Arizona History* 26 (Spring 1985): 41-52.

Wold, Frances M., comp. and ed. "The Letters of Effie Hanson, 1917- 1923: Farm Life in Troubled Times." *North Dakota History* 48 (Winter 1981): 20-43.

## Oral History

Allen, Marney. "Prairie Life: An Oral History of Greta Craig." *Atlantis* 7 (1982): 89-102.

Braxton, Joanne M. "Harriet Jacobs' *Incidents in the Life of a Slave Girl*: The Re-definition of the Slave-Girl Narrative." *Massachusetts Review* 27 (Summer 1986): 379-387.

Brooks, Maria. "Remembering the Reindeer Queen." *Frontiers* 6 (Fall 1981): 59-61.

Cook, Charles Orson, and James M. Poteet. "'Dem Was Black Times, Sure 'Nough': The Slave Narratives of Lydia Jefferson and Stephen Williams." *Louisiana History* 20 (Summer 1979): 281-292.

Elsasser, Nan, Kyle MacKenzie, and Yvonne Tixier y Vigil. "Excerpts from *Las Mujeres: Conversations from a Hispanic Community*." *Frontiers* 5 (Summer 1980): 38-47.

Hamilton, Paula. "'Inventing the Self': Oral History as Autobiography." *Hecate: An Interdisciplinary Journal of Women's Liberation* 16, no. 1/2 (1990): 128-133.

Henke, Suzette. "*Incidents in the Life of a Slave Girl*: Autobiography as Reconstruction." *Feminist Issues* 6 (Fall 1986): 33-39.

Ingrame, Ann G. "An Oral History Study of the Women's Equity Movement, University of Maryland, College Park." *Maryland History* 9, no. 2 (1978): 1-25.

Jones, Lu Ann. "'Mama Learned Us to Work': An Oral History of Virgie St. John Redmond." *Oral History Review* 17 (Fall 1989): 63-90.

McBane, Margo and Mary Winegarden. "Labor Pains: An Oral History of California Women Farm Workers." *California History* 58 (Summer 1979): 179-181.

Nelson, Kathryn. "Excerpts from *Los Testamentos*: Hispanic Women Folk Artists of the San Luis Valley, Colorado. Oral History from Eppie Archuleta." *Frontiers* 5 (Fall 1980): 34-43.

Plummer, Stephen and Suzanne Julin. "Lucy Swan, Sioux Woman: An Oral History." *Frontiers* 6 (Fall 1981): 29-32.

Shostak, Marjorie. "What the Wind Won't Take Away: The Oral History of an African Foraging Woman." *International Journal of Oral History* 8 (November 1987): 171-181.

Wolverton, Terry and Christine Wong. "An Oral Herstory of Lesbianism."
    *Frontiers* 4 (Fall 1979): 52-53.

## Theory

Alexander, Ziggi. "Let It Lie upon the Table: The Status of Black Women's
    Biography in the UK." *Gender & History* 2 (Spring 1990): 22-33.
Apthorp, Elaine Sargent. "Speaking of Silence: Willa Cather and the 'Problem'
    of Feminist Biography." *Women's Studies* 18, no. 1 (1990): 1-12.
Armitage, Susan. "Common Ground--Introduction to 'American Women's
    Narratives.'" *Women's Studies* 14, no. 1 (1987): 1-4.
Barr, Marleen. "Deborah Norris Logan, Feminist Criticism, and Identity Theory:
    Interpreting a Woman's Diary without the Danger of Separatism." *Biography*
    8 (Winter 1985): 12-24.
Barry, Kathleen. "Biography and the Search for Women's Subjectivity." *Women's
    Studies International Forum* 12, no. 6 (1989): 561-578.
-----. "The New Historical Synthesis: Women's Biography." *Journal of Women's
    History* 1 (Winter 1990): 75-105.
Bassett, Mark T. "Man-Made Tales: Deconstructing Biography as a Feminist
    Act." *Auto/Biography Studies* 3 (Fall 1987): 46-56.
Bloom, Lynn Z. "Shaping Women's Lives." *Auto/Biography Studies* 4 (Fall
    1988): 17-27.
Chevigny, Bell Gale. "Daughters Writing: Toward a Theory of a Women's
    Biography." *Feminist Studies* 9 (Spring 1983): 79-102.
Daniels, Elizabeth A., Anne Constantinople, and Marque Miringoff. "The
    Intersection of Biography and History: The Vassar Class of 1935."
    *International Journal of Oral History* 9 (June 1988): 125-130.
Feldman, Yael S. "Gender In/Difference in Contemporary Hebrew Fictional
    Autobiographies." *Biography* 11 (Summer 1988): 189-209.
Fox-Genovese, Elizabeth. "Myth and History: Discourse of Origins in Zora Neal
    Hurston and Maya Angelou." *Black American Literature Forum* 24 (Summer
    1990): 221-236.
Gadlin, Howard. "Scars and Emblems: Paradoxes of American Life." *Journal of
    Social History* 11 (Spring 1978): 305-327.
Gower, Herschel. "Beersheba Springs, and L. Virginia French: The Novelist as
    Historian." *Tennessee History Quarterly* 42 (Summer 1983): 115-137.
Hall, Jacquelyn Dowd. "Second Thoughts: On Writing a Feminist Biography."
    *Feminist Studies* 13 (Spring 1987): 19-37.
Huff, Cynthia. "Writer at Large: Culture and Self in Victorian Women's Travel
    Diaries." *Auto/Biography Studies* 4 (Winter 1988): 118-129.
Israel, Kali A. K. "Writing inside the Kaleidoscope: Re-Representing Victorian
    Women Public Figures." *Gender & History* 2 (Spring 1990): 40-48.
Joseph, Lawrence. "Catherine Pozzi's 'Agnes': Writing as Self-Construction."
    *Biography* 11 (Winter 1988): 47-59.
Keyser, Elizabeth Lennox. "Woman in the Twentieth Century: Margaret Fuller

and Feminist Biography." *Biography* 11 (1988): 283-302.

Kolias, Helen. "Empowering the Minor: Translating Women's Autobiography." *Journal of Modern Greek Studies* 8 (October 1990): 213-222.

Lidoff, Joan. "Autobiography in a Different Voice: Maxine Hong Kingston's *The Woman Warrior*." *Auto/Biography Studies* 3 (Fall 1987): 29-35.

Maiz, Magdalena and Luis H. Pena. "Between Lines: Construction the Political Self." *Auto/Biography Studies* 3 (Summer 1988): 23-36.

Matthews, Jean V. "'Woman's Place' and the Search for Identity in Ante-Bellum America." *Canadian Review of American Studies* 10 (Winter 1979): 289-304.

Mitchell, Catherine C. "The Place of Biography in the History of News Women." *American Journalism* 7 (Winter 1990): 23-32.

Perreault, Jeanne. "'That the Pain Not Be Wasted': Audre Lorde and the Written Self." *Auto/Biography Studies* 4 (Fall 1988): 1-16.

Perry, Ruth. "Some Methodological Implications of the Study of Women's Writing." *Harvard Library Journal* 35 (Spring 1987).

Quilligan, Maureen. "Rewriting History: The Difference of Feminist Biography." *Yale Review* 77 (Winter 1988): 259-286.

Rooke, Patricia T., and R. L. Schnell. "The Making of a Feminist Biography: Reflections on a Miniature Passion." *Atlantis: A Women's Studies Journal* 15 (Fall 1989): 56-64.

Smith, Sidonie. "The Impact of Critical Theory on the Study of Autobiography: Marginality, Gender, and Autobiographical Practice." *Auto/Biography Studies* 3 (Fall 1987): 1-12.

-----. "Self, Subject, and Resistance: Marginalities and Twentieth-Century Autobiographical Practice." *Tulsa Studies in Women's Literature* 9 (Spring 1990): 11-24.

Stanley, Liz. "Moments of Writing: Is There a Feminist Auto/Biography?" *Gender & History* 2 (Spring 1990): 58-67.

Wilkerson, Margaret B. "Excavating Our History: The Importance of Biographies of Women of Color." *Black American Literature Forum* 24 (Spring 1990): 73-84.

Woodress, James. "The Uses of Biography: The Case of Willa Cather." *Great Plains Quarterly* 2 (Fall 1982): 195-203.

# BIRTH CONTROL

## Abortion

Acevedo, Zoila. "Abortion in Early America." *Women and Health* 4 (1979): 159-167.

Backhouse, Constance. "Involuntary Motherhood: Abortion, Birth Control and the Law in 19th Century Canada." *Windsor Yearbook of Access to Justice* 3 (1983): 61-130.

Cassidy, Keith. "The Abortion Controversy as a Problem in Contemporary American History: Some Suggestions for Research." *Journal of Policy History*

1, no. 4 (1989): 440-460.

Cvornyek, Robert L., and Dorothy L. Cvornyek. "'I Know Something Awful Is Going to Happen': Abortion in Early Twentieth Century Alabama." *Southern Studies* 24 (Summer 1985): 229-232.

Dayton, Cornelia Hughes. "Taking the Trade: Abortion and Gender Relations in an Eighteenth-Century New England Village." *William and Mary Quarterly* 48 (January 1991): 19-49.

Dellapenna, Joseph W. "The Historical Case Against Abortion." *Continuity, A Journal of History* no. 13 (Spring/Fall 1989): 59-84.

-----. "The History of Abortions: Technology, Morality, and Law." *University of Pittsburgh Law Review* 40 (Spring 1979): 359-428.

Dewhurst, Sir John. "The Alleged Miscarriages of Catherine of Aragon and Anne Boleyn." *Medical History* 28 (January 1984): 49-56.

Donovan, James M. "Abortion, the Law, and the Juries in France, 1825-1920." *Western Society for French History* 15 (November 1987): 217.

Gavigan, Shelley A. M. "On 'Bringing on the Menses': The Criminal Liability of Women and the Therapeutic Exception in Canadian Abortion Law." *Canadian Journal of Women and the Law/Revue Juridique 'La Femme et le droit'* 1, no. 2 (1986): 279-312.

Glen, Kristin Booth. "Abortion in the Courts: A Laywoman's Historical Guide to the New Disaster Area." *Feminist Studies* 4 (February 1978): 1-26.

Grossman, Atina. "Abortion and Economic Crisis: The 1931 Campaign Against #218 in Germany." *New German Critique* 14 (1978): 119-137.

Hippler, Arthur E. "Psychodynamics, Psychohistory and Abortion." *Journal of Psychohistory* 13 (Fall 1985): 175-188.

McLaren, Angus. "Abortion in France: Women and the Regulation of Family Size." *French Historical Studies* 10 (Spring 1978): 461-485.

-----. "Birth Control and Abortion in Canada, 1870-1920." *Canadian Historical Review* 59 (September 1978): 319-340.

Mohr, James C. "Iowa's Abortion Battles of the Late 1960s and Early 1970s: Long-term Perspectives and Short-term Analyses." *Annals of Iowa* 50 (Summer 1989): 63-89.

Olasky, Marvin. "Advertising Abortion During the 1830s and 1840s: Madame Restell Builds a Business." *Journalism History* 13 (Summer 1986): 49-55.

Petchesky, Rosalind. "Antiabortion, Antifeminism, and the Rise of the New Right." *Feminist Studies* 7 (1981): 206-246.

Reagan, Leslie J. "'About to Meet Her Maker': Women, Doctors, Dying Declarations, and the State's Investigation of Abortion, Chicago, 1867-1940." *Journal of American History* 77 (March 1991): 1240-1264.

Sands, Diane. "Using Oral History to Chart the Course of Illegal Abortions in Montana." *Frontiers* 7, no. 1 (1983): 32-37.

Tien, H. Yuan. "Abortion in China: Incidence and Implications." *Modern China* 13 (October 1987): 441-468.

Usborne, Cornelie. "Abortion in Weimar Germany--the Debate Amongst the Medical Profession." *Continuity and Change* 5, no. 2 (1990): 199-224.

# Fertility

Bacci, Massimo Livi and Marco Breschi. "Italian Fertility: An Historical Account." *Journal of Family History* 15, no. 4 (1990): 385-408.

Bean, Lee L., Geraldine P. Mineau, Douglas L. Anderton, and Yung-chang Hsueh. "The Fertility Effects of Marriage Patterns in a Frontier American Population." *Historical Methods* 20 (Fall 1987): 161-171.

Ben-Barak, Shalvia. "Fertility Patterns Among Soviet Immigrants to Israel: The Role of Cultural Variables." *Journal of Family History* 15, no.1 (1990): 87-100.

Briggs, John W. "Fertility and Cultural Change Among Families in Italy and America." *American Historical Review* 91 (December 1986): 1129-1145.

Buckley, Thomas. "Menstruation and the Power of Yurok Women: Methods in Cultural Reconstruction." *American Ethnologist* 9, no. 1 (1982): 47-60.

Byers, Edward. "Fertility Transition in a New England Commercial Center: Nantucket, Massachusetts, 1680-1840." *Journal of Interdisciplinary History* 13 (Summer 1982): 17-40.

Crafts, N. F. R. "Duration of Marriage, Fertility and Women's Employment Opportunities in England and Wales in 1911." *Population Studies* 43 (1989): 325-335.

Feeney, Griffith, and Hamano Kiyoshi. "Rice Price Fluctuations and Fertility in Late Tokugawa Japan." *Journal of Japanese Studies* 16 (Winter 1990): 1-30.

Fialova, Ludmila, Zdenek Pavlik, and Pavel Veres. "Fertility Decline in Czechoslovakia During the Last Two Centuries." *Population Studies* 44 (March 1990): 89-106.

Folbre, Nancy. "Of Patriarchy Born:   The Political Economy of Fertility Decisions." *Feminist Studies* 9 (1983): 261-284.

Guest, Avery M. "What We Can Learn About Fertility Transitions from the New York State Census of 1865?" *Journal of Family History* 15, no. 1 (1990): 49-70.

Guest, Avery M., and Stewart E. Tolnay. "Children's Roles and Fertility: Late Nineteenth Century United States." *Social Science History* 7 (Fall 1983): 355-380.

-----. "Urban Industrial Structure and Fertility:   The Case of Large American Cities." *Journal of Interdisciplinary History* 13 (Winter 1983): 387-409.

Gutmann, Myron P. "Denomination and Fertility Decline: The Catholics and Protestants of Gillespie County, Texas." *Continuity and Change* 5, no. 3 (1990): 391-416.

Haines, Michael R. "American Fertility in Transition: New Estimates of Birth Rates in the United States, 1900-1910." *Demography* 26 (February 1989): 137-148.

-----. "Fertility and Marriage in a Nineteenth Century Industrial City: Philadelphia, 1850-1880." *Journal of Economic History* 40 (March 1980): 151-158.

-----. "Western Fertility in Mid-Transition: Fertility and Nuptiality in the United States and Selected Nations at the Turn of the Century." *Journal of Family*

*History* 15, no. 1 (1990): 23-48.

Hirschman, Charles, and Philip Guest. "Multilevel Models of Fertility Determination in Four Southeast Asian Countries: 1970 and 1980." *Demography* 27 (August 1990): 397-412.

Jackson, Hugh. "Fertility Decline in New South Wales: The Mackellar Royal Commission Reconsidered." *Australian Historical Studies* 23 (April 1989): 260-273.

Johnson, Judith M., Susan L. Thompson, and Gerald J. Perry. "Juju-Soup: The Witch Herbalist's Solution for Infertility." *African Studies Review* 33 (April 1990): 55-64.

Katz, Michael, and Mark Stern. "Fertility, Class, and Industrial Capitalism: Erie County, New York, 1855-1915." *American Quarterly* 33 (Spring 1981): 63-92.

King, M., and S. Ruggles. "American Immigration, Fertility and Race Suicide at the Turn of the Century." *Journal of Interdisciplinary History* 20 (Winter 1990): 347-370.

Klein, Herbert S., and Stanley L. Engerman. "Fertility Differentials Between Slaves in the United States and the British West Indies: A Note on Lactation Practices and Their Possible Implications." *William and Mary Quarterly* 35 (April 1978): 357-374.

Kudlien, Fridolf. "The German Response to the Birth-Rate Problem During the Third Reich." *Continuity and Change* 5, no. 2 (1990): 225-248.

Lantz, Herman and Lewellyn Hendrix. "Black Fertility and the Black Family in the Nineteenth Century: A Re-Examination of the Past." *Journal of Family History* 3 (Fall 1978): 251-261.

Lavely, William, and Ronald Freedman. "The Origins of the Chinese Fertility Decline." *Demography* 27 (August 1990): 357-368.

Lithell, Ulla-Britt. "Breast-Feeding Habits and Their Relation to Infant Mortality and Marital Fertility." *Journal of Family History* 6 (Summer 1981): 182-194.

Livi-Bacci, Massimo. "Fertility, Nutrition, and Pellagra: Italy During the Vital Revolution." *Journal of Interdisciplinary History* 16 (Winter 1986): 431-454.

Logue, Barbara J. "The Whaling Industry and Fertility Decline: Nantucket, Massachusetts, 1660-1850." *Social Science History* 7 (Fall 1983): 427-456.

McConnachie, Kathleen. "A Note on Fertility Rates Among Married Women in Toronto, 1871." *Ontario History* 75 (March 1983): 87-97.

McLaren, Dorothy. "Nature's Contraceptive. Wet-Nursing and Prolonged Lactation: The Case of Chesham, Buckinghamshire, 1578-1601." *Medical History* 23 (October 1979): 426-441.

Menken, Jane, James Trussell, and Susan Watkins. "The Nutrition Fertility Link: An Evaluation of the Evidence." *Journal of Interdisciplinary History* 11 (Winter 1981): 425-441.

Mineau, Geraldine P., Lee L. Bean, and Douglas L. Anderson. "Description and Evaluation of Linkage of the 1880 Census to Family Genealogies: Implications for Utah Fertility Research." *Historical Methods* 22 (Fall 1989): 144-157.

-----. "Migration and Fertility: Behavioral Change on the American Frontier." *Journal of Family History* 14, no. 1 (1989): 43-54.

Modell, John. "An Ecology of Family Decisions: Suburbanization, Schooling, and Fertility in Philadelphia, 1880-1920." *Journal of Urban History* 6 (August 1980): 397-418.

Mosk, Carl. "Fertility and Occupation: Mining Districts in Prewar Japan." *Social Science History* 5 (Summer 1981): 293-316.

Mroz, Thomas A., and David R. Weir. "Structural Change in Life Cycle Fertility During the Fertility Transition: France Before and After the Revolution of 1789." *Population Studies* 44 (March 1990): 61-88.

Olney, Martha L. "Fertility and the Standard of Living in Early Modern England: In Consideration of Wrigley and Schofield." *Journal of Economic History* 43 (March 1983): 71-78.

Parkerson, Donald H., and Jo Ann Parkerson. "'Fewer Children of Greater Spiritual Quality': Religion and the Decline of Fertility in Nineteenth-Century America." *Social Science History* 12 (Spring 1988): 49-70.

Pillai, Vijayan K. "The Postwar Rise and Decline of American Fertility: The Pace of Transition to Motherhood Among 1950-1969 Marital Cohorts of White Women." *Journal of Family History* 12, no. 4 (1987): 421-436.

Reynolds, Sian. "Who Wanted the Creches? Working Mothers and the Birth-Rate in France 1900-1950." *Continuity and Change* 5, no. 2 (1990): 173-198.

Robin, Jean. "Prenuptial Pregnancy in a Rural Area of Devonshire in the Mid-Nineteenth Century: Colyton, 1851-1881." *Continuity and Change* 1, no. 1 (1986): 113-124.

Ross, G. Alexander. "Delaying the Fertility Decline: German Women in Saginaw County, Michigan, 1850-1880." *Journal of Family History* 14, no. 2 (1989): 157-170.

-----. "Fertility Change on the Michigan Frontier: Saginaw County, 1840-1850." *Michigan Historical Review* 12 (Fall 1986): 69-85.

Sandelowski, Margarete J. "Failures of Volition: Female Agency and Infertility in Historical Perspective." *Signs* 15 (Spring 1990): 475-499.

Seccombe, Wally. "Starting to Stop: Working-Class Fertility Decline in Britain." *Past & Present* no. 126 (February 1990): 151-188.

Simkins, Charles, and Elizabeth van Heyningen. "Fertility, Morality, and Migration in the Cape Colony, 1891-1904." *The International Journal of African Historical Studies* 22, no. 1 (1989): 79-112.

Sprague, Rosamond Kent. "Metaphysics and Multiple Births." *Apeiron: Journal for Ancient Philosophy and Science* 20 (1987): 97-102.

Steckel, Richard H. "Antebellum Southern White Fertility: A Demographic and Economic Analysis." *Journal of Economic History* 40 (June 1980): 331-350.

Stenflo, Gun Alm. "Parity-Dependent Fertility in a Population with Natural Fertility in Northern Sweden 1720-1900." *Journal of Family History* 14, no. 3 (1989): 211-228.

Thane, P. M. "The Debate on the Declining Birth-Rate in Britain: The 'Menace' of an Ageing Population, 1920s-1950s." *Continuity and Change* 5, no. 2 (1990): 283-306.

Vinovskis, Maris A. "An 'Epidemic' of Adolescent Pregnancy? Some Historical

Considerations." *Journal of Family History* 6 (Summer 1981): 205-230.
Williams, Linda B., and Basil G. Zimmer. "The Changing Influence of Religion on U.S. Fertility: Evidence From Rhode Island." *Demography* 27 (August 1990): 475-483.
Witkowski, J. A. "Optimistic Analysis--Chemical Embryology in Cambridge 1920-42." *Medical History* 31 (July 1987): 247-268.

## Infanticide

Behlmer, George K. "Deadly Motherhood: Infanticide and Medical Opinion in Mid-Victorian England." *Journal of the History of Medicine and Allied Sciences* 34 (October 1979): 403-427.
Burton, June K. "Infanticide in Napoleonic France: The Law, the Medical Profession, and the Murdering Mother." *Western Society for French History* 14 (November 1986): 183.
Giladi, Avner. "Some Observations on Infanticide in Medieval Muslim Society." *International Journal of Middle East Studies* 22 (May 1990): 185-200.
Gilje, Paul A. "Infant Abandonment in Early Nineteenth-Century New York City." *Signs* 8 (Spring 1983): 580-590.
Higgenbotham, A. R. "Sin of the Age: Infanticide and Illegitimacy in Victorian London." *Victorian Studies* 32 (Spring 1989): 319-338.
Johnson, Michael P. "Smothered Slave Infants: Were Slave Mothers at Fault?" *Journal of Southern History* 47 (November 1981): 493-520.
Lee, Bernice J. "Female Infanticide in China." *Historical Reflections/Reflexions Historiques* 8 (Fall 1981): 163-178.
Masters, Ardyce L. "Infanticide: The Primate Data." *Journal of Psychohistory* 18 (Summer 1990): 99-108.
Ulbricht, Otto. "The Debate about Foundling Hospitals in Enlightenment Germany: Infanticide, Illegitimacy, and Infant Mortality Rates." *Central European History* 18 (September/December 1985): 211-256.
Wright, Mary Ellen. "Unnatural Mothers: Infanticide in Halifax, 1850-1875." *Nova Scotia Historical Review* 7, no. 2 (1987): 13-29.

## Material Culture

Bullough, Vern L. "A Brief Note on Rubber Technology and Contraception: The Diaphragm and the Condom." *Technology and Culture* 22, no. 1 (1981): 104-111.
-----. "Merchandising the Sanitary Napkin: Lillian Gilbreth's 1927 Survey." *Signs* 10, no. 3 (Spring 1985): 615-627.
Dellapenna, Joseph W. "The History of Abortions: Technology, Morality, and Law." *University of Pittsburgh Law Review* 40 (Spring 1979): 359-428.
Weiner, Nella Fermi. "Of Feminism and Birth Control Propaganda (1790-1840)." *International Journal of Women's Studies* 3 (September/October 1980): 411-430.

## Reproductive Rights and Options

Back, Kurt W. "Myth in the Lives of Leaders of Social Movements: The Case of the Family Planning Movement." *Biography* 11 (Spring 1988): 95-107.

Baehr, Ninia. "Women Making a Choice: The Long Quest for Reproductive Rights." *Radical America* 22, no. 5 (1989): 44-49.

Biller, P. A. "Birth-Control in the West in the Thirteenth and Early Fourteenth Centuries." *Past and Present* no. 94 (February 1982): 3-26.

Bishop, Mary F. "The Early Birth Controllers of B.C." *B.C. Studies* 61 (Spring 1984): 64-84.

Bock, Gisela. "Racism and Sexism in Nazi Germany: Motherhood, Compulsory Sterilization, and the State." *Signs* 8 (Spring 1983): 400-421.

Borell, Merriley. "Biologists and the Promotion of Birth Control Research." *Journal of the History of Biology* 20 (Spring 1987): 51-87.

Brown, Barbara B. "Facing the 'Black Peril': The Politics of Population Control in South Africa." *Journal of South African Studies* 13 (April 1987): 256-273.

Clarke, Adele E. "Controversy and the Development of Reproductive Sciences." *Social Problems* 37 (February 1990): 18-37.

Dodd, Dianne. "The Hamilton Birth Control Clinic of 1930s." *Ontario History* 75 (March 1983): 71-86.

Gordon, Linda. "The Long Struggle for Reproductive Rights." *Radical America* 15 (Spring 1981): 75-88.

-----. "Who Is Frightened of Reproductive Freedom for Women and Why? Some Historical Answers." *Frontiers* 9, no. 1 (1986): 23-26.

Heinsohn, Funnar, and Otto Steiger. "The Elimination of Medieval Birth Control and the Witch Trials of Modern Times." *International Journal of Women's Studies* 5 (May/June 1982): 193-214.

Huenemann, Ralph W. "Family Planning in Taiwan: The Conflict Between Ideologues and Technocrats." *Modern China* 16 (April 1990): 173-189.

Lane, Ann J. "The Politics of Birth Control." *Marxist Perspectives* 2 (Fall 1979): 160-169.

Lewis, Jan, and Kenneth A. Lockridge. "'Sally Has Been Sick': Pregnancy and Family Limitation Among Virginia Gentry Women, 1780-1830." *Journal of Social History* 22 (Fall 1988): 5-20.

Lewis, Jane. "The Ideology and Politics of Birth Control in Inter-war England." *Women's Studies* 2, no. 1 (1979): 33-48.

Logue, Barbara J. "The Case for Birth Control Before 1850: Nantucket Reexamined." *Journal of Interdisciplinary History* 15 (Winter 1985): 371-391.

Love, Rosaleen. "'Alice in Eugenics-Land': Feminism and Eugenics in the Scienctific Careers of Alice Lee and Ethel Elderton." *Annals of Science* 36 (1979): 145-158.

McLaren, Angus. "Contraception and Its Discontent: Sigmund Freud and Birth Control." *Journal of Social History* 12 (Summer 1979): 513-530.

-----. "The Creation of a Haven for 'Human Thoroughbreds': The Sterilization of the Feeble-Minded and the Mentally Ill in British Columbia." *Canadian*

*Historical Review* 67 (June 1986): 127-150.

-----. "The First Campaigns for Birth Control Clinics in British Columbia." *Journal of Canadian Studies/Revue d'etudes canadiennes* 19 (Fall 1984): 50-64.

-----. "'What Has This To Do With Working Class Women': Birth Control and the Canadian Left, 1900-1939." *Histoire sociale/Social History* 14 (November 1981): 435-454.

Neuman, R. "Working Class Birth Control in Wilhelmine Germany." *Comparative Studies in Society and History* 20 (1978): 408-428.

Nicoll, Christine E., and Robert G. Weisbord. "The Early Years of the Rhode Island Birth Control League." *Rhode Island History* 45 (November 1986): 111-125.

Ramusack, Barbara N. "Embattled Advocates: The Debate over Birth Control in India, 1920-1940." *Journal of Women's History* 1 (Fall 1989): 34-64.

Ray, Joyce M. "American Physicians and Birth Control, 1936-1947." *Journal of Social History* 18 (Spring 1985): 399-411.

Reed, James. "Public Policy on Human Reproduction and the Historian." *Journal of Social History* 18 (Spring 1985): 383-398.

Reilly, Philip R. "Involuntary Sterilization in the United States: A Surgical Solution." *Quarterly Review of Biology* 62 (1987): 153-170.

Schwartz, Gerald. "Walter M. Pierce and the Birth Control Movement." *Oregon Historical Quarterly* 88 (Winter 1987): 371-384.

Solinger, Rickie. "The Girl Nobody Loved: Psychological Explanations for White Single Pregnancy in the Pre-*Roe v. Wade* Era, 1945-1965." *Frontiers* 11, no. 2 & 3 (1990): 45-54.

Weindling, Paul. "Compulsory Sterilisation in National Socialist Germany." *German History* no. 5 (Autumn 1987): 10-24.

Weingart, Peter. "The Rationalization of Sexual Behavior: The Institutionalization of Eugenic Thought in Germany." *Journal of the History of Biology* 20 (1987): 159-193.

# CANADA

Abbott, John. "Accomplishing 'A Man's Task': Rural Women Teachers, Male Culture, and the School Inspectorate in Turn-of-the-Century Ontario." *Ontario History* 78 (December 1986): 313-330.

Abbott, Ruth K., and R. A. Young. "Cynical and Deliberate Manipulation? Child Care and the Reserve Army of Female Labour in Canada." *Journal of Canadian Studies/Revue d'études canadiennes* 24 (Summer 1989): 22-38.

Abeele, Cynthia R. "'The Infant Soldier':The Great War and the Medical Campaign for Child Welfare." *Canadian Bulletin of Medical History/Bulletin canadien d'histoire de la medicine* 5 (Winter 1988): 99-119.

-----. "'The Mothers of the Land Must Suffer': Child and Maternal Welfare in Rural and Outpost Ontario, 1918-1940." *Ontario History* 80 (September 1988): 183-205.

Andrews, Margaret W. "Attitudes in Canadian Women's History, 1945-1975." *Journal of Canadian Studies/Revue d'études canadiennes* 12 (Summer 1977): 69-78.

Bacchi, Carol. "'First Wave' Feminism in Canada: The Ideas of the English-Canadian Suffragists, 1877-1918." *Women's Studies* 5, no. 6 (1982): 575-584.

Backhouse, Constance. "Involuntary Motherhood: Abortion, Birth Control and the Law in 19th Century Canada." *Windsor Yearbook of Access to Justice* 3 (1983): 61-130.

-----. "Married Women's Property Law in Nineteenth-Century Canada." *Law and History Review* 6 (Fall 1988): 211-258.

-----. "Nineteenth Century Canadian Prostitution Law. Reflections on a Discriminatory Society." *Histoire sociale/Social History* 18 (November 1985): 387-423.

-----. "'Pure Patriarchy': Nineteenth-Century Canadian Marriage." *McGill Law Journal* 31 (March 1986): 264-312.

-----. "The Tort of Seduction: Fathers and Daughters in Nineteenth Century Canada." *Dalhousie Law Journal* 10 (June 1986): 45-80.

Backhouse, Frances M. "Women of the Klondike." *The Beaver* 68 (December 1988/January 1989): 30-36.

Baeyer, Edwinna Von. "The Horticultural Odyssey of Isabella Preson." *Canadian Horticultural History* 1, no. 3 (1987): 125-175.

Ball, Christine. "Female Sexual Ideologies in Mid- to Later Nineteenth-Century Canada." *Canadian Journal of Women and the Law/Revue juridique 'La femme et le droit'* 1, no. 2 (1986): 324-338.

Ballstadt, Carl Michael Peterman, and Elizabeth Hopkins. "'A Glorious Madness': Susanna Moodie and the Spiritualist Movement." *Journal of Canadian Studies/Revue d'études canadiennes* 17 (Winter 1983): 88-101.

Barber, Marilyn. "The Women Ontario Welcomed: Immigrant Domestics for Ontario Homes, 1870-1930." *Ontario History* 72 (September 1980): 148-172.

Bashevkin, Sylvia. "Political Participation, Ambition, and Feminism: Women in the Ontario Party Elites." *American Review of Canadian Studies* 15 (Winter 1985): 465-480.

-----. "Social Change and Political Partisanship, The Development of Women's Attitudes in Quebec, 1965-1979." *Comparative Political Studies* 16 (July 1983): 147-172.

-----. "Women's Participation in the Ontario Political Parties, 1971-1981." *Journal of Canadian Studies/Revue d'études canadiennes* 17 (Summer 1982): 44-54.

Bates, Christina. "Blue Monday: A Day in the Life of a Washerwoman, 1840." *Canadian Collector* (July/August 1985): 44-48.

Batts, John Stuart. "Saskatchewan and *The Pink Lady*." *Saskatchewan History* 40 (Autumn 1987): 114-119.

Beaudoin-Ross, Jacqueline. "'A la Canadienne' Once More: Some Insights into Quebec Rural Female Dress." *Dress* 7 (1981): 69-81.

-----. "A la Canadienne: Some Aspects of 19th Century Habitant Dress." *Dress* 6

(1980): 71-82.

Bedford, Judy. "Prostitution in Calgary, 1905-1914." *Alberta History* 29 (Spring 1981): 1-11.

Beeby, Dean. "Women in the Ontario C.C.F. 1940-1950." *Ontario History* 74 (December 1982): 258-283.

Biggs, C. Lesley. "The Case of the Missing Midwives: A History of Midwifery in Ontario from 1795-1900." *Ontario History* 75 (March 1983): 21-35.

Bishop, Mary F. "The Early Birth Controllers of B.C." *B.C. Studies* 61 (Spring 1984): 64-84.

Boutelle, Ann Edwards. "Frances Brooke's Emily Montague (1769): Canada and Woman's Rights." *Women's Studies* 12, no. 1 (1986): 7-16.

Bradbury, Bettina. "Surviving as a Widow in Nineteenth-Century Montreal." *Urban History Review* 17 (February 1989): 148-160.

-----. "Women and Wage Labour in a Period of Transition: Montreal, 1861-1881." *Histoire sociale/Social History* 17 (May 1984): 115-131.

Bramadat, I. J., and K. I. Chalmers. "Nursing Education in Canada: Historical 'Progress'--Contemporary Issues." *Journal of Advanced Nursing* 14 (1989): 719-726.

Brandt, Gail Cuthbert. "'Weaving It Together': Life Cycle and the Industrial Experience of Female Cotton Workers in Quebec, 1910-1950." *Labour/Le Travail* 7 (Spring 1981): 113-126.

-----. "Women in the Quebec Cotton Industry, 1890-1950." *Material History Bulletin* [Canada] 31 (Spring 1990): 99-105.

Brodribb, Somer. "The Traditional Roles of Native Women in Canada and the Impact of Colonization." *Canadian Journal of Native Studies* 4, no. 1 (1984): 85-103.

Brookes, Alan A., and Catharine A. Wilson. "'Working Away' from the Farm: The Young Women of North Huron, 1910-1930." *Ontario History* 77 (December 1985): 281-300.

Brower, Ruth Compton. "Moral Nationalism in Victorian Canada: The Case of Agnes Machar." *Journal of Canadian Studies/Revue d'études canadiennes* 20 (Spring 1985): 90-108.

Brown, Jennifer S. H. "Woman as Centre and Symbol in the Emergence of Metis Communities." *Canadian Journal of Native Studies* 3, no. 1 (1983): 39-46.

Buckley, Suzann, and Janice Dickin McGinnis. "Venereal Disease and Public Health Reform in Canada." *Canadian Historical Review* 63 (September 1982): 337-354.

Bullen, John. "Child Labour and the Family Economy in Late Nineteenth-Century Urban Ontario." *Labour/Le Travail* 18 (Fall 1986): 163-187.

-----. "Hidden Workers: Child Labour and the Family Economy in Late Nineteenth Century Urban Ontario." *Labour/Le Travail* 18 (Fall 1986): 163-188.

-----. "J. J. Kelso and the 'New' Child-Savers: The Genesis of the Children's Aid Movement in Ontario." *Ontario History* 82 (June 1990): 107-128.

Bumsted, J. M., and Wendy Owen. "The Victorian Family in Canada in Historical Perspective: The Ross Family of Red River and the Jarvis Family of Prince

Edward Island." *Manitoba History* 13 (Spring 1987): 12-18.

Buzek, Beatrice Ross. "'By Fortune Wounded': Loyalist Women in Nova Scotia." *Nova Scotia Historical Review* 7, no. 2 (1987): 45-62.

Bystydzienski, Jill. "Minority Women of North America: A Comparison of French-Canadian and Afro-American Women." *American Review of Canadian Studies* 15 (Winter 1985): 465-480.

Campbell, Ellen K. "More Than Just a Roof: Housing at the YWCA." *Canadian Housing/Habitation canadienne* 4 (Winter/Hiver 1987): 24-28.

Campbell, Gail G. "Canadian Women's History: A View From Atlantic Canada." *Acadiensis* 20 (Autumn 1990): 184-199.

-----. "Disfranchised but Not Quiescent: Women Petitioners in New Brunswick in the Mid-19th Century." *Acadiensis* 18 (Spring 1989): 22-54.

Carroll, William K., and Rennie Warburton. "Feminism, Class Consciousness and Household-Work Linkages Among Registered Nurses in Victoria." *Labour/Le Travail* 24 (Fall 1989): 131-146.

Castellano, Marlene Brant. "Women in Huron and Ojibwa Societies." *Canadian Woman Studies/Les cahiers de la femme* 10 (Summer/Fall 1989): 45-48.

Champion, Brian. "Mormon Polygamy: Parliamentary Comments 1889-90." *Alberta History* 35 (Spring 1987): 10-17.

Chapman, Terry L. "'Til Death Do Us Part,' Wife Beating in Alberta, 1905-1920." *Alberta History* 36 (Autumn 1988): 13-22.

-----. "Women, Sex and Marriage in Western Canada, 1890-1920." *Alberta History* 33 (Autumn 1985): 1-12.

Coates, Colin. "Authority and Illegitimacy in New France: The Burial of Bishop Saint-Vallier and Madeleine de Vercheres vs. the Priest of Batiscan." *Histoire sociale/Social History* 22 (May 1989): 65-90.

Cohen, Marjorie Griffin. "The Decline of Women in Canadian Dairying." *Histoire sociale/Social History* 17 (November 1984): 307-334.

Coldwell, Judith. "The Role of Women in the Nineteenth Century Church of Ontario." *Canadian Society of Church History Papers* 15 (1985): 31-57.

Conrad, Margaret. "The Re-Birth of Canada's Past: A Decade of Women's History." *Acadiensis* 12 (Spring 1983): 140-162.

Crowley, Terry. "Ada Mary Brown Courtice: Pacifist, Feminist and Educational Reformer in Early Twentieth Century Canada." *Studies in History and Politics* 1 (Fall 1980): 76-114.

-----. "Madonnas Before Magdalenes: Adelaide Hoodless and the Making of the Canadian Gibson Girl." *Canadian Historical Review* 67 (December 1986): 520-547.

Danylewycz, Marta. "Changing Relationships: Nuns and Feminists in Montreal, 1890-1925." *Histoire sociale/Social History* 14 (November 1981): 413-434.

Danylewycz, Marta, Beth Light, and Alison Prentice. "The Evolution of the Sexual Division of Labour in Teaching: A Nineteenth Century Ontario and Quebec Case Study." *Histoire sociale/Social History* 16 (May 1983): 81-109.

Danylewycz, Marta, and Alison Prentice. "Teachers, Gender and Bureaucratizing School Systems in Nineteenth Century Montreal and Toronto." *History of*

*Education Quarterly* 24 (Spring 1984): 75-100.

Davy, Shirley. "Why Church Women's Organizations Thrived." *Canadian Woman Studies/Les cahiers de la femme* 2 (Winter 1983): 59-61.

Dawson, N. M. "The Filles-du-Ray Sent to New France: French Women in 17th Century Canada--Protestant, Prostitute or Both." *Historical Reflections/Reflexions Historiques* 16 (Spring 1989): 55-78.

Day, Moira, and Marilyn Potts. "Elizabeth Sterling Haynes: Initiator of Alberta Theatre." *Theatre History in Canada* 8 (Spring 1987): 8-35.

De la Cour, Lykke. "The 'Other' Side of Psychology: Women Psychologists in Toronto from 1920 to 1945." *Canadian Woman Studies/Les cahiers de la femme* 8 (Winter 1987): 44-46.

De la Cour, Lykke, and Rose Sheinin. "The Ontario Medical College for Women, 1883 to 1906: Lessons from Gender-Separatism in Medical Education." *Canadian Woman Studies/Les cahiers de la femme* 7 (Fall 1986): 73-77.

Dembski, Peter E. Paul. "Jenny Kidd Trout and the Founding of the Women's Medical Colleges at Kingston and Toronto." *Ontario History* 77 (September 1985): 183-206.

Dempsey, Hugh A., ed. "Confessions of a Calgary Stenographer." *Alberta History* 36 (Spring 1988): 1-15.

Dennis, Thelma. "Eaton's Catalogue: Furnishings for Rural Alberta, 1886-1930." *Alberta History* 37 (Spring 1989): 21-31.

Dodd, Dianne. "The Canadian Birth Control Movement on Trial, 1936-1937." *Histoire sociale/Social History* 16 (November 1983): 411-428.

-----. "The Hamilton Birth Control Clinic of 1930s." *Ontario History* 75 (March 1983): 71-86.

Dryden, Jean E., and Sandra L. Myres. "The Letters of Barbara Alice Slater: Homesteading on the Canadian Prairies, 1909-1918." *Montana* 37 (Winter 1987): 14-33.

Emery, George. "Incomplete Registration of Births in Civil Systems: The Example of Ontario, Canada, 1900-1960." *Historical Methods* 23 (Winter 1990): 5-21.

Epp, Marlene. "Women in Canadian Mennonite History: Uncovering the 'Underside.'" *Journal of Mennonite Studies* 5 (1987): 90-107.

Fairbanks, Carol. "Lives of Girls and Women on the Canadian and American Prairies." *International Journal of Women's Studies* 2 (September/October 1979): 452-472.

Ferland, Jacques. "'In Search of the Unbound Prometheia': A Comparative View of Women's Activism in Two Quebec Industries, 1869-1908." *Labour/Le Travail* 24 (Fall 1989): 11-44.

"The First Mission of the Sisters Faithful Companions of Jesus in the North-West Territories, 1883." *Saskatchewan History* 36 (Spring 1983): 70-77.

Forestell, Nancy M. "Times Were Hard: The Pattern of Women's Paid Labour in St. John's Between the Two World Wars." *Labour/Le Travail* 24 (Fall 1989): 147-166.

Fox, Bonnie J., and John Fox. "Occupational Gender Segregation in the Canadian Labour Force, 1931-1981." *Canadian Review of Sociology and*

*Anthropology/Revue canadienne de Sociologie et d'Anthropologie* 24 (August 1987): 374-397.

Gavigan, Shelley A. M. "On 'Bringing on the Menses': The Criminal Liability of Women and the Therapeutic Exception in Canadian Abortion Law." *Canadian Journal of Women and the Law/Revue juridique 'La femme et le droit'* 1, no. 2 (1986): 279-312.

Gee, Ellen M. T. "Marriage in Nineteenth Century Canada." *Canadian Review of Sociology and Anthropology/Revue canadienne de Sociologie et d'Anthropologie* 19 (August 1982): 311-325.

Gibson, Dale. "A Scandal at Red River: The Judge and the Serving Girl." *Beaver* 70 (October/November 1990): 30-38.

Gould, Karen. "Spatial Poetics, Spatial Politics: Quebec Feminists on the City and the Countryside." *American Review of Canadian Studies* 12 (Spring 1982): 1-9.

Green, Gretchen. "Molly Brant, Catharine Brant, and Their Daughters: A Study in Colonial Acculturation." *Ontario History* 81 (September 1989): 235-250.

Green, Mary Jean. "The 'Literary Feminists' and the Fight for Women's Writing in Quebec." *Journal of Canadian Studies/Revue d'études canadiennes* 21 (Spring 1986): 128-143.

-----, Paula Gilbert Lewis, and Karen Gould. "Inscriptions of the Feminine: A Century of Women Writing in Quebec." *American Review of Canadian Studies* 15 (Winter 1985): 361-388.

Harney, Robert F. "Men without Women: Italian Migrants in Canada, 1885-1930." *Canadian Ethnic Studies/Etudes Ethniques Au Canada* 11, no. 1 (1979): 29-47.

Harrigan, Patrick J. "The Schooling of Boys and Girls in Canada." *Journal of Social History* 23 (Summer 1990): 803-816.

Hayden, Michael. "Women and the University of Saskatchewan: Pattern of a Problem." *Saskatchewan History* 40 (Spring 1987): 72-82.

Holford, Mary. "Dress and Society in Upper Canada, 1791-1841." *Costume* 17 (1983): 78-88.

Hood, Adrienne. "Early Canadian Quilts: Marriage of Art and Utility." *Rotunda* 17, no. 3 (1984-85): 28-35.

Horn, Michiel. "More Than Cigarettes, Sex, and Chocolate: The Canadian Army in the Netherlands, 1944-1945." *Journal of Canadian Studies/Revue d'études canadiennes* 16 (Fall/Winter 1981): 156-173.

Horodyski, Mary. "Women and the Winnipeg General Strike of 1919." *Manitoba History* 11 (Spring 1986): 28-37.

Howard, Irene. "The Mother's Council of Vancouver: Holding the Fort for the Unemployed, 1935-38." *B.C. Studies* 69-70 (Spring/Summer 1986): 249-287.

Iacovetta, Franca. "Trying to Make Ends Meet: An Historical Look at Italian Immigrant Women, the State and Family Survival Strategies in Post-War Toronto." *Canadian Woman Studies/Les cahiers de la femme* 8 (Summer 1987): 6-11.

Ilcan, Suzan M. "Women and Casual Work in the Nova Scotia Fish Processing Industry." *Atlantis* 11, no. 2 (1986): 23-34.

Indra, Doreen Marie. "The Invisible Mosaic: Women, Ethnicity and the Vancouver Press, 1900-1976." *Canadian Ethnic Studies/Etudes Ethniques Au Canada* 13 (1981): 63-74.

Irvine, Lorna. "Surfacing, Surviving, Surpassing: Canada's Women Writers." *Journal of Popular Culture* 15 (Winter 1981): 70-79.

Jardine, Pauline O. "An Urban Middle-Class Calling: Women and the Emergence of Modern Nursing Education at the Toronto General Hospital, 1881-1914." *Urban History Review* 17 (February 1989): 177-190.

Jones, David C. "'From Babies to Buttonholes': Women's Work at Agricultural Fairs." *Alberta History* 29 (Autumn 1981): 26-32.

Kaplan, Sidney. "Historical Efforts to Encourage White-Indian Intermarriage in the United States and Canada." *International Social Sciences Review* 65 (Summer 1990): 126-132.

Kealey, Linda. "Canadian Socialism and the Woman Question, 1900-1914." *Labour/Le Travail* 13 (Spring 1984): 77-100.

Kechnie, Margaret. "The United Farm Workers of Ontario: Developing a Political Consciousness." *Ontario History* 77 (December 1985): 267-280.

Keddy, B. "Nursing in Canada in the 1920s and 1930s: Powerful while Powerless." *History of Nursing* 2, no. 9 (1989): 1-7.

Keller, Betty C. "The Chastely Voluptuous Weblings." *The Beaver* 66 (April/May 1986): 13-18.

Kennedy, Joan E. "Jane Soley Hamilton, Midwife." *Nova Scotia Historical Review* 2 (1982): 6-29.

Kernaghan, Lois D. "A Man and His Mistress: J. F. W. DesBarres and Mary Cannon." *Acadiensis* 11 (Autumn 1981): 23-42.

Kirk, Sylvia Van. "The Role of Native Women in the Fur Trade Society of Western Canada, 1670-1830." *Frontiers* 7, no. 3 (1984): 9-13.

Kohn, Walter S. G. "Women in the Canadian House of Commons." *American Review of Canadian Studies* 14 (Fall 1984): 298-311.

Lambert, Ronald D., and James E. Curtis. "Quebecois and English Canadian Opposition to Racial and Religious Intermarriage, 1968-1983." *Canadian Ethnic Studies/Etudes Ethniques Au Canada* 16 (1984): 30-46.

Lamerson, C. D. "The Evolution of a Mixed-Gender Canadian Forces." *Minerva: Quarterly Report on Women and the Military* 7 (Fall/Winter 1989): 19-24.

Lawrence, R. "Lillie Langtry in Canada and the USA, 1882-1917." *Theatre History in Canada* 10 (Spring 1989): 30-42.

Lenskyi, Helen. "Femininity First: Sport and Physical Education for Ontario Girls, 1890-1930." *Canadian Journal of the History of Sport* 13 (December 1982): 4-17.

-----. "A 'Servant Problem' or a 'Servant-Mistress Problem'? Domestic Service in Canada, 1890-1930." *Atlantis* 7 (1981): 3-11.

Levesque, A. "Turning Off the Red Light: Reformers and Prostitution in Montreal 1865-1925." *Urban History Review* 17 (February 1989): 191-202.

Lewis, Norah L. "Creating the Little Machine: Child Rearing in British Columbia, 1919 to 1939." *B.C. Studies* 56 (Winter 1982-1983): 44-60.

Li, Peter S. "Immigration Laws and Family Patterns: Some Demographic Changes Among Chinese Families in Canada, 1885-1971." *Canadian Ethnic Studies/Etudes Ethniques Au Canada* 12, no. 1 (1980): 58-73.

Lowe, Graham. "Class, Job, and Gender in the Canadian Office." *Labour/Le Travail* 10 (Autumn 1982): 11-38.

-----. "Women, Work and the Office: The Feminization of Clerical Occupations in Canada, 1901-1930." *Canadian Journal of Sociology* 5 (1980): 361-381.

Manley, John. "Women and the Left in the 1930s: The Case of the Toronto C.C.F. Women's Joint Committee." *Atlantis* 5 (Spring 1980): 100-119.

Marks, Lynne. "Kale Meydelach or Shulamith Girls: Cultural Change and Continuity among Jewish Parents and Daughters--A Case Study of Toronto's Harbord Collegiate Institute in the 1920s." *Canadian Woman Studies/Les cahiers de la femme* 7 (Fall 1986): 85-89.

Marks, Lynne, and Chad Gaffield. "Women at Queen's University, 1895-1905: A Little Sphere All Their Own?" *Ontario History* 78 (December 1986): 331-350.

Martin, Ged. "Queen Victoria and Canada." *The American Review of Canadian Studies* 13 (Autumn 1983): 215-234.

McCallum, Margaret E. "Keeping Women in Their Place: The Minimum Wage in Canada, 1910-1925." *Labour/Le Travail* 17 (Spring 1986): 29-56.

-----. "Separate Spheres: The Organization of Work in a Confectionery Factory: Ganong Bros., St. Stephen, New Brunswick." *Labour/Le Travail* 24 (Fall 1989): 69-90.

McConnachie, Kathleen. "A Note on Fertility Rates Among Married Women in Toronto, 1871." *Ontario History* 75 (March 1983): 87-97.

McDonald, Cheryl. "The Angel in the House." *The Beaver* 66 (August/September 1986): 22-29.

McDonald, Lynn. "The Evolution of the Women's Movement in Canada, Part 1." *Branching Out* 6, no. 1 (1979): 39-43.

-----. "The Evolution of the Women's Movement in Canada, Part 2." *Branching Out* 6, no. 2 (1979): 31-35.

McLaren, Angus. "Birth Control and Abortion in Canada, 1870-1920." *Canadian Historical Review* 59 (September 1978): 319-340.

-----. "The Creation of a Haven for 'Human Thoroughbreds': The Sterilization of the Feeble-Minded and the Mentally Ill in British Columbia." *Canadian Historical Review* 67 (June 1986): 127-150.

-----. "The First Campaigns for Birth Control Clinics in British Columbia." *Journal of Canadian Studies/Revue d'études canadiennes* 19 (Fall 1984): 50-64.

-----. "'What Has This To Do With Working Class Women': Birth Control and the Canadian Left, 1900-1939." *Histoire sociale/Social History* 14 (November 1981): 435-454.

McLaren, John P. S. "Chasing the Social Evil: Moral Fervour and the Evolution of Canada's Prostitution Laws, 1867-1917." *Canadian Journal of Law and Society* 1 (1986): 125-165.

McPherson, K., and Veronica Strong-Boag. "The Confinement of Women:

Childbirth and Hospitalization in Vancouver, 1919-1939." *B.C. Studies* 69/70 (Spring/Summer 1986): 142-174.

Medjuck, Sheva. "Family and Household Composition in the Nineteenth Century: The Case of Moncton, New Brunswick, 1851 to 1871." *Canadian Journal of Sociology* 4 (Summer 1979): 275-286.

Miedema, Baukje, and Nancy Nason-Clark. "Second Class Status: An Analysis of the Lived Experiences of Immmigrant Women in Fredericton." *Canadian Ethnic Studies/Etudes Ethniques Au Canada* 21, no. 2 (1989): 63-73.

Mitchinson, Wendy. "Gynecological Operations on Insane Women: London, Ontario, 1895-1901." *Journal of Social History* 15 (Spring 1982): 467-484.

-----. "Hysteria and Insanity in Women: A Nineteenth-Century Canadian Perspective." *Journal of Canadian Studies/Revue d'études canadiennes* 21 (Fall 1986): 87-105.

-----. "A Medical Debate in Nineteenth Century English Canada: Ovariotomies." *Histoire sociale/Social History* 17 (May 1984): 133-147.

-----. "The Medical View of Women: The Case of Late Nineteenth-Century Canada." *Canadian Bulletin of Medical History/Bulletin canadien d'histoire de la medicine* 3 (Winter 1986): 207-224.

-----. "Medical Perceptions of Healthy Women: The Case of Late Nineteenth-Century Canada." *Canadian Woman Studies/Les cahiers de la femme* 8 (Winter 1987): 42-43.

Morrow, Don. "Sweetheart Sport: Barbara Ann Scott and the Post-World War II Image of the Female Athlete in Canada." *Canadian Journal of the History of Sport* 8 (May 1987): 36-54.

Moss, Jane. "Filial (Im)Pieties: Mothers and Daughters in Quebec Women's Theatre." *The American Review of Canadian Studies* 19 (Summer 1989): 177-186.

Muszynski, Alicja. "The Organization of Women and Ethnic Minorities in a Resource Industry: A Case Study of the Unionization of Shoreworkers in the B.C. Fishing Industry 1937-1949." *Journal of Canadian Studies/Revue d'études canadiennes* 19 (Spring 1984): 89-107.

Nicks, Trudy. "Mary Anne's Dilemma: The Ethnohistory of an Ambivalent Identity." *Canadian Ethnic Studies/Etudes Ethniques Au Canada* 17, no. 2 (1985): 103-114.

Noether, Emiliana P. "'Morally Wrong' or 'Politically Right'? Espionage in Her Majesty's Post Office, 1844-45." *Canadian Journal of History* 22 (April 1987): 41-58.

Nolan, Shelagh. "A Young Girl in the Old West." *The Beaver* 66 (August/September 1986): 4.

Olsen, Karen. "Native Women and the Fur Industry." *Canadian Woman Studies/Les cahiers de la femme* 10 (Summer/Fall 1989): 55-57.

Oppenheimer, Jo. "Childbirth in Ontario: The Transition from Home to Hospital in the Early Twentieth Century." *Ontario History* 75 (March 1983): 36-60.

Parr, Joy. "Rethinking Work and Kinship in a Canadian Hosiery Town, 1910-1950." *Feminist Studies* 13 (Spring 1987): 137-162.

Pedersen, Diana. "The Photographic Record of the Canadian YWCA, 1890-1930: A Visual Source for Women's History." *Archivaria* 24 (Summer 1987): 10-35.

Perry, Beulah Gullison. "Remembering: Growing Up as a Sea Captain's Daughter." *Nova Scotia Historical Review* 7, no. 2 (1987): 31-44.

Philips, David. "Sex, Race, Violence and the Criminal Law in Victoria: Anatomy of a Rape Case in 1888." *Labour History* 52 (May 1987): 30-49.

Pierson, Ruth Roach. "Canadian Women and Canadian Mobilization During the Second World War." *Revue Internationale d'Histoire Militaire* 51 (1982): 181-207.

-----. "The Double Bind of the Double Standard: VD Control and the CWAC in World War II." *Canadian Historical Review* 62 (March 1981): 31-58.

-----. "Gender and the Unemployment Insurance Debates in Canada, 1934-40." *Labour/Le Travail* 25 (Spring 1990): 77-104.

Pivato, Joseph. "Italian-Canadian Women Writers Recall History." *Canadian Ethnic Studies/Etudes Ethniques Au Canada* 18, no. 1 (1986): 79-88.

Prang, Margaret. "'The Girl God Would Have Me Be': The Canadian Girls in Training 1915-39." *Canadian Historical Review* 66 (June 1985): 154-184.

Prentice, Alison, and Marta Danylewycz. "Teacher's Work: Changing Patterns in the Emerging School Systems of Nineteenth and Early Twentieth Century Central Canada." *Labour/Le Travail* 17 (Spring 1986): 59-80.

Prokop, Manfred. "Canadianization of Immigrant Children: Role of the Elementary School in Alberta, 1900-1930." *Alberta History* 37 (Spring 1989): 1-10.

Ransom, Diane. "'The Saskatoon Lily': A Biography of Ethel Catherwood." *Saskatchewan History* 41 (Autumn 1988): 81-98.

Reid, John G. "The Education of Women at Mount Allison, 1854-1914." *Acadiensis* 12 (Spring 1983): 3-33.

Reitsma-Street, Marge. "More Control Than Care: A Critique of Historical and Contemporary Laws for Delinquency and Neglect of Children in Ontario." *Canadian Journal of Women and the Law/Revue juridique 'La femme et le droit'* 3, no. 2 (1989-1990): 510-530.

Roberts, Barbara. "Sex, Politics and Religion: Controversies in Female Immigration Reform Work in Montreal, 1881-1919." *Atlantis* 6 (1980): 25-38.

Rooke, Patricia T., and R. L. Schnell. "Charlotte Whitton and the 'Babies for Export' Controversy, 1947-48." *Alberta History* 30 (Winter 1982): 11-16.

-----. "Charlotte Whitton Meets 'The Last Best West': The Politics of Child Welfare in Alberta, 1929-1949." *Prairie Forum* 6, no. 2 (Fall 1981): 143-162.

-----. "Chastity as Power: Charlotte Whitton and the Ascetic Ideal." *American Review of Canadian Studies* 15 (Winter 1985): 389-404.

-----. "'Making the Way More Comfortable': Charlotte Whitton's Child Welfare Career, 1920-48." *Journal of Canadian Studies/Revue d'études canadiennes* 17 (Winter 1983): 33-45.

Rosenthal, Star. "Union Maids: Organized Women Workers in Vancouver, 1900-1915." *B.C. Studies* 41 (1979): 36-55.

Salloum, Habeeb. "Reminiscences: The Urbanization of an Arab Homesteading

Family." *Saskatchewan History* 42 (Spring 1989): 79-83.

Sangster, Joan. "Finnish Women in Ontario, 1890-1930." *Polyphony* 3 (Fall 1981): 46-54.

-----. "Women and Unions in Canada: A Review of Historical Research." *Resources For Feminist Research* 10 (July 1981): 2-6.

Schneider, Elise. "Addressing the Issues: Two Women's Groups in Demonton, 1905-16." *Alberta History* 36 (Summer 1988): 15-22.

Schrodt, B. "Canadian Women at the Commonwealth Games: 1930-1974." *Cahper Journal* 44 (March/April 1978): 26-29.

Shadd, Adrienne. "Three Hundred Years of Black Women in Canadian History: Circa 1700 to 1980." *Tiger Lily* 1, no. 2 (1987).

Sheehan, Nancy M. "The Red Cross and Relief in Alberta, 1920s-1930s." *Prairie Forum* 12 (Fall 1987): 277-294.

-----. "Temperance, Education and the WCTU in Alberta 1905-1930." *Journal of Educational Thought* 14 (August 1980): 108-124.

-----. "The WCTU and Educational Strategies on the Canadian Prairie." *History of Education Quarterly* 24 (Spring 1984): 101-120.

-----. "The WCTU on the Prairies, 1886-1930: An Alberta-Saskatchewan Comparison." *Prairie Forum* 6 (1981): 17-33.

Shortt, Mary. "Touring Theatrical Families in the Canada West: The Hills and the Herons." *Ontario History* 74 (March 1982): 3-25.

-----. "Victorian Temptations." *The Beaver* 68 (December 1988/January 1989): 4-13.

Silverman, Elaine Leslau. "Writing Canadian Women's History 1970-1982: An Historiographical Analysis." *Canadian Historical Review* 63 (December 1982): 513-533.

Simmons, Christina. "'Helping the Poorer Sisters': The Women of the Jost Mission, Halifax, 1905-1945." *Acadiensis* 14 (Autumn 1984): 3-27.

Smillie, Christine. "The Invisible Workforce: Women Workers in Saskatchewan from 1905 to World War II." *Saskatchewan History* 34 (Summer 1986): 62-78.

Smith, Michael J. "Graceful Athleticism or Robust Womanhood: The Sporting Culture of Women in Victorian Nova Scotia, 1870-1914." *Journal of Canadian Studies/Revue d'études canadiennes* 23 (Spring/Summer 1988): 120-137.

Snell, James G. "The International Border as a Factor in Marital Behaviour: A Historical Case Study." *Ontario History* 81 (December 1989): 289-302.

-----. "Marital Cruelty: Women and the Nova Scotia Divorce Court, 1900-1939." *Acadiensis* 18 (Autumn 1988): 3-32.

-----. "'The White Life for Two': The Defence of Marriage and Sexual Morality in Canada, 1890-1914." *Histoire sociale/Social History* 16 (May 1983): 111-128.

Snell, James G., and Cynthia Comacchio Abeele. "Regulating Nuptiality: Restricting Access to Marriage in Early Twentieth-Century English-Speaking Canada." *Canadian Historical Review* 69 (December 1988): 466-489.

Spencer, Samia I. "Women in Government in Quebec." *Proceedings of the Annual Meeting of the French Colonial Historical Society* 13 (1986): 271-275.

Stone, Olive M. "Canadian Women as Legal Persons: How Alberta Combined Judicial, Executive and Legislative Powers to Win Full Legal Personality For All Canadian Women." *Alberta Law Review* 17, no. 3 (1979): 331-371.

Strong-Boag, Veronica. "Canadian Feminism in the 1920s: The Case of Nellie L. McClung." *Journal of Canadian Studies/Revue d'études canadiennes* 12 (Summer 1977): 58-68.

-----. "The Girl of the New Day: Canadian Working Women in the 192Os." *Labour/Le Travail* 4 (1979): 131-164.

-----. "Mapping Women's Studies in Canada: Some Signposts." *Journal of Educational Thought* 17 (August 1983): 94-111.

-----. "Mothers' Allowances and the Beginnings of Social Security in Canada." *Journal of Canadian Studies/Revue d'études canadiennes* 14 (Spring 1979): 24-34.

-----. "Pulling in Double Harness or Hauling a Double Load: Women, Work, and Feminism on the Canadian Prairie." *Journal of Canadian Studies/Revue d'études canadiennes* 21 (Fall 1986): 32-52.

-----. "'Wages for Housework': Mothers' Allowances and the Beginnings of Social Security in Canada." *Journal of Canadian Studies/Revue d'études canadiennes* 14 (Spring 1979): 24-34.

-----. "Working Women and the State: The Case of Canada, 1889-1945." *Atlantis* 6 (Spring 1981): 1-10.

Struthers, James. "A Profession in Crisis: Charlotte Whitton and Canadian Social Work in the 1930's." *Canadian Historical Review* 62 (June 1981): 169-185.

Taft, Michael. "Folk Drama on the Great Plains: The Mock Wedding in Canada and the United States." *North Dakota History* 56 (Fall 1989): 16-23.

Tavill, A. A. "Early Medical Co-Education and Women's Medical College, Kingston, Ontario 1880-1894." *Historic Kingston* 30 (January 1982): 68-89.

Thierry, Joyce. "Northern Bride, 1947." *The Beaver* 69 (August/September 1989): 27-33.

Thomas, John D. "Servants of the Church: Canadian Methodist Deaconess Work, 1890-1926." *Canadian Historical Review* 65 (September 1984): 371-395.

Toth, Emily. "Fatherless and Dispossessed: Grace Metalious as a French-Canadian Writer." *Journal of Popular Culture* 15 (Winter 1981): 28-38.

Trofimenkoff, Susan Mann. "Nationalism, Feminism and Canadian Intellectual History." *Canadian Literature* 83 (Winter 1979): 7-20.

-----. "Thérese Casgrain and the CCF in Quebec." *Canadian Historical Review* 66 (June 1985): 125-153.

Van Kirk, Sylvia, ed. "Canadian Women's History: Teaching and Research." *Resources for Feminist Research* 7 (July 1979): 5-71.

Ward, Peter. "Courtship and Social Space in Nineteenth-Century English Canada." *Canadian Historical Review* 68 (March 1987): 35-62.

Ward, Peter, and Patricia C. Ward. "Infant Birth Weight and Nutrition in Industrializing Montreal." *American Historical Review* 89 (April 1984): 324-345.

Whiteley, Marilyn. "Modest, Unaffected and Fully Consecrated: Lady Evangelists in Canadian Methodism, 1884-1900." *Canadian Methodist Historical Society Papers* 6 (1987).

Wright, Mary Ellen. "Unnatural Mothers: Infanticide in Halifax, 1850-1875." *Nova Scotia Historical Review* 7, no. 2 (1987): 13-29.

Yee, May. "Chinese Canadian Women: Our Common Struggle." *Canadian Ethnic Studies/Etudes Ethniques Au Canada* 19, no. 3 (1987): 174-184.

## ECONOMICS (see also Work)

# Africa

Alpers, E. A. "State, Merchant Capital, and Gender Relations in Southern Mozambique to the End of the Nineteenth Century." *African Economic History* 13 (1984): 23-55.

Caplan, Patricia. "Gender, Ideology and Modes of Production on the Coast of East Africa." *Paideuma* 28 (1982): 29-43.

Ciancanelli, Penelope. "Exchange, Reproduction and Sex Subordination Among the Kikuyu of East Africa." *Review of African Political Economy* 12 (Summer 1980): 25-36.

Cowan, Nicole. "Women in Eritrea: An Eye-Witness Account." *Review of African Political Economy* 27/28 (1983): 143-152.

Hetherington, Penelope. "Generational Change and Class Formation in Kenya: The Kamore Family." *Australian Journal of Politics and History* 36, no. 1 (1990): 51-61.

Johnson, Marion. "Cloth as Money: The Cloth Strip Currencies of Africa." *Textile History* 11 (1980): 193-202.

Mandala, Elias. "Capitalism, Kinship, and Gender in the Lower Tchiri (Shire) Valley of Malawi, 1860-1960: An Alternative Theoretical Framework." *African Economic History* 13 (1984): 137-169.

Urdang, Stephanie. "The Last Transition? Women and Development in Mozambique." *Review of African Political Economy* 27/28 (1983): 8-32.

# Asia

Agarwal, Bina. "Women, Poverty and Agricultural Growth in India." *Journal of Peasant Studies* 13 (July 1986): 165-220.

Bhargava, Ashok. "Indian Economy During Mrs. Gandhi's Regime." *Journal of Asian and African Studies* 22 (July/October 1987): 193-216.

Dutt, Ashok K., Allen G. Noble, and Satish K. Davgun. "Socio-Economic Factors Affecting Marriage Distance in Two Sikh Villages of Punjab." *Journal of Cultural Geography* 2 (Fall/Winter 1981): 13-26.

Feeney, Griffith, and Hamano Kiyoshi. "Rice Price Fluctuations and Fertility in Late Tokugawa Japan." *Journal of Japanese Studies* 16 (Winter 1990): 1-30.

Gallen, Rita S. "Women, Family and the Political Economy of Taiwan." *Journal of Peasant Studies* 12 (October 1984): 76-92.

Haruko, Wakita. "Marriage and Property in Premodern Japan from the Perspective of Women's History." *Journal of Japanese Studies* 10 (Winter 1984): 73-100.

Holmgren, J. "Observations on Marriage and Inheritance Practices in Early Mongol and Yuan Society, with Particular Reference to the Leviate." *Journal of Asian History* 20, no. 2 (1986): 127-192.

-----. "Wei-shu Records on the Bestowal of Imperial Princesses During the Northern Wei Dynasty." *Papers on Far Eastern History* no. 27 (March 1983): 21-98.

Mariko, Fujita. "'It's All Mother's Fault': Childcare and Socialization of Working Mothers in Japan." *Journal of Japanese Studies* 15 (Winter 1989): 67-92.

Roth, Martha T. "The Dowries of the Women of the Itti-Marduk-balatu Family." *Journal of the American Oriental Society* 111 (January/March 1991): 19-37.

Wakita, Haruko. "Marriage and Property in Premodern Japan from the Perspective of Women's History." *Journal of Japanese Studies* 10 (Winter 1984): 73-99.

Walthall, Anne. "The Family Ideology of the Rural Entrepeneurs in Nineteenth Century Japan." *Journal of Social History* 23 (Spring 1990): 463-484.

## Australia

Johnson, Penelope. "Gender, Class and Work: The Council of Action for Equal Pay and the Equal Pay Campaign in Australia During World War II." *Labour History* 50 (May 1986): 132-146.

Smart, Judith. "Feminists, Food and the Fair Price: The Cost of Living Demonstrations in Melbourne, August-September 1917." *Labour History* 50 (May 1986): 113-131.

## Europe

Bonfield, Lloyd. "Marriage Settlements and the 'Rise of Great Estates': The Demographic Aspect." *Economic History Review* 32 (November 1979): 483-493.

Campbell, Elizabeth. "Of Mothers and Merchants: Female Economics in Christina Rossetti's 'Goblin Market.'" *Victorian Studies* 33 (Spring 1990): 393-410.

Chabot, Isabelle. "Poverty and the Widow in Late Medieval Florence." *Continuity and Change* 3, no. 2 (1988): 291-311.

Collins, James B. "The Economic Role of Women in Seventeenth-Century France." *French Historical Studies* 16 (Fall 1989): 436-470.

Crane, Elaine Forman. "The Socioeconomics of a Female Majority in Eighteenth-Century Bermuda." *Signs* 15 (Winter 1990): 231-258.

Egerbladh, Inez. "From Complex to Simple Family Households: Peasant Households in Northern Coastal Sweden 1700-1900." *Journal of Family History* 14, no. 3 (1989): 241-264.

Grossman, Atina. "Abortion and Economic Crisis: The 1931 Campaign Against

#218 in Germany." *New German Critique* 14 (1978): 119-137.

Guest, Harriet. "A Double Lustre: Femininity and Sociable Commerce, 1730-60." *Eighteenth-Century Studies* 23 (Summer 1990): 479-501.

Harris, Barbara J. "Property, Power, and Personal Relations: Elite Mothers and Sons in Yorkist and Early Tudor England." *Signs* 15 (Spring 1990): 606-632.

Hind, Robert J. "The Loss of English Working-Class Parents' Control over Their Children's Education: The Role of Property-Holders." *Historical Reflections/Reflexions Historiques* 12 (Spring 1985): 77-108.

Hughes, Diane Owen. "From Brideprice to Dowry." *Journal of Family History* 3 (Fall 1978): 262-296.

Humphries, Jane. "Enclosures, Common Rights, and Women: The Proletarianization of Families in the Late Eighteenth and Early Nineteenth Centuries." *Journal of Economic History* 50 (March 1990): 17-42.

Kirshner, Julius, and Anthony Molho. "The Dowry Fund and the Marriage Market in Early Quattrocentro Florence." *Journal of Modern History* 50 (September 1978): 403-438.

Kuehn, T. "Some Ambiguities of Female Inheritance Ideology in the Renaissance." *Continuity and Change* 2 (1987): 11-36.

Levine, David. "Education and Family Life in Early Industrial England." *Journal of Family History* 4 (Winter 1979): 368-380.

-----. "Illiteracy and Family Life During the First Industrial Revolution." *Journal of Social History* 14 (Fall 1980): 25-44.

Mate, Mavis. "Profit and Productivity on the Estates of Isabella de Fory (1260-92)." *Economic History Review* 33 (August 1980): 326-334.

Medjuck, Sheva. "Women's Response to Economic and Social Change in the Nineteenth Century: Moncton Parish, 1851 to 1891." *Atlantis* 11 (Fall 1985): 7-21.

Murray, Mary. "Property and 'Patriarchy' in English History." *Journal of Historical Sociology* 2 (December 1989): 303-327.

Ogilvie, Sheilagh C. "Coming of Age in a Coporate Society: Capitalism, Pietism and Family Authority in Rural Wurttemberg, 1590-1740." *Continuity and Change* 1, no. 3 (1986): 279-332.

Olney, Martha L. "Fertility and the Standard of Living in Early Modern England: In Consideration of Wrigley and Schofield." *Journal of Economic History* 43 (March 1983): 71-78.

Rainwater, Lee. "Mothers' Contribution to the Family Money Economy in Europe and the United States." *Journal of Family History* 4 (Summer 1979): 198-210.

Shaffer, John W. "Family, Class, and Young Women: Occupational Expectations in Nineteenth-Century Paris." *Journal of Family History* 3 (Spring 1978): 62-77.

Stuard, Susan Mosher. "Dowry Inflation and Increments in Wealth in Medieval Ragusa (Dubrovnik)." *Journal of Economic History* 41 (December 1981): 795-812.

Summerfield, Penelope. "Women, Work, and Welfare: A Study of Child Care and Shopping in Britain in the Second World War." *Journal of Social History* 17

(Winter 1983): 249-270.

Sundin, Jan. "Family Building in Paternalistic Proto-Industries: A Cohort Study from Nineteenth-Century Swedish Iron Foundries." *Journal of Family History* 14, no. 3 (1989): 265-289.

Watt, Jeffrey R. "Marriage Contract Disputes in Early Modern Neuchatel, 1547-1806." *Journal of Social History* 22 (Fall 1988): 129-148.

Weatherill, Lorna. "A Possession of One's Own: Women and Consuming Behavior in England, 1660-1740." *Journal of British Studies* 25 (April 1986): 131-156.

Weinburger, Stephen. "Women, Property and Poetry in Eleventh Century Provence." *Western Society for French History* 8 (October 1980): 24-33.

Wikander, Ulla. "On Women's History and Economic History." *Scandinavian Economic History Review & Economy and History* 38, no. 2 (1990): 65-71.

Winter, James. "Widowed Mothers and Mutual Aid in Early Victorian Britain." *Journal of Social History* 17 (Fall 1983): 115-125.

## Latin America

Coutourier, Edith, and Asuncion Lavrin. "Dowries and Wills: A View of Women's Socioeconomic Role in Colonial Guadelajara and Puebla." *Hispanic American Historical Review* 59 (May 1979): 280-304.

Flusche, Della M., and Eugene H. Korth. "A Dowry Office in Seventeenth-Century Chile." *The Historian* 49 (February 1987): 204-222.

Hahner, June E. "'Women's Place' in Politics and Economics in Brazil since 1964." *Luso-Brazilian Review* 19, no. 1 (1982): 83-91.

Kicza, John E. "The Role of the Family in Economic Development in Nineteenth-Century Latin America." *Journal of Family History* 10 (Fall 1985): 235-246.

Kuznesof, Elizabeth Anne. "Household Composition and Headship as Related to Changes in Mode of Production: Sao Paulo 1765-1836." *Comparative Studies in Society and History* 22, no. 1 (1980): 78-108.

Lavrin, Asuncion, and Edith Couturier. "Dowries and Wills: A View of Women's Socioeconomic Role in Colonial Guadalajara and Puebla, 1640-1790." *Hispanic American Historical Review* 59, no.2 (1979): 280-304.

León de Leal, Magdalena, and Carmen Diana Deere. "Rural Women and the Development of Capitalism of Colombian Agriculture." *Signs* 5 (Autumn 1979): 60-77.

Mallon, Florencia E. "Gender and Class in the Transition to Capitalism. Household and Mode of Production in Central Peru." *Latin American Perspectives* 13 (Winter 1986): 147-174.

Tutino, John. "Family Economies in Agrarian Mexico, 1750-1910." *Journal of Family History* 10 (Fall 1985): 258-271.

-----. "Power, Class, and Family: Men and Women in the Mexican Elite, 1750-1810." *Americas* 39 (1982): 359-382.

Wells, Allen. "Family Elites in a Boom and Bust Economy: The Molinas and

Peons of Porfirian Yucatan." *Hispanic American Historical Review* 62, no. 2 (1982): 224-253.

## Middle East/Near East

Ahanzar, Atlaf Hussain. "Inheritance Rights of Muslim Women under Kashmir Customary Law." *Islamic and Comparative Law Quarterly* 7 (1987): 217-239.

Batto, B. F. "Land Tenure and Women at Mari." *Journal of the Economic and Social History of the Orient* 23 (October 1980): 209-239.

Ben-Barak, Zafrira. "Inheritance by Daughters in the Ancient Near East." *Journal of Semitic Studies* 25 (Spring 1980): 22-33.

Marcus, Abraham. "Men, Women and Property: Dealers in Real Estate in 18th Century Aleppo." *Journal of the Economic and Social History of the Orient* 26 (May 1983): 137-163.

Mernissi, Fatima. "Women and the Impact of Capitalist Devolopment in Morocco, Part I." *Feminist Issues* 2, no. 2 (1982): 69-104.

Shatzmiller, M. "Aspects of Women's Participation in the Economic Life of Later Medieval Islam: Occupations and Mentalities." *Arabica* 35 (1988): 36-58.

Tavakolian, Bahram. "Women and the Socioeconomic Change Among Sheikhanzai Nomads of Western Afghanistan." *Middle East Journal* 38 (Summer 1984): 433-453.

Tucker, Judith. "Decline of the Family Economy in Mid-Nineteenth Century Egypt." *Arab Studies Quarterly* 1, no. 3 (1979): 245-271.

## North America

Adrian, Lynne M. "'Butter and Egg Money' Indeed!" *Canadian Review of American Studies* 20 (Summer 1989): 107-110.

Ahlborn, Richard Eighme. "The Will of a Woman in 1762." *New Mexico Historical Review* 65 (July 1990): 319-356.

Aldridge, Delores. "African-American Women in the Economic Marketplace: A Continuing Struggle." *Journal of Black Studies* 20 (December 1989): 129-154.

Allen, Walter R. "The Social and Economic Statuses of Black Women in the United States." *Phylon* (March 1981): 26-40.

Anderson, Karen. "Commodity Exchange and Subordination: Montagnais-Naskapi and Huron Women, 1600-1650." *Signs* 11 (Autumn 1985): 48-62.

Arendell, Terry J. "Women and the Economics of Divorce in the Contemporary United States." *Signs* 13 (Autumn 1987): 121-135.

Bauer, Arnold J. "Millers and Grinders: Technology and Household Economy in Meso-America." *Agricultural History* 64 (Winter 1990): 1-17.

Bennett, Sheila Kishler, and Glen H. Elder, Jr. "Women's Work in the Family Economy:  A Study of Depression Hardship in Women's Lives." *Journal of Family History* 4 (Summer 1979): 153-176.

Biemer, Linda, ed. "Business Letters of Alida Schuyler Livingston, 1680-1726." *New York History* 63 (April 1982): 183-207.

Billings, Dwight B., and Kathleen M. Blee. "Family Strategies in a Subsistence Economy: Beech Creek, Kentucky, 1850-1942." *Sociological Perspectives* 33 (Spring 1990): 63-88.

Bishop, Joan. "Game of Freeze-Out: Marguerite Greenfield and Her Battle with the Great Northern Railway, 1920-1929." *Montana* 35 (Summer 1985): 14-27.

Bolin, Winifred D. Wandersee. "The Economics of Middle-Income Family Life: Working Women During the Great Depression." *Journal of American History* 65 (June 1978): 60-74.

Braund, Kathryn E. Holland. "Guardians of Tradition and Handmaidens to Change: Women's Roles in Creek Economic and Social Life During the Eighteenth Century." *American Indian Quarterly* 14 (Summer 1990): 239-258.

Bullen, John. "Child Labour and the Family Economy in Late Nineteenth-Century Urban Ontario." *Labour/Le Travail* 18 (Fall 1986): 163-187.

Cohen, Marjorie. "The Razor's Edge Invisible: Feminism's Effect on Economics." *International Journal of Women's Studies* 8, no. 3 (1985): 286-298.

Corter, Susan B. "Occupational Segregation, Teachers' Wages, and American Economic Growth." *Journal of Economic History* 46 (June 1986): 373-384.

Cross, Gary, and Peter R. Shergold. "The Family Economy and the Market: Wages and Residence of Pennsylvania Women in the 1890s." *Journal of Family History* 11 (July 1986): 245-265.

Devine, Joel A., Joseph F. Sheley, and M. Dwayne Smith. "Macroeconomic and Social-Control Policy Influences on Crime-Rate Changes, 1948-1985." *American Sociological Review* 53 (June 1988): 407-420.

Fellman, Michael. "Getting Right with the Poor White." *Canadian Review of American Studies* 18 (Winter 1987): 527-540.

Folbre, Nancy. "The Unproductive Housewife: Her Evolution in Nineteenth-Century Economic Thought." *Signs* 16 (Spring 1991): 463-484.

Fox-Genovese, Elizabeth. "Property and Patriarchy in Classical Bourgeois Political Theory." *Radical History Review* 4 (1977): 36-59.

Gallagher, Teresa. "From Family Helpmeet to Independent Professional: Women In American Pharmacy, 1870-1940." *Pharmacy in History* 31 (1989): 60-77.

Ginsberg, Caren A., and Alan C. Swedlund. "Sex-Specific Mortality and Economic Opportunities: Massachusetts, 1860-1899." *Continuity and Change* 1, no. 3 (1986): 415-446.

Goldin, Claudia. "The Changing Economic Role of Women: A Quantitative Approach." *Journal of Interdisciplinary History* 13 (Spring 1983): 707-733.

-----. "The Economic Status of Women in the Early Republic: Quantitative Evidence." *Journal of Interdisciplinary History* 16 (Winter 1986): 375-404.

Grigg, Susan. "Women and Family Property: A Review of U.S. Inheritance Studies." *Historical Methods* 22 (Summer 1989): 116-122.

Hine, Darlene Clark. "Female Slave Resistance: The Economics of Sex." *Western Journal of Black Studies* 3 (Summer 1979): 123-127.

Iacovetta, Franca. "Trying to Make Ends Meet: An Historical Look at Italian Immigrant Women, the State and Family Survival Strategies in Post-War Toronto." *Canadian Woman Studies/Les cahiers de la femme* 8 (Summer 1987):

6-11.

Jones, Jacqueline. "'My Mother Was Much of a Woman': Black Women, Work, and the Family under Slavery." *Feminist Studies* 8 (Summer 1982): 235-270.

Juteau, Danielle, and Nicole Laurin. "From Nuns to Surrogate Mothers: Evolution of the Forms of the Appropriation of Women." *Feminist Issues* 9 (Spring 1989): 13-40.

King, Gail Buchwalter. "Women and Social Security: An Applied History." *Social Science History* 6 (Spring 1982): 227-232.

Land, Hilary. "State Income Maintenance Policies for Working-Class Wives and Mothers." *Society for the Study of Labour History* 48 (Spring 1984): 10.

Landale, Nancy. "Agricultural Opportunity and Marriage: The United States at the Turn of the Century." *Demography* 26 (May 1989): 203-218.

Littlefield, Daniel C. "Plantations, Paternalism, and Profitability:    Factors Affecting African Demography in the Old British Empire." *Journal of Southern History* 47 (May 1981): 167-182.

Mabee, Carleton. "Sojourner Truth Fights Dependence on Government: Moves Freed Slaves Off Welfare in Washington to Jobs in Upstate New York." *Afro-Americans in New York Life and History* 14 (January 1990): 7-26.

May, Elaine Tyler. "The Pressure to Provide: Class, Consumerism, and Divorce in Urban America 1880-1920." *Journal of Social History* 12 (Winter 1978): 180-193.

May, Martha. "The 'Good Managers': Married Working Class Women and Family Budget Studies, 1895-1915." *Labor History* 25 (Summer 1984): 351-372.

McMahon, Sarah F. "Provisions Laid Up for the Family: Towards a History of Diet in New England, 1650-1850." *Historical Methods* 14 (Winter 1981): 4-21.

Mercier, Laurie K. "Women's Economic Role in Montana Agriculture: 'You Had to Make Every Minute Count.'" *Montana* 38 (Autumn 1988): 50-61.

Needleman, Ruth. "A World in Transition: Women and Economic Change." *Labor Studies Journal* 10 (Winter 1985): 207-228.

O'Donnel, Margaret G. "Charlotte Perkins Gilman's Economic Interpretation of the Role of Women at the Turn of the Century." *Social Science Quarterly* 69, no. 1 (1988): 177-192.

Olasky, Marvin. "Advertising Abortion During the 1830s and 1840s: Madame Restell Builds a Business." *Journalism History* 13 (Summer 1986): 49-55.

Petrik, Paula. "Capitalists with Rooms: Prostitution in Helena, Montana, 1865-1900." *Montana* 31 (April 1981): 28-41.

Pool, Carolyn Garrett. "Reservation Policy and the Economic Position of Wichita Women." *Great Plains Quarterly* 8 (Summer 1988): 158-171.

Quadagno, Jill. "Race, Class, and Gender in the U.S. Welfare State: Nixon's Failed Family Assistance Plan." *American Sociological Review* 55 (February 1990): 11-28.

Reiff, Janice L., Michael R. Dahlin, and Daniel Scott Smith. "Rural Push and Urban Pull: Work and Family Experiences of Older Black Women in Southern Cities, 1880-1900." *Journal of Social History* 16 (Summer 1983): 39-48.

Rotella, Elyce J. "Women's Labor Force Participation and the Decline of the Family Economy in the United States." *Explorations in Economic History* 17, no. 2 (1980): 95-117.

Russell, Scott C., and Mark B. McDonald. "The Economic Contributions of Women in a Rural Western Navajo Community." *American Indian Quarterly* 6 (Fall/Winter 1982): 262-282.

Salmon, Marylynn. "Women and Property in South Carolina: The Evidence from Marriage Settlements, 1730-1830." *William and Mary Quarterly* 39 (October 1982): 655-685.

Schneyer, Mark. "Mothers and Children, Poverty and Morality: A Social Worker's Priorities, 1915." *Pennsylvania Magazine of History and Biography* 112 (April 1988): 209-226.

Schweninger, Loren. "Property-Owning Free African-American Women in the South, 1800-70." *Journal of Women's History* 1 (Winter 1990): 13-44.

Shankman, Arnold. "The Five-Day Plan and the Depression." *The Historian* 43 (May 1981): 393-409.

Snell, K. D. M., and J. Millar. "Lone-Parent Families and the Welfare State: Past and Present." *Continuity and Change* 2, no. 3 (1987): 387-422.

Sorensen, Annette, and Sara McLanahan. "Married Women's Economic Dependency, 1940-1980." *American Journal of Sociology* 93 (November 1987): 659-687.

Speth, Linda. "More Than Her 'Thirds': Wives and Widows in Colonial Virginia." *Women and History* 4 (1982): 5-41.

Spring, Eileen. "The Family, Strict Settlement and Historians." *Canadian Journal of History* 18 (December 1983): 379-398.

Steckel, Richard H. "Antebellum Southern White Fertility: A Demographic and Economic Analysis." *Journal of Economic History* 40 (June 1980): 331-350.

Swain, Martha H. "'The Forgotten Woman': Ellen S. Woodward and Women's Relief in the New Deal." *Prologue* 15 (Winter 1983): 201-213.

Thomson, Ross. "Learning by Selling and Invention: The Case of the Sewing Machine." *Journal of Economic History* 47 (June 1987): 433-446.

Tickamyer, Ann R., and Cecil H. Tickamyer. "Gender and Poverty in Central Appalachia." *Social Science Quarterly* 69 (December 1988): 874-891.

Tilly, Charles, and Louise Tilly. "Stalking the Bourgeois Family." *Social Science History* 4 (Spring 1980): 251-260.

Waters, John L. "Family, Inheritance, and Migration in Colonial New England: The Evidence from Guilford, Connecticut." *William and Mary Quarterly* 39 (January 1982): 64-86.

White, William W. "Marriage Insurance: The Mississippi Bubble of 1882." *Journal of Mississippi History* 46 (May 1984): 108-119.

Wright, Mary C. "Economic Development and Native American Women in the Early Nineteenth Century." *American Quarterly* 33 (Winter 1981): 525-536.

Ybarra, Lea. "When Wives Work: The Impact on the Chicano Family." *Journal of Marriage and Family* 44 (February 1982): 169-178.

## Soviet Union

Hudson, Hugh D., Jr. "Urban Estate Engineering in Eighteenth-Century Russia: Catherine the Great and the Elusive Meshchanstvo." *Canadian-American Slavic Studies/Revue canadienne-americaine d'etudes slaves* 18 (Winter 1984): 393-410.

Levin, Eve. "Women and Property in Medieval Novgorod: Dependence and Independence." *Russian History* 10, Part 2 (1983): 154-169.

Levy, Sandry. "Women and the Control of Property in Sixteenth-Century Muscovy." *Russian History* 10, Part 2 (1983): 201-212.

## EDUCATION

## Methods

Albisetti, James C. "The Reform of Female Education in Prussia, 1899-1908: A Study in Compromise and Containment." *German Studies Review* 8 (February 1985): 11-42.

Bailey, Beth L. "Scientific Truth . . . and Love:   The Marriage Education Movement in the United States." *Journal of Social History* 20 (Summer 1987): 711-732.

Barlow, William, and David O. Powell. "Homeopathy and Sexual Equality: The Controversy over Coeducation at Cincinnati's Pulte Medical College, 1873-1879." *Ohio History* 90 (Spring 1981): 101-113.

Bartow, Beverly. "Isabel Bevier at the University of Illinois and the Home Economics Movement." *Journal of the Illinois State Historical Society* 72 (February 1979): 21-38.

Belcher, Dixie. "A Democratic School for Democratic Women." *Chronicles of Oklahoma* 61 (Winter 1983): 414-421.

Belding, Robert E. "The Dubuque Female Seminary: Catherine Beecher's Blueprint for 19th-Century Women's Education." *Palimpsest* 63 (March/April 1982): 34-41.

Bender, Norman J. "'We Surely Gave Them an Uplift.'" *Chronicles of Oklahoma* 61 (Summer 1983): 180-193.

Berkeley, Kathleen Christine. "'The Ladies Want to Bring about Reform in the Public Schools': Public Education and Women's Rights in the Post-Civil War South." *History of Education Quarterly* (Spring 1984): 45-58.

Bernstein, George, and Lottelore Bernstein. "Attitudes toward Women's Education in Germany, 1870-1914." *International Journal of Women's Studies* 2 (September/October 1979): 473-488.

Bonner, T. N. "Pioneering in Women's Medical Education in the Swiss Universities 1864-1914." *Gesnerus* 45 (1988): 461-473.

-----. "Rendezvous in Zurich: Seven Who Made a Revolution in Women's Medical Education, 1864-1874." *Journal of the History of Medicine* 44, no. 1 (1989): 7-27.

Boris, Eileen. "Social Reproduction and the Schools: 'Educational House-keeping.'" *Signs* 4 (Spring 1979): 814-820.

Bourke, Joanna. "'The Health Caravan': Domestic Education and Female Labor in Rural Ireland, 1890-1914." *Eire-Ireland* 24 (Winter 1989): 7-20.

Bramadat, I. J., and K. I. Chalmers. "Nursing Education in Canada: Historical 'Progress'--Contemporary Issues." *Journal of Advanced Nursing* 14 (1989): 719-726.

Brown, Victoria Bissell. "The Fear of Feminization: Los Angeles High Schools in the Progressive Era." *Feminist Studies* 16 (Fall 1990): 493-518.

Castle, Alfred L. "Harriet Castle and the Beginnings of Progressive Kindergarten Education in Hawai'i 1894-1900." *Hawaiian Journal of History* 23 (1989): 119-136.

Chitty, Arthur Ben. "Women and Black Education: Three Profiles." *Historical Magazine of the Protestant Episcopal Church* 52 (June 1983): 153-165.

Cohen, Miriam. "Changing Education Strategies Among Immigrant Generations: New York Italians in Comparative Perspective." *Journal of Social History* 15 (Spring 1982): 443-466.

Crowder, Beth Jersey. "The Lux School: A Little Gem of Education for Women." *California History* 65 (Sept 1986): 208-213.

De la Cour, Lykke, and Rose Sheinin. "The Ontario Medical College for Women, 1883 to 1906: Lessons from Gender-Separatism in Medical Education." *Canadian Woman Studies/Les cahiers de la femme* 7 (Fall 1986): 73-77.

DeMadariaga, Isabel. "The Foundation of the Russian Educational System by Catherine II." *Slavonic and East European Review* 57 (July 1979): 369-395.

Dyehouse, C. "Towards a 'Feminine' Curriculum for English Schoolgirls: The Demands of Ideology 1870-1963." *Women's Studies International Quarterly* 1, no. 4 (1978): 297-330.

Edwards, Elizabeth. "Educational Institutions or Extended Families? The Reconstruction of Gender in Women's Colleges in the Late Nineteenth and Early Twentieth Centuries." *Gender and Education* 2, no. 1 (1990): 17-36.

Ellis, Rose Herlong. "The Calhoun School, Miss Charlotte Thorn's 'Lighthouse on the Hill' in Lowndes County, Alabama." *Alabama Review* 37 (July 1984): 183-201.

Engelmeyer, Bridget Mavie. "A Maryland First." *Maryland Historical Magazine* (Fall 1983): 186-204.

Epstein, Sandra P. "Women and Legal Education: The Case of Boalt Hall." *Pacific Historian* 28 (Fall 1984): 4-22.

Fitzpartick, David. "'A Share of the Honeycomb': Education, Emigration and Irishwomen." *Continuity and Change* 1, no. 2 (1986): 217-234.

Fleet, Betsy. "'If There Is No Bright Side, Then Polish Up the Dark One': Maria Louisa Fleet and the Green Mount Home School for Young Ladies." *Virginia Cavalcade* 29 (Winter 1980): 100-107.

Fleming, Juliet. "*The French Garden*: An Introduction to Women's French." *ELH* 56 (Spring 1989): 19-52.

Gibson, Joan. "Educating for Silence: Renaissance Women and the Language

Arts." *Hypatia* 4 (Spring 1989): 9-27.

Gordon, Lynn D. "Annie Nathan Meyer and Barnard College: Mission and Identity in Women's Higher Education, 1889-1950." *History of Education Quarterly* 26 (Winter 1986): 503-522.

-----. "Female Gothic: Writing the History of Women's Colleges." *American Quarterly* 37 (Summer 1985): 299-304.

Gray, Ricky Harold. "Corona Female College." *Journal of Mississippi History* (May 1980): 129-134.

Green, Nancy. "Female Education and School Competition, 1820-1850." *History of Education Quarterly* 18 (Summer 1978): 129-142.

Guy-Sheftall, Beverly. "Black Women and Higher Education:   Spelman and Bennett Colleges Revisited." *Journal of Negro Education* (Summer 1982): 278-287.

Handl, Johann. "Educational Chances and Occupational Opportunities of Women: A Sociohistorical Analysis." *Journal of Social History* 17 (Spring 1984): 463-487.

Hanft, Sheldon. "Mordecai's Female Academy." *American Jewish History* 79 (Autumn 1989): 72-93.

Harrington, Ann M. "Women and Higher Education in the Japanese Empire (1895-1945)." *Journal of Asian History* 21, no. 2 (1987): 169-186.

Hayden, Michael. "Women and the University of Saskatchewan: Pattern of a Problem." *Saskatchewan History* 40 (Spring 1987): 72-82.

Hind, Robert J. "The Loss of English Working-Class Parents' Control over their Children's   Education:   The   Role   of   Property-Holders."   *Historical Reflections/Reflexions Historiques* 12 (Spring 1985): 77-108.

Hine, Darlene Clark. "Opportunity and Fulfillment: Sex, Race, and Class in Health Care Education." *Sage* 2 (Fall 1985): 14-19.

Horowitz, Helen Lefkowitz. "Designing for the Genders: Curricula and Architecture at Scripps College and the California Institute of Technology." *Pacific Historical Review* 54 (November 1985): 439-461.

Jardine, Pauline O. "An Urban Middle-Class Calling: Women and the Emergence of Modern Nursing Education at the Toronto General Hospital, 1881-1914." *Urban History Review* 17 (February 1989): 177-190.

Jensen, Joan M. "Crossing Ethnic Barriers in the Southwest:   Women's Agricultural Extension Education, 1914-1940." *Agricultural History* 60 (Spring 1986): 169-181.

Jordahl, Donald C. "John Brown White and Early Women's Education: A History of Almira College." *Journal of the Illinois State Historical Society* 72 (May 1979): 101-110.

Jupp, Gertrude B.   "The   Heritage   of   Milwaukee-Downer   College:   A Reaffirmation." *Milwaukee History* 4 (Summer 1981): 43-47.

Koehler, Lyle. "Women's Rights, Society, and the Schools: Feminist Activities in Cincinnati, Ohio, 1864-1880." *Queen City Heritage* 42 (Winter 1984): 3-17.

Kolmerten, Carol A. "Egalitarian Promises and Inegalitarian Practices: Women's Roles in the American Owenite Communities, 1824-1828." *Journal of General*

*Education* 33 (Spring 1981): 31-44.

Leloudis, James L. I. "School Reform in the New South: The Woman's Association for the Betterment of Public School Houses in North Carolina, 1902-1919." *Journal of American History* (March 1983): 886-909.

Lenskyi, Helen. "Femininity First: Sport and Physical Education for Ontario Girls, 1890-1930." *Canadian Journal of the History of Sport* 13 (December 1982): 4-17.

Levine, David. "Education and Family Life in Early Industrial England." *Journal of Family History* 4 (Winter 1979): 368-380.

-----. "Illiteracy and Family Life During the First Industrial Revolution." *Journal of Social History* 14 (Fall 1980): 25-44.

Mabee, Carleton. "Margaret Mead and a 'Pilot Experiment' in Progressive and Interracial Education: The Downtown Community School." *New York History* 65 (January 1984): 5-31.

MacLeod, R., and R. Moseley. "Fathers and Daughters: Reflections on Women, Science and Victorian Cambridge." *History of Education Journal* 8 (1979): 321-333.

Mathews, Jill. "Education for Femininity: Domestic Arts Education in South Australia." *Labour History* 45 (November 1983): 30-53.

McAninch, Stuart A. "The Educational Theory of Mary Sheldon Barnes: Inquiry Learning as Indoctrination in History Education." *Educational Theory* 40 (Winter 1990): 45-52.

McCandless, Amy M. "'From Pedestal to Mortarboard': Higher Education for Women in South Carolina from 1920 to 1940." *Southern Studies* 23 (Winter 1984): 348-362.

-----. "Maintaining the Spirit and Tone of Robust Manliness: The Battle Against Coeducation at Southern Colleges and Universities, 1890-1940." *NWSA Journal* 2, no. 2 (Spring 1990): 199-216.

McCarthy, Wendy. "Education: What's in It for Women and Girls?" *Labour History* 48 (May 1985): 94-100.

McCrone, Kathleen E. "Play Up! Play Up! And Play the Game! Sport at the Late Victorian Girls' Public School." *Journal of British Studies* 23 (Spring 1984): 106-134.

Melder, Keith. "Ipswich Female Seminary: An Educational Experiment." *Essex Institute Historical Collections* 120 (October 1984): 223-240.

Merguerian, Barbara J. "Mt. Holyoke Seminary in Bitlis: Providing an American Education for Armenian Women." *Armenian Review* 43 (Spring 1990): 31-65.

Merrill, Marlene D. "Daughters of America Rejoice: The Oberlin Experiment." *Timeline* 4 (October/November 1987): 12-21.

Modell, John. "An Ecology of Family Decisions: Suburbanization, Schooling, and Fertility in Philadelphia, 1880-1920." *Journal of Urban History* 6 (August 1980): 397-418.

Mullaney, Marie Marmo. "The New Jersey College for Women: Middle Class Respectability and Proto-Feminism, 1911-1918." *Journal of Rutgers University Library* 42, no. 1 (1980): 26-39.

Nash, Carol S. "Educating New Mothers: Women and the Enlightenment in Russia." *History of Education Quarterly* 21 (Fall 1981): 301-316.

Nerad, Maresi. "Gender Stratification in Higher Education: The Department of Home Economics at the University of California, Berkeley, 1916-1962." *Women's Studies* 10, no. 2 (1987): 157-164.

Neverdon-Morton, Cynthia. "Self-Help Programs as Educative Activities of Black Women in the South, 1895-1925: Focus on Four Key Areas." *Journal of Negro Education* 51 (Summer 1982): 207-221.

Offen, Karen. "The Second Sex and the Baccalaureat in Republican France, 1880-1924." *French Historical Studies* 13 (Fall 1983): 252-286.

Perkins, Linda M. "Heed Life's Demands: The Educational Philosophy of Fanny Jackson Coppin." *Journal of Negro Education* 51 (Summer 1982): 181-190.

Perlmann, Joel and Dennis Shirley. "When Did New England Women Acquire Literacy?" *William and Mary Quarterly* 48 (January 1991): 50-67.

Peterson, Richard H. "Philanthropic Phoebe: The Educational Charity of Phoebe Apperson Hearst." *California History* 64 (Fall 1985): 284-289.

Petschauer, Peter. "Eighteenth-Century German Opinions about Education for Women." *Central European History* 19 (September 1986): 262-292.

Pinderhughes, Dianne M. "Black Women and National Educational Policy." *Journal of Negro Education* (Summer 1982): 301-308.

Pollock, Linda. "'Teach Her to Live under Obedience': The Making of Women in the Upper Ranks of Early Modern England." *Continuity and Change* 4 (August 1989): 231-258.

Purvis, J. "Towards a History of Women's Education in Nineteenth Century Britain: A Sociological Analysis." *Westminster Studies in Education* 4 (1981): 45-79.

Pusey, William Webb, III. "Lexington's Female Academy." *Virginia Cavalcade* (Summer 1982): 41-47.

Rapley, Elizabeth. "Fenelon Revisited: A Review of Girls' Education in Seventeenth-Century France." *Histoire sociale/Social History* 20 (November 1987): 299-313.

Reid, John G. "The Education of Women at Mount Allison, 1854-1914." *Acadiensis* 12 (Spring 1983): 3-33.

Rury, John, and Glenn Harper. "The Trouble with Coeducation: Mann and Women at Antioch, 1853-1860." *History of Education Quarterly* 26 (Winter 1986): 481-502.

Sawards, J. K. "Erasmus and the Education of Women." *Sixteenth Century Journal* 13 (Winter 1982): 77-89.

Schumacher, Carolyn Sutcher. "The Open Gate." *Western Pennsylvania Historical Magazine* 69 (October 1986): 295-326.

Schwager, Sally. "Educating Women in America." *Signs* 12 (Winter 1987): 333-372.

Schweider, Dorothy. "Education and Change in the Lives of Iowa Farm Women, 1900-1940." *Agricultural History* 60 (Spring 1986): 200-215.

Scott, Anne Firor. "The Ever Widening Circle: The Diffusion of Feminist Values from the Troy Female Seminary, 1822-1872." *History of Education Quarterly* 19 (Spring 1979): 3-25.

Sedlak, Michael W. "Young Women and the City: Adolescent Deviance and the Transformation of Education Policy, 1870-1960." *History of Education Quarterly* 23 (Spring 1983): 1-28.

Shackleton, J. R. "Jane Marcet and Harriet Martineau: Pioneers of Economics Education." *History of Education* 19 (December 1990): 283-298.

Sheehan, Nancy M. "Women's Organizations and Educational Issues, 1900-1930." *Canadian Woman Studies/Les cahiers de la femme* 7 (Fall 1986): 90-95.

Shelton, Brenda K. "Organized Mother Love: The Buffalo Women's Educational and Industrial Union, 1885-1915." *New York History* 67 (April 1986): 155-176.

Sinkoff, Nancy B. "Educating for 'Proper' Jewish Womanhood: A Case Study in Domesticity and Vocational Training, 1897-1926." *American Jewish History* 77, no. 4 (1988): 572-599.

Smock, Pamela J. "Remarriage Patterns of Black and White Women: Reassessing the Role of Educational Attainment." *Demography* 27 (August 1990): 467-474.

Spencer, Samia I. "Women and Education in Eighteenth-Century France." *Western Society for French History* 10 (October 1982): 274-284.

Steedman, Carolyn. "'The Mother Made Conscious': The Historical Development of a Primary School Pedagogy." *History Workshop* 20 (Autumn 1985): 149-163.

Steinson, Barbara J. "Sisters and Soldiers: American Women and the National Service Schools, 1916-1917." *Historian* 43 (February 1981): 23-35.

Stepan, Nancy Leys. "Women and Natural Knowledge: The Role of Gender in the Making of Modern Science." *Gender & History* 2 (Autumn 1990): 337-342.

Stephenson, William E. "The Davises, the Southalls, and the Founding of Wesleyan Female College, 1854-1859." *North Carolina Historical Review* 57 (July 1980): 257-279.

Tavill, A. A. "Early Medical Co-Education and Women's Medical College, Kingston, Ontario 1880-1894." *Historic Kingston* 30 (January 1982): 68-89.

Theobald, Marjorie R. "The PLC Mystique: Reflections on the Reform of Female Education in Nineteenth Century Australia." *Australian Historical Studies* 23 (April 1989): 241-259.

van Krieken, Robert. "Towards 'Good and Useful Men and Women': The State and Childhood in Sydney, 1840-1890." *Australian Historical Studies* 23 (October 1989): 405-425.

Vigue, Charles L. "Eugenics and the Education of Women in the United States." *Journal of Education Administration and History* 19, no. 2 (1987): 51-55.

Vinovskis, Maris A., and Richard M. Bernard. "Beyond Catharine Beecher: Female Education in the Antebellum Period." *Signs* 3 (Summer 1978): 856-869.

Walsh, Mary Roth, and Francis R. Walsh. "Integrating Men's Colleges at the Turn of the Century." *Historical Journal of Massachusetts* 10 (June 1982): 4-16.

Weis, Lois. "Women and Education in Ghana: Some Problems of Assessing the

Change." *International Journal of Women's Studies* 3, no. 5 (1980): 431-453.

Weiss, Janice. "Educating for Clerical Work: The Nineteenth-Century Private Commercial School." *Journal of Social History* 14 (Spring 1981): 407-423.

Whitley, Edna Talbott. "Mary Beck and the Female Mind." *Register of the Kentucky History Society* 77 (Winter 1979): 15-24.

Wieder, Alan. "One Who Stayed: Margaret Conner and the New Orleans School Crisis (1960)." *Louisiana History* 26 (Winter 1985): 194-201.

Windschuttle, Elizabeth. "Discipline, Domestic Training and Social Control: The Female School of Industry, Sydney, 1826-1847." *Labour History* 39 (November 1980): 1-14.

Yeager, Gertude M. "Women's Role in Nineteenth-Century Chile: Public Education Records, 1843-1883." *Latin American Research Review* 18, no. 3 (1983): 149-156.

Zschoche, Sue. "Dr. Clarke Revisited: Science, True Womanhood, and Female Collegiate Education." *History of Education Quarterly* 29 (Winter 1989): 545-569.

## Students

Abbott, Devon. "Ann Florence Wilson: Matriarch of the Cherokee Female Seminary." *Chronicles of Oklahoma* 67 (Winter 1989/90): 426-437.

Albert, Judith Strong. "Margaret Fuller's Row at the Greene Street School: Early Female Education in Providence, 1837-1839." *Rhode Island History* 42 (May 1983): 43-55.

Antler, Joyce. "'After College, What?': New Graduates and the Family Claim." *American Quarterly* 32 (Fall 1980): 409-434.

Auwers, Linda. "Reading the Marks of the Past: Exploring Female Literacy in Colonial Windsor, Connecticut." *Historical Methods* 13 (Fall 1980): 204-214.

Barthel, Diane L. "Women's Educational Experience under Colonialism: Toward a Diachronic Model." *Signs* 7, no. 1 (1985): 137-154.

Beasley, Maurine. "Women in Journalism Education: The Formative Period, 1908-1930." *Journalism History* 13 (Spring 1986): 10-18.

Bell, J. H., and U. S. Pandey. "The Exclusion of Women from Australian Post-Secondary Agricultural Education and Training 1880-1969." *Australian Journal of Politics and History* 36, no. 2 (1990): 205-216.

Black, J. L. "Educating Women in Eighteenth-Century Russia: Myths and Realities." *Canadian Slavic Papers* 20 (March 1978): 23-43.

Blackmore, Jill. "Schooling for Work: Gender Differentiation in Commercial Education in Victoria 1935-1960." *History of Education Review* [Australia] 16, no. 1 (1987).

Bohjalian, Christopher A. "Educating Gentlewomen." *Hayes Historical Journal* 4 (Fall 1984): 48-67.

Brisbay, Erin. "College Women in the 1930s: The Possibilities and the Realities." *Filson Club History Quarterly* 64 (January 1990): 32-59.

Britt, Judith S. "Lessons for Martha's Children: Music in George Washington's

Family." *Virginia Cavalcade* 35 (Spring 1986): 172-183.

Campbell, Debra. "Part-Time Female Evangelists of the Thirties and Forties: The Rosary College Catholic Evidence Guild." *U.S. Catholic Historian* 5 (Summer/Fall 1986): 371-383.

Carson, Mina J. "Agnes Hamilton of Fort Wayne: The Education of a Christian Settlement Worker." *Indiana Magazine of History* 80 (March 1984): 1-34.

Catlett, Judith. "After the Goodbyes: A Long-Term Look at the Southern School for Union Women." *Labor Journal* 10 (1986): 300-311.

Christensen, Lawrence O. "Being Special: Women Students at the Missouri School of Mines and Metallurgy." *Missouri Historical Review* 83 (October 1988): 17-35.

Clark, Linda L. "The Socialization of Girls in the Primary Schools of the Third Republic." *Journal of Social History* 15 (Summer 1982): 685-698.

-----. "The Socialization of Girls in the Primary Schools of the Third Republic." *Western Society for French History* 8 (October 1980): 437.

Clinton, Catherine. "Equally Their Due: The Education of the Planter Daughter in the Early Republic." *Journal of the Early Republic* 2 (Spring 1980): 39-60.

Cole, Stephen. "Sex Discrimination and Admission to Medical School, 1929-1984." *American Journal of Sociology* 92 (November 1986): 549-567.

Daniels, Elizabeth A., Anne Constantinople, and Marque Miringoff. "The Intersection of Biography and History: The Vassar Class of 1935." *International Journal of Oral History* 9 (June 1988): 125-130.

DeBlasio, Donna. "'The Greatest Woman In the Reserve': Betsy Mix Cowles, Feminist, Abolitionist, Educator." *Old Northwest* 13 (Fall/Winter 1987): 223-236.

Delpar, Helen. "Coeds and the 'Lords of Creation': Women Students at the University of Alabama, 1893-1930." *Alabama Review* 42 (October 1989): 292-312.

Dudgeon, Ruth A. "The Forgotten Minority: Women Students in Imperial Russia, 1872-1917." *Russian History* 9, no. 1 (1982): 1-26.

Engel, Barbara Alpern. "Women Medical Students in Russia, 1872-1882: Reformers or Rebels?" *Journal of Social History* 12 (Spring 1979): 394-414.

Fitzpatrick, Sheila. "Sex and Revolution: An Examination of Literacy and Statistical Data on the Mores of Soviet Students in the 1920s." *Journal of Modern History* 50 (June 1978): 252-278.

Gordon, Lynn D. "The Gibson Girl Goes to College: Popular Culture and Women's Higher Education in the Progressive Era, 1890-1920." *American Quarterly* 39 (Summer 1987): 211-230.

-----. "In the Shadow of SDS: Writing the History of Twentieth-Century College Students." *History of Education Quarterly* 26 (Spring 1986): 131-139.

Graham, Patricia Abjerg. "Expansion and Exclusion: A History of Women in American Higher Education." *Signs* 3 (Summer 1978): 759-773.

Gunnerson, Dolores. "Esther Gunnison: A Nebraskan at Oxford, 1920-1921." *Nebraska History* 59 (Spring 1978): 1-30.

Gunter, Helen Clifford. "A Young Latin Scholar: University Life in the 1920s."

*Palimpsest* 71 (Spring 1990): 38-48.

Harrigan, Patrick J. "The Schooling of Boys and Girls in Canada." *Journal of Social History* 23 (Summer 1990): 803-816.

Howard-Vital, Michelle R. "African-American Women in Higher Education: Struggling to Gain Identity." *Journal of Black Studies* 20 (December 1989): 180-191.

King, Patricia M. "The Campaign for Higher Education for Women in 19th Century Boston." *Proceedings of the Massachusetts Historical Society* 93 (1981): 59-79.

Kowaleski-Wallace, Beth. "Milton's Daughters: The Education of Eighteenth-Century Women Writers." *Feminist Studies* 12 (Summer 1986): 275-294.

Lawson, Ellen N., and Marlene Morrell. "Antebellum Black Coeds at Oberlin College." *Oberlin Alumni* 60 (Winter 1980): 8-11.

Lee, Sally J., and Jeffrey P. Brown. "Women at New Mexico State University: The Early Years, 1888-1920." *New Mexico Historical Review* 64 (January 1989): 77-94.

Maloney, Joan M. "Mary Toppan Pickman: The Education of a Salem Gentlewoman, 1820-1850." *Essex Institute Historical Collections* 123 (January 1987): 1-28.

Marks, Lynne. "Kale Meydelach or Shulamith Girls: Cultural Change and Continuity Among Jewish Parents and Daughters--A Case Study of Toronto's Harbord Collegiate Institute in the 1920s." *Canadian Woman Studies/Les cahiers de la femme* 7 (Fall 1986): 85-89.

Marks, Lynne, and Chad Gaffield. "Women at Queen's University, 1895-1905: A Little Sphere All Their Own?" *Ontario History* 78 (December 1986): 331-350.

Millstone, Amy B. "Behind Closed Doors: A Girl's Liberal Home Education under the Second Empire." *Western Society for French History* 15 (November 1987): 303-312.

Morrow, Sean. "'No Girl Leaves the School Unmarried': Mabel Shaw and the Education of Girls at Mbereshi, Northern Rhodesia, 1915-1940." *International Journal of African Historical Studies* 19, no. 4 (1986): 601-635.

Opheim, Teresa. "Portias of the Prairie: Early Women Graduates of the University Law Department." *Palimpsest* 67 (January/February 1986): 28-36.

Palmieri, Patricia A. "Women at Wellesley College, 1880-1920." *Frontiers* 5, no. 1 (1980): 63-67.

Porter, Kenneth Wiggins, ed. "Catherine Emma Wiggins, Pupil and Teacher in Northwest Kansas, 1888-1895." *Kansas History* 1 (Spring 1978): 16-38.

Proefriedt, William A. "The Education of Mary Antin." *Journal of Ethnic Studies* 17 (Winter 1990): 81-100.

Prokop, Manfred. "Canadianization of Immigrant Children: Role of the Elementary School in Alberta, 1900-1930." *Alberta History* 37 (Spring 1989): 1-10.

Requardt, Cynthia Horsburgh. "Alternative Professions for Goucher College

Graduates, 1892-1910." *Maryland Historical Magazine* 74, no. 3 (1979): 274-281.

Rossiter, Margaret W. "Doctorates for American Women, 1868-1907." *History of Education Quarterly* 22 (Summer 1982): 159-183.

Rury, John. "Urban Structure and School Participation: Immigrant Women in 1900." *Social Science History* 8 (Summer 1984): 219-242.

Sloan, Patricia E. "Early Black Nursing Schools and Responses of Black Nurses to Their Educational Programs." *Western Journal of Black Studies* 9 (Fall 1985): 158-172.

Szasz, Margaret Connell. " 'Poor Richard' Meets the Native American: Schooling for Young Indian Women in Eighteenth-Century Connecticut." *Pacific Historical Review* 49 (May 1980): 215-235.

Thompson, Delores, and Lyle Koehler. "Educated Pioneers: Black Woman at the University of Cincinnati, 1897-1940." *Queen City Heritage* 43 (Winter 1985): 21-28.

Trennert, Robert A. "Educating Indian Girls at Nonreservation Boarding Schools, 1878-1920." *Western Historical Quarterly* 13 (July 1982): 271-290.

Weinberg, Sydney Stahl. "Longing to Learn: The Education of Jewish Immigrant Women in New York City, 1900-1934." *Journal of American Ethnic History* 8 (Spring 1989): 108-126.

Yost, Nellie Snyder. "Nebraska's Scholarly Athlete: Louise Pound, 1872-1958." *Nebraska History* 64 (Winter 1983): 477-490.

## Teachers

Abbott, Devon. "'Commendable Progress': Acculturation at the Cherokee Female Seminary." *American Indian Quarterly* 11 (Summer 1987): 187-201.

Abbott, John. "Accomplishing 'A Man's Task': Rural Women Teachers, Male Culture, and the School Inspectorate in Turn-of-the-Century Ontario." *Ontario History* 78 (December 1986): 313-330.

Ahlquist, Roberta, and Ivan B. Kolozsvari. "Fragments From the Past: A New Teacher in a Frontier Town." *California History* 67, no. 2 (1988): 108-117.

Arnez, Nancy L. "Selected Black Female Superintendents of Public School Systems." *Journal of Negro Education* (Summer 1982): 309-317.

Balanoff, Elizabeth. "The Gary School Crisis of the 1950s: A Personal Memoir." *Indiana Magazine of History* 83 (March 1987): 65-73.

Berry, Mary Frances. "Twentieth-Century Black Women in Education." *Journal of Negro Education* (Summer 1982): 288-300.

Brink, J. R. "Bathsua Makin: Scholar and Educator of the Seventeenth Century." *International Journal of Women's Studies* 1 (July/August 1978): 417-426.

Burrage, Hilary F. "Women University Teachers of Natural Science, 1971-72: An Empirical Survey." *Social Studies of Science* 13 (February 1983): 147-160.

Carroll, Rosemary F. "A Plantation Teacher's Perceptions of the Impending Crisis." *Southern Studies* 18 (Fall 1979): 339-350.

Carter, Susan B. "Occupational Segregation, Teachers' Wages, and American

Economic Growth." *Journal of Economic History* 46 (June 1986): 373-384.

-----. "Academic Women Revisited: An Empirical Study of Changing Patterns in Women's Employment as College and University Faculty, 1890-1963." *Journal of Social History* 14 (Summer 1981): 675-699.

Christie, Jean. "'An Earnest Enthusiasm for Education': Sarah Christie Stevens, Schoolwoman." *Minnesota History* 48 (Summer 1983): 245-254.

Collier-Thomas, Bettye. "The Impact of Black Women in Education: An Historical Overview." *Journal of Negro Education* 51 (Summer 1982): 173-180.

Cordier, Mary Hurlbut. "Prairie Schoolwomen, Mid-1850s to 1920s, in Iowa, Kansas, and Nebraska." *Great Plains Quarterly* 8 (Spring 1988): 102-119.

Danylewycz, Marta, Beth Light, and Alison Prentice. "The Evolution of the Sexual Division of Labour in Teaching: A Nineteenth Century Ontario and Quebec Case Study." *Histoire sociale/Social History* 16 (May 1983): 81-109.

Danylewycz, Marta, and Alison Prentice. "Teachers, Gender and Bureaucratizing School Systems in Nineteenth Century Montreal and Toronto." *History of Education Quarterly* 24 (Spring 1984): 75-100.

DeBlasio, Donna. "'The Greatest Woman in the Reserve': Betsy Mix Cowles, Feminist, Abolitionist, Educator." *Old Northwest* 13 (Fall/Winter 1987): 223-236.

Dembski, Peter E. Paul. "Jenny Kidd Trout and the Founding of the Women's Medical Colleges at Kingston and Toronto." *Ontario History* 77 (September 1985): 183-206.

Doherty, Robert E. "Tempest on the Hudson: The Struggle for 'Equal Pay for Equal Work' in the New York City Public Schools, 1907-1911." *History of Education Quarterly* 19, no. 4 (1979): 413-434.

Elias, Louis, Jr. "James Chappel Hardy (c. 1870-1924): Founder of Gulf Park College for Women." *Journal of Mississippi History* (August 1984): 213-226.

Elliott, Josephine Mirabella. "Madame Marie Fretageot: Communitarian Educator." *Communal Societies* 4 (Fall 1984): 167-182.

Falls, Helen E. "Agnes Graham: Educator in Chile." *Baptist History and Heritage* 23 (January 1988): 23-31.

Fergenson, Laraine R. "Margaret Fuller in the Classroom: The Providence Period." *Studies in the American Renaissance* (1987): 131-142.

Fingard, Judith. "Gender and Inequality at Dalhousie: Faculty Women Before 1950." *Dalhousie Review* 64 (Winter 1984/85): 687-703.

Fish, Virginia Kemp. "'More Than Lore': Marion Talbot and Her Role in the Founding Years of the University of Chicago." *International Journal of Women's Studies* 8 (May/June 1985): 228-249.

Fleet, Betsy. "'If There Is No Bright Side, Then Polish Up the Dark One': Maria Louisa Fleet and the Green Mount Home School for Young Ladies." *Virginia Cavalcade* 29 (Winter 1980): 100-107.

Foote, Cheryl J. "Alice Blake of Trementina: Mission Teacher of the Southwest." *Journal of Presbyterian History* 60 (Fall 1982): 228-242.

Fullard, Joyce. "Ann Preston: Pioneer of Medical Education and Women's Rights." *Pennsylvania Heritage* 8 (Winter 1982): 9-14.

Fuller, Rosalie Trail. "A Holdrege High School Teacher, 1900-1905: The Letters of Sadie B. Smith." *Nebraska History* 60 (Fall 1979): 372-400.

Gething, Judith Dean. "The Educational and Civic Leadership of Elsie Wilcox, 1920-1932." *Hawaiian Journal of History* 16 (1982): 184-202.

Harley, Sharon. "Beyond the Classroom: The Organizational Lives of Black Female Educators in the District of Columbia, 1890-1930." *Journal of Negro Education* (Summer 1982): 254-265.

Hickle, Evelyn Myers. "Ruth Iowa Jones Myers, 1887-1974: Rural Iowa Educator." *Annals of Iowa* 45 (Winter 1980): 196-211.

Hoffert, Sylvia D. "Yankee Schoolmarms and the Domestication of the South." *Southern Studies* 24 (Summer 1985): 188-201.

Holmes, Madelyn. "The 'Unsung Heroines': Women Teachers in Salem Before the Civil War." *Esssex Institute Historical Collections* 122 (October 1986): 299-310.

Jayaweera, Swarna. "European Women Educators under the British Colonial Administration in Sri Lanka." *Women's Studies International Forum* 13, no. 4 (1990): 323-332.

Jefchak, Andrew. "Prostitutes and Schoolmarms: An Essay on Women in Western Films." *Heritage of the Great Plains* 16 (Summer 1983): 19-26.

Jensen, Joan M. "Not Only Ours but Others: The Quaker Teaching Daughters of the Mid-Atlantic, 1790-1850." *History of Education Quarterly* (Spring 1984): 3-19.

Jensen, Katherine. "Teachers and Progressives: The Navajo Day-School Experiment, 1935-1945." *Arizona and the West* 25 (Spring 1983): 49-62.

Johnson, Mary. "Antoinette Brevost: A Schoolmistress in Early Pittsburgh." *Winterthur Portfolio* 15 (Summer 1980): 151-168.

Jones, Jacqueline. "Women Who Were More Than Men: Sex and Status in Freedmen's Teaching." *History of Education Quarterly* (Spring 1979): 47-59.

Keller, Evelyn Fox, and Helene Moglen. "Competition and Feminism: Conflicts for Academic Women." *Signs* 12 (Spring 1987): 493-511.

Kennedy, Sally. "Useful and Expendable: Women Teachers in Western Australia in the 1920s and 1930s." *Labour History* 44 (May 1983): 18-26.

Klaus, Susan L., and Mary Porter Martin. "A Fair Chance: Virginia Randolph Ellett and Women's Education." *Virginia Cavalcade* 39 (Autumn 1989): 52-61.

Klotter, James C., and Freda Campbell. "Mary Desha, Alaskan Schoolteacher of 1888." *Pacific Northwest Quarterly* 71 (April 1980): 78-86.

Kyte, Elinor C. "A Tough Job for a Gentle Lady." *Journal of Arizona History* 25 (Winter 1984): 385-398.

Leiber, Justin, James Pickering, and Flora Bronson White, eds. "'Mother by the Tens': Flora Adelaide Holcomb Bronson's Account of Her Life as an Illinois Schoolteacher, Poet, and Farm Wife, 1851-1927." *Journal of the Illinois State Historical Society* 76 (Winter 1983): 283-307.

Leone, Janice. "Integrating the American Association of University Women, 1945-1949." *Historian* 51 (May 1989): 423-445.

Lief, Julia Wiech. "A Woman of Purpose: Julia B. Nelson." *Minnesota History*

47 (Winter 1981): 302-314.

Lubomudrov, Carol Ann. "A Woman State School Superintendent: Whatever Happened to Mrs. McVicker?" *Utah Historical Quarterly* 49 (Summer 1981): 254-261.

Menninger, Sally Ann, and Clare Rose. "Women Scientists and Engineers in American Academia." *International Journal of Women's Studies* 3 (May/June 1980): 292-299.

Moch, Leslie Page. "Government Policy and Women's Experience: The Case of Teachers in France." *Feminist Studies* 14 (Summer 1988): 301-324.

Nelms, Willie E. "Cora Wilson Stewart and the Crusade Against Illiteracy in Kentucky, 1916-1920." *Register of the Kentucky Historical Society* 82 (Spring 1984): 151-169.

Nelson, Margaret K. "Vermont Female Schoolteachers in the Nineteenth Century." *Vermont History* 49 (Winter 1981): 5-30.

Palmieri, Patricia A. "Here Was Fellowship: A Social Portrait of Academic Women at Wellesley College, 1895-1920." *History of Education Quarterly* 23 (Summer 1983): 195-214.

-----. "Patterns of Achievement of Single Academic Women at Wellesley College, 1880-1920." *Frontiers* 5 (Spring 1980): 63-67.

-----. "Women at Wellesley College, 1880-1920." *Frontiers* 5, no. 1 (1980): 63-67.

Pedersen, Joyce Senders. "Some Victorian Headmistresses: A Conservative Tradition of Social Reform." *Victorian Studies* 24 (Summer 1981): 463-488.

Pedersen, Sharon. "Married Women and the Right to Teach in St. Louis, 1941-1948." *Missouri Historical Review* 81 (January 1987): 141-158.

Perry, Elisabeth Israels. "Scholars Confront the ERA." *Canadian Review of American Studies* 18 (Fall 1987): 393-398.

Peterson, Susan. "'Holy Women' and Housekeepers: Women Teachers on South Dakota Reservations, 1885-1910." *South Dakota History* 13 (Fall 1983): 245-260.

Porter, Kenneth Wiggins, ed. "Catherine Emma Wiggins, Pupil and Teacher in Northwest Kansas, 1888-1895." *Kansas History* 1 (Spring 1978): 16-38.

Prentice, Alison, and Marta Danylewycz. "Teacher's Work: Changing Patterns in the Emerging School Systems of Nineteenth and Early Twentieth Century Central Canada." *Labour/Le travail* no. 17 (Spring 1986): 59-80.

Rankin, Charles C. "Teaching: Opportunity and Limitation for Wyoming Women." *Western Historical Quarterly* 21 (May 1990): 147-170.

Ransom, Lucy Adams. "Country Schoolma'am, 1907." Jay Ellis Ransom, ed. *Oregon Historical Quarterly* 87 (Spring 1986): 67-88.

-----. "Country Schoolma'am." Jay Ellis Ransom, ed. *Oregon Historical Quarterly* 86 (Winter 1985): 419-434.

-----. "Country Schoolma'am: Silver City: Closing the Wild West Era." Jay Ellis Ransom, ed. *Oregon Historical Quarterly* 87 (Summer 1986): 205-224.

Rector, Theresa A. "Black Nuns as Educators." *Journal of Negro Education* (Summer 1982): 238-253.

Roden, Donald. "From Old Miss to New Professional: A Portrait of Women Educators under the American Occupation of Japan 1945-1952." *History of Education Quarterly* 23 (Winter 1983): 469-489.

Ryesky, Diana. "Blanche Payne, Scholar and Teacher: Her Career in Costume History." *Pacific Northwest Quarterly* 77 (January 1986): 21-30.

Schrems, Suzanne H. "Teaching School on the Western Frontier: Acceptable Occupation for Nineteenth Century Women." *Montana* 37 (Summer 1987): 54-63.

Small, Sandra E. "The Schoolmarm in Freedmen's Schools: An Analysis of Attitudes." *Journal of Southern History* 45 (August 1979): 381-402.

Smith, Carol Hobson. "Black Female Achievers in Academe." *Journal of Negro Education* (Summer 1982): 318-341.

Smith, Joan K. "Progressive School Administration: Ella Flagg Young and the Chicago Schools, 1905-1915." *Journal of Illinois State Historical Society* 73 (Spring 1980): 27-44.

Smith, Sandra N., and Earle H. West. "Charlotte Hawkins Brown." *Journal of Negro Education* 51 (Summer 1982): 191-208.

Smyke, Raymond J. "Fatima Massaquoi Fahnbulleh (1912-1978) Pioneer Woman Educator." *Liberian Studies Journal* 15, no. 1 (1990): 48-73.

Southard, Barbara. "Bengal Women's Education League: Pressure Group and Professional Association." *Modern Asian Studies* 18, no. 1 (1984): 55-88.

Stahl, Ben. "The End of Segregation in Teacher Training in Delaware: Recollections of a Union Struggle, 1942-1946." *Labor's Heritage* 2 (January 1990): 24-33.

Stevenson, Louise L. "Sarah Porter Educates Useful Ladies, 1847-1900." *Winterthur Portfolio* 18 (Spring 1983): 39-60.

Strober, Myra H., and Audri Gordon Lanford. "The Feminization of Public School Teaching: Cross-sectional Analysis, 1850-1880." *Signs* 11 (Winter 1986): 212-235.

Tolan, Sally. "Margaret Hoben: Educator." *Milwaukee History* 8 (Spring 1985): 11-23.

Tomer, John S. "Scientist with a Gift for Teaching." *Chronicles of Oklahoma* 63 (Winter 1985/86): 397-411.

Turoff, Barbara Kivel. "Mary Beard: Feminist Educator." *Antioch Review* 37 (Summer 1979): 277-292.

Underwood, Kathleen. "The Pace of Their Own Lives: Teacher Training and the Life Course of Western Women." *Pacific Historical Review* 55 (November 1986): 513-530.

Vaughan, Mary Kay. "Women School Teachers in the Mexican Revolution: The Story of Reyna's Braids." *Journal of Women's History* 2 (Spring 1990): 143-168.

Vaughn-Roberson, Courtney Ann. "Having a Purpose in Life: Western Women Teachers in the Twentieth Century." *Great Plains Quarterly* 5 (Spring 1985): 107-124.

-----. "Sometimes Independent but Never Equal--Women Teachers, 1900-1950:

The Oklahoma Example." *Pacific Historical Review* 53 (February 1984): 39-58.

Wells, Carol. "Agnes Morris." *Louisiana History* 27 (Summer 1986): 261-272.

Williams-Burns, Winona. "Jane Ellen McAllister (b. 1899): Pioneer for Excellence in Teacher Education." *Journal of Negro Education* (Summer 1982): 342-357.

Williamson, Noeline. "The Employment of Female Teachers in the Small Bush Schools of New South Wales, 1880-1890: A Case of Stay Bushed or Stay Home." *Labour History* 43 (November 1982): 1-12.

You, Heng. "Alice M. Carpenter and the Ming Sum School for the Blind." *American Presbyterians* 68 (Winter 1990): 259-268.

# ETHNICITY

## Asian

Baum, Dale. "Woman Suffrage and the 'Chinese Question': The Limits of Radical Republicanism in Massachusetts, 1865-1876." *New England Quarterly* 56 (March 1983): 60-77.

Beesley, David. "From Chinese to Chinese American: Chinese Women and Families in a Sierra Nevada County." *California History* 67 (September 1988): 168-179.

Chacon, Ramon D. "The Beginning of Racial Segregation: The Chinese in West Fresno and Chinatown's Role as Red Light District, 1870s-1920s." *Southern California Quarterly* 70 (Winter 1988): 371-398.

Chai, Alice Yun. "Freed from the Elders but Locked into Labor: Korean Immigrant Women in Hawaii." *Women's Studies* 13, no. 3 (1987): 223-234.

Glenn, Evelyn Nakano. "The Dialectics of Wage Work: Japanese-American Women and Domestic Service, 1905-1940." *Feminist Studies* 6 (Fall 1980): 434-471.

-----. "Occupational Ghettoization: Japanese-American Women and Domestic Service, 1905-1970." *Ethnicity* 8 (December 1981): 352-386.

Gunson, Niel. "Sacred Women Chiefs and Female 'Headmen' in Polynesian History." *Journal of Pacific History* 22 (July 1987): 139-173.

Hemminger, Carol. "Little Manila: The Filipino in Stockton Prior to World War II, Part One." *Pacific Historian* 24 (Spring 1980): 21-34.

-----. "Little Manila: The Filipino in Stockton Prior to World War II, Part Two." *Pacific Historian* 24 (Summer 1980): 207-220.

Ichioka, Yuji. "*Amerika Nadeshiko*: Japanese Immigrant Women in the United States, 1900-1924." *Pacific Historical Review* 49 (May 1980): 339-357.

Lee, Mary Paik, and Sicheng Chan, eds. "A Korean-Californian Girlhood." *California History* 67, no. 1 (1988): 42-55.

Li, Peter S. "Immigration Laws and Family Patterns: Some Demographic Changes Among Chinese Families in Canada, 1885-1971." *Canadian Ethnic Studies/Etudes Ethniques Au Canada* 12, no. 1 (1980): 58-73.

Lim, Shirley Geok-lin. "Japanese American Women's Life Stories: Maternality in

Monica Sone's *Nisei Daughter* and Joy Kogawa's *Obasan." Feminist Studies* 16 (Summer 1990): 289-312.

Ling, S. "The Mountain Movers, Asian-American Women's Movement in Los Angeles." *Amerasia Journal* 15 (Spring 1989): 51-68.

Mathes, Valerie Sherer. "Annie E. K. Bidwell: Chico's Benefactress." *California History* 68 (Spring/Summer 1989): 14-25.

Matsumoto, Valerie. "Japanese American Women During World War II." *Frontiers* 8, no. 1 (1984): 6-14.

Nakano, Mei. "Japanese American Women: Three Generations." *History News* 45 (March/April 1990): 10-13.

Pascoe, Peggy. "Gender Systems in Conflict: The Marriages of Mission-Educated Chinese American Women, 1874-1939." *Journal of Social History* 22 (Summer 1989): 631-652.

Peffer, George Anthony. "Forbidden Families: Emigration Experiences of Chinese Women under the Page Law, 1875-1882." *Journal of American Ethnic History* 6 (Fall 1986): 28-46.

Shover, Michele. "Chico Women: Nemesis of a Rural Town's Anti-Chinese Campaigns, 1876-1888." *California History* 67 (December 1988): 228-243.

-----. "The Methodist Women and Molly White: A Chico Morality Tale." *Californians* 7 (September/October 1989): 26-31.

Tonai, Rosalyn. "Strength & Diversity: Japanese American Women 1885-1990." *History News* 45 (March/April 1990): 6-8.

## European

Birnbaum, Lucia Chiavola. "Earthmothers, Godmothers, & Radicals: The Inheritance of Sicilian-American Women." *Marxist Perspectives* 3 (Spring 1980): 128-141.

Bunting, Anne. "The American Molly Childers and the Irish Question." *Eire-Ireland* 23 (Summer 1988): 88-103.

Chapin, Helen Geracimos. "From Sparta to Spencer Street: Greek Women in Hawaii." *Hawaiian Journal of History* 13 (1979): 136-156.

Cohen, Miriam. "Changing Education Strategies Among Immigrant Generations: New York Italians in Comparative Perspective." *Journal of Social History* 15 (Spring 1982): 443-466.

Curtin, Emma. "Two British Gentlewomen." *Alberta History* 38 (Autumn 1990): 10-16.

Fielder, Mari Kathleen. "Chauncey Olcott: Irish-American Mother-Love, Romance and Nationalism." *Eire-Ireland* 22 (Summer 1987): 4-26.

-----. "Fatal Attraction: Irish-Jewish Romance in Early Film and Drama." *Eire-Ireland* 20 (Fall 1985): 6-18.

Fitzpatrick, David. "'A Share of the Honeycomb': Education, Emigration and Irishwomen." *Continuity and Change* 1, no. 2 (1986): 217-234.

Harney, Robert F. "Men Without Women: Italian Migrants in Canada, 1885-1930." *Canadian Ethnic Studies/Etudes Ethniques Au Canada* 11, no. 1

(1979): 29-47.

Harper, Jared V. "Marriage as an Adaptive Strategy Among Irish Travelers in South Carolina." *Southern Studies* 20 (Summer 1981): 174-184.

Iacovetta, Franca. "Trying to Make Ends Meet: An Historical Look at Italian Immigrant Women, the State and Family Survival Strategies in Post-War Toronto." *Canadian Woman Studies/Les cahiers de la femme* 8 (Summer 1987): 6-11.

Johnson, Loretta T. "Charivari/Shivaree: A European Folk Ritual on the American Plains." *Journal of Interdisciplinary History* 20 (Winter 1990): 371-388.

Meagher, Timothy J. "Sweet Good Mothers and Young Women out in the World: The Roles of Irish American Women in Late Nineteenth and Early Twentieth Century Worcester, Massachusetts." *U.S. Catholic Historian* 5 (Summer/Fall 1986): 325-344.

Mormino, Gary R., and George E. Pozzetta. "Immigrant Women in Tampa: The Italian Experience, 1890-1930." *Florida History Quarterly* (January 1983): 296-312.

-----. "Immigrant Women in Tampa: The Italian Experience, 1890-1930." *OAH Magazine of History* 4 (Spring 1990): 19-28.

Pivato, Joseph. "Italian-Canadian Women Writers Recall History." *Canadian Ethnic Studies/Etudes Ethniques Au Canada* 18, no. 1 (1986): 79-88.

Rainwater, Lee. "Mothers' Contribution to the Family Money Economy in Europe and the United States." *Journal of Family History* 4 (Summer 1979): 198-210.

Riley, Glenda. "From Ireland to Illinois: The Life of Helen Rose Hall." *Illinois Historical Journal* 81 (Autumn 1988): 162-180.

Scarpaci, J. Vincenza. "La Contadina: The Plaything of the Middle Class Woman Historian." *Journal of Ethnic Studies* 9 (Summer 1981): 21-38.

Sullivan, Mary Louise. "Mother Cabrini: Missionary to Italian Immigrants." *U.S. Catholic Historian* 6, no. 4 (1987): 265-279.

Vecchio, Diane C. "Italian Women in Industry: The Shoeworkers of Endicott, New York, 1914-1935." *Journal of American Ethnic History* 8 (Spring 1989): 60-86.

## General

Benmayor, Rina. "For Every Story There Is Another Story Which Stands Before It." *Oral History Review* 16 (Fall 1988): 1-14.

Bravo, Anna. "Solidarity and Loneliness: Piedmontese Peasant Women at the Turn of the Century." *International Journal of Oral History* 3 (June 1982): 76-91.

Burton, Antoinette M. "The White Woman's Burden: British Feminists and the Indian Woman, 1865-1915." *Women's Studies International Forum* 13, no. 4 (1990): 295-308.

Candelaria, Cordelia. "La Malinche, Feminist Prototype." *Frontiers* 5, no. 2 (1980): 1-6.

Coburn, Carol K. "Ethnicity, Religion, and Gender: The Women of Block, Kansas, 1868-1940." *Great Plains Quarterly* 8 (Fall 1988): 222-232.

D'Andrea, Vaneeta Marie. "Ethnic Women: A Critique of Literature, 1971-1981."

*Ethnic and Racial Studies* 9 (1986): 235-246.

Dill, Bonnie Thornton. "Our Mothers' Grief: Racial Ethnic Women and the Maintenance of Families." *Journal of Family History* 13, no. 4 (1988): 415-431.

Hardaway, Roger D. "Prohibiting Interracial Marriages: Miscegenation Laws in Wyoming." *Annals of Wyoming* 52 (Spring 1980): 55-60.

Hurtado, Albert L. "'Hardly a Farm House--A Kitchen without Them': Indian and White Households on the California Borderland Frontier in 1860." *Western Historical Quarterly* 13 (July 1982): 245-270.

Indra, Doreen Marie. "The Invisible Mosaic: Women, Ethnicity and the Vancouver Press, 1900-1976." *Canadian Ethnic Studies/Etudes Ethniques Au Canada* 13 (1981): 63-74.

Juarbe, Ana. "Anastasia's Story: A Window Into the Past, A Bridge to the Future." *Oral History Review* 16 (Fall 1988): 15-22.

Kellogg, Susan. "Exploring Diversity in Middle-Class Families: The Symbolism of American Ethnic Identity." *Social Science History* 14 (Spring 1990): 27-42.

Koonz, Claudia. "A Response to Eve Rosenhaft." *Radical History Review* 43 (Winter 1989): 81-85.

Kraut, Alan M. "'My Daughter Tells Me You're Ethnic.'" *Journal of American Ethnic History* 7 (Fall 1987): 74-82.

Lambert, Ronald D., and James E. Curtis. "Quebecois and English Canadian Opposition to Racial and Religious Intermarriage, 1968-1983." *Canadian Ethnic Studies/Etudes Ethniques Au Canada* 16, no. 2 (1984): 30-46.

Lindgren, H. Elaine. "Ethnic Women Homesteading on the Plains of North Dakota." *Great Plains Quarterly* 9 (Summer 1989): 157-173.

Ling, Amy. "Revelation and Mask: Autobiographies of the Eaton Sisters." *Auto/Biography Studies* 3 (Summer 1987): 46-52.

Mabee, Carleton. "Margaret Mead and a 'Pilot Experiment' in Progressive and Interracial Education: The Downtown Community School." *New York History* 65 (January 1984): 5-31.

-----. "Margaret Mead's Approach to Controversial Public Issues: Racial Boycotts in the AAAS." *The Historian* 48 (February 1986): 191-208.

Miller, Sally M. "Different Accents of Labor." *Labor's Heritage* 2 (July 1990): 62-75.

Nicks, Trudy. "Mary Anne's Dilemma: The Ethnohistory of an Ambivalent Identity." *Canadian Ethnic Studies/Etudes Ethniques Au Canada* 17, no. 2 (1985): 103-114.

Norkunas, Martha K. "Women, Work and Ethnic Identity: Personal Narratives and the Ethnic Enclaves in the Textile City of Lowell, Massachusetts." *Journal of Ethnic Studies* 15 (Fall 1987): 27-48.

Proefriedt, William A. "The Education of Mary Antin." *Journal of Ethnic Studies* 17 (Winter 1990): 81-100.

Scheffel, David. "From Polygamy to Cousin Marriage? Acculturation and Marriage in 19th Century Labrador Inuit Society." *Etudes inuit/Inuit Studies* 8 (1985): 61-76.

Shadd, Adrienne. "Three Hundred Years of Black Women in Canadian History: Circa 1700 to 1980." *Tiger Lily* 1, no. 2 (1987).

Thompson, Margaret Susan. "Sisterhood and Power: Class, Culture, and Ethnicity in the American Convent." *Colby Library Quarterly* 25 (September 1989): 149-175.

Waldowski, Paula. "Alice Brown Davis: A Leader of Her People." *Chronicles of Oklahoma* 58 (Winter 1980-81): 455-463.

White, W. Thomas. "Race, Ethnicity, and Gender in the Railroad Work Force: The Case of the Far Northwest, 1883-1918." *Western Historical Quarterly* 16 (July 1985): 265-284.

## Immigrants

Bannan, H. M. "Warrior Women: Immigrant Mothers in the Works of Their Daughters." *Women's Studies* 6 (Winter 1979): 165-177.

Barber, Marilyn. "The Women Ontario Welcomed: Immigrant Domestics for Ontario Homes, 1870-1930." *Ontario History* 72 (September 1980): 148-172.

Bergland, Betty. "Immigrant History and the Gendered Subject: A Review Essay." *Ethnic Forum* 8, no. 2 (1988): 24-39.

Bloom, Florence Teicher. "Struggling and Surviving: The Life Style of European Immigrant Breadwinning Mothers in American Industrial Cities, 1900-1930." *Women's Studies* 8, no. 6 (1985): 609-620.

Borst, Charlotte G. "Wisconsin's Midwives as Working Women: Immigrant Midwives and the Limits of a Traditional Occupation, 1870-1920." *Journal of American Ethnic History* 8 (Spring 1989): 24-59.

Browner, Carole H., and Dixie L. King, eds. "Cross-Cultural Perspectives on Women and Immigration." *Women's Studies* 17, nos. 1-2 (1989): 49-70.

Declercq, Eugene and Richard Lacroix. "The Immigrant Midwives of Lawrence: The Conflict Between Law and Culture in Early Twentieth-Century Massachusetts." *Bulletin of the History of Medicine* 59 (Summer 1985): 232-246.

-----. "The Nature and Style of Practice of Immigrant Midwives in Early Twentieth Century Massachusetts." *Journal of Social History* 19 (Fall 1985): 113-130.

Dodyk, Delight, and Steven Golin. "The Paterson Silk Strike: Primary Materials for Studying about Immigrants, Women, and Labor." *Social Studies* 78, no. 5 (1987): 206-209.

Edwards, Thomas S. "Strangers in a Strange Land: The Frontier Letters of John and Anna Graves." *Hayes Historical Journal* 6 (Summer 1987): 16-28.

Ewen, Elizabeth. "City Lights: Immigrant Women and the Rise of the Movies." *Signs* 5 (Spring 1980): 545-566.

Fitzpatrick, David. "'A Share of the Honeycomb': Education, Emigration and Irishwomen." *Continuity and Change* 1, no. 2 (1986): 217-234.

Gabaccia, Donna. "*The Transplanted*: Women and Family in Immigrant America." *Social Science History* 12 (Fall 1988): 243-254.

Gannage, Charlene. "Haven or Heartache: Immigrant Women Workers in the Household." *Anthropologica* 26, no. 2 (1984): 217-254.

Grubb, Farley. "Servant Auction Records and Immigration into the Delaware Valley, 1745-1831: The Proportion of Females Among Immigrant Servants." *Proceedings of the American Philosophical Society* 133 (June 1989): 154-169.

Hyman, Paula E. "Immigrant Women and Consumer Protest: The New York City Kosher Meat Boycott of 1902." *American Jewish History* 70 (September 1980): 91-105.

Jacoby, Susan. "World of Our Mothers: Immigrant Women, Immigrant Daughters." *Present Tense* 6, no. 3 (1979): 48-51.

Kessner, Thomas, and Betty Boyd Caroli. "New Immigrant Women at Work: Italians and Jews in New York City, 1880-1905." *Journal of Ethnic Studies* 5 (Winter 1978): 19-32.

King, M., and S. Ruggles. "American Immigration, Fertility and Race Suicide at the Turn of the Century." *Journal of Interdisciplinary History* 20 (Winter 1990): 347-370.

Li, Peter S. "Immigration Laws and Family Patterns: Some Demographic Changes Among Chinese Families in Canada, 1885-1971." *Canadian Ethnic Studies/Etudes Ethniques Au Canada* 12, no.1 (1980): 58-73.

Lissak, Rivka. "Myth and Reality: The Pattern of Relationship Between the Hull House Circle and the 'New Immigrants' on Chicago's West Side, 1890-1919." *Journal of American Ethnic History* 2 (Spring 1983): 21-50.

Miedema, Baukje, and Nancy Mason-Clark. "Second Class Status: An Analysis of the Lived Experiences of Immmigrant Women in Fredericton." *Canadian Ethnic Studies/Revue Ethnique Au Canada* 21 (1989): 63-73.

Miller, Sally M. "Other Socialists: Native-Born and Immigrant Women in the Socialist Party of America, 1901-1917." *Labor History* 24 (Winter 1983): 84-102.

Parr, Joy. "The Skilled Emigrant and Her Kin: Gender, Culture, and Labour Recruitment." *Canadian Historical Review* 68 (December 1987): 529-551.

Petterson, Lucille, ed. and trans. "Ephraim Is My Home Now: Letters of Anna and Anders Petterson, 1884-1889 (Part I)." *Wisconsin Magazine of History* 69 (Spring 1986): 187-210.

-----. "Ephraim Is My Home Now: Letters of Anna and Anders Petterson, 1884-1889 (Part II)." *Wisconsin Magazine of History* 69 (Summer 1986): 284-304.

-----. "Ephraim Is My Home Now: Letters of Anna and Anders Petterson, 1884-1889 (Part III)." *Wisconsin Magazine of History* 70 (Autumn 1986): 32-56.

-----. "Ephraim Is My Home Now: Letters of Anna and Anders Petterson, 1884-1889 (Part IV)." *Wisconsin Magazine of History* 70 (Winter 1986/87): 107-131.

Pickle, Linda Schelbitzki. "Women of the Saxon Immigration and Their Church." *Concordia Historical Institute Quarterly* 57 (Winter 1984): 146-161.

Prokop, Manfred. "Canadianization of Immigrant Children: Role of the

Elementary School in Alberta, 1900-1930." *Alberta History* 37 (Spring 1989): 1-10.

Rothbart, Ron. "'Homes Are What Any Strike Is About': Immigrant Labor and the Family Wage." *Journal of Social History* 23 (Winter 1989): 267-284.

Rury, John. "Urban Structure and School Participation: Immigrant Women in 1900." *Social Science History* 8 (Summer 1984): 219-242.

Salloum, Habeeb. "Reminiscences: The Urbanization of an Arab Homesteading Family." *Saskatchewan History* 42 (Spring 1989): 79-83.

Schenken, Suzanne O'Dea. "The Immigrants' Advocate: Mary Treglia and the Sioux City Community House, 1921-1959." *Annals of Iowa* 50 (Fall 1989/Winter 1990): 181-213.

Sinke, Suzanne. "A Historiography of Immigrant Women in the Nineteenth and Early Twentieth Centuries." *Ethnic Forum* 9, no. 1/2 (1989): 122-145.

Williams, Harvey. "Social Isolation and the Elderly Immigrant Woman." *Pacific Historian* 26 (Summer 1982): 15-23.

## Jewish

Abrams, Jeanne. "'For a Child's Sake': The Denver Sheltering Home for Jewish Children in the Progressive Era." *American Jewish History* 79 (Winter 1989-1990): 181-202.

-----. "Unsere Leit, ('Our People'): Anna Hillkowitz and the Development of the East European Jewish Woman Professional in America." *American Jewish Archives* 37 (November 1985): 275-278.

Arnstein, Flora J., and Susan B. Park. "The Godchaux Sisters." *Western States Jewish History* 15 (October 1982): 40-47.

Berrol, Selma. "Class or Ethnicity: The Americanized German Jewish Woman and Her Middle Class Sisters in 1895." *Jewish Social Studies* 47 (Winter 1985): 21-32.

-----. "When Uptown Met Downtown: Julia Richman's Work in the Jewish Community of New York, 1880-1912." *American Jewish History* 70 (September 1980): 35-51.

Boas, Jacob. "Etty Hillesum: From Amsterdam to Auschwitz." *Lilith* no. 23 (Spring 1989): 24-32.

Clar, Reva. "First Jewish Woman Physician of Los Angeles." *Western States Jewish Historical Quarterly* 14 (October 1981): 66-75.

-----. "Women in the Weekly *Gleaner*, Part I." *Western States Jewish History* 17 (July 1985): 333-346.

Clar, Reva, and William M. Kramer. "The Girl Rabbi of the Golden West: The Adventurous Life of Ray Frank in Nevada, California, and the Northwest, Part I." *Western States Jewish History* 18 (January 1986): 99-111.

-----. "The Girl Rabbi of the Golden West: The Adventurous Life of Ray Frank in Nevada, California, and the Northwest, Part II." *Western States Jewish History* 18 (April 1986): 223-236.

Cohn, Josephine. "Communal Life of San Francisco: Jewish Women in 1908."

*Western States Jewish History* 20 (October 1987): 15-36.

Drucker, Sally Ann. "'It Doesn't Say So in Mother's Prayerbook': Autobiographies in English by Immigrant Jewish Women." *American Jewish History* 79 (Autumn 1989): 55-71.

Ellman, Yisrael. "Intermarriage in the United States: A Comparative Study of Jews and Other Ethnic Groups." *Jewish Social Studies* 49 (Winter 1987): 1-26.

Feldman, Yael S. "Gender In/Difference in Contemporary Hebrew Fictional Autobiographies." *Biography* 11 (Summer 1988): 189-209.

Fielder, Mari Kathleen. "Fatal Attraction: Irish-Jewish Romance in Early Film and Drama." *Eire-Ireland* 20 (Fall 1985): 6-18.

"The First Jewish Wedding in the Territory of Arizona." *Western States Jewish History* 20, no. 2 (1988): 126-128.

Fridkis, Ari Lloyd. "Desertion in the American Jewish Immigrant Family: The Work of the National Desertion Bureau in Cooperation with the Industrial Removal Office." *American Jewish History* 71 (December 1981): 285-299.

Friedman, Reena Sigman. "'Send Me My Husband Who Is in New York City': Husband Desertion in the American Jewish Immigrant Community, 1900-1926." *Jewish Social Studies* 44 (Winter 1982): 1-18.

Golomb, Deborah Grand. "The 1893 Congress of Jewish Women: Evolution or Revolution in American Jewish Women's History." *American Jewish History* 70 (September 1980): 52-67.

Hagy, James W. "Her 'Scandalous Behavior': A Jewish Divorce in Charleston, South Carolina, 1788." *American Jewish Archives* 41 (Fall/Winter 1989): 185-198.

Hornbein, Marjorie. "Frances Jacobs: Denver's Mother of Charities." *Western States Jewish History* 15 (January 1983): 131-145.

Hurwitz, Henry. "A Mother Remembered." *American Jewish History* 70 (September 1980): 5-22.

Hyman, Paula E. "Immigrant Women and Consumer Protest: The New York City Kosher Meat Boycott of 1902." *American Jewish History* 70 (September 1980): 91-105.

Jacobs, Neil G. "Northeastern Yiddish Gender-Switch: Abstracting Dialect Features Regionally." *Diachronica: International Journal of Historical Linguistics* 7 (Spring 1990): 69-100.

Kaplan, Marion. "Prostitution, Morality Crusades and Feminism: German-Jewish Feminists and the Campaign Against White Slavery." *Women's Studies* 5, no. 6 (1982): 619-628.

Karsh, Audrey R. "Mothers and Daughters of Old San Diego." *Western States Jewish History* 19 (April 1987): 264-270.

Kramer, William M., and Norton B. Stern. "Birdie Stodel: Los Angeles Patriot." *Western States Jewish History* 20, no. 2 (1988): 109-116.

-----. "Hattie Sloss: Cultural Leader and Jewish Activist of Modern San Francisco." *Western States Jewish Historical Quarterly* 14 (April 1982): 207-215.

-----. "An Issue of Jewish Marriage and Divorce in Early San Francisco." *Western*

*States Jewish History* 21 (October 1988): 46-57.

-----. "A Woman who Pioneered Modern Fundraising in the West." *Western States Jewish History* 19 (July 1987): 335-345.

Lerner, Elinor. "Jewish Involvement in the New York City Woman Suffrage Movement." *American Jewish History* 70 (June 1981): 442-461.

Lipman, Rowena. "The Issac and Rebecca Harris Family of San Francisco." *Western States Jewish History* 23 (October 1990): 15-19.

Marks, Lara. "'Dear Old Mother Levy's': The Jewish Maternity Home and Sick Room Help Society 1895-1939." *Social History of Medicine* 3 (April 1990): 61-88.

Marks, Lynne. "Kale Meydelach or Shulamith Girls: Cultural Change and Continuity Among Jewish Parents and Daughters--A Case Study of Toronto's Harbord Collegiate Institute in the 1920s." *Canadian Woman Studies/Les cahiers de la femme* 7 (Fall 1986): 85-89.

Miller, Sally M. "From Sweatshop Worker to Labor Leader: Theresa Malkiel, a Case Study." *American Jewish History* 68 (December 1978): 189-205.

Mirelman, Victor A. "The Jewish Community versus Crime: The Case of White Slavery in Buenos Aires." *Jewish Social Studies* 46 (Spring 1984): 145-168.

Moore, Deborah Dash. "Reconsidering the Rosenbergs: Symbol and Substance in Second Generation Jewish Consciousness." *Journal of American Ethnic History* 8 (Fall 1988): 21-37.

Palmquist, Peter E., compiler. "Elizabeth Fleischmann-Aschheim, Pioneer X-ray Photographer." *Western States Jewish History* 23 (October 1990): 35-45.

Penkower, Monty N. "Eleanor Roosevelt and the Plight of World Jewry." *Jewish Social Studies* 49, no. 2 (1987): 125-136.

Porter, Jack Nusan. "Rosa Sonneschein and the American Jewess Revisited: New Historical Information on Early American Zionist and Jewish Feminist." *American Jewish Archives* 32 (November 1980): 125-131.

Pratt, Norma Fain. "Culture and Radical Politics: Yiddish Women Writers, 1890-1940." *American Jewish History* 70, no. 1 (1980): 68-90.

Raphael, Marc Lee. "From Marjorie to Tevya: The Image of the Jews in American Popular Literature, Theatre and Comedy, 1955-1965." *American Jewish History* 74 (September 1984): 66-72.

Rochlin, Harriet. "Riding High: Annie Oakley's Jewish Contemporaries--Was the West Liberating for Jewish Women." *Lilith* 14 (Fall 1985/Winter 1986): 14-18.

Rudd, Hynda. "The Unsinkable Anna Marks." *Western States Jewish Historical Quarterly* 10 ((April 1978): 234-237.

Schiff, Ellen. "What Kind of Way Is That for Nice Jewish Girls to Act?: Images of Jewish Women in Modern American Drama." *American Jewish History* 70 (September 1980): 106-118.

Schnur, Susan. "Badges of Shame." *Lilith* 14 (Fall 1989): 14-16.

Schoen, Carol. "Anzia Yezierska: New Light on the 'Sweatshop Cinderella.'" *Melus* 7 (1980): 3-11.

Seller, Maxine S. "Defining Socialist Womanhood: The Women's Page of the

*Jewish Daily Forward* in 1919." *American Jewish History* 76 (June 1987): 416-438.

-----. "World of Our Mothers: The Women's Page of the Jewish Daily Forward." *Journal of Ethnic Studies* 16, no. 2 (1988): 95-118.

Shoub, Myra Nelson. "Jewish Women's History: Development of a Critical Methodology." *Conservative Judaism* (January 1982): 33-46.

Sinkoff, Nancy B. "Educating for 'Proper' Jewish Womanhood: A Case Study in Domesticity and Vocational Training, 1897-1926." *American Jewish History* 77, no. 4 (1988): 572-599.

Sochen, June. "Jewish Women as Volunteer Activists." *American Jewish History* 70 (September 1980): 23-34.

-----. "Some Observations on the Role of American Jewish Women as Communal Volunteers." *American Jewish History* 70 (September 1980): 23-34.

Stern, Norton B. "The First Triplets Born in the West--1867." *Western States Jewish History* 19 (July 1987): 299-305.

-----. "Selma Gruenberg Lewis and Selma, California." *Western States Jewish History* 18 (October 1985): 22-29.

Stern, Norton B., and William M. Kramer. "The Phosphorescent Jewish Bride: San Francisco's Famous Murder Case." *Western States Jewish History* 13 (October 1980): 63-72.

Toll, William. "The Female Life Cycle and the Measure of Jewish Social Change: Portland, Oregon, 1880-1930." *American Jewish History* 72 (March 1983): 309-332.

-----. "A Quiet Revolution: Jewish Women's Clubs and the Widening Female Sphere, 1870-1920." *American Jewish Archives* 41 (Spring/Summer 1989): 7-26.

Tuerk, Richard. "Assimilation in Jewish-American Autobiography: Mary Antin and Ludwig Lewisohn." *Auto/Biography Studies* 3 (Summer 1987): 26-33.

Turitz, Leo E. "Amelia Greenwald (1886-1966): The Jewish Florence Nightingale." *American Jewish Archives* 37 (November 1985): 291-292.

Weinberg, Sydney Stahl. "Jewish Mothers and Immigrant Daughters: Positive and Negative Role Models." *Journal of American Ethnic History* 6 (Spring 1987): 39-55.

-----. "Longing to Learn: The Education of Jewish Immigrant Women in New York City, 1900-1934." *Journal of American Ethnic History* 8 (Spring 1989): 108-126.

Weissler, Chava. "'For Women and for Men Who Are like Women': The Construction of Gender in Yiddish Devotional Literature." *Journal of Feminist Studies in Religion* 5 (Fall 1989): 7-24.

Wenger, Beth S. "Jewish Women and Voluntarism: Beyond the Myth of Enablers." *American Jewish History* 79 (Autumn 1989): 16-36.

-----. "Jewish Women of the Club: The Changing Public Role of Atlanta's Jewish Women (1870-1930)." *American Jewish History* 76 (March 1987): 311-333.

-----. "Radical Politics in a Reactionary Age: The Unmaking of Rosika

Schwimmer, 1914-1930." *Journal of Women's History* 2 (Fall 1990): 66-99.

Wooden, Wayne S. "Edith Green: Television's Early Cook, 1949-1954." *Western States Jewish History* 19 (July 1987): 306-314.

Zandy, Janet. "Radical Jewish Women: Reclaiming Our Legacy." *Lilith* 22 (Winter 1989): 8-13.

Zmora, Nurith. "A Rediscovery of the Asylum: The Hebrew Orphan Asylum through the Lives of Its First Fifty Orphans." *American Jewish History* 77 (March 1988): 476-481.

## Latin American

Alvarez, Celia. "*El Hilo Que Nos Une*! The Thread That Binds Us: Becoming a Puerto Rican Woman." *Oral History Review* 16 (Fall 1988): 29-40.

Berge, Carol. "Dark Radiance: The Ancient Art of Maria Martinez, Legendary Matriarch of the Master Potters of San Ildefonso." *Art & Antiques* (September 1988): 104-107, 134.

Broyles-Gonzalez, Yolanda. "The Living Legacy of Chicana Performers: Preserving History through Oral Testimony." *Frontiers* 11, no. 1 (1990): 46-52.

Castaneda, Antonia I. "Gender, Race, and Culture: Spanish-Mexican Women in the Historiography of Frontier California." *Frontiers* 11, no. 1 (1990): 8-20.

Castillo-Speed, Lillian. "Chicana Studies: A Selected List of Materials since 1980." *Frontiers* 11, no. 1 (1990): 66-84.

Duron, Clementina. "Mexican Women and Labor Conflict in Los Angeles: The ILGWU Dressmakers' Strike of 1933." *Aztlan* (Spring 1984): 145-161.

Erazo, Blanca Vazquez. "The Stories Our Mothers Tell: Projections-of-Self in the Stories of Puerto Rican Garment Workers." *Oral History Review* 16 (Fall 1988): 23-28.

Fiol-Matta, Liza. "Naming Our World, Writing Our History: The Voices of Hispanic Feminist Poets." *Women's Studies Quarterly* 16 (Fall/Winter 1988): 68-80.

Garcia, Alma M. "The Development of Chicana Feminist Discourse, 1970-1980." *Gender & Society* 3 (June 1989): 217-238.

Garcia, Mario T. "The Chicana in American History: The Mexican Women of El Paso, 1880-1920--A Case Study." *Pacific Historical Review* 49 (May 1980): 315-337.

Gil, Carlos B. "Lydia Mendoza: Houstonian and First Lady of Mexican American Song." *Houston Review* (Summer 1981): 250-260.

Herrera-Sobek, Maria. "The Discourse of Love and *Despecho*: Representations of Women in the Chicano *Decima*." *Aztlan: International Journal of Chicano Studies Research* 18 (Spring 1987): 69-82.

-----. "The Treacherous Woman Archetype: A Structuring Agent in the Corrido." *Aztlan: International Journal of Chicano Studies Research* 13 (Spring/Fall 1982): 135-148.

Hewitt, Nancy A. "Women in Ybor City: An Interview with a Woman Cigar

Worker." *Tampa Bay History* 7 (Fall/Winter 1985): 161-165.

Jensen, Joan M. "Canning Comes to New Mexico, Women and the Agricultural Extension Service, 1914-1919." *New Mexico Historical Review* 57 (October 1982): 361-386.

-----. "Crossing Ethnic Barriers in the Southwest: Women's Agricultural Extension Education, 1914-1940." *Agricultural History* 60 (Spring 1986): 169-181.

Lecompte, Janet. "The Independent Women of Hispanic New Mexico, 1821-1846." *Western Historical Quarterly* 12 (January 1981): 17-36.

Loeb, Catherine. "La Chicana: A Bibliographic Survey." *Frontiers* 5 (Summer 1980): 59-74.

Lothrop, Gloria Ricci. "Introducing Seven Women of the Hispanic Frontier: A Series." *Californians* 8 (May/June 1990): 14.

Maiz, Magdalena, and Luis H. Pena. "Between Lines: Construction the Political Self." *Auto/Biography Studies* 3 (Summer 1988): 23-36.

Miller, Darlis A. "Cross-Cultural Marriages in the Southwest: The New Mexico Experience, 1846-1900." *New Mexico Historical Review* 57 (October 1982): 335-360.

Mindiola, Tatcho. "The Cost of Being a Mexican Female Worker in the 1970 Houston Labor Market." *Aztlan: International Journal of Chicano Studies Research* 11 (Fall 1980): 231-248.

Miranda, Gloria E. "*Gente de Razon* Marriage Patterns in Spanish and Mexican California: A Case Study of Santa Barbara and Los Angeles." *Southern California Quarterly* 63 (Spring 1981): 1-22.

-----. "Hispano-Mexican Childrearing Practices in Pre-American Santa Barbara." *Southern California Quarterly* 65 (Winter 1983): 307-320.

Monray, Douglas. "'Our Children Get So Different Here': Film, Fashion, Popular Culture and the Process of Cultural Syncretization in Mexican Los Angeles, 1900-1935." *Aztlan: International Journal of Chicano Studies Research* 19 (1988/1990): 79-108.

Myres, Sandra L. "Mexican Americans and Westering Anglos: A Feminine Perspective." *New Mexico Historical Review* 57 (October 1982): 317-334.

Pena, Devon Gerardo. "Las Maquiladoras: Mexican Women and Class Struggle in the Border Industries." *Aztlan: International Journal of Chicano Studies Research* 11 (Fall 1980): 159-230.

Rios, Palmiran. "Export-Oriented Industrialization and the Demand for Female Labor: Puerto Rican Women in the Manufacturing Sector, 1952-1980." *Gender & Society* 4 (September 1990): 321-337.

Rock, Rosalind Z. "'Pido Y Suplico': Women and the Law in Spanish New Mexico." *New Mexico Historical Review* 65 (April 1990): 145-160.

Romero, Mary. "Domestic Service in the Transition from Rural to Urban Life: The Case of La Chicana." *Women's Studies* 13, no. 3 (1987): 199-222.

Rose, Margaret. "'From the Fields to the Picket Line: Huelga Women and the Boycott,' 1965-1975." *Labor History* 31 (Summer 1990): 271-293.

Ruiz, Vicki L. "Texture, Text and Context: New Approaches in Chicano

Historiography." *Mexican Studies/Estudios Mexicanos* 2 (Winter 1986): 145-152.

Safa, Helen. "Female Employment and the Social Reproduction of the Puerto Rican Working Class." *International Migration Review* 18, no. 4 (1984): 1168-1187.

Sanchez Korrol, Virginia. "In Search of Unconventional Women: Histories of Puerto Rican Women in Religious Vocations Before Mid-Century." *Oral History Review* 16 (Fall 1988): 47-64.

-----. "On the Other Side of the Ocean: The Experience of Early Puerto Rican Migrant Women." *Caribbean Review* 7 (January/March 1979): 22-28.

Segura, Denise. "Labor Market Stratification: The Chicana Experience." *Berkeley Journal of Sociology* 29 (1984): 57-91.

Simon, Rita, and Margo Deley. "The Work Experience of Undocumented Mexican Women Migrants in Los Angeles." *International Migration Review* 18, no. 4 (1984): 1212-1229.

Stoller, Marianne L. "The Hispanic Women Artists of New Mexico: Present and Past." *El Palacio* 92 (Summer/Fall 1986): 21-25.

Taylor, Paul S. "Mexican Women in Los Angeles Industry in 1928." *Aztlan: International Journal of Chicano Studies Research* 11 (Spring 1980): 99-132.

Tykal, Jack B. "Taos to St. Louis: The Journey of Maria Rosa Villalpando." *New Mexico Historical Review* 65 (April 1990): 161-174.

Weber, Devra Anne. "*Raiz Fuerte*: Oral History and Mexicana Farmworkers." *Oral History Review* 17 (Fall 1989): 47-62.

Ybarra, Lea. "When Wives Work: The Impact on the Chicano Family." *Journal of Marriage and Family* 44 (February 1982): 169-178.

Zavella, Patricia. "'Abnormal Intimacy': The Varying Networks of Chicana Cannery Workers." *Feminist Studies* 11 (Fall 1985): 541-557.

# EUROPE

## Central Europe

Albisetti, James C. "The Fight for Female Physicians in Imperial Germany." *Central European History* 15 (June 1982): 99-123.

-----. "The Reform of Female Education in Prussia, 1899-1908: A Study in Compromise and Containment." *German Studies Review* 8 (February 1985): 11-42.

Allen, Ann Taylor. "German Radical Feminism and Eugenics, 1900-1918." *German Studies Review* 11 (February 1988): 31-56.

-----. "Mothers of the New Generation: Adele Schreiber, Helene Stocker, and the Evolution of a German Idea of Motherhood, 1900-1914." *Signs* 10 (Spring 1985): 418-438.

Arend, Angelika. "Humor and Irony in Annette Von Droste-Hulshoff's 'Heidebilder' Cycle." *German Quarterly* 63 (Winter 1990): 50-58.

Bernstein, George, and Lottelore Bernstein. "Attitudes toward Women's Education in Germany, 1870-1914." *International Journal of Women's Studies* 2 (September/October 1979): 473-488.

Blum, Stella. "The Idyllic Fashions of the Austro-Hungarian Empire, 1867-1918." *Dress* 6 (1980): 57-70.

Boak, Helen L. "Our Last Hope: Women's Votes for Hitler, A Reappraisal." *German Studies Review* 12 (May 1989): 311-332.

-----. "Women in Weimar Politics." *European History Quarterly* 20 (July 1990): 369-400.

Boas, Jacob. "Etty Hillesum: From Amsterdam to Auschwitz." *Lilith* 14 (Spring 1989): 24-32.

Bock, Gisela. "Racism and Sexism in Nazi Germany: Motherhood, Compulsory Sterilization, and the State." *Signs* 8 (Spring 1983): 400-421.

Bullough, Vern L. "The Fielding H. Garrison Lecture: The Physician and Research into Human Sexual Behavior in Nineteenth-Century Germany." *Bulletin of the History of Medicine* 63 (Summer 1989): 247-267.

Chickering, Roger. "'Casting Their Gaze More Broadly': Women's Patriotic Activism in Imperial Germany." *Past & Present* no. 118 (February 1988): 156-185.

Crew, David F. "German Socialism, the State and Family Policy, 1918-33." *Continuity and Change* 1, no. 2 (1986): 235-264.

Doneson, Judith E. "American History of Anne Frank's Diary." *Holocaust and Genocide Studies* [Great Britain] 2, no. 1 (1987): 149-160.

"East German Feminists: The Lila Manifesto," Lisa DiCaprio, intro. *Feminist Studies* 16 (Fall 1990): 621-634.

Erickson, Brigette, trans. "A Lesbian Execution in Germany, 1721. The Trial Records." *Journal of Homosexuality* 6 (Fall 1980/Winter 1981): 27-40.

Evans, Richard J. "German Social Democracy on Women's Suffrage 1891-1918." *Journal of Contemporary History* 15 (July 1980): 533-558.

Field, Richard Henning. "Lunenburg-German Household Textiles: The Evidence from Lunenburg County Estate Inventories, 1780-1830." *Material History Bulletin* [Canada] no. 24 (1986): 16-23.

Gerhard, Ute. "A Hidden and Complex Heritage: Reflections on the History of Germany's Women's Movements." *Women's Studies* 5, no. 6 (1982): 561-568.

Gravois, Martha. "Military Families in Germany, 1946-1986: Why They Came and Why They Stay." *Parameters* 6 (Winter 1986): 57-67.

Grossman, Atina. "Abortion and Economic Crisis: The 1931 Campaign Against #218 in Germany." *New German Critique* 14 (1978): 119-137.

Harzig, Christiane. "The Role of German Women in the German-American Working Class Movement in Late Nineteenth-Century New York." *Journal of American Ethnic History* 8 (Spring 1989): 108-126.

Hertz, Deborah. "Intermarriage in the Berlin Salons." *Central European History* 16 (December 1983): 303-346.

Holland, Carolsue, and G. R. Garett. "The 'Skirt' of Nessus: Women and the German Opposition to Hitler." *International Journal of Women's Studies* 6 (September/October 1983): 363-381.

Honeycutt, Karen. "Socialism and Feminism in Imperial Germany." *Signs* 5 (Autumn 1979): 30-41.

Imhof, Arthur E. "An Approach to Historical Demography in Germany." *Social History* 4 (May 1979): 345-366.

Jarausch, Konrad H. "Students, Sex and Politics in Imperial Germany." *Journal of Contemporary History* 17 (April 1982): 285-304.

Jennings, Richard. "The Legal Position of Women in Kayseri, A Large Ottoman City, 1590-1630." *International Journal of Women's Studies* 3 (November/December 1980): 559-582.

Kaplan, Marion A. "Jewish Women in Nazi Germany: Daily Life, Daily Struggles, 1933-1939." *Feminist Studies* 16 (Fall 1990): 579-606.

-----. "Prostitution, Morality Crusades and Feminism: German-Jewish Feminists and the Campaign Against White Slavery." *Women's Studies* 5, no. 6 (1982): 619-628.

Kawan, Hildegard, and Barbara Weber. "Reflections on a Theme: The German Women's Movement, Then and Now." *Women's Studies* 4, no. 4 (1981): 421-434.

Kenney, Anne R. "'She Got to Berlin': Virginia Irwin, St. Louis Post-Dispatch War Correspondent." *Missouri Historical Review* 79 (July 1985): 456-479.

King, Lynda A. "The Woman Question and Politics in Austrian Interwar Literature." *German Studies Review* 6 (February 1983): 75-100.

Kintner, Hallie J. "Trends and Regional Differences in Breastfeeding in Germany from 1871 to 1937." *Journal of Family History* 10 (Summer 1985): 163-182.

Kleinman, Ruth. "Social Dynamics at the French Court: The Household of Anne of Austria." *French Historical Studies* 16 (Spring 1990): 517-535.

Knodel, John, and Susan DeVos. "Preferences for the Sex of Offspring and Demographic Behavior in Eighteenth- and Nineteenth-Century Germany: An Examination of Evidence from Village Genealogies." *Journal of Family History* 5 (Summer 1980): 145-166.

Kudlien, Fridolf. "The German Response to the Birth-Rate Problem During the Third Reich." *Continuity and Change* 5, no. 2 (1990): 225-248.

Kuhn, Annette. "Power and Powerlessness: Women after 1945, or the Continuity of the Ideology of Femininity." *German History* 7 (April 1989): 35-46.

Lehmann, Hartmut. "The Persecution of Witches as Restoration to Order: The Case of Germany, 1590s-1650s." *Central Europe History* 21 (June 1988): 107-121.

Lilienthal, Georg. "The Illegitimacy Question in Germany, 1900-1945: Areas of Tension in Social and Population Policy." *Continuity and Change* 5, no. 2 (1990): 249-282.

Lindemann, Mary. "Love for Hire: The Regulation of the Wet-Nursing Business in Eighteenth-Century Hamburg." *Journal of Family History* 6 (Winter 1981): 379-395.

-----. "Maternal Politics: The Principles and Practice of Maternity Care in Eighteenth-Century Hamburg." *Journal of Family History* 9 (Spring 1984): 44-63.

Linton, Derek S. "Between School and Marriage, Workshop and Household: Young Working Women as a Social Problem in Late Imperial Germany." *European History Quarterly* 18 (October 1988): 387-408.

Lovin, Clifford R. "Farm Women in the Third Reich." *Agricultural History* 60 (Summer 1986): 105-123.

Melching, Willem. "'A New Morality': Left-Wing Intellectuals on Sexuality in Weimar Germany." *Journal of Contemporary History* 25 (January 1990): 69-86.

Neuman, R. "Working Class Birth Control in Wilhelmine Germany." *Comparative Studies in Society and History* 20 (1978): 408-428.

Nolan, Mary. "'Housework Made Easy': The Taylorized Housewife in Weimar Germany's Rationalized Economy." *Feminist Studies* 16 (Fall 1990): 549-578.

Obermeier, K. "Afro-German Women: Recording Their Own History." *New German Critique* no. 46 (Winter 1989): 172-180.

Petschauer, Peter. "Eighteenth-Century German Opinions about Education for Women." *Central European History* 19 (September 1986): 262-292.

-----. "Growing Up Female in Eighteenth-Century Germany." *Journal of Psychohistory* 11 (Fall 1983): 167-208.

Quataert, Jean H. "A Source Analysis in German Women's History: Factory Inspectors' Reports and the Shaping of Working Class Lives, 1878-1914." *Central European History* 16 (June 1983): 99-121.

Roper, Lyndal. "Discipline and Respectability: Prostitution and Reformation in Augsburg." *History Workshop* 19 (Spring 1985): 3-28.

-----. "Housework and Livelihood: Towards the *Alltagsgeschichte* of Women." *German History* no. 2 (Summer 1985): 3-9.

-----. "Mothers of Debauchery: Procuresses in Reformation Augsburg." *German History* 6 (April 1988): 1-19.

-----. "Will and Honor: Sex, Words and Power in Augsburg Criminal Trials." *Radical History Review* 43 (Winter 1989): 45-71.

Rosenhaft, Eve. "Inside the Third Reich: What Is the Woman's Story?" *Radical History Review* 43 (Winter 1989): 72-80.

Rupp, Leila J. "Women, Class and Mobilization in Nazi Germany." *Science and Society* 43 (Spring 1979): 51-69.

Schlegel, Katharina. "Mistress and Servant in Nineteenth Century Hamburg." *History Workshop* 15 (Spring 1983): 60-77.

Seider, Reinhard. "'*Vata, derf i aufstehn?*': Childhood Experiences in Viennese Working-Class Families around 1900." *Continuity and Change* 1, no. 1 (1986): 53-88.

Shorter, E. "Women and Jews in a Private Nervous Clinic in Late Nineteenth Century Vienna." *Medical History* 33 (1989): 149-183.

Stark, Gary D. "Pornography, Society, and the Law in Imperial Germany." *Central European History* 14 (September 1981): 200-229.

Stephenson, Jill. "Middle-Class Women and National Socialist 'Service.'" *History* 67 (February 1982): 32-44.

-----. "Women's Labor Service in Nazi Germany." *Central European History* 15

(September 1982): 241-265.

Ulbricht, Otto. "The Debate about Foundling Hospitals in Enlightenment Germany: Infanticide, Illegitimacy, and Infant Mortality Rates." *Central European History* 18 (September/December 1985): 211-256.

Usborne, Cornelie. "Abortion in Weimar Germany--the Debate Amongst the Medical Profession." *Continuity and Change* 5, no. 2 (1990): 199-224.

Wagener, Mary L. "Berta Zuckerkandl: Viennese Journalist and Publicist of Modern Art and Culture." *European Studies Review* 12 (October 1982): 425-444.

-----. "Fashion and Feminism in Fin-de-Siècle Vienna." *Woman's Art Journal* 10 (Fall/Winter 1990): 29-33.

Wegs, J. Robert. "Working Class Respectability: The Viennese Experience." *Journal of Social History* 15 (Summer 1982): 621-636.

Weindling, Paul. "Compulsory Sterilisation in National Socialist Germany." *German History* no. 5 (Autumn 1987): 10-24.

Westphal-Wihl, Sarah. "The Ladies' Tournament: Marriage, Sex, and Honor in Thirteenth-Century Germany." *Signs* 14 (Winter 1989): 371-398.

Wierling, Dorothee. "Women Domestic Servants in Germany at the Turn of the Century." *Oral History* no. 2 (Autumn 1982): 47-57.

Wiesner, Merry E. "Guilds, Male Bonding and Women's Work in Early Modern Germany." *Gender & History* 1 (Summer 1989): 125-137.

Willmot, Louise. "The Debate on the Introduction of an Auxiliary Military Service Law for Women in the Third Reich and Its Consequences, August 1944-April 1945." *German History* no. 2 (Summer 1985): 10-20.

Zucker, Stanley. "German Women and the Revolution of 1848: Kathinka Zitz-Halein and Humania Association." *Central European History* 13 (September 1980): 237-254.

## Eastern Europe

Dygo, M. "The Political Role of the Cult of the Virgin Mary in Teutonic Prussia in the Late 14th Century and the 15th Century." *Journal of Medieval History* 15 (March 1989): 63-80.

Fialova, Ludmila, Zdenek Pavlik, and Pavel Veres. "Fertility Decline in Czechoslovakia During the Last Two Centuries." *Population Studies* 44 (March 1990): 89-106.

Frankel, G. "Notes on the Costume of the Jewish Woman in Eastern Europe." *Journal of Jewish Art* no. 7 (1980): 50-51.

Moskoff, William. "Sex Discrimination, Commuting and the Role of Women in Rumanian Development." *Slavic Review* 37 (September 1978): 440-456.

Pabis-Braunstein, M. "The First Polish Women Pharmacists." *Pharmacy in History* 31, no. 1 (1989): 12-15.

Quataert, Jean H. "The Politics of Rural Industrialization: Class, Gender, and Collective Protest in the Saxon Oberlausitz of the Late Nineteenth Century." *Central European History* 20 (June 1987): 91-124.

-----. "The Shaping of Women's Work in Manufacturing: Guilds, Households, and the State in Central Europe, 1648-1870." *American Historical Review* 90 (December 1985): 1122-1148.

Sandler, Stephanie. "Embodied Words: Gender in Cvetaeva's Reading of Pushkin." *Slavic & East European Review* 34 (Summer 1990): 139-157.

Sklevicky, Lydia. "More Horses Than Women: On the Difficulties of Founding Women's History in Yugoslavia." *Gender & History* 11 (Spring 1989): 68-75.

Stuard, Susan Mosher. "Dowry Inflation and Increments in Wealth in Medieval Ragusa (Dubrovnik)." *Journal of Economic History* 41 (December 1981): 795-812.

Todorova, Maria. "Myth-Making in European Family History: The Zadruga Revisted." *East European Politics and Societies* 4 (Winter 1990): 30-76.

Vasary, Ildiko. "'The Sin of Transdanubia': The One-Child System in Rural Hungary." *Continuity and Change* 4 (December 1989): 429-468.

Vukanovic, T. P. "Witchcraft in the Central Balkans I: Characteristics of Witches." *Folklore* 100, no. 1 (1989): 9-24.

-----. "Witchcraft in the Central Balkans II: Protection Against Witches." *Folklore* 100, no. 2 (1989): 221-236.

Waters, Elizabeth. "Restructuring the 'Woman Question': *Perestroika* and Prostitution." *Feminist Review* no. 33 (Autumn 1989): 3-19.

Wolchick, Sharon L. "Ideology and Equality: The Status of Women in Eastern and Western Europe." *Comparative Political Studies* 13 (January 1981): 445-476.

-----. "The Status of Women in a Socialist Order: Czechoslovakia, 1948-1978." *Slavic Review* 38 (December 1979): 583-602.

Worobec, Christine D. "Temptress or Virgin? The Precarious Sexual Position of Women in Postemancipation Ukrainian Peasant Society." *Slavic Review* 49 (Summer 1990): 227-238.

# France

Aries, Philippe. "Indissoluble Marriage." *Western Society for French History* 9 (October 1981): 26-36.

Benhamou, Reed. "The Verdigris Industry in Eighteenth-Century Languedoc: Women's Work, Women's Art." *French Historical Studies* 16 (Spring 1990): 560-575.

Berenson, Edward. "The Politics of Divorce in France of the Belle Epoque: The Case of Joseph and Henriette Caillaux." *American Historical Review* 93 (February 1988): 31-55.

Blackley, F. D. "Isabella of France, Queen of England 1308-1358 and the Late Medieval Cult of the Dead." *Canadian Journal of History* 15 (April 1980): 23-48.

Bohanan, Donna. "Matrimonial Strategies Among the Nobles of Seventeenth-Century Aix-en-Provence." *Western Society for French History* 11 (November 1983): 122-129.

Bouton, Cynthia A. "Gendered Behavior in Subsistence Riots: The French Flour

War of 1775." *Journal of Social History* 23 (Summer 1990): 735-754.

Boxer, Marilyn J. "'First-Wave' Feminism in Nineteenth-Century France: Class, Family, and Religion." *Women's Studies International Forum* 5, no. 6 (1982): 551-559.

-----. "Protective Legislation and Home Industry: The Marginalization of Women Workers in Late Nineteenth-Early Twentieth-Century France." *Journal of Social History* 20 (Fall 1986): 45-65.

Burke, Janet M. "Through Friendship to Feminism: The Growth in Self Awareness Among Eighteenth-Century Women Freemasons." *Western Society for French History* 14 (November 1986): 187-196.

Burton, June K. "Infanticide in Napoleonic France: The Law, the Medical Profession, and the Murdering Mother." *Western Society for French History* 14 (November 1986): 183.

Cameron, Vivian. "Gender and Power: Images of Women in Late 18th-Century France." *History of European Ideas* 10, no. 3 (1989): 309-332.

Chapco, Ellen J. "Women at Court in Seventeenth-Century France: Madame de La Fayette and the Concept of Honne tête." *Western Society for French History* 11 (November 1983): 122-129.

Clark, Linda L. "A Battle of the Sexes in a Professional Setting: The Introduction of Inspectrices Primaires, 1889-1914." *French Historical Studies* 16 (Spring 1989): 96-125.

-----. "The Socialization of Girls in the Primary Schools of the Third Republic." *Western Society for French History* 8 (October 1980): 437.

Cohen, Elizabeth. "Fond Fathers, Devoted Daughters? Family Sentiment in Seventeenth Century France." *Histoire sociale/Social History* 19 (November 1986): 343-363.

Collins, James B. "The Economic Role of Women in Seventeenth-Century France." *French Historical Studies* 16 (Fall 1989): 436-470.

Colwill, Elizabeth. "Just Another Citoyenne? Marie-Antionette on Trial, 1790-1793." *History Workshop* no. 28 (Autumn 1989): 63-87.

Conner, Susan P. "Politics, Prostitution, and the Pox in Revolutionary Paris, 1789-1799." *Western Society for French History* 14 (November 1986): 183.

-----. "Sexual Politics and Citizenship: Women in Eighteenth-Century France." *Western Society for French History* 10 (October 1982): 264-273.

Dahl, Kathleen. "The Political Activities of Women During the French Revolution." *Western Society for French History* 15 (November 1987): 129.

Darrow, Margaret H. "French Noblewomen and the New Domesticity, 1750-1850." *Feminist Studies* 5 (Spring 1979): 41-65.

-----. "Popular Concepts of Marital Choice in Eighteenth Century France." *Journal of Social History* 19 (Winter 1985): 261-272.

Dauphin, Cecile, Anette Farge, Genevieve Fraisse, et al. "Women's Culture and Women's Power: An Attempt at Historiography." *Journal of Women's History* 1 (Spring 1989): 63-88.

Davis, Natalie Zemon. "Women in the Crafts in Sixteenth-Century Lyon." *Feminist Studies* 8 (Spring 1982): 47-80.

Dekker, Rudolf M., and Lotte C. van de Pol. "Republican Heroines: Cross-Dressing Women in the French Revolutionary Armies." *History of European Idea* 10, no. 3 (1989): 353-364.

Desan, S. "The Role of Women in Religious Riots During the French Revolution." *Eighteenth-Century Studies* 22 (Spring 1989): 451-468.

Desroches, Richard. "Primitivism and Feminism in Utopia." *Western Society for French History* 15 (November 1987): 142.

Diefendorf, Barbara B. "Widowhood and Remarriage in Sixteenth-Century Paris." *Journal of Family History* 7 (Winter 1982): 379-395.

Dock, Terry Smiley. "The Encyclopedists' Woman." *Western Society for French History* 10 (October 1982): 255-263.

Donovan, James M. "Abortion, the Law, and the Juries in France, 1825-1920." *Western Society for French History* 15 (November 1987): 217.

Euvich, Amanda. "Women, Brokerage, and Aristocratic Service: The Case of Marguerite de Selne." *Western Society for French History* 15 (November 1987): 48.

Evans, Richard J. "Feminism & Anticlericalism in France, 1870-1922." *The Historical Journal* 25 (December 1982): 947-950.

Fairchilds, Cissie. "Masters and Servants in Eighteenth Century Toulouse." *Journal of Social History* 12 (Spring 1979): 368-393.

Feigenbaum-Knox, Rena. "Aesthetics and Ethics: A Study of Sexuality in Denis Diderot's Art Criticism." *Western Society for French History* 9 (October 1981): 226-237.

-----. "The Place of Woman in Cabanis' 'Science of Man.'" *Western Society for French History* 10 (October 1982): 298.

Frader, Laura Levine. "Comment on Session: From the Twilight of Patriarchy to Paternalism and Its Discontents in the Nineteenth Century." *Western Society for French History* 11 (November 1983): 282-284.

-----. "Women's Work and Family Labor in the Vineyards of Lower Languedoc: Coursan 1860-1913." *Western Society for French History* 7 (November 1979): 97-98.

Fuchs, Rachel G., and Paul E. Knepper. "Women in the Paris Maternity Hospital: Public Policy in the Nineteenth Century." *Social Science History* 13 (Summer 1989): 187-203.

Fuchs, Rachel G., and Leslie Page Moch. "Pregnant, Single, and Far from Home: Migrant Women in Nineteenth-Century Paris." *American Historical Review* 95 (October 1990): 1007-1031.

Goldstein, Jan. "The Hysteria Diagnosis and the Politics of Anti-Clericalism in the Early Third Republic." *Western Society for French History* 8 (October 1980): 403.

-----. "The Hysteria Diagnosis and the Politics of Anticlericalism in Late Nineteenth Century France." *Journal of Modern History* 54 (June 1982): 209-239.

Goodman, Dena. "Filial Rebellion in the Salon: Madame Geoffrin and Her Daughter." *French Historical Studies* 16 (Spring 1989): 28-47.

Gough, Austin. "French Workers and Their Wives in the Mid-Nineteenth Century." *Labour History* 42 (May 1982): 74-82.

Grieder, Joesphine. "Kingdoms of Women in French Fictions of the 1780s." *Eighteenth-Century Studies* 23 (Winter 1989-90): 140-156.

Grubitzsch, Helga. "Women's Projects and Co-operatives in France at the Beginning of the 19th Century." *Women's Studies* 8, no. 4 (1985): 287-290.

Haine, W. Scott. "Privacy in Public: The Compartment of Working-Class Women in Late Nineteenth-Century Parisian Proletarian Cafes." *Western Society for French History* 14 (November 1986): 204-211.

Hanley, Sarah. "Engendering the State: Family Formation and State Building in Early Modern France." *French Historical Studies* 16 (Spring 1989): 4-27.

Hanna, Martha. "Iconology and Ideology: Images of Joan of Arc in the Idiom of the Action Francaise." *French Historical Studies* 14 (Fall 1985): 215-239.

Harsin, Jill. "Syphilis, Wives, and Physicians: Medical Ethics and the Family in Late Nineteenth-Century France." *French Historical Studies* 16 (Spring 1989): 72-95.

Hause, Steven C. "Citizeness of the Republic: Class and Sex Identity in the Feminist Career of Hubertine Auclert, 1848-1914." *Western Society for French History* 12 (October 1984): 235-242.

-----. "The Failure of Feminism in Provincial France, 1890-1920." *Western Society for French History* 8 (October 1980): 423-435.

-----. "Women Who Rallied to the Tricolor: The Effects of World War I on the French Women's Suffrage Movement." *Western Society for French History* 6 (November 1978): 371-377.

Hause, Steven C., and Anne R. Kenney. "The Development of the Catholic Women's Suffrage Movement in France, 1896-1922." *Catholic Historical Review* 67 (January 1981): 11-30.

-----. "The Limits of Suffragist Behavior: Legalism and Militancy in France, 1876-1922." *American Historical Review* 86 (October 1981): 781-806.

Hertz, Michel. "New History, Old Literature: Interpreting Molière's Women." *Western Society for French History* 6 (November 1978): 90-91.

Hesse, C. "Reading Signatures: Female Authorship and Revolutionary Law in France, 1750-1850." *Eighteenth-Century Studies* 22 (Spring 1989): 469.

Higonnet, Anne. "Writing the Gender of the Image: Art Criticism in Late Nineteenth-Century France." *Genders* no. 6 (November 1989): 60-73.

Hilden, Patricia. "Class and Gender: Conflicting Components of Women's Behaviour in the Textile Mills of Lilli, Roubaix and Tourcoing, 1880-1914." *Historical Journal* [Great Britain] 27 (June 1984): 361-386.

-----. "Re-Writing the History of Socialism: Working Woman and the Parti Ouvrier Français." *European History Quarterly* 17 (July 1987): 285-306.

-----. "Women and the Labour Movement in France, 1869-1914." *Historical Journal* [Great Britain] 29 (December 1986): 809-832.

Hilgar, Marie-France. "Anne de Beaujeu, Unofficial Regent, 1483-1492." *Western Society for French History* 11 (November 1983): 53.

Hufton, Olwen. "Women without Men: Widows and Spinsters in Britain and

France in the Eighteenth Century." *Journal of Family History* (Winter 1984): 355-376.

Huss, Marie-Monique. "Pronatalism in the Inter-war Period in France." *Journal of Contemporary History* 25 (January 1990): 39-68.

Jacob, Margaret C. "Feminine Sociability in Eighteenth- and Nineteenth-Century France: Comment on Papers by Burke, Walton, and Haine." *Western Society for French History* 14 (November 1986): 212-214.

Jonas, Raymond A. "Equality in Difference? Patterns of Feminine Labor Militancy in Nineteenth-Century France." *Western Society for French History* 15 (November 1987): 291-298.

Kanipe, Esther S. "Working Class Women and the Social Question in Late 19th-Century France." *Western Society for French History* 6 (November 1978): 298-306.

Kelly, Joan. "Early Feminist Theory and the *Querelle des Femmes*, 1400-1789." *Signs* 8 (Autumn 1982): 4-28.

Kettering, Sharon. "The Patronage Power of Early Modern French Noblewomen." *The Historical Journal* 32, no. 4 (1989): 817-842.

Kleinman, Ruth. "Social Dynamics at the French Court: The Household of Anne of Austria." *French Historical Studies* 16 (Spring 1990): 517-535.

Kuehn, Elain Kruse. "Emancipation or Survival? The Parisian Woman and Divorce: 1792-1804." *Western Society for French History* 8 (October 1980): 279-280.

Lehning, James R. "The Timing and Prevalence of Women's Marriage in the French Department of the Loire, 1851-1891." *Journal of Family History* 13, no. 3 (1988): 307-328.

Leridon, Henri. "Cohabitation, Marriage, Separation: An Analysis of Life Histories of French Cohorts from 1968 to 1985." *Population Studies* 44 (March 1990): 127-144.

Lewis, H. D. "The Legal Status of Women in Nineteenth Century France." *Journal of European Studies* 10 (September 1980): 178-188.

Lightman, Harriet. "Political Power and the Queen of France." *Canadian Journal of History* 21 (December 1986): 299-312.

-----. "Queens and Minor Kings in French Constitutional Law." *Western Society for French History* 9 (October 1981): 26-36.

Lingo, Alison K. "Empirics and Charlatans in Early Modern France: The Genesis of the Classification of the 'Other' in Medical Practice." *Journal of Social History* 19 (Summer 1986): 583-604.

Lipton, Eunice. "The Laundress in Late Nineteenth-Century French Culture: Imagery, Ideology and Edgar Degas." *Art History* 3 (September 1980): 295-313.

Lynch, Katherine A. "Marriage Age Among French Factory Workers: An Alsatian Example." *Journal of Interdisciplinary History* 16 (Winter 1986): 405-429.

Major, J. R. "Bastard Feudalism and the Kiss: Changing Social Mores in Late Medieval and Early Modern France." *Journal of Interdisciplinary History* 17

(Winter 1987): 509-536.

Martin, Benjamin F. "Sex, Property, and Crime in the Third Republic: A Statistical Introduction." *Historical Reflections/Reflexions Historiques* 11 (Fall 1984): 323-350.

Martin, Michel L. "From Periphery to Center: Women in the French Military." *Armed Forces & Society* 8 (Winter 1982): 303-333.

Maza, S. "The Rose-Girl of Salency: Representations of Virtue in Prerevolutionary France." *Eighteenth-Century Studies* 22 (Spring 1989): 395-412.

McBride, Theresa. "Comment on Session: Class and Sex Identity in French Feminist Politics." *Western Society for French History* 12 (October 1984): 257-259.

McDougall, Mary Lynn. "The Meaning of Reform: The Ban on Women's Night Work, 1892-1914." *Western Society for French History* 10 (October 1982): 404-417.

-----. "Protecting Infants: The French Campaign for Maternity Leaves, 1890s-1913." *French Historical Studies* 13 (Spring 1983): 79-105.

-----. "Women's Work in Industrializing Britain and France." *Atlantis* 4 (Spring 1979): 143-151.

McLaren, Angus. "Abortion in France: Women and the Regulation of Family Size." *French Historical Studies* 10 (Spring 1978): 461-485.

McMillan, James F. "Clericals, Anticlericals, and the Women's Movement in France under the Third Republic." *The Historical Journal* 24 (June 1981): 361-376.

-----. "Women, Religion, and Politics: The Case of the *Ligue Patristique des Françaises*." *Western Society for French History* 15 (November 1987): 355-364.

Millstone, Amy B. "Behind Closed Doors: A Girl's Liberal Home Education under the Second Empire." *Western Society for French History* 15 (November 1987): 303-312.

Mitchell, Barbara. "Revolutionary Syndication and the Woman Question." *Western Society for French History* 8 (October 1980): 436.

Moch, Leslie Page. "Government Policy and Women's Experience: The Case of Teachers in France." *Feminist Studies* 14 (Summer 1988): 301-324.

-----. "Women on the Move: Migration and Urban Work for Women in the Late Nineteenth Century." *Western Society for French History* 8 (October 1980): 281-282.

Moses, Claire G. "Comment on Session: Women and the Arts in Eighteenth-Century France." *Western Society for French History* 11 (November 1983): 139.

-----. "Saint-Simonian Men/ Saint-Simonian Women: The Transformation of Feminist Thought in 1830's France." *Journal of Modern History* 54 (June 1982): 240-267.

Mroz, Thomas A., and David R. Weir. "Structural Change in Life Cycle Fertility During the Fertility Transition: France Before and After the Revolution of

1789." *Population Studies* 44 (March 1990): 61-88.

Neel, Carol. "The Origins of the Beguines." *Signs* 14 (Winter 1989): 321-341.

Neuschel, Kristen B. "Noble Households in the Sixteenth Century: Material Settings and Human Communities." *French Historical Studies* 15 (Fall 1988): 595-622.

Norberg, Kathryn. "Women, the Family, and the Counter-Reformation: Women's Confraternities in the 17th Century." *Western Society for French History* 6 (November 1978): 55-62.

O'Brien, Patricia. "The Kleptomania Diagnosis: Bourgeois Women and Theft in Late Nineteenth-Century France." *Journal of Social History* 17 (Fall 1983): 65-77.

Offen, Karen M. "The Beginnings of 'Scientific' Women's History in France." *Western Society for French History* 11 (November 1983): 255-264.

-----. "Depopulation, Nationalism, and Feminism in Fin-de-Siècle France." *American Historical Review* 89 (June 1984): 648-676.

-----. "Ernest Legouve and the Doctrine of 'Equality in Difference' for Women: A Case Study of Male Feminism in Nineteenth-Century French Thought." *Journal of Modern History* 58 (June 1986): 452-484.

-----. "'First Wave' Feminism in France: New Work and Resources." *Women's Studies International Forum* 5 (1982): 685-689.

-----. "A Nineteenth-Century French Feminist Rediscovered: Jenny P. d'Hericourt, 1809-1875." *Signs* 13 (Autumn 1987): 144-158.

-----. "The Second Sex and the Baccalaureat in Republican France, 1880-1924." *French Historical Studies* 13 (Fall 1983): 252-286.

-----. "Women's Memory, Women's History, Women's Political Action: The French Revolution in Retrospect, 1789-1889-1989." *Journal of Women's History* 1 (Winter 1990): 211-230.

Phillips, Roderick. "Women's Emancipation, the Family and Social Change in Eighteenth-Century France." *Journal of Social History* 12 (Summer 1979): 553-567.

Potter, David. "Marriage and Cruelty Among the Protestant Nobility in Sixteenth-Century France: Diane de Barbancon and Jean de Rohan, 1561-7." *European History Quarterly* 20 (January 1990): 5-38.

Rabine, Leslie W. "Textual Practice/Social Practice: Flora Tristan and the Problem of the Woman Activist-Writer." *Western Society for French History* 11 (November 1983): 272.

Rand, Erica. "Depoliticizing Women: Female Agency, the French Revolution, and the Art of Boucher and David." *Genders* 7 (March 1990): 47-68.

Rapley, Elizabeth. "Fenelon Revisited: A Review of Girls' Education in Seventeenth-Century France." *Histoire sociale/Social History* 20 (November 1987): 299-313.

Reinhardt, Steven G. "Gender and History: Comment on Papers by Rizzo, Dahl, and Truant." *Western Society for French History* 15 (November 1987): 139-140.

Reynolds, Sian. "Who Wanted the Creches? Working Mothers and the Birth-Rate in France 1900-1950." *Continuity and Change* 5, no. 2 (1990): 173-198.

Riley, Philip F. "Michel Foucault, Lust, Women, and Sin in Louis XIV's Paris." *Church History* 59 (March 1990): 35-50.

Rizzo, Tracy. "Sexual Violence in the Enlightenment: The State, the Bourgeoisie, and the Cult of the Vicitimized Woman." *Western Society for French History* 15 (November 1987): 122-128.

Roffman, Marion H. "As the Poet Saw Her: Images of Woman in the Pastorals and the Fabliaux." *Western Society for French History* 8 (October 1980): 33-41.

Rostenberg, Leona. "'Don't Go on the Stage': Advice from Paris." *Manuscripts* 40, no. 1 (1988): 35-40.

Rowan, Mary M. "Seventeenth-Century French Feminism: Two Opposing Attitudes." *International Journal of Women's Studies* 3 (May/June 1980): 273-291.

Russell, Lois Ann. "Challe and Diderot: Tales in Defense of Woman." *Western Society for French History* 9 (October 1981).

Sabin, Linda E. "The French Revolution: A Forgotten Era in Nursing History." *Nursing Forum* 20, no. 3 (1981): 224-243.

Schulkind, Eugene. "Socialist Women During the 1871 Paris Commune." *Past and Present* no. 106 (February 1985): 124-163.

Schwartz, Paula. "Partisanes and Gender Politics in Vichy France." *French Historical Studies* 16 (Spring 1989): 126-151.

Scott, Joan Wallach. "New Documents on the Lives of French Women: The Journal of Caroline B., 1864-1868." *Signs* 12 (Spring 1987): 568-572.

Shaffer, John W. "Family, Class, and Young Women: Occupational Expectations in Nineteenth-Century Paris." *Journal of Family History* 3 (Spring 1978): 62-77.

Shapiro, Ann-Louise. "Disordered Bodies/Disorderly Acts: Medical Discourse and the Female Criminal in Nineteenth Century Paris." *Genders* no. 4 (March 1989): 68-86.

Smith, Bonnie G. "The History of Women's History in Nineteenth-Century France." *Western Society for French History* 11 (November 1983): 265-271.

Sowerwine, Charles. "Socialism, Feminism, and Violence: The Analysis of Madeleine Pellelier." *Western Society for French History* 8 (October 1980): 415-422.

Spencer, Samia I. "Women and Education in Eighteenth-Century France." *Western Society for French History* 10 (October 1982): 274-284.

-----. "Women Cabinet Members: Ornaments of Government?" *Western Society for French History* 12 (October 1984): 243-256.

Steele, Valerie. "The Social and Political Significance of Macaroni Fashion." *Costume* 19 (1985): 94-109.

Strumingher, Laura S. "'A Bas Les Pretres! A Bas Les Couvents!': The Church and the Workers in 19th Century Lyon." *Journal of Social History* 11 (Summer 1978): 546-552.

-----. "Flora Tristan and the Right to Work." *Western Society for French History*

11 (November 1983): 272.

-----. "L'Ange de la Maison: Mothers and Daughters in Nineteenth-Century France." *International Journal of Women's Studies* 2 (January/February 1979): 51-61.

Stuard, Susan Mosher. "The Annales School and Feminist History: Opening Dialog with the American Stepchild." *Signs* 7 (Autumn 1981): 135-143.

Sweeter, Marie-Odile. "Women and Power: Reflections on Some Queens in French Classical Tragedy." *Western Society for French History* 10 (October 1982): 60-67.

Thomas, Chantal. "Heroism in the Feminine: The Examples of Charlotte Corday and Madame Roland." *Eighteenth Century* [Lubbock] Special Issue: The French Revolution 1789-1989 (1989): 67-82.

Traville, Mary. "Revolution in The Boudoir: Mme. Roland's Subversion of Rousseau's Feminine Ideals." *Eighteenth-Century Life* 13 (May 1989): 65-86.

Truant, Cynthia M. "The Guildswomen of Paris: Gender, Power and Sociability in the Old Regime." *Western Society for French History* 15 (November 1987): 130-138.

Walton, Whitney. "Feminine Hospitality in the Bourgeois Home of Nineteenth-Century France." *Western Society for French History* 14 (November 1986): 197-203.

-----. "Working Women, Gender, and Industrialization in Nineteenth-Century France: The Case of Lorraine Embroidery Manufacturing." *Journal of Women's History* 2 (Fall 1990): 42-65.

Weinburger, Stephen. "Women, Property and Poetry in Eleventh Century Provence." *Western Society for French History* 8 (October 1980): 24-33.

White, Sarah Melhado. "Sexual Language and Human Conflict in Old French Fabliaux." *Comparative Studies in Society and History* 24, no. 2 (1982): 185-210.

## General

Atkinson, Clarissa W. "Precious Balsam in a Fragile Glass: The Ideology of Virginity in the Later Middle Ages." *Journal of Family History* 8 (Summer 1983): 131-143.

Atkinson, Colin B., and William P. Stoneman. "'These Griping Greeffes and Pinching Pange': Attitudes to Childbirth in Thomas Bentley's *The Monument of Matrones* (1582)." *Sixteenth Century Journal* 21 (Summer 1990): 193-204.

Barkai, Ron. "A Medieval Hebrew Treatise on Obstetrics." *Medical History* 33 (January 1989): 96-119.

Barstow, Anne Llewellyn. "On Studying Witchcraft as Women's History: A Historiography of the European Witch Persecutions." *Journal of Feminist Studies in Religion* 4 (Fall 1988): 7-20.

Bell, Susan Groag. "Medieval Women Book Owners: Arbiters of Lay Piety and Ambassadors of Culture." *Signs* 7 (Summer 1982): 742-768.

Benton, John F. "Trotula, Women's Problems, and the Professionalization of

Medicine in the Middle Ages." *Bulletin of the History of Medicine* 59 (Spring 1985): 30-53.

Biller, P. A. "Birth-Control in the West in the Thirteenth and Early Fourteenth Centuries." *Past and Present* no. 94 (February 1982): 3-26.

Bonfield, Lloyd. "Marriage Settlements and the 'Rise of Great Estates': The Demographic Aspect." *Economic History Review* 32 (November 1979): 483-493.

Boswell, John Eastburn. "*Exposito* and *Oblatio*: The Abandonment of Children and the Ancient and Medieval Family." *American Historical Review* 89 (February 1984): 10-33.

Burke, Janet M. "Freemasonry, Friendship and Noblewomen: The Role of the Secret Society in Bringing Enlightenment Thought to Pre-Revolutionary Women Elites." *History of European Ideas* 10, no. 3 (1989): 283-294.

Clawson, Mary Ann. "Early Modern Fraternalism and the Patriarchal Family." *Feminist Studies* 6 (Summer 1980): 368-391.

Collomp, Alain. "From Stem Family to Nuclear Family: Changes in the Coresident Domestic Group in Haute Provence Between the End of the Eighteenth and the Middle of the Nineteenth Centuries." *Continuity and Change* 3, no. 1 (1988): 65-82.

Dresch, Catherine. "Maternal Nutrition and Infant Mortality Rates: An Evaluation of the Bourgeoisie of 18th-Century Montheliard." *Food & Foodways* 4, no. 1 (1990): 1-38.

Estes, Leland. "Reginald Scot and his *Discoverie Of Witchcraft*: Religion and Science in Opposition to the European Witch Craze." *Church History* 52 (December 1983): 444-456.

Everson, Michael. "Tenacity in Religion, Myth, and Folklore: The Neolithic Goddess of Old Europe Preserved in a non-Indo-European Setting." *Journal of Indo-European Studies* 17 (Fall/Winter 1989): 277-296.

Franklin, Peter. "Peasant Widows' 'Liberation' and Remarriage Before the Black Death." *Economic History Review* 39 (May 1986): 186-204.

Fries, Maureen. "Feminae Populi: Popular Images of Women in Medieval Literature." *Journal of Popular Culture* 14 (Summer 1980): 77-86.

Garrett, Eilidh M. "The Trials of Labour: Motherhood versus Employment in a Nineteenth-Century Textile Centre." *Continuity and Change* 5, no. 1 (1990): 121-154.

Gaskin, Katharine. "Age at First Marriage in Europe Before 1850: A Summary of Family Reconstitution Data." *Journal of Family History* 3 (Spring 1978): 23-36.

Gillespie, James L. "Ladies of the Fraternity of Saint George and of the Society of the Garter." *Albion* 17 (Fall 1985): 259-278.

Greenshields, Malcolm. "Women, Violence, and Criminal Justice Records in Early Modern Haute Auvergne (1587-1664)." *Canadian Journal of History* 22 (August 1987): 175-194.

Guinsburg, Arlene Miller. "The Counterthrust to Sixteenth Century Misogyny: The Work of Agrippa and Paracelsus." *Historical Reflections/Reflexions*

*Historiques* 8 (Spring 1981): 3-28.

Hacker, Barton C. "Women and Military Institutions in Early Modern Europe: A Reconnaissance." *Signs* 6 (Summer 1981): 643-671.

Hajdu, Robert. "The Position of Noblewomen in the Pays des Costumes, 1100-1300." *Journal of Family History* 5 (Summer 1980): 122-144.

Hatem, Mervat. "Through Each Other's Eyes: Egyptian, Levantine-Egyptian, and European Women's Images of Themselves and of Each Other (1862-1920)." *Women's Studies International Forum* 12, no. 2 (1989): 183-198.

Hirshfield, Claire. "Liberal Women's Organizations and the War Against the Boers, 1899-1902." *Albion* 14 (Spring 1982): 27-49.

Horsley, Richard A. "Who Were the Witches? The Social Roles of the Accused in the European Witch Trials." *Journal of Interdisciplinary History* 9 (Spring 1979): 689-715.

Hossain, Mary. "Women and Paradise." *Journal of European Studies* 19 (December 1989): 293-310.

Hufton, Olwen. "Early Modern Europe." *Past & Present* no. 101 (November 1983): 125-140.

Hyam, R. "Empire and Sexual Opportunity." *The Journal of Imperial and Commonwealth History* 1, no. 2 (1986): 34-90.

Johnson, P. D. "Agnes of Burgundy, an 11th Century Woman as Monastic Patron." *Journal of Medieval History* 15 (June 1989): 93-104.

Karras, Ruth Mazo. "Holy Harlots: Prostitute Saints in Medieval Legend." *Journal of the History of Sexuality* 1 (July 1990): 3-32.

Kertzer, David I. "The Joint Family Household Revisited: Demographic Constraints and Household Complexity in the European Past." *Journal of Family History* 14, no. 1 (1989): 1-16.

Klassen, John. "The Development of the Conjugal Bond in Late Medieval Bohemia." *Journal of Medieval History* 13 (June 1987): 161-178.

-----. "Household Composition in Medieval Bohemia." *Journal of Medieval History* 16 (March 1990): 55-76.

Kowaleski, Maryanne, and Judith M. Bennett. "Crafts, Guilds, and Women in the Middle Ages: Fifty Years after Marian K. Dale." *Signs* 14 (Winter 1989): 474-501.

Kuehn, T. "Some Ambiguities of Female Inheritance Ideology in the Renaissance." *Continuity and Change* 2, no. 1 (1987): 11-36.

Land, Hilary. "The Changing Place of Women in Europe." *Daedalus* 108 (Spring 1979): 73-94.

Laquer, Thomas W. "The Queen Caroline Affair: Politics as Art in the Reign of George IV." *Journal of Modern History* 54 (September 1982): 417-466.

Laslett, Peter. "Family, Kinship and Collectivity as Systems of Support in Pre-Industrial Europe: A Consideration of the 'Nuclear-Hardship' Hypothesis." *Continuity and Change* 3, no. 2 (1988): 153-176.

Lemay, Helen Rodnite. "Some Thirteenth and Fourteenth Century Lectures on Female Sexuality." *International Journal of Women's Studies* 1 (July/August 1978): 391-400.

Marchalouis, Shirley. "Above Rubies: Popular Views of Medieval Women." *Journal of Popular Culture* 14 (Summer 1980): 87-93.

Mate, Mavis. "Profit and Productivity on the Estates of Isabella de Fory (1260-92)." *Economic History Review* 33 (August 1980): 326-334.

Matter, E. Ann. "My Sister, My Spouse: Women-Identified Women in Medieval Christianity." *Journal of Feminist Studies in Religion* 2 (Fall 1986): 81-94.

McLaughlin, Mary Martin. "Creating and Recreating Communities of Women: The Case of Corpus Domini, Ferrara, 1406-1452." *Signs* 14 (Winter 1989): 293-320.

Michel, Sonya, and Seth Koven. "Womanly Duties: Maternalist Politics and the Origins of Welfare States in France, Germany, Great Britain, and the United States, 1880-1920." *American Historical Review* 95 (October 1990): 1076-1108.

Park, Roberta J. "Sport, Gender and Society in a Transatlantic Perspective." *British Journal of Sports History* 2, no. 1 (1985): 5-28.

Parker, Geoffrey. "The European Witchcraze Revisited." *History Today* 30 (November 1980): 23-24.

Payer, Pierre J. "Early Medieval Regulations Concerning Marital Sexual Relations." *Journal of Medieval History* 6 (December 1980): 353-376.

Reineke, Martha J. "'This is My Body': Reflections on Abjection, Anorexia, and Medieval Women Mystics." *Journal of the American Academy of Religion* 58 (Summer 1990): 245-266.

Riley, Glenda. "European Views of White Women in the American West." *Journal of the West* 21 (April 1982): 71-81.

-----. "Some European (Mis)Perceptions of American Indian Women." *New Mexico Historical Review* 59 (July 1984): 237-266.

Robin, Jean. "Illegitimacy in Colyton, 1851-1881." *Continuity and Change* 2, no. 2 (1987): 307-342.

Robisheaux, Thomas. "Peasants and Pastors: Rural Youth Control and the Reformation in Hohenlohe, 1540-1680." *Social History* 6 (October 1981): 281-300.

Rusinowa, Izabella. "European Utopians in America: The Diary of Kalikst Wolski." *Quaderno* 1 (1988).

Scalingi, Paula Louise. "The Scepter or the Distaff: The Question of Female Sovereignty, 1516-1607." *The Historian* 41 (November 1978): 59-75.

Schulenburg, Jane Tibbetts. "Sexism and the Celestial Gynaeceum--from 500 to 1200." *Journal of Medieval History* 4 (June 1978): 117-134.

-----. "Women's Monastic Communities, 500-1100: Patterns of Expansion and Decline." *Signs* 14 (Winter 1989): 261-292.

Schwoerner, Lois G. "Women and the Glorious Revolution." *Albion* 18 (Summer 1986): 195-218.

Seccombe, Wally. "The Western European Marriage Pattern in Historical Perspective: A Response to David Levine." *Journal of Historical Sociology* 3 (March 1990): 50-74.

Shahar, Shulamith. "Infants, Infant Care, and Attitudes toward Infancy in the

Medieval Lives of Saints." *Journal of Psychohistory* 10 (Winter 1983): 281-310.

Siegfried, Michael. "The Skewed Sex Ration in a Medieval Population: A Reinterpretation." *Social Science History* 10 (Summer 1986): 195-204.

Smith, Bonnie. "The Contribution of Women to Modern Historiography in Great Britain, France and the United States 1750-1940." *American Historical Review* 89 (June 1984): 709-732.

Song, Cheunsoon, and Lucy Roy Sibley. "The Vertical Headdress of Fifteenth-Century Northern Europe." *Dress* 16 (1990): 4-15.

Stafford, Pauline. "The King's Wife in Wessex 800-1066." *Past and Present* no. 91 (May 1981): 3-27.

Summers, Anne. "Pride & Prejudice: Ladies and Nurses in the Crimean War." *History Workshop* 16 (Autumn 1983): 33-56.

Truax, Jean A. "Augustine of Hippo: Defender of Women's Equality?" *Journal of Medieval History* 16 (December 1990): 279-300.

Tuten, Jeff M. "Women in Military Service." *Armed Forces & Society* 8 (Fall 1981): 160-163.

Vega, Judith. "Feminist Republicanism: Etta Palm-Aelders on Justice, Virtue and Men." *History of European Ideas* 10, no. 3 (1989): 333-352.

Warner, Patricia Campbell. "Fetters of Gold: The Jewelry of Renaissance Saxony in the Portraits of Cranach the Elder." *Dress* 16 (1990): 16-27.

Watt, Jeffrey R. "Divorce in Early Modern Neuchatel, 1547-1806." *Journal of Family History* 14, no. 2 (1989): 137-156.

-----. "Marriage Contract Disputes in Early Modern Neuchatel, 1547-1806." *Journal of Social History* 22 (Fall 1988): 129-148.

Wemple, Suzanne F., and Denise A. Kaiser. "Dealth's Dance of Women." *Journal of Medieval History* 12 (December 1986): 333-344.

Wolchick, Sharon L. "Ideology and Equality: The Status of Women in Eastern and Western Europe." *Comparative Political Studies* 13 (January 1981): 445-476.

Wood, Charles T. "The Doctor's Dilemma: Sin, Salvation, and the Menstrual Cycle in Medieval Thought." *Speculum* 56 (1981): 710-727.

Yandell, Cathy. "Of Lice and Women: Rhetoric and Gender in *La Puce de Madame des Roches.*" *Journal of Medieval and Renaissance Studies* 20 (Spring 1990): 123-136.

Ziegler, J. E. "The Medieval Virgin as Object: Art or Anthropology?" *Historical Reflections/Reflexions Historiques* 16 (Summer & Fall 1989): 251-264.

## Great Britain

Abel, Trudi. "The Diary of a Poor Quaker Seamstress: Needles and Penury in Nineteenth Century London." *Quaker History* 75 (Fall 1986): 102-114.

Abelove, Henry. "Some Speculations on the History of Sexual Intercourse During the Long Eighteenth Century in England." *Genders* no. 6 (November 1989): 125-130.

Alberti, Johanna. "Inside Out: Elizabeth Haldane as a Women's Suffrage Survivor in the 1920s and 1930s." *Women's Studies International Forum* 13, no. 1/2 (1990): 117-127.

Alexander, Ziggi. "Let It Lie upon the Table: The Status of Black Women's Biography in the UK." *Gender & History* 2 (Spring 1990): 22-33.

Anderson, Michael. "Household, Families and Individuals: Some Preliminary Results from the National Sample from the 1851 Census of Great Britain." *Continuity and Change* 3, no. 3 (1988): 421-438.

-----. "The Social Position of Spinsters in Mid-Victorian Britain." *Journal of Family History* 9 (Winter 1984): 377-393.

Anderson, Nancy F. "The 'Marriage with a Deceased Wife's Sister Bill' Controversy: Incest Anxiety and the Defense of Family Purity in Victorian England." *The Journal of British Studies* 21 (Spring 1982): 67-86.

Andre, Caroline S. "Some Selected Aspects of the Role of Women in Sixteenth Century England." *International Journal of Women's Studies* 4 (January/February 1981): 76-88.

Anthony, Ilid. "Clothing Given to a Late Sixteenth-Century Servant in Wales." *Costume* 14 (1980): 32-40.

Arnstein, W. L. "Queen Victoria Opens Parliament: The Disinvention of Tradition." *Historical Research* 63 (June 1990): 178-194.

Atkinson, Colin B., and Jo Atkinson. "Maria Edgeworth, Belinda, and Women's Rights." *Eire-Ireland* 19 (Winter 1984): 94-118.

Bailey, Peter. "Parasexuality and Glamour: The Victorian Barmaid as Cultural Prototype." *Gender & History* 2 (Summer 1990): 148-172.

Ballard, Catherine. "Arranged Marriages in the British Context." *New Community* 6, no. 3 (1978): 181-196.

Bauer, Carol, and Lawrence Ritt. "'A Husband Is a Beating Animal': Frances Power Cobbe Confronts the Wife-Abuse Problem in Victorian England." *International Journal of Women's Studies* 6 (March/April 1983): 99-118.

-----. "Wife-Abuse, Late Victorian English Feminists, and the Legacy of Frances Power Cobbe." *International Journal of Women's Studies* 6 (May/June 1983): 195-207.

Behlmer, George K. "Deadly Motherhood: Infanticide and Medical Opinion in Mid-Victorian England." *Journal of the History of Medicine and Allied Sciences* 34 (October 1979): 403-427.

Bennett, Judith M. "Spouses, Siblings and Surnames: Reconstructing Families from Medieval Village Court Rolls." *The Journal of British Studies* 23 (Fall 1983): 26-46.

Betel, Lisa M. "Women's Monastic Enclosures in Early Ireland." *Journal of Medieval History* 12 (March 1986): 15-36.

Blackley, F. D. "Isabella of France, Queen of England 1308-1358 and the Late Medieval Cult of the Dead." *Canadian Journal of History* 15 (April 1980): 23-48.

Bland, Lucy. "Rational Sex or Spiritual Love?: The Men and Women's Club of the 1880s." *Women's Studies International Forum* 13, no. 1/2 (1990): 33-48.

Blum, Dilys E. "Englishwomen's Dress in Eighteenth-Century India: The Margaret Fowke Correspondence (1776-1786)." *Costume* 17 (1983): 47-58.

Bohstedt, John. "Gender, Household and Community Politics: Women in English Riots 1790-1810." *Past & Present* no. 120 (August 1988): 88-122.

Bourke, Joanna. "'The Health Caravan': Domestic Education and Female Labor in Rural Ireland, 1890-1914." *Eire-Ireland* 24 (Winter 1989): 7-20.

Brewer, Betty Webb. "'She Was Part of It': Emily Lawless (1845-1913)." *Eire-Ireland* 18 (Winter 1983): 119-131.

Brown, Irene Q. "Domesticity, Feminism, and Friendship: Female Aristocratic Culture and Marriage in England, 1660-1760." *Journal of Family History,* 4 (Winter 1982): 406-424.

Buckley, Cheryl. "Women Designers in the English Pottery Industry, 1919-1939." *Woman's Art Journal* 5 (Fall 1984/Winter 1985): 11-15.

Burton, Antoinette M. "The White Woman's Burden: British Feminists and the Indian Woman, 1865-1915." *Women's Studies International Forum* 13, no. 4 (1990): 295-308.

Caine, Barbara. "Feminism, Suffrage and the Nineteenth-Century English Women's Movement." *Women's Studies International Forum* 5, no. 6 (1982): 537-550.

Campbell, L. "Wet-Nurses in Early Modern England: Some Evidence from the Townshend Archives." *Medical History* 33 (1989): 360-370.

Carlton, Charles. "The Widow's Tale: Male Myths and Female Reality in Sixteenth and Seventeenth Century England." *Albion* 10 (Summer 1978): 118-129.

Carter, John Marshall. "The Status of Rape in Thirteenth-Century England: 1218-1275." *International Journal of Women's Studies* 7 (May/June 1984): 248-259.

Chandler, Victoria. "Ada de Warenne, Queeen Mother of Scotland (c. 1123-1178)." *Scottish Historical Review* 60 (October 1981): 119-139.

Clark, Anna. "Queen Caroline and the Sexual Politics of Popular Culture in London, 1820." *Representations* no. 31 (Summer 1990): 47-68.

Clark, Elaine. "City Orphans and Custody Laws in Medieval England." *American Journal of Legal History* 34 (April 1990): 168-187.

Conley, Caroline A. "Rape and Justice in Victorian England." *Victorian Studies* 29 (Summer 1986): 519-536.

Copelman, D. M. "Liberal Ideology, Sexual Difference, and the Lives of Women: Recent Works in British History." *Journal of Modern History* 62 (June 1990): 315-345.

Crafts, N. F. R. "Duration of Marriage, Fertility and Women's Employment Opportunities in England and Wales in 1911." *Population Studies* 43 (1989): 325-335.

Crawford, Patricia. "Attitudes to Menstruation in Seventeenth-Century England." *Past and Present* no. 91 (May 1981): 47-73.

Dailey, Barbara Ritter. "The Visitation of Sarah Wight: Holy Carnival and the Revolution of the Saints in Civil War London." *Church History* 55 (December

1986): 438-455.

Davidoff, Leonore. "Class and Gender in Victorian England: The Diaries of Arthur J. Munby and Hannah Cullwick." *Feminist Studies* 5 (Spring 1979): 87-141.

Davin, Anna. "London Feminist History." *History Workshop* 9 (Spring 1980): 192-195.

Davis, John. "Joan of Kent, Lollardy and the English Reformation." *Journal of Ecclesiastical History* 33 (April 1982): 225-233.

Dawson, Jane E. A. "Mary Queen of Scots, Lord Darnley, and Anglo-Scottish Relations." *The International Review of History* 8 (February 1986): 1-24.

DeAragon, RaGena C. "In Pursuit of Aristocratic Women: A Key to Success in Norman England." *Albion* 14 (Fall-Winter 1982): 258-267.

Delacy, Margaret. "Puerperal Fever in Eighteenth Century Britain." *Bulletin of the History of Medicine* 63 (Winter 1989): 521-556.

Dimond, Frances. "Queen Victoria and Fashions for the Young." *Costume* 22 (1988): 1-12.

Donovan, Grace. "An American Catholic in Victorian England: Louisa, Duchess of Leeds, and the Carroll Family Benefice." *Maryland Historical Magazine* 84 (Fall 1989): 223-234.

Doran, Susan. "Religion and Politics at the Court of Elizabeth I: The Habsburg Marriage Negotiations of 1559-1567." *English Historical Review* 104 (October 1989): 908-926.

Dowling, Maria. "Anne Boleyn and Reform." *Journal of Ecclesiastical History* 35 (January 1984): 30-46.

Durham, Martin. "Women and the British Union of Fascists, 1932-1940." *Immigrants & Minorities* 8 (March 1989): 3-18.

Dwork, Deborah. "The Milk Option: An Aspect of the History of the Infant Welfare Movement in England 1898-1908." *Medical History* 31 (January 1987): 51-69.

Dyehouse, Carol. "Towards a 'Feminine' Curriculum for English Schoolgirls: The Demands of Ideology 1870-1963." *Women's Studies International Quarterly* 1 (1978): 297-330.

-----. "Working-Class Mothers and Infant Mortality in England, 1895-1914." *Journal of Social History* 12 (Winter 1978): 248-267.

Earle, Peter. "The Female Labour Market in London in the Late Seventeenth and Early Eighteenth Centuries." *The Economic History Review* 42 (August 1989): 328-353.

Engel, Arthur. "Immoral Intentions: The University of Oxford and the Problem of Prostitution, 1827-1914." *Victorian Studies* 23 (1979): 79-107.

Erickson, Amy Louise. "Common Law versus Common Practice: The Use of Marriage Settlements in Early Modern England." *The Economic History Review* 43 (February 1990): 21-39.

Erikson, Carolly. "Bloody Mary: Images of Burning Flesh and Grim-Eyed Vengeance." *In Britain* 34 (April 1979): 30-33.

Fallon, Charlotte. "The Civil War Hungerstrikes: Women and Men." *Eire-Ireland*

22 (Fall 1987): 75-91.

Fielder, Mari Kathleen. "Fatal Attraction: Irish-Jewish Romance in Early Film and Drama." *Eire-Ireland* 20 (Fall 1985): 6-18.

Figbie, Karl. "Chlorosis and Chronic Disease in Nineteenth-Century Britain: The Social Constitution of Somatic Illness in a Capitalist Society." *Social History* 3 (May 1978): 167-197.

Fildes, Valerie. "The English Wet-Nurse and Her Role in Infant Care 1538-1800." *Medical History* 32 (April 1988): 142-173.

Finkel, Alicia. "Le Bal Costume: History and Spectacle in the Court of Queen Victoria." *Dress* 10 (1984): 64-72.

Fitzpatrick, David. "Divorce and Separation in Modern Irish History." *Past and Present* no. 114 (February 1987): 172-196.

Floud, Roderick, and Pat Thane. "Debate: The Incidence of Civil Marriage in Victorian England and Wales." *Past and Present* 84 (August 1979): 146-154.

Forbes, Thomas R. "Births and Deaths in a London Parish: The Record from the Registers, 1654-1693." *Bulletin of the History of Medicine* 55 (Fall 1981): 371-391.

-----. "Deadly Parents: Child Homicide in Eighteenth and Nineteenth Century England." *Journal of the History of Medicine and Allied Sciences* 41 (April 1986): 175-199.

Freeman, Ruth, and Patricia Klaus. "Blessed or Not? The New Spinster in England and the United States in the Late Nineteenth and Early Twentieth Centuries." *Journal of Family History* 9 (Winter 1984): 394-414.

Furdell, Elizabeth Lane. "The Medical Personnel at the Court of Queen Anne." *The Historian* 48 (May 1986): 412-429.

Gavigan, Shelley A. M. "Petit Treason in Eighteenth Century England: Women's Inequality Before the Law." *Canadian Journal of Women and the Law/Revue juridique 'La femme et le droit'* 3, no. 2 (1989/90): 335-374.

Gillis, John R. "Servants, Sexual Relations, and the Risks of Illegitimacy in London, 1801-1900." *Feminist Studies* 5 (Spring 1979): 142-173.

Gorham, Deborah. "The 'Maiden Tribute of Modern Babylon' Reexamined: Child Prostitution and the Ideas of Childhood in Late-Victorian England." *Victorian Studies* 21 (Spring 1978): 353-369.

Greaves, Richard L. "The Role of Women in Early English Noncomformity." *Church History* 52 (September 1983): 299-311.

Grube, Alberta Fabris, and Jacques Portes, eds. "An English Lady Looks at America: Frances Trollope's Domestic Manners of the Americans." *Europe and America: Criss-Crossing Perspectives, 1788-1848* (1987): 105-128.

Haggis, Jane. "Gendering Colonialism or Colonising Gender? Recent Women's Studies Approaches to White Women and the History of British Colonialism." *Women's Studies International Forum* 13, no. 1/2 (1990): 105-116.

Harris, Barbara J. "Marriage Sixteenth-Century Style: Elizabeth Stafford and the Third Duke of Norfolk." *Journal of Social History* 15 (Spring 1982): 371-382.

-----. "Power, Profit, and Passion: Mary Tudor, Charles Brandon, and the Arranged Marriage in Early Tudor England." *Feminist Studies* 15 (Spring

1989): 59-88.

-----. "Property, Power, and Personal Relations: Elite Mothers and Sons in Yorkist and Early Tudor England." *Signs* 15 (Spring 1990): 606-632.

-----. "Women and Politics in Early Tudor England." *Historical Journal* [Great Britain] 33, no. 2 (1990): 259-282.

Harrison, Brian. "Women in the Men's House: The Women M.P.s, 1919-1945." *The Historical Journal* 29 (September 1986): 623-654.

Harvey, Clodagh Brennan. "Some Irish Women Storytellers and Reflections on the Role of Women in the Storytelling Tradition." *Western Folklore* 48 (April 1989): 109-128.

Hayton, David. "The Crisis in Ireland and the Disintegration of Queen Anne's Last Ministry." *Irish Historical Studies* 22 (March 1981).

Heeney, Brian. "The Beginnings of Church Feminism: Women and the Councils of the Church of England 1897-1919." *Journal of Ecclesiastical History* 33 (January 1982): 89-110.

-----. "Women's Struggles for Professional Work and Status in the Church of England, 1900-1930." *The Historical Journal* 26 (June 1983): 229-348.

Heisch, Alison. "Queen Elizabeth I and the Persistence of Patriarchy." *Feminist Review* no. 4 (1980): 45-56.

Helterline, Marilyn. "The Emergence of Modern Motherhood: Motherhood in England 1899 to 1959." *International Journal of Women's Studies* 3 (November/December 1980): 590-614.

Hester, Marianne. "The Dynamics of Male Domination Using the Witch Craze in 16th- and 17th- century England as a Case Study." *Women's Studies International Forum* 13, no. 1/2 (1990).

Higgenbotham, A. R. "Sin of the Age: Infanticide and Illegitimacy in Victorian London." *Victorian Studies* 32 (Spring 1989): 319-338.

Higgs, Edward. "Domestic Servants and Households in Victorian England." *Social History* 8 (May 1983): 201-210.

Hilton, Rodney. "Women Traders in Medieval England." *Women's Studies* 11, no. 1/2 (1984): 139-156.

Hind, Robert J. "The Loss of English Working-Class Parents' Control over Their Children's Education: The Role of Property-Holders." *Historical Reflections/Reflexions Historiques* 12 (Spring 1985): 77-108.

Hinde, P. R. A. "Household Structure, Marriage and the Institution of Service in Nineteenth Century Rural England." *Local Population Studies* no. 35 (Autumn 1985): 43-51.

Hindson, James. "The Marriage Duty Acts and the Social Topography of the Early Modern Town: Shrewsbury, 1695-8." *Local Population Studies* no. 31 (Autumn 1983): 21-28.

Hirshfield, Claire. "A Fractured Faith: Liberal Party Women and the Suffrage Issue in Britain, 1892-1914." *Gender & History* 2 (Summer 1990): 173-197.

Holcomb, Adele M. "Anna Jameson: The First Professional English Art Historian." *Art History* 6 (June 1983): 171-187.

Holtzman, Ellen M. "The Pursuit of Married Love: Women's Attitudes toward Sexuality and Marriage in Great Britain, 1918-1959." *Journal of Social History* 16 (Winter 1982): 39-52.

Horn, James P. P. "'The Bare Necessities': Standards of Living in England and the Chesapeake, 1650-1700." *Historical Archaeology* 22, no. 2 (1988): 74-91.

Howell, Margaret. "The Resources of Eleanor of Provence as Queen Consort." *English Historical Review* 102 (April 1987): 372-393.

Howlett, Neil. "Family and Household in a Nineteenth Century Devon Village." *Local Population Studies* no. 30 (Spring 1983): 42-48.

Howsam, Leslie. "'Sound-Minded Women': Eliza Orme and the Study and Practice of Law in Late-Victorian England." *Atlantis* 15 (Fall 1989): 44-55.

Huff, Cynthia. "Private Domains: Queen Victoria and Women's Diaries." *Auto/Biography Studies* 4 (Fall 1988): 46-52.

Hufton, Olwen. "Women without Men: Widows and Spinsters in Britain and France in the Eighteenth Century." *Journal of Family History* (Winter 1984): 355-376.

Humphries, Jane. "'...The Most Free From Objection...': The Sexual Division of Labor and Women's Work in Nineteenth-Century England." *Journal of Economic History* 47 (December 1987): 929-950.

Hunt, Felecity. "The London Trade in the Printing and Binding of Books: An Experience in Exclusion, Dilution and De-skilling for Women Workers." *Women's Studies International Forum* 6, no. 5 (1983): 517-524.

Hurwitz B., and R. Richardson. "Inspector General James Barry, M.D.: Putting the Woman in Her Place." *British Medical Journal* 298 (1989): 299-305.

Jayaweera, Swarna. "European Women Educators under the British Colonial Administration in Sri Lanka." *Women's Studies International Forum* 13, no. 4 (1990): 323-332.

Jones, Judith P., and Sherianne Sellers Seibel. "Thomas More's Feminism: To Reform as Re-Form." *Albion* 10 (1978): 67-77.

Jones, Norman L. "Elizabeth, Edification, and the Latin Prayer Book of 1560." *Church History* 53 (June 1984): 174-186.

Jordan, Ellen. "The Exclusion of Women from Industry in Nineteenth-Century Britain." *Comparative Studies in Society and History* 31 (April 1989): 273-296.

Kain, Edward L., and Niall Bolger. "Social Change and Women's Work and Family Experience in Ireland and the United States." *Social Science History* 10 (Summer 1986): 171-194.

Karras, Ruth Mazo. "The Regulation of Brothels in Later Medieval England." *Signs* 14 (Winter 1989): 399-433.

Kastan, David Scott. "Shakespeare and 'The Way of Womenkind.'" *Daedalus* 111 (Summer 1982): 115-130.

Kelly, John D. "Fear of Culture: British Regulation of Indian Marriage in Post-Indenture Fiji." *Ethnohistory* 36 (Autumn 1989): 392-410.

Kenneally, James J. "Sexism, the Church, Irish Women." *Eire-Ireland* 21 (Fall 1986): 3-16.

Kent, D. A. "Ubiquitous but Invisible: Female Domestic Servants in Mid-Eighteenth Century London." *History Workshop* no. 28 (Autumn 1989): 111-128.

Khanna, Lee Cullen. "Images of Women in Thomas More's Poetry." *Albion* 10 (1978): 78-88.

King, John N. "Queen Elizabeth I: Representations of the Virgin Queen." *Renaissance Quarterly* 43 (Spring 1990): 30-74.

Kinnaird, Joan K. "Mary Astell and the Conservative Contribution to English Feminism." *The Journal of British Studies* 19 (Fall 1979): 53-75.

Klench, Anne L. "Anglo Saxon Women and the Law." *Journal of Medieval History* 8 (June 1982): 107-122.

Knox, Bruce. "The Queen's Letter of 1865 and British Policy towards Emancipation and Indentured Labour in the West Indies, 1830-1865." *The Historical Journal* 29 (June 1986): 345-368.

Kowaleski-Wallace, Beth. "Hannah and Her Sister: Women and Evangelism in Early Nineteenth-Century England." *Nineteenth-Century Contexts* 12, no. 2 (1988): 29-52.

Kubek, Elizabeth Bennett. "London as Text: Eighteenth-Century Women Writers and Reading the City." *Women's Studies* 17, no. 3/4 (1990): 303-340.

Kunze, Bonnelyn Young. "'Poore and in Necessity': Margaret Fell and Quaker Female Philanthropy in Northwest England in the Late Seventeenth Century." *Albion* 21 (Winter 1989): 559-580.

Kushner, Tony. "Politics and Race, Gender and Class: Refugees, Fascists and Domestic Service in Britain, 1933-1940." *Immigrants & Minorities* 8 (March 1989): 49-60.

Lambertz, Jan. "Feminist History in Britain." *Radical History Review* 19 (1979): 137-142.

-----. "Sexual Harassment in the Nineteenth Century English Cotton Industry." *History Workshop* 19 (Spring 1985): 29-61.

Lance, Keith Curray. "Strategy Choices of the British Women's Social and Political Union, 1903-1918." *Social Science Quarterly* 60 (June 1979): 51-61.

Lance, N. "Historical Lessons? The State Enrolled Nurse." *History of Nursing* 2, no. 9 (1989): 21-15.

Larner, C. "Witch Beliefs and Witch-Hunting in England and Scotland." *History Today* 31 (1981): 32-36.

Lee, M. "The Daughter of Debate: Mary Queen-of-Scots after 400 Years." *Scottish Historical Review* 68 (April 1989): 70-79.

Lee, Patricia-Ann. "A Bodye Politique to Governe: Aylmer, Knox and the Debate on Queenship." *Historian* 52 (February 1990): 242-261.

Leedom, Joe W. "Lady Matilda Holland, Henry of Lancaster and the Manor of Melbourne." *American Journal of Legal History* 31 (April 1987): 118-125.

Leneman, Leah, and Rosalind Mitchison. "Scottish Illegitimacy Ratios in the Early Modern Period." *Economic History Review* 40 (February 1987): 41-63.

Levack, B. P. "The Great Scottish Witch Hunt of 1661-1662." *Journal of British Studies* 20 (1981): 90-108.

Levin, Carole. "Women in The Book of Martyrs as Models of Behavior in Tudor England." *International Journal of Women's Studies* 4 (March/April 1981): 196-207.

-----. "'Would I Could Give You Help and Succor': Elizabeth I and the Politics of Touch." *Albion* 21 (Summer 1989): 191-205.

Levine, David. "Education and Family Life in Early Industrial England." *Journal of Family History* 4 (Winter 1979): 368-380.

Levine, Philppa. "Love, Friendship, and Feminism in Later 19th-Century England." *Women's Studies International Forum* 13, no. 1/2 (1990): 63-78.

Lewis, Jane. "The Ideology and Politics of Birth Control in Inter-war England." *Women's Studies* 2, no. 1 (1979): 33-48.

Lewis, Judith Schneid. "Maternal Health in the English Aristocracy: Myths and Realities 1790-1840." *Journal of Social History* 17 (Fall 1983): 97-114.

Loades, David. "The Reign of Mary Tudor: Historiography and Research." *Albion* 21 (Winter 1989): 547-558.

Lynch, Michael. "Queen Mary's Triumph: The Baptismal Celebrations at Stirling in December 1566." *Scottish Historical Review* 69 (April 1990): 1-21.

Mack, Phyllis. "Women as Prophets During the English Civil War." *Feminist Studies* 8 (Spring 1982): 19-46.

Mahood, Linda. "The Magdalene's Friend: Prostitution and Social Control in Glasgow, 1869-1890." *Women's Studies International Forum* 13, no. 1/2 (1990): 49-62.

Malcolmson, Patricia E. "Laundresses and the Laundry Trade in Victorian England." *Victorian Studies* 24 (Summer 1981): 439-462.

Marcus, Jane. "Transatlantic Sisterhood: Labor and Suffrage Links in the Letters of Elizabeth Robbins and Emmeline Pankhurst." *Signs* 3 (Spring 1978): 744-755.

Mason, Francis M. "The Newer Eve: The Catholic Women's Suffrage Society in England, 1911-1923." *Catholic Historical Review* 72 (October 1986): 620-638.

Mayall, David. "Rescued from the Shadows of Exile: Nellie Driver, Autobiography and the British Union of Fascists." *Immigrants & Minorities* 8 (March 1989): 19-39.

McClure, Peter, and Peter Headlam Wells. "Elizabeth I as a Second Virgin Mary." *Renaissance Studies* 4 (March 1990): 38-70.

McCrone, Kathleen E. "Play Up! Play Up! And Play the Game! Sport at the Late Victorian Girls' Public School." *Journal of British Studies* 23 (Spring 1984): 106-134.

McDougall, Mary Lynn. "Women's Work in Industrializing Britain and France." *Atlantis* 4 (Spring 1979): 143-151.

McEntee, Ann Marie. "The 1579 Masque of Amazons and Knights: A Coalescence of Elizabeth I's Gendered and Political Identities." *Journal of Unconventional History* 1 (Spring 1990): 53-65.

McKillen, Beth. "Irish Feminism and Nationalist Separatism, 1914-1923, Part I." *Eire-Ireland* 17 (Fall 1982): 52-67.

-----. "Irish Feminism and Nationalist Separatism, 1914-1923, Part II."

*Eire-Ireland* 17 (Winter 1982): 72-90.

McLaren, Dorothy. "Nature's Contraceptive. Wet-Nursing and Prolonged Lactation: The Case of Chesham, Buckinghamshire, 1578-1601." *Medical History* 23 (October 1979): 426-441.

McLaughlin, Megan. "The Woman Warrior: Gender, Warfare and Society in Medieval Europe." *Women's Studies* 17, no. 3/4 (1990): 193-210.

Meteyard, Belinda. "Illegitimacy and Marriage in Eighteenth-Century England." *Journal of Interdisciplinary History* 10 (Winter 1980): 479-489.

Michel, Robert H. "English Attitudes Towards Women, 1640-1700." *Canadian Journal of History* 13 (April 1978): 35-60.

Moore, Lindy. "Feminists and Femininity: A Case-Study of WSPU Propaganda and Local Response at a Scottish By-Election." *Women's Studies* 5, no. 6 (1982): 675-684.

Morgan, V., and W. Macafee. "Household and Family Size and Structure in County Antrim." *Continuity and Change* 2, no. 3 (1987): 455-476.

Murray, Mary. "Property and 'Patriarchy' in English History." *Journal of Historical Sociology* 2 (December 1989): 303-327.

Nord, Deborah Epstein. "'Neither Pairs Nor Odd': Female Community in Late Nineteenth-Century London." *Signs* 15 (Summer 1990): 733-754.

O'Brien, Susan. "Terra Incognita: The Nun in Nineteenth-Century England." *Past & Present* no. 121 (November 1988): 110-140.

Olney, Martha L. "Fertility and the Standard of Living in Early Modern England: In Consideration of Wrigley and Schofield." *Journal of Economic History* 43 (March 1983): 71-78.

Park, Jihang. "The British Suffrage Activists of 1913:  An Analysis." *Past & Present* no. 120 (August 1988): 147-162.

Paxton, Nancy L. "Feminism Under the Raj: Complicity and Resistance in the Writings of Flora Annie Steel and Annie Besant." *Women's Studies International Forum* 13, no. 4 (1990): 333-346.

Pedersen, Susan. "The Failure of Feminism in the Making of the British Welfare State." *Radical History Review* 43 (Winter 1989): 86-104.

-----. "Gender, Welfare, and Citizenship in Britain During the Great War." *American Historical Review* 95 (Ocotber 1990): 983-1006.

-----. "Hannah More Meets Simple Simon: Tracts, Chapbooks, and Popular Culture in Late Eighteenth-Century England." *The Journal of British Studies* 25 (January 1986): 84-113.

Penn, Simon A. C. "Female Wage-Earners in Late Fourteenth-Century England." *Agricultural History Review* 35, no. 1 (1987): 1-14.

Peterson, M. Jeanne. "Dr. Acton's Enemy: Medicine, Sex, and Society in Victorian England." *Victorian Studies* 29 (Summer 1986): 569-590.

-----. "No Angels in the House: The Victorian Myth and the Paget Women." *American Historical Review* 89 (June 1984): 677-708.

Pointon, M. "Factors Influencing the Participation of Women and Girls in Physical Education, Physical Recreation and Sport in Great Britain During the Period 1850-1920." *History of Education Bulletin* no. 24 (Autumn 1979): 46-56.

Pollock, Linda. "'Teach Her to Live Under Obedience': The Making of Women in the Upper Ranks of Early Modern England." *Continuity and Change* 4 (August 1989): 231-258.

Pratt, Linda Ray. "Lady Gregory's Memories of Robert Gregory." *Eire-Ireland* 24 (Winter 1989): 54-74.

Prochaska, F. K. "Female Philanthropy and Domestic Service in Victorian England." *Bulletin of the Institute of Historical Research* 54, no. 129 (1981): 78-85.

Pugh, Evelyn L. "The First Woman Candidate for Parliament: Helen Rayor and the Election of 1885." *International Journal of Women's Studies* 1 (July/August 1978): 378-390.

-----. "Florence Nightingale and J. S. Mill Debate Women's Rights." *Journal of British Studies* (Spring 1982): 118-138.

-----. "John Stuart Mill and the Women's Question in Parliament, 1865-1868." *The Historian* 42 (May 1980): 399-418.

Purvis, J. "Towards a History of Women's Education in Nineteenth Century Britain: A Sociological Analysis." *Westminster Studies in Education* 4 (1981): 45-79.

Ramusack, Barbara N. "Cultural Missionaries, Maternal Imperialists, Feminist Allies: British Women Activists in India, 1865-1945." *Women's Studies International Forum* 13, no. 4 (1990): 309-322.

Rasmussen, Jorgen S. "The Political Integration of British Women: The Response of a Traditional System to a Newly Emergent Group." *Social Science History* 7 (Winter 1983): 61-96.

Riley, Denise. "The Free Mothers: Protonationalism and Working-Class Mothers in Industry at the End of the Last War in Britain." *History Workshop* 11 (Spring 1981): 59-119.

Robin, Jean. "Prenuptial Pregnancy in a Rural Area of Devonshire in the Mid-Nineteenth Century: Colyton, 1851-1881." *Continuity and Change* 1, no. 1 (1986): 113-124.

Roebuck, Janet, and Jane Slaughter. "Ladies and Pensioners: Stereotypes and Public Policy Affecting Old Women in England, 1880-1940." *Journal of Social History* 13 (Fall 1979): 105-114.

Rose, Sonya O. "Gender Segregation in the Transition to the Factory: The English Hosiery Industry, 1850-1910." *Feminist Studies* 13 (Spring 1987): 163-184.

Rosenthal, Joel T. "Aristocratic Marriage and the English Peerage, 1350-1500: Social Institution and Personal Bond." *Journal of Medieval History* 10 (September 1984): 181-194.

-----. "Other Victims: Peeresses as War Widows, 1450-1500." *History* 72 (June 1987): 213-230.

Ross, Ellen. "'Fierce Questions and Taunts': Married Life in Working-Class London, 1870-1914." *Feminist Studies* 8 (Fall 1982): 575-602.

-----. "Women's Neighborhood Sharing in London Before World War One." *History Workshop* 15 (Spring 1983): 4-27.

Ross, Margaret Clunies. "Concubinage in Anglo-Saxon England." *Past and Present* no. 108 (August 1985): 3-34.

Rowbotham, Sheila. "Women and Radical Politics in Britain 1830-1914." *Radical History Review* 19 (Winter 1978/79): 149-159.

Schnouenberg, Barbara Brandon. "The Brood Hen of Faction: Mrs. Macaulay and Radical Politics, 1765-1775." *Albion* 11 (Spring 1979): 33-45.

Schroeder, Natalie. "Regina Maria Roche and the Early Nineteenth Century Irish Novel." *Eire-Ireland* 19 (Summer 1984): 116-130.

Schwoerner, Lois G. "Seventeenth-Century English Women Engraved in Stone?" *Albion* 16 (Winter 1984): 389-403.

Searle, Eleanor. "Seigneurial Control of Women's Marriage: The Antecedents and Function of *Merchet* in England." *Past and Present* no. 82 (Februrary 1979): 3-43.

Seccombe, Wally. "Starting to Stop: Working-Class Fertility Decline in Britain." *Past & Present* no. 126 (February 1990): 151-188.

Sellar, W. D. H. "Marriage, Divorce and Concubinage in Gaelic Scotland." *Trans Gaelic Soc. Inverness* 1 (1978/80): 464-493.

Shammas, Carole. "The Domestic Environment in Early Modern England and America." *Journal of Social History* 14 (Fall 1980): 3-24.

-----. "English Inheritance Law and Its Transfer to the Colonies." *American Journal of Legal History* 31 (April 1987): 145-163.

Sharpe, J. A. "Domestic Homicide in Early Modern England." *The Historical Journal* 24 (March 1981): 29-48.

Shteir, Ann B. "Botanical Dialogues: Maria Jacson and Women's Popular Science Writing in England." *Eighteenth-Century Studies* 23 (Spring 1990): 301-317.

Sigl, Patricia. "Prince Hoare's *Artist* and Anti-Theatrical Polemics in the Early 1800s: Mrs. Inchbald's Contribution." *Theatre Notebook* 44, no. 2 (1990): 62-73.

Sloan, Barry. "Mrs. Hall's Ireland." *Eire-Ireland* 19 (Fall 1984): 18-30.

Smith, Harold. "Sex vs. Class: British Feminists and the Labour Movement, 1919-1929." *The Historian* 47 (November 1984): 19-37.

-----. "The Womanpower Problem in Britain During the Second World War." *The Historical Journal* 27 (December 1984): 925-946.

Smith, Ruth L., and Deborah M. Valenze. "Mutuality and Marginality: Liberal Moral Theory and Working-Class Women in Nineteenth-Century England." *Signs* 13 (Winter 1988): 277-298.

Smuts, R. M. "The Puritan Followers of Henrietta Maria in the 1630s." *English Historical Review* 93 (January 1978): 26-45.

Souden, David. "'Rogues, Whores, and Vagabonds'?    Indentured Servant Emigrants to North America, and the Case of Mid-Seventeenth-Century Bristol." *Social History* 3 (January 1978): 23-41.

Spall, Richard Francis, Jr. "The Bedchamber Crisis and the Hastings Scandal: Morals, Politics, and the Press at the Beginning of Victoria's Reign." *Canadian Journal of History* 22 (April 1987): 19-40.

Spielmann, Richard M. "The Beginning of Clerical Marriage in the English

Reformation: The Reigns of Edward and Mary." *Anglican and Episcopal History* 56 (September 1987): 251-264.

Stanley, Liz. "British Feminist Histories: An Editorial Introduction." *Women's Studies International Forum* 13, no. 1/2 (1990): 3-8.

Stevens, Carolyn. "The History of Sexuality in Britain and America, 1800-1975: Course Method and Bill of Rights." *Women's Studies Quarterly* 16 (Spring/Summer 1988): 87-96.

Summerfield, Penelope. "Women, Work, and Welfare: A Study of Child Care and Shopping in Britain in the Second World War." *Journal of Social History* 17 (Winter 1983): 249-270.

Summers, A. "The Mysterious Demise of Sarah Gamp: The Domiciliary Nurse and Her Detractors, c. 1830-1860." *Victorian Studies* 32 (Spring 1989): 365-386.

Sydie, Rosalind. "Women Painters in Britain, 1768-1848." *Atlantis* 5 (April 1980): 144-175.

Taylor, Barbara. "'The Men Are as Bad as Their Masters . . .': Socialism, Feminism, and Sexual Antagonism in the London Tailoring Trade in the Early 1830s." *Feminist Studies* 5 (Spring 1979): 7-40.

Taylor, Lou. "Marguerite Shoobert, London Fashion Model, 1906-1917." *Costume* 17 (1983): 105-110.

Thane, Pat M. "The Debate on the Declining Birth-Rate in Britain: The 'Menace' of an Ageing Population, 1920s-1950s." *Continuity and Change* 5, no. 2 (1990): 283-306.

-----. "Women and the Poor Law in Victorian and Edwardian England." *History Workshop* 6 (Autumn 1978): 29-51.

Tomes, Nancy. "A 'Torrent of Abuse': Crimes of Violence Between Working-Class Men and Women in London 1840-1875." *Journal of Social History* 11 (Spring 1978): 328-345.

Treble, J. "The Seasonal Demand for Adult Labour in Glasgow, 1890-1914." *Social History* 3 (January 1978): 43-60.

Vaughan, Virginia Mason. "Daughters of the Game: Troilus and Cressida and the Sexual Discourse of 16th-Century England." *Women's Studies International Forum* 13, no. 3 (1990): 209-220.

Voris, Jacqueline Van. "Daniel O'Connell and Women's Rights, One Letter." *Eire-Ireland* 17 (Fall 1982): 35-39.

Walby, Sylvia. "From Private to Public Patriarchy: The Periodisation of British History." *Women's Studies International Forum* 13, no. 1/2 (1990): 91-105.

Walker, Sue Sheridan. "Convicted Ravishers: Statutory Strictures and Actual Practice in Thirteenth and Fourteenth-Century England." *Journal of Medieval History* 13 (September 1987): 237-250.

-----. "Free Consent and the Marriage of Feudal Wards in Medieval England." *Journal of Medieval History* 8 (June 1982): 123-134.

Walkowitz, Judith R. "Male Vice and Feminist Virtue: Feminism and the Politics of Prostitution in Nineteenth Century Britain." *History Workshop* 13 (Spring 1982): 77-93.

Wall, Alison. "Elizabethan Precept and Feminine Practice: The Thynne Family of Longleat." *History* 75 (February 1990): 23-38.

Warnicke, Retha M. "Anne Boleyn's Childhood and Adolescence." *The Historical Journal* 28 (December 1985): 939-952.

-----. "The Eternal Triangle and Court Politics: Henry VIII, Anne Boleyn, and Sir Thomas Wyatt." *Albion* 18 (Winter 1986): 565-580.

-----. "The Fall of Anne Boleyn: A Reassessment." *History* 70 (February 1985): 1-15.

-----. "Sexual Heresy at the Court of Henry VIII." *The Historical Journal* 30 (June 1987): 247-268.

Weatherill, Lorna. "A Possession of One's Own: Women and Consuming Behavior in England, 1660-1740." *Journal of British Studies* 25 (April 1986): 131-156.

Weinstein, Minna F. "Reconstructing Our Past: Reflections on Tudor Women." *International Journal of Women's Studies* 1 (March/April 1978): 133-140.

Weir, Angela, and Elizabeth Wilson. "The British Women's Movement." *New Left Review* no. 158 (1984): 74-103.

Wilcox, Penelope. "Marriage, Mobility and Domestic Service in Victorian Cambridge." *Local Population Studies* no. 29 (Autumn 1982): 19-34.

Willen, Diane. "Guildswomen in the City of York, 1560-1700." *The Historian* 46 (February 1984): 204-218.

Williams, Carolyn. "The Changing Face of Change: Fe/male In/constancy." *British Journal for Eighteenth-Century Studies* 12 (Spring 1989): 12-28.

Williams, John. "Irish Female Convicts and Tasmania." *Labour History* 44 (May 1983): 1-17.

Wilson, Adrian. "Illegitimacy and Its Implications in Mid-Eighteenth-Century London: The Evidence of the Foundling Hospital." *Continuity and Change* 4 (May 1989): 103-164.

Winter, James. "Widowed Mothers and Mutual Aid in Early Victorian Britain." *Journal of Social History* 17 (Fall 1983): 115-125.

Witkowski, J. A. "Optimistic Analysis--Chemical Embryology in Cambridge 1920-42." *Medical History* 31 (July 1987): 247-268.

Wolf, Toni Lesser. "Women Jewelers of the British Arts and Crafts Movement." *The Journal of Decorative and Propaganda Arts* 14 (Fall 1989): 28-45.

Woolf, D. R. "Two Elizabeths? James I and the Late Queen's Famous Memory." *Canadian Journal of History* 20 (August 1985): 167-192.

Worsnop, Judith. "A Reevaluation of 'the Problem of Surplus Women' in 19th-Century England: The Case of the 1851 Census." *Women's Studies International Forum* 13, no. 1/2 (1990): 21-32.

Yost, John K. "The Reformation Defense of Clerical Marriage in the Reigns of Henry VIII and Edward VI." *Church History* 50 (June 1981): 152-165.

Zimmeck, Meta. "Strategies and Stratagems for the Employment of Women in the British Civil Service, 1919-1939." *The Historical Journal* 27 (December 1984): 901-924.

# Northern Europe

Aberg, I. "Revivalism, Philanthropy and Emancipation: Women's Liberation and Organization in the Early Nineteenth-Century." *Scandinavian Journal of History* 13, no. 4 (1988).

Blom, Ida. "A Centenary of Organized Feminism in Norway." *Women's Studies* 5, no. 6 (1982): 569-574.

-----. "Changing Gender Identities in an Industrializing Society: The Case of Norway c. 1870-c. 1914." *Gender & History* 2 (Summer 1990): 131-147.

Bonner, T. N. "Pioneering in Women's Medical Education in the Swiss Universities 1864-1914." *Gesnerus* 45 (1988): 461-473.

-----. "Rendezvous in Zurich: Seven Who Made a Revolution in Women's Medical Education, 1864-1874." *Journal of the History of Medicine* 44, no. 1 (1989): 7-27.

Chapman, Dana Lacy, and Lois E. Dickey. "A Study of Costume through Art: An Analysis of Dutch Women's Costumes from 1600-1650." *Dress* 16 (1990): 28-37.

Christopherson, K. E. "Lady Inger and Her Family: Norway's Exemplar of Mixed Motives in the Reformation." *Church History* 55 (March 1986): 21-38.

Dukes, Paul. "The Leslie Family in the Swedish Period (1630-5) of the Thirty Years' War." *European Studies Review* 12 (October 1982): 401-424.

Egerbladh, Inez. "From Complex to Simple Family Households: Peasant Households in Northern Coastal Sweden 1700-1900." *Journal of Family History* 14, no. 3 (1989): 241-264.

Faber, Fokje. "Gender and Occupational Prestige. Some Observations about 'Sullerot's Law.'" *Netherlands' Journal of Social Sciences* 26 (April 1990): 51-66.

Gijswijt-Hofstra, Marijke. "The European Witchcraft Debate and the Dutch Variant." *Social History* 15 (May 1990): 181-194.

Hansen, Botil K. "Rural Women in Late Nineteenth-Century Denmark." *Journal of Peasant Studies* 9 (January 1982): 225-240.

Harbison, Craig. "Sexuality and Social Standing in Jan van Eyck's Arnolfini Double Portrait." *Renaissance Quarterly* 43 (Summer 1990): 249-291.

Ingelman, Ingrid. "Women Artists in Sweden: A Two-Front Struggle." *Woman's Art Journal* 5 (Spring/Summer 1984): 1-7.

Jochens, Jenny M. "The Church and Sexuality in Medieval Iceland." *Journal of Medieval History* 6 (December 1980): 377-392.

Johansson, Ella. "Beautiful Men, Fine Women and Good Workpeople: Gender and Skill in Northern Sweden, 1850-1950." *Gender & History* 1 (Summer 1989): 200-212.

Karras, Ruth Mazo. "Concubinage and Slavery in the Viking Age." *Scandinavian Studies* 62 (Spring 1990): 141-162.

Katz, David S. "Menasseh ben Israel's Mission to Queen Christina of Sweden, 1651-1655." *Jewish Social Studies* 45 (Winter 1983): 57-72.

Krotzl, C. "Parent-Child Relations in Medieval Scandinavia according to

Scandinavian Miracle Collections." *Scandinavian Journal of History* 14, no. 1 (1989): 21-38.

Lee, James, and Jon Gjerde. "Comparative Household Morphology of Stem, Joint and Nuclear Household Systems: Norway, China, and the United States." *Continuity and Change* 1, no. 1 (1986): 89-112.

Lieburg, M. J. van, and H. Morland. "Midwife Regulation, Education and Practice in the Netherlands During the Nineteenth Century." *Medical History* 33 (1989): 296-317.

Linke, Uli. "Women, Androgynes, and Models of Creation in Norse Mythology." *Journal of Psychohistory* 16 (Winter 1988): 231-262.

Matovic, Margareta R. "The Stockholm Marriage: Extra-Legal Family Formation in Stockholm, 1860-1890." *Continuity and Change* 1, no. 3 (1986): 385-414.

Monter, E. William. "Women in Calvinist Geneva (1550-1800)." *Signs* 6 (Winter 1980): 189-208.

Polasky, Janet. "Women in Revolutionary Belgium: From Stone Throwers to Hearth Tenders." *History Workshop* 21 (Spring 1986): 87-104.

Roodenburg, Herman W. "The Autobiography of Isabella DeMoerloose: Sex, Childrearing and Popular Belief in Seventeenth Century Holland." *Journal of Social History* 18 (Summer 1985): 517-540.

Skard, Torild, and Elina Haavio-Mannila. "Equality Between the Sexes--Myth or Reality in Norden?" *Daedalus* 113 (Winter 1984): 141-168.

Spierenburg, Pieter. "Imprisonment and the Family: An Analysis of Petitions for Confinement in Holland, 1680-1805." *Social Science History* 10 (Summer 1986): 115-146.

Stenflo, Gun Alm. "Parity-Dependent Fertility in a Population with Natural Fertility in Northern Sweden 1720-1900." *Journal of Family History* 14, no. 3 (1989): 211-228.

Sundin, Jan. "Family Building in Paternalistic Proto-Industries: A Cohort Study from Nineteenth-Century Swedish Iron Foundries." *Journal of Family History* 14, no. 3 (1989): 265-289.

Sundstrom, G. "A Haven in a Heartless World? Living With Parents in Sweden and the United States, 1880-1982." *Continuity and Change* 2, no. 1 (1987): 145-188.

Talberg, Marianne. "Nursing and Medical Care in Finland from the Eighteenth to the Late Nineteenth Century." *Scandinavian Journal of History* 14, no. 4 (1989): 269-284.

Watkins, Susan Cotts, and James McCarthy. "The Female Life Cycle in a Belgian Commune: La Hulpe, 1847-1866." *Journal of Family History* 5 (Summer 1980): 167-179.

Wirmark, Margareta. "Christina: Pandora or Eve." *Scandinavian Studies* 62 (Winter 1990): 116-122.

Wyntjes, Sherrin Marshall. "Survivors and Status: Widowhood and Family in the Early Modern Netherlands." *Journal of Family History* 7 (Winter 1982): 396-405.

## Southern Europe

Brennan, Brian. "'Episcipae': Bishops' Wives Viewed in Sixth-Century Gaul." *Church History* 54 (September 1985): 311-323.

Briggs, John W. "Fertility and Cultural Change Among Families in Italy and America." *American Historical Review* 91 (December 1986): 1129-1145.

Brown, Judith C. "Lesbian Sexuality in Renaissance Italy: The Case of Sister Benedetta Carline." *Signs* 9 (Summer 1984): 751-758.

Brown, Judith C., and Jordan Goodman. "Women and Industry in Florence." *Journal of Economic History* 40 (March 1980): 73-80.

Brundage, James A. "Matrimonial Politics in Thirteenth-Century Aragon: Moncada v. Urgel." *Journal of Ecclesiastical History* 31 (July 1980): 271-282.

-----. "Sumptuary Laws and Prostitution in Late Medieval Italy." *Journal of Medieval History* 13 (December 1987): 343-356.

Bullard, Melissa Meriam. "Marriage Politics and the Family in Florence: The Strozzi-Medici Alliance in 1508." *American Historical Review* 84 (June 1979): 668-687.

Chabot, Isabelle. "Poverty and the Widow in Late Medieval Florence." *Continuity and Change* 3, no. 2 (1988): 291-311.

Cicioni, Mirna. "'Love and Respect, Together': The Theory and Practice of *Affidamento* in Italian Feminism." *Australian Feminist Studies* no. 10 (Summer 1989): 71-84.

Cohen, Elizabeth S., and Thomas V. Cohen. "Camilla the Go-Between: The Politics of Gender in a Roman Household (1559)." *Continuity and Change* 4 (May 1989): 53-78.

Dillard, Heath. "Medieval Women in Castilian Town Communities." *Women's Studies* 11, no. 1/2 (1984): 115-138.

Eads, Valerie. "The Campaigns of Matilda of Tuscany." *Minerva: Quarterly Report on Women and the Military* 4 (Spring 1986): 167-181.

Gibson, Mary S. "The 'Female Offender' and the Italian School of Criminal Anthropology." *Journal of European Studies* 12 (September 1982): 155-165.

-----. "On the Insensitivity of Women: Science and the Woman Question in Liberal Italy, 1890-1910." *Journal of Women's History* 2 (Fall 1990): 11-41.

Grieve, Patricia E. "Mothers and Daughters in Fifteenth-Century Spanish Sentimental Romances: Implications for *Celestina.*" *Bulletin of Hispanic Studies* 67 (October 1990): 345-356.

Hart, Janet C. "Redeeming the Voices of a 'Sacrificed Generation': Oral Histories of Women in the Greek Resistance." *International Journal of Oral History* 10 (February 1989): 3-30.

Hughes, Diane Owen. "Representing the Family: Portraits and Purposes in Early Modern Italy." *Journal of Interdisciplinary History* 17 (Summer 1986): 7-38.

Kaplan, Temma. "Female Consciousness and Collective Action: The Case of Barcelona, 1910-1918." *Signs* 7 (Spring 1982): 545-566.

Keene, Judith. "A Spanish Springtime: Arleen Palmer and the Spanish Civil War." *Labour History* 52 (May 1987): 75-87.

Kirshner, Julius and Anthony Molho. "The Dowry Fund and the Marriage Market in Early Quattrocentro Florence." *Journal of Modern History* 50 (September 1978): 403-438.

Kuehn, Thomas. "'As If Conceived within a Legitimate Marriage' A Dispute Concerning Legitimation in Quattrocento Florence." *American Journal of Legal History* 29 (October 1985): 275-300.

Livi-Bacci, Massimo. "Fertility, Nutrition, and Pellagra: Italy During the Vital Revolution." *Journal of Interdisciplinary History* 16 (Winter 1986): 431-454.

Martin, John. "Out of the Shadow: Heretical and Catholic Women in Renaissance Venice." *Journal of Family History* 10 (Spring 1985): 21-33.

Reher, D. S. "Old Issues and New Perspectives: Household and Family within an Urban Context in Nineteenth Century Spain." *Continuity and Change* 2, no. 1 (1987): 103-144.

Robbert, Louise Buenger. "Twelfth-Century Italian Prices: Food and Clothing in Pisa and Venice." *Social Science History* 7 (Fall 1983): 381-404.

Romano, Dennis. "Gender and the Urban Geography of Renaissance Venice." *Journal of Social History* 23 (Winter 1989): 339-354.

Sealey, Raphael. "On Lawful Concubinage in Athens." *Classical Antiquity* 3 (April 1984): 111-133.

Sturcken, H. T. "The Unconsummated Marriage of Jaime of Aragon and Leonor of Castile (Oct 1319)." *Journal of Medieval History* 5 (September 1979): 185-202.

Sydie, R. A. "Humanism, Patronage and the Question of Women's Artistic Genius in the Italian Renaissance." *Journal of Historical Sociology* 2 (September 1989): 175-205.

Wells, Wendy. "Mercenary Prostitution in Ancient Greece." *Quest* 5 (Summer 1979): 76-80.

Welters, Linda. "The Transition from Folk to Fashionable Dress in Attica, Greece." *Dress* 11 (1985): 57-67.

## FAMILY

## Childbirth

Atkinson, Colin B., and William P. Stoneman. "'These Griping Greeffes and Pinching Pange': Attitudes to Childbirth in Thomas Bentley's *The Monument of Matrones* (1582)." *Sixteenth Century Journal* 21 (Summer 1990): 193-204.

Barkai, Ron. "A Medieval Hebrew Treatise on Obstetrics." *Medical History* 33 (January 1989): 96-119.

Bell, John. "Giving Birth to the New Soviet Man: Politics and Obstetrics in the USSR." *Slavic Review* 40 (Spring 1981): 1-16.

Biggs, C. Lesley. "The Case of the Missing Midwives: A History of Midwifery in Ontario from 1795-1900." *Ontario History* 75 (March 1983): 21-35.

Bogdan, Janet. "Care or Cure? Childbirth Practices in Nineteenth-Century America." *Feminist Studies* 4 (June 1978): 92-98.

Borst, Charlotte G. "Wisconsin's Midwives as Working Women: Immigrant Midwives and the Limits of a Traditional Occupation, 1870-1920." *Journal of American Ethnic History* 8 (Spring 1989): 24-59.

Cutright, Phillips, and Edward Shorter. "The Effects of Health on the Completed Fertility of Nonwhite and White U.S. Women Born Between 1867 and 1935." *Journal of Social History* 13 (Winter 1979): 191-218.

Declercq, Eugene, and Richard Lacroix. "The Immigrant Midwives of Lawrence: The Conflict Between Law and Culture in Early Twentieth-Century Massachusetts." *Bulletin of the History of Medicine* 59 (Summer 1985): 232-246.

-----. "The Nature and Style of Practice of Immigrant Midwives in Early Twentieth Century Massachusetts." *Journal of Social History* 19 (Fall 1985): 113-130.

Delacy, Margaret. "Puerperal Fever in Eighteenth Century Britain." *Bulletin of the History of Medicine* 63 (Winter 1989): 521-556.

Dewhurst, Sir John. "The Alleged Miscarriages of Catherine of Aragon and Anne Boleyn." *Medical History* 28 (January 1984): 49-56.

Dick, Kriste Lindenmeyer. "The Silent Charity: A History of the Cincinnati Maternity Society." *Queen City Heritage* 43 (Winter 1985): 29-33.

Dobbie, B. M. Willmott. "An Attempt to Estimate the True Rate of Maternal Mortality, Sixteenth to Eighteenth Centuries." *Medical History* 26 (January 1982): 79-89.

Dye, Nancy Schrom. "Modern Obstetrics and Working-Class Women: The New York Midwifery Dispensary, 1890-1920." *Journal of Social History* 20 (Spring 1987): 549-564.

Elder, Glen H. "Scarcity and Prosperity in Postwar Childbearing: Explorations from a Life Course Perspective." *Journal of Family History* 6 (Winter 1981): 410-433.

Fitzpatrick, Ellen. "Childbirth and an Unwed Mother in Seventeenth-Century New England." *Signs* 8 (Summer 1983): 744-749.

Forbes, Thomas R. "A Jury of Matrons." *Medical History* 32 (January 1988): 23-33.

Fuchs, Rachel G., and Paul E. Knepper. "Women in the Paris Maternity Hospital: Public Policy in the Nineteenth Century." *Social Science History* 13 (Summer 1989): 187-203.

Furth, Charlotte. "Concepts of Pregnancy, Childbirth and Infancy in Ch'ing Dynasty China." *Journal of Asian Studies* 46 (February 1987): 7-37.

Gorham, Deborah. "Birth and History." *Histoire sociale/Social History* 17 (November 1984): 383-394.

Hanson, Ann Ellis. "The Eight Months' Child and the Etiquette of Birth: *Obsit Omen!*" *Bulletin of the History of Medicine* 61 (Winter 1987): 589-602.

Ispa, Jean. "Soviet and American Childbearing Experiences and Attitudes: A Comparison." *Slavic Review* 42 (Spring 1983): 1-13.

Knodel, John, and Susan DeVos. "Preferences for the Sex of Offspring and Demographic Behavior in Eighteenth- and Nineteenth-Century Germany: An

Examination of Evidence from Village Genealogies." *Journal of Family History* 5 (Summer 1980): 145-166.

Kruk, R. "Pregnancy and Its Social Consequences in Mediaeval and Traditional Arab Society." *Quaderni di Studi Arabi* 5/6 (1987/1988): 418-430.

Landry, Donna, and Gerald MacLean. "Of Forceps, Patents and Paternity: *Tristram Shandy*." *Eighteenth-Century Studies* 23 (Summer 1990): 522-541.

Lansing, Dorothy I., W. Robert Penman, and Dorland J. Davis. "Puerperal Fever and the Group B Beta Hemolytic Streptococcus." *Bulletin of the History of Medicine* 57 (Spring 1983): 70-80.

Lantz, Herman, and Lewellyn Hendrix. "Black Fertility and the Black Family in the Nineteenth Century: A Re-Examination of the Past." *Journal of Family History* 3 (Fall 1978): 251-261.

Leavitt, Judith Walzer. "Under the Shadow of Maternity: American Women's Responses to Death and Debility Fears in Nineteenth-Century Childbirth." *Feminist Studies* 12 (Spring 1986): 129-154.

Lewis, Jan, and Kenneth A. Lockridge. "'Sally Has Been Sick': Pregnancy and Family Limitation Among Virginia Gentry Women, 1780-1830." *Journal of Social History* 22 (Fall 1988): 5-20.

Lindemann, Mary. "Maternal Politics: The Principles and Practice of Maternity Care in Eighteenth-Century Hamburg." *Journal of Family History* 9 (Spring 1984): 44-63.

Litoff, Judy Barett. "Forgotten Women: American Midwives at the Turn of the Twentieth Century." *Historian* 40 (February 1978): 235-251.

Loudon, Irvine. "Deaths in Childbed from the Eighteenth Century to 1935." *Medical History* 30 (January 1986): 1-41.

MacPike, Loralee. "The New Woman, Childbearing, and the Reconstruction of Gender, 1880-1900." *NWSA Journal* 1 (Spring 1989): 368-397.

McLaren, Angus. "Abortion in France: Women and the Regulation of Family Size." *French Historical Studies* 10 (Spring 1978): 461-485.

McPherson, K., and Veronica Strong-Boag. "The Confinement of Women: Childbirth and Hospitalization in Vancouver, 1919-1939." *B.C. Studies* 69/70 (Spring/Summer 1986): 142-174.

Mitchinson, Wendy. "Historical Attitudes toward Women and Childbirth." *Atlantis* 4 (1979): 13-34.

Oppenheimer, Jo. "Childbirth in Ontario: The Transition from Home to Hospital in the Early Twentieth Century." *Ontario History* 75 (March 1983): 36-60.

Silberman, Sara Lee. "Pioneering in Family-Centered Maternity and Infant Care: Edith B. Jackson and the Yale Rooming-In Research Project." *Bulletin of the History of Medicine* 64 (Summer 1990): 262-287.

Suitor, J. Jill. "Husbands' Participation in Childbirth: A Nineteenth-Century Phenomenon." *Journal of Family History* 6 (Fall 1981): 278-293.

Teachman, Jay D. "Historical and Subgroup Variations in the Association Between Marriage and First Childbirth: A Life-Course Perspective." *Journal of Family History* 10 (Winter 1985): 379-401.

Ulrich, Laurel Thatcher. "'The Living Mother of a Living Child': Midwifery and

Mortality in Post-Revolutionary New England." *William and Mary Quarterly* 66 (January 1989): 27-48.

Ward, W. Peter, and Patricia C. Ward. "Infant Birth Weight and Nutrition in Industrializing Montreal." *American Historical Review* 89 (April 1984): 324-345.

Weiner, Nella Fermi. "Baby Bust and Baby Boom: A Study of Family Size in a Group of University of Chicago Faculty Wives Born 1900-1934." *Journal of Family History* 8 (Fall 1983): 279-291.

## Childcare

Abbott, Ruth K., and R. A. Young. "Cynical and Deliberate Manipulation? Child Care and the Reserve Army of Female Labour in Canada." *Journal of Canadian Studies* 24 (Summer 1989): 22-38.

Apple, Rima D. "'To Be Used Only under the Direction of a Physician': Commercial Infant Feeding and Medical Practice, 1870-1940." *Bulletin of the History of Medicine* 54 (Fall 1980): 402-417.

Armitage, Susan. "Household Work and Childrearing on the Frontier: The Oral History Record." *Sociology and Social Research* 63 (April 1979): 467-474.

Austin, Linda T. "Babies for Sale: Tennessee's Children Adoption Scandal." *Tennessee Historical Quarterly* 49 (Summer 1990): 91-102.

Bardaglio, Peter W. "Challenging Parental Custody Rights: The Legal Reconstruction of Parenthood in the Nineteenth Century American South." *Continuity and Change* 4 (August 1989): 259-292.

Bishop, M. Guy. "Preparing to 'Take the Kingdom': Childrearing Directives in Early Mormonism." *Journal of the Early Republic* 7 (Fall 1987): 275-290.

Bridgeforth, Lucie Robertson. "The 'New' Woman in an Old Role: Maternal-Child Care in Memphis." *West Tennessee Historical Society Papers* 40 (December 1986): 45-54.

Broder, Sherri. "Child Care or Child Neglect? Baby Farming in Late-Nineteenth-Century Philadelphia." *Gender & Society* 2, no. 2 (1988): 128-148.

Campbell, L. "Wet-Nurses in Early Modern England: Some Evidence from the Townshend Archives." *Medical History* 33 (1989): 360-370.

Carson, S. L. "Presidential Children: Abandonment, Hysteria and Suicide." *Journal of Psychohistory* 11 (Spring 1984): 533-544.

Clark, Elaine. "City Orphans and Custody Laws in Medieval England." *American Journal of Legal History* 34 (April 1990): 168-187.

Clark, Gillian. "A Study of Nurse Children." *Local Population Studies* no. 39 (Autumn 1987): 8-23.

Crawford, Patricia. "'The Sucking Child': Adult Attitudes to Child Care in the First Year of Life in Seventeenth Century England." *Continuity and Change* 1, no. 1 (1986): 23-52.

Davis, Lynne. "Minding Children or Minding Machines . . . Women's Labour and Child Care During World War II." *Labour History* 53 (November 1987): 85-98.

Dwork, Deborah. "The Milk Option: An Aspect of the History of the Infant Welfare Movement in England 1898-1908." *Medical History* 31 (January 1987): 51-69.

Fildes, Valerie. "The English Wet-Nurse and Her Role in Infant Care 1538-1800." *Medical History* 32 (April 1988): 142-173.

Golden, J. "From Wet Nurse Directory to Milk Bank: The Delivery of Human Milk in Boston, 1909-1927." *Bulletin of the History of Medicine* 62 (1988): 589-605.

Grossberg, Michael. "Who Gets the Child? Custody, Guardianship, and Rise of Judicial Patriarchy in Nineteenth-Century America." *Feminist Studies* 9 (1983): 235-260.

Helvenston, Sally. "Advice to American Mothers on the Subject of Children's Dress 1800-1920." *Dress* 7 (1981): 31-46.

Herdman, Pam. "The Steward of Her Soul: Elsie Dinsmore and the Training of a Victorian Child." *American Studies* 29 (Fall 1988): 69-90.

Hind, Robert J. "The Loss of English Working-Class Parents' Control over Their Children's Education: The Role of Property-Holders." *Historical Reflections/Reflexions Historiques* 12 (Spring 1985): 77-108.

Horn, Margo. "The Moral Message of Child Guidance 1925-1945." *Journal of Social History* 18 (Fall 1984): 25-36.

Hunt, Marion. "Women and Childsaving: St. Louis Children's Hospital 1879-1979." *Bulletin of the Missouri Historical Society* 36 (January 1980): 65-79.

Jones, Kathleen W. "Sentiment and Science: The Late Nineteenth Century Pediatrician as Mother's Advisor." *Journal of Social History* 17 (Fall 1983): 79-96.

Kintner, Hallie J. "Trends and Regional Differences in Breastfeeding in Germany from 1871 to 1937." *Journal of Family History* 10 (Summer 1985): 163-182.

Lewis, Milton. "The Problem of Infant Feeding: The Australian Experience from the Mid-Nineteenth Century to the 1920s." *Journal of the History of Medicine and Allied Sciences* 35 (April 1980): 174-186.

Lewis, Norah L. "Creating the Little Machine: Child Rearing in British Columbia, 1919 to 1939." *B.C. Studies* 56 (Winter 1982/83): 44-60.

Lindemann, Mary. "Love for Hire: The Regulation of the Wet-Nursing Business in Eighteenth-Century Hamburg." *Journal of Family History* 6 (Winter 1981): 379-395.

Lithell, Ulla-Britt. "Breast-Feeding Habits and Their Relation to Infant Mortality and Marital Fertility." *Journal of Family History* 6 (Summer 1981): 182-194.

Lothrop, Gloria Ricci. "Nurturing Society's Children." *California History* 65 (December 1986): 274-283, 313-314.

Mariko, Fujita. "'It's All Mother's Fault': Childcare and Socialization of Working Mothers in Japan." *Journal of Japanese Studies* 15 (Winter 1989): 67-92.

McDougall, Mary Lynn. "Protecting Infants: The French Campaign for Maternity Leaves, 1890s-1913." *French Historical Studies* 13 (Spring 1983): 79-105.

McMillen, Sally. "Mother's Sacred Duty: Breast-feeding Patterns Among Middle-

and Upper-Class Women in the Antebellum South." *Journal of Southern History* 51 (August 1985): 333-356.

Miranda, Gloria E. "Hispano-Mexican Childrearing Practices in Pre-American Santa Barbara." *Southern California Quarterly* 65 (Winter 1983): 307-320.

Modell, John. "An Ecology of Family Decisions: Suburbanization, Schooling, and Fertility in Philadelphia, 1880-1920." *Journal of Urban History* 6 (August 1980): 397-418.

Reinier, Jacqueline. "Rearing the Republican Child: Attitudes and Practices in Post-Revolutionary Philadelphia." *William and Mary Quarterly* 39 (January 1982): 150-163.

Renne, Elisha P. "'If Men Are Talking, They Blame It on Women': A Nigerian Woman's Comments on Divorce and Child Custody." *Feminist Issues* 10 (Spring 1990): 37-49.

Rodgers, Daniel. "Socializing Middle-Class Children: Institutions, Fables, and Work Values in 19th Century America." *Journal of Social History* 13 (1980): 354-367.

Roodenburg, Herman W. "The Autobiography of Isabella DeMoerloose: Sex, Childrearing and Popular Belief in Seventeenth Century Holland." *Journal of Social History* 18 (Summer 1985): 517-540.

Seider, Reinhard. "'Vata, derf i aufstehn?': Childhood Experiences in Viennese Working-Class Families around 1900." *Continuity and Change* 1, no. 1 (1986): 53-88.

Shahar, Shulamith. "Infants, Infant Care, and Attitudes toward Infancy in the Medieval Lives of Saints." *Journal of Psychohistory* 10 (Winter 1983): 281-310.

Silberman, Sara Lee. "Pioneering in Family-Centered Maternity and Infant Care: Edith B. Jackson and the Yale Rooming-In Research Project." *Bulletin of the History of Medicine* 64 (Summer 1990): 262-287.

Summerfield, Penelope. "Women, Work, and Welfare: A Study of Child Care and Shopping in Britain in the Second World War." *Journal of Social History* 17 (Winter 1983): 249-270.

Swanson, Jenny. "Childhood and Childrearing in *ad status* Sermons by Later Thirteenth Century Friars." *Journal of Medieval History* 16 (December 1990): 309-332.

Treckel, Paula A. "Breast Feeding and Maternal Sexuality in Colonial America." *Journal of Interdisciplinary History* 20 (Summer 1989): 25-52.

Ward, W. Peter, and Patricia C. Ward. "Infant Birth Weight and Nutrition in Industrializing Montreal." *American Historical Review* 89 (April 1984): 324-345.

## Demographics

Aleksandrov, V. A. "Typology of the Russian Peasant Family in the Feudal Period." *Soviet Studies in History* 21 (Fall 1982): 26-62.

Anderson, Michael. "Household, Families and Individuals: Some Preliminary

Results from the National Sample from the 1851 Census of Great Britain."
*Continuity and Change* 3, no. 3 (1988): 421-438.

Angevine, Erma Miller. "Genealogical Research on Families of the District of
Columbia." *National Genealogical Society Quarterly* 78 (March 1990): 15-32.

Balmori, Diana, and Robert Oppenheimer. "Family Clusters: Generational
Nucleation in Nineteenth-Century Argentina and Chile." *Comparative Studies
in Society and History* [Great Britain] 21, no. 2 (1979): 136-158.

Barrett, Richard E. "Seasonality in Vital Processes in a Traditional Chinese
Population: Births, Deaths, and Marriages in Colonial Taiwan, 1906-1942."
*Modern China* 16 (April 1990): 190-225.

Blum, Alain, and Philippe Fargues. "Rapid Estimations of Maternal Mortality in
Countries with Defective Data. An Application to Bamako (1974-1985) and
Other Developing Countries." *Population Studies* 44 (March 1990): 155-171.

Briggs, John W. "Fertility and Cultural Change Among Families in Italy and
America." *American Historical Review* 91 (December 1986): 1129-1145.

Collomp, Alain. "From Stem Family to Nuclear Family: Changes in the
Coresident Domestic Group in Haute Provence Between the End of the
Eighteenth and the Middle of the Nineteenth Centuries." *Continuity and Change*
3, no. 1 (1988): 65-82.

Emery, George. "Incomplete Registration of Births in Civil Systems: The Example
of Ontario, Canada, 1900-1960." *Historical Methods* 23 (Winter 1990): 5-21.

Henderson, Rodger C. "Demographic Patterns and Family Structure in
Eighteenth-Century Lancaster County, Pennsylvania." *Pennsylvania Magazine
of History and Biography* 114 (July 1990): 349-383.

Howlett, Neil. "Family and Household in a Nineteenth Century Devon Village."
*Local Population Studies*, 30 (Spring 1983): 42-48.

Kertzer, David I. "The Joint Family Household Revisited: Demographic
Constraints and Household Complexity in the European Past." *Journal of
Family History* 14, no. 1 (1989): 1-16.

King, Miriam. "All in the Family? The Incompatibility and Reconciliation of
Family Demography and Family History." *Historical Methods* 23 (Winter
1990): 32-41.

Lee, James, and Robert Y. Eng. "Population and Family History in Eighteenth
Century Manchuria: Preliminary Results from Daoyi 1774-1798." *Late Imperial
China* 5 (June 1984): 1-55.

Lee, James, and Jon Gjerde. "Comparative Household Morphology of Stem, Joint
and Nuclear Household Systems: Norway, China, and the United States."
*Continuity and Change* 1, no. 1 (1986): 89-112.

Li, Peter S. "Immigration Laws and Family Patterns: Some Demographic Changes
Among Chinese Families in Canada, 1885-1971." *Canadian Ethnic
Studies/Etudes Ethniques Au Canada* 12, no. 1 (1980): 58-73.

Medjuck, Sheva. "Family and Household Composition in the Nineteenth Century:
The Case of Moncton, New Brunswick, 1851 to 1871." *Canadian Journal of
Sociology* 4 (Summer 1979): 275-286.

Mendels, Franklin F. "Notes on the Age of Maternity, Population Growth and

Family Structure in the Past." *Journal of Family History* 3 (Fall 1978): 236-250.

Mineau, Geraldine, Lee L. Bean, and Douglas L. Anderton. "Description and Evaluation of Linkage of the 1880 Census to Family Genealogies: Implications for Utah Fertility Research." *Historical Methods* 22 (Fall 1989): 144-157.

Morgan, V., and W. Macafee. "Household and Family Size and Structure in County Antrim." *Continuity and Change* 2, no. 3 (1987): 455-476.

Razzaque, Abdur, Nural Alam, Lokky Wai, and Andrew Foster. "Sustained Effects of the 1974-75 Famine on Infant and Child Mortality in a Rural Area of Bangaldesh." *Population Studies* 44 (March 1990): 145-154.

Ruggles, Steven. "Family Demography and Family History: Problems and Prospects." *Historical Methods* 23 (Winter 1990): 22-31.

Santi, Lawrence L. "Household Headship Among Unmarried Persons in the United States, 1970-1985." *Demography* 27 (May 1990): 219-232.

Smith, Daniel Blake. "The Study of the Family in Early America: Trends, Problems, and Prospects." *William and Mary Quarterly* 39 (January 1982): 3-28.

Teachman, Jay D. "Historical and Subgroup Variations in the Association Between Marriage and First Childbirth: A Life-Course Perspective." *Journal of Family History* 10 (Winter 1985): 379-401.

Vaughan, Megan. "Household Units and Historical Process in Southern Malawi." *Review of African Political Economy* 34 (December 1985): 35-45.

Waters, John L. "Family, Inheritance, and Migration in Colonial New England: The Evidence from Guilford, Connecticut." *William and Mary Quarterly* 39 (January 1982): 64-86.

Weiner, Nella Fermi. "Baby Bust and Baby Boom: A Study of Family Size in a Group of University of Chicago Faculty Wives Born 1900-1934." *Journal of Family History* 8 (Fall 1983): 279-291.

Wojtkiewicz, Roger A., Sara S. McLanahan, and Irwin Garfinkel. "The Growth of Families Headed by Women: 1950-1980." *Demography* 27 (February 1990): 19-30.

## Ethnicity

Ackerman, Lillian A. "The Effect of Missionary Ideals on Family Structure and Women's Roles in Plateau Indian Culture." *Idaho Yesterdays* 31 (Spring/Summer 1987): 64-74.

Bannan, H. M. "Warrior Women: Immigrant Mothers in the Works of Their Daughters." *Women's Studies* 6 (Winter 1979): 165-177.

Beesley, David. "From Chinese to Chinese American: Chinese Women & Families in a Sierra Nevada County." *California History* 67 (September 1988): 168-179.

Berlin, Ira, Steven F. Miller, and Leslie S. Rowland. "Afro-American Families in the Transition from Slavery to Freedom." *Radical History Review* 42 (1988): 89-121.

Bigham, Darrel E. "The Black Family in Evansville and Vanderburgh County, Indiana, in 1880." *Indiana Magazine of History* 75 (June 1979): 117-146.

Bloom, Florence Teicher. "Struggling and Surviving: The Life Style of European Immigrant Breadwinning Mothers in American Industrial Cities, 1900-1930." *Women's Studies* 8, no. 6 (1985): 609-620.

Borst, Charlotte G. "Wisconsin's Midwives as Working Women: Immigrant Midwives and the Limits of a Traditional Occupation, 1870-1920." *Journal of American Ethnic History* 8 (Spring 1989): 24-59.

Declercq, Eugene and Richard Lacroix. "The Immigrant Midwives of Lawrence: The Conflict Between Law and Culture in Early Twentieth-Century Massachusetts." *Bulletin of the History of Medicine* 59 (Summer 1985): 232-246.

-----. "The Nature and Style of Practice of Immigrant Midwives in Early Twentieth Century Massachusetts." *Journal of Social History* 19 (Fall 1985): 113-130.

Dill, Bonnie Thornton. "Our Mothers' Grief: Racial Ethnic Women and the Maintenance of Families." *Journal of Family History* 13, no. 4 (1988): 415-431.

Fielder, Mari Kathleen. "Chauncey Olcott: Irish-American Mother-Love, Romance and Nationalism." *Eire-Ireland* 22 (Summer 1987): 4-26.

Gabaccia, Donna. "*The Transplanted*: Women and Family in Immigrant America." *Social Science History* 12 (Fall 1988): 243-254.

Hampsten, Elizabeth. "A German-Russian Family in North Dakota." *Heritage of the Great Plains* 20 (Winter 1987): 15-20.

Harris, William G. "Research on the Black Family: Mainstream and Dissenting Perspectives." *Journal of Ethnic Studies* 6 (Winter 1979): 45-64.

Hurtado, Albert L. "'Hardly a Farm House--A Kitchen without Them': Indian and White Households on the California Borderland Frontier in 1860." *Western Historical Quarterly* 13 (July 1982): 245-270.

Hurwitz, Henry. "A Mother Remembered." *American Jewish History* 70 (September 1980): 5-22.

Jacoby, Susan. "World of Our Mothers: Immigrant Women, Immigrant Daughters." *Present Tense* 6, no. 3 (1979): 48-51.

Karsh, Audrey R. "Mothers and Daughters of Old San Diego." *Western States Jewish History* 19 (April 1987): 264-270.

Kellogg, Susan. "Exploring Diversity in Middle-Class Families: The Symbolism of American Ethnic Identity." *Social Science History* 14 (Spring 1990): 27-42.

LaBrack, Bruce and Karen Leonard. "Conflict and Compatibility in Punjabi-Mexican Immigrant Families in Rural California, 1915-1965." *Journal of Marriage and Family* 46 (August 1984): 527-537.

Li, Peter S. "Immigration Laws and Family Patterns: Some Demographic Changes Among Chinese Families in Canada, 1885-1971." *Canadian Ethnic Studies/Etudes Ethniques Au Canada* 12 (1980): 58-73.

Lipman, Rowena. "The Isaac and Rebecca Harris Family of San Francisco." *Western States Jewish History* 23 (October 1990): 15-19.

Marks, Lynne. "Kale Meydelach or Shulamith Girls: Cultural Change and Continuity Among Jewish Parents and Daughters--A Case Study of Toronto's Harbord Collegiate Institute in the 1920s." *Canadian Woman Studies/Les cahiers de la femme* 7 (Fall 1986): 85-89.

Meagher, Timothy J. "Sweet Good Mothers and Young Women out in the World: The Roles of Irish American Women in Late Nineteenth and Early Twentieth Century Worcester, Massachusetts." *U.S. Catholic Historian* 5 (Summer/Fall 1986): 325-344.

Medicine, Bea. "American Indian Family: Cultural Change and Adaptive Strategies." *Journal of Ethnic Studies* 8 (Winter 1981): 13-23.

Peffer, George Anthony. "Forbidden Families: Emigration Experiences of Chinese Women under the Page Law, 1875-1882." *Journal of American Ethnic History* 6 (Fall 1986): 28-46.

Russell-Wood, A. J. R. "The Black Family in the Americas." *Societas* 8 (Winter 1978): 1-38.

Salloum, Habeeb. "Reminiscences: The Urbanization of an Arab Homesteading Family." *Saskatchewan History* 42 (Spring 1989): 79-83.

Weinberg, Sydney Stahl. "Jewish Mothers and Immigrant Daughters: Positive and Negative Role Models." *Journal of American Ethnic History* 6 (Spring 1987): 39-55.

## General

Bahr, Howard M. "Ups and Downs: Three Middletown Families." *Wilson Quarterly* 11 (Winter 1987): 128-135.

Balmori, Diana A. "Family and Politics: Three Generations (1790-1890)." *Journal of Family History* 10 (Autumn 1985): 247-257.

Bate, Kerry William. "Family History: Some Answers, Many Questions." *Oral History Review* 16 (Spring 1988): 127-130.

Becnel, Thomas A. "The Ellenders: Pioneer Terrebonne Parish Family, 1840-1924." *Louisiana History* 26 (Spring 1985): 117-128.

Bernhard, Mary Elizabeth Kromer. "Portrait of A Family: Emily Dickinson's Norcross Connection." *New England Quarterly* 60 (September 1987): 363-381.

Bjorkman, Gwen Boyer. "Hannah (Baskel) Phelps Hill: A Quaker Woman and Her Offspring." *Southern Friend* 11 (Spring 1989): 10-30.

Boxer, Marilyn J. "'First-Wave' Feminism in Nineteenth-Century France: Class, Family, and Religion." *Women's Studies International Forum* 5, no. 6 (1982): 551-559.

Burdick, John. "From Virtue to Fitness: The Accommodation of a Planter Family to Postbellum Virginia." *Virginia Magazine of History and Biography* 93 (January 1985): 14-35.

Chapman, Berlin B. "The Neal Family and OAMC." *Chronicles of Oklahoma* 68 (Winter 1990/91): 340-359.

Cornell, L. L. "Analyzing the Consequences of Family Structure with Event-History Methods." *Historical Methods* 23 (Spring 1990): 53-62.

Courtwright, David. "New England Families in Historical Perspective." *Dublin Seminar for New England Folklife* (1985): 11-23.

Davis, Rodney O., ed. "A Hoosier Family Moves West, 1868-1895: Part I." *Indiana Magazine of History* 86 (March 1990): 50-93.

-----. "A Hoosier Family Moves West, 1868-1895: Part II." *Indiana Magazine of History* 86 (June 1990): 131-177.

Devereux, George. "The Family: Historical Function, Dysfunction, Lack of Function, and Schizophrenia." *Journal of Psychohistory* 8 (Fall 1980): 183-194.

Dubnoff, Steven. "Gender, the Family, and the Problem of Work Motivation in a Transition to Industrial Capitalism." *Journal of Family History* 4 (Summer 1979): 121-136.

Easton, Barbara. "Feminism and the Contemporary Family." *Socialist Review* 8 (May/June 1978): 11-36.

Epstein, Amy K. "Multifamily Dwellings and the Search for Respectability: Origins of the New York Apartment House." *Urbanism Past and Present* 5 (1980): 29-39.

Finkelstein, Barbara. "Tolerating Ambiguity in Family History: A Guide to Some Materials." *Journal of Psychohistory* 11 (Summer 1983): 117-128.

Hareven, Tamara K. "Family History at the Crossroads." *Journal of American History* 12, no. 1-3 (1987): ix-xxiii.

-----. "The History of the Family and the Complexity of Social Change." *American Historical Review* 96 (February 1991): 95-124.

Herring, Reuben. "Southern Baptist Convention Resolutions on the Family." *Baptist History and Heritage* 17 (January 1982): 36-45, 64.

Hickey, James T. "A Family Album: The Dressers of Springfield." *Journal of Illinois State Historical Society* 75 (Winter 1982): 309-319.

Hurtado, Albert L. "'Hardly a Farm House--A Kitchen without Them': Indian and White Households on the California Borderland Frontier in 1860." *Western Historical Quarterly* 13 (July 1982): 245-270.

Hutchinson, William Earl. "American Families: The Maurys of Virginia." *Manuscripts* 42 (Fall 1990): 293-302.

Kelley, Mary. "The Sentimentalists: Promise and Betrayal in the Home." *Signs* 4 (Spring 1979): 434-446.

Kellogg, Susan. "Exploring Diversity in Middle-Class Families: The Symbolism of American Ethnic Identity." *Social Science History* 14 (Spring 1990): 27-42.

Lazarus, Barbara, and John Modell. "Legacies: An Audiocourse on the History of Women and Families in America 1607-1870." *Social Science History* 12 (Spring 1988): 87-92.

Leboutte, Rene Georger Alter, and Myron Gutmann. "Analysis of Reconstituted Families: A Package of SAS Programs." *Historical Methods* 20 (Winter 1987): 29-34.

Lewis, Jan. "Domestic Tranquility and the Management of Emotion Among the Gentry of Pre-Revolutionary Virginia." *William and Mary Quarterly* 39 (January 1982): 135-149.

Lovell, Margaretta M. "Reading Eighteenth-Century American Family Portraits:

Social Images and Self-Images." *Winterthur Portfolio* 22 (Winter 1987): 243-264.

Macdougall, Elisabeth Blair. "A Circus, a Wild Man and a Dragon: Family History and the Villa Mattei." *Journal of the Society of Architectural Historians* 42 (May 1983): 121-130.

McClymer, John F. "The 'American Standard' of Living: Family Expectations and Strategies for Getting and Spending in the Gilded Age." *Hayes Historical Journal* 9 (Spring 1990): 20-43.

Matthews, Fred. "The Utopia of Human Relations: The Conflict-Free Family in American Social Thought, 1930-1960." *Journal of the History of the Behavioral Sciences* 24 (1988): 343-362.

Mintz, Steven. "Regulating the American Family." *Journal of Family History* 14, no. 4 (1989): 387-408.

Moran, Gerald F., and Maris Vinoskies. "The Puritan Family and Religion: A Critical Reappraisal." *William and Mary Quarterly* 39 (January 1982): 29-63.

Otto, John Solomon, and Ben Wayne Banks. "The Banks Family of Yell County, Arkansas: A 'Plain Folk' Family of the Highland South." *Arkansas Historical Quarterly* 41 (Summer 1982): 146-167.

Rapp, Rajna, Ellen Ross, and Renate Bridenthal. "Examining Family History." *Feminist Studies* 5 (Spring 1979): 174-200.

Robbert, Louise Buenger. "Lutheran Families in St. Louis and Perry County, Missouri, 1839-1870." *Missouri Historical Review* 82 (July 1988): 424-438.

Ryan, Mary P. "The Explosion of Family History." *Reviews in American History* 10 (December 1982): 181-195.

-----. "A Woman's Awakening: Evangelical Religion and the Families of Utica, New York, 1800-1840." *American Quarterly* 30 (1978): 602-633.

Samuels, Shirley. "The Family, the State, and the Novel in the Early Republic." *American Quarterly* 38, no. 3 (1986): 381-395.

Shurden, Kay. "The Impact of Southern Baptist Women on Social Issues: Three Viewpoints: Family Issues." *Baptist History and Heritage* 22 (July 1987): 33-36.

Sommerville, C. John. "The Family Fights Back: Its Struggle with Religious Movements." *Fides et Historia* 15 (Fall-Winter 1982): 6-23.

Spierenburg, Pieter. "Imprisonment and the Family: An Analysis of Petitions for Confinement in Holland, 1680-1805." *Social Science History* 10 (Summer 1986): 115-146.

Sverdlov, M. B. "Family and Commune in Ancient Russia." *Soviet Studies in History* 21 (Fall 1982): 1-25.

Tilly, Louise A. "Women's History and Family History: Fruitful Collaboration or Missed Connection?" *Journal of Family History* 12, no. 1/3 (1987): 303-318.

Tilly, Louise A., and Miriam Cohen. "Does the Family Have a History? A Review of Theory & Practice in Family History." *Social Science History* 6 (Spring 1982): 131-180.

Walton, Whitney. "Feminine Hospitality in the Bourgeois Home of

Nineteenth-Century France." *Western Society for French History* 14 (November 1986): 197-203.

## Infant Mortality

Behlmer, George K. "Deadly Motherhood: Infanticide and Medical Opinion in Mid-Victorian England." *Journal of the History of Medicine and Allied Sciences* 34 (October 1979): 403-427.

Buchanan, I. "Infant Mortality and Social Policy: The Eugenists and the Social Ameliorators, 1900-1914." *Society for the Social History of Medicine Bulletin* 27 (1980): 5-8.

Dresch, Catherine. "Maternal Nutrition and Infant Mortality Rates: An Evaluation of the Bourgeoisie of 18th-Century Montheliard." *Food & Foodways* 4, no. 1 (1990): 1-38.

Dye, Nancy Schrom, and Daniel Blake Smith. "Mother Love and Infant Death, 1750-1920." *Journal of American History* 73 (September 1986): 329-353.

Dyehouse, Carol. "Working-Class Mothers and Infant Mortality in England, 1895-1914." *Journal of Social History* 12 (Winter 1978): 248-267.

Hoffert, Sylvia D. "'A Very Peculiar Sorrow': Attitudes toward Infant Death in the Urban Northeast, 1800-1860." *American Quarterly* 39 (1987): 601-616.

Johnson, Michael P. "Smothered Slave Infants: Were Slave Mothers at Fault?" *Journal of Southern History* 47 (November 1981): 493-520.

Lithell, Ulla-Britt. "Breast-Feeding Habits and Their Relation to Infant Mortality and Marital Fertility." *Journal of Family History* 6 (Summer 1981): 182-194.

Ulbricht, Otto. "The Debate about Foundling Hospitals in Enlightenment Germany: Infanticide, Illegitimacy, and Infant Mortality Rates." *Central European History* 18 (September/December 1985): 211-256.

## International

Andreeva, I. S. "Sociophilosophical Problems of Sex, Marriage, and the Family." *Soviet Review* 22 (1981/82): 20-43.

Anees, Munawar Ahmad. "Study of Muslim Woman and Family: A Bibliography." *Muslim World Book Review* 8, no. 2 (1988): 59-67.

Arrom, Silvia M. "Changes in Mexican Family Law the Nineteenth Century: The Civil Codes of 1870 and 1884." *Journal of Family History* 10 (Autumn 1985): 305-317.

Barbagli, Marzio and David Kertzer. "An Introduction to the History of Italian Family Life." *Journal of Family History* 15, no. 4 (1990): 369-384.

Bell, John. "Giving Birth to the New Soviet Man: Politics and Obstetrics in the USSR." *Slavic Review* 40 (Spring 1981): 1-16.

Brown, Elizabeth A. R. "Authority, the Family, and the Dead in Late Medieval France." *French Historical Studies* 16 (Fall 1990): 803-832.

Bumsted, J. M., and Wendy Owen. "The Victorian Family in Canada in Historical Perspective: The Ross Family of Red River and the Jarvis Family of Prince

Edward Island." *Manitoba History* 13 (Spring 1987): 12-18.

Carlitz, Katherine N. "Family, Society, and Tradition in Jin ping mei." *Modern China* 10 (October 1984): 387-414.

Chandler, David S. "Family Bonds and the Bondsman: The Slave Family in Colonial Colombia." *Latin American Research Review* 16 (1981): 107-131.

Christopherson, K. E. "Lady Inger and Her Family: Norway's Exemplar of Mixed Motives in the Reformation." *Church History* 55 (March 1986): 21-38.

Couturier, Edith. "Women and the Family in Eighteenth-Century Mexico: Law and Practice." *Journal of Family History* 10 (Fall 1985): 294-304.

Crew, David F. "German Socialism, the State and Family Policy, 1918-33." *Continuity and Change* 1, no. 2 (1986): 235-264.

Donovan, Grace. "An American Catholic in Victorian England: Louisa, Duchess of Leeds, and the Carroll Family Benefice." *Maryland Historical Magazine* 84 (Fall 1989): 223-234.

Duben, Alan. "Understanding Muslim Households and Families in Late Ottoman Istanbul." *Journal of Family History* 15, no. 1 (1990): 71-86.

Ebrey, Patricia. "Conceptions of the Family in the Sung Dynasty." *Journal of Asian Studies* 43 (February 1984): 219-246.

Hanley, Sarah. "Engendering the State: Family Formation and State Building in Early Modern France." *French Historical Studies* 16 (Spring 1989): 4-27.

Hughes, Diane Owen. "Representing the Family: Portraits and Purposes in Early Modern Italy." *Journal of Interdisciplinary History* 17 (Summer 1986): 7-38.

Kaiser, Daniel H. "Soviet Studies on the History of the Family." *Soviet Studies in History* 21 (Fall 1982): v-xvi.

Kuznesof, Elizabeth Anne, and Robert Oppenheimer. "The Family and Society in Nineteenth-Century Latin America: An Historiographical Introduction." *Journal of Family History* 10 (Autumn 1985): 215-234.

Lavrin, Asuncion. "Women, the Family and Social Change in Latin America." *World Affairs* 150 (Fall 1987): 108-128.

Oppo, Anna. "'Where There's No Woman There's No Home': Profile of the Agro-Pastoral Family in Nineteenth-Century Sardinia." *Journal of Family History* 15, no. 4 (1990): 483-502.

Phillips, Roderick. "Women's Emancipation, the Family and Social Change in Eighteenth-Century France." *Journal of Social History* 12 (Summer 1979): 553-567.

Rabinovich, M. G. "The Russian Urban Family at the Beginning of the Eighteenth Century." *Soviet Studies in History* 21 (Fall 1982): 63-87.

Rassam, Amal. "Women and Domestic Power in Morocco." *International Journal of Middle East Studies* 7, no. 2 (1980): 171-179.

Reher, D. S. "Old Issues and New Perspectives: Household and Family within an Urban Context in Nineteenth Century Spain." *Continuity and Change* 2, no. 1 (1987): 103-144.

Saller, Richard. "*Patria Potestas* and the Stereotype of the Roman Family." *Continuity and Change* 1, no. 1 (1986): 7-22.

Shortt, Mary. "Touring Theatrical Families in Canada West: The Hills and the

Herons." *Ontario History* 74 (March 1982): 3-25.

Smith, Robert J. "Making Village Women into 'Good Wives and Wise Mothers' in Prewar Japan." *Journal of Family History* 8 (Spring 1983): 70-84.

Szuchman, Mark D. "Household Structure and Political Crisis: Buenos Aires, 1810-1860." *Latin American Research Review* 21 (1986): 55-93.

Todorova, Maria. "Myth-Making in European Family History: The Zadruga Revisted." *East European Politics and Societies* 4 (Winter 1990): 30-76.

Underwood, Malcolm G. "Politics and Piety in the Household of Lady Margaret Beaufort." *Journal of Ecclesiastical History* 38 (January 1987): 39-52.

Vasary, Ildiko. "'The Sin of Transdanubia': The One-Child System in Rural Hungary." *Continuity and Change* 4 (December 1989): 429-468.

Viazzo, Pier Paolo and Dionigi Albera. "The Peasant Family in Northern Italy, 1750-1930: A Reassessment." *Journal of Family History* 15, no. 4 (1990): 461-482.

Wall, Alison. "Elizabethan Precept and Feminine Practice: The Thynne Family of Longleat." *History* 75 (February 1990): 23-38.

Walton, Linda. "Kinship, Marriage, and Status in Song China: A Study of the Lou Lineage of Ningbo, c. 1050-1250." *Journal of Asian History* 18, no. 1 (1984): 1-34.

## Kinship

Ackerman, Lillian A. "The Effect of Missionary Ideals on Family Structure and Women's Roles in Plateau Indian Culture." *Idaho Yesterdays* 31 (Spring/Summer 1987): 64-74.

Allured, Janet. "Ozark Women and the Companionate Family in the Arkansas Hills, 1870-1910." *Arkansas Historical Quarterly* 47 (Autumn 1988): 230-256.

Antler, Joyce. "'After College, What?': New Graduates and the Family Claim." *American Quarterly* 32 (Fall 1980): 409-434.

Bennett, Judith M. "Spouses, Siblings and Surnames: Reconstructing Families From Medieval Village Court Roles." *The Journal of British Studies* 23 (Fall 1983): 26-46.

Blackburn, George, and Sherman L. Richards. "The Mother-Headed Family Among Free Negroes in Charleston, South Carolina, 1850-1860." *Phylon* 42 (March 1981): 11-25.

Caine, Barbara. "Family History as Women's History: The Sisters of Beatrice Webb." *Feminist Studies* 12 (Summer 1986): 295-320.

Calvert, Karin. "Children in American Family Portraiture, 1670-1810." *William and Mary Quarterly* 39 (January 1982): 87-113.

Cashin, Joan E. "The Structure of Antebellum Planter Families: 'The Ties That Bound Us Was Strong.'" *Journal of Southern History* 56 (February 1990): 55-70.

Clawson, Mary Ann. "Early Modern Fraternalism and the Patriarchal Family." *Feminist Studies* 6 (Summer 1980): 368-391.

Cody, Cheryll Ann. "Naming, Kinship, and Estate Dispersal: Notes on Slave

Family Life on a South Carolina Plantation, 1786 to 1833." *William and Mary Quarterly* 39 (January 1982): 192-211.

Cohen, Elizabeth. "Fond Fathers, Devoted Daughters? Family Sentiment in Seventeenth Century France." *Histoire sociale/Social History* 19 (November 1986): 343-363.

Cohen, Elizabeth, and Thomas V. Cohen. "Camilla the Go-Between: The Politics of Gender in a Roman Household (1559)." *Continuity and Change* 4 (May 1989): 53-78.

Craton, Michael. "Changing Patterns of Slave Families in the British West Indies." *Journal of Interdisciplinary History* 10 (Summer 1979): 1-35.

Dolensky, Suzanne T. "The Daughters of Jefferson Davis: A Study of Contrast." *Mississippi History* 51 (November 1989): 313-340.

Ebrey, Patricia. "Women in the Kinship System of the Southern Song Upper Class." *Historical Reflections/Reflexions Historiques* 8 (Fall 1981): 113-128.

------. "The Women in Liu Kezhuang's Family." *Modern China* 10, 4 (October 1984): 415-440.

Eisenmann, Linda. "Sisterhood and the Family Claim in Nineteenth Century America." *History of Education Quarterly* 29 (Fall 1989): 465-473.

Embry, Jessie L., and Martha S. Bradley. "Mothers and Daughters in Polygamy." *Dialogue* 18 (Fall 1985): 99-107.

Farnsworth, Beatrice. "The Litigious Daughter-in-law: Family Relations in Rural Russia in the Second Half of the Nineteenth Century." *Slavic Review* 45 (Spring 1986): 49-64.

Fellman, Anita Clair. "Laura Ingalls Wilder and Rose Wilder Lane: The Politics of a Mother-Daughter Relationship." *Signs* 15 (Spring 1990): 535-561.

Goodman, Dena. "Filial Rebellion in the Salon: Madame Geoffrin and Her Daughter." *French Historical Studies* 16 (Spring 1989): 28-47.

Green, Gretchen. "Molly Brant, Catharine Brant, and Their Daughters: A Study in Colonial Acculturation." *Ontario History* 81 (September 1989): 235-250.

Hanchett, Catherine M. "'What Sort of People and Families . . .': The Edmondson Sisters." *Afro-Americans in New York Life and History* 6 (July 1982): 21-38.

Hauser, William B. "Why So Few?: Women Household Heads in Osaka Chonin Families." *Journal of Family History* 11, no. 4 (1986): 343-352.

Hawks, Joanne Varner. "Like Mother, Like Daughter: Nellie Nugent Somerville and Lucy Somerville Howorth." *Journal of Mississippi History* 45 (May 1983): 116-128.

Horn, Margo E. "'Sisters Worthy of Respect': Family Dynamics and Women's Roles in the Blackwell Family." *Journal of Family History* 8 (Winter 1983): 367-382.

Jacoby, Susan. "World of Our Mothers: Immigrant Women, Immigrant Daughters." *Present Tense* 6, no. 3 (1979): 48-51.

Judd, Ellen R. "*Niangji*: Chinese Women and Their Natal Families." *Journal of Asian Studies* 48 (August 1989): 525-544.

Karsh, Audrey R. "Mothers and Daughters of Old San Diego." *Western States*

*Jewish History* 19 (April 1987): 264-270.

Kertzer, David I. and Dennis P. Hogan. "Household Organization and Migration in Nineteenth-Century Italy." *Social Science History* 14 (Winter 1990): 483-506.

Kim, Susie. "Two Women Under the Same Roof: The Family in Transitional Korean Society." *American Asian Review* 9 (Spring 1991): 65-80.

Klassen, John. "Household Composition in Medieval Bohemia." *Journal of Medieval History* 16 (March 1990): 55-76.

Koch, Mary Levin. "Letters from LaGrange:  The Correspondence of Caroline Haralson and Her Daughters (1844-51)." *Georgia History Quarterly* 66 (Spring 1982): 33-46.

Krotzl, C. "Parent-Child Relations in Medieval Scandinavia according to Scandinavian Miracle Collections." *Scandinavian Journal of History* 14, no. 1 (1989): 21-38.

Kuznesof, Elizabeth Anne. "The Role of the Female-Headed Household in Brazilian Modernization: Sao Paulo 1765 to 1836." *Journal of Social History* 13 (Summer 1980): 589-613.

Laslett, Peter. "Family, Kinship and Collectivity as Systems of Support in Pre-Industrial Europe: A Consideration of the 'Nuclear-Hardship' Hypothesis." *Continuity and Change* 3, no. 2 (1988): 153-176.

Lebsock, Suzanne. "'We Have Not Lived for Ourselves Alone':  Women and Domesticity in Antebellum Petersburg." *Virginia Cavalcade* 33 (Autumn 1983): 53-63.

-----. "Free Black Women and the Question of Matriarchy:  Petersburg, Virginia, 1784-1820." *Feminist Studies* 8 (Summer 1982): 271-292.

Levi, Giovanni. "Family and Kin--a Few Thoughts." *Journal of Family History* 15, no. 4 (1990): 567-580.

Levine, David. "Recombinant Family Formation Strategies." *Journal of Historical Sociology* 2 (June 1989): 89-115.

Logue, Larry M. "Modernization Arrested: Child Naming and the Family in a Utah Town." *Journal of American History* 74 (June 1987): 131-138.

Malone, Ann Patton. "Searching for the Family and Household Structure of Rural Louisiana Slaves, 1810-1864." *Louisiana History* 28 (Fall 1987): 357-380.

Marks, Lynne. "Kale Meydelach or Shulamith Girls: Cultural Change and Continuity Among Jewish Parents and Daughters--A Case Study of Toronto's Harbord Collegiate Institute in the 1920s." *Canadian Woman Studies/Les cahiers de la femme* 7 (Fall 1986): 85-89.

Maskiell, Michelle. "Gender, Kinship and Rural Work in Colonial Punjab." *Journal of Women's History* 2 (Spring 1990): 35-72.

Michie, Helena. "'There Is No Friend like a Sister': Sisterhood as Sexual Difference." *ELH* 56 (Summer 1989): 401-422.

Moss, Jane. "Filial (Im)Pieties: Mothers and Daughters in Quebec Women's Theatre." *The American Review of Canadian Studies* 19 (Summer 1989): 177-186.

Okin, Susan Moller. "Women and the Making of the Sentimental Family."

*Philosophy and Public Affairs* 11 (Winter 1982): 65-88.

Parr, Joy. "Rethinking Work and Kinship in a Canadian Hosiery Town, 1910-1950." *Feminist Studies* 13 (Spring 1987): 137-162.

Peters, Bette D. "Colorado's 'Mother Cawker' and Her Offspring." *National Genealogical Society Quarterly* 78 (June 1990): 115-134.

Petrik, Paula. "Mothers and Daughters of Eldorado: The Fisk Family of Helena, Montana, 1867-1902." *Montana* 32 (Summer 1982): 50-63.

Pyenson, Lewis. "Einstein's Natural Daughter." *History of Science* 28 (December 1990): 365-379.

Ross, Frances Mitchell, ed. "'A Tie Between Us That Time Cannot Sever': Latta Family Letters, 1855-1872." *Arkansas Historical Quarterly* 40 (Spring 1981): 31-78.

Rotter, Andrew J. "'Matilda for Gods Sake Write': Women and Families on the Argonaut Mind." *California History* 58 (Summer 1979): 128-141.

Sandburg, Helga. "Eyeing the World with All Delight: Helga Sandburg Looks Back at Her Family." *Illinois Historical Journal* 81 (Summer 1988): 82-94.

Smith, Daniel Scott, Michel Dahlin, and Mark Friedberger. "The Family Structure of the Older Black Population in the American South in 1880-1900." *Sociology and Social Research* 63, no. 3 (1979): 544-565.

Smith, Eleanor. "African American Women and the Extended Family: A Sociohistorical Review." *Western Journal of Black Studies* 13 (Winter 1989): 179-184.

Smith, Eleanor, and Paul M. Smith, Jr. "The Black Female Single-Parent Family Condition." *Journal of Black Studies* 17 (September 1986): 125-134.

Stowe, Steven M. "The Rhetoric of Authority: The Making of Social Values in Planter Family Correspondence." *Journal of American History* 73 (March 1987): 916-933.

Szuchman, Mark D. "Household Structure and Political Crisis: Buenos Aires, 1810-1860." *Latin American Research Review* 21 (1986): 55-93.

Toliver, Susan D. "20/20 Vision: A Perspective on Women's Changing Roles and the Structure of American Families, Past and Future." *Frontiers* 9, no. 1 (1986): 25-31.

Walters, J., and L. H. Walters. "Parent-child Relationships: A Review, 1970-1979." *Journal of Marriage and Family* 42, no. 4 (1980): 807-822.

Walton, Linda. "Kinship, Marriage, and Status in Song China: A Study of the Lou Lineage of Ningbo, c. 1050-1250." *Journal of Asian History* 18, no. 1 (1984): 1-34.

Weinberg, Sydney Stahl. "Jewish Mothers and Immigrant Daughters: Positive and Negative Role Models." *Journal of American Ethnic History* 6 (Spring 1987): 39-55.

Winsser, Johan. "Mary (Dyre) Ward: Mary (Barrett) Dyre's Missing Daughter Traced." *New England Historical and Genealogical Register* 145 (January 1991): 22-28.

# Motherhood

Allen, Ann Taylor. "Mothers of the New Generation: Adele Schreiber, Helene Stocker, and the Evolution of a German Idea of Motherhood, 1900-1914." *Signs* 10 (Spring 1985): 418-438.

Behlmer, George K. "Deadly Motherhood: Infanticide and Medical Opinion in Mid-Victorian England." *Journal of the History of Medicine and Allied Sciences* 34 (October 1979): 403-427.

Blackburn, George, and Sherman L. Richards. "The Mother-Headed Family Among Free Negroes in Charleston, South Carolina, 1850-1860." *Phylon* 42 (March 1981): 11-25.

Bland, Sue. "Henrietta the Homemaker and Rosie the Riveter: Images of Women in Advertising 1939-1950." *Atlantis* 8 (Spring 1983): 61-86.

Bloch, Ruth H. "American Feminine Ideals in Transition: The Rise of the Moral Mother, 1785-1815." *Feminist Studies* 4 (June 1978): 100-126.

Bloom, Florence Teicher. "Struggling and Surviving: The Life Style of European Immigrant Breadwinning Mothers in American Industrial Cities, 1900-1930." *Women's Studies* 8, no. 6 (1985): 609-620.

Bock, Gisela. "Racism and Sexism in Nazi Germany: Motherhood, Compulsory Sterilization, and the State." *Signs* 8 (Spring 1983): 400-421.

Boris, Eileen. "Regulating Industrial Homework: The Triumph of 'Sacred Motherhood'." *Journal of American History* 71 (March 1985): 745-763.

Bridgeforth, Lucie Robertson. "The 'New' Woman in an Old Role: Maternal-Child Care in Memphis." *West Tennessee Historical Society Papers* 40 (December 1986): 45-54.

Burton, June K. "Infanticide in Napoleonic France: The Law, the Medical Profession, and the Murdering Mother." *Western Society for French History* 14 (November 1986): 183.

Clark, James. "A Mother's Plea." *Civil War Times* (February 1985): 40-42.

Conner, Valerie J. "'The Mothers of the Race' in World War I: The National War Labor Board and Women in Industry." *Labor History* 21, no.1 (1980): 31-54.

Cookingham, Mary E. "Combining Marriage, Motherhood, and Jobs Before World War II: Women College Graduates, Classes of 1905-1935." *Journal of Family History* 9 (Summer 1984): 178-195.

-----. "Working after Childbearing in Modern America." *Journal of Interdisciplinary History* 14 (Spring 1984): 773-792.

Cooney, Bob, and Sayre Cooney Dodgson. "Fanny Cory Cooney: Montana Mother and Artist." *Montana* 30 (July 1980): 2-17.

Cown, Ruth Schwartz. "Less Work for Mother." *American Heritage* 38 (September/October 1987): 68-76.

Davin, Anna. "Imperialism and Motherhood." *History Workshop* 5 (Spring 1978): 9-66.

Dobler, Grace. "Oil Field Camp Wives and Mothers." *Kansas History* 10 (Spring 1987): 29-42.

Dye, Nancy Schrom, and Daniel Blake Smith. "Mother Love and Infant Death,

1750-1920." *Journal of American History* 73 (September 1986): 329-353.

Dyehouse, Carol. "Working-Class Mothers and Infant Mortality in England, 1895-1914." *Journal of Social History* 12 (Winter 1978): 248-267.

Ebrahim, Abul Fadl Mohsin. "Islamic Teachings and Surrogate Motherhood." *Journal for the Study of Religion* 3 (March 1990): 35-46.

Evans, Janet. "The Communist Party of the Soviet Union and the Women's Question: The Case of the 1936 Decree 'In Defence of Mother and Child.'" *Journal of Contemporary History* 16 (October 1981): 757-776.

Fielder, Mari Kathleen. "Chauncey Olcott: Irish-American Mother-Love, Romance and Nationalism." *Eire-Ireland* 22 (Summer 1987): 4-26.

Fitzpatrick, Ellen. "Childbirth and an Unwed Mother in Seventeenth-Century New England." *Signs* 8 (Summer 1983): 744-749.

Gaitskell, Deborah. "Housewives, Maids or Mothers: Some Contradictions of Domesticity for Christian Women in Johannesburg, 1903-39." *Journal of African History* 24, no. 2 (1983): 241-256.

Ganson, Barbara J. "Following Their Children into Battle: Women at War in Paraguay, 1864-1870." *The Americas* 46 (January 1990): 335-372.

Garrett, Eilidh M. "The Trials of Labour: Motherhood versus Employment in a Nineteenth-Century Textile Centre." *Continuity and Change* 5, no. 1 (1990): 121-154.

Gay, Judith. "'Mummies and Babies' and Friends and Lovers in Lesotho." *Journal of Homosexuality* 11, no. 3/4 (1985): 97-116.

Gear, Josephine. "The Baby's Picture: Woman as Image Maker in Small-Town America." *Feminist Studies* 13 (Summer 1987): 419-442.

Grimshaw, Patricia. "'Christian Woman, Pious Wife, Faithful Mother, Devoted Missionary': Conflicts in Roles of American Missionary Women in Nineteenth-Century Hawaii." *Feminist Studies* 9 (Summer 1983): 489-522.

Helterline, Marilyn. "The Emergence of Modern Motherhood: Motherhood in England 1899 to 1959." *International Journal of Women's Studies* 3 (November/December 1980): 590-614.

Hoffnung, Michele. "Teaching about Motherhood: Close Kin and the Transition of Motherhood." *Women's Studies Quarterly* 16 (Fall/Winter 1988): 48-57.

Hurwitz, Henry. "A Mother Remembered." *American Jewish History* 70 (September 1980): 5-22.

Huss, Marie-Monique. "Pronatalism in the Inter-war Period in France." *Journal of Contemporary History* 25 (January 1990): 39-68.

Johnson, James P. "Death, Grief, and Motherhood: The Woman Who Inspired Mother's Day." *West Virginia History* 39 (January/April 1978): 187-194.

Juteau, Danielle, and Nicole Laurin. "From Nuns to Surrogate Mothers: Evolution of the Forms of the Appropriation of Women." *Feminist Issues* 9 (Spring 1989): 13-40.

Killingsworth, Myrth Jimmie. "Whitman and Motherhood: A Historical View." *American Literature* 54 (March 1982): 28-43.

Leiber, Justin, James Pickering, and Flora Bronson White, eds. "'Mother by the Tens': Flora Adelaide Holcomb Bronson's Account of Her Life as an Illinois

Schoolteacher, Poet, and Farm Wife, 1851-1927." *Journal of the Illinois State Historical Society* 76 (Winter 1983): 283-307.

Lewis, Jane. "Motherhood Issues During the Late Nineteenth and Early Twentieth Centuries: Some Recent Viewpoints." *Ontario History* 75 (March 1983): 4-20.

List, Karen K. "The Post-Revolutionary Woman Idealized: Philadelphia Media's 'Republican Mother.'" *Journalism Quarterly* 66 (Spring 1989): 65-75.

Mackie, Vera. "Motherhood and Pacificism in Japan, 1900-1937." *Hecate* 14 (Winter 1989): 28-49.

Mannard, Joseph G. "Maternity . . . of the Spirit: Nuns and Domesticity in Antebellum America." *U.S. Catholic Historian* 5 (Summer 1986): 305-324.

Meagher, Timothy J. "Sweet Good Mothers and Young Women out in the World: The Roles of Irish American Women in Late Nineteenth and Early Twentieth Century Worcester, Massachusetts." *U.S. Catholic Historian* 5 (Summer/Fall 1986): 325-344.

Meckel, Richard A. "Educating a Ministry of Mothers: Evangelical Maternal Associations, 1815-1860." *Journal of the Early Republic* 2 (Winter 1982): 403-423.

Nash, Carol S. "Educating New Mothers: Women and the Enlightenment in Russia." *History of Education Quarterly* 21 (Fall 1981): 301-316.

Olwig, Karen Fog. "Women, 'Matrifocality' and Systems of Exchange: An Ethnohistorical Study of the Afro-American Family on St. John, West Indies." *Ethnohistory* 28 (Winter 1981): 59-81.

Omolade, Barbara. "The Unbroken Circle: A Historical and Contemporary Study of Black Single Mothers and Their Families." *Wisconsin Women's Law Journal* 3 (1987): 239-274.

Porterfield, Amanda. "The Mother in Eighteenth-Century American Conceptions of Man and God." *Journal of Psychohistory* 15 (Fall 1987): 189-206.

Rabinovitz, Lauren. "Sitcoms and Single Moms: Representations of Feminism on American TV." *Cinema Journal* 29 (Fall 1989): 3-19.

Ravenal, Carol M. "Three Faces of Mother: Madonna, Martyr, Medusa in the Art of Edvard Munch." *Journal of Psychohistory* 13 (Spring 1986): 371-412.

Riley, Denise. "The Free Mothers: Protonationalism and Working Class Mothers in Industry at the End of the Last War in  Britain." *History Workshop* 11 (Spring 1981): 59-119.

Schneyer, Mark. "Mothers and Children, Poverty and Morality: A Social Worker's Priorities, 1915." *Pennsylvania Magazine of History and Biography* 112 (April 1988): 209-226.

Shelton, Brenda K. "Organized Mother Love: The Buffalo Women's Educational and Industrial Union, 1885-1915." *New York History* 67 (April 1986): 155-176.

Simonds, Wendy. "Confessions of Loss: Maternal Grief in *True Story*, 1920-1985." *Gender & Society* 2, no. 2 (1988): 149-171.

Slotkin, Wendy. "Maternity and Sexuality in the 1890s." *Woman's Art Journal* 1 (Spring/Summer 1980): 13-19.

Smith, Robert J. "Making Village Women into 'Good Wives and Wise Mothers' in Prewar Japan." *Journal of Family History* 8 (Spring 1983): 70-84.

Smithson, Isaiah. "Great Mothers, Son Lovers and Patriarchy." *Journal of American Culture* 4 (Summer 1981): 23-36.

Steinson, Barbara J. "Memories of Hoosier Homemakers: A Review Essay." *Indiana Magazine of History* 86 (June 1990): 197-222.

Strumingher, Laura S. "L'Ange de la Maison: Mothers and Daughters in Nineteenth-Century France." *International Journal of Women's Studies* 2 (January/February 1979): 51-61.

Swetnam, Susan H. "Turning to the Mothers: Mormon Women's Biographies of Their Female Forebears and the Mormon Church's Expectations for Women." *Frontiers* 10, no. 1 (1988): 1-6.

Taves, Ann. "Mothers and Children and the Legacy of Mid-Nineteenth Century American Christianity." *Journal of Religion* 67 (April 1987): 203-219.

Taylor, Karen. "Blessing the House: Moral Motherhood and the Suppression of Physical Punishment." *Journal of Psychohistory* 15 (Summer 1987): 431-454.

White, Merry. "The Virtue of Japanese Mothers: Cultural Definitions of Women's Lives." *Daedalus* 116 (Summer 1987): 149-164.

Williams, Linda. "'Something Else besides a Mother': *Stella Dallas* and the Maternal Melodrama." *Cinema Journal* 24 (Fall 1984): 2-27.

Wrobel, Arthur. "'Noble American Motherhood': Whitman, Women, and the Ideal Democracy." *American Studies* 21 (Fall 1980): 7-25.

# FEMINISM

## Biography

Alexander, Ruth Ann. "Elaine Goodale Eastman and the Failure of the Feminist Protestant Ethic." *Great Plains Quarterly* 8 (Spring 1988): 89-101.

-----. "A Feminist Memoir, 1964-1989." *South Dakota History* 19 (Winter 1989): 538-555.

Antler, Joyce. "Feminism as Life-Process: The Life and Career of Lucy Sprague Mitchell." *Feminist Studies* 7 (Spring 1981): 134-157.

Berkeley, Kathleen Christine. "Elizabeth Avery Meriwether, 'An Advocate for Her Sex': Feminism and Conservatism in the Post-Civil War South." *Tennessee Historical Quarterly* 43 (Winter 1984): 390-407.

Buell, Janet W. "Alva Belmont: From Socialite to Feminist." *Historian* 52 (February 1990): 219-241.

Campbell, K. K. "Stanton and the Solitude of Self: A Rationale for Feminism." *Quarterly Journal of Speech* 66, no. 3 (1980): 304-312.

Chevigny, Bell Gale. "To the Edges of Ideology: Margaret Fuller's Centrifugal Evolution." *American Quarterly* 38 (Summer 1986): 173-201.

Cooksey, Alice J. "A Woman of Her Time: Birdie Robertson Johnson (1868-1926; Texas feminist)." *East Texas History Journal* 24, no. 2 (1986): 33-45.

Corwin, Margaret. "Minna Schmidt: Businesswoman, Feminist, and Fairy Godmother to Chicago." *Chicago History* 7 (Winter 1978/79): 226-235.

Crawford, Virginia L. "Transcendental Woman: Margaret Fuller's Feminist Vision." *State University of New York at Buffalo Studies in History* 4 (1982-1983).

DeBlasio, Donna. "'The Greatest Woman in the Reserve': Betsy Mix Cowles, Feminist, Abolitionist, Educator." *Old Northwest* 13 (Fall/Winter 1987): 223-236.

Eaton, Jeffrey C. "Simone Weil and Feminist Spirituality." *Journal of the American Academy of Religion* 54 (Winter 1986): 691-704.

Frankel, Lois. "Damaris Cudworth Masham: A Seventeenth Century Feminist Philosopher." *Hypatia* 4 (Spring 1989): 80-90.

Gates, Joanne E. "Stitches in a Critical Time: The Diaries of Elizabeth Robins, American Feminist in England, 1907-1924." *Auto/Biography Studies* 4 (Winter 1988): 130-139.

Hause, Steven C. "Citizeness of the Republic: Class and Sex Identity in the Feminist Career of Hubertine Auclert, 1848-1914." *Western Society for French History* 12 (October 1984): 235-242.

Hewitt, Marsha. "Emma Goldman: The Case for Anarchofeminism." *Our Generation* 17 (Fall 1985/Winter 1986): 167-175.

Hill, Mary A. "Charlotte Perkins Gilman: A Feminist's Struggle with Womanhood." *Massachusetts Review* 21 (Fall 1980): 503-526.

Japp, Phyllis M. "Esther or Isaiah?: The Abolitionist-Feminist Rhetoric of Angelina Grimke." *Quarterly Journal of Speech* 71 (August 1985): 335-348.

Juncker, Clara. "Grace King: Feminist, Southern Style." *Southern Quarterly* 26 (Spring 1988): 15-30.

Keyser, Elizabeth Lennox. "Woman in the Twentieth Century: Margaret Fuller and Feminist Biography." *Biography* 11, no. 4 (1988): 283-302.

Lapsansky, Emma Jones. "Feminism, Freedom, and Community: Charlotte Forten and Women Activists in Nineteenth Century Philadelphia." *Pennsylvania Magazine of History and Biography* 113 (January 1989): 3-20.

Love, Myra. "Christa Wolf and Feminism: Breaking the Patriarchial Connection." *New German Critique* 16 (Winter 1979): 31-53.

McFadden, Margaret. "Anna Doyle Wheeler: Philosopher, Socialist, Feminist." *Hypatia* 4 (Spring 1989): 91-101.

McKinley, Blaine. "Free Love and Domesticity: Lizzie M. Holmes, *Hagar Lyndon* (1893), and the Anarchist-Feminist Imagination." *Journal of American Culture* 13 (Spring 1990): 55-62.

Miller, Sally M. "Kate Richards O'Hare: Progression toward Feminism." *Kansas History* 7 (Winter 1984/85): 263-279.

Offen, Karen. "A Nineteenth-Century French Feminist Rediscovered: Jenny P. d'Hericourt, 1809-1875." *Signs* 13 (Autumn 1987): 144-158.

Okonkwo, Rina. "Adelaide Casely Hayford (1868-1960): Cultural Nationalist and Feminist (Gold Coast)." *Phylon* (March 1981): 41-51.

Oppenheim, J. "The Odyssey of Anne Besant: Victorian Radical, Feminist, Spiritualist." *History Today* 39 (September 1989): 12-18.

Perry, Ruth. "Mary Astell and the Feminist Critique of Possessive Individualism."

*Eighteenth-Century Studies* 23 (Summer 1990): 444-457.

Reiss, Mary-Ann. "Rosa Mayreder: Pioneer of Austrian Feminism." *International Journal of Women's Studies* 7 (May/June 1984): 207-216.

Rooke, Patricia T., and R. T. Schnell. "'An Idiot's Flowerbed': A Study of Charlotte Whitton's Feminist Thought, 1941-50." *International Journal of Women's Studies* 5 (January/February 1982): 29-46.

Roth, N. "The Roots of Mary Wollstonecraft's Feminism." *Journal of the American Academy of Psychoanalysis* 7 (1979): 67-78.

Sangster, Joan. "The Making of a Socialist-Feminist: The Early Career of Beatrice Brigden, 1888-1941." *Atlantis* 13 (Fall 1987): 13-28.

Scharnhorst, Gary. "Making Her Fame: Charlotte Perkins Gilman in California." *California History* 64 (Summer 1985): 192-201.

Shulman, Alix Kate. "Dancing in the Revolution: Emma Goldman's Feminism." *Socialist Review* no. 62 (1982): 31-44.

Treckel, Paula A. "Jane Grey Swisshelm and Feminism in Early Minnesota." *Midwest Review* 2 (Spring 1980): 1-17.

Waitt, Alden. "Katharine Anthony: Feminist Biographer with the 'Warmth of an Advocate.'" *Frontiers* 10, no. 1 (1988): 72-76.

Wexler, Alice, ed. "Emma Goldman on Mary Wollstonecraft." *Feminist Studies* 7 (Spring 1981): 113-134.

## General

Banner, Lois. "Feminism in America, 1848-1986." *Wilson Quarterly* 10 (Autumn 1986): 90-98.

Bennett, Judith M. "Feminism and History." *Gender & History* 1 (Autumn 1989): 251-272.

Butler, Melissa. "Early Roots of Feminism: John Locke and the Attack on Patriarchy." *American Political Science Review* 72 (March 1979): 135-150.

Candelaria, Cordelia. "La Malinche, Feminist Prototype." *Frontiers* 5, no. 2 (1980): 1-6.

Easton, Barbara. "Feminism and the Contemporary Family." *Socialist Review* 8 (May/June 1978): 11-36.

Ferguson, Moira. "The Discovery of Mary Wollstonecraft's The Female Reader." *Signs* 3 (Summer 1978): 945-957.

Fishbein, Leslie. "The Failure of Feminism in Greenwich Village Before World War I." *Women's Studies* 9, no. 3 (1982): 275-289.

Hilden, P. "Feminism's Past." *The Historical Journal* 32 (June 1989): 489-498.

Jones, Phyllis. "Ragtime: Feminist, Socialist and Black Perspectives on the Self-Made Man." *Journal of American Culture* 2 (Spring 1979): 17-28.

Kashdin, Gladys S. "Women Artists and the Institution of Feminism in America." *Proceedings of the Southeastern American Studies Association* (1979).

Kleinbaum, Abby Wettan. "Amazon Dreams: Feminism and the Amazon Image." *Minerva: Quarterly Report on Women and the Military* 3 (Spring 1985): 95-106.

Kramer, Rita. "Feminism in America, 1848-1986: The Third Wave." *Wilson Quarterly* 10 (Autumn 1986): 110-129.

Lagerfeld, Steven. "Feminism in America, 1848-1986: Measuring the Effects." *Wilson Quarterly* 10 (Autumn 1986): 130-138.

Michel, Sonya. "Feminism, Film and Public History." *Radical History Review* 25 (October 1981): 46-61.

Plutzer, Eric. "Work Life, Family Life and Women's Support of Feminism." *American Sociological Review* 53 (1988): 640-649.

Stern, Madeleine B. "A Feminist Association." *Manuscripts* 35 (Spring 1983): 113-117.

-----. "A Feminist's Testament." *Manuscripts* 36 (Summer 1984): 216-223.

Stetson, Erlene. "Black Feminism in Indiana, 1893-1933." *Phylon* 44 (December 1983): 292-298.

Walker, Nancy. "Humor and Gender Roles: The 'Funny' Feminism of the Post-World War II Suburbs." *American Quarterly* 37 (Spring 1985): 98-113.

Wall, Helena M. "Feminism and the New England Hospital, 1949-1961." *American Quarterly* 32 (Fall 1980): 435-452.

## International

Afary, Janet. "On the Origins of Feminism in Early 20th-Century Iran." *Journal of Women's History* 1 (Fall 1989): 65-87.

Badran, Margot. "Islam, Patriarchy, and Feminism in the Middle East." *Trends in History* 4, no. 1 (1985): 49-71.

Boxer, Marilyn J. "'First-Wave' Feminism in Nineteenth-Century France: Class, Family, and Religion." *Women's Studies International Forum* 5, no. 6 (1982): 551-559.

Brown, Irene Q. "Domesticity, Feminism, and Friendship: Female Aristocratic Culture and Marriage in England, 1660-1760." *Journal of Family History* (Winter 1982): 406-424.

Burke, Janet M. "Through Friendship to Feminism: The Growth in Self Awareness Among Eighteenth-Century Women Freemasons." *Western Society for French History* 14 (November 1986): 187-196.

Burton, Antoinette M. "The White Woman's Burden: British Feminists and the Indian Woman, 1865-1915." *Women's Studies International Forum* 13, no. 4 (1990): 295-308.

Caine, Barbara. "Feminism, Suffrage and the Nineteenth-Century English Women's Movement." *Women's Studies International Forum* 5, no. 6 (1982): 537-550.

Carroll, William K., and Rennie Warburton. "Feminism, Class Consciousness and Household-Work Linkages Among Registered Nurses in Victoria." *Labour/Le Travail* 24 (Fall 1989): 131-146.

Cicioni, Mirna. "'Love and Respect, Together': The Theory and Practice of *Affidamento* in Italian Feminism." *Australian Feminist Studies* no. 10 (Summer 1989): 71-84.

Cole, Juan R. "Feminism, Class, and Islam in Turn-of-the-Century Egypt." *International Journal of Middle East Studies* 19 (1981): 387-407.

Danylewycz, Marta. "Changing Relationships: Nuns and Feminists in Montreal, 1890-1925." *Histoire sociale/Social History* 14 (November 1981): 413-434.

Evans, Richard J. "Feminism and Anticlericalism in France, 1870-1922." *The Historical Journal* 25 (December 1982): 947-950.

Forbes, Geraldine. "Caged Tigers: 'First Wave' Feminists in India." *Women's Studies International Forum* 5, no. 6 (1982): 525-536.

Gould, Karen. "Spatial Poetics, Spatial Politics: Quebec Feminists on the City and the Countryside." *American Review of Canadian Studies* 12 (Spring 1982): 1-9.

Green, Mary Jean. "The 'Literary Feminists' and the Fight for Women's Writing in Quebec." *Journal of Canadian Studies/Revue d'études canadiennes* 21 (Spring 1986): 128-143.

Habibuddin, S. M. "A Comparative Appraisal of the Role of Indian Feminists in the Peace Movement Between Two World Wars." *Quarterly Review of Historical Studies* [Calcutta] 23 (April/June 1983): 44-53.

Hahner, June E. "Feminism, Women's Rights and the Suffrage Movement in Brazil, 1850-1932." *Latin American Research Review* 15, no. 1 (1980): 65-111.

Hause, Steven. "The Failure of Feminism in Provincial France, 1890-1920." *Western Society for French History* 8 (October 1980): 423-435.

Honeycutt, Karen. "Socialism and Feminism in Imperial Germany." *Signs* 5 (Autumn 1979): 30-41.

Jones, Judith P., and Sherianne Sellers Seibel. "Thomas More's Feminism: To Reform as Re-Form." *Albion* 10 (1978): 67-77.

Kinnaird, Joan K. "Mary Astell and the Conservative Contribution to English Feminism." *The Journal of British Studies* 19 (Fall 1979): 53-75.

Kuninobu, Junko Wada. "The Development of Feminism in Modern Japan." *Feminist Issues* 4 (Fall 1984): 3-22.

Levine, Philippa. "Love, Friendship, and Feminism in Later 19th-Century England." *Women's Studies International Forum* 13, no. 1/2 (1990): 63-78.

McKillen, Beth. "Irish Feminism and Nationalist Separatism, 1914-1923." *Eire-Ireland* 17 (Fall 1982): 52-67.

-----. "Irish Feminism and Nationalist Separatism, 1914-1923." *Eire-Ireland* 17 (Winter 1982): 72-90.

Molyneux, Maxine. "No God, No Boss, No Husband: Anarchist Feminism in Nineteenth-Century Argentina." *Latin American Perspectives* 13 (Winter 1986): 119-145.

Moore, Lindy. "Feminists and Femininity: A Case-Study of WSPU Propaganda and Local Response at a Scottish By-Election." *Women's Studies* 5, no. 6 (1982): 675-684.

Moses, Claire G. "Saint-Simonian Men/Saint-Simonian Women: The Transformation of Feminist Thought in 1830's France." *Journal of Modern History* 54 (June 1982): 240-267.

Nelson, Cynthia. "The Voices of Doria Shafik: Feminist Consciousness in Egypt, 1940-1960." *Feminist Issues* 6 (1986): 16-31.

Offen, Karen M. "Depopulation, Nationalism, and Feminism in Fin-de-Siècle France." *American Historical Review* 89 (June 1984): 648-676.

-----. "Ernest Legouve and the Doctrine of 'Equality in Difference' for Women: A Case Study of Male Feminism in Nineteenth-Century French Thought." *Journal of Modern History* 58 (June 1986): 452-484.

-----. "'First Wave' Feminism in France: New Work and Resources." *Women's Studies International Forum* 5 (1982): 685-689.

Okhamafe, E. Imafedia. "African-Style Feminism in Contemporary African Literature." *Africa Today* 37, no. 1 (1990): 73-75.

Paxton, Nancy L. "Feminism under the Raj: Complicity and Resistance in the Writings of Flora Annie Steel and Annie Besant." *Women's Studies International Forum* 13, no. 4 (1990): 333-346.

Rowan, Mary M. "Seventeenth-Century French Feminism: Two Opposing Attitudes." *International Journal of Women's Studies* 3 (May/June 1980): 273-291.

Smart, Judith. "Feminists, Food and the Fair Price: The Cost of Living Demonstrations in Melbourne, August-September 1917." *Labour History* 50 (May 1986): 113-131.

Smith, Harold. "Sex vs. Class: British Feminists and the Labour Movement, 1919-1929." *The Historian* 47 (November 1984): 19-37.

Strong-Boag, Veronica. "Pulling in Double Harness or Hauling a Double Load: Women, Work, and Feminism on the Canadian Prairie." *Journal of Canadian Studies* 21 (Fall 1986): 32-52.

Zarrow, Peter. "He Zhen and Anarcho-Feminism in China." *Journal of Asian Studies* 47 (November 1988): 796-813.

## Organizations

Allen, Judith. "The Feminisms of the Early Women's Movements, 1850-1920." *Refractory Girl* 17 (1979): 10-17.

Blom, Ida. "A Centenary of Organized Feminism in Norway." *Women's Studies* 5, no. 6 (1982): 569-574.

Chafetz, Janet Saltzman, and Gary Dworkin. "In the Face of Threat: Organized Antifeminism in Comparative Perspective." *Gender & Society* 1 (1987): 33-60.

Connelly, Patricia M. and Linda Christiansen-Ruffman. "The Transformation of the Old Feminist Movement." *Quarterly Journal of Speech* 67 (1981): 284-297.

Davis, Beverly. "To Seize the Moment: A Retrospective on the National Black Feminist Organization." *Sage* 5 (Fall 1988): 43-47.

Davis, M. "Modern Feminism and Women's Organization." *World Marxist Review* 24, no. 7 (1981): 104.

Echols, Alice. "Cultural Feminism: Feminist Capitalism and the Anti-Pornography Movement." *Social Text* 7 (1983): 34-53.

Export, Valie. "Aspects of Feminist Actionism." *New German Critique* no. 47 (Spring/Summer 1989): 69-92.

Foppa, Alaide. "The First Feminist Congress in Mexico, 1916." *Signs* 5 (Autumn

1979): 192-199.

Freedman, Estelle. "Separatism as Strategy: Female Institution Building and American Feminism, 1870-1930." *Feminist Studies* 5 (Fall 1979): 512-529.

Galush, William J. "Purity and Power: Chicago Polonian Feminists, 1880-1914." *Polish American Studies* 47 (Spring 1990): 5-24.

Kaplan, Temma. "Female Consciousness and Collective Action: The Case of Barcelona, 1910-1918." *Signs* 7 (Spring 1982): 545-566.

Katz, Sherry. "Francis Nocke Noel and 'Sister Movements': Socialism, Feminism, & Trade Unionism in Los Angeles, 1909-1916." *California History* 67 (September 1988): 180-190.

Leidner, Robin. "Stretching the Boundaries of Liberalism: Democratic Innovation in a Feminist Organization." *Signs* 16 (Winter 1991): 263-289.

Ling, S. "The Mountain Movers, Asian-American Women's Movement in Los Angeles." *Amerasia Journal* 15 (Spring 1989): 51-68.

Marshall, Susan E. "Ladies Against Women: Mobilization Dilemmas of Antifeminist Movements." *Social Problems* 32, no. 4 (1985): 348-362.

Marti, Donald B. "Sisters of the Grange: Rural Feminism in the Late Nineteenth Century." *Agricultural History* 58 (July 1984): 247-261.

Martin, Patricia Yancey. "Rethinking Feminist Organizations." *Gender & Society* 4 (June 1990): 182-206.

McCalman, Lain. "Females, Feminism, and Free Love in an Early Nineteenth Century Radical Movement." *Labour History* 38 (May 1980): 1-25.

Ross, Becki. "The House That Jill Built: Lesbian Feminist Organizing in Toronto, 1976-1980." *Feminist Review* no. 35 (Summer 1990): 75-91.

Salmon, Marilyn Hoder. "Myrtle Archer McDougal: Leader of Oklahoma's 'Timid Sisters.'" *Chronicles of Oklahoma* 60 (Autumn 1982): 332-343.

Schofield, Ann. "'To Do and to Be': Mary Frier, Pauline Newman, and the Psychology of Feminist Activism." *Psychohistory Review* 18 (Fall 1989): 33-55.

Sealander, Judith, and Dorothy Smith. "The Rise and Fall of Feminist Organizations in the 1970s: Dayton as a Case Study." *Feminist Studies* 12 (Summer 1986): 321-342.

## Politics

Allen, Ann Taylor. "German Radical Feminism and Eugenics, 1900-1918." *German Studies Review* 11 (February 1988): 31-56.

Badran, Margot. "Dual Liberation: Feminism and Nationalism in Egypt, 1870s-1925." *Feminist Issues* 8 (1988): 15-34.

Bashevkin, Sylvia. "Political Participation, Ambition, and Feminism: Women in the Ontario Party Elites." *American Review of Canadian Studies* 15 (Winter 1985): 465-480.

Bauer, Carol, and Lawrence Ritt. "Wife-Abuse, Late Victorian English Feminists, and the Legacy of Frances Power Cobbe." *International Journal of Women's Studies* 6 (May/June 1983): 195-207.

Brady, Marilyn Dell. "Populism and Feminism in a Newspaper by and for Women of the Kansas Farmers' Alliance, 1891-1894." *Kansas History* 7 (Winter 1984/85): 280-290.

Costin, Lela. "Feminism, Pacifism, Internationalism and the 1915 International Congress of Women." *Women's Studies* 5, no. 3/4 (1982): 301-316.

"East German Feminists: The Lila Manifesto." Lisa DiCaprio, intro. *Feminist Studies* 16 (Fall 1990): 621-634.

Evans, Sara M. "Toward a Usable Past: Feminism as History and Politics." *Minnesota History* 48 (Summer 1983): 230-235.

Frenier, Mariam Darce. "American Anti-Feminist Women: Comparing the Rhetoric of Opponents of the Equal Rights Amendment with That of Opponents of Women's Suffrage." *Women's Studies International Forum* 7, no. 6 (1984): 455-465.

Greenwald, Maurine Weiner. "Working-Class Feminism and the Family Wage Ideal: The Seattle Debate on Married Women's Right to Work, 1914-1920." *Journal of American History* 76 (June 1989): 118-149.

Kates, Carol. "Working Class Feminism and Feminist Unions: Title VII, the UAW and NOW." *Labor Studies Journal* 14 (Summer 1989): 28-45.

Katzenstein, Mary. "Feminism and the Meaning of the Vote." *Signs* 10 (1984): 4-26.

Lipschultz, Sybil. "Social Feminism and Legal Discourse: 1908-1923." *Yale Journal of Law and Feminism* 2 (Fall 1989): 131-160.

Loeffelholz, Mary. "Posing the Woman Citizen: The Contradictions of Stanton's Feminism." *Genders* 7 (March 1990): 87-98.

Marsden, Lorna, and Joan Busby. "Feminist Influence Through the Senate: The Case of Divorce, 1967." *Atlantis* 14 (Spring 1989): 72-81.

Matsuda, Mari J. "The West and the Legal State of Women: Explanations of Frontier Feminism." *Journal of the West* 24 (January 1985): 47-56.

McBride, Theresa. "Comment on Session: Class and Sex Identity in French Feminist Politics." *Western Society for French History* 12 (October 1984): 257-259.

Olson, Frances. "From False Paternalism to False Equality: Judicial Assaults on Feminist Community, Illinois 1869-1895." *Michigan Law Review* 84 (June 1986): 1518-1543.

Pedersen, Susan. "The Failure of Feminism in the Making of the British Welfare State." *Radical History Review* 43 (Winter 1989): 86-104.

Petchesky, Rosalind. "Antiabortion, Antifeminism, and the Rise of the New Right." *Feminist Studies* 7 (1981): 206-246

Schneer, Jonathon. "Politics and Feminism in 'Outcast London': George Lansbury and Jane Cobden's Campaign for the First London County Council." *Journal of British Studies* 30 (January 1991): 63-82.

Sealander, Judith. "Feminist Against Feminist: The First Phase of the Equal Rights Amendment Debate, 1923-1963." *South Atlantic Quarterly* 81 (Spring 1982): 147-161.

Strom, Sharon Hartman. "Challenging 'Woman's Place': Feminism, the Left and the Industrial Unionism in the 1930s." *Feminist Studies* 9 (Summer 1983): 359-386.

Vega, Judith. "Feminist Republicanism: Etta Palm-Aelders on Justice, Virtue and Men." *History of European Ideas* 10, no. 3 (1989): 333-352.

## Religion

Bauer, Carol P. "The Role of Religion in the Creation of a Philosophy of Feminism: The Case of Frances Power Cobbe." *Anima* 10 (Fall 1983): 59-70.

Boyer, Paul. "Minister's Wife, Widow, Reluctant Feminist: Catherine Marshall in the 1950s." *American Quarterly* 30 (Winter 1978): 703-721.

Foster, Lawrence. "Free Love and Feminism: John Humphrey Noyes and the Oneida Community." *Journal of the Early Republic* 1 (Summer 1981): 165-183.

Greene, Dana. "Quaker Feminism: The Case of Lucretia Mott." *Pennsylvania History* 48 (April 1981): 143-154.

Heeney, Brian. "The Beginnings of Church Feminism: Women and the Councils of the Church of England 1897-1919." *Journal of Ecclesiastical History* 33 (January 1982): 89-110.

Iversen, Joan. "Feminist Implications of Mormon Polygyny." *Feminist Studies* 10 (Fall 1984): 505-522.

Lindley, Susan H. "The Ambiguous Feminism of Mary Baker Eddy." *Journal of Religion* 64 (July 1984): 318-331.

McCants, David A. "Evangelicalism and Nineteenth Century Woman's Rights: A Case Study of Angelina E. Grimke." *Perspectives in Religious Studies* 14 (Spring 1987): 39-57.

O'Connor, June. "Feminist Research in Religion." *Women's Studies* 17, no. 1/2 (1989): 101-124.

Page, Ruth. "Re-review: Elizabeth Cady Stanton's *The Woman's Bible*." *Modern Churchman* 29, no. 4 (1987): 37-41.

Ruether, Rosemary Radford. "Prophets and Humanists: Types of Religious Feminism in Stuart England." *Journal of Religion* 70 (January 1990): 1-18.

Watts, Ruth. "Radical Dissent and the Emancipation of Women, 1780-1860." *Faith and Freedom* 38 (Summer 1985): 71-82.

Weaver, Mary Jo. "Feminist Perspectives and American Catholic History." *U.S. Catholic Historian* 5 (Summer/Fall 1986): 401-410.

White, O. Kendall, Jr. "A Feminist Challenge: 'Mormons for ERA' as an Internal Social Movement." *Journal of Ethnic Studies* 13 (Spring 1985): 29-50.

## Theory

Abrahams, Edward. "Randolph Bourne on Feminism and Feminists." *Historian* 43 (May 1981): 365-377.

Alcoff, Linda. "Cultural Feminism versus Post-Structuralism: The Identity Crisis in Feminist Theory." *Signs* 13 (Spring 1988): 405-436.

Armstrong, Hugh, and Pat Armstrong. "Comments: More on Marxist Feminism."

*Studies in Political Economy* 15 (1984): 179-184.

Billington, Rosamund. "Ideology and Feminism: Why the Suffragettes Were 'Wild Women.'" *Women's Studies International Forum* 5, no. 6 (1982): 663-674.

Birkett, Dea, and Julie Wheelwright. "'How Could She?' Unpalatable Facts and Feminists' Heroines." *Gender & History* 2 (Spring 1990): 49-57.

Bozzoli, Belinda. "Marxism, Feminism and South African Studies." *Journal of South African Studies* 9, no. 2 (1983): 139-171.

Burris, Val. "Who Opposed the ERA? The Social Bases of Feminism." *Social Science Quarterly* 64 (1983): 305-317.

Califia, Pat. "Feminism and Sadomasochism." *The CoEvolution Quarterly* (Spring 1982): 33-40.

Campbell, B. "Feminist Sexual Politics." *Feminist Review* 5 (1980): 1-18.

Campbell, Karlyn Kohrs. "Style and Content in the Rhetoric of Early Afro-American Feminists." *Quarterly Journal of Speech* 72 (November 1986): 434-445.

Cohen, Marjorie. "The Razor's Edge Invisible: Feminism's Effect on Economics." *International Journal of Women's Studies* 8, no. 3 (1985): 286-298.

Conway, Jill K. "Utopian Dream or Dystopian Nightmare? Nineteenth-Century Feminist Ideas about Equality." *Proceedings of the American Antiquarian Society* 96 (October 1986): 285-294.

Dallimore, Jonathon. "Shakespeare, Cultural Materialism, Feminism and Marxist Humanism." *New Literary History* 21 (Spring 1990): 471-494.

Desroches, Richard. "Primitivism and Feminism in Utopia." *Western Society for French History* 15 (November 1987): 142.

Dietz, Mary G. "Context Is All: Feminism and Theories of Citizenship." *Daedalus* 116 (Fall 1987): 1-24.

English, Deirdre, Amber Hollibough, and Gayle Rubin. "Talking Sex: A Conversation on Sexuality and Feminism." *Socialist Review* 11, no. 4 (1981): 43-62.

Ferguson, Kathy E. "Interpretation and Genealogy in Feminism." *Signs* 16 (Winter 1991): 322-339.

Fox-Genovese, Elizabeth. "Socialist-Feminist American Women's History." *Journal of Women's History* 1 (Winter 1990): 181-210.

Garcia, Alma M. "The Development of Chicana Feminist Discourse, 1970-1980." *Gender & Society* 3 (June 1989): 217-238.

Gordon, Linda. "Family Violence, Feminism, and Social Control." *Feminist Studies* 12 (Fall 1986): 453-478.

Gordon, Linda, and Ellen DuBois. "Seeking Ecstasy on the Battlefield: Danger and Pleasure in Nineteenth-Century Feminist Thought." *Feminist Studies* 9 (Spring 1983): 7-26.

Hartmann, Heidi. "The Unhappy Marriage of Marxism and Feminism: Towards a More Progressive Union." *Capital and Class* 8 (1979): 1-33.

Hunter, Jean E. "A Daring New Concept: *The Ladies' Home Journal* and Modern Feminism." *NWSA Journal* 2 (Autumn 1990): 583-602.

Jeffreys, Sheila. "The Spinster and Her Enemies: Sexuality and the Last Wave of

Feminism." *Scarlet Women* 13 (July 1981).

Kaplan, Carla. "Women's Writing and Feminist Strategy." *American Literary History* 2 (Summer 1990): 339-357.

Keller, Evelyn Fox, and Helene Moglen. "Competition and Feminism: Conflicts for Academic Women." *Signs* 12 (Spring 1987): 493-511.

King, Deborah K. "Multiple Jeopardy, Multiple Consciousness: The Context of a Black Feminist Ideology." *Signs* 14 (Autumn 1988): 42-72.

Lazreq, Marina. "Feminism and Difference: The Perils of Writing as a Woman on Women in Algeria." *Feminist Studies* 14 (Spring 1988): 81-107.

Leach, William. "Looking Forward Together: Feminists and Edward Bellamy." *Democracy* 2 (January 1982): 120-134.

Lima, Valentina da Rocha. "Women In Exile: Becoming Feminist." *International Journal of Oral History* 5 (June 1984): 81-99.

McDonald, Cheryl. "The Angel in the House." *The Beaver* 66 (August/September 1986): 22-29.

Olson, Richard. "Historical Reflections on Feminist Critiques of Science: The Scientific Background to Modern Feminism." *History of Science* 28 (June 1990): 125-147.

Pittenger, Mark. "Evolution, 'Woman's Nature,' and American Feminist Socialism, 1900-1915." *Radical History Review* 36 (1986): 46-61.

Rose, Gillian, and Miles Ogborn. "Feminism and Historical Geography." *Journal of Historical Geography* [Great Britain] 14, no. 4 (1988): 405-409.

Russo, Ann. "Conflicts and Contradictions Among Feminists over Issues of Pornography and Sexual Freedom." *Women's Studies International Forum* 10, no. 2 (1987): 103-112.

Scates, Bruce. "Socialism and Feminism: The Case of William Lane. A Reply to Marilyn Lake." *Labour History* no. 59 (November 1990): 45-58.

Sherwin, Susan. "Ethics, Feminism, and Caring." *Queen's Quarterly* 96 (Spring 1989): 3-13.

Smart, Carol. "Law's Power, the Sexed Body, and Feminist Discourse." *Journal of Law and Society* 17 (Summer 1990): 194-210.

Taylor, Verta. "Sisterhood, Solidarity and Modern Feminism: A Review Essay." *Gender and Society* 3 (1989): 277-286.

Trofimenkoff, Susan Mann. "Nationalism, Feminism and Canadian Intellectual History." *Canadian Literature* 83 (Winter 1979): 7-20.

Walkowitz, Judith, Myra Jehlen, and Bell Chevigny. "Patrolling the Borders: Feminist Historiography and the New Historicism." *Radical History Review* 43 (Winter 1989): 23-44.

# FRIENDSHIP

Brown, Irene Quenzler. "Death, Friendship, and Female Identity During New England's Second Great Awakening." *Journal of Family History* 12, no. 4 (1987): 367-388.

-----. "Domesticity, Feminism, and Friendship: Female Aristocratic Culture and

Marriage in England, 1660-1760." *Journal of Family History* (Winter 1982): 406-424.

Burgin, Diana Lewis. "After the Ball Is Over: Sophia Parnok's Creative Relationship with Marina Tsvetaeva." *Russian Review* 47, no. 4 (1988): 425-444.

Burke, Janet M. "Freemasonry, Friendship and Noblewomen: The Role of the Secret Society in Bringing Enlightenment Thought to Pre-Revolutionary Women Elites." *History of European Ideas* 10, no. 3 (1989): 283-294.

-----. "Through Friendship to Feminism: The Growth in Self Awareness Among Eighteenth-Century Women Freemasons." *Western Society for French History* 14 (November 1986): 187-196.

Coulter, Maureen. "'A Terrific Bond': The Spiritual Friendship of Caryll Houselander and Maisie Ward." *The Downside Review* 107 (April 1989): 106-118.

Elikins, William R., ed. "A Record of Friendship: Unpublished Letters from Allen White to Loverna (E.) Lawton Little Morris." *Heritage of the Great Plains* 15 (Winter 1982): 1-10.

Ford, Linda. "William Penn's Views on Women: Subjects of Friendship." *Quaker History* 72 (Fall 1983): 75-102.

Fryer, Judith. "What Goes on in the Ladies Room? Sarah Orne Jewett, Annie Fields, and Their Community of Women." *Massachusetts Review* 30 (Winter 1989): 610-628.

Gay, Judith. "'Mummies and Babies' and Friends and Lovers in Lesotho." *Journal of Homosexuality* 11, no. 3/4 (1985): 97-116.

Goldfarb, Clare R. "Female Friendship: An Alternative to Marriage and the Family in Henry James's Fiction?" *Colby Quarterly* 26 (December 1990): 205-212.

Gross, Robert A. "Lonesome in Eden: Dickinson, Thoreau and the Problem of Community in Nineteenth Century New England." *Canadian Review of American Studies* 14 (Spring 1983): 1-18.

Hewitt, Nancy A. "Feminist Friends: Agrarian Quakers and the Emergence of Woman's Rights in America." *Feminist Studies* 12 (Spring 1986): 27-50.

Jacob, Margaret C. "Feminine Sociability in Eighteenth- and Nineteenth-Century France: Comment on Papers by Burke, Walton, and Haine." *Western Society for French History* 14 (November 1986): 212-214.

Lacey, Barbara E. "The Bonds of Friendship: Sarah Osborn of Newport and the Reverend Joseph Fish of North Stonington, 1743-1779." *Rhode Island History* 45 (November 1986): 126-136.

Lapsansky, Emma Jones. "Friends, Wives, and Strivings: Networks and Community Values Among Nineteenth-Century Philadelphia Afroamerican Elites." *Pennsylvania Magazine of History and Biography* 108 (January 1984): 3-24.

Lasser, Carol. "'Let Us Be Sisters Forever': The Sororal Model of Nineteenth-Century Female Friendship." *Signs* 14 (Autumn 1988): 158-181.

Leites, Edmund. "The Duty to Desire: Love, Friendship and Sexuality to Some

Puritan Theories of Marriage." *Journal of Social History* 15 (Spring 1982): 383-408.

Levine, Philippa. "Love, Friendship, and Feminism in Later 19th-Century England." *Women's Studies International Forum* 13, no. 1/2 (1990): 63-78.

McLaughlin, Mary Martin. "Creating and Recreating Communities of Women: The Case of Corpus Domini, Ferrara, 1406-1452." *Signs* 14 (Winter 1989): 293-320.

Nord, Deborah Epstein. "'Neither Pairs Nor Odd': Female Community in Late Nineteenth-Century London." *Signs* 15 (Summer 1990): 733-754.

Palmer, Pamela Lynn. "Dorothy Scarborough and Karle Wilson Baker: A Literary Friendship." *Southwestern History Quarterly* 91 (July 1987): 19-32.

Palmer, Virginia A., ed. "'Faithfully Yours, Ellen C. Sabin': Correspondence Between Ellen C. Sabin and Lucia R. Briggs from January, 1921, to August, 1921." *Wisconsin Magazine of History* 67 (Autumn 1983): 17-41.

Palmieri, Patricia A. "Here Was Fellowship: A Social Portrait of Academic Women at Wellesley College, 1895-1920." *History of Education Quarterly* 23 (Summer 1983): 195-214.

Rooke, Patricia T. "Public Figure, Private Woman: Same-Sex Support Structures in the Life of Charlotte Whitton." *International Journal of Women's Studies* [Canada] 6 (November/December 1983): 412-428.

Ross, Ellen. "Women's Neighborhood Sharing in London Before World War One." *History Workshop* 15 (Spring 1983): 4-27.

Rupp, Leila J. "The Women's Community in the National Woman's Party, 1945 to the 1960s." *Signs* 10 (Summer 1985): 715-740.

Seeber, Frances. "Eleanor Roosevelt and Women in the New Deal: A Network of Friends." *Presidential Studies Quarterly* 20 (Fall 1990): 707-719.

Shammas, Carole. "The Female Social Structure of Philadelphia in 1775." *Pennsylvania Magazine of History and Biography* 107 (January 1983): 69-84.

Sheehan, Nancy M. "'Women Helping Women': The WCTU and the Foreign Population in the West, 1905-1930." *International Journal of Women's Studies* 6 (November/December 1983): 395-411.

Sklar, Kathryn Kish. "Hull House in the 1890s: A Community of Women Reformers." *Signs* 10 (Summer 1985): 658-677.

Spangler, Lynn C. "A Historical Overview of Female Friendships on Prime-Time Television." *Journal of Popular Culture* 22 (Spring 1989): 13-24.

Springer, Marlene. "Stowe and Eliot: An Epistolary Friendship." *Biography* 9 (Winter 1986): 59-81.

# HEALTH

## Health Care/Preventive Health Care

Abbott, Devon Irene. "Medicine for the Rosebuds: Health Care at the Cherokee Female Seminary, 1876-1909." *American Indian Culture and Research Journal* 12 (1988): 59-71.

Becker, Carl B. "Religious Healing in 19th Century 'New Religions': The Cases of Tenrikyo and Christian Science." *Religion* 20 (July 1990): 199-216.

Bularzik, Mary J. "The Dedham Temporary Asylum for Discharged Female Prisoners, 1864-1909." *Historical Journal of Massachusetts* 12 (January 1984): 28-35.

Byrde, Penelope. "'That Frightful Unbecoming Dress': Clothes for Spa Bathing at Bath." *Costume* 21 (1987): 44-56.

Cunningham, Patricia. "Annie Jenness Miller and Mabel Jenness: Promoters of Physical Culture and Correct Dress." *Dress* 16 (1990): 48-61.

Drachman, Virginia G. "Gynecological Instruments and Surgical Decisions at a Hospital in Late Nineteenth-Century America." *Journal of American Culture* 3 (Winter 1980): 660-672.

Hamilton, Diane. "The Cost of Caring: The Metropolitan Life Insurance Company's Visiting Nurse Service, 1909-1953." *Bulletin of the History of Medicine* 63 (Fall 1989): 414-434.

Herndl, Diane Price. "The Writing Cure: Charlotte Perkins Gilman, Anna O., and 'Hysterical' Writing." *NWSA Journal* 1 (Autumn 1988): 52-74.

Jones, C. "Sisters of Charity and the Ailing Poor." *Social History of Medicine* 2 (1989): 339-348.

Kloberdanz, Timothy J. "The Daughters of Shiphrah: Folk Healers and Midwives of the Great Plains." *Great Plains Quarterly* 9 (Winter 1989): 3-12.

Lingo, Alison K. "Empirics and Charlatans in Early Modern France: The Genesis of the Classification of the 'Other' in Medical Practice." *Journal of Social History* 19 (Summer 1986): 583-604.

Moldow, Gloria. "'For Women, by Women': Women's Dispensaries and Clinics in Washington, 1882-1900." *Records of the Columbia Historical Society of Washington, D.C.* 50 (1980).

Morantz, Regina Markell, and Sue Zschoche. "Professionalism, Feminism, and Gender Roles: A Comparative Study of Nineteenth-Century Medical Therapeutics." *Journal of American History* 67 (December 1980): 568-588.

Peterson, Susan C. "Adapting to Fill a Need: The Presentation Sisters and Health Care, 1901-1961." *South Dakota History* 17 (Spring 1987): 1-22.

Riddett, Lyn. "Sisters, Wives and Mothers: Settler Women as Healers and Preservers of Health in the N. T. During the 1930s." *Hecate* 15, no. 2 (1989): 7-22.

Schackel, Sandra K. "'The Tales Those Nurses Told!': Public Health Nurses Among the Pueblo and Navajo Indians." *New Mexico Historical Review* 65 (April 1990): 225-250.

Steckel, Richard H. "The Health and Mortality of Women and Children, 1850-1860." *Journal of Economic History* 48 (June 1988): 333-346.

Talberg, Marianne. "Nursing and Medical Care in Finland from the Eighteenth to the Late Nineteenth Century." *Scandinavian Journal of History* 14, no. 4 (1989): 269-284.

Thavenet, Dennis. "Tending Their Flock: Dirt, Hygiene, and Health for Nineteenth Century Reform Children." *Michigan Historical Review* 15 (Fall

1989): 23-46.

Vertinsky, Patricia. "God, Science and the Market Place: The Bases for Exercise Prescriptions for Females in Nineteenth Century North America." *Canadian Journal of the History of Sport* 17, no. 1 (1986): 38-44.

Wall, Helena M. "Feminism and the New England Hospital, 1949-1961." *American Quarterly* 32 (Fall 1980): 435-452.

Woodcock, John. "The Therapeutic Journals of Joanna Field and Etty Hillesum." *Auto/Biography Studies* 5 (Summer 1989): 15-25.

## Illness

Barker-Benfield, G. "'Mother Emancipator': The Meaning of Jane Addams' Sickness and Cure." *Journal of Family History* 4 (Winter 1979): 395-420.

Barton, Marcella Biro. "Saint Teresa of Avila: Did She Have Epilepsy?" *Catholic Historical Review* 68 (October 1982): 581-598.

Cayleff, S. E. "'Prisoners of Their Own Feebleness': Women, Nerves and Western Medicine--A Historical Overview." *Social Science Medicine* 26 (1988): 1199-1208.

Chauncey, George, Jr. "From Sexual Inversion to Homosexuality: Medicine and the Changing Conceptualization of Female Diseases." *Salmagundi* 58/59 (Fall/Winter 1983): 114-146.

Conner, Susan P. "Politics, Prostitution, and the Pox in Revolutionary Paris, 1789-1799." *Western Society for French History* 14 (November 1986): 183.

Crowley, John W. "Winifred Howells and the Economy of Pain." *Old Northwest* 10 (Spring 1984): 41-75.

Dorsey, Carolyn A. "Despite Poor Health: Olivia Davidson Washington's Story." *Sage* 11 (Fall 1985): 69-71.

Ebi-Kryston, Kristie L., Millicent W. Higgins, and Jacob B. Keller. "Health and Other Characteristics of Employed Women and Homemakers in Tecumseh, 1959-1978: I. Demographic Characteristics, Smoking Habits, Alcohol Consumption, and Pregnancy Outcomes and Conditions." *Women & Health* 16, no. 2 (1990): 5-22.

-----. "Health and Other Characteristics of Employed Women and Homemakers in Tecumseh, 1959-1978: II. Prevalence of Respiratory and Cardiovascular Symptoms and Illnesses, Mortality Rates and Physical and Physiological Measurements." *Women & Health* 16, no. 2 (1990): 23-40.

Figbie, Karl. "Chlorosis and Chronic Disease in Nineteenth-Century Britain: The Social Constitution of Somatic Illness in a Capitalist Society." *Social History* 3 (May 1978): 167-197.

Goldstein, Jan. "The Hysteria Diagnosis and the Politics of Anticlericalism in Late Nineteenth Century France." *Journal of Modern History* 54 (June 1982): 209-239.

-----. "The Hysteria Diagnosis and the Politics of Anti-Clericalism in the Early Third Republic." *Western Society for French History* 8 (October 1980): 403.

Hood, Brenda. "'This Worry I Have': Mary Herren Journal." *Oregon Historical*

*Quarterly* 80 (Fall 1979): 229-257.

Ineson, A. "Women's Work and Women's Health in the Munitions Industry in World War I." *Society for the Social History of Medicine Bulletin* no. 36 (1985): 44-47.

McGregor, Deborah Kuhn. "Female Disorders and 19th-Century Medicine: The Case of Vesico-Vaginal Fistula." *Caduceus: A Museum Quarterly for the Health Sciences* 3, no. 1 (1987): 1-31.

McReynolds, Rosalee. "The Sexual Politics of Illness in Turn of the Century Libraries." *Libraries & Culture* 25 (Spring 1990): 194-217.

Mercer, Caroline G., and Sarah D. Wangensteen. "'Consumption, Heart-Disease, or Whatever': Chlorosis, A Heroine's Illness in *The Wings of the Dove*." *Journal of the History of Medicine and Allied Sciences* 40 (July 1985): 259-285.

Micale, Mark. "Hysteria and Its Historiography: A Review of Past and Present Writings (II)." *History of Science* 27 (December 1989): 319-352.

Miller, Genevieve. "Putting Lady Mary in Her Place: A Discussion of Historical Causation." *Bulletin of the History of Medicine* 55 (Spring 1981): 2-16.

Padgug, Robert. "More Than the Story of a Virus: Gay History, Gay Communities and AIDS." *Radical America* 21 (March/April 1987): 35-42.

Paulshock, Bernadine Z. "'Let Every Reader Form His Own Conclusions': Doctor James A. Tilton's Case Report of a Delaware Woman Cured of Rabies." *Delaware History* 21 (Spring/Summer 1985): 186-196.

Smith, John H. "Abulia: Sexuality and Diseases of the Will in the Late Nineteenth Century." *Genders* no. 6 (November 1989): 102-124.

Stovall, Mary E. "'To Be, to Do, and to Suffer': Responses to Illness and Death in the Nineteenth-Century Central South." *Journal of Mississippi History* 52 (May 1990): 95-110.

Thomas, Samuel J. "Nostrum Advertising and the Image of Woman as Invalid in Late Victorian America." *Journal of American Culture* 5 (Fall 1982): 104-112.

Tintner, Adeline R., and Henry D. Janowitz. "Inoperable Cancer: An Alternate Diagnosis for Milly Theale's Illness." *Journal of the History of Medicine and Allied Sciences* 42 (January 1987): 77-82.

Van Deth, Ron and Walter Vandereycken. "Was Nervous Consumption a Precursor of Anorexia Nervosa?" *Journal of the History of Medicine and Allied Sciences* 46 (January 1991): 3-19.

## Maternity/Childbirth

Bogdan, Janet. "Care or Cure? Childbirth Practices in Nineteenth-Century America." *Feminist Studies* 4 (June 1978): 92-98.

Cutright, Phillips, and Edward Shorter. "The Effects of Health on the Completed Fertility of Nonwhite and White U.S. Women Born Between 1867 and 1935." *Journal of Social History* 13 (Winter 1979): 191-218.

Delacy, Margaret. "Puerperal Fever in Eighteenth Century Britain." *Bulletin of the History of Medicine* 63 (Winter 1989): 521-556.

Dobbie, B. M. Willmott. "An Attempt to Estimate the True Rate of Maternal

Mortality, Sixteenth to Eighteenth Centuries." *Medical History* 26 (January 1982): 79-89.

Fuchs, Rachel G., and Paul E. Knepper. "Women in the Paris Maternity Hospital: Public Policy in the Nineteenth Century." *Social Science History* 13 (Summer 1989): 187-203.

Hiddinga, Anja. "Obstetrical Research in The Netherlands in the Nineteenth Century." *Medical History* 31 (July 1987): 281-305.

Lane, Joan. "A Provincial Surgeon and His Obstetric Practice: Thomas W. Jones of Henley-in-Arden, 1764-1846." *Medical History* 31 (July 1987): 333-348.

Lansing, Dorothy I., W. Robert Penman, and Dorland J. Davis. "Puerperal Fever and the Group B Beta Hemolytic Streptococcus." *Bulletin of the History of Medicine* 57 (Spring 1983): 70-80.

Leavitt, Judith Walzer. "Birthing and Anesthesia: The Debate over Twilight Sleep." *Signs* 6 (Autumn 1980): 281-304.

-----."Under the Shadow of Maternity: American Women's Responses to Death and Debility Fears in Nineteenth-Century Childbirth." *Feminist Studies* 12 (Spring 1986): 129-154.

Lewis, Judith Schneid. "Maternal Health in the English Aristocracy: Myths and Realities 1790-1840." *Journal of Social History* 17 (Fall 1983): 97-114.

Lindemann, Mary. "Maternal Politics: The Principles and Practice of Maternity Care in Eighteenth-Century Hamburg." *Journal of Family History* 9 (Spring 1984): 44-63.

Longo, Lawrence D. "Electrotherapy in Gynecology: The American Experience." *Bulletin of the History of Medicine* 60 (Fall 1986): 343-366.

Loudon, Irvine. "Deaths in Childbed from the Eighteenth Century to 1935." *Medical History* 30 (January 1986): 1-41.

McPherson, K., and Veronica Strong-Boag. "The Confinement of Women: Childbirth and Hospitalization in Vancouver, 1919-1939." *B.C. Studies* 69/70 (Spring/Summer 1986): 142-174.

Oppenheimer, Jane M. "Basic Embryology and Clinical Medicine: A Case History in Serendipity." *Bulletin of the History of Medicine* 58 (Summer 1984): 236-240.

Oppenheimer, Jo. "Childbirth in Ontario: The Transition from Home to Hospital in the Early Twentieth Century." *Ontario History* 75 (March 1983): 36-60.

Siddell, A. Clair. "Bloodletting in American Obstetric Practice, 1800-1945." *Bulletin of the History of Medicine* 54 (Spring 1980): 101-110.

Stowe, Steven M. "Obstetrics and the Work of Doctoring in the Mid-Nineteenth-Century American South." *Bulletin of the History of Medicine* 64 (Winter 1990): 540-566.

Summey, Pamela S., and Marsha Hurst. "Ob/Gyn on the Rise: The Evolution of Professional Ideology in the Twentieth Century - Part I." *Women and Health* 11 (Spring 1986): 133-146.

-----. "Ob/Gyn on the Rise: The Evolution of Professional Ideology in the Twentieth Century - Part II." *Women and Health* 11 (Summer 1986): 103-122.

Ulrich, Laurel Thatcher. "'The Living Mother of a Living Child': Midwifery and

Mortality in Post-Revolutionary New England." *William and Mary Quarterly* 66 (January 1989): 27-48.

## Medical Issues

Axelson, Diana E. "Women as Victims of Medical Experimentation: J. Marion Sims' Surgery on Slave Women, 1845-1850." *Sage* 2 (Fall 1985): 10-13.

Bale, Anthony. "'Hope in Another Direction': Compensation for Work-Related Illness Among Women, 1900-1960--Part I." *Women & Health* 15, no. 1 (1989): 81-102.

Buckley, Suzann, and Jancie Dickin McGinnis. "Venereal Disease and Public Health Reform in Canada." *Canadian Historical Review* 63 (September 1982): 337-354.

Burton, June K. "Human Rights Issues Affecting Women in Legal Medical Textbooks." *History of European Ideas* 8 (1987): 427-434.

DeRocher, Gregory. "The Trouble with Women: Some Medical Musings from 16th-Century France." *Renaissance Papers* (1987): 39-47.

Draznin, Yaffa. "Did Victorian Medicine Crush Olive Schreiner's Creativity?" *Historian* 47 (February 1985): 196-207.

Fee, Elizabeth. "Nineteenth-Century Craniology: The Study of the Female Skull." *Bulletin of the History of Medicine* 53 (Fall 1979): 415-433.

Glazer, Nona Y. "The Home as Workshop: Women as Amateur Nurses and Medical Care Providers." *Gender & Society* 4 (December 1990): 479-499.

Gosling, F., and Joyce M. Ray. "The Right to Be Sick: American Physicians and Nervous Patients, 1885-1910." *Journal of Social History* 20 (Winter 1986): 251-267.

Harrison, B. "'Some of Them Gets Lead Poisoned': Occupational Lead Exposure in Women, 1880-1914." *Social History of Medicine* 2 (1989): 171-195.

Hurwitz B., and R. Richardson. "Inspector General James Barry, M.D.: Putting the Woman in Her Place." *British Medical Journal* 298 (1989): 299-305.

Kohlstedt, Sally Gregory. "Physiological Lectures for Women: Sarah Coates in Ohio, 1850." *Journal of the History of Medicine and Allied Sciences* 33 (January 1978): 75-81.

La Berge, Ann F. "Mothers and Infants, Nurses and Nursing: Alfred Donne and the Medicalization of Child-Care in Nineteenth-Century France." *Journal of the History of Medicine and Allied Sciences* 46 (January 1991): 20-43.

Lockwood, Rose Ann. "Birth, Illness, and Death in 18th-Century New England." *Journal of Social History* 12 (Fall 1978): 111-128.

Mitchinson, Wendy. "Gynecological Operations on Insane Women: London, Ontario, 1895-1901." *Journal of Social History* 15 (Spring 1982): 467-484.

-----. "Gynecological Operations on the Insane." *Archivaria* 10 (1980): 125-144.

-----. "A Medical Debate in Nineteenth Century English Canada: Ovariotomies." *Histoire sociale/Social History* 17 (May 1984): 133-147.

-----. "Medical Perceptions of Healthy Women: The Case of Late Nineteenth-Century Canada." *Canadian Woman Studies/Les cahiers de la femme* 8 (Winter 1987): 42-43.

-----. "The Medical View of Women: The Case of Late Nineteenth-Century Canada." *Canadian Bulletin of Medical History/Bulletin canadien d'histoire de la medicine* 3 (Winter 1986): 207-224.

Peterson, M. Jeanne. "Dr. Acton's Enemy: Medicine, Sex, and Society in Victorian England." *Victorian Studies* 29 (Summer 1986): 569-590.

Shapiro, Ann-Louise. "Disordered Bodies/Disorderly Acts: Medical Discourse and the Female Criminal in Nineteenth Century Paris." *Genders* no. 4 (March 1989): 68-86.

Verma, R. L. "Women's Role in Islamic Medicine Through the Ages." *Arab Historian* 22 (1982): 21-48.

Wood, Charles T. "The Doctor's Dilemma: Sin, Salvation, and the Menstrual Cycle in Medieval Thought." *Speculum* 56 (1981): 710-727.

## Psychology

Brown, Gillian. "The Empire of Agoraphobia." *Representations* 20 (Fall 1987): 134-157.

Carlson, Eric T. "The History of Multiple Personality in the United States: Mary Reynolds and Her Subsequent Reputation." *Bulletin of the History of Medicine* 58 (Spring 1984): 72-82.

Cohen, Alfred. "Prophecy and Madness: Women Visionaries During the Puritan Revolution." *Journal of Psychohistory* 11 (Winter 1984): 411-430.

Davies, Megan J. "Snapshots: Three Women and Psychiatry, 1920-1935." *Canadian Woman Studies/Les cahiers de la femme* 8 (Winter 1987): 47-48.

Decker, Hannah S. "Freud and Dora: Constraints on Medical Progress." *Journal of Social History* 14 (Spring 1981): 445-464.

Fishbein, Leslie. "Freud and the Radicals: The Sexual Revolution Comes to Greenwich Village." *Canadian Review of American Studies* 12 (Fall 1981): 173-190.

Freedman, Estelle B. "'Uncontrolled Desires': The Response to the Sexual Psychopath, 1920-1960." *Journal of American History* 74 (June 1987): 83-106.

Griswold, Robert L. "The Evolution of the Doctrine of Mental Cruelty in Victorian American Divorce, 1790-1900." *Journal of Social History* 20 (Fall 1986): 127-148.

Guttmann, A. "Freud Versus Feminism." *Dissent* 26 (1979): 204-212.

Haaken, Janice. "Field Dependence Research: A Historical Analysis of Psychological Construct." *Signs* 13 (Winter 1988): 311-330.

Kushner, Howard I. "Women and Suicide in Historical Perspective." *Signs* 10 (Spring 1985): 537-552.

Leibman, Nina C. "Sexual Misdemeanor/Psychoanalytic Felony." *Cinema Journal* 26 (Winter 1987): 27-38.

Lunbeck, Elizabeth. "'A New Gerneration of Women': Progressive Psychiatrists and the Hypersexual Female." *Feminist Studies* 13 (Fall 1987): 513-543.

McGovern, Constance M. "The Myths of Social Control and Custodial

Oppression: Patterns of Psychiatric Medicine in Late Nineteenth-Century Institutions." *Journal of Social History* 20 (Fall 1986): 3-23.

McLaren, Angus. "Contraception and Its Discontent: Sigmund Freud and Birth Control." *Journal of Social History* 12 (Summer 1979): 513-530.

-----. "The Creation of a Haven for 'Human Thoroughbreds': The Sterilization of the Feeble-Minded and the Mentally Ill in British Columbia." *Canadian Historical Review* 67 (June 1986): 127-150.

Micale, Mark. "Hysteria and Its Historiography: A Review of Past and Present Writings (II)." *History of Science* 27 (December 1989): 319-352.

Mitchinson, Wendy. "Gender and Insanity as Characteristics of the Insane: A Nineteenth-Century Case." *Canadian Bulletin of Medical History/Bulletin canadien d'histoire de la medicine* 4 (Winter 1987): 99-117.

-----. "Hysteria and Insanity in Women: A Nineteenth-Century Canadian Perspective." *Journal of Canadian Studies/Revue d'études canadiennes* 21 (Fall 1986): 87-105.

O'Brien, Patricia. "The Kleptomania Diagnosis: Bourgeois Women and Theft in Late Nineteenth-Century France." *Journal of Social History* 17 (Fall 1983): 65-77.

Pierce, Jennifer L. "The Relationship Between Emotion, Work, and Hysteria: A Feminist Reinterpretation of Freud's *Studies in Hysteria*." *Women's Studies* 16, no. 3/4 (1989): 255-270.

Russo, Nancy Felipe. "Barbara Strudler Wallston--Pioneer of Contemporary Feminist Psychology." *Psychology of Women Quarterly* 14 (June 1990): 277-287.

Seifert, Carolyn J. "Images of Domestic Madness in the Art and Poetry of American Women." *Woman's Art Journal* 1 (Fall 1980/Winter 1981): 1-6.

Shafter, R. "Women and Madness: A Social Historical Perspective." *Issues in Ego Psychology* 12 (1989): 72-82.

Shorter, Edward. "Paralysis: The Rise and Fall of a 'Hysterical' Symptom." *Journal of Social History* 19 (Summer 1986): 549-582.

-----. "Women and Jews in a Private Nervous Clinic in Late Nineteenth Century Vienna." *Medical History* 33 (1989): 149-183.

Showalter, Elaine. "Victorian Women and Insanity." *Victorian Studies* 23 (Winter 1980): 157-182.

Stephens, Jane. "Breezes of Discontent: A Historical Perspective of Anxiety Based Illnesses Among Women." *Journal of American Culture* 8 (Winter 1985): 11-16.

Theriot, Nancy M. "Psychosomatic Illness in History: The 'Green Sickness' Among Nineteenth-Century Adolescent Girls." *Journal of Psychohistory* 15 (Spring 1988): 461-480.

Warsh, Cheryl Krasnick. "The First Mrs. Rochester: Wrongful Confinement, Social Redundancy, and Commitment to the Private Asylum." *Historical Papers/Communications Historique* (1988): 145-167.

# LATIN AMERICA

Adams, Jane H. "The Decoupling of Farm and Household: Differential Consequences of Capitalist Development on Southern Illinois and Third World Family Farms." *Comparative Studies in Society and History* [Great Britain] 30, no. 3 (1988): 453-482.

Agosin, Marjorie. "Metaphors of Female Political Ideology: The Cases of Chile and Argentina." *Women's Studies International Forum* 10, no. 6 (1987): 571-577.

Angueira, Katherine. "To Make the Personal Political: The Use of Testimony as a Consciousness-Raising Tool Against Sexual Aggression in Puerto Rico." *Oral History Review* 16 (Fall 1988): 65-94.

Arenal, Electa, and Stacey Schlau. "Stratagems of the Strong, Stratagems of the Weak: Autobiographical Prose of the Seventeenth-Century Hispanic Convent." *Tulsa Studies in Women's Literature* 9 (Spring 1990): 25-42.

Arrom, Silvia M. "Changes in Mexican Family Law in the Nineteenth Century: The Civil Codes of 1870 and 1884." *Journal of Family History* 10 (Autumn 1985): 305-317.

-----. "Marriage Patterns in Mexico City, 1811." *Journal of Family History* 3 (Winter 1978): 376-391.

Arzipe, Lourdes. "Women in the Informal Labor Sector: The Case of Mexico City." *Signs* 3, no. 1 (1977): 25-37.

Azicri, Max. "Women's Development through Revolutionary Mobilization: A Study of the Federation of Cuban Women." *International Journal of Women's Studies* 2 (1979): 27-50.

Azize-Vargas, Yamila. "The Roots of Puerto Rico Feminism: The Struggle for Universal Suffrage." *Radical America* 23, no.1 (1989): 71-79.

Bailey, Samuel. "Marriage Patterns and Immigrant Assimilation in Buenos Aires, 1882-1923." *Hispanic American Historical Review* 60 (February 1980): 32-48.

Balmori, Diana, and Robert Oppenheimer. "Family Clusters: Generational Nucleation in Nineteenth-Century Argentina and Chile." *Comparative Studies in Society and History* [Great Britain] 21, no. 2 (1979): 136-158.

Barash, Carol. "The Character of Difference: The Creole Woman as Cultural Mediator in Narratives about Jamaica." *Eighteenth-Century Studies* 23 (Summer 1990): 407-423.

Behar, Ruth. "Rage and Redemption: Reading the Life Story of a Mexican Marketing Woman." *Feminist Studies* 16 (Summer 1990): 223-258.

Bengelsdorf, Carollee. "On the Problem of Studying Women in Cuba." *Race and Class* 27 (Autumn 1985): 35-50.

Blay, Eva Alterman. "The Political Participation of Women in Brazil: Female Mayors." *Signs* 5 (Autumn 1979): 42-59.

Bravo, Rosa, and Rosalba Todaro. "Chilean Women and the UN Decade for Women." *Women's Studies International Forum* 8, no. 2 (1985): 111-116.

Burkett, Elinor. "In Dubious Sisterhood: Class and Sex in Spanish South America." *Latin American Perspectives* 4 (Spring 1977): 18-26.

Burnard, Trevor. "Inheritance and Independence: Women's Status in Early Colonial Jamaica." *William and Mary Quarterly* 48 (January 1991): 93-115.

Bush, Barbara. "Towards Emancipation: Slave Women and Resistance to Coercive Labour Regimes in the British West Indian Colonies, 1790-1838." *Slavery and Abolition* 5 (December 1984): 222-243.

Butler, Flora Cornelia. "Socialist Feminism in Latin America." *Women & Politics* 4, no. 1 (1984): 69-93.

Campbell, Leon. "Women and the Great Rebellion in Peru, 1780-1783." *The Americas* 42 (October 1985): 163-196.

Catarella, Teresa. "Feminine Historicizing in the *Romancero Novelesco.*" *Bulletin of Hispanic Studies* 67 (October 1990): 331-344.

Chandler, David S. "Family Bonds and the Bondsman: The Slave Family in Colonial Colombia." *Latin American Research Review* 16, no. 2 (1981): 107-131.

-----. "The Montepios and Regulation of Marriage in the Mexican Bureaucracy, 1770-1821." *The Americas* 43 (July 1986): 47-68.

Ciria, Alberto. "Flesh and Fantasy: The Many Faces of Evita (and Juan Peron)." *Latin American Research Review* 18, no. 2 (1983): 150-165.

Clendinnen, Inga. "Yucatec Mayan Women and the Spanish Conquest: Role and Ritual in Historical Reconstruction." *Journal of Social History* (Spring 1982): 427-442.

Coutourier, Edith. "Women and the Family in Eighteenth-Century Mexico: Law and Practice." *Journal of Family History* 10 (Fall 1985): 294-304.

Coutourier, Edith, and Asuncion Lavrin. "Dowries and Wills: A View of Women's Socioeconomic Role in Colonial Guadalajara and Puebla." *Hispanic American Historical Review* 59 (May 1979): 280-304.

Craton, Michael. "Changing Patterns of Slave Families in the British West Indies." *Journal of Interdisciplinary History* 10 (Summer 1979): 1-35.

Cross, Harry. "Living Standards in Rural Nineteenth-Century Mexico: Zacatecas, 1820-1880." *Journal of Latin American Studies, Part 1* (May 1978): 1-19.

Falls, Helen E. "Agnes Graham: Educator in Chile." *Baptist History and Heritage* 23 (January 1988): 23-31.

Femenias, Blenda. "Peruvian Costume and European Perceptions in the Eighteenth Century." *Dress* 10 (1984): 52-63.

Figueiredo, Mariza. "The Socioeconomic Role of Women Heads of Family in a Brazilian Fishing Village." *Feminist Issues* 3 (Fall 1983): 83-103.

Florez, C. Elisa, and Dennis P. Hogan. "Demographic Transition and Life Course Change in Columbia." *Journal of Family History* 15, no. 1 (1990): 1-22.

Flusche, Della M., and Eugene H. Korth. "A Dowry Office in Seventeenth-Century Chile." *The Historian* 49 (February 1987): 204-222.

Foppa, Alaide. "The First Feminist Congress in Mexico, 1916." *Signs* 5 (Autumn 1979): 192-199.

Ganson, Barbara J. "Following Their Children into Battle: Women at War in

Paraguay, 1864-1870." *The Americas* 46 (January 1990): 335-372.

Gerardo Pena, Devon. "Las Maquiladoras: Mexican Women and the Class Struggles in the Border Industries." *Aztlan: International Journal of Chicano Studies Research* 11, no. 2 (1980): 159-229.

Gill, Lesley. "'Like a Veil to Cover Them': Women and the Pentecostal Movement in La Paz." *American Ethnologist* 17 (November 1990): 708-721.

Glickman, Nora. "The Jewish White Slave Trade in Latin American Writings." *American Jewish Archives* 34 (November 1982): 178-189.

Guy, Donna J. "Lower-Class Families, Women, and the Law in Nineteenth-Century Argentina." *Journal of Family History* 10 (Fall 1985): 318-330.

-----. "Public Health, Gender and Private Morality: Paid Labor and the Formation of the Body Politic in Buenos Aires." *Gender & History* 2 (Autumn 1990): 297-317.

-----. "The Rural Working-Class in Nineteenth-Century Argentina: Forced Plantation Labor in Tucuman." *Latin American Research Review* 13, no. 1 (1978): 135-145.

-----. "White Slavery, Public Health, and the Socialist Position on Legalized Prostitution in Argentina, 1913-1936." *Latin American Research Review* 23, no. 3 (1988): 60-80.

-----. "Women, Peonage, and Industrialization: Argentina, 1810-1914." *Latin American Research Review* 16, no. 3 (1981): 65-89.

Hagerman Johnson, Ann. "The Impact of Market Agriculture on Family and Household Structure in Nineteenth Century Chile." *Hispanic American Historical Review* 58, no. 4 (1978): 625-648.

Hahner, June E. "The Beginnings of the Women's Suffrage Movement in Brazil." *Signs* 5 (Fall 1979): 200-204.

-----. "Feminism, Women's Rights and the Suffrage Movement in Brazil, 1850-1932." *Latin American Research Review* 15, no. 1 (1980): 65-111.

-----. "Recent Research on Women in Brazil." *Latin American Research Review* 20, no. 3 (1985): 163-179.

-----. "Researching the History of Latin American Women: Past and Future Directions." *Revista Interamericana de Bibliografia* 33, no. 4 (1983): 545-552.

-----. "'Women's Place' in Politics and Economics in Brazil since 1964." *Luso-Brazilian Review* 19, no. 1 (1982): 83-91.

Hellbom, Anna-Britta. "The Life and Role of Women in the Aztec Culture." *Cultures* 8, no. 3 (1982): 55-65.

Keremitsis, Dawn. "Latin American Women Workers in Transition, Sexual Division of Labor Force in Mexico and Colombia in the Textile Industry." *The Americas* 40 (April 1984): 491-504.

Kicza, John E. "The Role of the Family in Economic Development in Nineteenth-Century Latin America." *Journal of Family History* 10 (Fall 1985): 235-246.

Kuznesof, Elizabeth A. "Household Composition and Headship as Related to Changes in Mode of Production: Saõ Paulo 1765-1836." *Comparative Studies in Society and History* 22, no. 1 (1980): 78-108.

------. "The Role of the Female-Headed Household in Brazilian Modernization: Sao Paulo, 1765-1836." *Journal of Social History* 13 (Summer 1980): 589-613.

Kuznesof, Elizabeth A., and Robert Oppenheimer. "The Family and Society in Nineteenth-Century Latin America: An Historiographical Introduction." *Journal of Family History* 10 (Autumn 1985): 215-234.

Lavrin, Asuncion. "Gender and Latin American History." *Cronicas* 29, no. 2 (1985): 213-225.

-----. "Unlike Sor Juana? The Model Nun in the Religious Literature of Colonial Mexico." *The University of Dayton Review* 16 (Spring 1983): 75-92.

-----. "Women in Latin American History." *History Teacher* 14 (May 1981): 387-400.

-----. "Women, the Family and Social Change in Latin America." *World Affairs* 150 (Fall 1987): 108-128.

-----. "Women, Labor, and the Left: Argentina and Chile, 1890-1925." *Journal of Women's History* 1 (Fall 1989): 88-116.

Lavrin, Asuncion, and Edith Coutourier. "Dowries and Wills: A View of Women's Socioeconomic Role in Colonial Guadalajara and Puebla, 1640-1790." *Hispanic American Historical Review* 59, no. 2 (1979): 280-304.

Leatham, Miquel. "*Indigenista* Hermeneutics and the Historical Meaning of Our Lady of Guadalupe of Mexico." *Folklore Forum* 22, no. 1/2 (1989): 27-39.

León de Leal, Magdalena, and Carmen Diana Deere. "Rural Women and the Development of Capitalism of Colombian Agriculture." *Signs* 5 (Autumn 1979): 60-77.

Love, Edgar F. "Marriage Patterns of Persons of African Descent in a Colonial Mexico City Parish." *Hispanic American Historical Review* 51, no. 1 (1971): 79-91.

Macias, Ana. "Women and the Mexican Revolution: 1910-1920." *Americas* 37 (July 1980): 53-81.

Mallon, Florencia E. "Gender and Class in the Transition to Capitalism. Household and Mode of Production in Central Peru." *Latin American Perspectives* 13 (Winter 1986): 147-174.

-----. "Studying Women's Work in Latin America: Reflections on the Direction of Feminist Scholarship." *Latin American Perspectives* 14 (Spring 1987): 255-261.

Matthews, Irene. "Woman as Myth: The 'Case' of Gabriela Mistral." *Bulletin of Hispanic Studies* 67 (January 1990): 57-70.

McCaa, Robert. "Modeling Social Interaction: Marital Miscegenation in Colonial Spanish America." *Historical Methods* 15 (1982): 45-66.

McCreery, David. "'This Life of Misery and Shame': Female Prostitution in Guatemala City, 1880-1920." *Journal of Latin American Studies* (November 1986): 333-353.

McGee, Sandra F. "The Visible and Invisible Liga Patriotica Argentina, 1919-1928: Gender Roles and the Right Wing." *Hispanic American Historical Review* 64, no. 2 (1984): 233-258.

Metcalf, Alida C. "Women and Means: Women and Family Property in Colonial

Brazil." *Journal of Social History* 24 (Winter 1990): 277-298.

Miller, Barbara Ann. "Women and Revolution: The Brigadas Femeninas and the Mexican Cristero Rebellion, 1926-1929." *Journal of Third World Studies* 15 (March 1981): 57-66.

Miller, Daniel. "Fashion and Ontology in Trinidad." *Culture & History* 7 (1990): 49-79.

Miller, Francesca. "The International Relations of Women of the Americas 1890-1928." *Americas* 43 (October 1986): 171-182.

Miller, Gary M. "Bourbon Social Engineering: Women and Conditions of Marriage in Eighteenth-Century Venezuela." *The Americas* 46 (January 1990): 261-290.

Mindiola, Tatcho. "The Cost of Being a Mexican Female Worker in the 1970 Houston Labor Market." *Aztlan: International Journal of Chicano Studies Research* 11 (Fall 1980): 231-248.

Mirelman, Victor A. "The Jewish Community versus Crime: The Case of White Slavery in Buenos Aires." *Jewish Social Studies* 46 (Spring 1984): 145-168.

Molyneux, Maxine. "Mobilization without Emancipation? Women's Interests, The State and Revolution in Nicaragua." *Feminist Studies* 11 (Summer 1985): 227-254.

-----. "No God, No Boss, No Husband: Anarchist Feminism in Nineteenth-Century Argentina." *Latin American Perspectives* 13 (Winter 1986): 119-145.

Nash, June. "The Aztecs and the Ideology of Male Dominance." *Signs* 4 (Winter 1978): 349-362.

Navarro, Marysa. "Evita and the Crisis of 17 October 1945: A Case Study of Peronist and Anti-Peronist Mythology." *Journal of Latin American Studies* 12 (May 1980): 127-138.

Nazzari, Muriel. "Parents and Daughters: Change in the Practice of Dowry in Sao Paulo (1600-1770)." *Hispanic American Historical Review* 70 (November 1990): 639-666.

Paz, Octavio. "Juana Ramirez." *Signs* 5, no.1 (1979): 80-97.

Pena, Devon Gerardo. "Las Maquiladoras: Mexican Women and Class Struggle in the Border Industries." *Aztlan: International Journal of Chicano Studies Research* 11 (Fall 1980): 159-230.

Ramos, Donald. "City and Country: The Family in Minas Gerais, 1804-1838." *Journal of Family History* 3 (Winter 1978): 361-375.

-----. "Marriage and the Family in Colonial Vila-Rica." *Hispanic American Historical Review* 55, no. 2 (1975): 200-225.

Rios, Palmiran. "Export-Oriented Industrialization and the Demand for Female Labor: Puerto Rican Women in the Manufacturing Sector, 1952-1980." *Gender & Society* 4 (September 1990): 321-337.

Russell-Wood, A. J. R. "The Black Family in the Americas." *Societas* 8 (Winter 1978): 1-38.

Safa, Helen. "Female Employment and the Social Reproduction of the Puerto Rican Working Class." *International Migration Review* 18, no. 4 (1984): 1168-1187.

-----. "Runaway Shops and Female Employment: The Search for Cheap Labor." *Signs* 7 (Winter 1981): 418-433.

-----. "Women's Social Movements in Latin America." *Gender & Society* 4 (September 1990): 354-369.

Sanchez, Virginia Korrol. "On the Other Side of the Ocean: The Experience of Early Puerto Rican Migrant Women." *Caribbean Review* 7 (January-March 1979): 22-28.

Sanlon, Geraldine M. "Class and Gender in Pardo Bazan's *La Tribuna.*" *Bulletin of Hispanic Studies* 67 (April 1990): 137-150.

Scott, Edith E. "Married Women's Rights under the Matrimonial Regimes of Chile and Colombia: A Comparative History." *Harvard Women's Law Journal* 7 (Spring 1984): 221-249.

Seed, Patricia. "The Church and the Patriarchal Family: Marriage Conflicts in the Sixteenth- and Seventeenth-Century New Spain." *Journal of Family History* 10 (Autumn 1985): 284-293.

-----. "Marriage Promises and the Value of a Woman's Testimony in Colonial Mexico." *Signs* 13 (Winter 1988): 253-276.

Silverblatt, Irene. "Andean Women in the Inca Empire." *Feminist Studies* 4 (Fall 1978): 37-61.

Simon, Rita, and Margo Deley. "The Work Experience of Undocumented Mexican Women Migrants in Los Angeles." *International Migration Review* 18, no. 4 (1984): 1212-1229.

Socolow, Susan Migden. "Marriage, Birth, and Inheritance: The Merchants of Eighteenth-Century Buenos Aires." *Hispanic American Historical Review* 60 (August 1980): 387-406.

-----. "Women and Crime: Buenos Aires, 1757-1797." *Journal of Latin American Studies* 12 (May 1980): 39-54.

Soeiro, Susan A. "The Social and Economic Role of the Convent: Women and Nuns in Colonial Bahia, 1677-1800." *Hispanic American Historical Review* 54, no. 2 (1974): 209-232.

Stafford, Susan Buchanon. "Haitian Immigrant Women: A Cultural Perspective." *Anthropologica* 26, no. 2 (1984): 171-190.

Stoner, K. Lynn. "Directions in Latin American Women's History, 1977-1985." *Latin American Research Review* 22 (Spring 1987): 101-134.

Szuchman, Mark D. "Household Structure and Political Crisis: Buenos Aires, 1810-1860." *Latin American Research Review* 21 (1986): 55-93.

Tiano, Susan. "Maquiladoras, Women's Work, and Unemployment in Northern Mexico." *Aztlan: International Journal of Chicano Studies Research* 15 (Fall 1985): 341-378.

Toman, Rene de la Pedraja. "Women in Colombian Organizations, 1900-1940: A Study in Changing Gender Roles." *Journal of Women's History* 2 (Spring 1990): 98-119.

Towner, Margaret. "Monopoly Capitalism and Women's Work During the Porfiriato." *Latin American Perspectives* 2, no. 1/2 (1979): 90-105.

Tutino, John. "Family Economies in Agrarian Mexico, 1750-1910." *Journal of*

*Family History* 10 (Fall 1985): 258-271.

-----. "Power, Class, and Family: Men and Women in the Mexican Elite, 1750-1810." *Americas* 39 (1982): 359-382.

Vasques de Miranda, Glaura. "Women's Labor Force Participation in a Developing Society: The Case of Brazil." *Signs* 3, no. 1 (1977): 261-274.

Vaughan, Mary Kay. "Women School Teachers in the Mexican Revolution: The Story of Reyna's Braids." *Journal of Women's History* 2 (Spring 1990): 143-168.

Wells, Allen. "Family Elites in a Boom and Bust Economy: The Molinas and Peons of Porfirian Yucatan." *Hispanic American Historical Review* 62, no. 2 (1982): 224-253.

Yeager, Gertrude M. "Women's Role in Nineteenth-Century Chile: Public Education Records, 1843-1883." *Latin American Research Review* 18, no. 3 (1983): 149-156.

Zulawski, Ann. "Social Differentiation, Gender and Ethnicity: Urban Indian Women in Colonial Bolivia, 1640-1725." *Latin American Research Review* 25, no. 2 (1990): 93-114.

# LAW/CRIME

## Courts, Trials, and Prisons

Booth, M. "Women's Prison Memoirs in Egypt and Elsewhere: Prison, Gender, Praxis." *MERIP Middle East Report* 149/17 (1987): 35-41.

Brown, Elizabeth Gaspar. "The Waukesha County Jail--Building, Administration, Inmates: 1901-1904." *American Journal of Legal History* 23 (1979): 236-264.

Bularzik, Mary J. "The Dedham Temporary Asylum for Discharged Female Prisoners, 1864-1909." *Historical Journal of Massachusetts* 12 (January 1984): 28-35.

Butler, Anne M. "Still in Chains: Black Women in Western Prisons, 1865-1910." *Western Historical Quarterly* 20 (February 1989): 19-35.

Cannon, Kenneth L. "A Strange Encounter: The English Courts and Mormon Polygamy." *Brigham Young University Studies* 22 (Winter 1982): 73-83.

Colwill, Elizabeth. "Just Another Citoyenne? Marie-Antionette on Trial, 1790-1793." *History Workshop* no. 28 (Autumn 1989): 63-87.

Cooper, R. A. "Jeremy Bentham, Elizabeth Fry, and English Prison Reform." *Journal of the History of Ideas* 42 (1981): 675-690.

Ewig, Rick. "Wyoming Women as Jurors." *Annals of Wyoming* 62 (Fall 1990): 140-143.

Foley, William E. "Slave Freedom Suits Before Dred Scott: The Case of Marie Jean Scypion's Descendants." *Missouri Historical Review* 79 (October 1984): 1-23.

Forbes, Thomas R. "A Jury of Matrons." *Medical History* 32 (January 1988): 23-33.

Freedman, Estelle B. "Sentiment and Discipline: Women's Prison Experiences in

Nineteenth Century America." *Prologue* 16 (Winter 1984): 249-259.

Gibson, Mary S. "The 'Female Offender' and the Italian School of Criminal Anthropology." *Journal of European Studies* 12 (September 1982): 155-165.

Greenshields, Malcolm. "Women, Violence, and Criminal Justice Records in Early Modern Haute Auvergne (1587-1664)." *Canadian Journal of History* 22 (August 1987): 175-194.

Hahn, Nicolas Fischer. "Female State Prisoners in Tennessee: 1831-1979." *Tennessee Historical Quarterly* 39 (Winter 1980): 485-497.

Hemphill, C. Dallett. "Women in Court: Sex-Role Differentiation in Salem, Massachusetts 1636 to 1683." *William and Mary Quarterly* 39 (January 1982): 164-175.

Howe, Adrian. "Prologue to a History of Women's Imprisonment: In Search of a Feminist Perspective." *Social Justice* 17 (Summer 1990): 5-22.

Kremer, Gary R. "Strangers to Domestic Virtues: Nineteenth-Century Women in the Missouri Prison." *Missouri Historical Review* 84 (April 1990): 293-310.

Martin, Charles H. "Race, Gender, and Southern Justice: The Rosa Lee Ingram Case." *American Journal of Legal History* 29 (July 1985): 251-268.

Schafer, Judith K. "'Open and Notorious Concubinage': The Emancipation of Slave Mistresses by Will and the Supreme Court in Antebellum Louisiana." *Louisiana History* 28 (Spring 1987): 165-182.

Schriber, Mary Suzanne. "Justice to Zenobia." *New England Quarterly* 55 (March 1982): 61-78.

Spindel, Donna J. "The Administration of Criminal Justice in North Carolina, 1720-1740." *American Journal of Legal History* 25 (1981): 24-47.

## Divorce, Family, and Marriage

Arrom, Silvia M. "Changes in Mexican Family Law in the Nineteenth Century: The Civil Codes of 1870 and 1884." *Journal of Family History* 10 (Autumn 1985): 305-317.

Backhouse, Constance B. "Married Women's Property Law in Nineteenth-Century Canada." *Law and History Review* 6 (Fall 1988): 211-258.

Bardaglio, Peter W. "Challenging Parental Custody Rights: The Legal Reconstruction of Parenthood in the Nineteenth Century American South." *Continuity and Change* 4 (August 1989): 259-292.

Basch, Norma. "Invisible Women: The Legal Fiction of Marital Unity in Nineteenth-Century America." *Feminist Studies* 5 (Fall 1979): 346-366.

-----. "Relief in the Premises: Divorce as a Woman's Remedy in New York and Indiana, 1815-1870." *Law and History Review* 8 (Spring 1990): 1-24.

Blackman, Charles F. "The Civil Sacrament: Law and Practice of Soviet Weddings." *American Journal of Comparative Law* 28 (1980): 555-576.

Brophy, Julia. "Parental Rights and Children's Welfare: Some Problems of Feminists' Strategy in the 1920s." *International Journal of the Sociology of Law* 10 (May 1982): 149-168.

Carroll, Lucy. "The Muslim Family Laws Ordinance, 1961: Provisions and

Procedures--A Reference Paper for Current Research." *Contributions to Indian Sociology* 13, no. 1 (1979): 117-143.

Chused, Richard H. "Late Nineteenth Century Married Women's Property Law: Reception of the Early Married Women's Property Acts by Courts and Legislatures." *American Journal of Legal History* 29 (January 1985): 3-35.

-----. "Married Women's Property and Inheritance by Widows in Massachusetts: A Study of Wills Probated Between 1800 and 1850." *Berkeley Women's Law Journal* 2 (Fall 1986): 42-88.

-----. "Married Women's Property Law: 1800-1850." *The Georgetown Law Journal* 71 (1983): 1359-1425.

-----. "The Oregon Donation Act of 1850 and Nineteenth Century Federal Married Women's Property Law." *Law and History Review* 2 (Spring 1984): 44-78.

Clark, Elaine. "City Orphans and Custody Laws in Medieval England." *American Journal of Legal History* 34 (April 1990): 168-187.

Clark, Elizabeth B. "Matrimonial Bonds: Slavery and Divorce in Nineteenth-Century America." *Law and History Review* 8 (Spring 1990): 25-54.

Coutourier, Edith. "Women and the Family in Eighteenth- Century Mexico: Law and Practice." *Journal of Family History* 10 (Fall 1985): 294-304.

Dougan, Michael B. "The Arkansas Married Woman's Property Law." *Arkansas Historical Quarterly* 46 (Spring 1987): 3-26.

Drake, W. Magruder, ed. "A Discourse on Divorce: Orleans Territorial Legislature 1806." *Louisiana History* 22 (Fall 1981): 434-437.

Erickson, Amy Louise. "Common Law versus Common Practice: The Use of Marriage Settlements in Early Modern England." *The Economic History Review* 43 (February 1990): 21-39.

Faith, Rosamond, Paul A. Grand and Paul R. Hyams. "Debate: 'Seigneurial Control of Women's Marriage.'" *Past & Present* no. 99 (May 1983): 123-147.

Feigenson, Neil R. "Extraterritorial Recognition of Divorce Decrees in the Nineteenth Century." *American Journal of Legal History* 34 (April 1990): 119-167.

Goodheart, Lawrence B., Neil Hanks, and Elizabeth Johnson. "'An Act for the Relief of Females . . .': Divorce and Changing Legal Status of Women in Tennessee, 1796-1860, Part I." *Tennessee Historical Quarterly* 44 (Fall 1985): 318-339.

-----. "'An Act for the Relief of Females . . .': Divorce and the Changing Legal Status of Women in Tennessee, 1796-1860, Part II." *Tennessee Historical Quarterly* 44 (Winter 1985): 402-416.

Griswold, Robert L. "Law, Sex Cruelty, and Divorce in Victorian America, 1840-1900." *American Quarterly* 38 (Winter 1986): 721-745.

Guy, Donna J. "Lower-Class Families, Women, and the Law in Nineteenth-Century Argentina." *Journal of Family History* 10 (Fall 1985): 318-330.

Hammerton, A. James. "Victorian Marriage and the Law of Matrimonial Cruelty." *Victorian Studies* 33 (Winter 1990): 269-292.

Hardaway, Roger D. "Prohibiting Interracial Marriages: Miscegenation Laws in

Wyoming." *Annals of Wyoming* 52 (Spring 1980): 55-60.

Hickling, R. H. "The Reception of English Divorce Law in Malaysia or the Misadventures of What Is Now Section 47 of Act 164." *Jurnal Undang-Undang/Journal of Malaysian and Comparative Law* [Kuala Lumpur] 10 (June-December 1983): 189-199.

Hindson, James. "The Marriage Duty Acts and the Social Topography of the Early Modern Town: Shrewsbury, 1695-8." *Local Population Studies* no. 31 (Autumn 1983): 21-28.

Ibrahim, Ahmad. "Plucking the Fruits of Divorce." *Jurnal Undang-Undang/Journal of Malaysian and Comparative Law* [Kuala Lumpur] 7 (1980): 127-137.

Jenson, Carol Elizabeth. "The Equity Jurisdiction and Married Women's Property in Ante-Bellum America: A Revisionist View." *International Journal of Women's Studies* 2 (March/April 1979): 144-154.

Kelly, John D. "Fear of Culture: British Regulation of Indian Marriage in Post-Indenture Fiji." *Ethnohistory* 36 (Autumn 1989): 392-410.

Linford, Orma. "The Mormons, the Law, and the Territory of Utah." *American Journal of Legal History* 23 (1979): 213-235.

Matovic, Margareta R. "The Stockholm Marriage: Extra-Legal Family Formation in Stockholm, 1860-1890." *Continuity and Change* 1, no. 3 (1986): 385-414.

Moncrief, Sandra. "The Mississippi Married Women's Property Act of 1839." *Journal of Mississippi History* 47 (May 1985): 110-125.

Mundy, Martha. "Women's Inheritance of Land in Highland Yemen." *Arabian Studies* 5 (1979): 161-187.

Peffer, George Anthony. "Forbidden Families: Emigration Experiences of Chinese Women under the Page Law, 1875-1882." *Journal of American Ethnic History* 6 (Fall 1986): 28-46.

Petrik, Paula. "If She Be Content: The Development of Montana Divorce Law, 1865-1907." *Western Historical Quarterly* 18 (July 1987): 261-292.

Pluss, Jacques Anthony. "Reading Case Law Historically: A *Consilium* of Baldus de Ubaldis on Widows and Dowries." *American Journal of Legal History* 30 (July 1986): 241-265.

Poovey, Mary. "Covered but Not Bound: Caroline Norton and the 1857 Matrimonial Causes Act." *Feminist Studies* 14 (Fall 1988): 467-486.

Saraceno, Chiara. "Women, Family, and the Law, 1750-1942." *Journal of Family History* 15, no. 4 (1990): 427-442.

Savage, Gail L. "The Operation of the 1857 Divorce Act, 1860-1910: A Research Note." *Journal of Social History* 16 (Summer 1983): 103-110.

Scott, Edith E. "Married Women's Rights under the Matrimonial Regimes of Chile and Colombia: A Comparative History." *Harvard Women's Law Journal* 7 (Spring 1984): 221-249.

Shammas, Carole. "English Inheritance Law and Its Transfer to the Colonies." *American Journal of Legal History* 31 (April 1987): 145-163.

Snell, James G., and Cynthia Comacchio Abeele. "Regulating Nuptiality: Restricting Access to Marriage in Early Twentieth-Century English-Speaking

Canada." *Canadian Historical Review* 69 (December 1988): 466-489.

Socolow, Susan Migden. "Marriage, Birth, and Inheritance: The Merchants of Eighteenth-Century Buenos Aires." *Hispanic American Historical Review* 60 (August 1980): 387-406.

Stanley, Mary Lyndon. "'One Must Ride Behind': Married Women's Rights and the Divorce Act of 1857." *Victorian Studies* 25 (Spring 1982): 355-376.

Walroth, Joanne Ruth. "Beyond Legal Remedy: Divorce in Seventeenth Century Woodbridge, New Jersey." *New Jersey History* 105 (Fall/Winter 1987): 1-36.

Wegner, Judith R. "The Status of Women in Jewish and Islamic Marriage and Divorce Law." *Harvard Women's Law Journal* 5 (Spring 1982): 1-34.

## Female Criminality

Austin, Linda T. "Babies for Sale: Tennessee's Children Adoption Scandal." *Tennessee Historical Quarterly* 49 (Summer 1990): 91-102.

Burton, June K. "Infanticide in Napoleonic France: The Law, the Medical Profession, and the Murdering Mother." *Western Society for French History* 14 (November 1986): 183.

Burton, William L. "Murder, Booze, and Sex: Three Perspectives on the Roaring Twenties." *Midwest Quarterly* 31 (Spring 1990): 374-395.

Coates, Colin. "Authority and Illegitimacy in New France: The Burial of Bishop Saint-Vallier and Madeleine de Vercheres vs the Priest of Batiscan." *Histoire sociale/Social History* 22 (May 1989): 65-90.

Dellapenna, Joseph W. "The History of Abortions: Technology, Morality, and Law." *University of Pittsburgh Law Review* 40 (Spring 1979): 359-428.

Devine, Joel A., Joseph F. Sheley, and M. Dwayne Smith. "Macroeconomic and Social-Control Policy Influences on Crime-Rate Changes, 1948-1985." *American Sociological Review* 53 (June 1988): 407-420.

Forbes, Thomas R. "Deadly Parents: Child Homicide in Eighteenth and Nineteenth Century England." *Journal of the History of Medicine and Allied Sciences* 41 (April 1986): 175-199.

Krone, K. A. "One Woman's Poisons: The Preferred Poisons of the Victorian Era." *Dark Lantern* 1 (1984): 19-27.

Leuchtenburg, William E. "The Case of the Chambermaid and the Nine Old Men." *American Heritage* 38 (December 1986): 34-41.

Rasche, Christine E. "Early Models for Contemporary Thought on Domestic Violence and Women Who Kill Their Mates: A Review of the Literature from 1895 to 1970." *Women & Criminal Justice* 1, no. 2 (1990): 31-54.

Rutenberg, D. "From Praise of Hanging to the Femme Fatale: Capital Punishment in Nineties Periodicals." *Victorian Periodicals Newsletter* 11 (1978): 95-104.

Sim, J. "Women in Prison: A Historical Analysis." *Abolitionist* 8 (1981): 14-18.

Thompson, Tommy R. "Feeblemindedness, Criminal Behavior, and Women: A Turn-of-the-Century Case Study." *Palimpsest* 71 (Fall 1990): 132-144.

## Lawyers

Elwood-Akers, Virginia. "Clara Shortridge Foltz, California's First Woman Lawyer." *Pacific Historian* 28 (Fall 1984): 23-29.

Epstein, Sandra P. "Women and Legal Education: The Case of Boalt Hall." *Pacific Historian* 28 (Fall 1984): 4-22.

Guyette, Elise A. "Myra Colby Bradwell: First Woman Lawyer from Vermont." *Vermont History News* 35 (September/October 1984).

Howsam, Leslie. "'Sound-Minded Women': Eliza Orme and the Study and Practice of Law in Late-Victorian England." *Atlantis* 15 (Fall 1989): 44-55.

Humme, June Hitchcock. "Almeda Eliza Hitchcock--Wahine Loio, or Lady Lawyer." *Hawaiian Journal of History* 20 (1986): 137-150.

Opheim, Teresa. "Portias of the Prairie: Early Women Graduates of the University Law Department." *Palimpsest* 67 (January/February 1986): 28-36.

Petrick, Barbara. "Right or Privilege? The Admission of Mary Philbrook to the Bar." *New Jersey History* 97 (Summer 1979): 91-104.

Polos, Nicholas C. "San Diego's 'Portia of the Pacific': California's First Woman Lawyer." *San Diego History* 2 (Summer 1980): 185-195.

Roeder, Richard B. "Crossing the Gender Line: Ella L. Knowles, Montana's First Woman Lawyer." *Montana* 32 (Summer 1982): 64-75.

## Reproductive Rights and Illegitimacy

Backhouse, Constance. "Involuntary Motherhood: Abortion, Birth Control and the Law in 19th Century Canada." *Windsor Yearbook of Access to Justice* 3 (1983): 61-130.

Baer, Judith A. "What We Know as Women: A New Look at *Roe v. Wade.*" *NWSA Journal* 2 (Autumn 1990): 558-582.

Binion, Gayle. "Reproductive Freedom and the Constitution: *The Limits of Choice.*" *Berkeley Women's Law Journal* 4 (1988-1989): 12-41.

Brumberg, Joan Jacobs. "'Ruined' Girls: Changing Community Responses to Illegitimacy in Upstate New York, 1890-1920." *Journal of Social History* 18 (Winter 1984): 247-272.

Dodd, Dianne. "The Canadian Birth Control Movement on Trial, 1936-1937." *Histoire sociale/Social History* 16 (November 1983): 411-428.

Donovan, James M. "Abortion, the Law, and the Juries in France, 1825-1920." *Western Society for French History* 15 (November 1987): 217.

Fairchilds, Cissie. "Female Sexuality and the Rise of Illegitimacy: A Case Study." *Journal of Interdisciplinary History* 8 (Spring 1978): 627-667.

Gavigan, Shelley A. M. "On 'Bringing on the Menses': The Criminal Liability of Women and the Therapeutic Exception in Canadian Abortion Law." *Canadian Journal of Women and the Law* 1, no. 2 (1986): 279-312.

Gillis, John R. "Servants, Sexual Relations, and the Risks of Illegitimacy in

London, 1801-1900." *Feminist Studies* 5 (Spring 1979): 142-173.

Glen, Kristin Booth. "Abortion in the Courts: A Laywoman's Historical Guide to the New Disaster Area." *Feminist Studies* 4 (February 1978): 1-26.

Gordon, Linda. "The Long Struggle for Reproductive Rights." *Radical America* 15 (Spring 1981): 75-88.

-----. "Who Is Frightened of Reproductive Freedom for Women and Why? Some Historical Answers." *Frontiers* 9, no. 1 (1986): 23-26.

Higgenbotham, A. R. "Sin of the Age: Infanticide and Illegitimacy in Victorian London." *Victorian Studies* 32 (Spring 1989): 319-338.

Kuehn, Thomas. "'As if Conceived within a Legitimate Marriage': A Dispute Concerning Legitimation in Quattrocento Florence." *American Journal of Legal History* 29 (October 1985): 275-300.

Leneman, Leah. "The Study of Illegitimacy from Kirk Session Records: Two Eighteenth Century Perthshire Parishes." *Local Population Studies* no. 31 (Autumn 1983): 29-33.

Leneman, Leah, and Rosalind Mitchison. "Scottish Illegitimacy Ratios in the Early Modern Period." *Economic History Review* 40 (February 1987): 41-63.

Lilienthal, Georg. "The Illegitimacy Question in Germany, 1900-1945: Areas of Tension in Social and Population Policy." *Continuity and Change* 5, no. 2 (1990): 249-282.

Meteyard, Belinda. "Illegitimacy and Marriage in Eighteenth-Century England." *Journal of Interdisciplinary History* 10 (Winter 1980): 479-489.

Ransel, David L. "Problems in Measuring Illegitimacy in Prerevolutionary Russia." *Journal of Social History* 16 (Winter 1982): 111-128.

Robin, Jean. "Illegitimacy in Colyton, 1851-1881." *Continuity and Change* 2, no. 2 (1987): 307-342.

Rogers, Nicholas. "Carnal Knowledge: Illegitimacy in Eighteenth-Century Westminster." *Journal of Social History* 23 (Winter 1989): 355-376.

Sands, Diane. "Using Oral History to Chart the Course of Illegal Abortions in Montana." *Frontiers* 7, no. 1 (1983): 32-37.

Ulbricht, Otto. "The Debate about Foundling Hospitals in Enlightenment Germany: Infanticide, Illegitimacy, and Infant Mortality Rates." *Central European History* 18 (September/December 1985): 211-256.

Wilson, Adrian. "Illegitimacy and Its Implications in Mid-Eighteenth-Century London: The Evidence of the Foundling Hospital." *Continuity and Change* 4 (May 1989): 103-164.

## Theories, and Other Issues

Ahlborn, Richard Eighme. "The Will of a Woman in 1762." *New Mexico Historical Review* 65 (July 1990): 319-356.

Backhouse, Constance B. "Nineteenth Century Canadian Prostitution Law: Reflections on a Discriminatory Society." *Histoire Sociale/Social History* 18 (November 1985): 387-423.

Basch, Norma. "The Emerging Legal History of Women in the United States:

Property, Divorce, and the Constitution." *Signs* 12 (Autumn 1986): 97-117.

Bowen, Donna Lee. "Muslim Juridical Opinions Concerning the Status of Women as Demonstrated by the Case of 'Azl." *Journal of Near Eastern Studies* 41 (1981): 323-329.

Brauer, Carl M. "Woman Activists, Southern Conservatives, and the Prohibition of Sex Discrimination in Title VII of the 1964 Civil Rights Act." *Journal of Southern History* 49 (February 1983): 37-56.

Brundage, James A. "Sumptuary Laws and Prostitution in Late Medieval Italy." *Journal of Medieval History* 13 (December 1987): 343-356.

Bynum, Victoria. "On the Lowest Rung: Court Control over Poor White and Free Black Women." *Southern Exposure* 12 (November/December 1984): 40-44.

Coleman, Willi. "Black Women and Segregated Public Transportation: Ninety Years of Resistance." *Truth* 8, no. 2 (1986): 3-10.

Forbes, Geraldine H. "In Pursuit of Justice: Women Organisations and Legal Reforms." *Samya Shakti* 1, no. 2 (1984): 33-54.

Gavigan, Shelley A. M. "Petit Treason in Eighteenth Century England: Women's Inequality Before the Law." *Canadian Journal of Women and the Law/Revue juridique 'La femme et le droit'* 3, no. 2 (1989/90): 335-374.

Graebner, William. "'Uncle Sam Just Loves the Ladies': Sex Discrimination in the Federal Government, 1917." *Labor History* 21, no. 1 (1980): 75-85.

Halila, Souad. "From Koranic Law to Civil Law: The Emancipation of Tunisian Women since 1956." *Feminist Issues* 4, no. 2 (1984): 23-44.

Hesse, C. "Reading Signatures: Female Authorship and Revolutionary Law in France, 1750-1850." *Eighteenth-Century Studies* 22 (Spring 1989): 469-487.

Hine, Darlene Clark. "An Angle of Vision: Black Women and the United States Constitution, 1787-1987." *OAH Magazine of History* 3 (Winter 1988): 7-14.

Hoff-Wilson, Joan. "The Unfinished Revolution: Changing Legal Status of U.S. Women." *Signs* 13 (Autumn 1987): 7-36.

-----. "Women and the Constitution." *APSA News* no. 46 (Summer 1985): 10-16.

Ibrahim, Ahmad. "Fasakh for Failure to Maintain." *Jurnal Undang-Undang/ Journal of Malaysian and Comparative Law* [Kuala Lumpur] 5 (1978): 329-346.

Jennings, Richard. "The Legal Position of Women in Kayseri, A Large Ottoman City, 1590-1630." *International Journal of Women's Studies* 3 (November/December 1980): 559-582.

Jones, Carolyn C. "Split Income and Separate Spheres: Tax Law and Gender Roles in the 1940s." *Law and History Review* 6 (Fall 1988): 259-310.

Klench, Anne L. "Anglo Saxon Women and the Law." *Journal of Medieval History* 8 (June 1982): 107-122.

Leedom, Joe W. "Lady Matilda Holland, Henry of Lancaster and the Manor of Melbourne." *American Journal of Legal History* 31 (April 1987): 118-125.

Lewis, H. D. "The Legal Status of Women in Nineteenth Century France." *Journal of European Studies* 10 (September 1980): 178-188.

Lightman, Harriet. "Queens and Minor Kings in French Constitutional Law."

*Western Society for French History* 9 (October 1981): 26-36.

Lipschultz, Sybil. "Social Feminism and Legal Discourse: 1908-1923." *Yale Journal of Law and Feminism* 2 (Fall 1989): 131-160.

Locke, Mamie E. "From Three-Fifths to Zero: Implications of the Constitution for African-American Women, 1787-1870." *Women & Politics* 10, no. 2 (1990): 33-46.

Matsuda, Mari J. "The West and the Legal State of Women: Explanations of Frontier Feminism." *Journal of the West* 24 (January 1985): 47-56.

McLaren, John P. S. "Chasing the Social Evil: Moral Fervour and the Evolution of Canada's Prostitution Laws, 1867-1917." *Canadian Journal of Law and Society* 1 (1986): 125-165.

Mezey, Susan Gluck. "When Should Difference Make a Difference: A New Approach to the Constitutionality of Gender-Based Laws." *Women & Politics* 10, no. 2 (1990): 105-120.

Olsen, F. "Feminism and Critical Legal Theory: An American Perspective." *International Journal of the Sociology of Law* 18 (May 1990): 199-216.

Olson, Frances. "From False Paternalism to False Equality: Judicial Assaults on Feminist Community, Illinois 1869-1895." *Michigan Law Review* 84 (June 1986): 1518-1543.

Pincetl, Stephanie S. "The Peculiar Legacy of Progressivism: Claire Dedrick's Encounter with Forest Practices Regulation in California." *Forest & Conservation History* 34 (January 1990): 26-34.

Rafter, Nicole Hahn, and Elena M. Natalizia. "Marxist Feminism: Implications for Criminal Justice." *Crime and Delinquency* 27 (January 1981): 81-98.

Ramadan, Said. "Women and Sharia." *Research Papers: Muslims in Europe* 18 (1983): 5-9.

Rapport, Sara. "The Freedman's Bureau as a Legal Agent for Black Men and Women in Georgia: 1865-1868." *Georgia Historical Quarterly* 73 (Winter 1989): 26-53.

Rock, Rosalind Z. "'*Pido y Suplico*': Women and the Law in Spanish New Mexico." *New Mexico Historical Review* 65 (April 1990): 145-160.

Salmon, Marylynn. "The Legal Status of Women in Early America: A Reappraisal." *Law and History Review* 1 (Spring 1983): 129-151.

Slavin, Sarah. "Authenticity and Fiction in Law: Contemporary Case Studies Exploring Radical Legal Feminism." *Journal of Women's History* 1 (Winter 1990): 123-159.

Smart, Carol. "Law's Power, the Sexed Body, and Feminist Discourse." *Journal of Law and Society* 17 (Summer 1990): 194-210.

Stevens, Carolyn. "The History of Sexuality in Britain and America, 1800-1975: Course Method and Bill of Rights." *Women's Studies Quarterly* 16 (Spring/Summer 1988): 87-96.

Stone, Olive M. "Canadian Women as Legal Persons: How Alberta Combined Judicial, Executive and Legislative Powers to Win Full Legal Personality for All Canadian Women." *Alberta Law Review* 17, no. 3 (1979): 331-371.

Thane, Pat. "Women and the Poor Law in Victorian and Edwardian England."

*History Workshop* 6 (Autumn 1978): 29-51.

West, Robin L. "The Difference in Women's Hedonic Lives: A Phenomenological Critique of Feminist Legal Theory." *Wisconsin Women's Law Journal* 3 (1987): 101-105.

Whisner, Mary. "Gender-Specific Clothing Regulation: A Study in Patriarchy." *Harvard Women's Law Journal* 5 (Spring 1982): 73-119.

## Work and Protective Legislation

Bale, Anthony. "'Hope in Another Direction': Compensation for Work-Related Illness Among Women, 1900-1960--Part I." *Women & Health* 15, no. 1 (1989): 81-102.

Boris, Eileen. "Looking at Women's Historians Looking at 'Difference.'" *Wisconsin Women's Law Journal* 3 (1987): 213-238.

Boxer, Marilyn J. "Protective Legislation and Home Industry: The Marginalization of Women Workers in Late Nineteenth - Early Twentieth-Century France." *Journal of Social History* 20 (Fall 1986): 45-65.

Brito, Patricia. "Protective Legislation in Ohio: The Inter-war Years." *Ohio History* 88 (Spring 1979): 173-197.

Declercq, Eugene, and Richard Lacroix. "The Immigrant Midwives of Lawrence: The Conflict Between Law and Culture in Early Twentieth-Century Massachusetts." *Bulletin of the History of Medicine* 59 (Summer 1985): 232-246.

Fox-Genovese, Elizabeth. "Women's Rights, Affirmative Action, and the Myth of Individualism." *George Washington Law Review* 54 (January/March 1986): 338-374.

Friesen, Jennifer, and Ronald K. L. Collins. "Looking Back on 'Muller v. Oregon.'" *American Bar Association Journal* 69 (March/April 1983): 294-298.

Gaudron, Mary. "Women in the Workforce and the Elimination of Discrimination--Whose Responsibility?" *Labour History* 42 (May 1982): 106-111.

Hall, Jacqueline Dowd, Sandi E. Cooper, Dr. Rosalind Rosenberg, and Alice Kessler-Harris. "Women's History Goes to Trial: EEOC v. Sears, Roebuck and Company." *Signs* 11 (Summer 1986): 751-779.

Harrison, Barbara. "'Some of Them Gets Lead Poisoned': Occupational Lead Exposure in Women, 1880-1914." *Social History of Medicine* 2 (1989): 171-195.

-----. "Suffer the Working Day: Women in the 'Dangerous Trades,' 1880-1914." *Women's Studies International Forum* 13, no. 1/2 (1990): 79-90.

Haskell, Thomas, and Sanford Levinson. "Academic Freedom and Expert Witnessing: Historians and the Sears Case." *Texas Law Review* 66 (1988): 301-331.

Hill, Ann Corinne. "Protection of Women Workers and the Courts: A Legal Case History." *Feminist Studies* 5 (Summer 1979): 247-273.

Hooker, Richard D., Jr. "Affirmative Action and Combat Exclusion: Gender

Roles in the U.S. Army." *Parameters* 19 (December 1989): 36-50.

Hunt, Vilma R. "A Brief History of Women Workers and Hazards in the Workplace." *Feminist Studies* 5 (Summer 1979): 274-285.

Kates, Carol. "Working Class Feminism and Feminist Unions: Title VII, the UAW and NOW." *Labor Studies Journal* 14 (Summer 1989): 28-45.

Kessler-Harris, Alice. "Equal Employment Opportunity Commission v. Sears, Roebuck and Company: A Personal Account." *Radical History Review* 35 (1986): 57-79.

Kirkby, Diane. "'The Wage Earning Woman and the State': The National Women's Trade Union League and Protective Legislation, 1903-1923." *Labor History* 28 (Winter 1987): 54-74.

Land, Hilary. "State Income Maintenance Policies for Working-Class Wives and Mothers." *Society for the Study of Labour History* 48 (Spring 1984): 10.

Lander, Byron G. "The Making of Missouri's Equal Pay Law and the Legislative Process." *Missouri Historical Review* 77 (1983): 310-327.

Landes, Elisabeth M. "The Effect of State Maximum-hour Laws on the Employment of Women in 1920." *Journal of Political Economics* 88, no. 3 (1980): 476-494.

Lehrer, Susan. "Origins of Protective Labor Legislation for Women, 1905-1925." *Berkeley Women's Law Journal* 3 (1987-88): 171-187.

Liebel, Helen P. "Free Trade and Protectionism under Maria Theresa and Joseph II." *Canadian Journal of History* 14 (December 1979): 355-374.

Lindenmeyer, Kristie. "Saving Mothers and Babies: The Sheppard-Towner Act in Ohio, 1921-1929." *Ohio History* 99 (Summer-Autumn 1990): 105-134.

Mabee, Carleton. "Sojourner Truth Fights Dependence on Government: Moves Freed Slaves off Welfare in Washington to Jobs in Upstate New York." *Afro-Americans in New York Life and History* 14 (January 1990): 7-26.

McCallum, Margaret E. "Keeping Women in Their Place: The Minimum Wage in Canada, 1910-1925." *Labour/Le Travail* 17 (Spring 1986): 29-56.

McDougall, Mary Lynn. "The Meaning of Reform: The Ban on Women's Night Work, 1892-1914." *Western Society for French History* 10 (October 1982): 404-417.

-----. "Protecting Infants:    The French Campaign for Maternity Leaves, 1890s-1913." *French Historical Studies* 13 (Spring 1983): 79-105.

Milkman, Ruth. "Women's History and the Sears Case." *Feminist Studies* 12 (Summer 1986): 375-400.

Pedersen, Sharon. "Married Women and the Right to Teach in St. Louis, 1941-1948." *Missouri Historical Review* 81 (January 1987): 141-158.

Pierson, Ruth Roach. "Gender and the Unemployment Insurance Debates in Canada, 1934-40." *Labour/Le Travail* 25 (Spring 1990): 77-104.

Strumingher, Laura. "Flora Tristan and the Right to Work." *Western Society for French History* 11 (November 1983): 272.

Swain, Martha H. "Organized Women in Mississippi: The Clash over Legal Disabilities in the 1920s." *Southern Studies* 23 (Spring 1984): 91-102.

Targ, Dena. "Women and the 'New Unemployment'." *Humboldt Journal of Social*

*Relations* 10 (Spring/Summer 1983): 47-60.

Tiano, Susan. "Maquiladoras, Women's Work, and Unemployment in Northern Mexico." *Aztlan: International Journal of Chicano Studies Research* 15 (Fall 1985): 341-378.

Willmot, Louise. "The Debate on the Introduction of an Auxiliary Military Service Law for Women in the Third Reich and Its Consequences, August 1944-April 1945." *German History* no. 2 (Summer 1985): 10-20.

## LIFESTAGES AND LIFESTYLES (except married)

# General

Boylan, Anne M. "Timid Girls, Venerable Widows and Dignified Matrons: Life Cycle Patterns Among Organized Women in New York and Boston, 1797-1840." *American Quarterly* 38 (Winter 1986): 779-797.

Brandt, Gail Cuthbert. "'Weaving It Together': Life Cycle and the Industrial Experience of Female Cotton Workers in Quebec, 1910-1950." *Labour/Le Travail* 7 (Spring 1981): 113-126.

Crawford, Patricia. "Attitudes to Menstruation in Seventeenth-Century England." *Past and Present* no. 91 (May 1981): 47-73.

Foss, Susan Moore. "She Who Sits as King." *African Arts* 12 (February 1979): 44-50.

Hutchens, Rose. "You Must Remember This . . ." *Women & Environments* 12 (May/June 1990): 20-21.

Murphy, Marjorie. "Gender Relations on an Urban Terrain: Locating Women in the City." *Journal of Urban History* 13 (February 1987): 197-206.

Pedersen, Diana. "'Building Today for Womenhood of Tomorrow': Businessmen, Boosters, and YMCA, 1890-1930." *Urban History Review* 15 (February 1987): 225-242.

Siegfried, Michael. "The Skewed Sex Ration in a Medieval Population: A Reinterpretation." *Social Science History* 10 (Summer 1986): 195-204.

# Life Courses

Behar, Ruth. "Rage and Redemption: Reading the Life Story of a Mexican Marketing Woman." *Feminist Studies* 16 (Summer 1990): 223-258.

Carr, A. "Coming of Age in Christianity: Women and the Churches." *The Furrow* 34 (June 1983): 345-358.

Chudacoff, Howard P. "The Life Course of Women:    Age and Age Consciousness, 1865-1915." *Journal of Family History* 5 (Fall 1980): 274-292.

Elder, Glen H., Jr. and Jeffrey K. Liker. "Hard Times in Women's Lives: Historical Influences across Forty Years." *American Journal of Sociology* 88 (September 1982): 241-269.

Florez, C. Elisa, and Dennis P. Hogan. "Demographic Transition and Life Course Change in Columbia." *Journal of Family History* 15, no. 1 (1990): 1-22.

Forbes, Thomas R. "Births and Deaths in a London Parish: The Record from the Registers, 1654-1693." *Bulletin of the History of Medicine* 55 (Fall 1981): 371-391.

Ginsberg, Caren A., and Alan C. Swedlund. "Sex-Specific Mortality and Economic Opportunities: Massachusetts, 1860-1899." *Continuity and Change* 1, no. 3 (1986): 415-446.

Goldberg, P. J. P. "Marriage, Migration, Servanthood and Life-Cycle in Yorkshire Towns of the Later Middle Ages." *Continuity and Change* 1, no. 2 (1986): 141-168.

Hill, Bridget. "The Marriage Age of Women and the Demographers." *History Workshop* no. 28 (Autumn 1989): 129-147.

Hoerning, Erika M. "Upward Mobility and Family Estrangement Among Females: What Happens When the 'Same Old Girl' Becomes the 'New Professional Woman'?" *International Journal of Oral History* 6 (June 1985): 104-117.

Jules-Rosette, Bennetta. "Changing Aspects of Women's Initiation in Southern Africa." *Canadian Journal of African Studies* 13, no. 3 (1980): 389-405.

Kattner, Lauren Ann. "Growing Up Female in New Braunfels: Social and Cultural Adaptation in a German-Texan Town." *Journal of American Ethnic History* 9 (Spring 1990): 49-72.

Moynihan, Ruth Barnes. "Coming of Age: Four Centuries of Connecticut Women and Their Choices." *The Connecticut Historical Society Bulletin* 53 (Winter/Spring 1988): 5-111.

Nakano, Mei. "Japanese American Women: Three Generations." *History News* 45 (March/April 1990): 10-13.

Petschauer, Peter. "Growing Up Female in Eighteenth-Century Germany." *Journal of Psychohistory* 11 (Fall 1983): 167-208.

Socolow, Susan Migden. "Marriage, Birth, and Inheritance: The Merchants of Eighteenth-Century Buenos Aires." *Hispanic American Historical Review* 60 (August 1980): 387-406.

Stansell, Christine. "Women, Children and the Uses of the Streets, Class and Gender Conflict in New York City, 1850-1860." *Feminist Studies* 8 (Summer 1982): 309-335.

Toll, William. "The Female Life Cycle and the Measure of Jewish Social Change: Portland, Oregon, 1880-1930." *American Jewish History* 72 (March 1983): 309-332.

Trussell, James, and Richard Steckel. "The Age of Slaves at Menarche and Their First Birth." *Journal of Interdisciplinary History* 8 (Winter 1978): 477-505.

Underwood, Kathleen. "The Pace of Their Own Lives: Teacher Training and the Life Course of Western Women." *Pacific Historical Review* 55 (November 1986): 513-530.

Vincent, David. "Love and Death and the Nineteenth-Century Working Class." *Social History* 5 (May 1980): 223-247.

Watkins, Susan Cotts, and James McCarthy. "The Female Life Cycle in a Belgian Commune: La Hulpe, 1847-1866." *Journal of Family History* 5 (Summer 1980): 167-179.

Wood, Charles T. "The Doctor's Dilemma: Sin, Salvation, and the Menstrual Cycle in Medieval Thought." *Speculum* 56 (1981): 710-727.

## Old Age

Premo, Terri L. "'Like a Being Who Does Not Belong': The Old Age of Deborah Norris Logan." *Pennsylvania Magazine of History and Biography* 107 (January 1983): 85-112.

Reiff, Janice L., Michael R. Dahlin, and Daniel Scott Smith. "Rural Push and Urban Pull: Work and Family Experiences of Older Black Women in Southern Cities, 1880-1900." *Journal of Social History* 16 (Summer 1983): 39-48.

Roebuck, Janet, and Jane Slaughter. "Ladies and Pensioners: Stereotypes and Public Policy Affecting Old Women in England, 1880-1940." *Journal of Social History* 13 (Fall 1979): 105-114.

Rose, Sonya O. "The Varying Household Arrangements of the Elderly in Three English Villages: Nottinghamshire, 1851-1881." *Continuity and Change* 3, no. 1 (1988): 101-122.

Stearns, Peter N. "Old Women: Some Historical Observations." *Journal of Family History* 5 (Spring 1980): 44-57.

Williams, Harvey. "Social Isolation and the Elderly Immigrant Woman." *Pacific Historian* 26 (Summer 1982): 15-23.

## Never-Married Women

Anderson, Michael. "The Social Position of Spinsters in Mid-Victorian Britain." *Journal of Family History* 9 (Winter 1984): 377-393.

Antler, Joyce. "'After College, What?': New Graduates and the Family Claim." *American Quarterly* 32 (Fall 1980): 409-434.

Bauman, Paula M. "Single Women Homesteaders in Wyoming, 1880-1930." *Annals of Wyoming* 58 (Spring 1986): 39-49.

Beattie, Betsy. "Dutiful Daughters: Maritime-Born Women in New England in the Late Nineteenth Century." *Retrospection* 2 (1989): 16-31.

Brandimarte, Cynthia A. "Somebody's Aunt and Nobody's Mother: The American China Painter and Her Work, 1870-1920." *Winterthur Portfolio* 23 (Winter 1988): 203-224.

Campbell, Ellen K. "More Than Just a Roof: Housing at the YWCA." *Canadian Housing/Habitation canadienne* 4 (Winter/hiver 1987): 24-28.

Chambers-Schiller, Lee. "'Woman Is Born to Love': The Maiden Aunt as Maternal Figure in Antebellum Literature." *Frontiers* 10 (1988): 34-43.

Freeman, Ruth, and Patricia Klaus. "Blessed or Not? The New Spinster in England and the United States in the Late Nineteenth and Early Twentieth Centuries." *Journal of Family History* 9 (Winter 1984): 394-414.

Fuchs, Rachel G., and Leslie Page Moch. "Pregnant, Single, and Far from Home: Migrant Women in Nineteenth-Century Paris." *American Historical Review* 95 (October 1990): 1007-1031.

Gillespie, Joanna. "Mary Briscoe Baldwin, 1811-1877, Single Woman Missionary and 'Very Much My Own Mistress'." *Anglican and Episcopal History* 57, no. 1 (1988): 63-92.

Goldin, Claudia. "The Work and Wages of Single Women, 1870-1920." *Journal of Economic History* 40 (March 1980): 81-88.

Hufton, Olwen. "Women without Men: Widows and Spinsters in Britain and France in the Eighteenth Century." *Journal of Family History* (Winter 1984): 355-376.

Jeffreys, Sheila. "The Spinster and Her Enemies: Sexuality and the Last Wave of Feminism." *Scarlet Women* 13 (July 1981).

Kelley, Mary. "A Woman Alone: Catharine Maria Sedgwick's Spinsterhood in Nineteenth-Century America." *New England Quarterly* 51 (June 1978): 209-225.

Linton, Derek S. "Between School and Marriage, Workshop and Household: Young Working Women as a Social Problem in Late Imperial Germany." *European History Quarterly* 18 (October 1988): 387-408.

Litchfield, R. Burr. "Single People in the Nineteenth-Century City: A Comparative Perspective on Occupations and Living Situations." *Continuity and Change* 3, no. 1 (1988): 83-100.

Meagher, Timothy J. "Sweet Good Mothers and Young Women out in the World: The Roles of Irish American Women in Late Nineteenth and Early Twentieth Century Worcester, Massachusetts." *U.S. Catholic Historian* 5 (Summer/Fall 1986): 325-344.

Meyerowitz, Joanne. "Women and Migration: Autonomous Female Migrants to Chicago, 1880-1930." *Journal of Urban History* 13 (February 1987): 147-168.

Moch, Leslie Page. "Women on the Move: Migration and Urban Work for Women in the Late Nineteenth Century." *Western Society for French History* 8 (October 1980): 281-282.

Morrow, Sean. "'No Girl Leaves the School Unmarried': Mabel Shaw and the Education of Girls at Mbereshi, Northern Rhodesia, 1915-1940." *International Journal of African Historical Studies* 19, no. 4 (1986): 601-635.

Omolade, Barbara. "The Unbroken Circle: A Historical and Contemporary Study of Black Single Mothers and Their Families." *Wisconsin Women's Law Journal* 3 (1987): 239-274.

Palazzi, Maura. "Female Solitude and Patrilineage: Unmarried Women and Widows during the Eighteenth and Nineteenth Centuries." *Journal of Family History* 15, no. 4 (1990): 443-460.

Palmieri, Patricia A. "Patterns of Achievement of Single Academic Women at Wellesley College, 1880-1920." *Frontiers* 5 (Spring 1980): 63-67.

Santi, Lawrence L. "Household Headship Among Unmarried Persons in the United States, 1970-1985." *Demography* 27 (May 1990): 219-232.

Seim, Turid Karlsen. "Ascetic Autonomy? New Perspectives on Single Women in the Early Church." *Studia Theologica: Scandinavian Journal of Theology* 43, no. 1 (1989): 125-140.

Sharpe, Pamela. "Literally Spinsters: A New Interpretation of Local Economy and

Demography in Colyton in the Seventeenth and Eighteenth Centuries."
*Economic History Review* 44 (February 1991): 46-65.

Thomas, Mary Martha. "The 'New Woman' in Alabama, 1890 to 1920." *Alabama Review* 43 (July 1990): 163-180.

Watkins, Susan Cotts. "Spinsters." *Journal of Family History* 9 (Winter 1984): 310-325.

Worsnop, Judith. "A Reevaluation of 'The Problem of Surplus Women' in 19th-Century England: the Case of the 1851 Census." *Women's Studies International Forum* 13, no. 1/2 (1990): 21-32.

## Widowhood

Bideau, Alain. "A Demographic and Social Analysis of Widowhood and Remarriage: The Example of the Castellany of Thoissey-en-Dombes, 1670-1840." *Journal of Family History* 5 (Spring 1980): 28-43.

Boulton, Jeremy. "London Widowhood Revisited: The Decline of Female Remarriage in the Seventeenth and Early Eighteenth Centuries." *Continuity and Change* 5, no. 3 (1990): 323-356.

Bradbury, Bettina. "Surviving as a Widow in Nineteenth-Century Montreal." *Urban History Review* 17 (February 1989): 148-160.

Briggs, John H Y. "She-Preachers, Widows, and Other Women: The Feminine Dimension in Baptist Life Since 1600." *Baptist Quarterly* 31 (July 1986): 337-352.

Carlton, Charles. "The Widow's Tale: Male Myths and Female Reality in Sixteenth and Seventeenth Century England." *Albion* 10 (Summer 1978): 118-129.

Chabot, Isabelle. "Poverty and the Widow in Late Medieval Florence." *Continuity and Change* 3, no. 2 (1988): 291-311.

Diefendorf, Barbara B. "Widowhood and Remarriage in Sixteenth-Century Paris." *Journal of Family History* 7 (Winter 1982): 379-395.

Franklin, Peter. "Peasant Widows' 'Liberation' and Remarriage Before the Black Death." *Economic History Review* 39 (May 1986): 186-204.

Gallagher, Gary W. "A Widow and Her Soldier: LaSalle Corbell Pickett as Author of the George E. Pickett Letters." *Virginia Magazine of History and Biography* 94 (July 1986): 329-344.

Gertzog, Irwin N. "The Matrimonial Connection: The Nomination of Congressmen's Widows for the House of Representatives." *Journal of Politics* 42 (August 1980): 820-833.

Goodrich, James W., and Donald B. Oster, eds. "'Few Men but Many Widows . . .': The Baniel Fogle Letters, August 8-September 4, 1867." *Missouri Historical Review* 20 (April 1986): 273-303.

Heaton, Tim B., and Caroline Hoppe. "Widowed and Married: Comparative Change in Living Arrangements." *Social Science History* 11 (Fall 1987): 261-280.

Henry, Susan. "Work, Widowhood and War: Hannah Bunce Watson, Connecticut

Printer." *Connecticut Historical Society Bulletin* 48 (Winter 1983): 25-39.

Holmgren, Jennifer. "Widow Chastity in the Northern Dynasties: The Lieh-nu Biographies in the Wei-shu." *Papers on Far Eastern History* no. 23 (March 1981): 165-186.

Hufton, Olwen. "Women without Men: Widows and Spinsters in Britain and France in the Eighteenth Century." *Journal of Family History* (Winter 1984): 355-376.

Leslie, I. Julia. "Suttee or Sati: Victim or Victor?" *Bulletin: Center for the Study of World Religions, Harvard University* 14, no. 2 (1987/88): 5-23.

MacDonald, Dennis R. "Virgins, Widows, and Paul in Second Century Asia Minor." *Society of Biblical Literature: Seminar Papers* no. 16 (1979): 169-184.

Mani, Lata. "Production of an Official Discourse on Sati in Early Nineteenth Century Bengal." *Economic and Political Weekly* 21 (April 26, 1986): WS-32--WS-40.

Mann, Susan. "Widows in the Kinship, Class, and Community Structures of Qing Dynasty China." *Journal of Asian Studies* 46 (February 1987): 37-57.

Mazumdar, Vina. "Comment on Suttee." *Signs* 4 (Winter 1978): 269-273.

McNamara, Jo Ann. "Wives and Widows in Early Christian Thought." *International Journal of Women's Studies* 2 (November/December 1979): 575-592.

McWilliams, Ruth. "Preparing for the Biographer: A Widow's Task." *Manuscripts* 36 (Summer 1984): 187-196.

Palazzi, Maura. "Female Solitude and Patrilineage: Unmarried Women and Widows during the Eighteenth and Nineteenth Centuries." *Journal of Family History* 15, no. 4 (1990): 443-460.

Pike, Martha. "'In Memory of : Artifacts Related to Mourning in Nineteenth-Century America." *Journal of American Culture* 3 (Winter 1980): 642-659.

Pluss, Jacques Anthony. "Reading Case Law Historically: *A Consilium* of Baldus de Ubaldis on Widows and Dowries." *American Journal of Legal History* 30 (July 1986): 241-265.

Rosenthal, Joel T. "Other Victims: Peeresses as War Widows, 1450-1500." *History* 72 (June 1987): 213-230.

Speth, Linda. "More Than Her 'Thirds': Wives and Widows in Colonial Virginia." *Women and History* 4 (1982): 5-41.

Waciega, Lisa Wilson. "A 'Man of Business': The Widow of Means in Southeastern Pennsylvania, 1750-1850." *William and Mary Quarterly* 44 (January 1987): 40-64.

Walker, Ronald W. "A Mormon 'Widow' in Colorado: The Exile of Emily Wells Grant." *Arizona and the West* 25 (Spring 1983): 5-22.

Waltner, Ann. "Widows and Remarriage in Ming and Early Qing China." *Historical Reflections/Reflexions Historiques* 8 (Fall 1981): 129-146.

Winter, James. "Widowed Mothers and Mutual Aid in Early Victorian Britain." *Journal of Social History* 17 (Fall 1983): 115-125.

Wyntjes, Sherrin Marshall. "Survivors and Status: Widowhood and Family in the

Early Modern Netherlands." *Journal of Family History* 7 (Winter 1982): 396-405.

Yang, Anand A. "Whose Sati? Widow Burning in Early 19th-Century India." *Journal of Women's History* 1 (Fall 1989): 8-33.

## Youth

Bardarson, Gertrude. "My Childhood Visit to Sweden." *Swedish-American Historical Quarterly* 41 (July 1990): 133-140.

Birch, Brian P. "Possessed of a Restless Spirit: A Young Girl's Memories of the Southern Iowa Frontier." *Palimpsest* 66 (September/October 1985): 174-184.

Brent, Elizabeth Reed. "Childhood on the Western Frontier." *Oregon Historical Quarterly* 83 (Summer 1982): 117-152.

Carson, S. L. "Presidential Children: Abandonment, Hysteria and Suicide." *Journal of Psychohistory* 11 (Spring 1984): 533-544.

Carter, Susan B., and Mark Prus. "The Labor Market and the American High School Girl, 1890-1928." *Journal of Economic History* 42 (March 1982): 163-172.

Clark, Robert D. "Ada Harris, Teenager: Oswego County, New York, 1873." *New York History* 66 (January 1985): 29-48.

Fleet, Betsy. "'If There Is No Bright Side, Then Polish Up the Dark One': Maria Louisa Fleet and the Green Mount Home School for Young Ladies." *Virginia Cavalcade* 29 (Winter 1980): 100-107.

Fredriksson, Kristine. "Growing Up on the Road: The Children of Wild West Shows and Rodeos." *Journal of American Culture* 8 (Summer 1985): 19-24.

Frost, Margaret Fullerton. "Small Girl in a New Town." *Great Plains Journal* 19 (1980): 2-73.

-----. "Small Girl in a New Town." *Great Plains Journal* 20 (1981): 3-71.

-----. "Small Girl in a New Town." *Great Plains Journal* 21 (1982): 3-80.

Guinnane, Timothy. "Coming of Age in Rural Ireland at the Turn of the Twentieth Century." *Continuity and Change* 5, no. 3 (1990): 443-472.

Hawes, Joseph M. "The Strange History of Female Adolescence in the United States." *Journal of Psychohistory* 13 (Summer 1985): 51-64.

Leaphart, Susan. "Frieda and Belle Fligelman: A Frontier-City Girlhood in the 1890's." *Montana* 32 (Summer 1982): 85-92.

Lee, Mary Paik, and Sicheng Chan, eds. "A Korean-Californian Girlhood." *California History* 67, no. 1 (1988): 42-55.

Light, Alison. "'Young Bess': Historical Novels and Growing Up." *Feminist Review* no. 33 (Autumn 1989): 57-72.

Lowe, Blanch Beal. "Growing Up in Kansas." *Kansas History* 8 (Spring 1985): 36-53.

McFadden, Margaret. "Boston Teenagers Debate the Woman Question, 1837-1838." *Signs* 15 (Summer 1990): 832-847.

Nolan, Shelagh. "A Young Girl in the Old West." *The Beaver* 66 (August/September 1986): 4.

Perry, Beulah Gullison. "Remembering: Growing Up as a Sea Captain's Daughter." *Nova Scotia Historical Review* 7, no. 2 (1987): 31-44.

Prang, Margaret. "'The Girl God Would Have Me Be': The Canadian Girls in Training 1915-39." *Canadian Historical Review* 66 (June 1985): 154-184.

Quinney, Valerie. "Childhood in a Southern Mill Village." *International Journal of Oral History* 3 (November 1982): 167-192.

Robisheaux, Thomas. "Peasants and Pastors: Rural Youth Control and the Reformation in Hohenlohe, 1540-1680." *Social History* 6 (October 1981): 281-300.

Rothschild, Mary Aickin. "To Scout or to Guide? The Girl Scout-Boy Scout Controversy, 1912-1941." *Frontiers* 6 (Fall 1981): 115-121.

Schlossman, Stephen, and Wallach, Stephanie. "The Crime of Precocious Sexuality: Female Juvenile Delinquency in the Progressive Era." *Harvard Educational Review* 48 (February 1978): 65-94.

Sedlak, Michael W. "Young Women and the City: Adolescent Deviance and the Transformation of Education Policy, 1870-1960." *History of Education Quarterly* 23 (Spring 1983): 1-28.

Seider, Reinhard. "'Vata, derf i aufstehn?': Childhood Experiences in Viennese Working-Class Families around 1900." *Continuity and Change* 1, no. 1 (1986): 53-88.

Sturdevant, Lynda M. "Girl Scouting in Stillwater, Oklahoma: A Case Study in Local History." *Chronicle of Oklahoma* 57 (Spring 1979): 34-48.

Wales, Martha Gray. "When I Was a Little Girl: Things I Remember From Living at Frontier Military Posts." Willard B. Pope, ed. *North Dakota History* 50 (Spring 1983): 12-22.

Welch, Edward Gibson, ed. "Childhood's Panorama: Mattie Gibson Welch's Poems and Drawings of the Western Experience." *South Dakota History* 11 (Spring 1981): 111-123.

West, Elliott. "Child's Play: Tradition and Adaptation on the Frontier." *Montana* 38 (Winter 1988): 2-15.

Wilson, Christine, ed. "Growing Up in Marion County: A Memoir by Eva Davis Beets." *Journal of Mississippi History* 48 (August 1986): 199-213.

Zmora, Nurith. "A Rediscovery of the Asylum: The Hebrew Orphan Asylum through the Lives of Its First Fifty Orphans." *American Jewish History* 77 (March 1988): 476-481.

# MARRIAGE/DIVORCE

## Courtship

Anderson, George M. "The Civil War Courtship of Richard Mortimer Williams and Rose Anderson of Rockville." *Maryland Historical Magazine* 80 (Summer 1985): 119-138.

-----. "An Early Commuter: The Letters of James and Mary Anderson." *Maryland Historical Magazine* 75 (Fall 1980): 217-232.

Balkan, Kemal. "Betrothal of Girls During Childhood in Ancient Assyria and Anatolia." *Assyriological Studies* 23 (1986): 1-9.

Davis, Stephen and Robert Pollard III. "Allen C. Redwood and Sophie Bledsoe Herrick: The Discovery of a Secret, Significant Relationship." *Maryland Historical Magazine* 85 (Fall 1990): 256-263.

Deutsch, Phyllis. "Theater of Mating: Jewish Summer Camps and Cultural Transformation." *American Jewish History* 75 (March 1986): 307-321.

Fielder, Mari Kathleen. "Fatal Attraction: Irish-Jewish Romance in Early Film and Drama." *Eire-Ireland* 20 (Fall 1985): 6-18.

Hamilton, Virginia Van der Veer, ed. "'So Much in Love . . .': The Courtship of a Bluegrass Belle--Rosalie Stewart's Diary, December 1890-July 1891." *Register of the Kentucky Historical Society* 1 (Winter 1990): 77-108.

Holtzman, Ellen M. "The Pursuit of Married Love: Women's Attitudes toward Sexuality and Marriage in Great Britain, 1918-1959." *Journal of Social History* 16 (Winter 1982): 39-52.

Johnson, Susan L. "Sharing Bed and Board: Cohabitation and Cultural Difference in Central Arizona Mining Towns." *Frontiers* 7, no. 3 (1984): 36-42.

Lundeen, Kathleen. "A Modest Proposal? Paradise Found in Jane Austen's Betrothal Scenes." *Review of English Studies* 41 (February 1990): 65-75.

McDaniel, Ruth Currie. "Courtship and Marriage in the Nineteenth Century: Albion and Emma Tourgee, a Case Study." *North Carolina Historical Review* 61 (July 1984): 285-310.

Mingus, Lorence, and George Geil. "Babe and Gabriel: An Oregon Courtship." *Oregon Historical Quarterly* 87 (Summer 1986): 117-166.

Moore, John C. "Courtly Love: A Problem in Terminology." *Journal of the History of Ideas* 40 (October/December 1979): 621-632.

Motz, Marilyn Ferris. "'Thou Art My Last Love': The Courtship and Remarriage of a Rural Texas Couple in 1892." *Southwestern Historical Quarterly* 93 (April 1990): 457-473.

Rothman, Ellen K. "Sex and Self-Control: Middle-Class Courtship in America, 1770-1870." *Journal of Social History* 15 (Spring 1982): 409-426.

Schaedel, Grace Logan. "The Story of Ernest and Lizzie Logan--A Frontier Courtship." *Annals of Wyoming* 54 (Fall 1982): 48-61.

Stowe, Steven M. "'The Thing, Not Its Vision': A Woman's Courtship and Her Sphere in the Southern Planter Class." *Feminist Studies* 9 (Spring 1983): 113-130.

Ward, Peter. "Courtship and Social Space in Nineteenth-Century English Canada." *Canadian Historical Review* 68 (March 1987): 35-62.

Wilson, Douglas L. "Abraham Lincoln, Ann Rutledge, and the Evidence of Herndon's Informants." *Civil War History* 36 (December 1990): 301-324.

## Demographics

Ambler, R. W. "Civil Registration and Baptism; Popular Perceptions of the 1836 Act for Registering Births, Deaths and Marriages." *Local Population Studies* no. 39 (Autumn 1987): 24-31.

Bailey, Samuel. "Marriage Patterns and Immigrant Assimilation in Buenos Aires, 1882-1923." *Hispanic American Historical Review* 60 (February 1980): 32-48.

Barrett, Richard E. "Seasonality in Vital Processes in a Traditional Chinese Population: Births, Deaths, and Marriages in Colonial Taiwan, 1906-1942." *Modern China* 16 (April 1990): 190-225.

Bean, Lee L., Geraldine P. Mineau, Douglas L. Anderton, and Yung-chang Hsueh. "The Fertility Effects of Marriage Patterns in a Frontier American Population." *Historical Methods* 20 (Fall 1987): 161-171.

Bennett, Neil G., David E. Bloom, and Patricia H. Craig. "The Divergence of Black and White Marriage Patterns." *American Journal of Sociology* 95 (November 1989): 692-722.

Bideau, Alain. "A Demographic and Social Analysis of Widowhood and Remarriage: The Example of the Castellany of Thoissey-en-Dombes, 1670-1840." *Journal of Family History* 5 (Spring 1980): 28-43.

Bonfield, Lloyd. "Marriage Settlements and the 'Rise of Great Estates': The Demographic Aspect." *Economic History Review* 32 (November 1979): 483-493.

Crafts, N. F. R. "Duration of Marriage, Fertility and Women's Employment Opportunities in England and Wales in 1911." *Population Studies* 43 (1989): 325-335.

Edwards, W. J. "Remarriage: Some Preliminary Findings." *Local Population Studies* no. 39 (Autumn 1987): 32-45.

Floud, Roderick, and Pat Thane. "Debate: The Incidence of Civil Marriage in Victorian England and Wales." *Past and Present* 84 (August 1979): 146-154.

Gallman, James M. "Determinants of Age at Marriage in Colonial Perquimans County, North Carolina." *William and Mary Quarterly* 39 (January 1982): 176-191.

-----. "Relative Ages of Colonial Marriage." *Journal of Interdisciplinary History* 14 (Winter 1984): 609-617.

Gaskin, Katharine. "Age at First Marriage in Europe Before 1850: A Summary of Family Reconstitution Data." *Journal of Family History* 3 (Spring 1978): 23-36.

Goldberg, P. J. P. "Marriage, Migration, Servanthood and Life-Cycle in Yorkshire Towns of the Later Middle Ages." *Continuity and Change* 1, no. 2 (1986): 141-168.

Haines, Michael R. "Fertility and Marriage in a Nineteenth Century Industrial City: Philadelphia, 1850-1880." *Journal of Economic History* 40 (March 1980): 151-158.

-----. "Western Fertility in Mid-Transition: Fertility and Nuptiality in the United States and Selected Nations at the Turn of the Century." *Journal of Family History* 15, no. 1 (1990): 23-48.

Hill, Bridget. "The Marriage Age of Women and the Demographers." *History Workshop* no. 28 (Autumn 1989): 129-147.

Hinde, P. R. A. "Household Structure, Marriage and the Institution of Service in

Nineteenth Century Rural England." *Local Population Studies* no. 35 (Autumn 1985): 43-51.

Hindson, James. "The Marriage Duty Acts and the Social Topography of the Early Modern Town: Shrewsbury, 1695-8." *Local Population Studies* no. 31 (Autumn 1983): 21-28.

Hunter, Alan. "Marriage Horizons and Seasonality: A Comparison." *Local Population Studies* no. 35 (Autumn 1985): 38-42.

Lehning, James R. "The Timing and Prevalence of Women's Marriage in the French Department of the Loire, 1851-1891." *Journal of Family History* 13, no. 3 (1988): 307-328.

Miranda, Gloria E. "*Gente de Razon* Marriage Patterns in Spanish and Mexican California: A Case Study of Santa Barbara and Los Angeles." *Southern California Quarterly* 63 (Spring 1981): 1-22.

Molloy, Maureen. "'No Inclination to Mix With Strangers': Marriage Patterns among Highland Scot Migrants to Cape Breton and New Zealand, 1800-1916." *Journal of Family History* 11 (July 1986): 221-243.

Pace, D. Gene. "Wives of Nineteenth Century Mormon Bishops: A Quantitative Analysis." *Journal of the West* 21 (April 1982): 49-57.

Seccombe, Wally. "The Western European Marriage Pattern in Historical Perspective: A Response to David Levine." *Journal of Historical Sociology* 3 (March 1990): 50-74.

Smock, Pamela J. "Remarriage Patterns of Black and White Women: Reassessing the Role of Educational Attainment." *Demography* 27 (August 1990): 467-474.

Swagerty, William R. "Marriage and Settlement Patterns of Rocky Mountain Trappers and Traders." *Western Historical Quarterly* 11 (April 1980): 159-180.

Teachman, Jay D. "Historical and Subgroup Variations in the Association between Marriage and First Childbirth: A Life-Course Perspective." *Journal of Family History* 10 (Winter 1985): 379-401.

Vinovskis, Maris A. "Marriage Patterns in Mid-Nineteenth-Century New York State: A Multivariate Analysis." *Journal of Family History* 3 (Spring 1978): 51-61.

Wilcox, Penelope. "Marriage, Mobility and Domestic Service in Victorian Cambridge." *Local Population Studies* no. 29 (Autumn 1982): 19-34.

## Divorce

Arendell, Terry J. "Women and the Economics of Divorce in the Contemporary United States." *Signs* 13 (Autumn 1987): 121-135.

Basch, Norma. "The Emerging Legal History of Women in the United States: Property, Divorce, and the Constitution." *Signs* 12 (Autumn 1986): 97-117.

Berenson, Edward. "The Politics of Divorce in France of the Belle Epoque: The Case of Joseph and Henriette Caillaux." *American Historical Review* 93 (February 1988): 31-55.

Censer, Jane Turner. "'Smiling through Her Tears': Ante-Bellum Southern

Women and Divorce." *American Journal of Legal History* 25 (January 1981): 24-47.

Clark, Elizabeth B. "Matrimonial Bonds: Slavery and Divorce in Nineteenth-Century America." *Law and History Review* 8 (Spring 1990): 25-54.

Cohen, Sheldon S. "The Broken Bond: Divorce in Providence County, 1749-1809." *Rhode Island History* 44 (August 1985): 67-80.

-----. "'To Parts of the World Unknown': The Circumstances of Divorce in Connecticut, 1750-1797." *Canadian Review of American Studies* 11 (Winter 1980): 275-294.

Cornell, Laurel L. "Peasant Women and Divorce in Preindustrial Japan." *Signs* 15 (Summer 1990): 710-732.

Drake, W. Magruder, ed. "A Discourse on Divorce: Orleans Territorial Legislature 1806." *Louisiana History* 22 (Fall 1981): 434-437.

Feigenson, Neil R. "Extraterritorial Recognition of Divorce Decrees in the Nineteenth Century." *American Journal of Legal History* 34 (April 1990): 119-167.

Fitzpatrick, David. "Divorce and Separation in Modern Irish History." *Past and Present* no. 114 (February 1987): 172-196.

Goodheart, Lawrence B., Neil Hanks and Elizabeth Johnson. "'An Act for the Relief of Females . . .': Divorce and Changing Legal Status of Women in Tennessee, 1796-1860, Part I." *Tennessee Historical Quarterly* 44 (Fall 1985): 318-339.

-----. "'An Act for the Relief of Females . . .': Divorce and the Changing Legal Status of Women in Tennessee, 1796-1860, Part II." *Tennessee Historical Quarterly* 44 (Winter 1985): 402-416.

Griswold, Robert L. "Apart but Not Adrift: Wives, Divorce, and Independence in California, 1850-1890." *Pacific Historical Review* 49 (May 1980): 265-283.

-----. "The Evolution of the Doctrine of Mental Cruelty in Victorian American Divorce, 1790-1900." *Journal of Social History* 20 (Fall 1986): 127-148.

-----. "Law, Sex Cruelty, and Divorce in Victorian America, 1840-1900." *American Quarterly* 38 (Winter 1986): 721-745.

-----. "Sexual Cruelty and the Case for Divorce in Victorian America." *Signs* 11 (Spring 1986): 529-541.

Hagy, James W. "Her 'Scandalous Behavior': A Jewish Divorce in Charleston, South Carolina, 1788." *American Jewish Archives* 41 (Fall/Winter 1989): 185-198.

Hickling, R. H. "The Reception of English Divorce Law in Malaysia or the Misadventures of What Is Now Section 47 of Act 164." *Jurnal Undang-Undang/Journal of Malaysian and Comparative Law* [Kuala Lumpur] 10 (June/December 1983): 189-199.

Kuehn, Elain Kruse. "Emancipation or Survival? The Parisian Woman and Divorce: 1792-1804." *Western Society for French History* 8 (October 1980): 279-280.

Marsden, Lorna, and Joan Busby. "Feminist Influence through the Senate: The

Case of Divorce, 1967." *Atlantis* 14 (Spring 1989): 72-81.

May, Elaine Tyler. "The Pressure to Provide: Class, Consumerism, and Divorce in Urban America 1880-1920." *Journal of Social History* 12 (Winter 1978): 180-193.

Pavalko, Eliza K., and Glen H. Elder, Jr. "World War II and Divorce: A Life-Course Perspective." *American Journal of Sociology* 95 (March 1990): 1213-1234.

Petrik, Paula. "If She Be Content: The Development of Montana Divorce Law, 1865-1907." *Western Historical Quarterly* 18 (July 1987): 261-292.

Renne, Elisha P. "'If Men Are Talking, They Blame It On Women': A Nigerian Woman's Comments on Divorce and Child Custody." *Feminist Issues* 10 (Spring 1990): 37-49.

Riley, Glenda. "Divorce in Oklahoma." *Chronicles of Oklahoma* 67 (Winter 1989/90): 392-413.

-----. "Divorce Records: Linn County, Iowa, 1928-1944." *Annals of Iowa* 50 (Winter 1991): 787-800.

-----. "Sara Bard Field, Charles Erskine Wood, and the Phenomenon of Migratory Divorce." *California History* 69 (Fall 1990): 250-259.

-----. "Torn Asunder: Divorce in Early Oklahoma Territory." *Chronicles of Oklahoma* 77 (Winter 1989/90): 392-413.

Savage, Gail L. "The Operation of the 1857 Divorce Act, 1860-1910: A Research Note." *Journal of Social History* 16 (Summer 1983): 103-110.

Schultz, Martin. "Divorce Patterns in Nineteenth-Century New England." *Journal of Family History* 15, no. 1 (1990): 101-124.

Snell, James. "Marital Cruelty: Women and the Nova Scotia Divorce Court, 1900-1939." *Acadiensis* 18 (Autumn 1988): 3-32.

Stanley, Mary Lyndon. "'One Must Ride Behind': Married Women's Rights and the Divorce Act of 1857." *Victorian Studies* 25 (Spring 1982): 355-376.

Verdon, Michel. "Divorce in Abutia." *Africa* 52, no. 4 (1982): 48-66.

Walroth, Joanne Ruth. "Beyond Legal Remedy: Divorce in Seventeenth Century Woodbridge, New Jersey." *New Jersey History* 105 (Fall/Winter 1987): 1-36.

Watt, Jeffrey R. "Divorce in Early Modern Neuchatel, 1547-1806." *Journal of Family History* 14, no. 2 (1989): 137-156.

Wegner, Judith R. "The Status of Women in Jewish and Islamic Marriage and Divorce Law." *Harvard Women's Law Journal* 5 (Spring 1982): 1-34.

## Ethnicity

Campbell, Randolph B., and Donald K. Pickens, eds. "'My Dear Husband': A Texas Slave's Love Letter, 1862." *Journal of Negro History* 65 (Fall 1980): 361- 364.

Ellman, Yisrael. "Intermarriage in the United States: A Comparative Study of Jews and Other Ethnic Groups." *Jewish Social Studies* 49 (Winter 1987): 1-26.

Fielder, Mari Kathleen. "Fatal Attraction: Irish-Jewish Romance in Early Film and

Drama." *Eire-Ireland* 20 (Fall 1985): 6-18.

"The First Jewish Wedding in the Territory of Arizona." *Western States Jewish History* 20, no. 2 (1988): 126-128.

Grimshaw, Patricia. "New England Missionary Wives, Hawaiian Women, and 'The Cult of True Womanhood.'" *Hawaiian Journal of History* 19 (1985): 71-100.

Grindal, Garcia. "The Americanization of the Norwegian Pastors' Wives." *Norwegian-American Studies* 32 (1989): 199-207.

Hagy, James W. "Her 'Scandalous Behavior': A Jewish Divorce in Charleston, South Carolina, 1788." *American Jewish Archives* 41 (Fall/Winter 1989): 185-198.

Harper, Jared V. "Marriage as an Adaptive Strategy Among Irish Travelers in South Carolina." *Southern Studies* 20 (Summer 1981): 174-184.

Hoig, Stan. "Diana, Tiana or Talihana? The Myth and Mystery of Sam Horton's Cherokee Wife." *Chronicles of Oklahoma* 64 (Summer 1986): 53-59.

Johnson, Loretta T. "Charivari/Shivaree: A European Folk Ritual on the American Plains." *Journal of Interdisciplinary History* 20 (Winter 1990): 371-388.

Kaplan, Sidney. "Historical Efforts to Encourage White-Indian Intermarriage in the United States and Canada." *International Social Sciences Review* 65 (Summer 1990): 126-132.

Kramer, William M., and Norton B. Stern. "An Issue of Jewish Marriage and Divorce in Early San Francisco." *Western States Jewish History* 21 (October 1988): 46-57.

Lambert, Ronald D., and James E. Curtis. "Quebecois and English Canadian Opposition to Racial and Religious Intermarriage, 1968-1983." *Canadian Ethnic Studies/Etudes Ethniques Au Canada* 16, no. 2 (1984): 30-46.

Miller, Darlis A. "Cross-Cultural Marriages in the Southwest: The New Mexico Experience, 1846-1900." *New Mexico Historical Review* 57 (October 1982): 335-360.

Pascoe, Peggy. "Gender Systems in Conflict: The Marriages of Mission-Educated Chinese American Women, 1874-1939." *Journal of Social History* 22 (Summer 1989): 631-652.

Rasmussen, Janet E. "'I met him at Normanna Hall': Ethnic Cohesion and Marital Patterns Among Scandiinavian Immigrant Women." *Norwegian-American Studies* 32 (1989): 71-92.

Salvaneschi, Lenore. "Die Frau Pastor: The Life of a Missouri Synod Lutheran Pastor's Wife in the First Half of the Twentieth Century." *Palimpsest* 67 (March/April 1986): 53-68.

Scheffel, David. "From Polygamy to Cousin Marriage? Acculturation and Marriage in 19th Century Labrador Inuit Society." *Etudes inuit/Inuit Studies* 8, no. 2 (1985): 61-76.

Schily, Thomas, and Jodye Lynn Dickson Schily. "Amazons, Witches, and Country Wives: Plains Indian Women in Historical Perspective." *Annals of Wyoming* 59 (Spring 1987): 48-56.

Smith, S. L. "A Window on Themselves--Perceptions of Indians by Military
    Officers and Their Wives." *New Mexico Historical Review* 64 (October 1989):
    447-462.
Smits, David D. "'Abominable Mixture': Toward the Repudiation of Anglo-Indian
    Intermarriage in Seventeenth Century Virginia." *Virginia Magazine of History
    and Biography* 95 (April 1987): 157-192.
Stern, Norton B., and William M. Kramer. "The Phosphorescent Jewish Bride:
    San Francisco's Famous Murder Case." *Western States Jewish History* 13
    (October 1980): 63-72.

## General

Bailey, Beth L. "Scientific Truth . . . and Love: The Marriage Education
    Movement in the United States." *Journal of Social History* 20 (Summer 1987):
    711-732.
Barstow, Anne Llewellyn. "The First Generations of Anglican Clergy Wives:
    Heroines or Whores?" *Historical Magazine of the Protestant Episcopal Church*
    52 (March 1983): 3-16.
Basch, Francoise. "Women's Rights and the Wrongs of Marriage in
    Mid-Nineteenth Century America." *History Workshop* 22 (Autumn 1986):
    56-69.
Battick, John F. "The Searsport 'Thirty-six': Seafaring Wives of a Maine
    Community in 1880." *American Neptune* 44 (Summer 1984): 149-154.
Bergman, David. "Marianne Moore and the Problem of 'Marriage.'" *American
    Literature* 60, no. 2 (1988): 241-254.
Bernhard, Virginia. "Cotton Mather's 'Most Unhappy Wife': Reflections on the
    Uses of Historical Evidence." *New England Quarterly* 60 (September 1987):
    341-362.
Bishop, M. Guy. "Eternal Marriages in Early Mormon Marital Beliefs." *Historian*
    52 (Autumn 1990): 77-88.
Boyd, Lois A. "Presbyterian Ministers' Wives--A Nineteenth-Century Portrait."
    *Journal of Presbyterian History* 59 (Spring 1981): 3-17.
Boyle, Susan C. "Did She Generally Decide? Women in Ste. Genevieve,
    1750-1805." *William and Mary Quarterly* 44 (October 1987): 775-789.
Buckley, Thomas E., ed. "The Duties of a Wife: Bishop James Madison to His
    Daughter, 1811." *Virginia Magazine of History and Biography* (January 1983):
    98-104.
Buecker, Thomas R., ed. "Letters From a Post Surgeon's Wife." *Annals of
    Wyoming* 53 (Fall 1981): 44-63.
Cancian, Francesca M., and Steven L. Gordon. "Changing Emotion Norms in
    Marriage: Love and Anger in U. S. Women's Magazines since 1900." *Gender
    & Society* 2, no. 3 (1988): 308-342.
Cetti, Luisa. "The Radicals and the Wrongs of Marriage: The Rutland Free
    Convention of 1858." *Quaderno* 1 (1988): 77-94.
Cherpak, Evelen M. "Remembering Days in Old China: A Navy Bride Recalls

Life on the Asiatic Station in the 1920s." *American Neptune* 44 (Summer 1984): 179-185.

Clark, Ricky. "A Bride's Quilt from New Connecticut: Rebellion or Reflection?" *Hayes Historical Journal* 6 (Summer 1987): 28-39.

Crook, Elizabeth. "Sam Houston and Eliza Allen: The Marriage and the Mystery." *Southwestern Historical Quarterly* 94 (July 1990): 1-36.

Dobler, Grace. "Oil Field Camp Wives and Mothers." *Kansas History* 10 (Spring 1987): 29-42.

Friedman, Alice T. "Portrait of a Marriage: The Willoughby Letters of 1585-1586." *Signs* 11 (Spring 1986): 529-541.

Gates, Susa Young. "From Impulsive Girl to Patient Wife: Lucy Bigelow Young." *Utah Historical Quarterly* 45 (Summer 1977): 270-288.

Gertzog, Irwin N. "The Matrimonial Connection: The Nomination of Congressmen's Widows for the House of Representatives." *Journal of Politics* 42 (August 1980): 820-833.

Gough, Robert J. "Close-Kin Marriage and Upper-Class Formation in Late-Eighteenth Century Philadelphia." *Journal of Family History* 14, no. 2 (1989): 119-136.

Gunn, Peter A. "Productive Cycles and the Season of Marriage: A Critical Test." *Journal of Interdisciplinary History* 21 (Autumn 1990): 217-243.

Heaton, Tim B., and Caroline Hoppe. "Widowed and Married: Comparative Change in Living Arrangements." *Social Science History* 11 (Fall 1987): 261-280.

Holder, Ray, ed. "My Dear Husband: Letters of a Plantation Mistress: Martha Dubose Winans to William Winans, 1834-44." *Journal of Mississippi History* 49 (November 1987): 301-324.

Howgill, Woodie. "Honeymoon across the Plains: The Ellen Bell Tootle Diary." *Heritage of the Great Plains* 16 (Summer 1983): 11-17.

Jensen, Carol. "Cleofas M. Jaramillo on Marriage in Territorial Northern New Mexico." *New Mexico Historical Review* 58 (April 1983): 153-172.

Jensen, Richard. "The Lynds Revisited." *Indiana Magazine of History* 75 (December 1979): 303-320.

Johnson, Kenneth R. "White Married Women in Antebellum Alabama." *The Alabama Review* 43 (January 1990): 3-17.

Lale, Max S., ed. "Letters from a Bride in Indian Territory, 1889." *Red River Valley History Review* 6 (Winter 1981): 12-24.

Lambert, Ronald D., and James E. Curtis. "Quebecois and English Canadian Opposition to Racial and Religious Intermarriage, 1968-1983." *Canadian Ethnic Studies/Etudes Ethniques Au Canada* 16, no. 2 (1984): 30-46.

Leites, Edmund. "The Duty to Desire: Love, Friendship and Sexuality to Some Puritan Theories of Marriage." *Journal of Social History* 15 (Spring 1982): 383-408.

Lewis, Jan. "The Republican Wife: Virtue and Seduction in the Early Republic." *William and Mary Quarterly* 44 (October 1987): 689-721.

Loesberg, Jonathon. "Deconstruction, Historicism, and Overdetermination:

Dislocations of the Marriage Plot in *Robert Elsmere* and *Dombey and Son.*"
*Victorian Studies* 33 (Spring 1990): 441-464.

Martin, Dorris B. "A Congressional Wife in Wartime Washington." *Palimpsest*
64 (March/April 1983): 34-44.

Mayberry, Virginia. "Draftee's Wife: A Memoir of World War II." *Indiana
Magazine of History* 79 (December 1983): 305-329.

Millard, Peggy. "Company Wife." *The Beaver* 315 (Spring 1985): 30-39.

Modell, John, ed., Kingsley Davis, and Amyra Grossbard-Shechtman. "Historical
Reflections on American Marriage." *Contemporary Marriage* (1985): 181-196.

-----. "Normative Aspects of American Marriage Timing since World War II."
*Journal of Family History* 5 (Summer 1980): 210-234.

Modell, John, and Duane Steffey. "Waging War and Marriage: Military Service
and Family Formation, 1940-1950." *Journal of Family History* 13, no. 2
(1988): 195-218.

Myres, Sandra L. "Romance and Reality on the American Frontier: View of
Army Wives." *Western Historical Quarterly* 13 (October 1982): 409-428.

Peterson, Richard H. "Comstock Couple: The Triumph and Tragedy of Sandy and
Eilley Bowers." *Californians* 7 (September/October 1989): 44-49.

Pieroth, Doris H. "Peace River Journey, 1916." *The Beaver* 71 (February/March
1991): 39-42.

Ransome, David R. "Wives for Virginia, 1621." *William and Mary Quarterly* 48
(January 1991): 3-18.

Renshaw, Patrick. "Rose of the World: The Pastor-Stokes Marriage and the
American Left, 1905-1925." *New York History* 62 (October 1981): 415-438.

Rubinger, Catherine. "Marriage and the Women of Louisbourg." *Dalhousie
Review* 60 (Autumn 1980): 445-461.

Scheffel, David. "From Polygamy to Cousin Marriage? Acculturation and
Marriage in 19th Century Labrador Inuit Society." *Etudes inuit/Inuit Studies* 8,
no. 2 (1985): 61-76.

Shanley, Mary Lyndon. "Marriage Contract and Social Contract in Seventeenth
Century Political Thought." *Western Political Quarterly* 32 (March 1979):
79-91.

Shover, Michele. "The Blockhead Factor: Marriage and the Fate of California
Daughters." *Californians* 7 (September/October 1989): 32-39.

Silverman, Jane L. "To Marry Again." *Hawaiian Journal of History* 17 (1983):
64-75.

Snell, James G. "Marriage Humour and Its Social Functions, 1900-1939." *Atlantis*
11 (Spring 1986): 70-85.

Tual, Jacques. "Sexual Equality and Conjugal Harmony: The Way to Celestial
Bliss. A View of Early Quaker Matrimony." *The Journal of the Friends'
Historical Society* 55, no. 6 (1988): 161-174.

## International

Andreeva, I. S. "Sociophilosophical Problems of Sex, Marriage, and the Family."

*Soviet Review* 22, no. 1 (1981/82): 20-43.

Aries, Philippe. "Indissoluble Marriage." *Western Society for French History* 9 (October 1981): 26-36.

Arrom, Silvia M. "Marriage Patterns in Mexico City, 1811." *Journal of Family History* 3 (Winter 1978): 376-391.

Atsumi, Reiko. "Dilemmas and Accommodations of Married Japanese Women in White Collar Employment." *Bulletin of Concerned Asian Scholars* 20 (July/September 1988): 54-63.

Ault, James M., Jr. "Making 'Modern' Marriage 'Traditional.'" *Theory and Society* 12 (March 1983): 181-210.

Backhouse, Constance. "'Pure Patriarchy': Nineteenth-Century Canadian Marriage." *McGill Law Journal* 31 (March 1986): 264-312.

Ballard, Catherine. "Arranged Marriages in the British Context." *New Community* 6, no. 3 (1978): 181-196.

Bartman, William J. "Korean War Brides, Prostitutes and Yellow Slavery." *Minerva: Quarterly Report on Women and the Military* 7 (Summer 1989): 16-25.

Beougher, Tim. "The Puritan View of Marriage: The Husband/Wife Relationship in Puritan England as Taught and Experienced by Richard Baxter." *Trinity Journal* 10 (Fall 1990): 131-160.

Blackman, Charles F. "The Civil Sacrament: Law and Practice of Soviet Weddings." *American Journal of Comparative Law* 28 (1980): 555-576.

Bohanan, Donna. "Matrimonial Strategies Among the Nobles of Seventeenth-Century Aix-en-Provence." *Western Society for French History* 11 (November 1983): 122-129.

Brennan, Brian. "'Episcipae': Bishops' Wives Viewed in Sixth-Century Gaul." *Church History* 54 (September 1985): 311-323.

Brown, Irene Q. "Domesticity, Feminism, and Friendship: Female Aristocratic Culture and Marriage in England, 1660-1760." *Journal of Family History* (Winter 1982): 406-424.

Brundage, J. A. "'Allas! That Evere Love Was Synne': Sex and Medieval Canon Law." *Catholic Historical Review* 72 (January 1986): 1-13.

-----. "Matrimonial Politics in Thirteenth-Century Aragon: Moncada v. Urgel." *Journal of Ecclesiastical History* 31 (July 1980): 271-282.

Bullard, Melissa Meriam. "Marriage Politics and the Family in Florence: The Strozzi-Medici Alliance in 1508." *American Historical Review* 84 (June 1979): 668-687.

Carroll, Lucy. "Talaq-i-Tafwid and Stipulations in Muslim Marriage Contracts: Important Means of Protecting the Position of the South Asian Muslim Wife." *Modern Asian Studies* 16, no. 2 (1982): 277-309.

Chandler, David S. "The Montepios and Regulation of Marriage in the Mexican Bureaucracy, 1770-1821." *The Americas* 43 (July 1986): 47-68.

Cohen, Shaye J D. "Solomon and the Daughter of the Pharoah: Intermarriage, Conversion, and the Impurity of Women." *Journal of the Ancient Near Eastern Society* 16-17 (1984-1985): 23-37.

Darrow, Margaret H. "Popular Concepts of Marital Choice in Eighteenth Century France." *Journal of Social History* 19 (Winter 1985): 261-272.

Diefendorf, Barbara B. "Widowhood and Remarriage in Sixteenth-Century Paris." *Journal of Family History* 7 (Winter 1982): 379-395.

Doran, Susan. "Religion and Politics at the Court of Elizabeth I: The Habsburg Marriage Negotiations of 1559-1567." *English Historical Review* 104 (October 1989): 908-926.

Edwards, Walter. "The Commercialized Wedding as Ritual: A Window on Social Values." *Journal of Japanese Studies* 13, no. 1 (Winter 1987): 51-78.

Evans, N. E. "The Anglo-Russian Royal Marriage Negotiations of 1600-1603." *The Slavic & East European Review* 61 (July 1983): 363-387.

Farmer, Sharon. "Persuasive Voices: Clerical Images of Medieval Wives." *Speculum* 61 (July 1986): 517-543.

Forbes, Geraldine. "Women and Modernity: The Issue of Child Marriage in India." *Women's Studies International Quarterly* 2, no. 4 (1979): 407-419.

Franklin, Peter. "Peasant Widows' 'Liberation' and Remarriage Before the Black Death." *Economic History Review* 39 (May 1986): 186-204.

Gee, Ellen M. T. "Marriage in Nineteenth Century Canada." *Canadian Review of Sociology and Anthropology/Revue canadienne de Sociologie et d'Anthropologie* 19 (August 1982): 311-325.

Geissler, Suzanne B. "Reflections on a Royal Wedding." *Historical Magazine of the Protestant Episcopal Church* 50 (June 1981): 171-176.

Gough, Austin. "French Workers and Their Wives in the Mid-Nineteenth Century." *Labour History* 42 (May 1982): 74-82.

Gudjonsson, Elsa E. "An Icelandic Bridal Costume from about 1800." *Costume* 23 (1989): 1-21.

Gullette, Margaret Morganroth. "The Puzzling Case of the Deceased Wife's Sister: Nineteenth-Century England Deals with a Second-Chance Plot." *Representations* no. 31 (Summer 1990): 142-166.

Harrington, Joel F. "Reformation, Statebuilding and the 'Secularization' of Marriage: Jurisdiction in the Palatinate, 1450-1619." *Fides et Historia* 22 (Fall 1990): 53-63.

Harris, Barbara J. "Marriage Sixteenth-Century Style: Elizabeth Stafford and the Third Duke of Norfolk." *Journal of Social History* 15 (Spring 1982): 371-382.

-----. "Power, Profit, and Passion: Mary Tudor, Charles Brandon, and the Arranged Marriage in Early Tudor England." *Feminist Studies* 15 (Spring 1989): 59-88.

Harth, Erica. "The Virtue of Love: Lord Hardwicke's Marriage Act." *Cultural Critique* no. 9 (Spring 1988): 87-122.

Haruko, Wakita. "Marriage and Property in Premodern Japan from the Perspective of Women's History." *Journal of Japanese Studies* 10 (Winter 1984): 73-100.

Hertz, Deborah. "Intermarriage in the Berlin Salons." *Central European History* 16 (December 1983): 303-346.

Holmgren, J. "Marriage and Political Power in Sixth Century China: A Study of the Kao Family of Northern Ch'i, c. 520-550." *Journal of Asian History* 16, no. 1 (1982): 1-50.

Kinsley, David. "Devotion as an Alternative to Marriage in the Lives of Some Hindu Women Devotees." *Journal of Asian and African Studies* 15 (January/April 1980): 83-93.

Klassen, John. "The Development of the Conjugal Bond in Late Medieval Bohemia." *Journal of Medieval History* 13 (June 1987): 161-178.

Leridon, Henri. "Cohabitation, Marriage, Separation: An Analysis of Life Histories of French Cohorts from 1968 to 1985." *Population Studies* 44 (March 1990): 127-144.

Litchfield, R., and David Gordon. "Closing the 'Tour': A Close Look at the Marriage Market, Unwed Mothers, and Abandoned Children in Mid-Nineteenth Century Amiens." *Journal of Social History* 13 (Spring 1980): 458-472.

Lynch, Katherine A. "Marriage Age among French Factory Workers: An Alsatian Example." *Journal of Interdisciplinary History* 16 (Winter 1986): 405-429.

Matovic, Margareta R. "The Stockholm Marriage: Extra-Legal Family Formation in Stockholm, 1860-1890." *Continuity and Change* 1, no. 3 (1986): 385-414.

McCaa, Robert. "Modeling Social Interaction: Marital Miscegenation in Colonial Spanish America." *Historical Methods* 15 (1982): 45-66.

McNamara, Jo Ann. "Wives and Widows in Early Christian Thought." *International Journal of Women's Studies* 2 (November/December 1979): 575-592.

Merzario, Raul. "Land, Kinship, and Consanguineous Marriage in Italy from the Seventeenth to the Nineteenth Centuries." *Journal of Family History* 15, no. 4 (1990): 529-546.

Meteyard, Belinda. "Illegitimacy and Marriage in Eighteenth-Century England." *Journal of Interdisciplinary History* 10 (Winter 1980): 479-489.

Miller, Gary M. "Bourbon Social Engineering: Women and Conditions of Marriage in Eighteenth-Century Venezuela." *The Americas* 46 (January 1990): 261-290.

Molloy, Maureen. "Considered Affinity: Kinship, Marriage, and Social Class in New France, 1640-1729." *Social Science History* 14 (Spring 1990): 1-26.

Mosk, Carl. "Nuptiality in Meiji Japan." *Journal of Social History* 13 (Spring 1980): 474-489.

Payer, Pierre J. "Early Medieval Regulations Concerning Marital Sexual Relations." *Journal of Medieval History* 6 (December 1980): 353-376.

Pearce, R. D. "Violet Bourdillon: Colonial Governor's Wife." *African Affairs* 82, no. 327 (1983): 267-277.

Rettaroli, Rosella. "Age at Marriage in Nineteenth-Century Italy." *Journal of Family History* 15, no. 4 (1990): 409-426.

Ritsuko, Yoshida. "Getting Married the Corporate Way." *Japan Quarterly* 37 (April/June 1990): 171-175.

Rosenthal, Joel T. "Aristocratic Marriage and the English Peerage, 1350-1500: Social Institution and Personal Bond." *Journal of Medieval History* 10 (September 1984): 181-194.

Ross, Ellen. "'Fierce Questions and Taunts': Married Life in Working-Class London, 1870-1914." *Feminist Studies* 8 (Fall 1982): 575-602.

Scott, Edith E. "Married Women's Rights under the Matrimonial Regimes of Chile and Colombia: A Comparative History." *Harvard Women's Law Journal* 7 (Spring 1984): 221-249.

Searle, Eleanor. "A Rejoinder [to 'Debate: Seigneurial Control of Women's Marriage']." *Past & Present* no. 99 (May 1983): 148-160.

-----. "Seigneurial Control of Women's Marriage: The Antecedents and Function of Merchet in England." *Past and Present* no. 82 (Februrary 1979): 3-43.

Seed, Patricia. "The Church and the Patriarchal Family: Marriage Conflicts in the Sixteenth- and Seventeenth-Century New Spain." *Journal of Family History* 10 (Autumn 1985): 284-293.

-----. "Marriage Promises and the Value of a Woman's Testimony in Colonial Mexico." *Signs* 13 (Winter 1988): 253-276.

Sellar, W. D. H. "Marriage, Divorce and Concubinage in Gaelic Scotland." *Trans. Gaelic Soc. Inverness* 1 (1978-80): 464-493.

Shanley, Mary Lyndon. "Marriage Contract and Social Contract in Seventeenth Century Political Thought." *Western Political Quarterly* 32 (March 1979): 79-91.

Sharma, Arvind. "Marriage in the Hindu Religious Tradition." *Journal of Ecumenical Studies* 22 (Winter 1985): 69-80.

Shimp, Robert E. "A Catholic Marriage for an Anglican Prince." *Historical Magazine of the Protestant Episcopal Church* 50 (March 1981): 3-18.

Smith, Robert J. "Making Village Women into 'Good Wives and Wise Mothers' in Prewar Japan." *Journal of Family History* 8 (Spring 1983): 70-84.

Snell, James G. "The International Border as a Factor in Marital Behaviour: A Historical Case Study." *Ontario History* 81 (December 1989): 289-302.

-----. "'The White Life for Two': The Defence of Marriage and Sexual Morality in Canada, 1890-1914." *Histoire sociale/Social History* 16 (May 1983): 111-128.

Snell, James G., and Cynthia Comacchio Abeele. "Regulating Nuptiality: Restricting Access to Marriage in Early Twentieth-Century English-Speaking Canada." *Canadian Historical Review* 69 (December 1988): 466-489.

Socolow, Susan Migden. "Marriage, Birth, and Inheritance: The Merchants of Eighteenth-Century Buenos Aires." *Hispanic American Historical Review* 60 (August 1980): 387-406.

Soulliere, E. "The Imperial Marriages of the Ming Dynasty." *Papers on Far Eastern History* no. 37 (March 1988): 15-42.

Spearritt, Katie. "The Market for Marriage in Colonial Queensland." *Hecate: An Interdisciplinary Journal of Women's Liberation* 16, no. 1/2 (1990): 23-42.

Spielmann, Richard M. "The Beginning of Clerical Marriage in the English Reformation: The Reigns of Edward and Mary." *Anglican and Episcopal History* 56 (September 1987): 251-264.

Sturcken, H. T. "The Unconsummated Marriage of Jaime of Aragon and Leonor of Castile (Oct 1319)." *Journal of Medieval History* 5 (September 1979): 185-202.

Taft, Michael. "Folk Drama on the Great Plains: The Mock Wedding in Canada and the United States." *North Dakota History* 56 (Fall 1989): 16-23.

Thierry, Joyce. "Northern Bride, 1947." *The Beaver* 69 (August/September 1989): 27-33.

Walker, Sue Sheridan. "Free Consent and the Marriage of Feudal Wards in Medieval England." *Journal of Medieval History* 8 (June 1982): 123-134.

Waltner, Ann. "Widows and Remarriage in Ming and Early Qing China." *Historical Reflections/Reflexions Historiques* 8 (Fall 1981): 129-146.

Walton, Linda. "Kinship, Marriage, and Status in Song China: A Study of the Lou Lineage of Ningbo, c. 1050-1250." *Journal of Asian History* 18, no. 1 (1984): 1-34.

Westphal-Wihl, Sarah. "The Ladies' Tournament: Marriage, Sex, and Honor in Thirteenth-Century Germany." *Signs* 14 (Winter 1989): 371-398.

Wright, Marcia. "Technology, Marriage and Women's Work in the History of Maize Growers in Mazabuka, Zambia: A Reconnaissance." *Journal of South African Studies* 10 (October 1983): 71-85.

Yost, John K. "The Reformation Defense of Clerical Marriage in the Reigns of Henry VIII and Edward VI." *Church History* 50 (June 1981): 152-165.

## Polygamy

Bennett, Dana. "Mormon Polygamy in Early Southeastern Idaho." *Idaho Yesterdays* 28 (Spring 1984): 24-30.

Bennion, Lowell Ben. "The Incidence of Mormon Polygamy in 1880: 'Dixie' versus Davis Stake." *Journal of Mormon History* 11 (1984): 27-42.

Champion, Brian. "Mormon Polygamy: Parliamentary Comments 1889-90." *Alberta History* 35 (Spring 1987): 10-17.

Driggs, Ken. "After the Manifesto: Modern Polygamy and Fundamentalist Mormons." *Journal of Church and State* 32 (Spring 1990): 367-389.

Dunfey, Julie. "'Living the Principle' of Plural Marriage: Mormon Women, Utopia, and Female Sexuality in the Nineteenth Century." *Feminist Studies* 10 (Fall 1984): 523-536.

Embry, Jessie L. "Effects of Polygamy on Mormon Women." *Frontiers* 7, no. 3 (1984): 56-61.

Embry, Jessie L., and Martha S. Bradley. "Mothers and Daughters in Polygamy." *Dialogue* 18 (Fall 1985): 99-107.

Foster, Lawrence. "Polygamy and the Frontier: Mormon Women in Early Utah." *Utah Historical Quarterly* 50 (Summer 1982): 268-289.

Iversen, Joan. "Feminist Implications of Mormon Polygyny." *Feminist Studies* 10 (Fall 1984): 505-522.

James, Kimberly Jensen. "'Between Two Fires': Women on the 'Underground' of Mormon Polygamy." *Journal of Mormon History* 8 (1981): 49-62.

Lewis, David Rich. "'For Life, the Resurrection, and the Life Everlasting': James

J. Strang and Strangite Mormon Polygamy, 1849-1856." *Wisconsin Magazine of History* 66 (Summer 1983): 274-291.

Linford, Orma. "The Mormons, the Law, and the Territory of Utah." *American Journal of Legal History* 23 (1979): 213-235.

Logue, Larry. "A Time of Marriage: Monogamy and Polygamy in a Utah Town." *Journal of Mormon History* 11 (1984): 3-26.

Madsen, Carol Cornwall. "Mormon Missionary Wives in Nineteenth Century Polynesia." *Journal of Mormon History* 13 (1986-87): 61-88.

Mehr, Kahilile. "Women's Response to Plural Marriage." *Dialogue* 18 (Fall 1985): 84-97.

Scheffel, David. "From Polygamy to Cousin Marriage? Acculturation and Marriage in 19th Century Labrador Inuit Society." *Etudes inuit/Inuit Studies* 8, no. 2 (1985): 61-76.

Shipps, Jan. "The Principle Revoked: A Closer Look at the Demise of Plural Marriage." *Journal of Mormon History* 11 (1984): 65-78.

Whittaker, David J. "The Bone in the Throat: Orson Pratt and the Public Announcement of Plural Marriage." *Western Historical Quarterly* 18 (July 1987): 293-314.

-----. "Early Mormon Polygamy Defenses." *Journal of Mormon History* 11 (1984): 43-64.

## MATERIAL AND POPULAR CULTURE

### Architecture/City Planning/Neighborhoods

Allport, Carolyn. "Left Off the Agenda: Women, Reconstruction and New Order Housing." *Labour History* 46 (May 1984): 1-20.

Anderson, M. Christine. "Home and Community for a Generation of Women: A Case Study of the Cincinnati Y.W.C.A. Residence, 1920-1940." *Queen City Heritage* 43 (Winter 1985): 34-41.

Archer, John. "Country and City in the American Romantic Suburb." *Journal of the Society of Architectural Historians* 42 (May 1983): 139-158.

Bailey, Kristin Szylvian. "Defense Housing in Greater Pittsburgh, 1945-1955." *Pittsburgh History* 73 (Spring 1990): 16-29.

Barrows, Robert G. "'The Homes of Indiana': Albion Fellows Bacon and Housing Reform Legislation, 1907-1917." *Indiana Magazine of History* 81 (December 1985): 309-350.

Birchman, Sandra. "The Mitchell House." *History News* (February 1984): 12-15.

Blair, Karen J. "The Limits of Sisterhood: The Woman's Building in Seattle, 1908-1921." *Frontiers* 8, no. 1 (1984): 45-52.

Brewer, Priscilla J. "'We Have Got a Very Good Cooking Stove': Advertising, Design, and Consumer Response to the Cookstove, 1815-1880." *Winterthur Portfolio* 25 (Spring 1990): 35-54.

Brown, Elizabeth Gaspar. "The Waukesha County Jail--Building, Administration, Inmates: 1901-1904." *American Journal of Legal History* 23 (1979): 236-264.

Cohen, Lizabeth A. "Embellishing a Life of Labor: An Interpretation of the Material Culture of American Working Class Homes, 1885-1915." *Journal of American Culture* (Winter 1980): 752-775.

Cranz, Galen. "Women in Urban Parks." *Signs* 5 (Spring 1980): 579-595.

de Bretteville, Shelia Leurant. "The 'Parlorization' of Our Homes and Ourselves." *Chrysalis* 8 (Summer 1979).

Dennis, Thelma. "Eaton's Catalogue: Furnishings for Rural Alberta, 1886-1930." *Alberta History* 37 (Spring 1989): 21-31.

Ellis, Anita J. "Cincinnati Art Furniture: Woman as Beautifier." *Queen City Heritage* 42 (Winter 1984): 19-26.

Epstein, Amy K. "Multifamily Dwellings and the Search for Respectability: Origins of the New York Apartment House." *Urbanism Past and Present* 5, no. 2 (1980): 29-39.

Feller, John Quentin. "Julia Dent Grant and the Mikado Porcelain." *Winterthur Portfolio* 24 (Summer/Autumn 1989): 165-174.

Forman, Benno M. "Furniture for Dressing in Early America, 1650-1730: Forms, Nomenclature, and Use." *Winterthur Portfolio* 22 (Summer/Autumn 1987): 149-164.

Gordon, Jean, and Jan McArthur. "Interior Decorating Advice as Popular Culture: Women's Views Concerning Wall and Window Treatments, 1870-1920." *Journal of American Culture* 9 (Fall 1986): 15-24.

Gould, Karen. "Spatial Poetics, Spatial Politics: Quebec Feminists on the City and the Countryside." *American Review of Canadian Studies* 12 (Spring 1982): 1-9.

Haine, W. Scott. "Privacy in Public: The Compartment of Working-Class Women in Late Nineteenth-Century Parisian Proletarian Cafes." *Western Society for French History* 14 (November 1986): 204-211.

Hayden, Dolores. "Charlotte Perkins Gilman and the Kitchenless House." *Radical History Review* 21 (Fall 1979): 225-247.

-----. "Two Utopian Feminists and Their Campaigns for Kitchenless Houses." *Signs* 4, no. 2 (Winter 1978): 274-290.

Heisner, Beverly. "Harriet Morrison Irwin's Hexagonal House: An Invention to Improve Domestic Dwellings." *North Carolina Historical Review* 58 (Spring 1981): 105-123.

Horn, James P. P. "'The Bare Necessities': Standards of Living in England and the Chesapeake, 1650-1700." *Historical Archaeology* 22, no. 2 (1988): 74-91.

Horowitz, Helen Lefkowitz. "Hull House as Women's Space." *Chicago History* 12 (Winter 1983/84): 40-55.

Jacobsen, Mary Ann, and Ruth E. Gates. "Norwegian American Ethnicity and Ethnic Clothing, Textiles, and Household Objects." *Ethnicity* 6 (1979): 215-221.

Kinnane, Adrian J. "A House United: Morality and Invention in the Wright Brothers' Home." *Psychohistory Review* 16 (Spring 1988): 367-397.

Lewis, Johanna Miller. "A Social and Architectural History of the Girls' Boarding School Building at Salem, North Carolina." *North Carolina Historical Review* 66 (April 1989): 125-148.

Lyle, Royster, Jr. "Of Manor Houses and Gardens: Edith Sale (1876-1932), Pioneer in the Study of Virginia Mansions." *Virginia Cavalcade* 34 (Winter 1985): 126-135.

Macdougall, Elisabeth Blair. "A Circus, a Wild Man and a Dragon: Family History and the Villa Mattei." *Journal of the Society of Architectural Historians* 42 (May 1983): 121-130.

Matelic, Candace Tangorra. "Living History Farms." *Museum News* 58 (March/April 1980): 36-45.

Matthew, Alva T. "Emily W. Roebling: One of the Builders of the Bridge." *Annals of the New York Academy of Sciences* 424 (May 1984).

Mazey, Mary Ellen, and Theresa Seiler. "Women in Suburbia." *Journal of Cultural Geography* 3 (Fall/Winter 1982): 122-130.

McClaugherty, Martha Crabill. "Household Art: Creating the Artistic Home, 1868-1893." *Winterthur Portfolio* 18 (Spring 1983): 1-26.

McGahan, Elizabeth W. "Inside the Hallowed Walls: Convent Life through Material History." *Material History Bulletin* 25 (Spring 1987): 1-9.

McMurry, Sally. "City Parlor, Country Sitting Room: Rural Vernacular Design and the American Parlor, 1840-1900." *Winterthur Portfolio* 20 (Winter 1985): 261-280.

Meyerowitz, Joanne. "Sexual Geography and Gender Economy: The Furnished Room Districts of Chicago, 1890-1930." *Gender & History* 2 (Autumn 1990): 274-296.

Neuschel, Kristen B. "Noble Households in the Sixteenth Century: Material Settings and Human Communities." *French Historical Studies* 15 (Fall 1988): 595-622.

Patton, June O. "Moonlight and Magnolias in Southern Education: The Black Mammy Memorial Institute." *Journal of Negro History* (Spring 1980): 149-155.

Pohl, Frances K. "Historical Reality or Utopian Ideal? The Woman's Building at the World's Columbian Exposition, Chicago, 1893." *International Journal of Women's Studies* 5 (September/October 1982): 289-311.

Roth, Darlene. "Feminine Marks on the Landscape: An Atlanta Inventory." *Journal of American Culture* 3 (Winter 1980): 673-685.

Scharff, Virginia. "Of Parking Spaces and Women's Places: The Los Angeles Parking Ban of 1920." *NWSA Journal* 1 (Autumn 1988): 37-51.

Schwartz, Joel. "Home as Haven, Cloister, and Winnebago." *American Quarterly* 39 (Fall 1987): 467-473.

Scott, Anne Firor. "Women and Libraries." *Journal of Library History* 21 (Spring 1986): 400-405.

Shammas, Carole. "The Domestic Environment in Early Modern England and America." *Journal of Social History* 14 (Fall 1980): 3-24.

Thatcher, Elaine. "'Some Chairs For My Family': Furniture in Nineteenth Century Cache Valley." *Utah Historical Quarterly* 56 (Fall 1988): 331-351.

Wharton, Annabel. "Gender, Architecture, and Institutional Self-Presentation: The Case of Duke University." *South Atlantic Quarterly* 90 (Winter 1991): 175-218.

## Books/Literary Images/Literature

Abraham, Mildred K. "The Library of Lady Jean Skipwith: A Book Collection from the Age of Jefferson." *Virginia Magazine of History and Biography* 91 (July 1983): 296-347.

Armstrong, Frances. "Gender and Miniaturization: Games of Littleness in Nineteenth-Century Fiction." *English Studies in Canada* 16 (December 1990): 403-416.

Brown, William R. "The American Girl and the Christmas Tree: World War II Soldier Poets Look at What the G.I.s Were Fighting For." *Journal of American Culture* 7 (Summer 1985): 38-48.

Cherry, Deborah, and Griselda Pollock. "Woman as Sign in Pre-Raphaelite Literature: A Study of the Representation of Elizabeth Siddall." *Art History* 7 (June 1984): 206-227.

DeShazer, Mary K. "'Sisters in Arms': The Warrior Construct in Writings by Contemporary U.S. Women of Color." *NWSA Journal* 2 (Summer 1990): 349-373.

Flaumenhaft, Eugene, and Carol Flaumenhaft. "Four Books that Changed Nursing." *Journal of the History of Medicine and Allied Sciences* 42 (January 1987): 54-72.

Fries, Maureen. "Feminae Populi: Popular Images of Women in Medieval Literature." *Journal of Popular Culture* 14 (Summer 1980): 77-86.

Gibbs, Phillip A. "Self Control and Male Sexuality in the Advice Literature of Nineteenth Century America, 1830-1860." *Journal of American Culture* 9 (Summer 1986): 37-41.

Gilman, Amy. "'Cogs to the Wheels': The Ideology of Women's Work in Mid-Nineteenth-Century Fiction." *Science and Society* 47 (Summer 1983): 178-204.

Gordon, Jean, and Joan McArthur. "Living Patterns in Antebellum Rural America as Depicted by Nineteenth-Century Women Writers." *Winterthur Portfolio* 19 (Summer/Autumn 1984): 177-192.

Grant, Barbara L. "Five Liturgical Songs by Hildegard von Bingen." *Signs* 5 (Spring 1980): 557-567.

Hanna, Martha. "Iconology and Ideology: Images of Joan of Arc in the Idiom of the Action Francaise." *French Historical Studies* 14 (Fall 1985): 215-239.

Heil, Jo Ellen. "When Hymns Were Hers." *Daughters of Sarah* 15 (July/August 1989): 16-19.

Hertz, Michel. "New History, Old Literature: Interpreting Molière's Women." *Western Society for French History* 6 (November 1978): 90-91.

Hooker, Jessica. "The Hen Who Sang: Swordbearing Women in Eastern European Fairytales." *Folklore* 110, no. 2 (1990): 178-184.

Hovet, Grace Ann. "Studies of Popular Fiction for Women." *American Studies* 27 (Fall 1986): 51-53.

Huttenback, Robert A. "The Perpetuation of Two Stereotypes--Racism and Sexism in the Imperial Adventure Story." *Bengal Past and Present* 101,

Parts 1/2 (1984): 49-60.

Jeffrey, Julie Roy. "'There Is Some Splendid Scenery': Women's Responses to the Great Plains Landscape." *Great Plains Quarterly* 8 (Spring 1988).

Khanna, Lee Cullen. "Images of Women in Thomas More's Poetry." *Albion* 10 (1978): 78-88.

Light, Alison. "'Young Bess': Historical Novels and Growing Up." *Feminist Review* no. 33 (Autumn 1989): 57-72.

Linke, Uli. "Women, Androgynes, and Models of Creation in Norse Mythology." *Journal of Psychohistory* 16 (Winter 1988): 231-262.

Mulhern, Chieko Irie. "Japanese Harlequin Romances as Transcultural Women's Fiction." *Journal of Asian Studies* 48 (February 1989): 50-71.

Murray, Gail S. "Rational Thought and Republican Virtues: Children's Literature, 1789-1820." *Journal of the Early Republic* 8 (Summer 1988): 159-178.

Murray, J. H. "Class vs. Gender Indentification in the *Englishwoman's Review* of the 1880's." *Victorian Periodicals Review* 8 (1985): 138-142.

Nestor, P. "A New Departure in Women's Publishing: The *English Woman's Journal* and *The Victorian Magazine*." *Victorian Periodicals Review* 15 (1982): 93-106.

Oehlschaeger, Fritz H. "Civilization as Emasculation: The Threatening Role of Women in the Frontier Fiction of Harold Bell Wright and Zane Grey." *Midwest Quarterly* 22 (Summer 1981): 346-360.

Raphael, Marc Lee. "From Marjorie to Tevya: The Image of the Jews in American Popular Literature, Theatre and Comedy, 1955-1965." *American Jewish History* 74 (September 1984): 66-72.

Ridgley, Ronald. "'History with a Heart'--A Frontier Historian Looks at the 'Little House' Books of Laura Ingalls Wilder." *Heritage of the Great Plains* 20 (Winter 1987): 21-27.

Roberts, Robin. "The Female Alien: Pulp Science Fiction's Legacy to Feminists." *Journal of Popular Culture* 21, no. 2 (1987): 33-52.

Roffman, Marion H. "As the Poet Saw Her: Images of Woman in the Pastorals and the Fabliaux." *Western Society for French History* 8 (October 1980): 33-41.

Russell, Lois Ann. "Challe and Diderot: Tales in Defense of Woman." *Western Society for French History* 9 (October 1981): 216-225.

Samuels, Shirley. "The Family, the State, and the Novel in the Early Republic." *American Quarterly* 38, no. 3 (1986): 381-395.

Seifert, Carolyn J. "Images of Domestic Madness in the Art and Poetry of American Women." *Woman's Art Journal* 1 (Fall 1980/Winter 1981): 1-6.

Shumaker, Conrad. "'A Daughter of the Puritans': History in Hawthorne's *The Marble Faun*." *New England Quarterly* 57 (March 1984): 65-83.

-----. "'Too Terribly Good to Be Printed': Charlotte Gilman's 'The Yellow Wallpaper'." *American Literature* 57 (December 1985): 588-599.

Silver, Brenda R. "The Authority of Anger: *Three Guineas* as Case Study." *Signs* 16 (Winter 1991): 340-370.

Sweeter, Marie-Odile. "Women and Power: Reflections on Some Queens in

French Classical Tragedy." *Western Society for French History* 10 (October 1982): 60-67.

Taylor, Peter, and Hermann Rebel. "Hessian Peasant Women, Their Families, and the Draft: A Social-Historical Interpretation of Four Tales from the Grimm Collection." *Journal of Family History* 6 (Winter 1981): 347-378.

Trompf, G. W. "On Attitudes towards Women in Paul and Paulinist Literature: 1 Cor. 11:2-16 and Its Context." *Catholic Biblical Quarterly* 42 (1980): 196-215.

Underwood, June O. "Western Women and True Womanhood: Culture and Symbol in History and Literature." *Great Plains Quarterly* 5 (Spring 1985): 93-106.

Walker, Nancy. "Feminist or Naturalist: The Social Context of Kate Chopin's *The Awakening*." *Southern Quarterly* (Winter 1979): 95-103.

Wan, Ning. "Desire and Desperation: An Analysis of the Female Characters in Cao's Yu's Play *The Thunderstorm*." *Chinese Studies in History* 20, no. 2 (Winter 1986/87): 75-90.

Welch, Edward Gibson, ed. "Childhood's Panorama: Mattie Gibson Welch's Poems and Drawings of the Western Experience." *South Dakota History* 11 (Spring 1981): 111-123.

Wilson, Douglas L. "Sowerby Revisited: The Unfinished Catalogue of Thomas Jefferson's Library." *William and Mary Quarterly* 41 (October 1984): 615-628.

## Crafts/Quilts/Embroidery

Blaski, Steven. "Quilts Reveal Lives of Early Iowans." *Palimpsest* 71 (Spring 1990): 33-34.

Brackman, Barbara. "Quilts on the Kansas Frontier." *Kansas History* 13 (Spring 1990): 13-22.

Brandimarte, Cynthia A. "Somebody's Aunt and Nobody's Mother: The American China Painter and Her Work, 1870-1920." *Winterthur Portfolio* 23 (Winter 1988): 203-224.

Chinn, Jennie A. "'Some Ladies Make Quilts, but They Aren't Quilt Makers': Aesthetic Principles in Quilt Making." *Kansas History* 13 (Spring 1990): 32-44.

Clark, Ricky. "A Bride's Quilt from New Connecticut: Rebellion or Reflection?" *Hayes Historical Journal* 6 (Summer 1987): 28-39.

-----. "A Quilting in Strongsville." *Timeline* 3 (August/September 1986): 50-53.

Connolly, Loris, and Agatha Huepenbecker. "Home Weaving in Southeast Iowa, 1833-1870." *Annals of Iowa* 48 (Summer/Fall 1985): 3-31.

Cunningham, Patricia A. "The Woven Record: Nineteenth-Century Coverlets and Textile Industries in Northwest Ohio." *Northwest Ohio Quarterly* 56 (Spring 1984): 43-76.

Davis, Gayle R. "Women in the Quilt Culture: An Analysis of Social Boundaries and Role Satisfaction." *Kansas History* 13 (Spring 1990): 5-12.

Dewhurst, C. Kurt, Betty MacDowell, and Marsha MacDowell. "A Stitch or Sketch in Time: Michigan's Women Folk Artists." *Michigan History* 66

(July/August 1982): 8-13.

Hedges, Elaine. "The 19th Century Diarist and Her Quilts." *Feminist Studies* 8 (Summer 1982): 293-299.

Hilts, Victor L., and Patricia A. Hilts. "Not for Pioneers Only: The Story of Wisconsin's Spinning Wheels." *Wisconsin Magazine of History* 66 (Autumn 1982): 3-24.

Hood, Adrienne. "Early Canadian Quilts: Marriage of Art and Utility." *Rotunda* 17, no. 3 (1984-85): 28-35.

Kelly, Mary B. "Goddess Embroideries of Russia and the Ukraine." *Woman's Art Journal* 4 (Fall 1983/Winter 1984): 10-13.

Kogan, Lee. "The Quilt Legacy of Elizabeth, New Jersey." *The Clarion, America's Folk Art Magazine* 15 (Winter 1990): 58-64.

Levinsohn, Rhoda. "Rural Kwazulu Beadwork." *Ornament* 4 (September 1980): 38-41.

Levinsohn, Rhoda, and Morris Levinsohn. "Symbolic Significance of Traditional Zulu Beadwork." *Black Art* 3, no. 4 (1979): 29-35.

Mack, John. "Bakuba Embroidery Patterns: A Commentary on Their Social and Political Implications." *Textile History* 11 (1980): 163-174.

Madden, Mary W. "The Kansas Quilt Project: Piecing Together Our Past." *Kansas History* 13 (Spring 1990): 2-4.

-----. "Textile Diaries: Kansas Quilt Memories." *Kansas History* 13, 1 (Spring 1990): 45-78.

Neaher, Nancy C. "Igbo Carved Doors." *African Arts* 15 (November 1981): 49-55.

Rowen, Mary Margaret. "Group Quilting in Kansas." *Kansas History* 13 (Spring 1990): 23-31.

Ruckman, Jo Ann. "'Knit, Knit, and Then Knit': The Women of Pocatello and the War Effort of 1917-1918." *Idaho Yesterdays* 26 (Spring 1982): 26-36.

Sherman, Ruth Wilder. "The Mary Atwood Sampler." *New England Historical and Genealogical Register* 194 (January 1990): 23-28.

Spencer, Carole A. "Victorian Crazy Quilts." *Palimpsest* 71 (Spring 1990): 16-32.

Trifonoff, Karen M. "Amish Culture as Preserved in Quilts." *Journal of Cultural Geography* 10 (Winter 1989): 63-74.

## Fashion/Textiles/Beauty Culture

Adaskina, Natalia. "Constructivist Fabrics and Dress Design." *The Journal of Decorative and Propaganda Arts* no. 5 (Summer 1987): 144-159.

Adler, Shane. "A Diary and A Dress." *Dress* 6 (1980): 83-88.

Albrecht, Juliana, Jane Farrell-Beck, and Geitel Winakor. "Function, Fashion, and Convention in American Women's Riding Costumes, 1880-1930." *Dress* 14 (1988): 56-67.

Anderson, Marcia G. "Munsingwear, An Underwear for America." *Minnesota History* 50 (Winter 1986): 152-163.

Anthony, Ilid. "Clothing Given to a Late Sixteenth-Century Servant in Wales."

*Costume* 14 (1980): 32-40.

Arnold, Janet. "Jane Lambarde's Mantle." *Costume* 14 (1980): 56-72.

Baron, B. "Unveiling in Early Twentieth Century Eqypt: Practical and Symbolic Considerations." *Middle Eastern Studies* 25 (1989): 370-386.

Beaudoin-Ross, Jacqueline. "'A la Canadienne' Once More: Some Insights into Quebec Rural Female Dress." *Dress* 7 (1981): 69-81.

-----. "A la Canadienne: Some Aspects of 19th Century Habitant Dress." *Dress* 6 (1980): 71-82.

Behling, Dorothy. "Fashion Change in a Northwoods Lumbering Town, 1915-1925." *Dress* 9 (1983): 32-40.

Berch, Bettina. "Scientific Management in the Home: The Empress's New Clothes." *Journal of American Culture* 3 (Fall 1980): 440-445.

Biebuyck, Daniel P. "Lega Dress as Cultural Artifact." *African Arts* 15 (May 1982): 59-65, 92.

Bliss, Frank. "Bahriyan Jewelry and Its Relation to the Nile Valley." *Ornament* 6 (December 1982): 10-14, 44-45.

Blum, Dilys E. "Englishwomen's Dress in Eighteenth-Century India: The Margaret Fowke Correspondence (1776-1786)." *Costume* 17 (1983): 47-58.

Blum, Stella. "The Idyllic Fashions of the Austro-Hungarian Empire, 1867-1918." *Dress* 6 (1980): 57-70.

Brackenbury, Terry. "A Fashion History of Knitting." *Textiles* 19, no.1 (1990): 8-12, 17-18.

Brett-Smith, Sarah C. "Symbolic Blood: Cloths for Excised Women." *RES* 3 (Spring 1982): 15-31.

Buck, Anne M. "Clothes in Fact and Fiction, 1825-1865." *Costume* 17 (1983): 89-104.

Buck, Anne M., and Harry Matthews. "Pocket Guides to Fashion." *Costume* 18 (1984): 35-58.

Burt, Eugene C. "Eroticism in Baluyia Body Arts." *African Arts* 15 (February 1982): 68-69, 88.

Byrde, Penelope. "'That Frightful Unbecoming Dress': Clothes for Spa Bathing at Bath." *Costume* 21 (1987): 44-56.

Carter, Alison J. "Mary Tudor's Wardrobe." *Costume* 18 (1984): 9-28.

Chapman, Dana Lacy, and Lois E. Dickey. "A Study of Costume Through Art: An Analysis of Dutch Women's Costumes from 1600-1650." *Dress* 16 (1990): 28-37.

Clark, Sallye. "Carrie Taylor, Kentucky Dressmaker." *Dress* 6 (1980): 13-23.

Cohen-Stratyner, Barbara. "Fashion Fillers in Silent Film Periodicals." *Performing Arts Resources* 14 (1989): 127-142.

Coleman, Elizabeth Ann. "Fashions of the Opulent Era." *Vintage Fashions* 1 (January/February 1990): 26-29.

Coleman, Evelyn J. "Boston's Atheneum for Fashions." *Dress* 5 (1979): 25-32.

-----. "Fashions as Seen Through Fashion Plates." *Vintage Fashions* 1 (March/April 1990): 48-53.

Cooper, Arlene. "La Camargo's Skirt: The Eighteenth Century Ballet

Re-Dressed." *Dress* 10 (1984): 33-42.

-----. "Casual, But Not That Casual: Some Fashions of the 1950s." *Dress* 11 (1985): 47-56.

Cumming, Valerie. "Ellen Terry: An Aesthetic Actress and Her Costumes." *Costume* 21 (1987): 67-74.

Cunningham, Patricia. "Annie Jenness Miller and Mabel Jenness: Promoters of Physical Culture and Correct Dress." *Dress* 16 (1990): 48-61.

Daily, Christie. "A Woman's Concern: Millinery in Century Iowa, 1870-1880." *Journal of the West* 21 (April 1982): 20-32.

Dekker, Rudolf M., and Lotte C. van de Pol. "Republican Heroines: Cross-Dressing Women in the French Revolutionary Armies." *History of European Idea* 10, no. 3 (1989): 353-364.

Dimond, Frances. "Queen Victoria and Fashions for the Young." *Costume* 22 (1988): 1-12.

Doering, Mary D. "American Red Cross Uniforms." *Dress* 5 (1979): 33-48.

Drucker, Alison R. "The Influence of Western Women on the Anti-Footbinding Movement 1840-1911." *Historical Reflections/Reflexions Historiques* 8 (Fall 1981): 179-200.

Dublin, Thomas. "Gender and Textiles: A Personal Overview." *Material History Bulletin* [Canada] 31 (Spring 1990): 75-78.

Duquette, Danielle Gallois. "Women Power and Initiation in the Bisagos Islands." *African Arts* 12 (May 1979): 31-35.

Eastwood, Gillian. "A Medieval Face-Veil from Egypt." *Costume* 17 (1983): 33-38.

Edwards, Lesley. "'Dres't Like a May-Pole.'" *Costume* 19 (1985): 75-93.

Eicher, Joanne, Tonye Victor Erekosima, and Carl Liedholm. "Cut and Drawn: Textile Work from Nigeria." *Craft International* 2 (Summer 1982): 16-19.

Evans, Valerie. "In Mourning." *Material History Bulletin* 23 (Spring 1986): 49-52.

Ewers, John C. "Climate, Acculturation, and Costume: A History of Women's Clothing Among the Indians of the Southern Plains." *Plains Anthropologist* 25, no. 7 (1980): 63-82.

Farrell, Jane A. "Clothing for Adults in Iowa, 1850-1899." *Annals of Iowa* 46 (Fall 1981): 100-120.

Feather, Betty L., and Lucy R. Sibley. "Overlooked Pages of North American Clothing History." *Dress* 5 (1979): 63-73.

Femenias, Blenda. "Peruvian Costume and European Perceptions in the Eighteenth Century." *Dress* 10 (1984): 52-63.

Field, Richard Henning. "Lunenburg-German Household Textiles: The Evidence from Lunenburg County Estate Inventories, 1780-1830." *Material History Bulletin* [Canada] 24 (1986): 16-23.

Finkel, Alicia. "Le Bal Costume: History and Spectacle in the Court of Queen Victoria." *Dress* 10 (1984): 64-72.

Flawers, Judi. "Mourning Clothes." *Vintage Fashions* 1 (September/October 1990): 6-12.

Foote, Shelly. "Bloomers." *Dress* 6 (1980): 1-12.

Frankel, G. "Notes on the Costume of the Jewish Woman in Eastern Europe." *Journal of Jewish Art* no. 7 (1980): 50-51.

Gibson, Gail. "Costume and Fashion in Charleston, 1769-1782." *South Carolina Historical Magazine* 82 (July 1981): 225-247.

Gjergji, Andromaqi. "Aprons in Albanian Popular Costume." *Costume* 20 (1986): 44-62.

Glover, Jean M. "'In Consideration of Her Most Praiseworthy Conduct.'" *Costume* 14 (1980): 110-116.

Gordon, Beverly. "Dress in American Communal Societies." *Communal Societies* 5 (Fall 1985): 122-136.

Gordon, Eleanor, and Jean Nerenberg. "Everywoman's Jewelry: Early Plastics and Equality in Fashion." *Journal of Popular Culture* 13 (Spring 1980): 629-644.

Grootkerk, Paul. "The Beauty Parlor Mirror: Reflections of Tradition." *Journal of American Culture* 11 (Summer 1988): 11-16.

Grossbard, Judy, and Robert S. Merkel. "'Modern' Wheels Liberated 'The Ladies' 100 Years Ago." *Dress* 16 (1990): 70-80.

Gudjonsson, Elsa E. "An Icelandic Bridal Costume from about 1800." *Costume* 23 (1989): 1-21.

Hamer, Louise. "The Cullercoats Fishwife." *Costume* 18 (1984): 66-73.

Hanson, Karen. "Dressing Down Dressing Up--The Philosophic Fear of Fashion." *Hypatia* 5 (Summer 1990): 107-121.

Harris, Jennifer. "'Thieves, Harlots and Stinking Goats': Fashionable Dress and Aesthetic Attitudes in Romanesque Art." *Costume* 21 (1987): 4-15.

Hayden, Peter. "Elizabeth's Jervis's Clothing." *Costume* 22 (1988): 32-38.

Helvenston, Sally. "Advice to American Mothers on the Subject of Children's Dress 1800-1920." *Dress* 7 (1981): 31-46.

-----. "Popular Advice for the Well Dressed Woman in the 19th Century." *Dress* 6 (1980): 31-46.

Holford, Mary. "Dress and Society in Upper Canada, 1791-1841." *Costume* 17 (1983): 78-88.

Hood, Adrienne D. "Material Culture and Textiles: An Overview." *Material History Bulletin* [Canada] 31 (Spring 1990): 5-10.

-----. "North American Textiles: A Selected Bibliography." *Material History Bulletin* [Canada] 31 (Spring 1990): 11-13.

Hope, Christine. "Caucasian Female Body Hair and American Culture." *Journal of American Culture* 5 (Spring 1982): 93-99.

Jacobsen, Mary Ann, and Ruth E. Gates. "Norwegian American Ethnicity and Ethnic Clothing, Textiles, and Household Objects." *Ethnicity* 6 (1979): 215-221.

Jerde, Judith. "Mary Molloy: St. Paul's Extraordinary Dressmaker." *Dress* 7 (1981): 82-89.

Johnson, Marion. "Cloth as Money: The Cloth Strip Currencies of Africa." *Textile History* 11 (1980): 193-202.

Kendall, Joan. "The Development of a Distinctive Form of Quaker Dress." *Costume* 19 (1985): 58-74.

Klumpp, Donna Rey. "An Historical Overview of Masai Dress." *Dress* 7 (1981): 95-102.

Lansdell, Avril. "Costume for Oarswomen, 1919-1979." *Costume* 13 (1979): 73-79.

Lauer, Jeanette C., and Robert H. Lauer. "The Battle of the Sexes: Fashion in 19th Century America." *Journal of Popular Culture* 13 (Spring 1980): 581-589.

Lebing, Wendy. "The Rustle of Her Dress: The Sounds of Late 19th and Early 20th Century Clothing." *Dress* 11 (1985): 90-101.

-----. "Sink or Swimwear." *Vintage Fashions* 1 (January/February 1990): 18-21.

Lemire, Beverly. "The Theft of Clothes and Popular Consumerism in Early Modern England." *Journal of Social History* 24 (Winter 1990): 255-276.

Lewis, J. M. "Caucasian Body Hair Management: A Key to Gender and Species Identification in U.S. Culture?" *Journal of American Culture* 10 (Spring 1987): 7-14.

Lothrop, Gloria Ricci. "How a Trio of Tinseltown Mermaids Invented Southern California's Sportswear Industry." *Californians* 7 (January/February 1989): 32-39.

Lucas, Catherine. "Postmen and Postwomen in Rural Areas." *Costume* 13 (1979): 52-53.

Mactaggart, Ann, and Peter Mactaggart. "Ease, Convenience and Stays, 1750-1850." *Costume* 13 (1979): 41-51.

Martin, Richard. "'The New Soft Look': Jackson Pollack, Cecil Beaton, and American Fashion in 1951." *Dress* 7 (1981): 1-8.

Matthews, Jill. "They Had Such a Lot of Fun: The Women's League of Health and Beauty." *History Workshop* 30 (Autumn 1990): 22-54.

Maynard, M. "A Dream of Fair Women--Revival Dress and the Formation of Late Victorian Images of Feminity." *Art History* 12 (September 1989): 322-341.

McCracken, Grant. "Textile History and the Consumer Epidemic: An Anthropological Approach to Popular Consumption and the Mass Market." *Material History Bulletin* [Canada] 31 (Spring 1990): 59-63.

Miller, Daniel. "Fashion and Ontology in Trinidad." *Culture & History* 7 (1990): 49-79.

Neaher, Nancy C. "Igbo Carved Doors." *African Arts* 15 (November 1981): 49-55.

Noun, Louise. "Amelia Bloomer, A Biography: Part I, The Lily of Seneca Falls." *Annals of Iowa* 47 (Winter 1985): 575-617.

Orayan, Susanna. "Black: The Basic Outline." *Vintage Fashions* 1 (March/April 1990): 6-9.

Paoletti, Jo Barraclough. "The Role of Choice in the Democratization of Fashion." *Dress* 6 (1980): 47-56.

Peacock, Primrose. "Buttons on the Dress of Household Servants." *Costume* 13 (1979): 54-57.

Peiss, Kathy. "Making Faces: The Cosmetics Industry and the Cultural Construction of Gender, 1890-1930." *Genders* 7 (March 1990): 143-169.

Picton, John. "Women's Weaving: The Manufacture and Use of Textiles Among the Igbirra People of Nigeria." *Textile History* 11 (1980): 63-88.

Platt, Elizabeth E. "Jewelry of Bible Times and the Catalog of Isa 3:18-23, Part 1." *Andrews University Seminary Studies* 17 (Spring 1979): 71-84.

-----. "Jewelry of Bible Times and the Catalog of Isa 3:18-23, Part 2." *Andrews University of Seminary Studies* 17 (Autumn 1979): 189-202.

Potts, Alex. "Beautiful Bodies and Dying Heroes." *History Workshop* 30 (Autumn 1990): 1-21.

Poyner, Robin. "Traditional Textiles in Owo, Nigeria." *African Arts* 14 (November 1980): 47-51, 88.

Prellwitz, Marcia, and Marcia D. Metcalf. "The Documentation of 19th Century American Costume." *Dress* 6 (1980): 24-30.

Rabun, Josette H., and Mary Frances Drake. "Warmth in Clothing: A Victorian Perspective." *Dress* 9 (1983): 24-31.

Rendell, T. Joan. "Fashions of a Wedmore Family, 1816-1916." *Costume* 16 (1982): 47-56.

Ribeiro, Aileen. "Dress in Utopia." *Costume* 21 (1987): 26-33.

Richard, K. Keith. "Of 'Gingham,' 'Barn Doors,' and 'Exquisites': George H. Hines on Pioneer Fashion." *Oregon Historical Quarterly* 90 (Winter 1989): 385-393.

Robbert, Louise Buenger. "Twelfth-Century Italian Prices: Food and Clothing in Pisa and Venice." *Social Science History* 7 (Fall 1983): 381-404.

Rolley, Katrina. "Cutting a Dash: The Dress of Radclyffe Hall and Una Troubridge." *Feminist Review* no. 35 (Summer 1990): 54-66.

-----. "Fashion, Femininity and the Fight for the Vote." *Art History* 13 (March 1990): 47-71.

Ryesky, Diana. "Blanche Payne, Scholar and Teacher: Her Career in Costume History." *Pacific Northwest Quarterly* 77 (January 1986): 21-30.

Sanderson, Elizabeth. "The Edinburgh Milliners, 1720-1820." *Costume* 20 (1986): 18-28.

Sawyer, Corinne Holt. "Men in Skirts and Women in Trousers, from Achilles to Victoria Grant: One Explanation of a Comedic Paradox." *Journal of Popular Culture* 21, no. 2 (1987): 1-16.

Scarce, Jennifer. "Turkish Fashion in Transition." *Costume* 14 (1980): 144-167.

Sherman, Mimi. "Elizabeth and John Freake: Fashions of the Times." *The Clarion* 15 (Winter 1990-1991): 42-48.

Shine, Carolyn R. "Hunting Shirts and Silk Stockings: Clothing Early Cincinnati." *Queen City Heritage* 45 (Fall 1987): 23-48.

-----. "Scalping Knives and Silk Stockings: Clothing the Frontier, 1780-1795." *Dress* 14 (1988): 39-47.

Shonfield, Zuzanna. "Miss Marshall and the Cimabue Browns." *Costume* 13 (1979): 62-72.

Smith, Fred T. "Frafra Dress." *African Arts* 15 (May 1982): 36-42, 92.

Smith, Fred T., and Joanne B. Eicher. "The Systematic Study of African Dress and Textiles." *African Arts* 15 (May 1982): 28.

Song, Cheunsoon, and Lucy Roy Sibley. "The Vertical Headdress of Fifteenth Century Northern Europe." *Dress* 16 (1990): 4-15.

Spainhour, Judi. "Waistlines and Fashions." *Vintage Fashions* 1 (March/April 1990): 10-12.

Stage, Sarah. "Seeing through American Beauty." *American Quarterly* 36 (Summer 1984): 297-302.

Staniland, Kay. "Medieval Courtly Splendour." *Costume* 14 (1980): 7-23.

-----. "The Wedding Dresses of H. R. H. The Princess of Wales (1981) and H. R. H. The Duchess of York (1986)." *Costume* 21 (1987): 94-96.

Staniland, Kay, and Santina M. Levey. "Queen Victoria's Wedding Dress and Lace." *Costume* 17 (1983): 1-32.

Steele, Valerie. "Fashion in China." *Dress* 9 (1983): 8-15.

-----. "The Social and Political Significance of Macaroni Fashion." *Costume* 19 (1985): 94-109.

Stewart, Imogen. "Betsy Sheridan's Journal." *Costume* 22 (1988): 39-43.

Storm, Penny A. "A Thought on the Origin and Function of Dress since They Weren't Naked After All." *Dress* 7 (1981): 90-94.

Sutton, Anne. "The Coronation Robes of Richard III and Anne Neville." *Costume* 13 (1979): 8-16.

Tandberg, Gerilyn. "Clothing for Conformity: A Study of the Brethren Sect." *Costume* 20 (1986): 63-71.

-----. "Field Hand Clothing in Louisiana and Mississippi During the Ante-Bellum Period." *Dress* 6 (1980): 89-103.

-----. "Sinning for Silk--Dress-for-Success Fashions of the New Orleans Storyville Prostitute." *Women's Studies International Forum* 13, no. 3 (1990): 229-248.

-----. "Towards Freedom in Dress for 19th Century Women." *Dress* 11 (1985): 11-30.

Tandberg, Gerilyn, and Sally Graham Durand. "Dress-up Clothes for Field Slaves of Ante-Bellum Louisiana and Mississippi." *Costume* 15 (1981): 40-48.

Tansug, Sabiha. "'A Thousand and One Flowers' on Turkish Women's Traditional Headware and Dress." *Turkish Review* 2 (1987): 73-86.

Tarrant, Naomi E. A. "A Maternity Dress of about 1845-50." *Costume* 14 (1980): 117-120.

Taylor, Lou. "Marguerite Shoobert, London Fashion Model, 1906-1917." *Costume* 17 (1983): 105-110.

Tinling, Marion. "Bloomerism Comes to California." *California History* 61 (Spring 1982): 18-25.

Trautman, Pat. "Personal Clothiers: A Demographic Study of Dressmakers, Seamstresses, and Tailors." *Dress* 5 (1979): 74-83.

van Ierlant, Marie J. Ghering. "Anglo-French Fashion, 1786." *Costume* 17 (1983): 64-77.

Wagener, M. L. "Fashion and Feminism in Fin-de-Siècle Vienna." *Woman's Art Journal* 10 (Fall/Winter 1990): 29-33.

Walasek, Richard A. "Will Miss Montana Ever Be Chosen?" *North American Culture* 5, no. 1 (1989): 51-66.

Walden, Keith. "The Road to Fat City: An Interpretation of the Development of Weight Consciousness in Western Society." *Historical Reflections/Reflexions Historiques* 12 (Fall 1985): 331-374.

Walkley, Christina. "Charity and the Victorian Needlewoman." *Costume* 14 (1980): 136-143.

Walsh, Margaret. "The Democratization of Fashion: The Emergence of the Women's Dress Pattern Industry." *Journal of American History* 66 (September 1979): 299-313.

Warner, Patricia Campbell. "Fetters of Gold: The Jewelry of Renaissance Saxony in the Portraits of Cranach the Elder." *Dress* 16 (1990): 16-27.

-----. "Public and Private: Men's Influence on American Women's Dress for Sport and Physical Education." *Dress* 14 (1988): 48-55.

Wehrle, Louise, and Jo Paoletti. "What Do We Wear to the Wedding Now That the Funeral Is Over? A Look at Advice and Etiquette Literature, and Practice During the Years 1880-1910 in America." *Dress* 16 (1990): 81-88.

Weimann, Jeanne Madeline. "Fashion and the Fair." *Chicago History* 12 (Fall 1983).

Weir, Shelagh. "Palestinian Costume." *British Museum Society Bulletin* no. 62 (Winter 1989): 34-40.

Welters, Linda. "The Transition from Folk to Fashionable Dress in Attica, Greece." *Dress* 11 (1985): 57-67.

Whisner, Mary. "Gender-Specific Clothing Regulation: A Study in Patriarchy." *Harvard Women's Law Journal* 5 (Spring 1982): 73-119.

Whyte, Ann W. "Helen Bagrie, Costumiere, 343 Union Street, Aberdeen." *Costume* 16 (1982): 71-85.

William, Albert E. "Pretty Is as Pretty Says: The Rhetoric of Beauty Salon Names." *Names* 36, no. 1/2 (1988): 61-68.

Wilson, Elizabeth. "Deviant Dress." *Feminist Review* no. 35 (Summer 1990): 67-74.

Wilson, Laurel. "Anna Gove: 'Lady, Female Doctress:' Social Non-conformist and Clothing Conservative." *Dress* 16 (1990): 62-69.

Wipper, Audrey. "African Women, Fashion and Scapegoating." *Canadian Journal of African Studies* 6, no. 2 (1972): 329-349.

## Food

Bynum, Caroline Walker. "Fast, Feast, and Flesh: The Religious Significance of Food to Medieval Women." *Representations* 11 (1985): 1-25.

Conlin, Joseph R. "Eating on the Run: Organizing Meals on the Overland Trail." *California History* 64 (Summer 1985): 218-225.

Hartwell, Marcia Byrom. "Researching Food in American History." *History News* 42 (November/December 1987): 18-20.

Levenstein, Harvey. "The 'Servant Problem' and American Cookery." *Revue française d'études américaines* no. 27/28 (1986): 127-135.

Levine, Phillipa. "'The Humanising Influences of Five O'Clock Tea': Victorian Feminist Periodicals." *Victorian Studies* 33 (Winter 1990): 293-306.

Marling, Karal Ann. "'She Brought Forth Butter in a Lordly Dish': The Origins of Minnesota Butter Sculpture." *Minnesota History* 50 (Summer 1987): 218-228.

McMahon, Sarah F. "Provisions Laid Up for the Family: Towards a History of Diet in New England, 1650-1850." *Historical Methods* 14 (Winter 1981): 4-21.

Robbert, Louise Buenger. "Twelfth-Century Italian Prices: Food and Clothing in Pisa and Venice." *Social Science History* 7 (Fall 1983): 381-404.

Robinson, Lisa Mae. "Regulating What We Eat: Mary Engle Pennington and the Food Research Laboratory." *Agricultural History* 64 (Spring 1990): 143-153.

Stedman, Jane W. "Edna Ferber and Menus with Meaning." *Journal of American Culture* 2 (Fall 1979): 454-462.

## General

Batts, John Stuart. "Saskatchewan and *The Pink Lady.*" *Saskatchewan History* 40 (Autumn 1987): 114-119.

Harries, Patrick. "Symbols and Sexuality: Culture and Identity on the Early Witwatersrand Gold Mines." *Gender & History* 2 (Autumn 1990): 318-336.

Higham, John. "Indian Princess and Roman Goddess: The First Female Symbols of America." *Proceedings of the American Antiquarian Society* 100, no. 1 (1990): 45-80.

Iovine, Julie V. "The Impeccable Gardner." *American Heritage* 37 (June/July 1986): 66-77.

Maza, S. "The Rose-Girl of Salency: Representations of Virtue in Prerevolutionary France." *Eighteenth-Century Studies* 22 (Spring 1989): 395-412.

Pike, Martha. "'In Memory Of : Artifacts Related to Mourning in Nineteenth-Century America." *Journal of American Culture* 3 (Winter 1980): 642-659.

Riley, Barbara. "Domestic Work: Oral History and Material Culture." *Canadian Oral History Association Journal* 8 (1985): 9-14.

Rogers, Gayle J. "The Changing Image of the Southern Woman: A Performer on a Pedestal." *Journal of Popular Culture* (Winter 1982): 60-67.

Schnur, Susan. "Badges of Shame." *Lilith* 14 (Fall 1989): 14-16.

Senelick, Laurence. "Ladykillers and Lady Killers: Recent Popular Victoriana." *Victorian Studies* 21 (Summer 1978): 493-526.

Shaffer, Kelly I., and Frank Kurtik. "Images of Women: Outside the Home." *Western Pennsylvania Historical Magazine* 69 (October 1986): 327-342.

Sill, Louise Morgan. "Through Inland Seas (Through a Woman's Eyes in 1904)." *Inland Seas* 44 (Fall 1988): 190-196.

Walker, Nancy. "Wit, Sentimentality and the Image of Women in the Nineteenth Century." *American Studies* (Fall 1981): 5-22.

Willard, Charity Cannon. "Early Images of the Female Warrior: Minerva, the Amazons, Joan of Arc." *Minerva: Quarterly Report on Women and the Military* 6 (Fall 1988): 1-11.

## Photographs/Paintings/Visual Images/Movies

Anderson, Amanda S. "D. G. Rossetti's 'Jenny': Agency, Intersubjectivity, and the Prostitute." *Genders* no. 4 (March 1989): 103-121.

Armitage, Susan. "Women and Men in Western History: A Stereoptical Vision." *Western Historical Quarterly* 16 (October 1985): 381-396.

Bell, Susan Groag. "Women Create Gardens in Male Landscapes: A Revisionist Approach to Eighteenth Century English Garden History (Art Essay)." *Feminist Studies* 16 (Fall 1990): 471-492.

Benes, Peter. "Decorated Family Records from Coastal Massachusetts, New Hampshire, and Connecticut." *Dublin Seminar for New England Folklife* (1985): 91-147.

Bonfante, Larissa. "Nudity as Costume in Classical Art." *American Journal of Archaeology* 93 (October 1989): 543-570.

Bonney, Claire. "The Nude Photograph: Some Female Perspectives." *Woman's Art Journal* 6 (Fall 1985/Winter 1986): 9-14.

Brown, Jean Lucas. "Miji Kenda Grave and Memorial Sculptures." *African Arts* 13 (August 1980): 36-69, 99.

Calvert, Karin. "Children in American Family Portraiture, 1670-1810." *William and Mary Quarterly* 39 (January 1982): 87-113.

Carlson, Dick. "Women in San Diego . . . a History in Photographs." *Journal of San Diego History* 24 (Summer 1978): 311-342.

Cheney, Liana. "Lavinia Fontana, Boston 'Holy Family.'" *Woman's Art Journal* 5 (Spring/Summer 1984): 12-15.

Crosthwaite, Jane F. "'A White and Seamless Robe': Celibacy and Equality in Shaker Art and Theory." *Colby Library Quarterly* 25 (September 1989): 188-198.

Curtis, James C. "Dorothea Lange, Migrant Mother, and the Culture of the Great Depression." *Winterthur Portfolio* 21 (Spring 1986): 1-20.

Darby, Elizabeth. "John Gibson, Queen Victoria and the Idea of Sculptural Polychromy." *Art History* 4 (March 1981): 37-53.

Dawkins, Heather. "The Diaries and Photographs of Hannah Cullwick." *Art History* 10 (June 1987): 154-187.

Doss, Erika L. "Images of American Women in the 1930s: Reginald Marsh and 'Paramount Picture.'" *Woman's Art Journal* 4 (Fall 1983/Winter 1984): 1-4.

Edelstein, T. J. "They Sang 'The Song of the Shirt': The Visual Iconology of the Seamstress." *Victorian Studies* 23 (Winter 1980): 183-210.

Erikson, Carolly. "Bloody Mary: Images of Burning Flesh and Grim-Eyed Vengeance." *In Britain* 34 (April 1979): 30-33.

Ferree, Myra Marx and Elaine J. Hall. "Visual Images of American Society: Gender and Race in Introductory Sociology Textbooks." *Gender & Society* 4

(December 1990): 500-533.

Fielder, Mari Kathleen. "Fatal Attraction: Irish-Jewish Romance in Early Film and Drama." *Eire-Ireland* 20 (Fall 1985): 6-18.

Fischer, Lucy. "Two-Faced Women: The 'Double' in Women's Melodrama of the 1940s." *Cinema Journal* 23 (Fall 1983): 24-43.

Foote, Cheryl J. "Changing Images of Women in the Western Film." *Journal of the West* 22 (October 1983): 64-71.

Foss, Susan Moore. "She Who Sits as King." *African Arts* 12 (February 1979): 44-50.

Garb, Tamar. "Renoir and the Natural Woman." *The Oxford Art Journal* 8, no. 2 (1985): 3-15.

Gershman, Elizabeth, and Joyce Pendery. "Women at Work: How Stamford's Exhibit Traces the Professional Development of Women." *History News* 35 (August 1980): 12-15.

Gronberg, Theresa Ann. "Femmes de Brasserie." *Art History* 7 (September 1984): 329-344.

Groseclose, Barbara S. "Harriet Hosmer's Tomb to Judith Falconnet: Death and the Maiden." *The American Art Journal* 12 (Spring 1980): 78-89.

Hansen, Miriam. "Pleasure, Ambivalence, Identification: Valentino and Female Spectatorship." *Cinema Journal* 25 (Summer 1986): 6-32.

Harbison, Craig. "Sexuality and Social Standing in Jan van Eyck's Arnolfini Double Portrait." *Renaissance Quarterly* 43 (Summer 1990): 249-291.

Hills, Patricia. "Eastman Johnson's 'The Field Hospital,' the U.S. Sanitary Commission, and Women in the Civil War." *The Minneapolis Institute of Arts Bulletin* 65 (1981/82): 66-81.

Hults, Linda C. "Durer's *Lucretia*: Speaking the Silence of Women." *Signs* 16 (Winter 1991): 205-237.

Inglis, Ken. "Men, Women, and War Memorials: Anzac Australia." *Daedalus* 116 (Fall 1987): 35-60.

Jacobs, Lea. "The Censorship of *Blonde Venus*: Textual Analysis and Historical Methods." *Cinema Journal* 27 (Spring 1988): 21-31.

Jefchak, Andrew. "Prostitutes and Schoolmarms: An Essay on Women in Western Films." *Heritage of the Great Plains* 16 (Summer 1983): 19-26.

Jirat-Wasiutynski, Vojtech. "Paul Gauguin's Self-Portraits and 'Oviri': The Image of the Artist, Eve, and the Fatal Woman." *The Art Quarterly* 2, no. 2 (1979): 172-190.

Kalisch, Philip A., and Beatrice J. Kalisch. "When Nurses Were National Heroines: Images of Nursing in American Film, 1942-1945." *Nursing Forum* 20, no. 1 (1981): 14-61.

King, John N. "Queen Elizabeth I: Representations of the Virgin Queen." *Renaissance Quarterly* 43 (Spring 1990): 30-74.

Kirk, Martha A. "Art for Worship, Women as Imaged, Women as Image Makers." *Journal of Women and Religion* 3 (Summer 1984): 51-58.

Kitch, Sally L. "'As a Sign That All May Understand': Shaker Gift Drawings and Female Spiritual Power." *Winterthur Portfolio* 24 (Spring 1989): 1-28.

Leader, Bernice Kramer. "Antifeminism in the Paintings of the Boston School." *Arts Magazine* 56, no. 5 (1982): 112-119.

Leja, Michael. "'Le Vieux Marcheur' and 'Les Deux Risques': Picasso, Prostitution, Venereal Disease, and Maternity, 1899-1907." *Art History* 8 (March 1985): 66-81.

Lipton, Eunice. "The Laundress in Late Nineteenth-Century French Culture: Imagery, Ideology and Edgar Degas." *Art History* 3 (September 1980): 295-313.

-----. "Women, Pleasure, and Painting (e.g., Boucher)." *Genders* 7 (March 1990): 69-86.

Lovell, Margaretta M. "Reading Eighteenth-Century American Family Portraits: Social Images and Self-Images." *Winterthur Portfolio* 22 (Winter 1987): 243-264.

Marsh, Jan. "Pre-Raphaelite Women." *New Society* 67 (February 1984): 279-282.

Michel, Sonya. "Feminism, Film and Public History." *Radical History Review* 25 (October 1981): 46-61.

Modleski, Tania. "Time and Desire in the Woman's Film." *Cinema Journal* 23 (Spring 1984): 19-30.

Motz, Marilyn F. "Visual Autobiography: Photograph Albums of Turn-of-the-Century Midwestern Women." *American Quarterly* 41 (March 1989): 63-92.

Movshovitz, Howard. "The Still Point: Women in the Westerns of John Ford." *Frontiers* 7, no. 3 (1984): 68-72.

Naficy, Hamid. "History, Memory, and Film: Voices from Inside Lebanon." *Jusur* 3 (1987): 95-102.

Nead, Lynda. "Seduction, Prostitution, Suicide: 'On the Brink' by Alfred Elmore." *Art History* 5 (September 1982): 310-322.

Oshana, Maryann. "Native American Women in Westerns: Reality and Myth." *Frontiers* 6 (Fall 1981): 46-50.

Ostendorf, Lloyd. "A New Mary Todd Lincoln Photograph: A Tour of the White Mountains in Summer, 1863." *Illinois Historical Journal* 83 (Summer 1990): 109-112.

Pedersen, Diana. "The Photographic Record of the Canadian YWCA, 1890-1930: A Visual Source for Women's History." *Archivaria* 24 (Summer 1987): 10-35.

"Photographic Portfolio: Cleopatra's Needle." *Hayes Historical Journal* 8 (Winter 1989): 23-36.

Prince, Stephen. "The Pornographic Image and the Practice of Film Theory." *Cinema Journal* 27 (Winter 1988): 27-39.

Ramirez, Jan Seidler. "The 'Lovelorn Lady': A New Look at William Wetmore Story's 'Sappho.'" *The American Art Journal* 15 (Summer 1983): 80-90.

Rand, Erica. "Depoliticizing Women: Female Agency, the French Revolution, and the Art of Boucher and David." *Genders* 7 (March 1990): 47-68.

Ravenal, Carol M. "Three Faces of Mother: Madonna, Martyr, Medusa in the Art of Edvard Münch." *Journal of Psychohistory* 13 (Spring 1986): 371-412.

Reilly, Joan. "Many Brides: 'Mistress and Maid' on Athenian *Lekythoi*." *Hesperia*

58 (October/December 1989): 411-444.

Rugh, Thomas F. "Emmy Hennings and the Emergence of Zurich Dada." *Woman's Art Journal* 2 (Spring/Summer 1981): 1-6.

Sayer, Karen. "'Utterly Shameless Women': Images of Women Field Workers." *Labour History Review* 55 (Spring 1990): 11-12.

Seifert, Carolyn J. "Images of Domestic Madness in the Art and Poetry of American Women." *Woman's Art Journal* 1 (Fall 1980/Winter 1981): 1-6.

Skaggs, Merrill. "Submission and Fidelity, Assertion and Surprise: Two 'Southern Woman' Films." *Southern Quarterly* 24 (Spring 1986): 5-13.

Sloan, Kay. "Sexual Warfare in the Silent Cinema: Comedies and Melodramas of Woman Suffragism." *American Quarterly* 33 (Fall 1981): 412-436.

Slusser, Cathy. "Women of Tampa Bay: A Photo Essay." *Tampa Bay History* 5 (Fall/Winter 1983): 47-65.

Springer, Julie Anne. "Art and The Feminine Muse: Women in Interiors by John White Alexander." *Woman's Art Journal* 6 (Fall 1985/Winter 1986): 1-8.

Sund, Judy. "Favoured Fictions: Women and Books in the Art of Van Gogh." *Art History* 11 (June 1988): 255-267.

Waldman, Diane. "'At Last I Can Tell It to Someone!': Feminine Point of View and Subjectivity in the Gothic Romance Film of the 1940s." *Cinema Journal* 23 (Winter 1984): 29-40.

Walsh, Lorena S. "Women, History, and History Museums: An Exhibition Review." *Winterthur Portfolio* 21 (Spring 1986): 65-69.

Welch, Edward Gibson, ed. "Childhood's Panorama: Mattie Gibson Welch's Poem and Drawings of the Western Experience." *South Dakota History* 11 (Spring 1981): 111-123.

Werness, Hope B. "The Modest Maiden in 19th-Century Art: Evolution of a Theme." *Woman's Art Journal* 5 (Fall 1984/Winter 1985): 7-10.

White, Mimi. "Representing Romance: Reading/Writing/Fantasy and the 'Liberated' Heroine of Recent Hollywood Films." *Cinema Journal* 28 (Spring 1989): 41-56.

Williams, Linda. "'Something Else Besides a Mother': *Stella Dallas* and the Maternal Melodrama." *Cinema Journal* 24 (Fall 1984): 2-27.

Zemel, Carol. "Sorrowing Women, Rescuing Men: Van Gogh's Images of Women and Family." *Art History* 10 (September 1987): 351-368.

Ziegler, J. E. "The Medieval Virgin as Object: Art or Anthropology?" *Historical Reflections/Reflexions Historiques* 16 (Summer & Fall 1989): 251-264.

## Popular Culture/Mass Media/Advertising

Bakker, Jan. "Caroline Gilman and the Issue of Slavery in the Rose Magazines, 1832-1839." *Southern Studies* 24 (Fall 1985): 273-283.

Brooks, Lynn Matluck. "Emblem of Gaiety, Love, and Legislation: Dance in Eighteenth-Century Philadelphia." *Pennsylvania Magazine of History and Biography* 65 (January 1991): 63-88.

Cancian, Francesca M., and Steven L. Gordon. "Changing Emotion Norms in

Marriage: Love and Anger in U.S. Women's Magazines Since 1900." *Gender & Society* 2, no. 3 (1988): 308-342.

Cordato, Mary Frances. "Toward a New Century: Women and the Philadelphia Centennial Exhibition, 1876." *Pennsylvania Magazine of History and Biography* 107 (January 1983): 113-136.

Curtin, Michael. "A Question of Manners: Status and Gender in Etiquette and Courtesy." *Journal of Modern History* 57 (September 1985): 395-423.

Dalstrom, E. Kay, and Harl A. Dalstrom. "From the Skylon Ballroom to Oscar's Palladium: Dancing in Nebraska, 1948-1957." *Nebraska History* 65 (Fall 1984): 366-386.

Davis, Rodney O. "Earnest Elmo Calkins and Pheobe Snow." *Railroad History* 163 (Autumn 1990): 88-92.

Emlen, Robert P. "Wedding Silver for the Browns: A Rhode Island Family Patronizes A Boston Goldsmith." *The American Art Journal* 16 (Spring 1984): 39-50.

Ewen, Elizabeth. "City Lights: Immigrant Women and the Rise of the Movies." *Signs* 5 (Spring 1980): 545-566.

Faderman, Lillian. "Lesbian Magazine Fiction in the Early Twentieth Century." *Journal of Popular Culture* (Spring 1978): 800-817.

Gardner, John. "Contradances and Cotillions: Dancing in Eighteenth-Century Delaware." *Delaware History* 22 (Spring/Summer 1986): 39-47.

Grossbard, Judy, and Robert S. Merkel. "'Modern' Wheels Liberated 'The Ladies' 100 Years Ago." *Dress* 16 (1990): 70-80.

Hasna, Begum. "Mass Media and Women in Bangladesh." *South Asia* 9 (June 1986): 15-23.

Held, Jutta. "Between Bourgeois Enlightenment and Popular Culture: Goya's Festivals, Old Women, Monsters and Blind Men." *History Workshop* 23 (Spring 1987): 39-58.

Honey, Maureen. "Recruiting Women for War Work: OWI and the Magazine Industry During World War II." *Journal of American Culture* 3 (Spring 1980): 47-52.

Huffman, James R., and Julie L. Huffman. "Sexism and Cultural Lag: The Rise of the Jailbait Songs, 1955-1985." *Journal of Popular Culture* 21, no. 2 (1987): 65-83.

Jennings, Susan E. "'As American as Hot Dogs, Apple Pie, and Chevrolet': The Desegregation of Little League Baseball." *Journal of American Culture* 4 (Winter 1981): 81-91.

Jones, Phyllis. "Ragtime: Feminist, Socialist and Black Perspectives on the Self-Made Man." *Journal of American Culture* 2 (Spring 1979): 17-28.

Langlois, Karen S. "A Fresh Voice from the West: Mary Austin, California, and American Literary Magazines, 1892-1910." *California History* 69 (Spring 1990): 22-35.

Leach, William R. "Transformations in a Culture of Consumption: Women and Department Stores, 1890-1925." *Journal of American History* 71 (September 1984): 319-342.

Ling, P. "Sex and the Automobile in the Jazz-Age." *History Today* 39 (November 1989): 18-24.

Lisenby, Foy. "American Women in Magazine Cartoons." *American Journalism* 2 (1985): 130-134.

List, Karen K. "Magazine Portrayals of Women's Role in the New Republic." *Journalism History* 13 (Summer 1986): 64-70.

Marks, Patricia. "Mrs. Wettin Meets a Chum. Life's View of Victoria, 1883-1901." *Journal of American Culture* 3 (Spring 1980): 80-94.

Masel-Walters, Lynne. "To Hustle with the Rowdies: The Organization and Functions of the American Woman Suffrage Press." *Journal of American Culture* 3 (Spring 1980): 167-183.

Masters, Ardyce. "The Doll as Delegate and Disguise." *Journal of Psychohistory* 13 (Winter 1986): 293-308.

McBride, Theresa. "A Woman's World: Department Stores and the Evolution of Women's Employment, 1870-1920." *French Historical Studies* 10 (Fall 1978): 664-683.

McCall, Laura. "'The Reign of Brute Force Is Now Over': A Content Analysis of *Godey's Lady's Book*, 1830-1860." *Journal of the Early Republic* 9 (Summer 1989): 217-236.

Moseley, Caroline. "'The Maids of Dear Columbia': Images of Young Women in Victorian American Parlor Song." *Journal of American Culture* 6 (Spring 1983): 18-31.

Neal, Arthur G., and Helen L. Youngelson. "The Folklore of Wall Street: Gamesmanship, Gurus, and the Myth-Making Process." *Journal of American Culture* 11 (Spring 1988): 55-62.

Nord, David P. "A Republican Literature: A Study of Magazine Reading and Readers in Late Eighteenth-Century New York." *American Quarterly* 40 (March 1988): 42-64.

Pedersen, Susan. "Hannah More Meets Simple Simon: Tracts, Chapbooks, and Popular Culture in Late Eighteenth-Century England." *The Journal of British Studies* 25 (January 1986): 84-113.

Rabinovitz, Lauren. "Sitcoms and Single Moms: Representations of Feminism on American TV." *Cinema Journal* 29 (Fall 1989): 3-19.

Robinson, Gertrude. "The Media and Social Change: 30 Years of Magazine Coverage of Women and Work (1950-1977)." *Atlantis* 8 (Spring 1983): 87-112.

Sanford, Charles L. "'Woman's Place' in American Car Culture." *Michigan Quarterly Review* 19-20 (Fall 1980-Winter 1981): 532-547.

Scheurer, Timothy E. "Goddesses and Golddiggers: Images of Women in Popular Music of the 1930s." *Journal of Popular Culture* 24 (Summer 1990): 23-38.

Shay, Anthony. "Fandangos and Bailes: Dancing and Dance Events in Early California." *Southern California Quarterly* 64 (Summer 1982): 99-114.

Simonds, Wendy. "Confessions of Loss: Maternal Grief in *True Story*, 1920-1985." *Gender & Society* 2, no. 2 (1988): 149-171.

Spangler, Lynn C. "A Historical Overview of Female Friendships on Prime-Time Television." *Journal of Popular Culture* 22 (Spring 1989): 13-24.

Taylor, Dorothy Loring. "Olive Beaupre Miller and *My Book House*." *Illinois Historical Journal* 78 (Winter 1985): 273-288.

Thomas, Samuel J. "Nostrum Advertising and the Image of Woman as Invalid in Late Victorian America." *Journal of American Culture* 5 (Fall 1982): 104-112.

Walden, Keith. "Speaking Modern: Language, Culture, and Hegemony in Grocery Window Displays, 1887-1920." *Canadian Historical Review* 70 (September 1989): 285-310.

Waller-Zuckerman, Mary Ellen. "The Business Side of Media Development: Popular Women's Magazines in the Late Nineteenth Century." *Essays in Economic and Business History* 7 (1989): 40-59.

Weiner, Nella Fermi. "Of Feminism and Birth Control Propaganda (1790-1840)." *International Journal of Women's Studies* 3 (September/October 1980): 411-430.

Wilkinson, Doris Y. "The Doll Exhibit: A Psycho-Cultural Analysis of Black Female Role Stereotypes." *Journal of Popular Culture* 21, no. 2 (1987): 19-29.

## Science and Technology

Bose, Christine E. "Technology and Changes in the Division of Labor in the American Home." *Women's Studies* 2, no. 3 (1979): 295-304.

Bose, Christine E., Philip L. Bereano, and Mary Malloy. "Household Technology and the Social Construction of Housework." *Technology and Culture* 25 (January 1984): 53-82.

Bourque, Susan C., and Kay B. Warren. "Technology, Gender, and Development." *Daedalus* 116 (Fall 1987): 173-198.

Bullough, Vern L. "A Brief Note on Rubber Technology and Contraception: The Diaphragm and the Condom." *Technology and Culture* 22, no. 1 (1981): 104-111.

-----. "Merchandising the Sanitary Napkin: Lillian Gilbreth's 1927 Survey." *Signs* 10 (Spring 1985): 615-627.

Bushman, Richard L., and Claudia L. Bushman. "The Early History of Cleanliness in America." *Journal of American History* 74 (March 1988): 1213-1238.

Carrell, Kimberly W. "The Industrial Revolution Comes to the Home: Kitchen Design Reform and Middle-Class Women." *Journal of American Culture* (Fall 1979): 488-499.

Cowan, Ruth Schwartz. "From Virginia Dare to Virginia Slims: Women and Technology in American Life." *Technology and Culture* 20 (January 1979): 51-63.

Dellapenna, Joseph W. "The History of Abortions: Technology, Morality, and Law." *University of Pittsburgh Law Review* 40 (Spring 1979): 359-428.

Douglas, Diane M. "The Machine in the Parlor: A Dialectical Analysis of the Sewing Machine." *Journal of American Culture* 5 (Spring 1982): 20-29.

Drachman, Virginia G. "Gynecological Instruments and Surgical Decisions at a Hospital in Late Nineteenth-Century America." *Journal of American Culture*

3 (Winter 1980): 660-672.

Fox, Bonnie J. "Selling the Mechanized Household: 70 Years of Ads in Ladies Home Journal." *Gender & Society* 4 (March 1990): 25-40.

Golden, J. "From Wet Nurse Directory to Milk Bank: The Delivery of Human Milk in Boston, 1909-1927." *Bulletin of the History of Medicine* 62 (1988): 589-605.

Greene, Sally. "Operator--Could You Please Ring? A History of Rural Telephone Service to Kendrick and Juliatta, Idaho." *Idaho Yesterdays* 31 (Fall 1987): 2-10.

Hettrick, Jane Schatkin. "She Drew an Angel Down: The Role of Women in the History of the Organ, 300 B.C. to 1900 A.D." *American Organist* 13 (November 1979): 39-45.

Jaki, Stanley L. "The Virgin Birth and the Birth of Science." *The Downside Review* 107 (October 1989): 255-273.

Jellison, Katherine. "Women and Technology on the Great Plains, 1910-1940." *Great Plains Quarterly* 8 (Summer 1988): 145-157.

Mueller, Milton. "The Switchboard Problem: Scale, Signaling, and Organization in Manual Telephone Switching, 1877-1897." *Technology and Culture* 30 (July 1989): 534-560.

Oudshoorn, Nelly. "On Measuring Sex Hormones: The Role of Biological Assays in Sexualizing Chemical Substances." *Bulletin of the History of Medicine* 64 (Summer 1990): 243-261.

Schiebinger, Linda. "The Anatomy of Difference: Race and Sex in Eighteenth-Century Science." *Eighteenth-Century Studies* 23 (Summer 1990): 387-406.

-----. "The History and Philosophy of Women in Science." *Signs* 12 (Winter 1987): 305-332.

Shields, Stephanie. "The Variability Hypothesis: The History of a Biological Model of Sex Differences in Intelligence." *Signs* 7 (Summer 1982): 769-782.

Stone, May N. "The Plumbing Paradox: American Attitudes toward Late Nineteenth-Century Domestic Sanitary Arrangements." *Winterthur Portfolio* 14 (Autumn 1979): 283-310.

Thomson, Ross. "Learning by Selling and Invention: The Case of the Sewing Machine." *Journal of Economic History* 47 (June 1987): 433-446.

## MIDDLE EAST/NEAR EAST

Abadan-Unat, Nermin. "Implication of Migration on Emancipation and Pseudo-Emancipation of Turkish Women." *International Migration Review* 11, no. 1 (1977): 31-58.

-----. "The Modernization of Turkish Women." *Middle East Journal* 32, no. 3 (1978): 291-306.

Abbott, Nabia. "Women and the State in Early Islam, I. Muhannad and the First Four Caliphs." *Journal of Near Eastern Studies* 1 (1942): 106-126.

-----. "Women and the State in Early Islam, II. The Umayyads." *Journal of Near*

*Eastern Studies* 1 (1942): 341-361.

-----."Women and the State on the Eve of Islam." *The American Journal of Semitic Languages and Literatures* 58 (January/October 1941): 259-285.

Afary, Janet. "On the Origins of Feminism in Early 20th-Century Iran." *Journal of Women's History* 1 (Fall 1989): 65-87.

Ahmed, Leila. "Arab Culture and Writing Women's Bodies." *Feminist Issues* 9 (Spring 1989): 41-55.

-----. "Western Ethnocentrism and Perceptions of the Harem." *Feminist Studies* 8 (Fall 1982): 521-524.

-----. "Women and the Advent of Islam." *Signs* 11 (Summer 1986): 665-691.

Akgun, S. "Women's Emancipation in Turkey." *Turkish Studies Association Bulletin* 10 (1986): 1-10.

Al-Hibri, Azizah. "A Study of Islamic Herstory: Or How Did We Ever Get into This Mess?" *Women's Studies* 5, no. 2 (1982): 207-220.

Allam, S. "Women as Holders of Rights in Ancient Egypt (During the Late Period)." *Journal of the Economic and Social History of the Orient* 33 (February 1990): 1-34.

Badran, Margot. "Dual Liberation: Feminism and Nationalism in Egypt, 1870s-1925." *Feminist Issues* 8, no. 1 (1988): 15-34.

-----. "Islam, Patriarchy, and Feminism in the Middle East." *Trends in History* 4, no. 1 (1985): 49-71.

-----. "Women and Production in the Middle East." *Trends in History* 2, no. 3 (1982): 59-88.

Baer, Gabriel. "Women and Waqf: An Analysis of the Istanbul Tahrir of 1546." *Asian and African Studies* 17, no. 1/3 (1983): 9-28.

Balkan, Kemal. "Betrothal of Girls During Childhood in Ancient Assyria and Anatolia." *Assyriological Studies* 23 (1986): 1-9.

Batto, B. F. "Land Tenure and Women at Mari." *Journal of the Economic and Social History of the Orient* 23 (October 1980): 209-239.

Becker, Gary S. "Human Capital, Effort, and the Sexual Division of Labor." *Journal of Labor Economics* 3, no. 1 (1985): S33-S59.

Ben-Barak, Shalvia. "Fertility Patterns Among Soviet Immigrants to Israel: The Role of Cultural Variables." *Journal of Family History* 15, no. 1 (1990): 87-100.

Benallegue, Nora. "Algerian Women in the the Struggle for Independence and Reconstruction." *International Social Science Journal* 35, no. 4 (1983): 703-717.

Bernstein, Deborah. "The Plough Woman Who Cried into the Pots: The Position of Women in the Labor Force in Pre-State Israeli Society." *Jewish Social Studies* 45 (Winter 1983): 43-56.

-----. "The Women Workers' Movement in Pre-State Israel, 1919-1939." *Signs* 12 (Spring 1987): 454-470.

Bianchi, Robert Steven. "Cleopatra, Woman of the Twenty-First Century." *Botswana Review* 1 (Summer 1989): 41-44.

Bliss, Frank. "Bahriyan Jewelry and Its Relation to the Nile Valley." *Ornament*

6 (December 1982): 10-14, 44-45.

Bowen, Donna Lee. "Muslim Juridical Opinions Concerning the Status of Women as Demonstrated by the Case of 'Azl." *Journal of Near Eastern Studies* 41 (1981): 323-329.

Camp, C. V. "The Wise Women of 2 Samuel: A Role Model for Women in Early Israel." *Catholic Biblical Quarterly* 43 (1981): 14-29.

Charrad, Mounira. "State and Gender in Maghrib." *Middle East Report* 163 (March/April 1990): 19-24.

Cole, Juan R. "Feminism, Class, and Islam in Turn-of-the-Century Egypt." *International Journal of Middle East Studies* 19 (1981): 387-407.

Daleb, Nuha. "Palestinian Women and Their Role in the Revolution." *Peuples Mediterraneans* 5 (1978): 35-47.

Diakonoff, I. M. "Women in Old Babylonia Not under Patriarchial Authority." *Journal of the Economic and Social History of the Orient* 29 (October 1986): 225-238.

Dodd, Peter C. "Youth and Women's Emancipation in the United Arab Republic." *Middle East Journal* 22, no. 2 (1968): 159-172.

Duben, Alan. "Understanding Muslim Households and Families in Late Ottoman Istanbul." *Journal of Family History* 15, no. 1 (1990): 71-86.

Eastwood, Gillian. "A Medieval Face-Veil from Egypt." *Costume* 17 (1983): 33-38.

Ebeid, Joan. "Women at the Centre of Social Change--An Egyptian Case." *British Society for Middle Eastern Studies Bulletin* 12 (1985): 42-44.

El Guindi, Fadwa. "Veiled Activism: Egyptian Women in the Contemporary Islamic Movement." *Mediterranean Peoples* 22/23 (1983): 78-89.

Eliraz, Giora. "Egyptian Intellectuals and Women's Emancipation, 1919-1939." *Asian and African Studies* 16, no. 1 (1982): 95-120.

Fensham, F. Charles. "Widow, Orphan, and the Poor in Ancient Near Eastern Legal and Wisdom Literature." *Journal of Near Eastern Studies* 221 (1962): 129-139.

Finkelstein, J. J. "Sex Offence in Sumerian Laws." *Journal of the American Oriental Society* 86 (1966): 355-372.

Giladi, Avner. "Some Observations on Infanticide in Medieval Muslim Society." *International Journal of Middle East Studies* 22 (May 1990): 185-200.

Haim, Sylvia G. "The Situation of Arab Women in the Mirror of Literature." *Middle Eastern Studies* 17, no. 4 (1981): 510-530.

Halila, Souad. "From Koranic Law to Civil Law: The Emancipation of Tunisian Women since 1956." *Feminist Issues* 4, no. 2 (1984): 23-44.

Hammam, Mona. "Women and Industrial Work in Egypt: The Chubra El-Kheima Case." *Arab Studies Quarterly* 2, no. 1 (1980): 50-69.

Hasna, Begum. "Mass Media and Women in Bangladesh." *South Asia* 9 (June 1986): 15-23.

Hatem, Mervat. "Egyptian Upper- and Middle-Class Women's Early Nationalist Discourses on National Liberation and Peace in Palestine (1922-1944)." *Women & Politics* 9, no. 3 (1989): 49-70.

-----. "Egypt's Middle Class in Crisis: The Sexual Division of Labor." *Middle East Journal* 42 (Summer 1988): 407-422.

-----. "The Enduring Alliance of Nationalism and Patriarchy in Muslim Personal Status Laws: The Case of Modern Egypt." *Feminist Issues* 6, no. 1 (1986): 19-43.

-----. "The Politics of Sexuality and Gender in Segregated Patriarchal Systems: The Case of Eighteenth- and Nineteenth-Century Egypt." *Feminist Studies* 12, no. 2 (Summer 1986): 251-274.

-----. "Through Each Other's Eyes: Egyptian, Levantine-Egyptian, and European Women's Images of Themselves and of Each Other (1862-1920)." *Women's Studies International Forum* 12, no. 2 (1989): 183-198.

Heggoy, Alf Andrew. "Algerian Women and the Right to Vote: Some Colonial Anomalies." *Muslim World* 64, no. 3 (1974): 228-235.

-----. "Cultural Disrespect: European and Algerian Views on Women in Colonial and Independent Algeria." *Muslim World* 62, no. 4 (1972): 323-335.

Heussler, Robert. "Imperial Lady: Gertrude Bell and the Middle East, 1889-1926." *The British Studies Monitor* 9 (Summer 1979): 3-22.

Hoffman-Ladd, Valerie. "Polemics on the Modesty and Segregation of Women in Contemporary Egypt." *International Journal of Middle East Studies* 19 (1987): 23-50.

Howard-Merriam, Kathleen. "Women, Education, and the Professions in Egypt." *Comparative Education Review* 23 (1979): 256-270.

Ilan, Tal. "Notes on the Distribution of Jewish Women's Names in Palestine in the Second Temple and Mishnaic Periods." *Journal of Jewish Studies* 40 (Autumn 1989): 186-200.

Jastrow, M. "Veiling in Ancient Assyria." *Revue Archeologique* 14 (1921): 209-238.

Jennings, Ronald C. "Women in the Early Seventeenth-Century Ottoman Judicial Records: The Sharia Court of Anatolian Kayseri." *Journal of the Economic and Social History of the Orient* 28 (1975): 53-114.

Kandiyoti, Deniz. "Emancipated but Unliberated? Reflections on the Turkish Case." *Feminist Studies* 13 (Summer 1987): 317-338.

-----. "Sex Roles and Social Change: A Comparative Study of Turkey's Women." *Signs* 3, no. 1 (1977): 57-73.

-----. "Slave Girls, Temptresses, and Comrades: Images of Women in the Turkish Novel." *Feminist Issues* 8, no. 1 (1988): 35-50.

Katz, David S. "Menasseh ben Israel's Mission to Queen Christina of Sweden, 1651-1655." *Jewish Social Studies* 45 (Winter 1983): 57-72.

Keddie, Nikki. "The Past and Present of Women in the Muslim World." *Journal of World History* 1 (Spring 1990): 77-108.

Kraemer, Ross S. "Monastic Jewish Women in Greco-Roman Egypt: Philo Judeaus on the Therapeutrides." *Signs* 14 (Winter 1989): 342-370.

Kuhnke, Laverne. "The 'Doctoress' on a Donkey: Women Health Officers in Nineteenth-Century Egypt." *Clio Medica* 9, no. 3 (1974): 193-205.

Lassner, J. "Why Did the Caliph al-Mansur Build ar-Rusafa?" *Journal of Near*

*Eastern Studies* 24 (1965): 95-99.

Lazreg, Marnia. "Feminism and Difference: The Perils of Writing as a Woman on Women in Algeria." *Feminist Studies* 14 (Spring 1988): 81-107.

-----. "Gender and Politics in Algeria: Unraveling the Religious Paradigm." *Signs* 15 (Summer 1990): 755-780.

Lerner, Gerda. "The Origin of Prostitution in Ancient Mesopotamia." *Signs* 11 (Winter 1986): 236-254.

Lutfi, Huda. "Al-Sakhawi's Kitab al-nisa' as a Source for the Social and Economic History of Muslim Women During the Fifteenth-Century A. D." *Muslim World* 71 (April 1981): 104-124.

-----. "A Study of Six Fourteenth Century Iqrars from al-Quds Relating to Muslim Women." *Journal of the Economic and Social History of the Orient* 26 (October 1983): 246-294.

Mahdavi, Shireen. "Women and Ideas in Qagar Iran." *Asian and African Studies* 9 (1985): 187-197.

-----. "Women and the Shii Ulama in Iran." *Middle Eastern Studies* 19, no. 1 (1983): 17-27.

Marcus, Abraham. "Men, Women and Property: Dealers in Real Estate in 18th Century Aleppo." *Journal of the Economic and Social History of the Orient* 26 (May 1983): 137-163.

Marshall, Susan E. "Politics and Female Status in North Africa: A Reconsideration of Development Theory." *Economic Development and Cultural Change* 32, no. 3 (1984): 499-524.

Meltzer, Edmund S. "Queens, Goddesses, and Other Women of Ancient Egypt." *Journal of the American Oriental Society* 110 (July/September 1990): 503-509.

Mernissi, Fatima. "Women and the Impact of Capitalist Devolopment in Morocco, Part I." *Feminist Issues* 2, no. 2 (1982): 69-104.

Moore, Andrew M. "The Development of Neolithic Societies in the Near East." *Advances in World Archaeology* 4 (1985): 1-68.

Mundy, Martha. "Women's Inheritance of Land in Highland Yemen." *Arabian Studies* 5 (1979): 161-187.

Nair, Janaki. "Uncovering the Zenana: Visions of Indian Womanhood in Englishwomen's Writings: 1813-1940." *Journal of Women's History* 2 (Spring 1990): 8-34.

Nelson, Cynthia. "Public and Private Politics: Women in the Middle Eastern World." *American Ethnologist* 1 (1974): 551-563.

-----. "The Voices of Doria Shafik: Feminist Consciousness in Egypt, 1940-1960." *Feminist Issues* 6, no. 2 (1986): 16-31.

Patai, Raphael. "Nomadism: Middle Eastern and Central Asian." *Southwestern Journal of Anthropology* 7 (1951): 401-414.

Peterson, J. E. "The Political Status of Women in the Arab Gulf States." *Middle East Journal* 43 (Winter 1989): 34-50.

Philipp, Thomas. "Women in the Historical Perspective of an Early Arab Modernist (Gurgi Zaidan)." *Welt des Islam* 18, no. 1/2 (1977): 65-83.

Pomeroy, Sarah B. "The Persian King and the Queen Bee." *American Journal of*

*Ancient History* 9, no. 2 (1984): 98-108.

Ramazani, Nesta. "Arab Women in the Gulf." *Middle East Journal* 39 (Spring 1985): 258-276.

-----. "Behind the Veil: Status of Women in Revolutionary Iran." *Journal of South Asia and Middle Eastern Studies* 4, no. 2 (1980): 27-36.

Rassam, Amal. "Women and Domestic Power in Morocco." *International Journal of Middle East Studies* 7, no. 2 (1980): 171-179.

Rorlich, Azade-Ayse. "The 'Sli Bayramov' Club, the Journal *Sharg Gadini* and the Socialization of Azeri Women: 1920-1930." *Central Asian Survey* 5 (1986): 221-239.

Roth, Martha T. "Age of Marriage and the Household: A Study of Neo-Babylonian and Neo-Assyrian Forms." *Comparative Studies in Society and History* [Great Britain] 29, no. 4 (1987): 715-747.

-----. "'She Will Die by the Iron Dagger': Adultery and Neo-Babylonian Marriage." *Journal of the Economic and Social History of the Orient* 31 (June 1988): 186-206.

Sayigh, Rosemary. "Roles and Functions of Arab Women." *Arab Studies Quarterly* 3, no. 3 (1981): 259-274.

Shahidian, Hammed. "The Education of Women in the Islamic Republic of Iran." *Journal of Women's History* 2 (Winter 1991): 6-38.

Shoaee, Rokhsareh S. "The Mujahid Women of Iran: Reconciling 'Culture' and 'Gender.'" *Middle East Journal* 41 (Autumn 1987): 519-537.

Smyke, Raymond J. "Fatima Massaquoi Fahnbulleh (1912-1978) Pioneer Woman Educator." *Liberian Studies Journal* 15, no. 1 (1990): 48-73.

Sprengling, M. "From Persian to Arabic." *American Journal of Semitic Languages* 55/56 (1938-39): 175-225.

Stone, Elizabeth C. "The Social Role of the Naditu Women in Old Babylon Nippur." *Journal of the Economic and Social History of the Orient* 25 (February 1982): 50-70.

Tavakolian, Bahram. "Women and the Socioeconomic Change Among Sheikhanzai Nomads of Western Afghanistan." *Middle East Journal* 38 (Summer 1984): 433-453.

Tucker, Judith. "Decline of the Family Economy in Mid-Nineteenth Century Egypt." *Arab Studies Quarterly* 1, no. 3 (1979): 245-271.

-----. "Problems in the Historiography of Women in the Middle East: The Case of Nineteenth Century Egypt." *International Journal of Middle East Studies* 15, no. 3 (1983): 321-336.

Waltz, Susan E. "Another View of Feminine Networks: Tunisian Women and the Development of Political Efficacy." *International Journal of Middle East Studies* 22 (February 1990): 21-36.

Wegner, Judith R. "The Status of Women in Jewish and Islamic Marriage and Divorce Law." *Harvard Women's Law Journal* 5 (Spring 1982): 1-34.

Weir, Shelagh. "Palestinian Costume." *British Museum Society Bulletin* no. 62 (Winter 1989): 34-40.

Westenholz, Joan Goodnick. "Towards a New Conceptualization of the Female

Role in Mesopotamian Society." *Journal of the American Oriental Society* 110 (July/September 1990): 510-522.

Youssef, Nadia Haggag. "Women and Agricultural Production in Muslim Societies." *Comparative International Development* 3, no. 1 (1977): 41-88.

## MILITARY/WAR

## Home Front

Abeele, Cynthia R. "'The Infant Soldier': The Great War and the Medical Campaign for Child Welfare." *Canadian Bulletin of Medical History/Bulletin canadien d'histoire de la medicine* 5 (Winter 1988): 99-119.

Anderson, George M. "The Civil War Courtship of Richard Mortimer Williams and Rose Anderson of Rockville." *Maryland Historical Magazine* 80 (Summer 1985): 119-138.

Arnston, Laurie. "Civil War Fictional Propaganda: Mary Anne Cruse's *Cameron Hall.*" *Southern Historian* 9 (Spring 1989): 66-77.

Bacevich, Andrew J., Jr. "Family Matters: American Civilian and Military Elites in the Progressive Era." *Armed Forces & Society* 8 (Spring 1982): 405-418.

Bartman, William J. "Korean War Brides, Prostitutes and Yellow Slavery." *Minerva: Quarterly Report on Women and the Military* 7 (Summer 1989): 16-25.

Beauchamp, Virginia Walcott. "Madge Preston's Private War." *Maryland Historical Magazine* 82 (Spring 1987): 69-81.

-----. "The Sisters and the Soldiers." *Maryland Historical Magazine* 81 (Summer 1986): 117-133.

Bland, Sue. "Henrietta the Homemaker and Rosie the Riveter: Images of Women in Advertising 1939-1950." *Atlantis* 8 (Spring 1983): 61-86.

Bloch, Ruth H. "The Gendered Meanings of Virtue in Revolutionary America." *Signs* 13 (Autumn 1987): 37-58.

Boak, H. L. "Our Last Hope: Women's Votes for Hitler, A Reappraisal." *German Studies Review* 12 (May 1989): 311-332.

Brandt, Gail Cuthbert. "'Pigeon-Holed and Forgotten': The Work of the Subcommittee on the Post-War Problems of Women, 1943." *Histoire sociale/Social History* 15 (May 1982): 239-259.

Breen, William J. "Black Women and the Great War: Mobilization and Reform in the South." *Journal of Southern History* 44 (August 1978): 421-440.

-----. "Southern Women in the War: The North Carolina Woman's Committee, 1917-1919." *North Carolina Historical Review* 55 (Summer 1978): 251-283.

Brown, William R. "The American Girl and the Christmas Tree: World War II Soldier Poets Look at What the G.I.s Were Fighting for." *Journal of American Culture* 7 (Summer 1985): 38-48.

Carroll, Rosemary F. "A Plantation Teacher's Perceptions of the Impending Crisis." *Southern Studies* 18 (Fall 1979): 339-350.

Champion, Elizabeth, ed. "The Home Front in America During the Great War:

The 1918 Correspondence of Florence Davenport Hollis (1849-1954)." Lee W. Formwalt, intro. *Journal of Southwest Georgia History* 5 (Fall 1987): 38-63.

Clark, James. "A Mother's Plea." *Civil War Times* (February 1985): 40-42.

Coalier, Paula. "Beyond Sympathy: The St. Louis Ladies' Union Aid Society and the Civil War." *Gateway Heritage* 11 (Summer 1990): 38-51.

Conner, Susan P. "Politics, Prostitution, and the Pox in Revolutionary Paris, 1789-1799." *Western Society for French History* 14 (November 1986): 183.

Conner, Valerie J. "'The Mothers of the Race' in World War I: The National War Labor Board and Women in Industry." *Labor History* 21, no. 1 (1980): 31-54.

Dahl, Kathleen. "The Political Activities of Women During the French Revolution." *Western Society for French History* 15 (November 1987): 129.

Dailey, Barbara Ritter. "The Visitation of Sarah Wight: Holy Carnival and the Revolution of the Saints in Civil War London." *Church History* 55 (December 1986): 438-455.

Darst, W. Maury, ed. "The Vicksburg Diary of Mrs. Alfred Ingraham (May 2-June 13, 1863)." *Journal of Mississippi History* 44 (May 1982): 148-179.

Davis, Curtis Carroll. "Mrs. Warner's Winter Warfare: A Memento of Arnold's Campaign." *Journal of the Lancaster County Historical Society* 84, no. 3 (1981): 125-129.

Desan, S. "The Role of Women in Religious Riots During the French Revolution." *Eighteenth-Century Studies* 22 (Spring 1989): 451-468.

Doneson, Judith E. "American History of Anne Frank's Diary." *Holocaust and Genocide Studies* [Great Britain] 2, no. 1 (1987): 149-160.

Dukes, Paul. "The Leslie Family in the Swedish Period (1630-5) of the Thirty Years' War." *European Studies Review* 12 (October 1982): 401-424.

Elder, Glen H. "Scarcity and Prosperity in Postwar Childbearing: Explorations from a Life Course Perspective." *Journal of Family History* 6 (Winter 1981): 410-433.

Endres, Kathleen L. "The Women's Press in the Civil War: A Portrait of Patriotism, Propaganda, and Prodding." *Civil War History* 30 (March 1984): 31-53.

Fallon, Charlotte. "The Civil War Hungerstrikes: Women and Men." *Eire-Ireland* 22 (Fall 1987): 75-91.

Fischer, LeRoy H., ed. "A Civil War Experience of Some Arkansas Women in Indian Territory." *Chronicles of Oklahoma* 57 (Summer 1979): 137-163.

Foote, Cheryl J. "'My Husband Was a Madman and a Murderer': Josephine Clifford McCrackin, Army Wife, Writer, and Conservationist." *New Mexico Historical Review* 65 (April 1990): 199-224.

Gallagher, Gary W. "A Widow and Her Soldier: LaSalle Corbell Pickett as Author of the George E. Pickett Letters." *Virginia Magazine of History and Biography* 94 (July 1986): 329-344.

Graham, Masako Nakagawa. "The Consort and the Warrior: *Yokihi Monogatari.*" *Monumenta Nipponica* 45 (Spring 1990): 1-26.

Gravois, Martha. "Military Families in Germany, 1946-1986: Why They Came and Why They Stay." *Parameters* 6 (Winter 1986): 57-67.

Greene, Dana. "Evelyn Underhill and Her Response to War." *Anglican and Episcopal History* 55 (June 1986): 127-136.

Gundersen, Joan R. "Independence, Citizenship, and the American Revolution." *Signs* 13 (Autumn 1987): 59-77.

Hales, Jean Gould. "'Co-Laborers in the Cause': Women in the Ante-bellum Nativist Movement." *Civil War History* 25 (June 1979): 119-138.

Hause, Steven C. "Women Who Rallied to the Tricolor: The Effects of World War I on the French Women's Suffrage Movement." *Western Society for French History* 6 (November 1978): 371-377.

Hirshfield, Claire. "Liberal Women's Organizations and the War Against the Boers, 1899-1902." *Albion* 14 (Spring 1982): 27-49.

Holland, Carolsue, and G. R. Garett. "The 'Skirt' of Nessus: Women and the German Opposition to Hitler." *International Journal of Women's Studies* 6 (September/October 1983): 363-381.

Holt, Daniel D. and Marilyn Irvin Holt. "'The Pleasures of Female Society' at Cantonment Leavenworth." *Kansas History* 8 (Spring 1985): 21-35.

Hoobler, James A. "The Civil War Diary of Louisa Brown Pearl." *Tennessee Historical Quarterly* 38 (Fall 1979): 308-321.

Hutchens, Rose. "You Must Remember This . . ." *Women & Environments* 12 (May/June 1990): 20-21.

Inglis, Ken. "Men, Women, and War Memorials: Anzac Australia." *Daedalus* 116 (Fall 1987): 35-60.

Jones, Anne Goodwyn. "Gender and the Great War: The Case of Faulkner and Porter." *Women's Studies* 13, no. 1, 2 (1986): 134-148.

Juncker, Clara. "Writing Herstory: Mary Chesnut's Civil War." *Southern Studies* 26 (Spring 1987): 18-27.

Kalisch, Philip A., and Beatrice J. Kalisch. "When Nurses Were National Heroines: Images of Nursing in American Film, 1942-1945." *Nursing Forum* 20, no. 1 (1981): 14-61.

Karolevitz, Robert F. "Life on the Home Front: South Dakota in World War II." *South Dakota History* 19 (Fall 1989): 392-423.

Kenney, Anne R. "'She Got to Berlin': Virginia Irwin, St. Louis Post-Dispatch War Correspondent." *Missouri Historical Review* 79 (July 1985): 456-479.

Kerber, Linda K. "'I Have Don . . . Much to Carrey on the Warr': Women and the Shaping of Republican Ideology after the American Revolution." *Journal of Women's History* 1 (Winter 1990): 231-243.

King, Lynda A. "The Woman Question and Politics in Austrian Interwar Literature." *German Studies Review* 6 (February 1983): 75-100.

Kleinbaum, Abby Wettan. "Amazon Dreams: Feminism and the Amazon Image." *Minerva: Quarterly Report on Women and the Military* 3 (Spring 1985): 95-106.

Laas, Virginia Jeans, ed. "Elizabeth Blair Lee: Union Counterpart of Mary Boykin Chesnut." *Journal of Southern History* 50 (August 1984): 385-406.

-----. "'On the Qui Vive for the Long Letter': Washington Letters from a Navy Wife, 1861." *Civil War History* 29 (March 1983): 28-52.

Lacey, Barbara E. "Women in the Era of the American Revolution: The Case of Norwich, Connecticut." *New England Quarterly* 53 (December 1980): 527-543.

Lady, Claudia Lynn. "Five Tri-State Women During the Civil War: Day-to-Day Life." *West Virginia History* 43 (Spring 1982): 189-226.

-----. "Five Tri-State Women During the Civil War: Views on the War." *West Virginia History* 43 (Summer 1982): 303-321.

Leslie, James W., ed. "Arabella Lanktree Wilson's Civil War Letter." *Arkansas Historical Quarterly* 47 (Autumn 1988): 257-272.

Lewis, Jane. "The Ideology and Politics of Birth Control in Inter-war England." *Women's Studies* 2, no. 1 (1979): 33-48.

Litoff, Judy Barrett, and David C. Smith. "Since You Went Away: The World War II Letters of Barbara Woodall Taylor." *Women's Studies* 17, no. 3-4 (1990): 249-276.

Litoff, Judy Barrett, David C. Smith, and Martha Swain. "'Dear Boys': The Wartime Letters of Mrs. Keith Frazier Somerville, 1943-1945." *Journal of Mississippi History* 52 (May 1990): 77-94.

Mabee, Carleton. "Margaret Mead and Behavioral Scientists in World War II: Problems in Responsibility, Truth, and Effectiveness." *Journal of the History of the Behavioral Sciences* 23 (January 1987): 3-13.

Mackin, Sister Aloysius. "Wartime Scenes from Convent Windows: St. Cecilia, 1860-1865." *Tennessee Historical Quarterly* 39 (Winter 1980): 401-422.

Manion, Richard L., ed. "The Civil War Homefront in Seneca County: Two Letters of Sophia Clark Dunn." *Northwest Ohio Quarterly* 62 (Winter/Spring 1990): 11-16.

Manley, Kathleen B. "Women of Los Alamos During World War II: Some of Their Views." *New Mexico Historical Review* 65 (April 1990): 251-266.

Martin, Dorris B. "A Congressional Wife in Wartime Washington." *Palimpsest* 64 (March/April 1983): 34-44.

Matsumoto, Valerie. "Japanese American Women During World War II." *Frontiers* 8, no. 1 (1984): 6-14.

Mayberry, Virginia. "Draftee's Wife: A Memoir of World War II." *Indiana Magazine of History* 79 (December 1983): 305-329.

McArthur, Judith N. "From Rosie the Riveter to the Feminine Mystique: An Historiographical Survey of American Women and World War II." *Bulletin of Bibliography* 44 (March 1987): 10-18.

Moneyhon, Carl H., ed. "Life in Confederate Arkansas: The Diary of Virginia Davis Gray, 1863-1865, Part I." *Arkansas Historical Quarterly* 42 (Spring 1983): 47-85.

-----. "Life in Confederate Arkansas: The Diary of Virginia Davis Gray, 1863-1866, Part II." *Arkansas Historical Quarterly* 42 (Spring 1983): 134-169.

Myres, Sandra L. "Army Women's Narratives as Documents of Social History: Some Examples from the Western Frontier, 1840-1900." *New Mexico Historical Review* 65 (April 1990): 175-198.

-----. "Romance and Reality on the American Frontier: View of Army Wives." *Western Historical Quarterly* 13 (October 1982): 409-428.

Nelson, James. "'My Dear Son': Letters to a Civil War Soldier." *Filson Club History Quarterly* 56 (April 1982): 151-169.

Offen, Karen. "Women's Memory, Women's History, Women's Political Action: The French Revolution in Retrospect, 1789-1889-1989." *Journal of Women's History* 1 (Winter 1990): 211-230.

Pavalko, Eliza K., and Glen H. Elder, Jr. "World War II and Divorce: A Life-Course Perspective." *American Journal of Sociology* 95 (March 1990): 1213-1234.

Pedersen, Susan. "Gender, Welfare, and Citizenship in Britain during the Great War." *American Historical Review* 95 (Ocotber 1990): 983-1006.

Roden, Donald. "From Old Miss to New Professional: A Portrait of Women Educators Under the American Occupation of Japan 1945-1952." *History of Education Quarterly* 23 (Winter 1983): 469-489.

Ross, Ellen. "Women's Neighborhood Sharing in London before World War One." *History Workshop* 15 (Spring 1983): 4-27.

Ruckman, Jo Ann. "'Knit, Knit, and Then Knit': The Women of Pocatello and the War Effort of 1917-1918." *Idaho Yesterdays* 26 (Spring 1982): 26-36.

Smith, C. Calvin. "Diluting an Institution: The Social Impact of World War II on the Arkansas Family." *Arkansas Historical Quarterly* 39 (Spring 1980): 21-34.

Summerfield, Penelope. "Women, Work, and Welfare: A Study of Child Care and Shopping in Britain in the Second World War." *Journal of Social History* 17 (Winter 1983): 249-270.

Tiesheng, Rong. "The Women's Movement in China Before and After the 1911 Revolution." *Chinese Studies in History* 16 (Spring/Summer 1983): 159-200.

Vaughan, Mary Kay. "Women School Teachers in the Mexican Revolution: The Story of Reyna's Braids." *Journal of Women's History* 2 (Spring 1990): 143-168.

Wales, Martha Gray. "When I Was a Little Girl: Things I Remember From Living at Frontier Military Posts." Willard B. Pope, ed. *North Dakota History* 50 (Spring 1983): 12-22.

Westbrook, Robert B. "'I Want a Girl, Just Like the Girl That Married Harry James': American Women and the Problem of Political Obligation in World War II." *American Quarterly* 42 (December 1990): 587-614.

White, Luise. "Prostitution, Identity and Class Consciousness in Nairobi During World War II." *Signs* 11 (Winter 1986): 255-273.

Williams, Emma Inman, ed. "Hettie Wisdom Tapp's Memoirs (Civil War)." *West Tenneesse History Society Papers* 36 (1982): 117-123.

Willmot, Louise. "The Debate on the Introduction of an Auxiliary Military Service Law for Women in the Third Reich and Its Consequences, August 1944-April 1945." *German History* no. 2 (Summer 1985): 10-20.

Wister, Fanny Kemble. "Sarah Butler Wister's Civil War Diary." *Pennsylvania Magazine of History and Biography* 102 (July 1978): 271-327.

# Jobs

Anderson, Karen T. "Last Hired, First Fired: Black Women Workers During World War II." *Journal of American History* 69 (June 1982): 86-97.

-----. "Teaching About Rosie the Riveter: The Role of Women During World War II." *OAH Magazine of History* 3 (Summer/Fall 1988): 35-37.

Carruthers, Susan L. "'Manning the Factories': Propaganda and Policy on the Employment of Women, 1939-1947." *History* 75 (June 1990): 232-256.

Clive, Alan. "Women Workers in World War II: Michigan as a Test Case." *Labor History* 20 (Winter 1979): 44-72.

Conner, Valerie J. "'The Mothers of the Race' in World War I: The National War Labor Board and Women in Industry." *Labor History* 21, no. 1 (1980): 31-54.

Croucher, Richard. "Women and Militancy in the Munitions Industries 1935-45." *Society for the Study of Labour History* 38 (Spring 1979): 8-9.

Davis, Lynne. "Minding Children or Minding Machines . . . Women's Labour and Child Care During World War II." *Labour History* 53 (November 1987): 85-98.

Forestell, Diane G. "The Necessity of Sacrifice for the Nation at War: Women's Labour Force Participation, 1939-1946." *Histoire sociale/Social History* 22 (November 1989): 333-348.

Gabin, Nancy. "Women Workers and the UAW in the Post-World War II Period: 1945-1954." *Labor History* 21 (Winter 1979/80): 5-30.

Gluck, Sherna Berger. "Interlude or Change: Women and the World War II Work Experience: A Feminist Oral History." *International Journal of Oral History* 3 (June 1982): 92-113.

Henry, Susan. "Work, Widowhood and War: Hannah Bunce Watson, Connecticut Printer." *Connecticut Historical Society Bulletin* 48 (Winter 1983): 25-39.

Hirshfield, Deborah Scott. "Women Shipyard Workers in the Second World War." *International History Review* 11 (August 1989): 478-485.

Honey, Maureen. "Recruiting Women for War Work: OWI and the Magazine Industry During World War II." *Journal of American Culture* 3 (Spring 1980): 47-52.

Johnson, Penelope. "Gender, Class and Work: The Council of Action for Equal Pay and the Equal Pay Campaign in Australia During World War II." *Labour History* 50 (May 1986): 132-146.

Keene, Judith. "A Spanish Springtime: Arleen Palmer and the Spanish Civil War." *Labour History* 52 (May 1987): 75-87.

Mack, Phyllis. "Women as Prophets During the English Civil War." *Feminist Studies* 8 (Spring 1982): 19-46.

Milkman, Ruth. "Redefining 'Women's Work': The Sexual Division of Labor in the Auto Industry During World War II." *Feminist Studies* 8 (Summer 1982): 337-372.

Montgomerie, Deborah. "Men's Jobs and Women's Work: The New Zealand Women's Land Service in World War II." *Agricultural History* 63 (Summer 1989): 1-14.

More, Ellen S. "A Certain Restless Ambition: Women Physicians and World War I." *American Quarterly* 41 (December 1989): 636-660.

Nash, Michael. "Women and the Pennsylvania Railroad: The World War II Years." *Labor History* 30 (Autumn 1989): 608-621.

Reekie, Gail. "Industrial Action by Women Workers in Western Australia During World War II." *Labour History* 49 (November 1985): 75-82.

Riley, Denise. "The Free Mothers: Protonationalism and Working Class Mothers in Industry at the End of the Last War in Britain." *History Workshop* 11 (Spring 1981): 59-119.

Sabin, Linda E. "The French Revolution: A Forgotten Era in Nursing History." *Nursing Forum* 20, no.3 (1981): 224-243.

Schweitzer, Mary M. "World War II and Female Labor Force Participation Rates." *Journal of Economic History* 40 (March 1980): 89-95.

Smillie, Christine. "The Invisible Workforce: Women Workers in Saskatchewan from 1905 to World War II." *Saskatchewan History* 34 (Summer 1986): 62-78.

Smith, Harold L. "The Womanpower Problem in Britain During the Second World War." *The Historical Journal* 27 (December 1984): 925-946.

Stephenson, Jill. "Women's Labor Service in Nazi Germany." *Central European History* 15 (September 1982): 241-265.

Sullivan, Jean, and Susan Allen. "'An Odd Lot? Self-Help, Women, and War.'" *Labour History* 41 (November 1981): 118-131.

Thomas, Mary Martha. "Rosie the Alabama Riveter." *Alabama Review* 39 (July 1986): 196-212.

## Peace Activism

Abrams, Irwin. "Bertha von Suttner (1845-1914): Bibliographic Notes." *Peace & Change* 16 (January 1991): 64-73.

Alonso, Harriet Hyman. "Jeannette Rankin and the Women's Peace Union." *Montana* 29 (Spring 1989): 34-49.

-----. "Suffragists for Peace during the Interwar Years, 1919-1941." *Peace & Change* 14 (July 1989): 243-262.

Arrington, Leonard J. "Modern Lysistratas: Mormon Women in the International Peace Movement, 1899-1939." *Journal of Mormon History* 15 (1989): 89-104.

Braker, Regina. "Bertha van Suttner as Author: The Harriet Beecher Stowe of the Peace Movement." *Peace & Change* 16 (January 1991): 74-96.

Brooks, Juanita, and Janet G. Butler, eds. "Utah's Peace Advocate, the 'Mormona': Elise Furer Musser." *Utah Historical Quarterly* 46 (Spring 1978): 151-166.

Brown, Freda. "Towards the World Assembly for Peace and Life--The Noble Mission of Ael Women." *World Marxist Review* 26, no. 3 (1983): 23-27.

Carroll, Berenice A. "The Outsiders: Comments on Fukuda Hideko, Catherine

Marshall and Dorothy Detzer." *Peace and Change* 4 (Fall 1977): 23-26.

Cooper, Matthew. "Living Together: How Communal Were the Children of Peace?" *Ontario History* 79 (March 1987): 3-17.

Cooper, Sandi. "The Work of Women in Nineteenth Century Continental European Peace Movements." *Peace and Change* 9 (Winter 1984): 11-28.

Costin, Lela. "Feminism, Pacifism, Internationalism and the 1915 International Congress of Women." *Women's Studies* 5, no. 3/4 (1982): 301-316.

Craig, John M. "Redbaiting, Pacifism, and Free Speech: Lucia Ames Mead and Her 1926 Lecture Tour in Atlanta and the Southeast." *Georgia Historical Quarterly* 71 (Winter 1987): 601-622.

Crangle, John V., and Joseph O. Baylen. "Emily Hobhousen's Peace Mission, 1916." *Journal of Contemporary History* 14 (October 1979): 731-743.

Crowley, Terry. "Ada Mary Brown Courtice: Pacifist, Feminist and Educational Reformer in Early Twentieth Century Canada." *Studies in History and Politics* 1 (Fall 1980): 76-114.

Curti, Merle. "Reflections on the Genesis and Growth of Peace History." *Peace and Change* 11 (Spring 1985): 1-18.

Early, Frances H. "Feminism, Peace, and Civil Liberties: Women's Role in the Origins of the World War I Civil Liberties Movement." *Women's Studies* 18, no. 2/3 (1990): 155-176.

Fieseler, Beate and Ulrike Lodwig. "Women and the Peace Movement in the Federal Republic of Germany." *Frontiers* 8, no. 2 (1985): 59-64.

Gordon, Linda. "The Peaceful Sex? On Feminism and the Peace Movement." *NWSA Journal* 2 (Autumn 1990): 624-634.

Gray, John S. "The Story of Mrs. Picotte-Galpin, a Sioux Heroine: Eagle Woman Becomes a Trader and Counsels for Peace, 1868-1888." *Montana* 36 (Summer 1986): 2-21.

Habibuddin, S. M. "A Comparative Appraisal of the Role of Indian Feminists in the Peace Movement Between Two World Wars." *Quarterly Review of Historical Studies* [Calcutta] 23 (April/June 1983): 44-53.

Hanley, Marla Martin. "The Children's Crusade of 1922: Katie O'Hare and the Campaign to Free Radical War Dissenters in the Era of America's First Red Scare." *Gateway Heritage* 10 (Summer 1989): 34-43.

Hatem, Mervat. "Egyptian Upper- and Middle-Class Women's Early Nationalist Discourses on National Liberation and Peace in Palestine (1922-1944)." *Women & Politics* 9, no. 3 (1989): 49-70.

Henle, Ellen Langenheim. "Clara Barton, Soldier or Pacifist?" *Civil War History* 24 (June 1978): 152-160.

Hoff-Wilson, Joan. "'Peace Is a Woman's Job . . .'--Jeanette Rankin and American Foreign Policy: Her Lifework as a Pacifist." *Montana* 30 (Spring 1980): 38-53.

-----. "'Peace Is a Woman's Job . . .': Jeannette Rankin and American Foreign Policy: The Origins of Her Pacifism." *Montana* 30 (Winter 1980): 28-41.

Jensen, Joan M. "When Women Worked: Helen Marston and the California Peace Movement, 1915-1945." *California History* 67 (June 1988): 118-131.

McDonagh, Celia. "The Women's Peace Movement in Britain." *Frontiers* 8, no. 2 (1985): 53-58.

Mackie, Vera. "Motherhood and Pacifism in Japan, 1900-1937." *Hecate* 14 (Winter 1989): 28-49.

Maga, Timothy. "Humanism and Peace: Eleanor Roosevelt's Mission to the Pacific, August-September, 1943." *Maryland Historian* 19 (Fall/Winter 1988): 33-47.

Mellown, Muriel. "One Woman's Way to Peace: The Development of Vera Brittain's Pacifism." *Frontiers* 8, no. 2 (1985): 1-6.

Newberry, Jo Vellacott. "Women and War in England: The Case of Catherine E. Marshall and World War I." *Peace and Change* 4 (Fall 1977): 13-17

Perry, Elizabeth Israels. "Industrial Reform in New York City: Belle Moskowitz and the Protocol of Peace, 1913-1916." *Labor History* 23 (Winter 1982): 5-31.

Pois, Anne Marie. "The U.S. Women's International League for Peace and Freedom and American Neutrality, 1935-1939." *Peace & Change* 14 (July 1989): 263-284.

Rainbolt, Rosemary. "Women and War in the United States: The Case of Dorothy Detzer, National Secretary Women's International League for Peace and Freedom." *Peace and Change* 4 (Fall 1977): 18-22.

Roberts, Nancy L. "Journalism and Activism: Dorothy Day's Response to the Cold War." *Peace and Change* 12, no. 1/2 (1987): 13-28.

Sager, E. W. "The Social Origins of Victorian Pacifism." *Victorian Studies* 23 (1980): 211-236.

Schott, Linda. "The Woman's Peace Party and the Moral Basis for Women's Pacifism." *Frontiers* 8, no. 2 (1985): 18-24.

Sowerwine, Charles. "Women Against the War: A Feminine Basis for Internationalism and Pacifism?" *Western Society for French History* 6 (November 1978): 361-370.

Stevenson, Janet. "Lola Maverick Lloyd: 'I Must Do Something for Peace.'" *Chicago History* 9, no. 1 (1980): 47-57.

Swerdlow, Amy. "Ladies Day at the Capitol: Women Strike for Peace versus HUAC." *Feminist Studies* 8 (Fall 1982): 493-520.

Takenaka, Chiharu. "Peace, Democracy and Women in Postwar Japan." *Peace and Change* 12, no. 3/4 (1987): 69-78.

Ushioda, Sharlie Conroy. "Women and War in Meiji Japan: The Case of Fukuda Hideko (1865-1927)." *Peace and Change* 4 (Fall 1977): 9-12.

Zeiger, S. "Finding a Cure for War: Women's Politics and the Peace Movement in the 1920s." *Journal of Social History* 24 (Autumn 1990): 69-86.

## War Service

Abed, Ali J. "An Army Career: 1945-1968: An Interview with Major Edith N. Straw, USA (Ret)." *Minerva: Quarterly Report on Women and the Military* 3 (Fall 1985): 95-126.

Akers, Regina T. "Female Naval Reservists During World War II: A

Historiographical Essay." *Minerva: Quarterly Report on Women and the Military* 8 (Summer 1990): 55-61.

Allen, Ann. "The News Media and the Women's Army Auxiliary Corps: Protagonists for a Cause." *Military Affairs* 50 (April 1986): 77-83.

Allen, Margaret. "The Domestic Ideal and the Mobilization of Womanpower in World War II." *Women's Studies* 6, no. 4 (1983): 401-412.

Alsmeyer, Marie Bennett. "A Preliminary Survey of Literature about World War II Women in the Navy." *Minerva: Quarterly Report on Women and the Military* 1 (Winter 1983): 71-76.

Ambrose, Stephen E. "Sidesaddle Soldier: Libbie Custer's Partnership in Glory." *Timeline* 3 (April/May 1986): 3-12.

Attebury, Mary Ann. "Women and Their Wartime Roles." *Minerva: Quarterly Report on Women and the Military* 8 (Spring 1990): 11-28.

Berube, Allan, and John D'Emilio. "The Military and Lesbians During the McCarthy Years." *Signs* 9 (Summer 1984): 759-775.

Boas, Jacob. "Etty Hillesum: From Amsterdam to Auschwitz." *Lilith* no. 23 (Spring 1989): 24-32.

Bombard, Charles F., Wynona M. Bice-Stephens, and Karen L. Ferguson. "The Soldiers' Nurse: Colonel Florence A. Blanchfield." *Minerva: Quarterly Report on Women and the Military* 6 (Winter 1988): 43-50.

Brown, Sharon A. "Recovering the History of Western Military Women." *Minerva: Quarterly Report on Women and the Military* 2 (Spring 1984): 83-97.

Buffalohead, Priscilla K. "Farmers, Warriors, Traders: A Fresh Look at Ojibway Women." *Minnesota History* 48 (Summer 1983): 236-244.

Bynum, Victoria. "'War Within a War': Women's Participation in the Revolt of the North Carolina Piedmont, 1863-1865." *Frontiers* 9, no. 3 (1987): 43-49.

Campbell, D'Ann. "Servicewomen of World War II." *Armed Forces & Society* 16 (Winter 1990): 251-270.

Christides, Michelle A. "Women Veterans of the Great War: Oral Histories." *Minerva: Quarterly Report on Women and the Military* 3 (Summer 1985): 103-127.

Clements, Barbara Evans. "Working-Class and Peasant Women in the Russian Revolution, 1917-1923." *Signs* 8 (Winter 1982): 215-235.

Cottam, K. Jean. "Soviet Women in Combat in World War II: The Ground Forces and the Navy." *International Journal of Women's Studies* 3 (July/August 1980): 345-357.

-----. "Soviet Women in Combat in World War II: The Rear Services, Resistance Behind Enemy Lines and Political Workers." *International Journal of Women's Studies* 5 (September/October 1982): 363-378.

Davis, Curtis Carroll. "A 'Gallantress' Gets Her Due: The Earliest Published Notice of Deborah Sampson." *Proceedings of the American Antiquarian Society* 91 (October 21, 1981): 319-323.

De Pauw, Linda Grant. "Women in Combat: The Revolutionary War Experience." *Armed Forces & Society* 7 (Winter 1980): 209-226.

Dekker, Rudolf M., and Lotte C. van de Pol. "Republican Heroines:

Cross-Dressing Women in the French Revolutionary Armies." *History of European Ideas* 10, no. 3 (1989): 353-364.

Dengler, Brenda. "Acceptance and Avoidance: The Woman Vietnam Vet." *Minerva: Quarterly Report on Women and the Military* 5 (Summer 1987): 72-96.

Duke, David C. "Spy Scares, Scapegoats, and the Cold War." *South Atlantic Quarterly* 79 (Summer 1980): 245-278.

Dunn, Joe P. "Women and The Vietnam War: A Bibliographic Review." *Journal of American Culture* 12 (Spring 1989): 79-86.

Eads, Valerie. "The Campaigns of Matilda of Tuscany." *Minerva: Quarterly Report on Women and the Military* 4 (Spring 1986): 167-181.

Edwards, John C. "Atlanta's Prodigal Daughter: The Turbulent Life of Jane Anderson (1893-1942) as Expatriate and Nazi Propagandist." *Atlanta History Journal* 28 (Summer 1984): 23-41.

Emo, Dretha M., Sharon Hall, and Darlene Kern. "1964: Vietnam and Army Nursing." *Minerva: Quarterly Report on Women and the Military* 8 (Spring 1990): 49-67.

Enloe, Cynthia, and Harold Jordan. "Black Women in the Military." *Minerva: Quarterly Report on Women and the Military* 3 (Winter 1985): 108-116.

Frank, Mary E. V. "Army and Navy Nurses Held as Prisoners of War During World War II." *Minerva: Quarterly Report on Women and the Military* 6 (Summer 1988): 82-90.

Frankel, Noralee. "The Southern Side of 'Glory': Mississippi African-American Women During the Civil War." *Minerva: Quarterly Report on Women and the Military* 8 (Fall 1990): 28-37.

Ganson, Barbara J. "Following Their Children into Battle: Women at War in Paraguay, 1864-1870." *The Americas* 46 (January 1990): 335-372.

Godfrey, Audrey M. "Housewives, Hussies, and Heroines, or the Women of Johnston's Army." *Utah Historical Quarterly* 54 (Spring 1986): 157-178.

Goodson, Susan H. "Capt. Joy Bright Hancock and the Role of Women in the U.S. Navy." *New Jersey History* 105 (Spring/Summer 1987): 1-18.

Green, Anne Bosanko. "Private Bosanko Goes to Basic: A Minnesota Woman in World War II." *Minnesota History* 51 (Fall 1989): 246-258.

Greene, Rebecca S. "The United States: Women in World War II." *Trends in History* 2 (Winter 1981).

Griesse, Anne Eliot, and L. CDR. Margaret A. Harlow, U.S.N. "Soldiers of Happenstance: Women in Soviet Uniform." *Minerva: Quarterly Report on Women and the Military* 3 (Fall 1985): 127-151.

Hacker, Barton C. "Where Have all The Women Gone? The Pre-Twentieth Century Sexual Division of Labor in Armies." *Minerva: Quarterly Report on Women and the Military* 3 (Spring 1985): 107-148.

-----. "Women and Military Institutions in Early Modern Europe: A Reconnaissance." *Signs* 6 (Summer 1981): 643-671.

Hamand, Wendy F. "'No Voice From England': Mrs. Stowe, Mr. Lincoln, and the British in the Civil War." *New England Quarterly* 61, no. 1 (1988): 3-24.

Hart, Janet C. "Redeeming the Voices of a 'Sacrificed Generation': Oral Histories of Women in the Greek Resistance." *International Journal of Oral History* 10 (February 1989): 3-30.

Hedin, Barbara A. "Through a Glass Darkly: Vietnam, Alienation, and Passion." *Minerva: Quarterly Report on Women and the Military* 6 (Winter 1988): 51-68.

Henle, Ellen Langenheim. "Clara Barton, Soldier or Pacifist?" *Civil War History* 24 (June 1978): 152-160.

Hills, Patricia. "Eastman Johnson's 'The Field Hospital,' the U.S. Sanitary Commission, and Women in the Civil War." *The Minneapolis Institute of Arts Bulletin* 65 (1981/82): 66-81.

Hine, Darlene Clark. "The Call That Never Came: Black Women Nurses and World War I, An Historical Note." *Indiana Military History Journal* 15 (January 1983): 23-27.

Hooker, Richard D., Jr. "Affirmative Action and Combat Exclusion: Gender Roles in the U.S. Army." *Parameters* 19 (December 1989): 36-50.

Hopkins, Counce. "Pauline Cushman: Actress in the Theatre of War." *American History Illustrated* 19, no. 9 (1985): 20-21.

Horn, Michiel. "More Than Cigarettes, Sex, and Chocolate: The Canadian Army in the Netherlands, 1944-1945." *Journal of Canadian Studies/Revue d'études canadiennes* 16 (Fall/Winter 1981): 156-173.

Hunter, Edna J., Sharon J. Rose, and J. Bradley Hamlin. "Women in the Military: An Annotated Bibliography." *Armed Forces & Society* 4 (Summer 1978): 695-716.

Johnson, Richard. "The Role of Women in the Russian Civil War, 1917-1921." *Conflict* 2, no. 2 (1980): 201-217.

Kalisch, Philip A., and Margaret Scobey. "Female Nurses in American Wars: Helplessness Suspended for the Duration." *Armed Forces & Society* 9 (Winter 1983): 215-244.

Kapur, Ashok. "Indian Security and Defense Policies under Indira Gandhi." *Journal of Asian and African Studies* 22 (July/October 1987): 175-192.

Kaufman, Janet E. "Under the Petticoat Flag: Women in the Confederate Army." *Southern Studies* 23 (Winter 1984): 363-375.

Knight, Amy. "Female Terrorists in the Russian Socialist Revolutionary Party." *The Russian Review* 38 (April 1979): 139-159.

Lamerson, C. D. "The Evolution of a Mixed-Gender Canadian Forces." *Minerva: Quarterly Report on Women and the Military* 7 (Fall/Winter 1989): 19-24.

Larson, C. Kay. "Bonny Yank and Ginny Reb." *Minerva: Quarterly Report on Women and the Military* 8 (Spring 1990): 33-48.

Leonard, Patrick L. "Deborah Sampson: Official Heroine of the State of Massachusetts." *Minerva: Quarterly Report on Women and the Military* 6 (Fall 1988): 61-66.

Macias, Ana. "Women and the Mexican Revolution: 1910-1920." *Americas* 37 (July 1980): 53-81.

Malcomsom, Robert. "Three British Women and the Battle of Lake Erie." *Inland Seas* 46 (Spring 1990): 11-17.

Martin, Michel L. "From Periphery to Center: Women in the French Military." *Armed Forces & Society* 8 (Winter 1982): 303-333.

Mathes, Valerie Sherer. "Native American Women in Medicine and the Military." *Journal of the West* 21 (April 1982): 41-48.

McGlashan, Zena Beth. "Women Witness the Russian Revolution: Analyzing Ways of Seeing." *Journalism History* 12 (Summer 1985): 54-61.

McKenney, Jancie E. "'Women in Combat': Comment." *Armed Forces & Society* 8 (Summer 1982): 686-692.

McLaughlin, Megan. "The Woman Warrior: Gender, Warfare and Society in Medieval Europe." *Women's Studies* 17, no. 3/4 (1990): 193-210.

Miller, Barbara Ann. "Women and Revolution: The Brigadas Femeninas and the Mexican Cristero Rebellion, 1926-1929." *Journal of Third World Studies* 15 (March 1981): 57-66.

Moore, Brenda L. "Black, Female and in Uniform: An African-American Woman in the United States Army 1973-1979." *Minerva: Quarterly Report on Women and the Military* 8 (Summer 1990): 62-66.

Moore, Margaret L. "Memories of a Woman Marine (1950-1957): An Oral History." *Minerva: Quarterly Report on Women and the Military* 3 (Summer 1985): 128-137.

Murphy, Miriam B. "'If Only I Shall Have the Right Stuff': Utah Women in World War I." *Utah Historical Quarterly* 58 (Fall 1990): 334-350.

Nau, Erika S. "The Spirit of Molly Marine." *Minerva: Quarterly Report on Women and the Military* 8 (Winter 1990): 23-29.

Newman, Debra L. "The Propaganda and the Truth: Black Women and World War II." *Minerva: Quarterly Report on Women and the Military* 4 (Winter 1986): 72-92.

Paquette, Patricia. "A Bandage in One Hand and a Bible in the Other: The Story of Captain Sally L. Tompkins." *Minerva: Quarterly Report on Women and the Military* 8 (Summer 1990): 47-54.

Perez, Julia. "'Be All That You Can Be': The 1958 Army." *Minerva: Quarterly Report on Women and the Military* 4 (Spring 1986): 157-166.

Peterson, Susan C., and Beverly Jensen. "The Red Cross Call to Serve: The Western Response from North Dakota Nurses." *Western Historical Quarterly* 21 (August 1990): 321-340.

Pierson, Ruth Roach. "Canadian Women and Canadian Mobilization During the Second World War." *Revue Internationale d'Histoire Militaire* 51 (1982): 181-207.

Polasky, Janet. "Women in Revolutionary Belgium: From Stone Throwers to Hearth Tenders." *History Workshop* 21 (Spring 1986): 87-104.

Pollard, Clarice F. "WAACs in Texas During the Second World War." *Southwestern Historical Quarterly* 93 (July 1989): 61-74.

Reeves, Connie L. "The Story of 'Yashika': Commander of the Russian Women's Battalion of Death." *Minerva: Quarterly Report on Women and the Military* 6 (Fall 1988): 67-73.

Rosenhaft, Eve. "Inside the Third Reich: What Is the Woman's Story." *Radical*

*History Review* 43 (Winter 1989): 72-80.

Rupp, Leila J. "Women, Class and Mobilization in Nazi Germany." *Science and Society* 43 (Spring 1979): 51-69.

Samuelson, Nancy B. "Employment of Female Spies in the American Civil War." *Minerva: Quarterly Report on Women and the Military* 7 (Fall/Winter 1989): 57-66.

-----. "The Fate Worse Than Death: Women Captives of the Indian Wars." *Minerva: Quarterly Report on Women and the Military* 3 (Winter 1985): 117-137.

-----. "Mother Bickerdyke: She Outranked Everybody but God." *Minerva: Quarterly Report on Women and the Military* 5 (Summer 1987): 11-25.

-----. "Revolutionary War Women and the Second Oldest Profession." *Minerva: Quarterly Report on Women and the Military* 7 (Summer 1989): 51-68.

Schulz, Constance B. "Daughters of Liberty: The History of Women in the Revolutionary War Pension Records." *Prologue* 16 (Fall 1984): 139-153.

Schwantes, Carlos A. "Western Women in Coxey's Army in 1894." *Arizona and the West* 26 (Spring 1984): 5-20.

Schwoerner, Lois G. "Women and the Glorious Revolution." *Albion* 18 (Summer 1986): 195-218.

Seigel, Peggy Brase. "She Went to War: Indiana Women Nurses in the Civil War." *Indiana Magazine of History* 86 (March 1990): 1-27.

Shermann, Janann. "'They Either Need These Women or They Do Not': Margaret Chase Smith and the Fight for Regular Status for Women in the Military." *Journal of Military History* 54 (January 1990): 47-78.

Smith, Nina B. "Men and Authority: The Union Army Nurse and the Problem of Power." *Minerva: Quarterly Report on Women and the Military* 6 (Winter 1988): 25-42.

Spelts, Doreen. "The Women Who Died in Vietnam." *Minerva: Quarterly Report on Women and the Military* 3 (Winter 1985): 89-96.

Speranskaya, E. "Christian Women in the Great Patriotic War." *Journal of the Moscow Patriarchate* no. 5 (1985): 44-46.

Stewart, Miller J. "Army Laundresses: Ladies of the 'Soap Suds Row.'" *Nebraska History* 61 (Winter 1980): 421-436.

Stoddard, Eleanor, interviewer. "One Woman's War: The Story of Joan Campbell, Member of the Women's Army Corps, World War II." *Minerva: Quarterly Report on Women and the Military* 4 (Summer 1986): 133-175.

-----. "One Woman's War: The Story of Joan Campbell, Member of the Women's Army Corps, World War II." *Minerva: Quarterly Report on Women and the Military* 4 (Spring 1986): 122-156.

-----. "Shore Duty: The Story of Frances Prindle Taft, Officer in the WAVES, World War II." *Minerva: Quarterly Report on Women and the Military* 5 (Spring 1987): 88-125.

Summers, Anne. "Pride & Prejudice: Ladies and Nurses in the Crimean War." *History Workshop* 16 (Autumn 1983): 33-56.

Tanner, Doris Brinker. "Cornelia Fort: A WASP in World War II, Part I."

*Tennessee Historical Quarterly* 40 (Winter 1981): 381-394.

-----. "Cornelia Fort: A WASP in World War II, Part II." *Tennessee Historical Quarterly* 41 (Spring 1982): 67-80.

Treadway, Sandra Gioia. "Anna Maria Lane: An Uncommon Common Soldier of the American Revolution." *Virginia Cavalcade* 37 (Winter 1988): 134-147.

Treeger, Karen. "No Supplies, No Benefits, but Earned Respect: The Dieticians of World War I." *Minerva: Quarterly Report on Women and the Military* 4 (Winter 1986): 93-104.

Tuten, Jeff M. "Women in Military Service." *Armed Forces & Society* 8 (Fall 1981): 160-163.

Willard, Charity Cannon. "Early Images of the Female Warrior: Minerva, the Amazons, Joan of Arc." *Minerva: Quarterly Report on Women and the Military* 6 (Fall 1988): 1-11.

Willenz, June A. "Women Veterans from the Vietnam War Through the Eighties." *Minerva: Quarterly Report on Women and the Military* 6 (Fall 1988): 61-66.

Woolley, Alma S. "A Hoosier Nurse in France: The World War I Diary of Maude Frances Essig." *Indiana Magazine of History* 82 (March 1986): 37-68.

Zucker, Stanley. "German Women and the Revolution of 1848: Kathinka Zitz-Halein and the Humania Association." *Central European History* 13 (September 1980): 237-254.

## General

Elshtain, Jean Bethke. "Women and War: An Excerpt from a New Book." *Books and Religion* 15 (March-April 1987): 1, 16-21, 24-28.

Kumin, Maxine. "'Stamping a Tiny Foot Against God': Some American Women Poets Writing Between the Two Wars." *Quarterly Journal of the Library of Congress* 39 (Winter 1982).

Kunkle, Camille. "'It Is What It Does to the Souls': Women's Views of the Civil War." *Atlanta History* 33 (Summer 1989): 56-70.

Lawson, Jacqueline E. "'She's a Pretty Woman . . . for a Gook': The Misogyny of the Vietnam War." *Journal of American Culture* 12 (Fall 1989): 55-66.

Modell, John, and Duane Steffey. "Waging War and Marriage: Military Service and Family Formation, 1940-1950." *Journal of Family History* 13, no. 2 (1988): 195-218.

O'Connor, Colleen M. "Imagine the Unimaginable: Helen Gahagan Douglas, Women, and the Bomb." *Southern California Quarterly* 67 (Spring 1985): 35-50.

Pierson, Ruth Roach. "The Double Bind of the Double Standard: VD Control and the CWAC in World War II." *Canadian Historical Review* 62 (March 1981): 31-58.

Rand, Erica. "Depoliticizing Women: Female Agency, the French Revolution, and the Art of Boucher and David." *Genders* 7 (March 1990): 47-68.

Sanasarian, Elizabeth. "Gender Distinctions in the Genocidal Process: A Preliminary Study of the Armenian Case." *Holocaust and Genocide Studies* 4, no. 4 (1989): 449-461.

Sharbach, Sarah E. "A Woman Acting Alone: Louise Olivereau and the First World War." *Pacific Northwest Quarterly* 78 (January/April 1987): 32-40.

Solterer, Helen. "Figures of Female Militancy in Medieval France." *Signs* 16 (Spring 1991): 522-549.

Sturma, Michael. "Public Health and Sexual Morality: Venereal Disease in World War II Australia." *Signs* 13 (Summer 1988): 725-740.

Taylor, Peter and Hermann Rebel. "Hessian Peasant Women, Their Families, and the Draft: A Social-Historical Interpretation of Four Tales from the Grimm Collection." *Journal of Family History* 6 (Winter 1981): 347-378.

Walker, Nancy. "Humor and Gender Roles: The 'Funny' Feminism of the Post-World War II Suburbs." *American Quarterly* 37 (Spring 1985): 98-113.

# POLITICS

## First Ladies

Anderson, Nancy Fix. "Feminist Revisionist Psychobiography: A New Interpretation of Mary Todd Lincoln." *Psychohistory Review* 17 (Fall 1988): 5-10.

Baker, Jean. "Writing Female Lives: The Case of Mary Todd Lincoln." *Psychohistory Review* 17 (Fall 1988): 33-48.

Beasley, Maurine, and Paul Belgrade. "Eleanor Roosevelt: First Lady as Radio Pioneer." *Journalism History* 11 (Autumn/Winter 1984): 42-45.

-----. "Media Coverage of a Silent Partner: Mamie Eisenhower as First Lady." *American Journalism* 3, no. 1 (1986): 39-49.

Benze, James G., Jr. "Nancy Reagan: China Doll or Dragon Lady?" *Presidential Studies Quarterly* 20 (Fall 1990): 777-790.

Bernhard, Virginia. "Ima Hogg: The Governor's Daughter." *East Texas History Journal* (Spring 1984): 19-32.

Black, Allida M. "Championing a Champion: Eleanor Roosevelt and the Marian Anderson 'Freedom Concert.'" *Presidential Studies Quarterly* 20 (Fall 1990): 719-736.

Bourne, Russell. "When the First Lady Speaks Her Mind." *American Heritage* 38 (September/October 1987): 108-109.

Burke, Frank G. "First Ladies as National Leaders." *Prologue* 19 (Summer 1987): 68-69.

Gelles, Edith B. "'The Anchor of Our Hope': Abigail Adams and Religion." *Religion and Public Education* 14 (Fall 1987): 359-364.

Gould, Lewis L. "First Ladies." *American Scholar* 55 (Autumn 1986): 528-535.

-----. "First Ladies and the Presidency." *Presidential Studies Quarterly* 20 (Fall 1990): 677-684.

-----. "Modern First Ladies: An Institutional Perspective." *Prologue* 19 (Summer 1987): 70-83.

-----. "Modern First Ladies in Historical Perspective." *Presidential Studies*

*Quarterly* 15 (Summer 1985): 532-540.

Jensen, Faye Lind. "An Awesome Responsibility: Rosalynn Carter as First Lady." *Presidential Studies Quarterly* 20 (Fall 1990): 769-776.

Maga, Timothy. "Humanism and Peace: Eleanor Roosevelt's Mission to the Pacific, August-September, 1943." *Maryland Historian* 19 (Fall/Winter 1988): 33-47.

Mayer, Dale C. "An Uncommon Woman: The Quiet Leadership Style of Lou Henry Hoover." *Presidential Studies Quarterly* 20 (Fall 1990): 685-698.

Melosh, Barbara, and Christina Simmons. "From Martha Washington to Alice Paul in Our Nation's Capital." *Radical History Review* no. 25 (October 1981): 100-113.

Mezzack, Janet L. "'Without Manners You Are Nothing': Lady Bird Johnson, Eartha Kitt, and the Women Doers' Luncheon of January 18, 1968." *Presidential Studies Quarterly* 20 (Fall 1990): 745-760.

Minor, Michael, and Larry F. Vryalik. "A Study in Tragedy: Jane Means Pierce, First Lady (1853-1857)." *Manuscripts* 40, no. 3 (1988): 177-189.

Ostromecki, Walter A., Jr. "Proxy First Ladies." *Manuscripts* 39 (Summer 1987): 211-218.

Penkower, Monty N. "Eleanor Roosevelt and the Plight of World Jewry." *Jewish Social Studies* 49, no. 2 (1987): 125-136.

Pratt, Rita. "Virginia Blackwell Docking: A Most Versatile First Lady." *Heritage of the Great Plains* 13 (Fall 1980): 33-44.

Rohrer, Karen M. "'If There Was Anything You Forgot to Ask . . .': The Papers of Betty Ford." *Prologue* 19 (Summer 1987): 142-153.

Saunders, Frances W. "'Dearest Ones': Edith Bolling Wilson's Letters from Paris, 1918-1919." *Virginia Cavalcade* 37, no. 2 (1987): 52-67.

Scharf, Lois. "First Ladies." *Reviews in American History* 14, no. 2 (1986): 181-189.

Schwartz, Thomas F. "Is A Psychobiography of Mary Todd Lincoln Possible?" *Psychohistory Review* 17 (Fall 1988): 25-32.

Seeber, Frances. "Eleanor Roosevelt and Women in the New Deal: A Network of Friends." *Presidential Studies Quarterly* 20 (Fall 1990): 707-719.

Smith, Nancy Kegan. "A Journey of the Heart: The Papers of Lady Bird Johnson." *Prologue* 19 (Summer 1987): 126-135.

-----. "On Being First Lady: An Interview with Lady Bird Johnson." *Prologue* 19 (Summer 1987): 136-141.

-----. "Private Reflections on a Public Life: The Papers of Lady Bird Johnson at the LBJ Library." *Presidential Studies Quarterly* 20 (Fall 1990): 737-744.

-----. "Women and the White House: A Look at Women's Papers in the Johnson Library." *Prologue* 18 (Summer 1986): 123-129.

Spence, Mary Lee. "Jessie Benton Frémont: First Lady of Arizona." *Journal of Arizona History* 24 (Spring 1983): 55-72.

Strozier, Charles B. "The Psychology of Mary Todd Lincoln." *Psychohistory Review* 17 (Fall 1988): 11-24.

Tobin, Leesa E. "Betty Ford as First Lady: A Woman for Women." *Presidential*

*Studies Quarterly* 20 (Fall 1990): 761-768.

Winfield, Betty Houchin. "Anna Eleanor Roosevelt's White House Legacy: The Public First Lady." *Presidential Studies Quarterly* 18 (1988): 331-345.

-----. "The Legacy of Eleanor Roosevelt." *Presidential Studies Quarterly* 20 (Fall 1990): 699-706.

## General

Babcock, Barbara A. "At Home, No Women Are Storytellers: Potteries, Stories, and Politics in Cochiti Pueblo." *Journal of the Southwest* 30 (Autumn 1988): 356-389.

Brigman, William. "Pornography as Political Expression." *Journal of Popular Culture* 17, no. 2 (1983): 129-134.

Cohen, Elizabeth S., and Thomas V. Cohen. "Camilla the Go-Between: The Politics of Gender in a Roman Household (1559)." *Continuity and Change* 4 (May 1989): 53-78.

Cott, Nancy. "Liberation Politics in Two Eras." *American Quarterly* 32 (1980): 96-105.

Cox, Cheryl Anne. "Incest, Inheritance and the Political Forum in Fifth-Century Athens." *The Classical Journal* 85 (October/November 1989): 34-46.

Gruenebaum, Jane. "Women in Politics." *Proceedings of the Academy of Political Science* 34, no. 2 (1981): 104-120.

Holtzman, Elizabeth, and Shirley Williams. "Women in the Political World: Observations." *Daedalus* 116 (Fall 1987): 25-34.

Renshaw, Patrick. "Rose of the World: The Pastor-Stokes Marriage and the American Left, 1905-1925." *New York History* 62 (October 1981): 415-438.

Thornton, Emma, and Pauline Adams. "Speaking to the People: 19th Century Populist Rhetoric." *Journal of Popular Culture* 13 (Spring 1980): 654-658.

## Government Policy

Blakeley, Brian L. "Women and Imperialism: The Colonial Office and Female Emigration to South Africa, 1901-1910." *Albion* 13 (Summer 1981): 131-149.

Bock, Gisela. "Racism and Sexism in Nazi Germany: Motherhood, Compulsory Sterilization, and the State." *Signs* 8 (Spring 1983): 400-421.

Boles, Janet K. "Systematic Factors Underlying Legislative Responses to Woman Suffrage and the Equal Rights Amendment." *Women & Politics* 2, no. 1/2 (1982): 5-22.

Bostick, Theodora P. "Women's Suffrage, the Press, and the Reform Bill of 1867." *International Journal of Women's Studies* 3 (July/August 1980): 373-390.

Brauer, Carl M. "Woman Activists, Southern Conservatives, and the Prohibition of Sex Discrimination in Title VII of the 1964 Civil Rights Act." *Journal of Southern History* 49 (February 1983): 37-56.

Brown, Barbara B. "Facing the 'Black Peril': The Politics of Population Control in South Africa." *Journal of South African Studies* 13 (April 1987): 256-273.

Carroll, Lucy. "The Muslim Family Laws Ordinance, 1961: Provisions and Procedures--A Reference Paper for Current Research." *Contributions to Indian Sociology* 13, no. 1 (1979): 117-143.

Carver, Joan S. "The Equal Rights Amendment and the Florida Legislature." *Florida Historical Quarterly* 60 (April 1982): 455-481.

Champion, Brian. "Mormon Polygamy: Parliamentary Comments 1889-90." *Alberta History* 35 (Spring 1987): 10-17.

Chandler, David S. "The Montepios and Regulation of Marriage in the Mexican Bureaucracy, 1770-1821." *The Americas* 43 (July 1986): 47-68.

Crew, David F. "German Socialism, The State and Family Policy, 1918-33." *Continuity and Change* 1, no. 2 (1986): 235-264.

Davin, Anna. "Imperialism and Motherhood." *History Workshop* 5 (Spring 1978): 9-66.

Duniway, Abigail Scott. "Abigail Scott Duniway Addresses the Idaho Constitutional Convention." *Idaho Yesterdays* 34 (Summer 1990): 21-27.

Graebner, William. "'Uncle Sam Just Loves the Ladies': Sex Discrimination in the Federal Government, 1917." *Labor History* 21, no. 1 (1980): 75-85.

Grant, Marilyn. "The 1912 Suffrage Referendum: An Exercise in Political Action." *Wisconsin Magazine of History* 64 (Winter 1980/81): 107-118.

Grant, Philip A., Jr. "Kansas and the Woman Suffrage Amendment, 1917-1919." *Heritage of the Great Plains* 19 (Fall 1986): 1-8.

Harrison, Cynthia E. "A 'New Frontier' for Women: The Public Policy of the Kennedy Administration." *Journal of American History* 67 (December 1980): 630-646.

Jackal, Patricia Stranahan. "Changes in Policy for Yanan Women, 1935-1947." *Modern China* 7 (January 1981): 83-112.

Koven, Seth, and Sonya Michel. "Womanly Duties: Maternalist Politics and the Origins of Welfate States in France, Germany, Great Britain, and the United States, 1880-1920." *American Historical Review* 95 (October 1990): 1076-1108.

Loveland, Anne C. "Lillian Smith and the Problem of Segregation in the Roosevelt Era." *Southern Studies* 22 (Spring 1983): 32-34.

Mabee, Carleton. "Margaret Mead's Approach to Controversial Public Issues: Racial Boycotts in the AAAS." *The Historian* 48 (February 1986): 191-208.

Moch, Leslie Page. "Government Policy and Women's Experience: The Case of Teachers in France." *Feminist Studies* 14 (Summer 1988): 301-324.

Perry, Elisabeth Israels. "Scholars Confront the ERA." *Canadian Review of American Studies* 18 (Fall 1987): 393-398.

## Political Participation

Allured, Janet. "Arkansas Baptists and Methodists and the Equal Rights Amendment." *Arkansas Historical Quarterly* 43 (Spring 1984): 55-66.

Alpern, Sara, and Dale Baum. "Female Ballots: The Impact of the Nineteenth Amendment." *Journal of Interdisciplinary History* 16 (Summer 1985): 43-67.

Andersen, Kristi, and Elizabeth A. Cook. "Women, Work, and Political Attitudes." *American Journal of Social Science* 29 (August 1985): 606-625.

Baskevkin, Sylvia. "Social Change and Political Partisanship, The Development of Women's Attitudes in Quebec, 1965-1979." *Comparative Political Studies* 16 (July 1983): 147-172.

Beeton, Beverly. "'I Am an American Woman': Charlotte Ives Cobb Godbe Kirby." *Journal of the West* 27 (April 1988): 13-19.

Bernstein, Alison. "A Mixed Record: The Political Enfranchisement of American Indian Women During the Indian New Deal." *Journal of the West* 23 (July 1984): 13-20.

Boak, Helen L. "Our Last Hope: Women's Votes for Hitler, A Reappraisal." *German Studies Review* 12 (May 1989): 311-332.

-----. "Women in Weimar Politics." *European History Quarterly* 20 (July 1990): 369-400.

Bohstedt, John. "Gender, Household and Community Politics: Women in English Riots 1790-1810." *Past & Present* no. 120 (August 1988): 88-122.

Boos, Florence, and William Boos. "Catharine Macaulay: Historian and Political Reformer." *International Journal of Women's Studies* 2 (September/October 1979): 473-488.

Bordin, Ruth. "Frances Willard and the Practice of Political Influence." *Hayes Historical Journal* 5 (Spring 1985): 18-28.

Bouton, Cynthia A. "Gendered Behavior in Subsistence Riots: The French Flour War of 1775." *Journal of Social History* 23 (Summer 1990): 735-754.

Brooks, Evelyn. "Religion, Politics, and Gender: The Leadership of Nannie Helen Burroughs." *Journal of Religious Thought* 44 (Winter/Spring 1988): 7-22.

Bryan, Dianetta Gail. "Her-Story Unsilenced: Black Female Activists in the Civil Rights Movement." *Sage* 5 (Fall 1988): 60-64.

Bullough, Vern, and Bonnie Bullough. "Nurses and Power: Professional Power vs Political Clout." *Women & Politics* 4, no. 4 (1984): 67-74.

Burris, Val. "Who Opposed the ERA? The Social Bases of Feminism." *Social Science Quarterly* 64 (1983): 305-317.

Campbell, Leon. "Women and the Great Rebellion in Peru, 1780-1783." *The Americas* 42 (October 1985): 163-196.

Carver, Joan S. "First League of Women Voters in Florida: Its Troubled History." *Florida Historical Quarterly* 63 (April 1985): 406-422.

-----. "Women in Florida." *Journal of Politics* (August 1979): 941-955.

Catlin, Robert A. "Organizational Effectiveness and Black Political Participation: The Case of Katie Hall." *Phylon* 46 (September 1985): 179-192.

Chesson, Michael B. "Harlots or Heroines? A New Look at the Richmond Bread Riot." *Virginia Magazine of History and Biography* 92 (April 1984): 131-175.

Chickering, Roger. "'Casting Their Gaze More Broadly': Women's Patriotic Activism in Imperial Germany." *Past & Present* no. 118 (February 1988): 156-185.

Crawford, Vicki. "Grassroots Activists in the Mississippi Civil Rights Movement." *Sage* 5 (Fall 1988): 24-29.

Dahl, Kathleen. "The Political Activities of Women During the French Revolution." *Western Society for French History* 15 (November 1987): 129.

Edwards, John C. "Atlanta's Prodigal Daughter: The Turbulent Life of Jane Anderson (1893-1942) as Expatriate and Nazi Propagandist." *Atlanta History Journal* 28 (Summer 1984): 23-41.

Everett, Jana Matson. "The Upsurge of Women's Activism in India." *Frontiers* 7, no. 2 (1983): 18-26.

Evins, Janie Synatzske. "Arkansas Women: Their Contribution to Society, Politics, and Business, 1865-1900." *Arkansas History Quarterly* 44 (Summer 1985): 118-133.

Frank, Dana. "Housewives, Socialists, and the Politics of Food: The 1917 New York Cost-of-Living Protests." *Feminist Studies* 11 (Summer 1985): 255-286.

Freeman, Jo. "Protest and Policy: Women Make Waves." *Prospects* 4 (1979): 595-610.

Frenier, Mariam Darce. "American Anti-Feminist Women: Comparing the Rhetoric of Opponents of the Equal Rights Amendment with That of Opponents of Women's Suffrage." *Women's Studies International Forum* 7, no. 6 (1984): 455-465.

Geiger, Susan. "Women in Nationalist Struggle: TANU Activists in Dar es Salaam." *International Journal of African Historical Studies* 20, no. 1 (1987): 1-26.

Gellott, Laura, and Michael Phayer. "Dissenting Voices: Catholic Women in Opposition to Fascism." *Journal of Contemporary History* 22 (January 1987): 91-114.

Gundersen, Joan R. "Independence, Citizenship, and the American Revolution." *Signs* 13 (Autumn 1987): 59-77.

Holland, Carolsue, and G. R. Garett. "The 'Skirt' of Nessus: Women and the German Opposition to Hitler." *International Journal of Women's Studies* 6 (September/October 1983): 363-381.

Hughes, Lindsey. "Sofiya Alekseyevna and the Moscow Rebellion of 1682." *Slavonic & East European Review* 63 (October 1985): 518-539.

Hyman, Paula E. "Immigrant Women and Consumer Protest: The New York City Kosher Meat Boycott of 1902." *American Jewish History* 70 (September 1980): 91-105.

Isaacman, Allen, and Barbara Isaacman. "The Role of Women in the Liberation of Mozambique." *Ufahamu* 13, no. 2/3 (1984): 128-185.

Jarausch, Konrad H. "Students, Sex and Politics in Imperial Germany." *Journal of Contemporary History* 17 (April 1982): 285-304.

Kaufman, Polly Welts. "Julia Harrington Duff: An Irish Woman Confronts the Boston Power Structure, 1900-1905." *Historical Journal of Massachusetts* 18 (Summer 1990): 113-137.

Kenneally, James J. "Women Divided: The Catholic Struggle for an Equal Rights Amendment, 1923-1945." *The Catholic Historical Review* 75 (April 1989): 249-263.

Kincheloe, Joe L., Jr. "Transcending Role Restrictions: Women at Camp Meetings and Political Rallies." *Tennessee History Quarterly* 40 (Summer 1981): 158-169.

Lapsansky, Emma Jones. "Feminism, Freedom, and Community: Charlotte Forten and Women Activists in Nineteenth Century Philadelphia." *Pennsylvania Magazine of History and Biography* 113 (January 1989): 3-20.

Long, David. "'We're Not Isolated Now!' Anna Boe Dahl and the ERA." *Montana* 39 (Spring 1989): 18-23.

McGovern, James R. "Helen Hunt West: Florida's Pioneer for ERA (1917-64)." *Florida History Quarterly* 57 (July 1978): 39-53.

Monoson, S. Sara. "The Lady and the Tiger: Women's Electoral Activism in New York City Before Suffrage." *Journal of Women's History* 2 (Fall 1990): 100-135.

Nelson, Anna Kasten. "Jane (McManus) Storms Cazneau (b. 1807): Disciple of Manifest Destiny." *Prologue* 18 (Spring 1986): 25-40.

Nichols, Carole. "Votes and More for Women: Suffrage and After in Connecticut." *Women and History* no. 5 (1983): 1-86.

Petchesky, Rosalind. "Antiabortion, Antifeminism, and the Rise of the New Right." *Feminist Studies* 7 (1981): 206-246

Pratt, Norma Fain. "Culture and Radical Politics: Yiddish Women Writers, 1890-1940." *American Jewish History* 70, no. 1 (1980): 68-90.

Prince, Vinton M. "Will Women Turn the Tide: Mississippi Women and the 1922 United States Senate Race." *Journal of Mississippi History* 42 (August 1980): 212-220.

-----. "The Woman Voter and Mississippi Elections in the Early Twenties." *Journal of Mississippi History* 49 (May 1987): 105-114.

-----. "Women, Politics, and the Press: The Mississippi *Woman Voter*." *Southern Studies* 19 (Winter 1980): 365-372.

Rowbotham, Sheila. "Women and Radical Politics in Britain 1830-1914." *Radical History Review* 19 (Winter 1978/79): 149-159.

Rubens, Lisa. "The Patrician Radical: Charlotte Anita Whitney." *California History* 65 (September 1986): 158-171.

Schneider, Elise. "Addressing the Issues: Two Women's Groups in Demonton, 1905-16." *Alberta History* 36 (Summer 1988): 15-22.

Sealander, Judith. "Feminist Against Feminist: The First Phase of the Equal Rights Amendment Debate, 1923-1963." *South Atlantic Quarterly* 81 (Spring 1982): 147-161.

Shankman, Arnold. "A Jury of Her Peers: The South Carolina Woman and Her Campaign for Jury Service." *South Carolina History Magazine* (April 1980): 102-121.

Shawhan, Dorothy. "Women behind the Woman Voter." *Journal of Mississippi History* 49 (May 1987): 115-128.

Sheppard, M. G. "The Effects of the Franchise Provisions on the Social and Sex Composition of the Municipal Electorate 1882-1914." *Society for the Study of Labour History* 45 (Autumn 1982): 19-25.

Smith, Jean M. "The Voting Women of San Diego, 1920." *Journal of San Diego*

*History* 26, no. 2 (1980): 133-154.

Stephenson, Jill. "Middle-Class Women and National Socialist 'Service.'" *History* 67 (February 1982): 32-44.

Tackett, Timothy. "Women and Men in Counterrevolution: The Somieres Riot of 1791." *Journal of Modern History* 59 (December 1987): 680-704.

Tyrell, Alex. "'Woman's Mission' and Pressure Group Politics in Britain (1825-1860)." *Bulletin of the John Rylands University Library of Manchester* 63 (Autumn 1980): 194-230.

## International Relations

Badran, Margot. "Dual Liberation: Feminism and Nationalism in Egypt, 1870s-1925." *Feminist Issues* 8, no. 1 (1988): 15-34.

Bell, John. "Giving Birth to the New Soviet Man: Politics and Obstetrics in the USSR." *Slavic Review* 40 (Spring 1981): 1-16.

Bhushan, Madhu. "Vimochana: Women's Struggles, Nonviolent Militancy and Direct Action in the Indian Context." *Women's Studies International Forum* 12, no. 1 (1989): 25-33.

Bravo, Rosa, and Rosalba Todaro. "Chilean Women and the UN Decade for Women." *Women's Studies International Forum* 8, no. 2 (1985): 111-116.

Chandler, David S. "The Montepios and Regulation of Marriage in the Mexican Bureaucracy, 1770-1821." *The Americas* 43 (July 1986): 47-68.

Charrad, Mounira. "State and Gender in Maghrib." *Middle East Report* 163 (March/April 1990): 19-24.

Clark, Carolyn M. "Land and Food, Women and Power, in Nineteenth Century Kikuyu." *Africa* 50, no. 4 (1980): 357-369.

Conner, Susan P. "Politics, Prostitution, and the Pox in Revolutionary Paris, 1789-1799." *Western Society for French History* 14 (November 1986): 183.

Crew, David F. "German Socialism, The State and Family Policy, 1918-33." *Continuity and Change* 1, no. 2 (1986): 235-264.

Diakonoff, I. M. "Women in Old Babylonia Not under Patriarchial Authority." *Journal of the Economic and Social History of the Orient* 29 (October 1986): 225-238.

Doran, Susan. "Religion and Politics at the Court of Elizabeth I: The Habsburg Marriage Negotiations of 1559-1567." *English Historical Review* 104 (October 1989): 908-926.

Eliraz, Giora. "Egyptian Intellectuals and Women's Emancipation, 1919-1939." *Asian and African Studies* 16, no. 1 (1982): 95-120.

Engels, Dagmar. "The Limits of Gender Ideology: Bengali Women, the Colonial State, and the Private Sphere, 1890-1930." *Women's Studies International Forum* 12, no. 4 (1989): 425-438.

Evans, N. E. "The Anglo-Russian Royal Marriage Negotiations of 1600-1603." *The Slavic & East European Review* 61 (July 1983): 363-387.

Foot, Rosemary. "Where are the Women? The Gender Dimension in the Study of International Relations." *Diplomatic History* 14 (Fall 1990): 615-622.

Gipoulon, Catherine. "The Emergence of Women in Politics in China, 1898-1927." *Chinese Studies in History* 23 (Winter 1989/90): 46-67.

Gould, Karen. "Spatial Poetics, Spatial Politics: Quebec Feminists on the City and the Countryside." *American Review of Canadian Studies* 12 (Spring 1982): 1-9.

Haggis, Jane. "Gendering Colonialism or Colonising Gender? Recent Women's Studies Approaches to White Women and the History of British Colonialism." *Women's Studies International Forum* 13, no. 1/2 (1990): 105-116.

Hahner, June E. "'Women's Place' in Politics and Economics in Brazil since 1964." *Luso-Brazilian Review* 19, no. 1 (1982): 83-91.

Hanley, Sarah. "Engendering the State: Family Formation and State Building in Early Modern France." *French Historical Studies* 16, no. 1 (Spring 1989): 4-27.

Hatem, Mervat. "The Enduring Alliance of Nationalism and Patriarchy in Muslim Personal Status Laws: The Case of Modern Egypt." *Feminist Issues* 6 (1986): 19-43.

Herda, Phyllis. "Gender, Rank and Power in 18th Century Tonga: The Case of Tupoumoheofo." *Journal of Pacific History* 22 (October 1987): 195-208.

Heussler, Robert. "Imperial Lady: Gertrude Bell and the Middle East, 1889-1926." *The British Studies Monitor* 9 (Summer 1979): 3-22.

Holmgren, J. "Marriage and Political Power in Sixth Century China: A Study of the Kao Family of Northern Ch'i, c. 520-550." *Journal of Asian History* 16, no. 1 (1982): 1-50.

Honeycutt, Karen. "Socialism and Feminism in Imperial Germany." *Signs* 5 (Autumn 1979): 30-41.

Hunt, Nancy Rose. "Domesticity and Colonialism in Belgian Africa: Usumbura's Foyer Social, 1946-1960." *Signs* 15 (Spring 1990): 447-474.

Kandiyoti, Deniz. "Emancipated but Unliberated? Reflections on the Turkish Case." *Feminist Studies* 13 (Summer 1987): 317-338.

Kushner, Tony. "Politics and Race, Gender and Class: Refugees, Fascists and Domestic Service in Britain, 1933-1940." *Immigrants & Minorities* 8 (March 1989): 49-60.

Lazreg, Marnia. "Gender and Politics in Algeria: Unraveling the Religious Paradigm." *Signs* 15 (Summer 1990): 755-780.

Maza, Sarah. "Domestic Melodrama as Political Ideology: The Case of the Comte de Sanais." *American Historical Review* 94 (December 1989): 1249-1264.

McBride, Theresa. "Comment on Session: Class and Sex Identity in French Feminist Politics." *Western Society for French History* 12 (October 1984): 257-259.

McGee, Sandra F. "The Visible and Invisible Liga Patriotica Argentina, 1919-1928: Gender Roles and the Right Wing." *Hispanic American Historical Review* 64, no. 2 (1984): 233-258.

McKillen, Beth. "Irish Feminism and Nationalist Separatism, 1914-1923." *Eire-Ireland* 17 (Fall 1982): 52-67.

-----. "Irish Feminism and Nationalist Separatism, 1914-1923." *Eire-Ireland* 17 (Winter 1982): 72-90.

McMillan, James. "Women, Religion, and Politics: The Case of the Ligue Patristique des Françaises." *Western Society for French History* 15 (November 1987): 355-364.

Michel, Sonya, and Seth Koven. "Womanly Duties: Maternalist Politics and the Origins of Welfare States in France, Germany, Great Britain, and the United States, 1880-1920." *American Historical Review* 95 (October 1990): 1076-1108.

Miller, Francesca. "The International Relations of Women of the Americas 1890-1928." *Americas* 43 (October 1986): 171-182.

Moore, Lindy. "Feminists and Femininity: A Case-Study of WSPU Propaganda and Local Response at a Scottish By-Election." *Women's Studies* 5, no. 6 (1982): 675-684.

Moskoff, William. "Sex Discrimination, Commuting and the Role of Women in Rumanian Development." *Slavic Review* 37 (September 1978): 440-456.

Murray-Hudson, Anne. "SWAPO: Solidarity with Our Sisters." *Review of African Political Economy* 27/28 (1983): 120-125.

Napierkowski, Thomas J. "Anne Pellowski: A Voice for Polonia." *Polish American Studies* 42 (Autumn 1985): 89-97.

Offen, Karen. "Depopulation, Nationalism, and Feminism in Fin-de-Siecle France." *American Historical Review* 89 (June 1984): 648-676.

Papachristou, Judith. "American Women and Foreign Policy, 1898-1905: Exploring Gender in Diplomatic History." *Diplomatic History* 14 (Fall 1990): 493-509.

Pedersen, Susan. "Gender, Welfare, and Citizenship in Britain During the Great War." *American Historical Review* 95 (October 1990): 983-1006.

Peterson, J. E. "The Political Status of Women in the Arab Gulf States." *Middle East Journal* 43 (Winter 1989): 34-50.

Ramphele, Mamphela. "The Dynamics of Gender Politics in the Hostels of Cape Town: Another Legacy of the South African Migrant Labour System." *Journal of South African Studies* 15 (April 1989): 393-414.

Ramusack, Barbara N. "Cultural Missionaries, Maternal Imperialists, Feminist Allies: British Women Activists in India, 1865-1945." *Women's Studies International Forum* 13, no. 4 (1990): 309-322.

Rasmussen, Jorgen S. "The Political Integration of British Women: The Response of a Traditional System to a Newly Emergent Group." *Social Science History* 7 (Winter 1983): 61-96.

Rogers, Susan G. "Anti-Colonial Protest in Africa: A Female Strategy Reconsidered." *Heresies* 3, no. 9 (1980): 22-25.

Schnouenberg, Barbara Brandon. "The Brood Hen of Faction: Mrs. Macaulay and Radical Politics, 1765-1775." *Albion* 11 (Spring 1979): 33-45.

Schoeffel, Penelope. "Rank, Gender and Politics in Ancient Samoa: The Genealogy of Salamasina *O Le Tafaifa*." *Journal of Pacific History* 22 (October 1987): 174-194.

Schwartz, Paula. "Partisanes and Gender Politics in Vichy France." *French Historical Studies* 16 (Spring 1989): 126-151.

Seidman, Gay W. "Women in Zimbabwe: Postindependence Struggles." *Feminist*

*Studies* 10 (Fall 1984): 419-440.

Shanley, Mary Lyndon. "Marriage Contract and Social Contract in Seventeenth Century Political Thought." *Western Political Quarterly* 32 (March 1979): 79-91.

Szuchman, Mark D. "Household Structure and Political Crisis: Buenos Aires, 1810-1860." *Latin American Research Review* 21 (1986): 55-93.

Toman, Rene de la Pedraja. "Women in Colombian Organizations, 1900-1940: A Study in Changing Gender Roles." *Journal of Women's History* 2 (Spring 1990): 98-119.

Tseggai, Araia. "Eritrean Women and Italian Soldiers: Status of Eritrean Women under Italian Rule." *Journal of Eritrean Studies* 4 (Summer 1989/Winter 1990): 7-12.

Underwood, Malcolm G. "Politics and Piety in the Household of Lady Margaret Beaufort." *Journal of Ecclesiastical History* 38 (January 1987): 39-52.

Waltz, Susan E. "Another View of Feminine Networks: Tunisian Women and the Development of Political Efficacy." *International Journal of Middle East Studies* 22 (February 1990): 21-36.

Wolchik, Sharon L. "The Status of Women in a Socialist Order: Czechoslovakia, 1948-1978." *Slavic Review* 38 (December 1979): 583-602.

Zimmerman, Judith E. "Natalie Herzen and the Early Intelligentsia." *The Russian Review* 41 (July 1982): 249-272.

## Monarchies

Abdurachman, Paramita R. "'Niachile pokaraga': A Sad Story of a Moluccan Queen." *Modern Asian Studies* 22, no. 3 (1988): 571-592.

Arnstein, W. L. "Queen Victoria Opens Parliament: The Disinvention of Tradition." *Historical Research* 63 (June 1990): 178-194.

Chandler, Victoria. "Ada de Warenne, Queen Mother of Scotland (c. 1123-1178)." *Scottish Historical Review* 60 (October 1981): 119-139.

Chung, Priscilla Ching. "Power and Prestige: Palace Women in the Northern Sung (960-1126)." *Historical Reflections/Reflexions Historiques* 8 (Fall 1981): 99-112.

Chung, Sue Fawn. "The Much Maligned Empress Dowager: A Revisionist Study of the Empress Dowager Tz'u-hsi (1835-1908)." *Modern Asian Studies* 13, no. 2 (1979): 177-196.

Dawson, Jane E. A. "Mary Queen of Scots, Lord Darnley, and Anglo-Scottish Relations." *The International Review of History* 8 (February 1986): 1-24.

Doran, Susan. "Religion and Politics at the Court of Elizabeth I: The Habsburg Marriage Negotiations of 1559-1567." *English Historical Review* 104 (October 1989): 908-926.

Ellem, Elizabeth Wood. "Queen Salote Tupou of Tonga as Tu'i Fefine." *Journal of Pacific History* 22 (October 1987): 209-227.

Evans, N. E. "The Anglo-Russian Royal Marriage Negotiations of 1600-1603." *The Slavic & East European Review* 61 (July 1983): 363-387.

Gunson, Niel. "Sacred Women Chiefs and Female 'Headmen' in Polynesian History." *Journal of Pacific History* 22 (July 1987): 139-173.

Harris, Barbara J. "Women and Politics in Early Tudor England." *Historical Journal* [Great Britain] 33, no. 2 (1990): 259-282.

Haugaard, William P. "Elizabeth Tudor's *Book of Devotions*: A Neglected Clue to the Queen's Life and Character." *Sixteenth Century Journal* 12, no. 2 (1981): 79-106.

Hayton, David. "The Crisis in Ireland and the Disintegration of Queen Anne's Last Ministry." *Irish Historical Studies* 22 (March 1981): 193-215.

Heisch, Alison. "Queen Elizabeth I and the Persistence of Patriarchy." *Feminist Review* no. 4 (1980): 45-56.

Holmgren, J. "The Harem in Northern Wei Politics--398-498 A.D.: A Study of T'o-pa Attitudes Towards the Institution of Empress, Empresss-Dowager, and Regency Governments in the Chinese Dynastic System During Early Northern Wei." *Journal of the Economic and Social History of the Orient* 26 (February 1983): 71-96.

Howell, Margaret. "The Resources of Eleanor of Provence as Queen Consort." *English Historical Review* 102 (April 1987): 372-393.

Katz, David S. "Menasseh ben Israel's Mission to Queen Christina of Sweden, 1651-1655." *Jewish Social Studies* 45 (Winter 1983): 57-72.

Kettering, Sharon. "The Patronage Power of Early Modern French Noblewomen." *The Historical Journal* 32, no. 4 (1989): 817-842.

Kleinman, Ruth. "Social Dynamics at the French Court: The Household of Anne of Austria." *French Historical Studies* 16 (Spring 1990): 517-535.

Knox, Bruce. "The Queen's Letter of 1865 and British Policy towards Emancipation and Indentured Labour in the West Indies, 1830-1865." *The Historical Journal* 29 (June 1986): 345-368.

Kumar, Ann. "Javanese Court Society and Politics in the Late Eighteenth Century: The Record of a Lady Soldier." *Indonesia* 29 (April 1980): 1-49.

-----. "Political Developments: The Courts and the Company, 1784-1791." *Indonesia* 30 (October 1980): 67-111.

Laquer, Thomas W. "The Queen Caroline Affair: Politics as Art in the Reign of George IV." *Journal of Modern History* 54 (September 1982): 417-466.

Lee, Patricia-Ann. "A Bodye Politique to Governe: Aylmer, Knox and the Debate on Queenship." *Historian* 52 (February 1990): 242-261.

Levin, Carole. "'Would I Could Give You Help and Succor': Elizabeth I and the Politics of Touch." *Albion* 21 (Summer 1989): 191-205.

Lightman, Harriet. "Political Power and the Queen of France." *Canadian Journal of History* 21 (December 1986): 299-312.

-----. "Queens and Minor Kings in French Constitutional Law." *Western Society for French History* 9 (October 1981): 26-36.

Loades, David. "The Reign of Mary Tudor: Historiography and Research." *Albion* 21 (Winter 1989): 547-558.

McEntee, Ann Marie. "The 1579 Masque of Amazons and Knights: A Coalescence of Elizabeth I's Gendered and Political Identities." *Journal of*

*Unconventional History* 1 (Spring 1990): 53-65.

Murray, Dian. "One Woman's Rise to Power: Cheng I's Wife and Pirates." *Historical Reflections/Reflexions Historiques* 8 (Fall 1981): 147-162.

Noether, Emiliana P. "'Morally Wrong' or 'Politically Right?' Espionage in Her Majesty's Post Office, 1844-45." *Canadian Journal of History* 22 (April 1987): 41-58.

Papmehl, K. A. "The Empress and 'Un Fanatique': A Review of Circumstances Leading to the Government Action Against Novikov in 1792." *Slavonic and East European Review* 68 (October 1990): 665-691.

Scalingi, Paula Louise. "The Scepter or the Distaff: The Question of Female Sovereignty, 1516-1607." *The Historian* 41 (November 1978): 59-75.

Spall, Richard Francis, Jr. "The Bedchamber Crisis and the Hastings Scandal: Morals, Politics, and the Press at the Beginning of Victoria's Reign." *Canadian Journal of History* 22 (April 1987): 19-40.

Ta Van Tai. "The Status of Women in Traditional Vietnam: A Comparison of the Code of the Le Dynasty (1428-1788) with the Chinese Codes." *Journal of Asian History* 15 (1981): 97-145.

Tsurumi, E. Patricia. "Japan's Early Female Emperors." *Historical Reflections/Reflexions Historiques* 8 (Spring 1981).

Underwood, Malcolm G. "Politics and Piety in the Household of Lady Margaret Beaufort." *Journal of Ecclesiastical History* 38 (January 1987): 39-52.

Warnicke, Retha M. "Anne Boleyn's Childhood and Adolescence." *The Historical Journal* 28 (December 1985): 939-952.

-----. "The Eternal Triangle and Court Politics: Henry VIII, Anne Boleyn, and Sir Thomas Wyatt." *Albion* 18 (Winter 1986): 565-580.

## Office Holders

Abramowitz, Benjamin L. "Anna Ella Carroll: Invisible Member of Lincoln's Cabinet." *Minerva: Quarterly Report on Women and the Military* 8 (Winter 1990): 30-43.

Bernstein, Robert A. "Why Are There So Few Women in the House?" *Western Political Quarterly* 39 (March 1986): 155-164.

Blay, Eva Alterman. "The Political Participation of Women in Brazil: Female Mayors." *Signs* 5 (Autumn 1979): 42-59.

Braitman, Jacqueline R. "A California Stateswoman: The Public Career of Katherine Philips Edson." *California History* 65 (June 1986): 82-95, 151-152.

Bridenstine, Ellenore M. "My Years as Montana's First Woman State Senator." *Montana* 39 (Winter 1989): 54-58.

Chunko, Mary T. "Call Her Madam Secretary." *Humanities* 8 (May/June 1987): 22-23.

Ciria, Alberto. "Flesh and Fantasy: The Many Faces of Evita (and Juan Peron)." *Latin American Research Review* 18, no. 2 (1983): 150-165.

Cobble, Dorothy Sue. "A Self-Possessed Woman: A View of FDR's Secretary of Labor, Madame Perkins." *Labor History* 29, no. 2 (1988): 225-229.

Dains, Mary K. "Women Pioneers in the Missouri Legislature." *Missouri Historical Review* 85 (October 1990): 40-52.

Deber, Raisa B. "'The Fault, Dear Brutus': Women as Congressional Candidates in Pennsylvania." *Journal of Politics* 44 (May 1982): 463-479.

Duffy, Joe. "Anna Dickinson and the 1863 Connecticut Gubernatorial Campaign." *Connecticut Historical Society Bulletin* 49 (Fall 1984): 165-174.

Ellis, Mary Carolyn, and Joanne V. Hawks. "Creating a Different Pattern: Florida's Women Legislators, 1928-1986." *Florida Historical Quarterly* 66 (July 1987): 68-83.

Foppa, Alaide. "The First Feminist Congress in Mexico, 1916." *Signs* 5 (Autumn 1979): 192-199.

Gehring, Lorraine A. "Women Officeholders in Kansas, 1872-1912." *Kansas History* 9 (Summer 1986): 48-57.

Gertzog, Irwin N. "The Matrimonial Connection: The Nomination of Congressmen's Widows for the House of Representatives." *Journal of Politics* 42 (August 1980): 820-833.

Gething, Judith Dean. "The Educational and Civic Leadership of Elsie Wilcox, 1920-1932." *Hawaiian Journal of History* 16 (1982): 184-202.

Gordon, P. "Lady Knightley and the South Northamptonshire Election of 1885." *Northamptonshire Past and Present* 6 (1981/1982): 265-273.

Hardaway, Roger D. "Jeannette Rankin: The Early Years." *North Dakota Quarterly* 48 (Winter 1980): 62-68.

-----. "New Mexico Elects a Congresswoman." *Red River Valley Historical Review* 4 (Fall 1979): 75-89.

Hardin, William H. "Elizabeth Kee: West Virginia's First Woman in Congress." *West Virginia History* 45, no. 1/4 (1984): 109-123.

Harrison, Brian. "Women in Men's House: The Women M.P.s, 1919-1945." *The Historical Journal* 29 (September 1986): 623-654.

Hawks, Joanne V. "A Challenge to Racism and Sexism: Black Women in Southern Legislatures, 1965-1986." *Sage* 5 (Fall 1988): 20-23.

-----. "Like Mother, Like Daughter: Nellie Nugent Somerville and Lucy Somerville Howorth." *Journal of Mississippi History* 45 (May 1983): 116-128.

-----. "A Select Few: Alabama's Women Legislators, 1922-83." *Alabama Review* 38 (July 1985): 175-201.

Hawks, Joanne V., Carolyn Ellis, and J. Byron Morris. "Women in the Mississippi Legislature." *Journal of Mississippi History* 43 (November 1981): 266-293.

James, Louise B. "Alice Mary Robertson--Anti-Feminist Congresswoman." *Chronicles of Oklahoma* 55 ((Winter 1977-78): 454-461.

Jensen, Joan M. "Pioneers in Politics." *El Palacio* 92 (Summer/Fall 1986): 12-19.

Jones, Kay F. "Ana Frohmiller: Watchdog of the Arizona Treasury." *Journal of Arizona History* 25 (Winter 1984): 349-368.

Kohn, Walter S. G. "Women in the Canadian House of Commons." *American Review of Canadian Studies* 14 (Fall 1984): 298-311.

Malik, Yogendra K. "Indira Gandhi: Personality, Political Power and Party

Politics." *Journal of Asian and African Studies* 22 (July/October 1987): 141-155.

Malik, Yogendra K., and Dhirendra K. Vajpeyi. "India: The Years of Indira Gandhi." *Journal of Asian and African Studies* 22 (July/October 1987): 135-140.

Marchildon, Rudy G. "The 'Persons' Controversy: The Legal Aspects of the Fight for Women Senators." *Atlantis* 6 (Spring 1981): 99-113.

Martin, Dorris B. "A Congressional Wife in Wartime Washington." *Palimpsest* 64 (March/April 1983): 34-44.

McManus, Susan A. "A City's First Female Officeholder: 'Coattails' for Future Female Officeholders." *Western Political Quarterly* 34 (March 1981): 88-99.

Melosh, Barbara, and Christina Simmons. "From Martha Washington to Alice Paul in Our Nation's Capital." *Radical History Review* no. 25 (October 1981): 100-113.

Miller, Kristie. "Ruth Hanna McCormick and the Senatorial Election of 1930." *Illinois Historical Journal* 81 (Autumn 1988): 191-210.

Mitchell, Gary. "Women Standing for Women: The Early Political Career of Mary T. Norton." *New Jersey History* 96 (Spring/Summer 1978): 27-42.

Morgan, Georgia Cook. "India Edwards: Distaff Politician of the Truman Era." *Missouri Historical Review* 78 (April 1984): 293-310.

Morris, Allen. "Florida's First Women Candidates." *Florida Historical Quarterly* 63 (April 1985): 406-422.

Navarro, Marysa. "Evita and the Crisis of 17 October 1945: A Case Study of Peronist and Anti-Peronist Mythology." *Journal of Latin American Studies* 12 (May 1980): 127-138.

Nichols, Carole and Joyce Pendery. "*Pro Bono Publico*: Voices of Connecticut's Political Women, 1915-1945." *Oral History Review* 11 (1983): 49-74.

Pieroth, Doris Hinson. "Bertha Knight Landes: The Woman Who Was Mayor." *Pacific Northwest Quarterly* 75 (July 1984): 117-127.

Pitzer, Paul C. "Dorothy McCullough Lee: The Successes and Failures of 'Dottie-Do-Good.'" *Oregon Historical Quarterly* 91 (Spring 1990): 5-42.

Pugh, Evelyn L. "The First Woman Candidate for Parliament: Helen Rayor and the Election of 1885." *International Journal of Women's Studies* 1 (July/August 1978): 378-390.

Rao, R. V. R. Chandrasekhara. "Mrs. Indira Gandhi and India's Constitutional Structures: An Era of Erosion." *Journal of Asian and African Studies* 22 (July/October 1987): 156-174.

Richter, William L. "Mrs. Gandhi's Neighborhood: Indian Foreign Policy Toward Neighboring Countries." *Journal of Asian and African Studies* 22 (July/October 1987): 249-264.

Scobie, Ingrid Winthur. "Helen Gahagan Douglas: Broadway Star as California Politician." *California History* 66 (December 1987): 242-261.

Segrest, Mab. "Barbara Deming: 1917-1984." *Southern Exposure* 13 (March/June 1985): 72-75.

Shkolnik, Esther Simon. "Petticoat Power: The Political Influence of Mrs.

Gladstone." *The Historian* 42 (August 1980): 631-647.

Spencer, Samia I. "Women Cabinet Members: Ornaments of Government?" *Western Society for French History* 12 (October 1984): 243-256.

-----. "Women in Government in Quebec." *Proceedings of the Annual Meeting of the French Colonial Historical Society* 13 (1986): 271-275.

Treadway, Sandra Gioia. "Sarah Lee Fain: Norfolk's First Woman Legislator." *Virginia Cavalcade* 30 (Winter 1981): 124-133.

Vial, Rebecca, and W. Calvin Dickinson. "Kate Bradford Stockton." *Tennessee Historical Quarterly* 49 (Fall 1990): 152-160.

Ward, Karen. "From Executive to Feminist: the Business Women's Legislative Council of Los Angeles, 1927-1932." *Essays in Economic and Business History* 7 (1989): 60-75.

Welch, Susan. "Congressional Nomination Procedures and the Representation of Women." *Congress & The Presidency* 16 (Autumn 1989): 121-135.

White, Kate. "May Holman: 'Australian Labor's Pioneer Woman Parliamentarian.'" *Labour History* 41 (November 1981): 110-117.

## Parties

Basen, Neil K. "Kate Richards O'Hare: The 'First Lady' of American Socialism, 1901-1917." *Labor History* 21 (Spring 1980): 165-199.

Bashevkin, Sylvia. "Political Participation, Ambition, and Feminism: Women in the Ontario Party Elites." *American Review of Canadian Studies* 15 (Winter 1985): 465-480.

-----. "Women's Participation in the Ontario Political Parties, 1971-1981." *Journal of Canadian Studies/Revue d'études canadiennes* 17 (Summer 1982): 44-54.

Bates, J. Leonard, and Vanette M. Schwartz. "The Golden Special Campaign Train: Republican Women Campaign for Charles Evans Hughes for President in 1916." *Montana* 37 (Summer 1987): 26-35.

Beeby, Dean. "Women in the Ontario C.C.F. 1940-1950." *Ontario History* 74 (December 1982): 258-283.

Belcher, Dixie. "A Democratic School for Democratic Women." *Chronicles of Oklahoma* 61 (Winter 1983): 414-421.

Brady, Marilyn Dell. "Populism and Feminism in a Newspaper by and for Women of the Kansas Farmers' Alliance, 1891-1894." *Kansas History* 7 (Winter 1984/85): 280-290.

Brower, Ruth Compton. "Moral Nationalism in Victorian Canada: The Case of Agnes Machar." *Journal of Canadian Studies/Revue d'études canadiennes* 20 (Spring 1985): 90-108.

Bunting, Anne. "The American Molly Childers and the Irish Question." *Eire-Ireland* 23 (Summer 1988): 88-103.

Butler Flores, Cornelia. "Socialist Feminism in Latin America." *Women & Politics* 4, no. 1 (1984): 69-93.

Buzek, Beatrice Ross. "'By Fortune Wounded': Loyalist Women in Nova Scotia." *Nova Scotia Historical Review* 7, no. 2 (1987): 45-62.

Collette, Christine. "Socialism and Scandal: The Sexual Politics of the Early Labour Movement." *History Workshop* 23 (Spring 1987): 102-111.

Cott, Nancy F. "Feminist Politics in the 1920s: The National Woman's Party." *Journal of Amercian History* 71 (June 1984): 43-68.

de Grazia, Victoria. "Women and Communism in Advanced Capitalist Societies: Readings and Resources." *Radical History Review* 23 (Spring 1980): 80-101.

Durham, Martin. "Women and the British Union of Fascists, 1932-1940." *Immigrants & Minorities* 8 (March 1989): 3-18.

Evans, Janet. "The Communist Party of the Soviet Union and the Women's Question: The Case of the 1936 Decree 'In Defence of Mother and Child.'" *Journal of Contemporary History* 16 (October 1981): 757-776.

Fiesler, Beate. "The Making of Russian Female Social Democrats, 1890-1917." *International Review of Social History* 34, no. 2 (1989): 193-226.

Fuller, Paul E. "An Early Venture of Kentucky Women in Politics: The Breckinridge Campaign of 1894." *The Filson Club History Quarterly* 63 (April 1989): 224-242.

Geidel, Peter. "The National Woman's Party and the Origins of the Equal Rights Amendment, 1920-1923." *Historian* 42 (August 1980): 557-582.

Gordon, Felice D. "After Winning: The New Jersey Suffragists in the Political Parties, 1920-1930." *New Jersey History* 101 (Fall/Winter 1983): 13-36.

Gundersen, Rae C. "Mary Elizabeth Lease: Voice of the Populists." *Heritage of the Great Plains* 13 (Fall 1980): 3-10.

Hilden, Patricia. "Re-Writing the History of Socialism: Working Woman and the Parti Ouvrier Francais." *European History Quarterly* 17 (July 1987): 285-306.

Hirshfield, Claire. "A Fractured Faith: Liberal Party Women and the Suffrage Issue in Britain, 1892-1914." *Gender & History* 2 (Summer 1990): 173-197.

Holmes, William F. "Ellen Dortch and the Farmer's Alliance." *Georgia Historical Quarterly* 69 (Summer 1985): 149-172.

Jones, David. "Women and Chartism." *History* 68 (February 1983): 1-21.

Klatch, Rebecca. "Coalition and Conflict Among Women of the New Right." *Signs* 13 (1988): 671-694.

Knight, Amy. "Female Terrorists in the Russian Socialist Revolutionary Party." *The Russian Review* 38 (April 1979): 139-159.

Kraft, James P. "The Fall of Job Harriman's Socialist Party: Violence, Gender, and Politics in Los Angeles, 1911." *Southern California Quarterly* 70, no. 1 (1988): 43-68.

Krieger, Nancy. "Queen of the Bolsheviks: The Hidden History of Dr. Marie Equi." *Radical America* 17 (September/October 1983): 55-73.

Kruks, Sonia, and Ben Wisner. "The State, The Party, and the Female Peasantry in Mozambique." *Journal of South African Studies* 11, no. 1 (1984): 106-127.

Lance, Keith Curray. "Strategy Choices of the British Women's Social and Political Union, 1903-1918." *Social Science Quarterly* 60 (June 1979): 51-61.

Manley, John. "Women and the Left in the 1930s: The Case of the Toronto C.C.F. Women's Joint Committee." *Atlantis* 5 (Spring 1980): 100-119.

Mason, Tim. "The Domestication of Female Socialist Icons: A Note in Reply to

Eric Hobsbawm." *History Workshop* 7 (Spring 1979): 170-175.

Mayo, Edith P. "Campaign Appeals to Women." *Journal of American Culture* 3 (Winter 1980): 722-742.

Miller, Sally M. "Other Socialists: Native-Born and Immigrant Women in the Socialist Party of America, 1901-1917." *Labor History* 24 (Winter 1983): 84-102.

Norton, Barbara T. "The Making of Female Marxist: E. D. Kuskova's Conversion to Russian Social Democracy." *International Review of Social History* 34, no. 2 (1989): 227-247.

Patterson, Cynthia M. "New Directions in the Political History of Women: A Case Study of the National Women's Party's Campaign for the Equal Rights Amendment, 1920-1927." *Women's Studies* 5, no. 6 (1982): 585-598.

Rupp, Leila J. "The Women's Community in the National Woman's Party, 1945 to the 1960s." *Signs* 10 (Summer 1985): 715-740.

Sangster, Joan. "The Communist Party and the Woman Question, 1900-1914." *Labour* 15 (Spring 1985): 25-56.

-----. "The Making of a Socialist-Feminist: The Early Career of Beatrice Brigden, 1888-1941." *Atlantis* 13 (Fall 1987): 13-28.

Schulkind, Eugene. "Socialist Women During the 1871 Paris Commune." *Past and Present* no. 106 (February 1985): 124-163.

Shaffer, Robert. "Women and the Communist Party, USA, 1930-1940." *Socialist Review* 45 (May/June 1979).

Shapcott, Jennifer. "The Red Chrysanthemum: Yamakawa Kikue and the Socialist Women's Movement in Pre-War Japan." *Papers on Far Eastern History* no. 35 (March 1987): 1-30.

Sillito, John R. "Women and the Socialist Party in Utah, 1900-1920." *Utah Historical Quarterly* 49 (Summer 1981): 220-238.

Snyder, Robert E. "Margaret Bourke-White and the Communist Witch Hunt." *Journal of American Studies* 19, no. 1 (April 1985): 5-25.

Starr, Karen. "Fighting for a Future: Farm Women of the Nonpartisan League." *Minnesota History* 48 (Summer 1983): 255-262.

Trofimenkoff, Susan Mann. "Thérèse Casgrain and the CCF in Quebec." *Canadian Historical Review* 66 (June 1985): 125-153.

Wheelwright, Julie. "'Colonel' Barker: A Case Study in the Contradictions of Fascism." *Immigrants & Minorities* 8 (March 1989): 40-48.

Zickefoose, Sandra. "Women and the Socialist Party of America, 1900-1915." *UCLA Historical Journal* 1 (1980): 26-41.

## Theories and Issues

Agosin, Marjorie. "Metaphors of Female Political Ideology: The Cases of Chile and Argentina." *Women's Studies International Forum* 10, no. 6 (1987): 571-577.

Baker, Paula. "The Domestication of Politics: Women and American Political Society 1780-1920." *American Historical Review* 89 (June 1984): 620-647.

Balmori, Diana A. "Family and Politics: Three Generations (1790-1890)." *Journal of Family History* 10 (Autumn 1985): 247-257.

Bergman, Jay. "The Political Thought of Vera Zasulich." *Slavic Review* 38 (June 1979): 243-258.

Brennan, Teresa, and Carole Pateman. "'Mere Auxiliaries to the Commonwealth': Women and the Origins of Liberalism." *Political Studies* 27 (June 1979): 183-200.

Brewster, Frieda Trubar. "A Personal View of the Early Left in Pittsburgh, 1907-1923." *Western Pennsylvania Historical Magazine* 69 (October 1986): 343-366.

Calhoun, Daniel H. "Eyes for the Jacksonian World: William C. Woodbridge and Emma Willard." *Journal of the Early Republic* 4 (Spring 1984): 1-26.

Caplan, Judith. "Woodrow Wilson and Women: The Formative Influences on Wilson's Attitudes toward Women." *New Jersey History* 104 (Spring/Summer 1986): 23-35.

Conway, Jill K. "Politics, Pedagogy, and Gender." *Daedalus* 116 (Fall 1987): 137-152.

Craig, John M. "Redbaiting, Pacifism, and Free Speech: Lucia Ames Mead and Her 1926 Lecture Tour in Atlanta and the Southeast." *Georgia Historical Quarterly* 71 (Winter 1987): 601-622.

Dietz, Mary G. "Context Is All: Feminism and Theories of Citizenship." *Daedalus* 116 (Fall 1987): 1-24.

Duke, David C. "Spy Scares, Scapegoats, and the Cold War." *South Atlantic Quarterly* 79 (Summer 1980): 245-256.

Evans, Sara M. "Toward a Usable Past: Feminism as History and Politics." *Minnesota History* 48 (Summer 1983): 230-235.

Fox-Genovese, Elizabeth. "The Personal Is Not Political Enough." *Marxist Perspectives* 2 (Winter 1979/80): 94-113.

-----. "Property and Patriarchy in Classical Bourgeois Political Theory." *Radical History Review* 4 (1977): 36-59.

Ginzberg, Lori D. "'Moral Suasion Is Moral Balderdash': Women, Politics, and Social Activism in the 1850s." *Journal of American History* 73 (December 1986): 601-622.

Hackett, David G. "The Social Origins of Nationalism: Albany, New York, 1754-1835." *Journal of Social History* 21 (Summer 1988): 659-682.

Hine, Darlene Clark. "An Angle of Vision: Black Women and the United States Constitution, 1787-1987." *OAH Magazine of History* 3 (Winter 1988): 7-14.

Jones, Kathleen B. "Citizenship in a Woman-friendly Polity." *Signs* 15 (Summer 1990): 781-812.

Kechnie, Margaret. "The United Farm Workers of Ontario: Developing a Political Consciousness." *Ontario History* 77 (December 1985): 267-280.

Kerber, Linda K. "'I Have Don...Much to Carrey on the Warr': Women and the Shaping of Republican Ideology after the American Revolution." *Journal of Women's History* 1 (Winter 1990): 231-243.

-----. "The Politicks of Housework." *Signs* 4 (Winter 1978): 402-406.

Marshall, Susan E. "Politics and Female Status in North Africa: A Reconsideration of Development Theory." *Economic Development and Cultural Change* 32, no. 3 (1984): 499-524.

Matthews, Jean. "Race, Sex, and the Dimensions of Liberty in Antebellum America." *Journal of the Early Republic* 6 (Fall 1986): 275-292.

May, Elaine Tyler. "Expanding the Past: Recent Scholarship on Women in Politics and Work." *Reviews in American History* 10 (December 1982): 216-233.

Mitchell, Claudine. "Madeleine Pelletier (1874-1939): The Politics of Sexual Oppression." *Feminist Review* no. 33 (Autumn 1989): 72-92.

Mullaney, Marie Marmo. "Gender and Revolution: Rosa Luxemburg and the Female Revolutionary Personality." *Journal of Psychohistory* 11 (Spring 1984): 463-476.

Nauright, Lynda. "Politics and Power: A New Look at Florence Nightingale." *Nursing Forum* 21, no. 1 (1984): 5-8.

O'Connor, Colleen M. "Imagine the Unimaginable: Helen Gahagan Douglas, Women, and the Bomb." *Southern California Quarterly* 67 (Spring 1985): 35-50.

Offen, Karen. "Women's Memory, Women's History, Women's Political Action: The French Revolution in Retrospect, 1789-1889-1989." *Journal of Women's History* 1 (Winter 1990): 211-230.

Papachristou, Judith. "American Women and Foreign Policy, 1898-1905: Exploring Gender in Diplomatic History." *Diplomatic History* 14 (Fall 1990): 493-509.

"The Political Application of Ideologies of Femininity: The Case of Marion Sparg." *Critical Arts* 5, no. 2 (1989): 55-57.

Prazniak, Roxann. "Weavers and Sorceresses of Chuansha: The Social Origins of Political Activism Among Rural Chinese Women." *Modern China* 12 (April 1986): 202-229.

Rand, Erica. "Depoliticizing Women: Female Agency, the French Revolution, and the Art of Boucher and David." *Genders* 7 (March 1990): 47-68.

Seller, Maxine S. "Defining Socialist Womanhood: The Women's Page of the *Jewish Daily Forward* in 1919." *American Jewish History* 76 (June 1987): 416-438.

Smith, Wallace. "The Birth of Petticoat Government." *American History Illustrated* 19, no. 3 (1984): 50-55.

Tansey, Richard. "Prostitution and Politics in Antebellum New Orleans." *Southern Studies* 18 (Winter 1979): 449-479.

Trimberger, Ellen Kay. "Women in the Old and New Left: The Evolution of a Politics of Personal Life." *Feminist Studies* 5 (Fall 1979): 432-450.

Tronto, Joan. "Changing Goals and Changing Strategies: Varieties of Women's Political Activities (Review Essay)." *Feminist Studies* 17 (Spring 1991): 85-104.

Vega, Judith. "Feminist Republicanism. Etta Palm-Aelders on Justice, Virtue and Men." *History of European Ideas* 10, no. 3 (1989): 333-352.

Walkowitz, Judith. "The Politics of Prostitution." *Signs* 6 (Autumn 1980): 123-135.

Wallace, Shelley Burtner. "Umatilla's 'Petticoat Government,' 1916-1920." *Oregon Historical Quarterly* 88 (Winter 1987): 385-402.

Wenger, Beth S. "Radical Politics in a Reactionary Age: The Unmaking of Rosika Schwimmer, 1914-1930." *Journal of Women's History* 2 (Fall 1990): 66-99.

## Women's Rights

Allam, S. "Women as Holders of Rights in Ancient Egypt (During the Late Period)." *Journal of the Economic and Social History of the Orient* 33 (February 1990): 1-34.

Anderson, Kathryn. "Anne Martin and the Dream of Political Equality for Women." *Journal of the West* 27 (April 1988): 28-34.

Andors, Phyllis. "Women's Liberation in China: A Continuing Struggle." *China Notes* 23 (Spring/Summer 1984): 287-293.

Andrews, Alice C. "The State of Women in the Americas." *Journal of Cultural Geography* 2 (Fall/Winter 1981): 27-44.

Atkinson, Colin B., and Jo Atkinson. "Maria Edgeworth, *Belinda*, and Women's Rights." *Eire-Ireland* 19 (Winter 1984): 94-118.

Azar, Robert. "The Liberation of Georgia Women for Jury Service." *Atlanta History Journal* (Fall 1980): 21-26.

Basch, Norma. "Equity vs. Equality: Emerging Concepts of Women's Political Status in the Age of Jackson." *Journal of the Early Republic* 3 (Fall 1983): 297-318.

Berger, Iris. "Gender, Race, and Political Empowerment: South African Canning Workers, 1940-1960." *Gender & Society* 4 (September 1990): 398-420.

Brown, Susan E. "'Rational Creatures and Free Citizens': The Language of Politics in the Eighteenth Century Debate on Women." *Historical Papers/Communications Historique* (1988): 35-47.

Caine, Barbara. "Beatrice Webb and the 'Woman Question.'" *History Workshop* 14 (Autumn 1982): 23-43.

-----. "Family History as Women's History: The Sisters of Beatrice Webb." *Feminist Studies* 12 (Summer 1986): 295-320.

Calman, Leslie J. "Women and Movement Politics in India." *Asian Survey* 29 (October 1989): 940-958.

Clark, E. Culpepper. "Sarah Morgan and Francis Dawson: Raising the Woman Question in Reconstruction South Carolina." *South Carolina Historical Magazine* 81 (January 1980): 8-23.

Conner, Susan P. "Sexual Politics and Citizenship: Women in Eighteenth-Century France." *Western Society for French History* 10 (October 1982): 264-273.

Costain, Anne N., and W. Douglas Costain. "Movements and Gatekeepers: Congressional Response to Women's Movement Issues, 1900-1982." *Congress and the Presidents* 12 (Spring 1985): 21-42.

Huff, Robert A. "Anne Miller and the Geneva Political Equality Club, 1897-1912." *New York History* 65 (October 1984): 324-348.

Jensen, Joan M. "'Disfranchisement Is a Disgrace': Women and Politics in New Mexico, 1900-1940." *New Mexico Historical Review* 56 (January 1981): 5-36.

Kealey, Linda. "Canadian Socialism and the Woman Question, 1900-1914." *Labour/Le Travail* 13 (Spring 1984): 77-100.

King, Lynda A. "The Woman Question and Politics in Austrian Interwar Literature." *German Studies Review* 6 (February 1983): 75-100.

Kinnaird, Joan K. "Mary Astell and the Conservative Contribution to English Feminism." *The Journal of British Studies* 19 (Fall 1979): 53-75.

Mitchell, Gary. "Women Standing for Women: The Early Political Career of Mary T. Norton." *New Jersey History* 96 (Spring-Summer 1978): 27-42.

Molyneux, Maxine. "Mobilization without Emancipation? Women's Interests, the State and Revolution in Nicaragua." *Feminist Studies* 11 (Summer 1985): 227-254.

Pugh, Evelyn L. "John Stuart Mill and the Women's Question in Parliament, 1865-1868." *The Historian* 42 (May 1980): 399-418.

-----. "John Stuart Mill, Harriet Taylor, and Women's Rights in America, 1850-1873." *Canadian Journal of History* 13 (December 1978): 423-442.

Rogers, Susan G. "Efforts toward Women's Development in Tanzania: Gender Rhetoric vs. Gender Realities." *Women and Politics* 2, no. 4 (1982): 23-41.

Rohrlich, Ruby. "State Formation in Sumer and the Subjugation of Women." *Feminist Studies* 6 (Spring 1980): 76-102.

Sauter-Bailliet, Theresia. "'Remember the Ladies': Emancipation Efforts of American Women from Independence to Seneca Falls." *European Contributions to American Studies* [Netherlands] 14 (1988): 271-279.

Voris, Jacqueline Van. "Daniel O'Connell and Women's Rights, One Letter." *Eire-Ireland* 17 (Fall 1982): 35-39.

Wellman, Judith. "Women's Rights, Republicanism, and Revolutionary Rhetoric in Ante-bellum New York State." *New York History* 69, no. 3 (1988): 353-384.

Wells, Julia. "Why Women Rebel: A Comparative Study of South African Women's Resistance in Bloemfontein (1913) and Johannesburg (1958)." *Journal of South African Studies* 10 (October 1983): 55-70.

# PORNOGRAPHY

Brigman, William. "Pornography as Political Expression." *Journal of Popular Culture* 17, no. 2 (1983): 129-134.

Champagne, Roland A. "The Engendered Blow Job: Bakhtin's Comic Dismemberment and the Pornography of Georges Bataille's 'Story of the Eye' (1928)." *Humor* 3, no. 2 (1990): 177-192.

Decew, Judith Wagner. "Violent Pornography: Censorship, Morality and Social Alternatives." *Journal of Applied Philosophy* 1, no. 1 (1984): 79-94.

Dworkin, Andrea. "Beaver and Male Power in Pornography." *New Political Science* 1, no. 4 (1980): 37-41.

Echols, Alice. "Cultural Feminism: Feminist Capitalism and the Anti-Pornography

Movement." *Social Text* 7 (1983): 34-53.

Ellis, Kate, Barbara O'Dair, and Abby Tallmer. "Feminism and Pornography." *Feminist Review* no. 36 (Autumn 1990): 15-18.

Garry, Ann. "Pornography and Respect for Women." *Social Theory and Practice* 4 (Summer 1978): 395-421.

Hommel, Teresa. "Images of Women in Pornography and Media." *New York University Review of Law and Social Change* 8, no. 2 (1978/79): 207-214.

Lansbury, Coral. "Gynaecology, Pornography, and the Antivivisection Movement." *Victorian Studies* 28 (Spring 1985): 413-438.

McCalman, I. "Unrespectable Radicalism, Infidels, and Pornography in Early 19th Century London." *Past & Present* no. 104 (1984): 74-110.

Nead, Lynda. "The Female Nude: Pornography, Art and Sexuality." *Signs* 15 (Winter 1990): 323-335.

Prince, Stephen. "The Pornographic Image and the Practice of Film Theory." *Cinema Journal* 27 (Winter 1988): 27-39.

Russo, Ann. "Conflicts and Contradictions Among Feminists over Issues of Pornography and Sexual Freedom." *Women's Studies International Forum* 10, no. 2 (1987): 103-112.

Segal, Lynne. "Pornography and Violence: What the 'Experts' Really Say." *Feminist Review* no. 36 (Autumn 1990): 29-41.

Smith-Rosenberg, Carroll. "Davy Crockett as Trickster: Pornography, Liminality and Symbolic Inversion in Victorian America." *Journal of Contemporary History* 17 (April 1982): 325-350.

Snitow, Ann B. "Mass Market Romance: Pornography for Women Is Different." *Radical History Review* 20 (Spring/Summer 1979): 141-161.

Stark, Gary D. "Pornography, Society, and the Law in Imperial Germany." *Central European History* 14 (September 1981): 200-229.

# PROFESSIONS

## Theory and Issues

Abrams, Jeanne. "Unsere Leit ('Our People'): Anna Hillkowitz and the Development of the East European Jewish Woman Professional in America." *American Jewish Archives* 37 (November 1985): 275-278.

Bartlett, Robin L., and Timothy I. Miller. "Executive Earnings by Gender: A Case Study." *Social Science Quarterly* 69 (December 1988): 892-909.

Brumberg, Joan Jacobs, and Nancy Tomes. "Women in the Professions: A Research Agenda for American Historians." *Reviews in American History* 10 (June 1982): 275-296.

Clark, Linda L. "A Battle of the Sexes in a Professional Setting: The Introduction of Inspectrices Primaires, 1889-1914." *French Historical Studies* 16 (Spring 1989): 96-125.

Cookingham, Mary E. "Combining Marriage, Motherhood, and Jobs Before World War II: Women College Graduates, Classes of 1905-1935." *Journal of*

*Family History* 9 (Summer 1984): 178-195.

Diner, Steven J. "George Herbert Mead's Ideas on Women and Careers: A Letter to His Daughter-in-Law, 1920." *Signs* 4 (Winter 1978): 407-409.

Gershman, Elizabeth, and Joyce Pendery. "Women at Work: How Stamford's Exhibit Traces the Professional Development of Women." *History News* 35 (August 1980):

Gilkes, Cheryl Townsend. "Successful Rebellious Professionals: The Black Woman's Professional Identity and Community Commitment." *Psychology of Women Quarterly* 6 (1982): 289-311.

Heeney, Brian. "Women's Struggles for Professional Work and Status in the Church of England, 1900-1930." *The Historical Journal* 26 (June 1983): 229-348.

Hoerning, Erika M. "Upward Mobility and Family Estrangement Among Females: What Happens When the 'Same Old Girl' Becomes the 'New Professional Woman'?" *International Journal of Oral History* 6 (June 1985): 104-117.

Kryder, LeeAnne Giannone. "Self-Assertion and Social Commitment: The Significance of Work to the Progressive Era's New Woman." *Journal of American Culture* 6 (Summer 1983): 25-30.

Mohraz, Judy Jolley. "The Equity Club: Community Building Among Professional Women." *Journal of American Culture* 5 (Winter 1982): 34-39.

Slater, Miriam, and Penina Migdal Glazer. "Prescriptions for Professional Survival." *Daedalus* 116 (Fall 1987): 119-136.

## General

Anderson, Kathie Ryckman. "Eva Bell Thompson: A North Dakota Daughter." *North Dakota History* 49 (Fall 1982): 11-18.

Chunko, Mary T. "Call Her Madam Secretary." *Humanities* 8 (May/June 1987): 22-23.

Cobble, Dorothy Sue. "A Self-Possessed Woman: A View of FDR's Secretary of Labor, Madame Perkins." *Labor History* 29, no. 2 (1988): 225-229.

Lapp, Rudolph M. "Mable Craft Deering: A Young Woman of Advanced Ideas." *California History* 66 (September 1987): 162-169.

Requardt, Cynthia Horsburgh. "Alternative Professions for Goucher College Graduates, 1892-1910." *Maryland Historical Magazine* 74, no. 3 (1979): 274-281.

Scott, Anne Firor. "Almira Lincoln Phelps: The Self-Made Woman in the Nineteenth Century." *Maryland Historical Magazine* 75, no. 3 (Fall 1980): 203-216.

Welter, Barbara. "She Hath Done What She Could: Protestant Women's Missionary Careers in Nineteenth-Century America." *American Quarterly* 30 (Winter 1978): 624-638.

Whiteley, Marilyn. "Modest, Unaffected and Fully Consecrated: Lady Evangelists in Canadian Methodism, 1884-1900." *Canadian Methodist Historical Society Papers* 6 (1987).

## Professional Career Choices

Albertine, Susan. "Breaking the Silent Partnership: Businesswomen in Popular Fiction." *American Literature* 62 (June 1990): 238-261.

Albisetti, James C. "The Fight for Female Physicians in Imperial Germany." *Central European History* 15 (June 1982): 99-123.

Aldrich, Michele L. "Women in Paleontology in the United States, 1840-1960." *Earth Sciences History* 1 (1982): 14-22.

Andrews, Janice L. "Female Social Workers in the Second Generation." *Affilia* 5 (Summer 1990): 46-59.

Babcock, Barbara, and Nancy Parezo. "The Leading Edge: Women Anthropologists in the Native Southwest, 1880-1945." *El Palacio* 92 (Summer/Fall 1986): 41-49.

Barlow, William, and David O. Powell. "Homeopathy and Sexual Equality: The Controversy over Coeducation at Cincinnati's Pulte Medical College, 1873-1879." *Ohio History* 90 (Spring 1981): 101-113.

Beasley, Maurine. "Women in Journalism: Contributors to Male Experience or Voices of Feminine Expression?" *American Journalism* 7 (Winter 1990): 39-54.

-----. "Women in Journalism Education: The Formative Period, 1908-1930." *Journalism History* 13 (Spring 1986): 10-18.

-----. "The Women's National Press Club: Case Study of Professional Aspirations." *Journalism History* 15 (Winter 1988): 112-121.

Bell, Maureen. "Hannah Allen and the Development of a Puritan Publishing Business, 1646-51." *Publishing History* 26 (1989): 5-66.

-----. "Mary Westwood, Quaker Publisher." *Publishing History* 23 (1988): 5-66.

Bennion, Sherilyn Cox. "Ada Chase Merritt and the Recorder: Pioneer Idaho Editor and Her Newspaper." *Idaho Yesterdays* 25 (Winter 1982): 22-30.

-----. "Enterprising Ladies: Utah's Nineteenth Century Women Editors." *Utah Historical Quarterly* 49 (1981): 291-304.

-----. "Lula Greene Richards: Utah's First Woman Editor." *Brigham Young University Studies* 21 (Spring 1981): 155-174.

-----. "Women Editors of California, 1854-1900." *Pacific Historian* 28 (Fall 1984): 30-43.

-----. "A Working List of Women Editors of the 19th-Century West." *Journalism History* 7, no. 2 (1980): 60-65.

Benton, John F. "Trotula, Women's Problems, and the Professionalization of Medicine in the Middle Ages." *Bulletin of the History of Medicine* 59 (Spring 1985): 30-53.

Berthoff, Rowland. "Conventional Mentality: Free Blacks, Women, and Business Corporations as Unequal Persons, 1820-1870." *Journal of American History* 76 (December 1989): 753-784.

Bickley, Ancella R. "Midwifery in West Virginia." *West Virginia History* 49 (1990): 55-67.

Blackstock, Joseph R. "Laura Scudder: Southern California's Potato Chip Pioneer Queen." *Californians* 7 (January/February 1990): 30-39.

Bleser, Carol K. "The Three Women Presidents of the Southern Historical Association: Ella Tonn, Kathryn Abby Hanna, and Mary Elizabeth Massey." *Southern Studies* 20 (Summer 1981): 101-121.

Bonner, T. N. "Pioneering in Women's Medical Education in the Swiss Universities 1864-1914." *Gesnerus* 45 (1988): 461-473.

-----. "Rendezvous in Zurich: Seven Who Made a Revolution in Women's Medical Education, 1864-1874." *Journal of the History of Medicine* 44, no. 1 (1989): 7-27.

Boos, Florence, and William Boos. "Catharine Macaulay: Historian and Political Reformer." *International Journal of Women's Studies* 2 (September/October 1979): 473-488.

Boyes, Georgina. "Alice Bertha Gomme (1852-1938): A Reassessment of the Work of a Folklorist." *Folklore* 110, no. 2 (1990): 198-208.

Bramadat, I. J., and K. I. Chalmers. "Nursing Education in Canada: Historical 'Progress'--Contemporary Issues." *Journal of Advanced Nursing* 14 (1989): 719-726.

Bratton, J. S. "Hesba Stretton's Journalism." *Victorian Periodicals Review* 12 (1979): 60-70.

Bridges, Lamar W. "Eliza Jane Nicholson and the *Daily Picayune*, 1876-1896." *Louisiana History* 30 (Summer 1989): 263-278.

Brody, David. "The Job of Nursing: Work and Work Culture in a Women's Trade." *Reviews in American History* 12 (1984): 115-118.

Bullough, Vern L. "American Nursing Leaders: A Comparative Study of Achievement." *Journal of Professional Nursing* 5, no. 4 (1989): 192-198.

Bullough, Vern L., and Bonnie Bullough. "Nurses and Power: Professional Power vs Political Clout." *Women & Politics* 4, no. 4 (1984): 67-74.

Campbell, Anne G. "Mary Breckenridge and the American Committee for Devastated France: The Foundations of the Frontier Nursing Service." *Register of the Kentucky Historical Society* 82 (Summer 1984): 257-276.

Cangi, Ellen Corwin. "A New Profession for Women: The Art and Science of Nursing in Cincinnati, 1889-1940." *Queen City Heritage* 41 (Winter 1983): 24-29.

-----. "Patrons and Proteges: Cincinnati's First Generation of Women Doctors, 1875-1910." *Cincinnati Historical Society Bulletin* 37 (Summer 1979): 89-114.

Carmichael, James V., Jr. "Tommie Dora Barker and the Atlanta Public Library 1915-1930: A Case Study in Female Professionalism." *Atlanta History* 34 (Spring 1990): 24-41.

Carroll, William K., and Rennie Warburton. "Feminism, Class Consciousness and Household-Work Linkages Among Registered Nurses in Victoria." *Labour/Le Travail* 24 (Fall 1989): 131-146.

Casey, Naomi Taylor. "Miss Edith Johnson: Pioneer Newspaper Woman." *Chronicles of Oklahoma* 60 (Spring 1982): 66-73.

Caswell, Lucy Shelton. "Edwina Dumm: Pioneer Woman Editorial Cartoonist, 1915-1917." *Journalism History* 15 (Spring 1988): 2-6.

-----. "The Lady Cartoonist." *Timeline* 6 (June/July 1989): 44-49.

Chabot, Jeanette Toudin. "Takamure Itsue: The First Historian of Japanese Women." *Women's Studies* 8, no. 4 (1985): 287-290.

Chambers, Clarke A. "Women in the Creation of the Profession of Social Work." *Social Service Review* 60 (March 1986): 1-33.

Chua, Wai-Fong, and Stewart Clegg. "Professional Closure: The Case of British Nursing." *Theory and Society* 19 (April 1990): 135-172.

Clar, Reva. "First Jewish Woman Physician of Los Angeles." *Western States Jewish Historical Quarterly* 14 (October 1981): 66-75.

Clevenger, Martha R. "From Lay Practitioner to Doctor of Medicine: Women Physicians in St. Louis, 1860-1920." *Gateway Heritage* 8 (Winter 1987/88): 12-21.

Coates, Mary Sue. "Women Geologists Work Toward Equality." *Geotimes* 31 (November 1986): 11-14.

Corwin, Margaret. "Minna Schmidt: Businesswoman, Feminist, and Fairy Godmother to Chicago." *Chicago History* 7 (Winter 1978/79): 226-235.

Cravens, Hamilton. "Establishing the Science of Nutrition at the USDA: Ellen Swallow Richards and Her Allies." *Agricultural History* 64 (Spring 1990): 122-133.

Crowe-Carraco, Carol. "Mary Breckenridge (d. 1965) and the Frontier Nursing Service." *Register of the Kentucky History Society* 76 (July 1978): 179-191.

Davis, Audrey B. "With Love and Money: Visiting Nursing in Buffalo, New York, 1885-1915." *New York History* 71 (January 1990): 45-67.

Davis, S. "Lucy Hobbs Taylor: The Mixed Blessing of Being First." *Journal of the American Dental Association* 117 (1988): 443.

De la Cour, Lykke. "The 'Other' Side of Psychology: Women Psychologists in Toronto from 1920 to 1945." *Canadian Woman Studies/Les cahiers de la femme* 8 (Winter 1987): 44-46.

De La Cour, Lykke, and Rose Sheinin. "The Ontario Medical College for Women, 1883 to 1906: Lessons from Gender-Separatism in Medical Education." *Canadian Woman Studies/Les cahiers de la femme* 7 (Fall 1986): 73-77.

Deegan, Mary Jo. "Early Women Sociologists and the American Sociological Society: The Patterns of Exclusion and Participation." *American Sociologist* 16 (February 1981): 14-24.

Dembski, Peter E. Paul. "Jenny Kidd Trout and the Founding of the Women's Medical Colleges at Kingston and Toronto." *Ontario History* 77 (September 1985): 183-206.

Dion, Susan. "Women in the Boston Gazette, 1755-1775." *Historical Journal of Massachusetts* 14 (June 1986): 87-102.

Drachman, Virginia G. "Female Solidarity and Professional Success: The Dilemma of Women Doctors in Late Nineteenth-Century America." *Journal of Social History* 15 (Summer 1982): 607-620.

-----. "The Limits of Progress: The Professional Lives of Women Doctors, 1881-1926." *Bulletin of the History of Medicine* 60 (Spring 1986): 58-72.

Dye, Nancy Schrom. "Mary Breckinridge, the Frontier Nursing Service and the

Introduction of Nurse-Midwifery in the United States." *Bulletin of the History of Medicine* 57 (Winter 1983): 485-507.

Ehrlich, George, and Sherry Piland. "The Architectural Career of Nelle Peters." *Missouri Historical Review* 83 (January 1989): 161-176.

Engel, Barbara Alpern. "Women Medical Students in Russia, 1872-1882: Reformers or Rebels?" *Journal of Social History* 12 (Spring 1979): 394-414.

Evins, Janie Synatzske. "Arkansas Women: Their Contribution to Society, Politics, and Business, 1865-1900." *Arkansas History Quarterly* 44 (Summer 1985): 118-133.

Fine, Lisa M. "Between Two Worlds: Business Women in a Chicago Boarding Home 1900-1930." *Journal of Social History* 19 (Spring 1986): 511-520.

Fish, Virginia Kemp. "Anne Marion MacLean: A Neglected Part of the Chicago School." *Journal of the History of Sociology* 3 (Spring 1981): 43-62.

-----. "'More Than Lore': Marion Talbot and Her Role in the Founding Years of the University of Chicago." *International Journal of Women's Studies* 8 (May/June 1985): 228-249.

Flaumenhaft, Eugene, and Carol Flaumenhaft. "American Nursing and the Road Not Taken." *Journal of the History of Medicine and Allied Sciences* 44 (January 1989): 72-89.

Ford, Charlotte A. "Eliza Frances Andrews, Practical Botanist, 1840-1931." *Georgia History Quarterly* 70 (Spring 1986): 63-80.

Fox, Robert, and Anna Guagnini. "Classical Values and Useful Knowledge: The Problem of Access to Technical Careers in Modern Europe." *Daedalus* 116, no. 4 (1987): 153-171.

Frankel, Lois. "Damaris Cudworth Masham: A Seventeenth Century Feminist Philosopher." *Hypatia* 4 (Spring 1989): 80-90.

Fullard, Joyce. "Ann Preston: Pioneer of Medical Education and Women's Rights." *Pennsylvania Heritage* 8 (Winter 1982): 9-14.

Furumoto, Laurel. "Mary Whitton Calkins, 1863-1930: Fourteenth President of the American Psychological Association." *Journal of the History of Behavioral Sciences* 15, no. 4 (1979): 346-356.

Gallagher, Teresa. "From Family Helpmeet to Independent Professional: Women in American Pharmacy, 1870-1940." *Pharmacy in History* 31 (1989): 60-77.

Gilley, B. H. "A Woman for Women: Eliza Nicholson, Publisher of the New Orleans *Daily Picayune*." *Louisiana History* 30 (Summer 1989): 233-248.

Gilmartin, Pat. "Fish and Fetishes--A Victorian Woman on African Rivers." *Women & Environments* 12 (May/June 1990): 10-12.

Green, Judy, and Jeanne LaDuke. "Women in the American Mathematical Community: The Pre-1940 Ph.D.'s." *Mathematical Intelligencer* 9, no. 1 (1987): 11-23.

Greene, J. "The Beginning of Community Psychiatric Nursing." *History of Nursing* 2, no. 9 (1989): 14-20.

Greentree, Carol. "Harriett Barnhart Wimmer: A Pioneer San Diego Woman Landscape Architect." *Journal of San Diego History* 34 (Summer 1988): 223-239.

Grinstein, Louise S. "Women in Physics and Astronomy: A Selected Bibliography." *School Science and Mathematics* 80 (May/June 1980): 384-398.

Guy, John R. "The Episcopal Licensing of Physicians, Surgeons and Midwives." *Bulletin of the History of Medicine* 56 (Winter 1982): 528-542.

Hahn, Gertrude, and Naomi Hahn. "Frieda M. Damm, Red Cross Nurse, 1917-1919." *Concordia Historical Institute Quarterly* 57 (Summer 1984): 53-59.

Hales, David A. "'There Goes Matilda': Millard County Midwife and Nurse." *Utah Historical Quarterly* 55 (Summer 1987): 278-293.

Hastings, Margaret, and Elisabeth Kimball. "Two Distinguished Medievalists-- Nellie Neilson and Bertha Putnam." *Journal of British Studies* 18 (Spring 1979): 142-159.

Hawkins, Joellen Beck W. "Public Health Nursing in Chicago in the 1920s: The Reminiscences of Lillian Beck Fuller, R.N." *Journal of Illinois State Historical Society* 76 (Autumn 1983): 195-204.

Heinz, Catharine. "Women Radio Pioneers." *Journal of Popular Culture* 12 (Fall 1978): 305-314.

Henry, Susan. "'Dear Companion, Ever-Ready Co-Worker': A Woman's Role in a Media Dynasty." *Journalism Quarterly* 64 (Summer/Autumn 1987): 301-312.

-----. "Exception to the Female Model: Colonial Printer Mary Crouch." *Journalism Quarterly* 62 (Winter 1985): 725-733, 749.

Hewitt, D. L. "Dentistry's First Lady: Lucy Hobbs Taylor." *Ohio Dentistry Journal* 62, no. 4 (1988): 28-31.

Hine, Darlene Clark. "The Ethel Johns Report: Black Women in the Nursing Profession, 1925." *Journal of Negro History* 67 (Fall 1982): 212-228.

-----. "From Hospital to College: Black Nurse Leaders and the Rise of Collegiate Nursing Schools." *Journal of Negro Education* 51 (Summer 1982): 222-237.

Howe, Barbara J. "Women in Historic Preservation: The Legacy of Ann Pamela Cunningham." *Public Historian* 12 (Winter 1990): 31-61.

Hunt, Marion. "Woman's Place in Medicine: The Career of Dr. Mary Hancock McClean." *Missouri Historical Society Bulletin* 36 (July 1980): 255-263.

James, Laurence P., and Sandra C. Taylor. "'Strong Minded Women': Desdemona Stott Beeson and Other Hard Rock Mining Entrepreneurs." *Utah Historical Quarterly* 46 (Spring 1978): 136-150.

Jardine, Pauline O. "An Urban Middle-Class Calling: Women and the Emergence of Modern Nursing Education at the Toronto General Hospital, 1881-1914." *Urban History Review* 17 (February 1989): 177-190.

Kalisch, Philip A., and Beatrice J. Kalisch. "When Nurses Were National Heroines: Images of Nursing in American Film, 1942-1945." *Nursing Forum* 20, no. 1 (1981): 14-61.

Kaufman, Polly Welts. "Challenging Tradition: Pioneer Women Naturalists in the National Park Service." *Forest & Conservation History* 34 (January 1990): 4-16.

Keddy, Barbara. "Nursing in Canada in the 1920s and 1930s: Powerful while Powerless." *History of Nursing* 2, no. 9 (1989): 1-7.

Keddy, Barbara, et al. "Nurses' Work World: Scientific or 'Womanly Ministering'?" *Resources for Feminist Research* [Canada] 16, no. 4 (1987): 37-39.

Keller, Evelyn Fox. "Women Scientists and Feminist Critics of Science." *Daedalus* 116 (Fall 1987): 77-92.

Kennedy, Joan E. "Jane Soley Hamilton, Midwife." *Nova Scotia Historical Review* 2 (1982): 6-29.

Kenney, Anne R. "'She Got to Berlin': Virginia Irwin, St. Louis Post-Dispatch War Correspondent." *Missouri Historical Review* 79 (July 1985): 456-479.

Kidwell, Peggy Aldrich. "Women Astronomers in Britain, 1780-1930." *Isis: An International Review Devoted to the History of Science and Its Cultural Influences* 75 (September 1984): 457-480.

King, M. G. "Nursing Shortage, circa 1915." *Image* 21, no. 3 (1989): 124-127.

Kloberdanz, Timothy J. "The Daughters of Shiphrah: Folk Healers and Midwives of the Great Plains." *Great Plains Quarterly* 9 (Winter 1989): 3-12.

Kohlstedt, Sally Gregory. "Maria Mitchell: The Advancement of Women in Science." *New England Quarterly* 51 (March 1978): 39-63.

Krishnaraj, Maithreyi. "The Status of Women in Science in India." *Journal of Higher Education* 5 (Spring 1980): 381-393.

Kunzel, Regina. "The Professionalization of Benevolence: Evangelicals and Social Workers in the Florence Crittenton Homes, 1915 to 1945." *Journal of Social History* 22 (Fall 1988): 21-44.

Lance, N. "Historical Lessons? The State Enrolled Nurse." *History of Nursing* 2, no. 9 (1989): 21-51.

Lapp, Rudolph M. "Mable Craft Deering: A Young Woman of Advanced Ideas." *California History* 66 (September 1987): 162-169.

Leone, Janice. "Integrating the American Association of University Women, 1945-1949." *Historian* 51 (May 1989): 423-445.

Lewin, Miriam. "Early Women Psychologists Challenge Sexism." *Women's Studies Quarterly* 16 (Fall/Winter 1988): 58-67.

Libby, Barbara S. "Women in the Economics Profession, 1900-1940: Factors in the Declining Visibility." *Essays in Economic and Business History* 8 (1990): 121-130.

Lieburg, M. J. van, and H. Morland. "Midwife Regulation, Education and Practice in the Netherlands During the Nineteenth Century." *Medical History* 33 (1989): 296-317.

Litoff, Judy Barett. "Forgotten Women: American Midwives at the Turn of the Twentieth Century." *Historian* 40 (February 1978): 235-251.

Lyons-Barrett, Mary. "The Omaha Visiting Nurses Association During the 1920s and 1930s." *Nebraska History* 70 (Winter 1988): 283-296.

Mabee, Carleton. "Margaret Mead and Behavioral Scientists in World War II: Problems in Responsibility, Truth, and Effectiveness." *Journal of the History of the Behavioral Sciences* 23 (January 1987): 3-13.

Marrett, Cora Bahley. "On the Evolution of Women's Medical Societies." *Bulletin of the History of Medicine* 53, no. 3 (1979): 434-448.

Marshall, Alice K. "'Little Doc,' Architect of Modern Nursing." *Pennsylvania Heritage* 10 (Spring 1984): 4-11.

Mathes, Valerie Sherer. "Native American Women in Medicine and the Military." *Journal of the West* 21 (April 1982): 41-48.

-----. "Susan LaFlesche Picotte: Nebraska's Indian Physician, 1865-1915." *Nebraska History* 63 (Winter 1982): 502-530.

McConnachie, Kathleen. "Methodology in the Study of Women in History: A Case Study of Helen MacMurchy, M.D." *Ontario History* 75 (March 1983): 61-70.

McDonell, Katherine Mandusic. "Women and Medicine in Early Nineteenth Century Indiana." *Indiana Medical History Quarterly* 6 (June 1980).

McFadden, Margaret. "Anna Doyle Wheeler: Philosopher, Socialist, Feminist." *Hypatia* 4 (Spring 1989): 91-101.

McGovern, Constance M. "Doctors or Ladies? Women Physicians in Psychiatric Institutions, 1872-1900." *Bulletin of the History of Medicine* 55 (Spring 1981): 88-107.

Menninger, Sally Ann, and Clare Rose. "Women Scientists and Engineers in American Academia." *International Journal of Women's Studies* 3 (May/June 1980): 292-299.

Mercier, Laurie K. "Montana at Work: Businesswomen in Agricultural Communities." *Montana* 40 (Summer 1990): 77-83.

Meredith, Lesley. "Working Our Way to the Bottom: Women and Nursing." *Labour History* 52 (May 1987): 96-102.

Miller, Elissa Lane. "Arkansas Nurses, 1895 to 1920: A Profile." *Arkansas Historical Quarterly* 47 (Summer 1988): 154-171.

Mitchell, Catherine C. "The Place of Biography in the History of News Women." *American Journalism* 7 (Winter 1990): 23-32.

-----. "Scholarship on Women Working in Journalism." *American Journalism* 7 (Winter 1990): 33-38.

Monteiro, Lois A. "On Separate Roads: Florence Nightingale and Elizabeth Blackwell." *Signs* 9 (Spring 1984): 520-533.

Morantz, Regina Markell. "Feminism, Professionalism, and Germs: The Thought of Mary Putnam Jacobi and Elizabeth Blackwell." *American Quarterly* 34 (Winter 1982): 459-478.

Morantz, Regina Markell, and Sue Zschoche. "Professionalism, Feminism, and Gender Roles: A Comparative Study of Nineteenth-Century Medical Therapeutics." *Journal of American History* 67 (December 1980): 568-588.

More, Ellen. "The Blackwell Medical Society and the Professionalization of Women Physicians." *Bulletin of the History of Medicine* 61 (Winter 1987): 603-628.

-----. "A Certain Restless Ambition: Women Physicians and World War I." *American Quarterly* 41 (December 1989): 636-660.

Morgan, J. Graham. "Women in American Sociology in the Nineteenth Century." *Journal of the History of Sociology* 2 (Spring 1980): 1-34.

Morgan, Paul. "Francis Wolfreston and 'Hor Bouks': A Seventeenth-Century

Woman Book-Collector." *The Library* 11 (September 1989): 197-219.

Muecke, M. A., and W. Srisuphan. "Born Female: The Development of Nursing in Thailand." *Social Science Medicine* 29 (1989): 643-652.

Murphy, Beatrice. "Diary of a Night Nurse, Butte, Montana, 1909." *Montana* 39 (Autumn 1989): 64-70.

Murphy, Lucy Eldersveld. "Business Ladies: Midwestern Women and Enterprise, 1850-1880." *Journal of Women's History* 3 (Spring 1991): 65-89.

-----. "Her Own Boss: Businesswomen and Separate Spheres in the Midwest, 1850-1880." *Illinois Historical Journal* 80 (Autumn 1987): 155-176.

Murphy, Miriam B. "The Working Women of Salt Lake City: A Review of the Utah Gazetteer, 1892-93." *Utah Historical Quarterly* 46 (Spring 1978): 121-135.

Nauright, Lynda. "Politics and Power: A New Look at Florence Nightingale." *Nursing Forum* 21, no. 1 (1984): 5-8.

Norman, Elizabeth M. "Who and Where Are Nursing's Historians." *Nursing Forum* 20, no. 2 (1981): 138-152.

Nostwich, T. D., ed. "Nellie Bly's Account of Her 1895 Visit to Drought-Stricken Nebraska and South Dakota." *Nebraska History* 67 (Spring 1986): 30-67.

O'Brien, Kevin H. F. "Irene Osgood, John Richmond Limited and the Wilde Circle." *Publishing History* no. 22 (1987): 73-93.

Okonkwo, Rina. "Adelaide Casely Hayford (1868-1960): Cultural Nationalist and Feminist (Gold Coast)." *Phylon* (March 1981): 41-51.

Pabis-Braunstein, M. "The First Polish Women Pharmacists." *Pharmacy in History* 31, no. 1 (1989): 12-15.

Palmquist, Peter E., comp. "Elizabeth Fleischmann-Aschheim, Pioneer X-ray Photographer." *Western States Jewish History* 23 (October 1990): 35-45.

Paradis, Roger. "Henriette, La capuche: The Portrait of a Frontier Midwife." *Canadian Folklore* 3, no. 2 (1981): 10-26.

Peebles, R. J. "Female Surgeons in the U.S.: An Eighteen Year Review." *Bulletin of American College Surgeons* 74, no. 11 (1989): 18-23.

Pendergrass, Lee F. "Dispelling Myths: Women's Contributions to the Forest Service in California." *Forest & Conservation History* 34 (January 1990): 17-25.

Peterson, Susan C., and Beverly Jensen. "The Red Cross Call to Serve: The Western Response from North Dakota Nurses." *Western Historical Quarterly* 21 (August 1990): 321-340.

Pursell, Carroll. "The Cover Design: Women Inventors in America." *Technology and Culture* 22 (July 1981): 545-549.

Quiroga, Virginia A. Metaxas. "Female Lay Managers and Scientific Pediatrics at Nursery and Child's Hospital, 1854-1910." *Bulletin of the History of Medicine* 60 (Summer 1986): 194-208.

Reese, Linda W. "'Dear Oklahoma Lady': Women Journalists Speak Out." *Chronicles of Oklahoma* 67 (Fall 1989): 264-295.

Rife, Gladys Talcott. "Personal Perspectives on the 1950s: Iowa's Rural Women Newspaper Columnists." *Annals of Iowa* 49 (Spring 1989): 661-682.

Roscher, Nina Matheny, and Phillip L. Ammons. "Early Women Chemists of the Northeast." *Journal of the Washington Academy of Sciences* 71 (December 1981): 177-182.

Rossiter, Margaret W. "Women and the History of Scientific Communication." *Journal of Library History* 21 (Winter 1986): 39-59.

-----. "'Women's Work' in Science, 1880-1910." *Isis: An International Review Devoted to the History of Science and Its Cultural Influences* 71, no. 258 (1980): 381-398.

Rothman, Patricia. "Genius, Gender, and Culture: Women Mathematicians of the 19th Century." *Interdisciplinary Science Reviews* 13 (1988): 64-72.

Sabin, Linda E. "The French Revolution: A Forgotten Era in Nursing History." *Nursing Forum* 20, no. 3 (1981): 224-243.

Schackel, Sandra K. "'The Tales Those Nurses Told!': Public Health Nurses Among the Pueblo and Navajo Indians." *New Mexico Historical Review* 65 (April 1990): 225-250.

Schiebinger, Linda. "The History and Philosophy of Women in Science." *Signs* 12 (Winter 1987): 305-332.

Scott, Robert C. "Adventures of the Bumming Botanists: From the Diary of Nelle Stevenson, 1907." *Essays and Monographs in Colorado History* 5 (1987): 67-77.

Sebire, Dawn. "'To Shield from Temptation': The Business Girl and the City." *Urban History Review* 17 (February 1989): 203-208.

Seigel, Peggy Brase. "She Went to War: Indiana Women Nurses in the Civil War." *Indiana Magazine of History* 86 (March 1990): 1-27.

Seraile, William. "Susan McKinney Steward: New York State's First African-American Woman Physician." *Afro-Americans in New York Life and History* 9 (July 1985): 27-44.

Sheppard, Alice. "There Were Ladies Present: American Women Cartoonists and Comic Artists in the Early Twentieth Century." *Journal of American Culture* 7 (Fall 1984): 38-48.

Sherwood, Midge. "Eliza Ann Otis, Co-Founder of the Los Angeles Times." *Pacific Historian* 28 (Fall 1984): 45-53.

Shteir, Ann B. "Botanical Dialogues: Maria Jacson and Women's Popular Science Writing in England." *Eighteenth-Century Studies* 23 (Spring 1990): 301-317.

Sloan, Patricia E. "Early Black Nursing Schools and Responses of Black Nurses to their Educational Programs." *Western Journal of Black Studies* 9 (Fall 1985): 158-172.

Smith, Beatrice Scheer. "Hannah English Williams: America's First Woman Natural History Collector." *South Carolina Historical Magazine* 87 (April 1986): 83-92.

Smith, Susan Hunter. "Women Architects in Atlanta, 1895-1979." *Atlanta History Journal* (Winter 1980): 85-106.

Steiner, Linda, and Susanne Gray. "Genevieve Forbes Herrick: A Front-Page Reporter 'Pleased to Write About Women.'" *Journalism History* 12 (Spring 1985): 8-16.

Stofer, Paula. "Angels of Mercy: Michigan's Midwives." *Michigan History* 73 (September/October 1989): 40-47.

Struthers, James. "A Profession in Crisis: Charlotte Whitton and Canadian Social Work in the 1930's." *Canadian Historical Review* 62 (June 1981): 169-185.

Summers, A. "Ministering Angels." *History Today* 39 (February 1989): 31-37.

-----. "The Mysterious Demise of Sarah Gamp: The Domiciliary Nurse and Her Detractors, c. 1830-1860." *Victorian Studies* 32 (Spring 1989): 365-386.

-----. "Pride & Prejudice: Ladies and Nurses in the Crimean War." *History Workshop* 16 (Autumn 1983): 33-56.

Talberg, Marianne. "Nursing and Medical Care in Finland from the Eighteenth to the Late Nineteenth Century." *Scandinavian Journal of History* 14, no. 4 (1989): 269-284.

Tavill, A. A. "Early Medical Co-Education and Women's Medical College, Kingston, Ontario 1880-1894." *Historic Kingston* 30 (January 1982): 68-89.

Thatcher, Linda, and John R. Sillito. "'Sisterhood and Sociability': The Utah Women's Press Club, 1891-1928." *Utah Historical Quarterly* 53 (Spring 1985): 144-156.

Tomer, John S. "Scientist with a Gift for Teaching." *Chronicles of Oklahoma* 63 (Winter 1985/86): 397-411.

Tucker, Sara W. "Opportunities for Women: The Development of Professional Women's Medicine in Canton, China, 1879-1901." *Women's Studies International Forum* 13, no. 4 (1990): 357-368.

Turitz, Leo E. "Amelia Greenwald (1886-1966): The Jewish Florence Nightingale." *American Jewish Archives* 37 (November 1985): 291-292.

Wade-Gayles, Gloria. "Black Women Journalists in the South, 1880-1905: An Approach to the Study of Black Women's History." *Callaloo* 9 (February/October 1981): 138-152.

Wagener, Mary L. "Berta Zuckerkandl Viennese Journalist and Publicist of Modern Art and Culture." *European Studies Review* 12 (October 1982): 425-444.

Walkowitz, Daniel J. "The Making of a Feminine Professional Identity: Social Workers in the 1920s." *American Historical Review* 95 (October 1990): 1051-1076.

Waller-Zuckerman, Mary Ellen. "Vera Connolly: Progressive Journalist." *Journalism History* 15 (Summer/Autumn 1988): 80-88.

Ward, Karen. "From Executive to Feminist: The Business Women's Legislative Council of Los Angeles, 1927-1932." *Essays in Economic and Business History* 7 (1989): 60-75.

Ward, P. S. "Hygeia's Sisters: A History of Women in Pharmacy." *Caduceus* 4, no. 3/4 (1988): 1-57.

Warner, Deborah. "Women Astronomers." *Natural History* 88 (May 1979): 12-26.

Weaver, Bill L., and James A. Thompson. "Women in Medicine and the Issue in Late Nineteenth-Century Alabama." *Alabama Historical Quarterly* 43 (Winter 1981): 292-314.

Whitman, Betsey S. "Women in the American Mathematical Society before 1900."

*Association for Women in Mathematics Newsletter* 13 (September/October 1983): 7-9.

Wiesner, Merry E. "Early Modern Midwifery: A Case Study." *International Journal of Women's Studies* 6 (January/February 1983): 26-43.

Wilson, Laurel. "Anna Gove: 'Lady, Female Doctress:' Social Non-conformist and Clothing Conservative." *Dress* 16 (1990): 62-69.

Wood, Sharon E. "Althea Sherman and the Birds of Prairie and Dooryard: A Scientist's Witness to Change." *Palimpsest* 70 (Winter 1989): 164-185.

Woolley, Alma S. "A Hoosier Nurse in France: The World War I Diary of Maude Frances Essig." *Indiana Magazine of History* 82 (March 1986): 37-68.

Wyman, A. L. "The Surgeoness: The Female Practitioner of Surgery 1400-1800." *Medical History* 28 (January 1984): 22-41.

Zschoche, Sue. "Dr. Clarke Revisited: Science, True Womanhood, and Female Collegiate Education." *History of Education Quarterly* 29 (Winter 1989): 545-569.

## White Collar Work

Adams, Carole Elizabeth. "White-Blouse and White-Collar: Work, Culture and Gender." *Gender & History* 2 (Autumn 1990): 343-348.

Andrews, Melodie. "'What the Girls Can Do': The Debate over the Employment of Women in the Early American Telegraph Industry." *Essays in Economic and Business History* 8 (1990): 109-120.

Aron, Cindy S. "To Barter Their Souls for Gold': Female Clerks in Federal Government Offices, 1862-1890." *Journal of American History* 67 (March 1981): 835-853.

Atsumi, Reiko. "Dilemmas and Accommodations of Married Japanese Women in White Collar Employment." *Bulletin of Concerned Asian Scholars* 20 (July/September 1988): 54-63.

Bruns, James H. "By the Seat of Their Pants: Flying the Mail." *Timeline* 4 (December 1987/January 1988): 20-32.

Corn, Joseph J. "Making Flying 'Thinkable': Women Pilots and the Selling of Aviation, 1927-1940." *American Quarterly* 31 (Fall 1979): 556-571.

Cross, Gary, and Peter Shergold. "'We Think We Are the Oppressed': Gender, White Collar Work, and Grievances of Late Nineteenth Century Women." *Labor History* 28 (Winter 1987): 23-53.

Dempsey, Hugh A., ed. "Confessions of a Calgary Stenographer." *Alberta History* 36 (Spring 1988): 1-15.

Hadley, Nancy. "The 'Hello' Girls of Houston." *Houston Review* 9, no. 2 (1987): 82-94.

Lowe, Graham. "Class, Job, and Gender in the Canadian Office." *Labour* 10 (Autumn 1982): 11-38.

-----. "Women, Work and the Office: The Feminization of Clerical Occupations in Canada, 1901-1930." *Canadian Journal of Sociology* 5 (1980): 361-381.

Mueller, Milton. "The Switchboard Problem: Scale, Signaling, and Organization in Manual Telephone Switching, 1877-1897." *Technology and Culture* 30 (July 1989): 534-560.

Ritter, Darlene. "Nebraska's First Aviatrix, Ethel Ives Tillotson: 1894-1928." *Nebraska History* 63 (Summer 1982): 152-163.

Vinson, Michael. "From Housework to Office Clerk: Utah's Working Women, 1870-1900." *Utah Historical Quarterly* 53 (Fall 1985): 326-335.

Weiss, Janice. "Educating for Clerical Work: The Nineteenth-Century Private Commercial School." *Journal of Social History* 14 (Spring 1981): 407-423.

Wharton, Amy, and Val Burris. "Office Automation and Its Impact on Women Workers." *Humboldt Journal of Social Relations* 10 (Spring/Summer 1983): 112-126.

Wright, Helena. "Sarah G. Bagley: A Biographical Note." *Labor History* 20, no. 3 (Summer 1979): 398-413.

Zimmeck, Meta. "Strategies and Stratagems for the Employment of Women in the British Civil Service, 1919-1939." *The Historical Journal* 27 (December 1984): 901-924.

# PROSTITUTION

Anderson, Amanda S. "D. G. Rossetti's 'Jenny': Agency, Intersubjectivity, and the Prostitute." *Genders* no. 4 (March 1989): 103-121.

Archer, Leonie. "Virgin and Harlot in the Writings of Formative Judaism." *History Workshop* 24 (Autumn 1987): 1-16.

Backhouse, Constance B. "Nineteenth Century Canadian Prostitution Law. Reflections on a Discriminatory Society." *Histoire Sociale/Social History* 18 (November 1985): 387-423.

Barstow, Anne Llewellyn. "The First Generations of Anglican Clergy Wives: Heroines or Whores?" *Historical Magazine of the Protestant Episcopal Church* 52 (March 1983): 3-16.

Bartman, William J. "Korean War Brides, Prostitutes and Yellow Slavery." *Minerva: Quarterly Report on Women and the Military* 7 (Summer 1989): 16-25.

Bedford, Judy. "Prostitution in Calgary, 1905-1914." *Alberta History* 29 (Spring 1981): 1-11.

Berg, Joel. "Careers in Brothel Prostitution: St. Paul, 1865-1883." *Journal of Interdisciplinary History* 12 (Spring 1982): 597-619.

Brumberg, Joan Jacobs. "'Ruined' Girls: Changing Community Responses to Illegitimacy in Upstate New York, 1890-1920." *Journal of Social History* 18 (Winter 1984): 247-272.

Brundage, James A. "Sumptuary Laws and Prostitution in Late Medieval Italy." *Journal of Medieval History* 13 (December 1987): 343-356.

Carlisle, Marcia. "Disorderly City, Disorderly Women: Prostitution in Ante-Bellum Philadelphia." *Pennsylvania Magazine of History and Biography* 110 (October 1986): 549-568.

Chacon, Ramon D. "The Beginning of Racial Segregation: The Chinese in West

Fresno and Chinatown's Role as Red Light District, 1870s-1920s." *Southern California Quarterly* 70 (Winter 1988): 371-398.

Chesson, Michael B. "Harlots or Heroines? A New Look at the Richmond Bread Riot." *Virginia Magazine of History and Biography* 92 (April 1984): 131-175.

Conner, Susan P. "Politics, Prostitution, and the Pox in Revolutionary Paris, 1789-1799." *Western Society for French History* 14 (November 1986): 183.

Dawson, N. M. "The Filles-du-Ray Sent to New France: French Women in 17th Century Canada--Protestant, Prostitute or Both." *Historical Reflections* 16 (Spring 1989): 55-78.

Diffendal, Anne P. "Prostitution in Grand Island Nebraska, 1870-1913." *Heritage of the Great Plains* 16 (Summer 1983): 1-9.

Engel, Arthur. "Immoral Intentions: The University of Oxford and the Problem of Prostitution, 1827-1914." *Victorian Studies* 23 (1979): 79-107.

Engel, Barbara Alpern. "St. Petersburg Prostitutes in the Late 19th-Century--A Personal and Social Profile." *Russian Review* 48 (January 1989): 21-44.

Engelstein, Laura. "Gender and the Juridical Subject: Prostitution and Rape in Nineteenth-Century Russian Criminal Codes." *The Journal of Modern History* 60 (September 1988): 458-495.

Fishbein, Leslie. "Harlot or Heroine? Changing Views of Prostitution, 1870-1920." *The Historian* 43 (November 1980): 23-35.

Foster, Craig L. "Tarnished Angels: Prostitution in Storyville, New Orleans, 1900-1910." *Louisiana History* 31 (Winter 1990): 387-397.

Gilfoyle, Timothy J. "Strumpets and Misogynists: Brothel 'Riots' and the Transformation of Prostitution in Antebellum New York City." *New York History* 68 (January 1987): 45-65.

-----. "The Urban Geography of Commericial Sex: Prostitution in New York City, 1790-1860." *Journal of Urban History* 13 (August 1987): 371-393.

Glickman, Nora. "The Jewish White Slave Trade in Latin American Writings." *American Jewish Archives* 34 (November 1982): 178-189.

Goldman, Marion. "Sexual Commerce on the Comstock Lode." *Nevada Historical Society Quarterly* 21 (Summer 1978): 98-129.

Gorham, Deborah. "The 'Maiden Tribute of Modern Babylon' Reexamined: Child Prostitution and the Ideas of Childhood in Late-Victorian England." *Victorian Studies* 21 (Spring 1978): 353-369.

Guy, Donna J. "White Slavery, Public Health, and the Socialist Position on Legalized Prostitution in Argentina, 1913-1936." *Latin American Research Review* 23, no. 3 (1988): 60-80.

Halperin, David M. "The Democratic Body: Prostitution and Citizenship in Classical Athens." *Differences* 2 (Spring 1990): 1-28.

Hapke, Laura. "The Late Nineteenth-Century Streetwalker: Images and Realities." *Mid-America* 65 (October 1983): 155-162.

-----. "Maggie's Sisters: Nineteenth-Century Literary Images of the American Streetwalker." *Journal of American Culture* 5 (Summer 1982): 29-35.

Humphrey, David C. "Prostitution and Public Policy in Austin, Texas, 1870-1915." *Southwestern Historical Quarterly* 86 (April 1983): 473-516.

Jefchak, Andrew. "Prostitutes and Schoolmarms: An Essay on Women in Western Films." *Heritage of the Great Plains* 16 (Summer 1983): 19-26.

Jones, Colin. "Prostitution and the Ruling Class in 18th-Century Montpellier." *History Workshop* 6 (Autumn 1978): 7-28.

Kaplan, Marion. "Prostitution, Morality Crusades and Feminism: German-Jewish Feminists and the Campaign Against White Slavery." *Women's Studies* 5, no. 6 (1982): 619-628.

Karras, Ruth Mazo. "Concubinage and Slavery in the Viking Age." *Scandinavian Studies* 62 (Spring 1990): 141-162.

-----. "Holy Harlots: Prostitute Saints in Medieval Legend." *Journal of the History of Sexuality* 1 (July 1990): 3-32.

-----. "The Regulation of Brothels in Later Medieval England." *Signs* 14 (Winter 1989): 399-433.

Kern, J. B. "The Fallen Woman, From the Perspective of Five Early Eighteenth-Century Women Novelists." *Studies in Eighteenth-Century Culture* 10 (1981): 457-468.

King, Donna. "'Prostitutes as Pariahs in the Age of Aids': A Content Analysis of Coverage of Women Prostitutes in *The New York Times* and the *Washington Post* September 1985-April 1988." *Women & Health* 16, no. 3/4 (1990): 155-176.

Langhauer, Laurie. "Dickens's Streetwalkers: Women and the Form of Romance." *ELH* 53 (Summer 1986): 411-432.

Leja, Michael. "'Le Vieux Marcheur' and 'Les Deux Risques': Picasso, Prostitution, Venereal Disease, and Maternity, 1899-1907." *Art History* 8 (March 1985): 66-81.

Leonard, Carol, and Isidor Wallimann. "Prostitution and Changing Morality in the Frontier Cattle Towns of Kansas." *Kansas History* 2 (Spring 1979): 34-53.

Lerner, Gerda. "The Origin of Prostitution in Ancient Mesopotamia." *Signs* 11 (Winter 1986): 236-254.

Levesque, A. "Turning Off the Red Light: Reformers and Prostitution in Montreal 1865-1925." *Urban History Review* 17 (February 1989): 191-202.

Lovejoy, Paul E. "Concubinage and the Status of Women Slaves in Early Colonial Northern Nigeria." *Journal of African History* 29 (1988): 245-266.

-----. "Concubinage in the Sokoto Caliphate (1804-1903)." *Slavery & Abolition* 11 (September 1990): 159-189.

Mahood, Linda. "The Magdalene's Friend: Prostitution and Social Control in Glasgow, 1869-1890." *Women's Studies International Forum* 13, no. 1/2 (1990): 49-62.

McCormick, John S. "Red Lights in Zion: Salt Lake City's Stockade, 1908-11." *Utah Historical Quarterly* 50 (Spring 1982): 168-181.

McCreery, David. "'This Life of Misery and Shame': Female Prostitution in Guatemala City, 1880-1920." *Journal of Latin American Studies* (November 1986): 333-353.

McKanna, Clare V., Jr. "Hold Back the Tide: Vice Control in San Diego, 1870-1930." *Pacific Historian* 28 (Fall 1984): 54-64.

McLaren, John P. S. "Chasing the Social Evil: Moral Fervour and the Evolution of Canada's Prostitution Laws, 1867-1917." *Canadian Journal of Law and Society* 1 (1986): 125-165.

Ming, Hanneke. "Barracks-Concubinage in the Indies, 1887-1920." *Indonesia* no. 35 (April 1983): 65-93.

Mirelman, Victor A. "The Jewish Community versus Crime: The Case of White Slavery in Buenos Aires." *Jewish Social Studies* 46 (Spring 1984): 145-168.

Murphy, Mary. "The Private Lives of Public Women: Prostitution in Butte, Montana, 1878-1917." *Frontiers* 7, no. 3 (1984): 30-35.

Nash, Stanley. "Prostitution and Charity: The Magdalen Hospital, A Case Study." *Journal of Social History* 17 (Summer 1984): 617-628.

Nead, Lynda. "Seduction, Prostitution, Suicide: 'On the Brink' by Alfred Elmore." *Art History* 5 (September 1982): 310-322.

Newman, Frances, and Elizabeth Cohen, with Patricia Tobin and Gail Mac Pherson. "Historical Perspectives on the Study of Female Prostitution." *International Journal of Women's Studies* 8 (January/February 1985): 78-84.

Oldenburg, Veena Talwar. "Lifestyle as Resistance: The Case of the Courtesans of Lucknow, India." *Feminist Studies* 16 (Summer 1990): 259-288.

Petrik, Paula. "Capitalists with Rooms: Prostitution in Helena, Montana, 1865-1900." *Montana* 31 (April 1981): 28-41.

-----. "Strange Bedfellows: Prostitution, Politicians, and Moral Reform in Helena, Montana, 1885-1887." *Montana* 35 (Summer 1985): 2-13.

Pivar, David J. "Cleansing the Nation: The War on Prostitution, 1917-1921." *Prologue* 12 (Spring 1980): 29-40.

Roper, Lyndal. "Discipline and Respectability: Prostitution and Reformation in Augsburg." *History Workshop* 19 (Spring 1985): 3-28.

-----. "Mothers of Debauchery: Procuresses in Reformation Augsburg." *German History* 6 (April 1988): 1-19.

Ross, Margaret Clunies. "Concubinage in Anglo-Saxon England." *Past and Present* no. 108 (August 1985): 3-34.

Ruggles, Steven. "Fallen Women: The Inmates of the Magdalen Society Asylum of Philadelphia, 1836-1908." *Journal of Social History* 16 (Summer 1983): 65-82.

Saxon, Gerald D., and John R. Summerville. "The Chicken Ranch: A Home on the Range." *Red River Valley Historical Review* 7 (Winter 1982): 33-44.

Schafer, Judith K. "'Open and Notorious Concubinage': The Emancipation of Slave Mistresses by Will and the Supreme Court in Antebellum Louisiana." *Louisiana History* 28 (Spring 1987): 165-182.

Sealey, Raphael. "On Lawful Concubinage in Athens." *Classical Antiquity* 3 (April 1984): 111-133.

Sellar, W. D. H. "Marriage, Divorce and Concubinage in Gaelic Scotland." *Trans. Gaelic Soc. Inverness* 1 (1978-80): 464-493.

Shumsky, Neil Larry. "Tacit Acceptance: Respectable Americans and Segregated Prostitution, 1870-1910." *Journal of Social History* 19 (Summer 1986): 655-680.

Shumsky, Neil Larry, and Larry M. Springer. "San Francisco's Zone of Prostitution, 1880-1934." *Journal of Historical Geography* [Great Britain] 7 (January 1981): 71-89.

Sneddeker, Duane R. "Regulating Vice: Prostitution and the St. Louis Social Evil Ordinance, 1870-1874." *Gateway Heritage* 11 (Fall 1990): 20-47.

Souden, David. "'Rogues, Whores, and Vagabonds?' Indentured Servant Emigrants to North America, and the Case of Mid-Seventeenth-Century Bristol." *Social History* 3 (January 1978): 23-41.

Tandberg, Gerilyn G. "Sinning for Silk--Dress-for-Success Fashions of the New Orleans Storyville Prostitute." *Women's Studies International Forum* 13, no. 3 (1990): 229-248.

Tansey, Richard. "Prostitution and Politics in Antebellum New Orleans." *Southern Studies* 18 (Winter 1979): 449-479.

Walkowitz, Judith R. "Male Vice and Feminist Virtue: Feminism and the Politics of Prostitution in Nineteenth Century Britain." *History Workshop* 13 (Spring 1982): 77-93.

-----. "The Politics of Prostitution." *Signs* 6 (Autumn 1980): 123-135.

Waters, Elizabeth. "Restructuring the 'Woman Question': *Perestroika* and Prostitution." *Feminist Review* no. 33 (Autumn 1989): 3-19.

Wegars, Priscilla. "'Inmates of Body Houses': Prostitution in Moscow, Idaho, 1885-1910." *Idaho Yesterdays* 33 (Spring 1989): 25-37.

Wells, Wendy. "Mercenary Prostitution in Ancient Greece." *Quest* 5 (Summer 1979): 76-80.

West, Elliott. "Scarlet West: The Oldest Profession in the Trans-Mississippi West." *Montana* 31 (April 1981): 16-27.

White, Luise. "Prostitutes, Reformers, and Historians." *Criminal Justice History* 6 (1985): 201-228.

-----. "Prostitution, Identity and Class Consciousness in Nairobi During World War II." *Signs* 11 (Winter 1986): 255-273.

## RELIGION

## Catholicism

Arenal, Electa, and Stacey Schlau. "Stratagems of the Strong, Stratagems of the Weak: Autobiographical Prose of the Seventeenth-Century Hispanic Convent." *Tulsa Studies in Women's Literature* 9 (Spring 1990): 25-42.

Babinsky, Ellen. "Marguerite Porete: An Intrepid Beguine of the Late Thirteenth Century." *Austin Seminary Bulletin* 104 (October 1988): 5-15.

Barton, Marcella Biro. "Saint Teresa of Avila: Did She Have Epilepsy?" *Catholic Historical Review* 68 (October 1982): 581-598.

Beauchamp, Virginia Walcott. "The Sisters and the Soldiers." *Maryland Historical Magazine* 81 (Summer 1986): 117-133.

Berten, Virginia. "The Sisters of St. Ursula, Seventy-Five Years of Service." *Queen City Heritage* 43 (Fall 1985): 40-48.

Betel, Lisa M. "Women's Monastic Enclosures in Early Ireland." *Journal of Medieval History* 12 (March 1986): 15-36.

Bonner, Thomas, Jr. "Christianity and Catholicism in the Fiction of Kate Chopin." *Southern Quarterly* 20 (Winter 1982): 118-125.

Bradshaw, Sue. "Catholic Sisters in China: An Effort to Raise the Status of Women." *Historical Reflections/Reflexions Historiques* 8 (Fall 1981): 201-214.

Brown, Judith C. "Lesbian Sexuality in Renaissance Italy: The Case of Sister Benedetta Carline." *Signs* 9 (Summer 1984): 751-758.

Brundage, James A. "'Allas! That Evere Love Was Synne': Sex and Medieval Canon Law." *Catholic Historical Review* 72 (January 1986): 1-13.

Bukowczyk, John J. "Mary the Messiah: Polish Immigrant Heresy and the Malleable Ideology of the Roman Catholic Church, 1880-1930." *Journal of American Ethnic History* 4 (Spring 1985): 5-32.

Burns, Jeffrey M. "Catholic Laywomen in the Culture of American Catholicism in the 1950s." *U.S. Catholic Historian* 5 (Summer/Fall 1986): 385-400.

Byrne, Patricia. "Sisters of St. Joseph: The Americanization of a French Tradition." *U.S. Catholic Historian* 5 (Summer/Fall 1986): 241-272.

Camp, C. V. "The Wise Women of 2 Samuel: A Role Model for Women in Early Israel." *Catholic Biblical Quarterly* 43 (1981): 14-29.

Camp, Richard L. "From Passive Subordination to Complementary Partnership: The Papal Conception of Women's Place in Church and Society since 1878." *Catholic Historical Review* 76 (July 1990): 506-525.

Campbell, Debra. "Part-Time Female Evangelists of the Thirties and Forties: The Rosary College Catholic Evidence Guild." *U.S. Catholic Historian* 5 (Summer/Fall 1986): 371-383.

Casteras, Susan P. "Virgin Vows: The Early Victorian Artists' Portrayal of Nuns and Novices." *Victorian Studies* 24 (Winter 1981): 157-184.

Chandler, Kenneth J. "Rose Philippine Duchesne: An American Saint." *Gateway Heritage* 9 (Summer 1988): 26-31.

Coates, Colin. "Authority and Illegitimacy in New France: The Burial of Bishop Saint-Vallier and Madeleine de Vercheres vs. the Priest of Batiscan." *Histoire sociale/Social History* 22 (May 1989): 65-90.

Creamer, Sister Mary Michael. "Mother Catherine Spalding--St. Catherine Street, Louisville, Kentucky." *The Filson Club History Quarterly* 63 (April 1989): 191-223.

Danylewycz, Marta. "Changing Relationships: Nuns and Feminists in Montreal, 1890-1925." *Histoire sociale/Social History* 14 (November 1981): 413-434.

Donovan, Grace. "An American Catholic in Victorian England: Louisa, Dutchess of Leeds, and the Carroll Family Benefice." *Maryland Historical Magazine* 84 (Fall 1989): 223-234.

-----. "The Caton Sisters: The Carrolls of Carrollton Two Generations Later." *U.S. Catholic Historian* 5 (Summer/Fall 1986): 291-303.

Dygo, M. "The Political Role of the Cult of the Virgin Mary in Teutonic Prussian in the Late 14th Century and the 15th Century." *Journal of Medieval History* 15 (March 1989): 63-80.

Farina, John. "Nineteenth Century American Interest in Saint Catherine of Genoa." *Catholic Historical Review* 70 (April 1984): 250-261.

Fields, Mary Jean. "Reminiscences of the Sisters of St. Joseph of Carondelet and the Academy of Our Lady of Peace, 1882-1982." *San Diego History* 28 (Summer 1982): 178-193.

Foss, David B. "From God as Mother to Priest as Mother: Julian of Norwich and the Movement for the Ordination of Women." *Downside Review* 104 (July 1986): 214-226.

Gellott, Laura, and Michael Phayer. "Dissenting Voices: Catholic Women in Opposition to Fascism." *Journal of Contemporary History* 22 (January 1987): 91-114.

Gillespie, James L. "Ladies of the Fraternity of S aint George and of the Society of the Garter." *Albion* 17 (Fall 1985): 259-278.

Hanna, Martha. "Iconology and Ideology: Images of Joan of Arc in the Idiom of the Action Francaise." *French Historical Studies* 14 (Fall 1985): 215-239.

Hause, Steven C., and Anne R. Kenney. "The Development of the Catholic Women's Suffrage Movement in France, 1896-1922." *Catholic Historical Review* 67 (January 1981): 11-30.

Holloway, Marcella M. "The Sisters of St. Joseph of Carondelet: 150 Years of Good Works in America." *Gateway Heritage* 7 (Fall 1986): 24-31.

Johnson, P. D. "Agnes of Burgundy, an 11th Century Woman as Monastic Patron." *Journal of Medieval History* 15 (June 1989): 93-104.

Jones, C. "Sisters of Charity and the Ailing Poor." *Social History of Medicine* 2 (1989): 339-348.

Kane, Paula M. "The Pulpit of the Hearthstone: Katherine Conway and Boston Catholic Women, 1900-1920." *U.S. Catholic Historian* 5 (Summer/Fall 1986): 355-370.

Kenneally, James. "Reflections on Historical Catholic Women." *U.S. Catholic Historian* 5 (Summer/Fall 1986): 411-418.

-----. "Women Divided: The Catholic Struggle for an Equal Rights Amendment, 1923-1945." *The Catholic Historical Review* 75 (April 1989): 249-263.

Kim, Ok-Hy. "Women in the History of Catholicism in Korea." *Korea Journal* 24 (August 1984): 28-40.

Kolmer, Elizabeth. "Catholic Women Religious and Women's History: A Survey of the Literature." *American Quarterly* 30 (Winter 1978): 639-651.

Lavrin, Asuncion. "Unlike Sor Juana? The Model Nun in the Religious Literature of Colonial Mexico." *The University of Dayton Review* 16 (Spring 1983): 75-92.

Letta, Corrado G. "Stigmatine Sisters: Pioneers of Women's Education in Albania (1875-1950)." *Albanian Catholic Bulletin* 10 (1989): 59-70.

Lynch, Michael. "Queen Mary's Triumph: The Baptismal Celebrations at Stirling in December 1566." *Scottish Historical Review* 69 (April 1990): 1-21.

Mackin, Sister Aloysius. "Wartime Scenes from Convent Windows: St. Cecilia, 1860-1865." *Tennessee Historical Quarterly* 39 (Winter 1980): 401-422.

Mannard, Joseph G. "Maternity . . . of the Spirit: Nuns and Domesticity

Antebellum America." *U.S. Catholic Historian* 5 (Summer 1986): 305-324.

Martin, John. "Out of the Shadow: Heretical and Catholic Women in Renaissance Venice." *Journal of Family History* 10 (Spring 1985): 21-33.

Mason, Francis M. "The Newer Eve: The Catholic Women's Suffrage Society in England, 1911-1923." *Catholic Historical Review* 72 (October 1986): 620-638.

Mathes, Valerie Sherer. "American Indian Women and the Catholic Church." *North Dakota History* 47 (Fall 1980): 20-25.

McClure, Peter, and Peter Headlam Wells. "Elizabeth I as a Second Virgin Mary." *Renaissance Studies* 4 (March 1990): 38-70.

McDonough, Peter. "Metamorphoses of the Jesuits: Sexual Identity, Gender Roles, and Hierarchy in Catholicism." *Comparative Studies in Society and History* [Great Britain] 32 (April 1990): 325-356.

McGahan, Elizabeth W. "Inside the Hallowed Walls: Convent Life Through Material History." *Material History Bulletin* 25 (Spring 1987): 1-9.

McNamara, JoAnn. "THe Ordeal of Community: Hagiography and Discipline in Merovingian Convents." *Vox Benedictina* 3 (October 1986): 293-326.

Metz, Judith. "150 Years of Caring: The Sisters of Charity in Cincinnati." *Cincinnati Historical Society Bulletin* 37 (Fall 1979): 151-174.

Neel, Carol. "The Origins of the Beguines." *Signs* 14 (Winter 1989): 321-341.

O'Brien, Susan. "Terra Incognita: The Nun in Nineteenth-Century England." *Past & Present* no. 121 (November 1988): 110-140.

Oates, Mary J., ed. "'Lowell': An Account of Convent Life in Lowell Massachusetts, 1852-1890." *New England Quarterly* 61 (March 1988):101-118.

-----. "The Role of Laywomen in American Catholic Philanthropy, 1820-1920." *U.S. Catholic Historian* 9 (Summer 1990): 249-260.

Peterson, Susan C. "From Paradise to Prairie: The Presentation Sisters in Dakota, 1880-1896." *South Dakota History* 10 (Summer 1980): 210-222.

-----. "Religious Communities of Women in the West: The Presentation Sister's Adaptation to the Northern Plains Frontier." *Journal of the West* 21 (April 1982): 65-70.

------. "A Widening Horizon: Catholic Sisterhoods on the Northern Plains, 1874-1910." *Great Plains Quarterly* 5 (Spring 1985): 125-132.

Quinn, Margaret. "Sylvia, Adele and Rosine Parmentier: 19th Century Women of Brooklyn." *U.S. Catholic Historian* 5 (Summer/Fall 1986): 345-354.

Rector, Theresa A. "Black Nuns as Educators." *Journal of Negro Education* (Summer 1982): 238-253.

Schulenburg, Jane Tibbets. "Women's Monastic Communities, 500-1100: Patterns of Expansion and Decline." *Signs* 14 (Winter 1989): 261-292.

Shimp, Robert E. "A Catholic Marriage for an Anglican Prince." *Historical Magazine of the Protestant Episcopal Church* 50 (March 1981): 3-18.

Sorrento, Audrey. "From the Middle Ages to the Modern World: Personal Experiences of a Roman Catholic Woman From the 1940s to the 1970s." *Drew Gateway* 48, no. 3 (1978): 62-71.

Strumingher, Laura S. "'À Bas Les Pretres! A Bas Les Couvents!': The Church and the Workers in 19th Century Lyon." *Journal of Social History* 11 (Summer

1978): 546-552.

Sullivan, Mary Louise. "Mother Cabrini: Missionary to Italian Immigrants." *U.S. Catholic Historian* 6, no. 4 (1987): 265-279.

Swidler, Arlene. "Women in American Catholic History." *Horizons: The Journal of the College Theology Society* 10 (Fall 1983): 334-340.

Thomas, Marie A. "Muscovite Convents in the Seventeenth Century." *Russian History* 10, part 2 (1983): 230-242.

Thomas, Samuel J. "Catholic Journalists and the Ideal Woman in Late Victorian America." *International Journal of Women's Studies* 4 (January/February 1981): 89-100.

Thompson, Margaret Susan. "Discovering Foremothers: Sisters, Society, and the American Catholic Experience." *U.S. Catholic Historian* 5 (Summer/Fall 1986): 273-290.

-----. "Sisterhood and Power: Class, Culture, and Ethnicity in the American Convent." *Colby Library Quarterly* 25 (September 1989): 149-175.

Trompf, G. W. "On Attitudes towards Women in Paul and Paulinist Literature: 1 Cor. 11:2-16 and Its Context." *Catholic Biblical Quarterly* 42 (1980): 196-215.

Weaver, Mary Jo. "Feminist Perspectives and American Catholic History." *U.S. Catholic Historian* 5 (Summer/Fall 1986): 401-410.

## Missions and Missionaries

Ackerman, Lillian A. "The Effect of Missionary Ideals on Family Structure and Women's Roles in Plateau Indian Culture." *Idaho Yesterdays* 31 (Spring/Summer 1987): 64-74.

Allen, Catherine B. "Ruth Pettigrew: Taking the Gospel to the Orient." *Baptist History and Heritage* 23 (January 1988): 13-22.

Bahr, Donald, and Susan Fenger. "Indians and Missions: Homage to and Debate with Ruport Costo and Jeanette Henry." *Journal of the Southwest* 31 (Autumn 1989): 300-321.

Bendroth, Margaret L. "Women and Missions: Conflict and Changing Roles in the Presbyterian Church in the United States of America, 1870-1935." *American Presbyterians* 65 (Spring 1987): 49-59.

Bradshaw, Sister Sue. "Religious Women in China: Understanding of Indigenization." *Catholic Historical Review* 68 (January 1982): 28-45.

Claw, Richmond L. "Mary Clementine Collins: Missionary at Standing Rock." *North Dakota History* 52 (Spring 1985): 10-17.

Copeland, Louise. "The Impact of the American Women's Liberation Movement on Protestant World Missions." *Japan Christian Quarterly* 46 (Summer 1980): 160-166.

David, S. Immanuel. "Women in Church and Mission (1800-1938)." *Indian Church History Review* 20 (December 1986): 104-152.

Donovan, Mary S. "Women and Mission: Towards a More Inclusive Historiography." *Historical Magazine of the Protestant Episcopal Church* 53

(December 1984): 297-306.

-----. "Zealous Evangelists: The Woman's Auxiliary to the Board of Missions."
    *Historical Magazine of the Protestant Episcopal Church* 51 (December 1982):
    371-384.

"The First Mission of the Sisters Faithful Companions of Jesus in the North-West
    Territories, 1883." *Saskatchewan History* 36 (Spring 1983): 70-77.

Flemming, Leslie A. "New Roles for Old: Presbyterian Women Missionaries and
    Women's Education in North India, 1910-1930." *Indian Church History Review*
    20 (December 1986): 127-142.

Foote, Cheryl J. "Alice Blake of Trementina: Mission Teacher of the Southwest."
    *Journal of Presbyterian History* 60 (Fall 1982): 228-242.

Forbes, Geraldine. "In Search of the 'Pure Heathen': Missionary Women in
    Nineteenth Century India." *Economic and Political Weekly* 21 (April 26,1986):
    WS-2--WS-8.

Gillespie, Joanna. "Mary Briscoe Baldwin, 1811-1877, Single Woman Missionary
    and 'Very Much My Own Mistress.'" *Anglican and Episcopal History* 57, no.
    1 (1988): 63-92.

Grimshaw, Patricia. "'Christian Woman, Pious Wife, Faithful Mother, Devoted
    Missionary': Conflicts in Roles of American Missionary Women in
    Nineteenth-Century Hawaii." *Feminist Studies* 9 (Summer 1983): 489-522.

-----. "New England Missionary Wives, Hawaiian Women, and 'The Cult of True
    Womanhood.'" *Hawaiian Journal of History* 19 (1985): 71-100.

Herring, Rebecca. "Their Work Was Never Done: Women Missionaries on the
    Kiowa-Comanche Reservation." *Chronicles of Oklahoma* 64 (Spring 1986):
    69-83.

Heuser, Frederick J., Jr. "Women's Work for Women: Belle Sherwood Hawkes
    and the East Persia Presbyterian Mission." *American Presbyterians* 65 (Spring
    1987): 7-17.

Horner, Patricia V. "Mary Richardson Walker: The Shattered Dreams of a
    Missionary Woman." *Montana* 32 (Summer 1982): 20-31.

Hoyt, Fredrick B. "'When a Field Was Found Too Difficult for a Man, a Woman
    Should Be Sent': Adele M. Fielde in Asia, 1865-1890." *The Historian* 44 (May
    1982): 314-334.

Hunt, Nancy Rose. "'Single Ladies on the Congo': Protestant Missionary Tensions
    and Voices." *Women's Studies International Forum* 13, no. 4 (1990): 395-404.

Huntley, Martha. "Presbyterian Women's Work and Rights in the Korean
    Mission." *American Presbyterians* 65 (Spring 1987): 37-48.

Jacobs, Sylvia M. "African-American Women Missionaries and European
    Imperialism in Southern Africa, 1880-1920." *Women's Studies International
    Forum* 13, no. 4 (1990): 381-394.

-----. "'Say Africa When You Pray': The Activities of Early Black Baptist Women
    Missionaries Among Liberian Women and Children." *Sage* 3 (Fall 1986):
    16-21.

Jeffrey, Julie Roy. "The Making of a Missionary: Narcissia Whitman and Her
    Vocation." *Idaho Yesterdays* 31 (Spring/Summer 1987): 75-85.

Keller, Rosemary Skinner. "Creating a Sphere for Women in the Church: How Consequential an Accommodation?" *Methodist History* 18 (January 1980): 83-94.

Langmore, D. "A Neglected Force: White Women Missionaries in Papua 1874-1914." *Journal of Pacific History* 17 (July 1982): 138-157.

Lodwik, Kathleen L. "Women at the Hainan Presbyterian Mission: Ministry and Diversion." *American Presbyterians* 65 (Spring 1987): 19-28.

Madsen, Carol Cornwall. "Mormon Missionary Wives in Nineteenth Century Polynesia." *Journal of Mormon History* 13 (1986-87): 61-88.

Massey, Barbara. "Training Children in Missions in South Baptist Churches." *Baptist History and Heritage* 25 (October 1990): 21-28.

Miller, Page Putnam. "Ann Breese's 'Address' to the Female Missionary Society of the Western District." *American Presbyterians* 65 (Spring 1987): 1-6.

Mondello, Salvatore. "Isabel Crawford: The Making of a Missionary, Part I." *Foundations* 21, no. 4 (1978): 322-339.

Motte, Mary. "The Involvement of Roman Catholic Women in Mission Since 1965." *International Bulletin of Missionary Research* 8 (January 1984): 9-10.

Papageorge, Linda Madson. "Feminism and Methodist Missionary Activity in China: The Experience of Atlanta's Laura Haygood, 1884-1900." *West Georgia College Studies in the Social Sciences* 22 (June 1983): 71-77.

Peterson, Susan C. "Challenging the Stereotypes: The Adaptation of the Sisters of St. Francis to South Dakota Indian Missions, 1885-1910." *Upper Midwest History* 4 (1984): 1-10.

-----. "Doing 'Women's Work': The Grey Nuns at Fort Totten Indian Reservation, 1874-1900." *North Dakota History* 52 (Spring 1985): 18-25.

-----. "'Holy Women' and Housekeepers: Women Teachers on South Dakota Reservations, 1885-1910." *South Dakota History* 13 (Fall 1983): 245-260.

Ridout, Katherine. "A Woman of Mission: The Religious and Cultural Odyssey of Agnes Wintemute Coates." *Canadian Historical Review* 71 (June 1990): 208-241.

Simmons, Christina. "'Helping the Poorer Sisters': The Women of the Jost Mission, Halifax, 1905-1945." *Acadiensis* 14 (Autumn 1984): 3-27.

Sorrill, Bobbie. "The History of the Week of Prayer for Foreign Missions." *Baptist History and Heritage* 15 (October 1980): 28-35.

Vickers, Gregory. "Models of Womanhood and the Early Woman's Missionary Union." *Baptist History and Heritage* 24 (January 1989): 41-53.

White, Ann. "Counting the Cost of Faith: America's Early Female Missionaries." *Church History* 57 (March 1988): 19-30.

## Other Religions

Abiodun, Rowland. "Women in Yoruba Religious Images." *African Languages and Cultures* 2, no. 1 (1989): 1-18.

Allen, Peter S., and A. Lily Macrakis, eds. "Greek Women and Men in History, Literature, and Religious Life." *Journal of Modern Greek Studies* 1 (May

1983): 7-155.

Allured, Janet. "Arkansas Baptists and Methodists and the Equal Rights Amendment." *Arkansas Historical Quarterly* 43 (Spring 1984): 55-66.

Alpers, Edward A. "'Ordinary Household Chores': Ritual and Power in a 19th-Century Swahili Women's Spirit Possession Cult." *International Journal of African Historical Studies* 17, no. 4 (1984): 677-702.

Anderson, Gary. "Celibacy or Consummation in the Garden? Reflections on Early Jewish and Christian Interpretations of the Garden of Eden." *Harvard Theological Review* 82 (April 1989): 121-148.

Archer, Leonie. "Virgin and Harlot in the Writings of Formative Judaism." *History Workshop* 24 (Autumn 1987): 1-16.

Baldwin, Lewis V. "Black Women and African Union Methodism, 1813-1983." *Methodist History* (July 1983): 225-237.

Ballstadt, Carl, Michael Peterman, and Elizabeth Hopkins. "'A Glorious Madness': Susanna Moodie and the Spiritualist Movement." *Journal of Canadian Studies/Revue d'études canadiennes* 17 (Winter 1983): 88-101.

Barber, Karin. "Oriki, Women and the Proliferation and Merging of Orisa." *Africa* 60, no. 3 (1990): 313-337.

Barfoot, Charles H. and Gerald T. Sheppard. "Prophetic vs. Priestly Religion: The Changing Role of Women Clergy in Classical Pentecostal Churches." *Review of Religious Research* 22 (September 1980): 2-17.

Barstow, Anne. "The Uses of Archaeology for Women's History: James Mellaarts's Work on the Neolithic Goddess at Catal Huyuk." *Feminist Studies* 4 (October 1978): 7-18.

Bednarowski, Mary Farrell. "Outside the Mainstream: Women's Religion and Women Religious Leaders in Nineteenth-Century America." *Journal of the American Academy of Religion* 48 (June 1980): 207-231.

-----. "Women in American Religious History." *American Theological Library Association: Proceedings* 34 (1980): 102-104.

Billington, Louis. "'Female Laborers in the Church': Women Preachers in the Northeastern United States, 1790-1840." *Journal of American Studies* 19 (December 1985): 369-394.

Blee, Kathleen M. "Women in the 1920's Ku Klux Klan Movement." *Feminist Studies* 17 (Spring 1991): 57-78.

Blum, Carol J. "The Cincinnati Women's Christian Association: A Study of Innovation and Change, 1868-1880." *Queen City Heritage* 41 (Winter 1983): 56-64.

Boyer, Paul. "Minister's Wife, Widow, Reluctant Feminist: Catherine Marshall in the 1950s." *American Quarterly* 30 (Winter 1978): 703-721.

Brooten, Bernadette J. "Jewish Women's History in the Roman Period: A Task for Christian Theology." *Harvard Theological Review* 79 (January-July 1986): 22-30.

-----. "Women and the Churches in Early Christianity." *Ecumenical Trends* 14 (April 1985): 51-54.

Brown, Douglass Summers. "Elizabeth Henry Campbell Russell: Patroness of

Early Methodism in the Highlands of Virginia." *Virginia Cavalcade* 30 (Winter 1981): 110-117.

Brown, Elsa B. "Womanist Consciousness: Maggie Lena Walker and the Independent Order of Saint Luke." *Signs* 14 (Winter 1989): 610-633.

Butler, Jonathon M. "Prophecy, Gender and Culture: Ellen Gould Harmon [White] and the Roots of Seventh-day Adventism." *Religion and American Culture* 1 (Winter 1991): 3-30.

Bynum, Carolyn Walker. "Women Mystics and Eucharistic Devotion in the Thirteenth Century." *Women's Studies* 2 (1984): 179-214.

Cahill, Suzanne. "Performers and Female Taoist Adepts: Hsi Wang Mu as the Patron Diety of Women in Medieval China." *Journal of the American Oriental Society* 106 (1986): 155-168.

Calabro, John A. "Susan Warner and Her Bible Classes." *Legacy* 4, no. 2 (1987): 45-52.

Campbell, Debra. "Hannah Whitall Smith (1832-1911): Theology of the Mother-hearted God." *Signs* 15 (Autumn 1989): 70-101.

Carpenter, Delores C. "Black Women in Religious Institutions: A Historical Summary from Slavery to the 1960s." *Journal of Religious Thought* 46 (Winter 1989/Spring 1990): 7-27.

Carroll, Lucy. "Nizam-i-Islam: Processes and Conflicts in Pakistan's Programme of Islamisation, with Special Reference to the Position of Women." *Journal of Commonwealth and Comparative Politics* 20 (March 1982): 57-95.

Carson, Mina J. "Agnes Hamilton of Fort Wayne: The Education of a Christian Settlement Worker." *Indiana Magazine of History* 80 (March 1984): 1-34.

Clar, Reva, and William M. Kramer. "The Girl Rabbi of the Golden West: The Adventurous Life of Ray Frank in Nevada, California, and the Northwest, Part I." *Western States Jewish History* 18 (January 1986): 99-111.

-----. "The Girl Rabbi of the Golden West: The Adventurous Life of Ray Frank in Nevada, California, and the Northwest, Part II." *Western States Jewish History* 18 (April 1986): 223-236.

Clark, David L. "'Miracles for a Dime'--From Chautauqua Tent to Radio Station with Sister Aimee." *California History* 57 (Winter 1978/79): 354-363.

Cohen, Alfred. "Prophecy and Madness: Women Visionaries During the Puritan Revolution." *Journal of Psychohistory* 11 (Winter 1984): 411-430.

Cohen, S. J. D. "Women in the Synagogues in Antiquity." *Conservative Judaism* 34 (1980): 23-29.

Cole, Juan R. "Feminism, Class, and Islam in Turn-of-the-Century Egypt." *International Journal of Middle East Studies* 19 (1981): 387-407.

Collins, Michael. "Sister Aimee." *The Beaver* 69 (June/July 1989): 28-32.

Coulter, Moureen. "'A Terrific Bond': The Spiritual Friendship of Caryll Houselander and Maisie Ward." *The Downside Review* 107 (April 1989): 106-118.

Dailey, Barbara Ritter. "The Visitation of Sarah Wight: Holy Carnival and the Revolution of the Saints in Civil War London." *Church History* 55 (December 1986): 438-455.

Deuchler, Martina. "Neo-Confuciansim: The Impulse for Action in Early Yi Korea." *Journal of Korean Studies* 2 (1980): 71-112.

Dieter, Melvin E. "Women and Ministry in the Methodist Tradition (1784-1880)." *Asbury Theological Journal* 39 (Spring 1985): 3-7.

Eaton, Jeffrey C. "Simone Weil and Feminist Spirituality." *Journal of the American Academy of Religion* 54 (Winter 1986): 691-704.

Ebrahim, Abul Fadl Mohsin. "Islamic Teachings and Surrogate Motherhood." *Journal for the Study of Religion* 3 (March 1990): 35-46.

Eller, Cynthia. "Relativizing the Patriarchy: The Sacred History of the Feminist Spirituality Movement." *History of Religions* 30 (February 1991): 279-295.

Engelmeyer, Bridget Mavie. "A Maryland First." *Maryland Historical Magazine* (Fall 1983): 186-204.

Epp, Marlene. "Women in Canadian Mennonite History: Uncovering the 'Underside.'" *Journal of Mennonite Studies* 5 (1987): 90-107.

Everson, Michael. "Tenacity in Religion, Myth, and Folklore: The Neolithic Goddess of Old Europe Preserved in a Non-Indo-European Setting." *Journal of Indo-European Studies* 17 (Fall/Winter 1989): 277-296.

Findly, Ellison Banks. "Religious Resources for Secular Power: The Case of Nur Jahan." *Colby Library Quarterly* 25 (September 1989): 129-148.

Gaitskell, Deborah. "'Christian Compounds for Girls': Church Hostels for African Women in Johannesburg, 1907-1970." *Journal of South African Studies* 61 (October 1979): 44-69.

-----. "Housewives, Maids or Mothers: Some Contradictions of Domesticity for Christian Women in Johannesburg, 1903-39." *Journal of African History* 24, no. 2 (1983): 241-256.

George, Carol V. R. "In the Beginning: Mother Bethel and the A. M. E. Church." *American Vision* 1, no. 6 (1986): 43-46.

Gifford, Carolyn DeSwarte. "Sisterhoods of Service and Reform: Organized Methodist Women in the Late Nineteenth Century, An Essay on the State of the Research." *Methodist History* 24 (October 1985): 15-30.

Gill, Lesley. "'Like a Veil to Cover Them': Women and the Pentecostal Movement in La Paz." *American Ethnologist* 17 (November 1990): 708-721.

Gillespie, Joanna B. "Many Gracious Providences: The Religious Cosmos of Martha Laurens Ramsay (1759-1811)." *Colby Library Quarterly* 25 (September 1989): 199-212.

-----. "Modesty Canonized: Female Saints in Antebellum Methodist Sunday School Literature." *Historical Reflections/Reflexions Historiques* 10 (Summer 1983): 195-220.

Goldsmith, Peter. "A Woman's Place Is in the Church: Black Pentecostalism on the Georgia Coast." *Journal of Religious Thought* 46 (Winter 1989/Spring 1990): 53-69.

Grindal, Garcia. "The Americanization of the Norwegian Pastors' Wives." *Norwegian-American Studies* 32 (1989): 199-207.

Hardesty, Nancy A. "'The Best Temperance Organization in the Land': Southern Methodists and the W.C.T.U. in Georgia." *Methodist History* 28 (April 1990):

187-194.

-----. "No Rights But Human Rights (Women in 19th Century American Revivals)." *Perkins School of Theology: Journal* 35 (Fall 1981): 58-62.

Harris, Rivkah. "Inanna-Ishtar as Paradox and Coincidence of Opposites." *History of Religions* 30 (February 1991): 261-278.

Hickey, Joseph V., and June O. Underwood. "In the Name of the Thurman Church: Women's Clubs and the Revitalization of a Flint Hills Neighborhood." *Locus* 1, no. 1 (1988): 65-83.

Hicks, M. A. "The Piety of Margaret, Lady Hungerford (d. 1478)." *Journal of Ecclesiastical History* 38 (January 1987): 19-38.

Hill, Patricia R. "Heathen Women's Friends: The Role of the Methodist Episcopal Women in the Women's Foreign Mission Movement." *Methodist History* 19, no. 3 (1981): 146-154.

Hollis, Susan Tower. "Women of Ancient Egypt and the Sky Goddess." *Journal of American Folklore* 100 (October-December 1987): 496-503.

Hopkins, Leroy T. "Freedom's Second Generation: Mrs. Maude Wilson Ball's Reminiscences of Bethel A.M.E. Church (1897-1935)." *Journal of the Lancaster County Historical Society* 91 (Michaelmas 1987/88): 173-183.

Ilan, Tal. "Notes on the Distribution of Jewish Women's Names in Palestine in the Second Temple and Mishnaic Periods." *Journal of Jewish Studies* 40 (Autumn 1989): 186-200.

Irvin, Dorothy. "The Ministry of Women in the Early Church: The Archaeological Evidence." *Duke Divinity School Review* 45, no. 2 (1980): 76-86.

Irwin, Lee. "Divinity and Salvation: The Great Goddesses of China." *Asian Folklore Studies* 49, no. 1 (1990): 53-68.

Jamal, Mieguel. "Shamaness Religion: History of Women and Religion." *Journal of Women and Religion* 1 (Spring 1981): 13-20.

Johnson, S. A. "The Distinctive Role of Women in Early Christianity and Islam." *International Journal of Islamic and Arabic Studies* 1 (1984): 97-111.

Johnston, Patricia Condon. "Reflected Glory: The Story of Ellen Ireland." *Minnesota History* 48 (Spring 1982): 13-23.

Kajiyama, Yuichi. "Women in Buddhism." *Eastern Buddhist* 15 (Autumn 1982): 53-70.

Kalugila, Leonidas. "Women in the Ministry of Priesthood in the Early Church: An Inquiry." *Africa Theological Journal* 14, no. 1 (1985): 35-45.

Kaplan, Marion A. "Jewish Women in Nazi Germany: Daily Life, Daily Struggles, 1933-1939." *Feminist Studies* 16 (Fall 1990): 579-606.

Keddie, Nikki. "The Past and Present of Women in the Muslim World." *Journal of World History* 1 (Spring 1990): 77-108.

Keller, Rosemary S. "Women and the Nature of Ministry in the United Methodist Tradition." *Methodist History* (January 1984): 99-114.

Kidder, J. Edward. "Problems of Cremation in Early Japan: The Role of Empress Jito." *Humanities, Christianity and Culture* 13 (March 1979): 191-201.

King, Richard. "Eleanor Dickinson: Religion and the Southern Artist." *Woman's Art Journal* 3 (Spring/Summer 1982): 1-5.

Kinsley, David. "Devotion as an Alternative to Marriage in the Lives of Some Hindu Women Devotees." *Journal of Asian and African Studies* 15 (January/April 1980): 83-93.

Klawiter, Frederick C. "The Role of Martyrdom and Persecution in Developing the Priestly Authority of Women in Early Christianity: A Case Study of Montanism." *Church History* 49 (September 1980): 251-261.

Klingelsmith, Sharon. "Women in the Mennonite Church, 1900-1930." *Mennonite Quarterly Review* 54 (July 1980): 163-207.

Knotts, Alice G. "Methodist Women and Interracial Fairness in the 1930s." *Methodist History* 27 (July 1989): 230-240.

Kraemer, Ross S. "Monastic Jewish Women in Greco-Roman Egypt: Philo Judeaus on the Therapeutrides." *Signs* 14 (Winter 1989): 342-370.

-----. "Women in the Religions of the Greco-Roman World." *Religious Studies Review* 9 (April 1983): 127-139.

Lang, Karen Christina. "Image of Women in Early Buddhism and Christian Gnosticism." *Buddhist Christian Studies* 2 (1982): 95-105.

Lazerow, Jama. "Religion and the New England Mill Girl: A New Perspective on an Old Theme." *New England Quarterly* 60 (September 1987): 429-453.

Lazreg, Marnia. "Gender and Politics in Algeria: Unraveling the Religious Paradigm." *Signs* 15 (Summer 1990): 755-780.

Levin, Carole. "Women in the Book of Martyrs as Models of Behavior in Tudor England." *International Journal of Women's Studies* 4 (March/April 1981): 196-207.

Lewis, Nantawan Boonprasat. "Asian Women Theology: A Historical and Theological Analysis." *Asian Journal of Theology* 4 (October 1986): 18-22.

Lindley, Susan H. "Women and the Social Gospel Novel." *Church History* 54 (March 1985): 56-73.

Lothrop, Gloria Ricci. "West of Eden: Pioneer Media Evangelist Aimee Semple McPherson in Los Angeles." *Journal of the West* 27 (April 1988): 50-59.

Lutfi, Huda. "A Study of Six Fourteenth Century Iqrars from al-Quds Relating to Muslim Women." *Journal of the Economic and Social History of the Orient* 26 (October 1983): 246-294.

Mani, Lata. "Production of an Official Discourse on Sati in Early Nineteenth Century Bengal." *Economic and Political Weekly* 21 (April 26, 1986): WS-32--WS-40.

Marcus, Ivan G. "Mothers, Martyrs and Moneymakers: Some Jewish Women in Medieval Europe." *Conservative Judaism* 38 (Spring 1986): 34-45.

Mazumdar, Vina. "Comment on Suttee." *Signs* 4 (Winter 1978): 269-273.

McGill, William J. "In Search of a Unicorn: Maria Theresa and the Religion of State." *The Historian* 42 (February 1980): 304-319.

McMillan, James. "Women, Religion, and Politics: The Case of the Ligue Patristique des Françaises." *Western Society for French History* 15 (November 1987): 355-364.

Michaels, J. Ramsey. "Images of Grace in Flannery O'Connor's Strong Women." *Daughters of Sarah* 16 (January/February 1990): 27-30.

Minault, Gail. "Making Invisible Women Visible: Studying the History of Muslim Women in South Asia." *South Asia* 9 (June 1986): 1-14.

Molinaro, Ursule. "A Christian Martyr in Reverse Hypatia: 370-415 A.D." *Hypatia* 4 (Spring 1989): 6-8.

Montgomery, Hugo. "Women and Status in the Greco-Roman World." *Studia Theologica: Scandinavian Journal of Theology* 43, no. 1 (1989): 115-124.

Morey, Ann-Janine. "The Reverend Idol and Other Parsonage Secrets: Women Write Romances About Ministers, 1880-1950." *Journal of Feminist Studies in Religion* 6 (Spring 1990): 87-104.

Murdoch, Norman H. "Female Ministry in the Thought of Catherine Booth." *Church History* 53 (September 1984): 348-362.

Neusner, Jacob. "Mishnah on Women: Thematic or Systematic Description." *Marxist Perspectives* 3 (Spring 1980): 78-99.

Newman, Harvey K. "The Role of Women in Atlanta's Churches, 1865-1906." *Atlanta History Journal* (Winter 1980): 17-30.

Newman, Josephine. "The Women's Movement in the Church and in the World." *Doctrine and Life* 34, no. 3 (1984): 108-118.

O'Connor, June. "Dorothy Day as Autobiographer." *Religion* 20 (July 1990): 275-296.

Oppenheim, J. "The Odyssey of Anne Besant: Victorian Radical, Feminist, Spiritualist." *History Today* 39 (September 1989): 12-18.

Overton, Betty J. "Black Women Preachers: A Literary Overview." *Southern Quarterly* 23 (Spring 1985): 157-166.

Packull, Werner O. "Anna Jansz of Rotterdam, a Historical Investigation of an Early Anabaptist Heroine." *Archiv fur Reformationsgeschichte* 78 (1987): 147-173.

Paper, Jordon. "The Persistence of Female Deities in Patriarchal China." *Journal of Feminist Studies in Religion* 6 (Spring 1990): 25-40.

Paquette, Patricia. "A Bandage in One Hand and a Bible in the Other: The Story of Captain Sally L. Tompkins." *Minerva: Quarterly Report on Women and the Military* 8 (Summer 1990): 47-54.

Perkins, Carol O. "The Pragmatic Idealism of Mary McLeod Bethune." *Sage* 5 (Fall 1988): 30-36.

Pernet, Henry. "Masks and Women: Towards a Reappraisal." *History of Religions* 22 (August 1982): 328-339.

Pickle, Linda Schelbitzki. "Women of the Saxon Immigration and Their Church." *Concordia Historical Institute Quarterly* 57 (Winter 1984): 146-161.

Pope, Barbara Corrado. "A Heroine without Heroics: The Little Flower of Jesus and Her Times." *Church History* 57 (March 1988): 46-60.

Prell, Riv-Ellen. "The Dilemma of Women's Equality in the History of Reform Judaism." *Judaism* 30 (Fall 1981): 418-426.

Pruitt, Linda Carlisle. "Ann Dumville: A Woman of Conviction." *Methodist History* 25, no. 3 (1987): 147-163.

Richardson, Peter. "From Apostles to Virgins: Romans 16 and the Roles of Women in the Early Church." *Toronto Journal of Theology* 2 (Fall 1986): 232-261.

Robbert, Louise Buenger. "Lutheran Families in St. Louis and Perry County, Missouri, 1839-1870." *Missouri Historical Review* 82 (July 1988): 424-438.

Roberts, Barbara. "Sex, Politics and Religion: Controversies in Female Immigration Reform Work in Montreal, 1881-1919." *Atlantis* 6 (1980): 25-38.

Salvaneschi, Lenore. "Die Frau Pastor: The Life of a Missouri Synod Lutheran Pastor's Wife in the First Half of the Twentieth Century." *Palimpsest* 67 (March/April 1986): 53-68.

Saum, Lewis O. "Florence Chance Huntley and Exotic Religion in the Gilded Age." *Hayes Historical Journal* 8 (Winter 1989): 5-22.

Saxon, A. H. "Olympia Brown in Bridgeport: 'Acts of Injustice' or a Failed Ministry?" *Proceedings of the Unitarian Universalist Historical Society* 21, no. 1 (1987/88): 55-65.

Shankman, Arnold. "Dorothy Tilly, Civil Rights, and the Methodist Church." *Methodist History* 18 (January 1980): 95-108.

Shiels, Richard D. "The Feminization of American Congregationalism 1730-1835." *American Quarterly* 33 (Spring 1981): 46-62.

Shover, Michele. "The Methodist Women and Molly White: A Chico Morality Tale." *Californians* 7 (September/October 1989): 26-31.

Simpson, Jane. "Women and Asceticism in the Fourth Century: A Question of Interpretation." *Journal of Religious History* 15 (June 1988): 38-60.

Stapleton, Carolyn L. "Belle Harris Bennett (1852-1922): Model of Holistic Christianity." *Methodist History* 21 (April 1983): 131-142.

Strayer, Brian E. "Sarah A. H. Lindsey: Advent Preacher on the Southern Tier." *Adventist Heritage* 11, no. 2 (1986): 16-25.

Stuckey-Kauffman, Priscilla. "A Woman's Ministry: Clara Brubaker Shank, 1869-1958." *Mennonite Quarterly Review* 60 (July 1986): 404-428.

Stump, Roger W. "Women Clergy in the United States: A Geographical Analysis of Religious Change." *Social Science Quarterly* 67 (June 1986): 337-352.

Sullivan, Mary C. "Catherine McAuley's Theological and Literary Debt to Alonso Rodriquez: The 'Spirit of the Institute' Parallels." *Recusant History* 20 (May 1990): 81-105.

Swain, Tony. "The Earth Mother From Northern Waters." *History of Religions* 30 (February 1991): 223-260.

Tandberg, Gerilyn. "Clothing for Conformity: A Study of the Brethren Sect." *Costume* 20 (1986): 63-71.

Thomas, John D. "Servants of the Church: Canadian Methodist Deaconess Work, 1890-1926." *Canadian Historical Review* 65 (September 1984): 371-395.

Topping, Eva Catafygiotu. "Thekla the Nun: In Praise of Women." *Greek-Orthodox Theological Review* 25 (Winter 1980): 353-370.

Trevett, Christine. "Woman, God and Mary Baker Eddy." *Religion* 14 (April 1984): 143-153.

Tsai, Kathryn A. "The Chinese Buddhist Monastic Order for Women: The First Two Centuries." *Historical Reflections/Reflexions Historiques* 8 (Fall 1981): 1-20.

Waldman, Marilyn Robinson. "Tradition as a Modality of Change: Islamic

Examples." *History of Religions* 25 (May 1986): 318-340.

Wasson, Margaret. "Texas Methodism's Other Half." *Methodist History* 19 (July 1981): 206-223.

Wegner, Judith R. "The Status of Women in Jewish and Islamic Marriage and Divorce Law." *Harvard Women's Law Journal* 5 (Spring 1982): 1-34.

Weissler, Chava. "'For Women and for Men Who Are Like Women': The Construction of Gender in Yiddish Devotional Literature." *Journal of Feminist Studies in Religion* 5 (Fall 1989): 7-24.

Whiteley, Marilyn Fardig. "'Doing Just About What They Please': Ladies' Aids in Ontario Methodism." *Ontario History* 82 (December 1990): 289-304.

Widmann, Ruth Dunn. "'Lost in the Immensity of God': A Pre-Civil War Methodist Woman's Experiences of the Presence and Power of God." *Methodist History* 25, no. 3 (1987): 164-175.

Williamson, Erik Lather. "'Doing What Had to Be Done': Norwegian Lutheran Ladies Aid Societies of North Dakota." *North Dakota History* 57 (Spring 1990): 2-13.

Wittenburg, Sister Mary Ste. Therese. "A California Girlhood: Reminiscences of Ascension Sepulveda y Avila." *Southern California Quarterly* 64 (Summer 1982): 133-140.

Wyntjes, Sherrin Marshall. "Women and Religious Choices in the 16th Century Netherlands." *Archiv für Reformationsgeschichte* 75 (1984): 276-289.

## Protestantism

Abel, Trudi. "The Diary of a Poor Quaker Seamstress: Needles and Penury in Nineteenth Century London." *Quaker History* 75 (Fall 1986): 102-114.

Alexander, Ruth Ann. "Elaine Goodale Eastman and the Failure of the Feminist Protestant Ethic." *Great Plains Quarterly* 8 (Spring 1988): 89-101.

Allen, Catherine B. "The Impact of Southern Baptist Women on Social Issues: Three Viewpoints: Other Issues Needing Attention." *Baptist History and Heritage* 22 (July 1987): 36-40.

Allured, Janet. "Arkansas Baptists and Methodists and the Equal Rights Amendment." *Arkansas Historical Quarterly* 43 (Spring 1984): 55-66.

Arrington, Leonard J. "Modern Lysistratas: Mormon Women in the International Peace Movement, 1899-1939." *Journal of Mormon History* 15 (1989): 89-104.

-----. "Persons for All Seasons: Women in Mormon History." *Brigham Young University Studies* 20 (Fall 1979): 39-58.

-----. "Rural Life Among Nineteenth-Century Mormons: The Woman's Experience." *Agricultural History* 58 (July 1984): 239-246.

Avery, Valeen Tippetts, and Linda King Newell. "The Lion and the Lady: Brigham Young and Emma Smith." *Utah Historical Quarterly* 48 (Winter 1980): 81-97.

Bacon, Margaret H. "Quaker Women and the Charge of Separatism." *Quaker History* 69 (Spring 1980): 23-26.

-----. "Quaker Women in Overseas Ministry." *Quaker History* 77 (Fall 1988): 93-109.

Barber, Ian J. "The Ecclesiastical Position of Women in Two Mormon Trajectories." *Journal of Mormon History* 14 (1988): 63-80.

Barstow, Anne Llewellyn. "The First Generations of Anglican Clergy Wives: Heroines or Whores?" *Historical Magazine of the Protestant Episcopal Church* 52 (March 1983): 3-16.

Beck, Rosalie, Kay Shurden, and Catherine B. Allen. "The Impact of Southern Baptist Women on Social Issues: Three Viewpoints." *Baptist History and Heritage* 22 (July 1987): 29-40.

Becker, Carl B. "Religious Healing in 19th Century 'New Religions': The Cases of Tenrikyo and Christian Science." *Religion* 20 (July 1990): 199-216.

Bederman, G. "The Women Have Had Charge of the Church Work Long Enough: The Men and Religion Forward Movement of 1911-12 and the Masculinization of Middle-Class Protestantism." *American Quarterly* 41 (September 1989): 432-465.

Beecher, Maureen Ursenbach. "The 'Leading Sisters': A Female Hierarchy in Nineteenth Century Mormon Society." *Journal of Mormon History* 9 (1982): 25-40.

-----. "Women's Work on the Mormon Frontier." *Utah Historical Quarterly* 49 (Summer 1981): 276-290.

Bell, Maureen. "Mary Westwood, Quaker Publisher." *Publishing History* no. 23 (1988): 5-66.

Bellamy, V. Nelle. "Participation of Women in the Public Life of the Church from Lambeth Conference 1867-1978." *Historical Magazine of the Protestant Episcopal Church* 51 (March 1982): 81-98.

Bennett, Dana. "Mormon Polygamy in Early Southeastern Idaho." *Idaho Yesterdays* 28 (Spring 1984): 24-30.

Bennion, Lowell Ben. "The Incidence of Mormon Polygamy in 1880: 'Dixie' versus Davis Stake." *Journal of Mormon History* 11 (1984): 27-42.

Bernhard, Virginia. "Cotton Mather's 'Most Unhappy Wife': Reflections on the Uses of Historical Evidence." *New England Quarterly* 60 (September 1987): 341-362.

Bishop, M. Guy. "Preparing to 'Take the Kingdom': Childrearing Directives in Early Mormonism." *Journal of the Early Republic* 7 (Fall 1987): 275-290.

Bitten, Davis, and Gary L. Bunker. "Double Jeopardy: Visual Images of Mormon Women to 1914." *Utah Historical Quarterly* 46 (Spring 1978): 184-202.

Bjorkman, Gwen Boyer. "Hannah (Baskel) Phelps Hill: A Quaker Woman and Her Offspring." *Southern Friend* 11 (Spring 1989): 10-30.

Blaisdell, Charmarie Jenkins. "Calvin's Letters to Women: The Courting of Ladies in High Places." *Sixteenth Century Journal* 13 (Fall 1982): 67-84.

Blevins, Carolyn DeArmond. "Patterns of Ministry Among Southern Baptist Women." *Baptist History and Heritage* 22 (July 1987): 41-49.

Blumhoffer, Edith L. "A Confused Legacy: Reflections on Evangelical Attitudes toward Ministering Women in the Past Century." *Fides et Historia* 22 (Winter/Spring 1990): 49-61.

Bonta, Marcia. "Graceanna Lewis: Portrait of a Quaker Naturalist." *Quaker History* 74 (Spring 1985): 27-40.

Boyd, Lois A. "Presbyterian Ministers' Wives--A Nineteenth-Century Portrait." *Journal of Presbyterian History* 59 (Spring 1981): 3-17.

-----. "Shall Women Speak? Confrontation in the Church, 1876." *Journal of Presbyterian History* 56 (Winter 1978): 271-296.

Boyd, Sandra Hughes. "The History of Women in the Episcopal Church: A Selected Annotated Bibliography." *History Magazine of the Protestant Episcopal Church* (December 1981): 423-433.

Boylan, Anne M. "Evangelical Womanhood in the Nineteenth Century: The Role of Women in Sunday Schools." *Feminist Studies* 4 (October 1978): 62-80.

Brackenridge, R. Douglas. "Equality for Women? A Case Study in Presbyterian Polity, 1926-1930." *Journal of Presbyterian History* 58 (Summer 1980): 142-165.

Brackenridge, R. Douglas, and Lois A. Boyd. "United Presbyterian Policy on Women and the Church—an Historical Overview." *Journal of Presbyterian History* 59 (Fall 1981): 383-407.

Bradley, Martha S. "The Women of Fundamentalism: Short Creek, 1953." *Dialogue* 23 (Summer 1990): 15-37.

Brennan, Brian. "'Episcipae': Bishops' Wives Viewed in Sixth-Century Gaul." *Church History* 54 (September 1985): 311-323.

Brooks, Juanita, and Janet G. Butler, eds. "Utah's Peace Advocate, the 'Mormona': Elise Furer Musser." *Utah Historical Quarterly* 46 (Spring 1978): 151-166.

Brower, Ruth Compton. "Presbyterian Women and the Foreign Missionary Movement 1876-1914: The Context of a Calling." *The Canadian Society of Presbyterian History Papers* (1985-85): 1-24.

Brown, Lawrence. "Texas Bishop Vetoes Women Council Delegates in 1921." *Historical Magazine of the Protestant Episcopal Church* 48, no. 1 (1979): 93-102.

Brumberg, Joan Jacobs. "Zenanas and Girlless Villages: The Ethnology of American Evangelical Women, 1870-1910." *Journal of American History* 69 (September 1982): 347-371.

Buell, Susan D. "Our Lady of Guadalupe: A Feminine Mythology for the New World." *Historical Magazine of the Protestant Episcopal Church* 51 (December 1982): 399-404.

Burkett, Randall K. "Elizabeth Mars Johnson Thomson, (1807-1864): A Research Note." *Historical Magazine of the Protestant Episcopal Church* 55 (March 1986): 21-30.

Carson, Mary Faith, and James J. H. Price. "The Ordination of Women and the Function of the Bible." *Journal of Presbyterian History* 59 (Summer 1981): 245-266.

Champion, Brian. "Mormon Polygamy: Parliamentary Comments 1889-90."

*Alberta History* 35 (Spring 1987): 10-17.

Coldwell, Judith. "The Role of Women in the Nineteenth Century Church of Ontario." *Canadian Society of Church History Papers* 15 (1985): 31-57.

Cole, Phyllis Blum. "The Divinity School Address of Mary Moody Emerson: Women's Silence and Speech in American Puritan Tradition." *Harvard Divinity Bulletin* 16 (December 1985-January 1986): 4-6.

Cooper, James F., Jr. "Anne Hutchinson and the 'Lay Rebellion' Against the Clergy." *New England Quarterly* 61 (September 1988): 381-397.

Dawson, N. M. "The Filles-du-Ray Sent to New France: French Women in 17th Century Canada--Protestant, Prostitute or Both." *Historical Reflections* 16 (Spring 1989): 55-78.

Derounian, Kathryn Zabelle. "Puritan Orthodoxy and the 'Survivor Syndrome' in Mary Rowlandson's Indian Captivity Narrative." *Early American Literature* 22, no. 1 (1987): 82-93.

Dickson, Charles Ellis. "And Ladies of the Church: The Origins of the Episcopal Congregation in Minot." *North Dakota History* 55 (Fall 1988): 8-19.

Donaldson, Margaret E. "The Invisible Factor: 19th Century Feminist Evangelical Concern for Human Rights." *Journal for the Study of Religion* 2 (September 1989): 3-15.

Driggs, Ken. "After the Manifesto: Modern Polygamy and Fundamentalist Mormons." *Journal of Church and State* 32 (Spring 1990): 367-389.

Dunfey, Julie. "'Living the Principle' of Plural Marriage: Mormon Women, Utopia, and Female Sexuality in the Nineteenth Century." *Feminist Studies* 10 (Fall 1984): 523-536.

Dunn, Mary Maples. "Saints and Sisters: Congregational and Quaker Women in the Early Colonial Period." *American Quarterly* 30 (Winter 1978): 582-601.

Embry, Jessie L. "Effects of Polygamy on Mormon Women." *Frontiers* 7, no. 3 (1984): 56-61.

Evans, Vella Neil. "The Mormon Women: Defined in Authoritative Church Discourse, 1830-1980." *Religious Studies and Theology* 7 (January 1987): 31-42.

Fielding, Lavinia. "Mary Fielding Smith: Her Ox Goes Marching On." *Dialogue* 14 (Winter 1981): 91-100.

Firmage, Mary Brown. "'Dear Sister Zina . . . Dear Brother Hugh. . . .'" *Dialogue* 21, no. 2 (1988): 29-50.

Ford, Linda. "William Penn's Views on Women: Subjects of Friendship." *Quaker History* 72 (Fall 1983): 75-102.

Foster, Lawrence. "From Frontier Activism to Neo-Victorian Domesticity: Mormon Women in the Nineteenth and Twentieth Centuries." *Journal of Mormon History* 6 (1979): 3-22.

-----. "Polygamy and the Frontier: Mormon Women in Early Utah." *Utah Historical Quarterly* 50 (Summer 1982): 268-289.

Fox, Margery. "Protest in Piety: Christian Science Revisited." *International Journal of Women's Studies* 1 (July/August 1978): 401-416.

Gillespie, Joanna B. "Carrie, or the Child in the Rectory: 19th-Century Episcopal

Sunday School Prototype." *Historical Magazine of the Protestant Episcopal Church* 51 (December 1982): 359-370.

Gimelli, Louis B. "Louisa Maxwell Cocke: An Evangelical Plantation Mistress in the Antebellum South." *Journal of the Early Republic* 9 (Spring 1989): 53-72.

Ginzberg, Lori D. "Women in an Evangelical Community: Oberlin, 1835-1850." *Ohio History* 89 (Winter 1980): 78-88.

Greene, Dana. "Quaker Feminism: The Case of Lucretia Mott." *Pennsylvania History* 48 (April 1981): 143-154.

Gundersen, Joan R. "The Local Parish as a Female Institution: The Experience of All Saints Episcopal Church in Frontier Minnesota." *Church History* 55 (September 1986): 307-322.

-----. "Parallel Churches?: Women and the Episcopal Church, 1850-1980." *Mid-America* 69 (April/July 1987): 87-97.

Hall, Lark. "The Other Side of the Coin: Reflections on Women in American Myth and Culture." *American Baptist Quarterly* (March 1983): 51-58.

Heeney, Brian. "The Beginnings of Church Feminism: Women and the Councils of the Church of England 1897-1919." *Journal of Ecclesiastical History* 33 (January 1982): 89-110.

-----. "Women's Struggles for Professional Work and Status in the Church of England, 1900-1930." *The Historical Journal* 26 (June 1983): 229-348.

Herring, Reuben. "Southern Baptist Convention Resolutions on the Family." *Baptist History and Heritage* 17 (January 1982): 36-45, 64.

Hewitt, Nancy A. "Feminist Friends: Agrarian Quakers and the Emergence of Woman's Rights in America." *Feminist Studies* 12 (Spring 1986): 27-50.

Hill, Bridget. "A Refuge from Men: The Idea of a Protestant Nunnery." *Past and Present* no. 117 (November 1987): 107-130.

Hill, Meredith. "The Women Workers of the Diocese of Athabasca; 1930-1970." *Journal of the Canadian Church Historical Society* 28 (October 1986): 63-74.

Hiner, N. Ray. "Cotton Mather and His Female Children: Notes on the Relationship Between Private Experience and Public Thought." *Journal of Psychohistory* 13 (Summer 1985): 33-50.

Hudson, Mary Lin. "'Shall Woman Preach?' Louisa Woosley and the Cumberland Presbyterian Church." *American Presbyterians* 68 (Winter 1990): 221-230.

Hudson, Winthrop S. "Early Nineteenth-Century Evangelical Religion and Women's Liberation." *Foundations* 23 (April/June 1980): 181-185.

Huyck, Heather. "Indelible Change: Woman Priests in the Episcopal Church." *Historical Magazine of the Protestant Episcopal Church* 51 (December 1982): 385-398.

Ingle, H. Larry. "A Quaker Woman on Women's Roles: Mary Penington to Friends, 1678." *Signs* 16 (Spring 1991): 587-596.

Ishikawa, Nancy Hiles. "Alice Smith Edwards: The Little Princess." *Journal of Mormon History* 6 (1979): 61-74.

Iversen, Joan. "Feminist Implications of Mormon Polygyny." *Feminist Studies* 10 (Fall 1984): 505-522.

James, Kimberly Jensen. "'Between Two Fires': Women on the 'Underground' of Mormon Polygamy." *Journal of Mormon History* 8 (1981): 49-62.

Jennings, Judith. "The Journal of Margaret Hoare Woods." *Quaker History* 75 (Spring 1986): 26-34.

Jensen, Joan M. "Not Only Ours but Others: The Quaker Teaching Daughters of the Mid-Atlantic, 1790-1850." *History of Education Quarterly* (Spring 1984): 3-19.

Karant-Nunn, Susan C. "Continuity and Change: Some Effects of the Reformation on the Women of Zwickau." *Sixteenth Century Journal* 13 (Summer 1982): 17-42.

Kendall, Joan. "The Development of a Distinctive Form of Quaker Dress." *Costume* 19 (1985): 58-74.

Kowaleski-Wallace, Beth. "Hannah and Her Sister: Women and Evangelism in Early Nineteenth-Century England." *Nineteenth-Century Contexts* 12, no. 2 (1988): 29-52.

Krugler, John D. and David Weinberg-Kinsey. "Equality of Leadership: The Ordinations of Sarah E. Dickson and Margaret E. Towner in the Presbyterian Church in the U.S.A." *American Presbyterians* 68 (Winter 1990): 245-258.

Kunze, Bonnelyn Young. "'Poore and in Necessity': Margaret Fell and Quaker Female Philanthropy in Northwest England in the Late Seventeenth Century." *Albion* 21 (Winter 1989): 559-580.

Kunzel, Regina. "The Professionalization of Benevolence: Evangelicals and Social Workers in the Florence Crittenton Homes, 1915 to 1945." *Journal of Social History* 22 (Fall 1988): 21-44.

Lewis, David Rich. "'For Life, the Resurrection, and the Life Everlasting': James J. Strang and Strangite Mormon Polygamy, 1849-1856." *Wisconsin Magazine of History* 66 (Summer 1983): 274-291.

Lieber, Constance L. "'The Goose Hangs High': Excerpts from the Letters of Martha Hughes Cannon." *Utah Historical Quarterly* 48 (Winter 1980): 37-48.

Linford, Orma. "The Mormons, the Law, and the Territory of Utah." *American Journal of Legal History* 23 (1979): 213-235.

Logue, Larry. "A Time of Marriage: Monogamy and Polygamy in a Utah Town." *Journal of Mormon History* 11 (1984): 3-26.

Maclear, J. F. "Anne Hutchinson and the Mortalist Heresy." *New England Quarterly* 54 (March 1981): 74-103.

Madsen, Carol Cornwall. "A Bluestocking in Zion: The Literary Life of Emmeline B. Wells." *Dialogue* 16 (Spring 1983): 126-140.

-----. "Emmeline B. Wells: 'Am I Not a Woman and a Sister.'" *Brigham Young University Studies* 22 (Spring 1982): 161-178.

-----. "Mormon Missionary Wives in Nineteenth Century Polynesia." *Journal of Mormon History* 13 (1986-87): 61-88.

-----. "Mormon Women and the Struggle for Definition." *Dialogue: A Journal of Mormon Thought* 14 (Winter 1981): 40-47.

Madsen, Carol Cornwall, and David J. Whittaker. "History's Sequel: A Source Essay on Women in Mormon History." *Journal of Mormon History* 6 (Spring 1980): 123-145.

Malmgreen, Gail. "Anne Knight and the Radical Subculture." *Quaker History* 71 (Fall 1982): 100-113.

McBeth, H. Leon. "The Changing Role of Women in Baptist History." *Southwestern Journal of Theology* 22 (Fall 1979): 84-96.

-----. "Perspectives on Women in Baptist Life." *Baptist History and Heritage* 22 (July 1987): 4-11.

McDonald, Jean A. "Mary Baker Eddy and the Nineteenth-Century 'Public' Woman: A Feminist Reappraisal." *Journal of Feminist Studies in Religion* 2 (Spring 1986): 89-111.

Meckel, Richard A. "Educating a Ministry of Mothers: Evangelical Maternal Associations, 1815-1860." *Journal of the Early Republic* 2 (Winter 1982): 403-423.

Monter, E. William. "Women in Calvinist Geneva (1550-1800)." *Signs* 6 (Winter 1980): 189-208.

Moran, Gerald F., and Maris Vinoskies. "The Puritan Family and Religion: A Critical Reappraisal." *William and Mary Quarterly* 39 (January 1982): 29-63.

Morgan, Cecilia. "Gender, Religion, and Rural Society: Quaker Women in Norwich, Ontario, 1820-1880." *Ontario History* 82 (December 1990): 273-288.

Moseley, Eva. "Labor Holdings at the Schlesinger Library, Radcliffe College." *Labor History* 31 (Winter/Spring 1990): 16-24.

-----. "One Half Our History." *Harvard Library Bulletin* 32 (Summer 1984): 274-311.

-----. "Sources for the 'New Women's History.'" *American Archivist* (Spring 1980): 180-190.

Newell, Linda King. "The Historical Relationship of Mormon Women and Priesthood." *Dialogue* 18 (Fall 1985): 21-32.

Newell, Linda King, and Valeen T. Avery. "New Light on the Sun: Emma Smith and the *New York Sun* Letter." *Journal of Mormon History* 6 (1979): 23-36.

Nudd, Rosemary SP. "The Parable of Mary Baker." *Daughters of Sarah* 15 (November/December 1989): 10-12.

Nutt, Rick. "Robert Lewis Dabney Presbyterians and Women's Suffrage." *Journal of Presbyterian History* 62 (Winter 1984): 339-353.

O'Brien, Patrick. "Lois Irwin, Barber College and Christian Altruism in Alabama, 1926-1927." *Journal of Presbyterian History* 62 (Winter 1984): 322-338.

Pace, D. Gene. "Wives of Nineteenth Century Mormon Bishops: A Quantitative Analysis." *Journal of the West* 21 (April 1982): 49-57.

Peterson, Levi S. "Juanita Brooks, My Subject, My Sister." *Dialogue* 22 (Spring 1989): 16-29.

Peterson, Susan C. "Adapting to Fill a Need: The Presentation Sisters and Health Care, 1901-1961." *South Dakota History* 17 (Spring 1987): 1-22.

Porterfield, Amanda. "Beames of Wrathe and Brides of Christ: Anger and Female Piety in Puritan New England." *Connecticut Review* 11 (Summer 1989): 1-12.

Prelinger, Catherine M. "Women and Religion, Women as Episcopalians: Some Methodological Observations." *Historical Magazine of the Protestant Episcopal Church* 52 (June 1983): 141-152.

Reed, John Shelton. "'A Female Movement': The Feminization of Nineteenth-Century Anglo-Catholicism." *Anglican and Episcopal History* 57 (June 1988): 199-238.

Roetger, R. W. "The Transformation of Sexual Morality in 'Puritan' New England: Evidence From New Haven Court Records, 1639-1690." *Canadian Review of American Studies* 15 (Fall 1984): 243-258.

Rogal, Samuel J. "The Epworth Women: Susanna Wesley and Her Daughters." *Wesleyan Theological Journal* 18 (Fall 1983): 80-89.

Rose, Susan D. "Conversations of Conversions: Interviewing American Evangelical Women." *International Journal of Oral History* 8 (February 1987): 171-181.

Ryan, Mary. "A Woman's Awakening: Evangelical Religion and the Families of Utica, New York, 1800-1840." *American Quarterly* 30 (1978): 602-633.

Santee, R. Virgil. "Sallie Paine Peck." *American Baptist Quarterly* 3 (September 1984): 225-234.

Scheffler, Judith. "Prison Writings of Early Quaker Women." *Quaker History* 74 (Fall 1984): 25-37.

Scott, Anne Firor. "Mormon Women, Other Women: Paradoxes and Challenges." *Journal of Mormon History* 13 (1986/87): 3-20.

Scott, Patricia Lyn, and Maureen Ursenbach Beecher. "Mormon Women: A Bibliography in Process, 1977-1985." *Journal of Mormon History* 12 (1985): 113-128.

Shipps, Jan. "The Principle Revoked: A Closer Look at the Demise of Plural Marriage." *Journal of Mormon History* 11 (1984): 65-78.

Shumaker, Conrad. "'A Daughter of the Puritans': History in Hawthorne's *The Marble Faun.*" *New England Quarterly* 57 (March 1984): 65-83.

Shurden, Kay. "The Impact of Southern Baptist Women on Social Issues: Three Viewpoints: Family Issues." *Baptist History and Heritage* 22 (July 1987): 33-36.

Smith, Frank. "Petticoat Presbyterianism: A Century of Debate in American Presbyterianism on the Issue of the Ordination of Women." *Westminster Theological Journal* 51 (Spring 1989): 51-76.

Smuts, R. M. "The Puritan Followers of Henrietta Maria in the 1630s." *English Historical Review* 93 (January 1978): 26-45.

Soderlund, Jean R. "Women's Authority in Pennsylvania and New Jersey Quaker Meetings, 1680-1760." *William and Mary Quarterly* 44 (October 1987): 722-749.

Sorrill, Bobbie. "Southern Baptist Laywomen in Missions." *Baptist History and Heritage* 22 (July 1987): 21-28.

Spielmann, Richard M. "The Beginning of Clerical Marriage in the English Reformation: The Reigns of Edward and Mary." *Anglican and Episcopal History* 56 (September 1987): 251-264.

Stehle, Eva. "Sappho's Gaze: Fantasies of a Goddess and Young Man." *Differences* 2 (Spring 1990): 88-125.

Swanson, Kimberly. "Eva Emery Dye and the Romance of Oregon History."

*Pacific Historian* 29 (Winter 1985): 59-68.

Swetnam, Susan H. "Turning to the Mothers: Mormon Women's Biographies of Their Female Forebears and the Mormon Church's Expectations for Women." *Frontiers* 10, no. 1 (1988): 1-6.

Thompsett, Fredrica Harris. "Women Inclined to Holiness: Our Reformation Ancestry." *Historical Magazine of the Protestant Episcopal Church* 51 (December 1982): 337-346.

Thompson, Evelyn Wings. "Southern Baptist Women as Writers and Editors." *Baptist History and Heritage* 22 (July 1987): 50-58.

Thorp, Malcolm R. "Winifred Graham and the Mormon Image." *Journal of Mormon History* 6 (1979): 107-122.

Todd, Margo. "Humanists, Puritans and the Spiritualized Household." *Church History* 49 (March 1980): 18-34.

Topping, Eva Catafygiotu. "Frances Wright: Petticoat Lecturer." *Cincinnati Historical Society Bulletin* 36 (Spring 1978): 43-56.

Trevett, Christine. "The Women around James Nayler, Quaker: A Matter of Emphasis." *Religion* 20 (July 1990): 249-274.

Tual, Jacques. "Sexual Equality and Conjugal Harmony: The Way to Celestial Bliss. A View of Early Quaker Matrimony." *The Journal of the Friends' Historical Society* 55, no. 6 (1988): 161-174.

Vickers, Gregory. "Southern Baptist Women and Social Concerns, 1910-1929." *Baptist History and Heritage* 23 (October 1988): 3-13.

Walker, Ronald W. "A Mormon 'Widow' in Colorado: The Exile of Emily Wells Grant." *Arizona and the West* 25 (Spring 1983): 5-22.

Weatherford, Carolyn. "Shaping of Leadership Among Southern Baptist Women." *Baptist History and Heritage* 22 (July 1987): 12-20.

Welter, Barbara. "She Hath Done What She Could: Protestant Women's Missionary Careers in Nineteenth-Century America." *American Quarterly* 30 (Winter 1978): 624-638.

Westerkamp, Marilyn J. "Anne Hutchinson, Sectarian Mysticism, and the Puritan Order." *Church History* 59 (December 1990): 482-496.

White, O. Kendall, Jr. "A Feminist Challenge: 'Mormons for ERA' as an Internal Social Movement." *Journal of Ethnic Studies* 13 (Spring 1985): 29-50.

Whiteley, Marilyn. "Modest, Unaffected and Fully Consecrated: Lady Evangelists in Canadian Methodism, 1884-1900." *Canadian Methodist Historical Society Papers* 6 (1987).

Whittaker, David J. "Early Mormon Polygamy Defenses." *Journal of Mormon History* 11 (1984): 43-64.

Wilson, Christine, ed. "Growing Up in Marion County: A Memoir by Eva Davis Beets." *Journal of Mississippi History* 48 (August 1986): 199-213.

Winsser, Johan. "Mary Dyer and the 'Monster' Story." *Quaker History* 79 (Spring 1990): 20-34.

# Religious Issues and Witchcraft

Arceneaux, Pamela D. "Guidebooks to Sin: The Blue Books of Storyville." *Louisiana History* 28 (Fall 1987): 397-405.

Barstow, Anne Llewellyn. "On Studying Witchcraft as Women's History: A Historiography of the European Witch Persecutions." *Journal of Feminist Studies in Religion* 4 (Fall 1988): 7-20.

Baym, Nina. "Onward Christian Women: Sarah J. Hale's History of the World." *New England Quarterly* 63 (June 1990): 249-270.

Le Beau, Bryan F. "Philip English and the Witchcraft Hysteria." *Historical Journal of Massachusetts* 15 (January 1987): 1-20.

Ben-Yehuda, Nachman. "Problems Inherent in Socio-historical Approaches to the European Witch Craze." *Journal for the Scientific Study of Religion* 20 (December 1981): 326-338.

Bendroth, Margaret L. "Millennial Themes and Private Visions: The Problem of 'Women's Place' in Religious History." *Fides et Historia* 20 (June 1988): 24-31.

Bewell, Alan J. "A 'Word Scarce Said': Hysteria and Witchcraft in Wordsworth's 'Experimental' Poetry of 1797-1798." *ELH* 53 (Summer 1986): 357-390.

Boxer, Marilyn J. "'First-Wave' Feminism in Nineteenth-Century France: Class, Family, and Religion." *Women's Studies International Forum* 5, no. 6 (1982): 551-559.

Brooks, Evelyn. "Religion, Politics, and Gender: The Leadership of Nannie Helen Burroughs." *Journal of Religious Thought* 44 (Winter/Spring 1988): 7-22.

Broshi, Magen. "Beware the Wiles of the Wanton Woman: Dead Sea Scroll Fragment Reflects Essene Fear of, and Contempt for, Women." *Biblical Archaeology Review* 9 (July/August 1983): 54-56.

Brown, Earl K. "Women in Church History: Stereotypes, Archetypes and Operational Modalities." *Methodist History* 18 (January 1980): 109-132.

Brown, Irene Quenzler. "Death, Friendship, and Female Identity During New England's Second Great Awakening." *Journal of Family History* 12, no. 4 (1987): 367-388.

Brower, Ruth Compton. "The 'Between-Age' Christianity of Agnes Machar." *Canadian Historical Review* 65 (September 1984): 529-552.

Burke, Janet M. "Freemasonry, Friendship and Noblewomen: The Role of the Secret Society in Bringing Enlightenment Thought to Pre-Revolutionary Women Elites." *History of European Ideas* 10, no. 3 (1989): 283-294.

Bynum, Caroline Walker. "Fast, Feast, and Flesh: The Religious Significance of Food to Medieval Women." *Representations* 11 (1985): 1-25.

Carr, A. "Coming of Age in Christianity: Women and the Churches." *The Furrow* 34 (June 1983): 345-358.

Castelli, Elizabeth. "Virginity and Its Meaning for Women's Sexuality in Early

Christianity." *Journal of Feminist Studies in Religion* 2 (Spring 1986): 61-88.

Christopherson, K. E. "Lady Inger and Her Family: Norway's Exemplar of Mixed Motives in the Reformation." *Church History* 55 (March 1986): 21-38.

Clark, Elizabeth A. "Ascetic Renunciation and Feminine Advancement: A Paradox of Late Ancient Christianity." *Anglican Theological Review* 63 (July 1981): 240-257.

-----. "Patrons, Not Priests: Gender and Power in Late Ancient Christianity." *Gender & History* 2 (Autumn 1990): 253-273.

Clark, Elizabeth B. "Religion, Rights, and Difference in the Early Woman's Rights Movement." *Wisconsin Women's Law Journal* 3 (1987): 29-58.

Clark, Stuart. "Inversion, Misrule, and the Meaning of Witchcraft." *Past and Present* 87 (May 1980): 98-127.

Coburn, Carol K. "Ethnicity, Religion, and Gender: The Women of Block, Kansas, 1868-1940." *Great Plains Quarterly* 8 (Fall 1988): 222-232.

Davies, Brian. "George Eliot and Christianity." *Downside Review* 100 (January 1982): 47-61.

Davis, Jacaleen. "Witchcraft and Superstitions of Torrance County." *New Mexico Historical Review* 54 (January 1979): 53-58.

Davis, John. "Joan of Kent, Lollardy and the English Reformation." *Journal of Ecclesiastical History* 33 (April 1982): 225-233.

Davy, Shirley. "Why Church Women's Organizations Thrived." *Canadian Women's Studies/Les cahiers de la femme* 2 (Winter 1983): 59-61.

Desan, S. "The Role of Women in Religious Riots During the French Revolution." *Eighteenth-Century Studies* 22 (Spring 1989): 451-468.

Dodson, Jualynne E. "Power and Surrogate Leadership: Black Women and Organized Religion." *Sage* 5 (Fall 1988): 37-42.

Doran, Susan. "Religion and Politics at the Court of Elizabeth I: The Habsburg Marriage Negotiations of 1559-1567." *English Historical Review* 104 (October 1989): 908-926.

Douglass, Jane Dempsey. "Christian Freedom: What Calvin Learned at the School of Women." *Church History* 53 (June 1984): 155-173.

Dowling, Maria. "Anne Boleyn and Reform." *Journal of Ecclesiastical History* 35 (January 1984): 30-46.

Estes, Leland. "Reginald Scot and His *Discoverie of Witchcraft*: Religion and Science in Opposition to the European Witch Craze." *Church History* 52 (December 1983): 444-456.

Evans, Richard J. "Feminism & Anticlericalism in France, 1870-1922." *The Historical Journal* 25 (December 1982): 947-950.

Fox-Genovese, Elizabeth. "Two Steps Forward, One Step Back: New Questions and Old Models in the Religious History of American Women." *Journal of the American Academy of Religion* 53 (September 1985): 465-471.

Frankforter, A. Daniel. "Elizabeth Bowes and John Knox: A Woman and Reformation Theology." *Church History* 56 (September 1987): 333-347.

French, Roderick S. "Liberation from Man and God in Boston: Abner Kneeland's

Free-Thought Campaign 1830-1839." *American Quarterly* 32 (Summer 1980): 202-221.

Geis, Gilbert. "Lord Hale, Witches and Rape." *British Journal of Law and Society* 5 (1978): 26-44.

Gijswijt-Hofstra, Marijke. "The European Witchcraft Debate and the Dutch Variant." *Social History* 15 (May 1990): 181-194.

Gildrie, Richard P. "Vision of Evil: Popular Culture, Puritanism, and the Massachusetts Witchcraft Crisis of 1692." *Journal of American Culture* 8 (Winter 1985): 17-34.

Gilkes, Cheryl Townsend. "'Together and in Harness': Women's Traditions in the Sanctified Church." *Signs* 10 (Summer 1985): 678-699.

Gillespie, Joanna Bowen. "'The Clear Leadings of Providence': Pious Memoirs and the Problems of Self-Realization for Women in the Early Nineteenth Century." *Journal of the Early Republic* 5 (Summer 1985): 197-222.

Goodman, D. "Enlightenment Salons: The Convergence of Female and Philosophic Ambitions." *Eighteenth Century Studies* 22 (Spring 1989): 329-350.

Goodrich, Michael. "The Contours of Female Piety in Later Medieval Hagiography." *Church History* 50 (March 1981): 20-32.

Grant, Barbara L. "Hildegard and Wisdom." *Anima* 6 (Spring 1980): 125-129.

Grant, Robert M. "A Woman of Rome: The Matron in Justin, 2 *Apology* 2.1-9." *Church History* 54 (December 1985): 461-472.

Greaves, Richard L. "The Role of Women in Early English Nonconformity." *Church History* 52 (September 1983): 299-311.

Gundersen, Joan R. "The Non-Institutional Church: The Religious Role of Women in Eighteenth-Century Virginia." *Historical Magazine of the Protestant Episcopal Church* 51 (December 1982): 347-358.

Hall, David D. "Witchcraft and the Limits of Interpretation." *New England Quarterly* 59 (June 1985): 253-281.

Harley, David. "Historians as Demonologists: The Myth of the Midwife-Witch." *Social History of Medicine* 3 (April 1990): 1-26.

Heinsohn, Gunnar, and Otto Steiger. "The Elimination of Medieval Birth Control and the Witch Trials of Modern Times." *International Journal of Women's Studies* 5 (May/June 1982): 193-214.

Hester, Marianne. "The Dynamics of Male Domination Using the Witch Craze in 16th- and 17th- Century England as a Case Study." *Women's Studies International Forum* 13, no. 1/2 (1990).

Horsley, Richard A. "Who Were the Witches? The Social Roles of the Accused in the European Witch Trials." *Journal of Interdisciplinary History* 9 (Spring 1979): 689-715.

House, H. Wayne. "A Biblical View of Women in the Ministry; pt. 5: Distinctive Roles for Women in the Second and Third Centuries." *Bibliotheca Sacra* 146 (January-March 1989): 41-54.

Hynes, P. "Women in the Church." *Doctrine and Life* 31, no. 8 (1981): 521-524.

Jaki, Stanley L. "The Virgin Birth and the Birth of Science." *The Downside*

*Review* 107 (October 1989): 255-273.

Jobe, Thomas Harmon. "The Devil in Restoration Science: The Glanvill-Webster Witchcraft Debate." *Isis: An International Review Devoted to the History of Science and Its Cultural Influences* 72 (September 1981): 343-356.

Jochens, Jenny M. "The Church and Sexuality in Medieval Iceland." *Journal of Medieval History* 6 (December 1980): 377-392.

Jones, Norman L. "Elizabeth, Edification, and the Latin Prayer Book of 1560." *Church History* 53 (June 1984): 174-186.

Karras, Ruth Mazo. "Holy Harlots: Prostitute Saints in Medieval Legend." *Journal of the History of Sexuality* 1 (July 1990): 3-32.

Kenneally, James J. "Sexism, The Church, Irish Women." *Eire-Ireland* 21 (Fall 1986): 3-16.

Kibbey, Ann. "Mutations of the Supernatural: Witchcraft, Remarkable Providences, and the Power of Puritan Men." *American Quarterly* 34 (Summer 1982): 125-148.

Lambert, Ronald D., and James E. Curtis. "Quebecois and English Canadian Opposition to Racial and Religious Intermarriage, 1968-1983." *Canadian Ethnic Studies/Etudes Ethniques Au Canada* 16, no. 2 (1984): 30-46.

Larner, Christina. "Was Witch-hunting Woman-hunting?" *New Society* 58 (October 1981): 11-12.

-----. "Witch Beliefs and Witch-Hunting in England and Scotland." *History Today* 31 (1981): 32-36.

Lehmann, Hartmut. "The Persecution of Witches as Restoration to Order: The Case of Germany, 1590s-1650s." *Central Europe History* 21 (June 1988): 107-121.

Leslie, I. Julia. "Suttee or Sati: Victim or Victor?" *Bulletin: Center for the Study of World Religions, Harvard University* 14 (1987/88): 5-23.

Levack, B. P. "The Great Scottish Witch Hunt of 1661-1662." *Journal of British Studies* 20 (1981): 90-108.

Martin, John Hilary. "The Injustice of Not Ordaining Women: A Problem for Medieval Theologians." *Theological Studies* 48 (June 1987): 303-316.

McLachlan, Hugh V., and J. K. Swales. "Witchcraft and Anti-feminism." *Scottish Journal of Sociology* 4 (May 1980): 141-166.

McNamara, Jo Ann. "Wives and Widows in Early Christian Thought." *International Journal of Women's Studies* 2 (November/December 1979): 575-592.

Miller, Page Putnam. "Women in the Vanguard of the Sunday School Movement." *Journal of Presbyterian History* 58 (Winter 1980): 311-325.

Moxnes, Halvor, ed. "Feminist Reconstruction of Early Christian History." *Studia Theologica: Scandinavian Journal of Theology* 43, no. 1 (1989): 1-163.

Norberg, Kathryn. "Women, the Family, and the Counter-Reformation: Women's Confraternities in the 17th Century." *Western Society for French History* 6 (November 1978): 55-62.

Norlin, Dennis A. "The Suffrage Movement and South Dakota Churches: Radicals and the Status Quo, 1890." *South Dakota History* 14 (Winter 1984): 308-334.

O'Connor, June. "Feminist Research in Religion." *Women's Studies* 17, no. 1-2 (1989): 101-124.

Oman, Susan Staker. "Nurturing LDS Primaries: Louis Felt and May Anderson, 1880-1940." *Utah Historical Quarterly* 49 (Summer 1981): 262-275.

Parker, Geoffrey. "The European Witchcraze Revisited." *History Today* 30 (November 1980): 23-24.

Parkerson, Donald H., and Jo Ann Parkerson. "'Fewer Children of Greater Spiritual Quality': Religion and the Decline of Fertility in Nineteenth-Century America." *Social Science History* 12 (Spring 1988): 49-70.

Porterfield, Amanda. "The Mother in Eighteenth-Century American Conceptions of Man and God." *Journal of Psychohistory* 15 (Fall 1987): 189-206.

Prochaska, F. K. "Body and Soul: Bible Nurses and the Poor in Victorian London." *Historical Research* 60 (1987): 336-348.

Reineke, Martha J. "'The Devils Are Come Down Upon Us': Myth, History, and the Witch as Scapegoat." *Union Seminary Quarterly Review* 44, no. 1-2 (1990): 55-83.

-----. "'This Is My Body': Reflections on Abjection, Anorexia, and Medieval Women Mystics." *Journal of the American Academy of Religion* 58 (Summer 1990): 245-266.

Riley, Philip F. "Michel Foucault, Lust, Women, and Sin in Louis XIV's Paris." *Church History* 59 (March 1990): 35-50.

Roccasabio, Joan L. "Churchwomen as Ministers in Eastern Christian Antiquity." *Diakonia* 21, no. 3 (1987): 164-174.

Rousselle, Robert. "The Dreams of Vibia Perpetua: Analysis of a Female Christian Martyr." *Journal of Psychohistory* 14 (Winter 1987): 193-206.

Sanchez, Virginia Korrol. "In Search of Unconventional Women: Histories of Puerto Rican Women in Religious Vocations Before Mid-Century." *Oral History Review* 16 (Fall 1988): 47-64.

Schmidt, Jean Miller. "Beyond Separate Spheres: Women, Religion and Social Change." *Drew Gateway* 57 (Fall 1987): 80-94.

Seed, Patricia. "The Church and the Patriarchal Family: Marriage Conflicts in the Sixteenth- and Seventeenth-Century New Spain." *Journal of Family History* 10 (Autumn 1985): 284-293.

Shahar, Shulamith. "Infants, Infant Care, and Attitudes toward Infancy in the Medieval Lives of Saints." *Journal of Psychohistory* 10 (Winter 1983): 281-310.

Shaner, Donald W. "Women in the Church: A Biblical Interpretation of an Ethical Problem." *Foundations* 23 (July-September 1980).

Shortt, Mary. "Victorian Temptations." *The Beaver* 68 (December 1988/January 1989): 4-13.

Smith, Bonnie G. "Religion & the Rise of Domesticity: Ladies of the Nord." *Marxist Perspectives* 2 (Summer 1979): 56-83.

Smith, Ruth L. "Moral Transcendence and Moral Space in the Historical Experiences of Women." *Journal of Feminist Studies in Religion* 4 (Fall 1988): 21-38.

Sommerville, C. John. "The Family Fights Back: Its Struggle with Religious Movements." *Fides et Historia* 15 (Fall/Winter 1982): 6-23.

Sweet, Leonard I. "The Female Seminary Movement and Woman's Mission in Antebellum America." *Church History* 54 (March 1985): 41-55.

Taves, Ann. "Spiritual Purity and Sexual Shame: Religious Themes in the Writings of Harriet Jacobs." *Church History* 56 (March 1987): 59-72.

Travis, Carol. "Rural Connecticut in 1840: The Pastor's Wife's Manuscript." *Manuscripts* 36 (Summer 1984): 197-202.

Underwood, Malcolm G. "Politics and Piety in the Household of Lady Margaret Beaufort." *Journal of Ecclesiastical History* 38 (January 1987): 39-52.

Vukanovic, T. P. "Witchcraft in the Central Balkans I: Characteristics of Witches." *Folklore* 100, no. 1 (1989): 9-24.

-----. "Witchcraft in the Central Balkans II: Protection Against Witches." *Folklore* 100, no. 2 (1989): 221-236.

Walker, Nancy. "Wit, Sentimentality and the Image of Women in the Nineteenth Century." *American Studies* 22 (Fall 1981): 5-22.

Walkowitz, Judith R. "Science and the Seance: Transgressions of Gender and Genre in Late Victorian London." *Representations* 22 (1988): 3-29.

White, Charles Edward. "The Beauty of Holiness: The Career of Phoebe Palmer." *Fides et Historia* 19 (February 1987): 22-34.

Williams, Linda B., and Basil G. Zimmer. "The Changing Influence of Religion on U.S. Fertility: Evidence from Rhode Island." *Demography* 27 (August 1990): 475-483.

Wire, Antoinette Clark. "Ancient Miracle Stories and Women's Social World." *Forum* 2 (December 1986): 77-84.

Yoder, R. Paul. "Clarissa Regained: Richardson's Redemption of Eve." *Eighteenth Century Life* 13 (May 1989): 87-99.

Yost, John K. "The Reformation Defense of Clerical Marriage in the Reigns of Henry VIII and Edward VI." *Church History* 50 (June 1981): 152-165.

## SEXUALITY

### Ideology

Anderson, Gary. "Celibacy or Consummation in the Garden? Reflections on Early Jewish and Christian Interpretations of the Garden of Eden." *Harvard Theological Review* 82 (April 1989): 121-148.

Andreeva, I. S. "Sociophilosophical Problems of Sex, Marriage, and the Family." *Soviet Review* 22, no. 1 (1981/82): 20-43.

Bailey, Peter. "Parasexuality and Glamour: The Victorian Barmaid as Cultural Prototype." *Gender & History* 2 (Summer 1990): 148-172.

Ball, Christine. "Female Sexual Ideologies in Mid to Later Nineteenth-Century Canada." *Canadian Journal of Women and the Law/Revue juridique 'La femme et le droit'* 1, no. 2 (1986): 324-338.

Blackwood, Evelyn. "Sexuality and Gender in Certain Native American Tribes:

The Case of Cross-Gender Females." *Signs* 10 (Autumn 1984): 27-42.

Bland, Lucy. "Protecting and Policing Female Sexuality." *Society for the Study of Labour History* 48 (Spring 1984): 16-17.

-----. "Rational Sex or Spiritual Love?: The Men and Women's Club of the 1880s." *Women's Studies International Forum* 13, no. 1/2 (1990): 33-48.

Bloch, Ruth H. "The Gendered Meanings of Virtue in Revolutionary America." *Signs* 13 (Autumn 1987): 37-58.

Brundage, James A. "'Allas! That Evere Love Was Synne': Sex and Medieval Canon Law." *Catholic Historical Review* 72 (January 1986): 1-13.

Campbell, B. "Feminist Sexual Politics." *Feminist Review* 5 (1980): 1-18.

Carby, Hazel V. "It Jus Be's Dat Way Sometime: The Sexual Politics of Women's Blues." *Radical America* 20, no. 4 (1986): 9-24.

Clark, Anna. "Queen Caroline and the Sexual Politics of Popular Culture in London, 1820." *Representations* no. 31 (Summer 1990): 47-68.

Collette, Christine. "Socialism and Scandal: The Sexual Politics of the Early Labour Movement." *History Workshop* 23 (Spring 1987): 102-111.

Conner, Susan P. "Sexual Politics and Citizenship: Women in Eighteenth-Century France." *Western Society for French History* 10 (October 1982): 264-273.

Cott, Nancy F. "Passionlessness: An Interpretation of Victorian Sexual Ideology, 1790-1850." *Signs* 4 (Winter 1978): 237-252.

D'Emilio, John, and Estelle B. Freedman. "A Response to Ann duCille's 'Othered Matters.'" *Journal of the History of Sexuality* 1 (July 1990): 128-130.

Dolan, Jill. "'What, No Beans?': Images of Women and Sexuality in Burlesque Comedy." *Journal of Popular Culture* 18 (Winter 1984): 37-48.

DuBois, Ellen Carol, and Linda Gordon. "Seeking Ecstasy on the Battlefield: Danger and Pleasure in Nineteenth-Century Feminist Sexual Thought." *Feminist Studies* 9 (Spring 1983): 7-25.

du Cille, Ann. "'Othered' Matters: Reconceptualizing Dominance and Difference in the History of Sexuality in America." *Journal of the History of Sexuality* 1 (July 1990): 102-127.

Engels, Dagmar. "The Age of Consent Act of 1891: Colonial Ideology in Bengal." *South Asia Research* 3 (November 1983): 107-134.

-----. "History and Sexuality in India: Discursive Trends." *Trends in History* 4, no. 4 (1990).

English, Deirdre, Amber Hollibough, and Gayle Rubin. "Talking Sex: A Conversation on Sexuality and Feminism." *Socialist Review* 11, no. 4 (1981): 43-62.

Epstein, Julia. "Either/Or--Neither/Both: Sexual Ambiguity and the Ideology of Gender." *Genders* 7 (March 1990): 99-142.

Feigenbaum-Knox, Rena. "Aesthetics and Ethics: A Study of Sexuality in Denis Diderot's Art Criticism." *Western Society for French History* 9 (October 1981): 226-237.

Fishbein, Leslie. "Freud and the Radicals: The Sexual Revolution Comes to Greenwich Village." *Canadian Review of American Studies* 12 (Fall 1981): 173-190.

Fitzpatrick, Sheila. "Sex and Revolution: An Examination of Literacy and Statistical Data on the Mores of Soviet Students in the 1920s." *Journal of Modern History* 50 (June 1978): 252-278.

Foster, Lawrence. "Free Love and Feminism: John Humphrey Noyes and the Oneida Community." *Journal of the Early Republic* 1 (Summer 1981): 165-183.

Freedman, Estelle B. "'Uncontrolled Desires': The Response to the Sexual Psychopath, 1920-1960." *Journal of American History* 74 (June 1987): 83-106.

Gay, P. "Victorian Sexuality: Old Texts and New Insights." *American Scholar* 49 (1980): 372-378.

Gibbs, Phillip A. "Self Control and Male Sexuality in the Advice Literature of Nineteenth Century America, 1830-1860." *Journal of American Culture* 9 (Summer 1986): 37-41.

Halperin, D. M. "Is There a History of Sexuality?" *History and Theory* 23, no. 3 (1989): 257-274.

Hansen, Karen Tranberg. "Body Politics: Sexuality, Gender, and Domestic Service in Zambia." *Journal of Women's History* 2 (Spring 1990): 120-142.

-----. "Negotiating Sex and Gender in Urban Zambia." *Journal of South African Studies* 10 (April 1984): 219-238.

Hansen, Miriam. "Pleasure, Ambivalence, Identification: Valentino and Female Spectatorship." *Cinema Journal* 25 (Summer 1986): 6-32.

Harbison, Craig. "Sexuality and Social Standing in Jan van Eyck's Arnolfini Double Portrait." *Renaissance Quarterly* 43 (Summer 1990): 249-291.

Hatem, Merrat. "The Politics of Sexuality and Gender in Segregated Patriarchal Systems: The Case of Eighteenth- and Nineteenth-Century Egypt." *Feminist Studies* 12 (Summer 1986): 251-274.

Heyns, Michiel. "The Steam-hammer and the Sugar-tongs: Sexuality and Power in Elizabeth Gaskell's *North and South*." *English Studies in Africa* 32, no. 2 (1989): 79-94.

Holtzman, Ellen M. "The Pursuit of Married Love: Women's Attitudes toward Sexuality and Marriage in Great Britain, 1918-1959." *Journal of Social History* 16 (Winter 1982): 39-52.

Horn, Margo. "The Moral Message of Child Guidance 1925-1945." *Journal of Social History* 18 (Fall 1984): 25-36.

Horn, Michiel. "More Than Cigarettes, Sex, and Chocolate: The Canadian Army in the Netherlands, 1944-1945." *Journal of Canadian Studies/Revue d'études canadiennes* 16 (Fall/Winter 1981): 156-173.

Jarausch, Konrad H. "Students, Sex and Politics in Imperial Germany." *Journal of Contemporary History* 17 (April 1982): 285-304.

Jeffreys, Sheila. "'Free from All Uninvited Touch of Man': Women's Campaigns around Sexuality 1880-1914." *Women's Studies International Forum* 5, no. 6 (1982): 629-645.

-----. "The Spinster and Her Enemies: Sexuality and the Last Wave of Feminism." *Scarlet Women* 13 (July 1981).

Jirat-Wasiutynski, Vojtech. "Paul Gauguin's Self-Portraits and 'Oviri': The Image of the Artist, Eve, and the Fatal Woman." *The Art Quarterly* 2, no. 2 (1979): 172-190.

Jochens, Jenny M. "The Church and Sexuality in Medieval Iceland." *Journal of Medieval History* 6 (December 1980): 377-392.

Johnson, Sonia. "Women, Desire, and History." *Woman of Power* no. 16 (Spring 1990): 73-77.

Kandiyoti, Deniz. "Slave Girls, Temptresses, and Comrades: Images of Women in the Turkish Novel." *Feminist Issues* 8, no. 1 (1988): 35-50.

Kern, Louis J. "Ideology and Reality: Sexuality and Women's Status in the Oneida Community." *Radical History Review* 20 (Spring/Summer 1979): 180-204.

Landale, Nancy S., and Avery M. Guest. "Ideology and Sexuality Among Victorian Women." *Social Science History* 10 (Summer 1986): 147-170.

Leites, Edmund. "The Duty to Desire: Love, Friendship and Sexuality to Some Puritan Theories of Marriage." *Journal of Social History* 15 (Spring 1982): 383-408.

Lemay, Helen Rodnite. "Some Thirteenth and Fourteenth Century Lectures on Female Sexuality." *International Journal of Women's Studies* 1 (July/August 1978): 391-400.

Lenhoff, Gail. "Hellenistic Erotica and the Kiev Cave Patericon 'Tale of Moses the Hungarian.'" *Russian History* 10, no. 2 (1983): 141-153.

Levesque, Andree. "Prescribers and Rebels: Attitudes to European Women's Sexuality in New Zealand 1860-1916." *Women's Studies* 4, no. 2 (1981): 133-144.

Lipton, Eunice. "Women, Pleasure, and Painting (e.g., Boucher)." *Genders* 7 (March 1990): 69-86.

Long, Diana E. "Moving Reprints: A Historian Looks at Sex Research Publications of the 1930s." *Journal of the History of Medicine and Allied Sciences* 45 (July 1990): 452-468.

Lunbeck, Elizabeth. "'A New Generation of Women': Progressive Psychiatrists and the Hypersexual Female." *Feminist Studies* 13 (Fall 1987): 513-543.

Mackinnon, Alison, and Carol Bacchi. "Sex, Resistance, and Power: Sex Reform in South Australia, c. 1905." *Australian Historical Studies* 23 (April 1988): 60-71.

Major, J. R. "Bastard Feudalism and the Kiss: Changing Social Mores in Late Medieval and Early Modern France." *Journal of Interdisciplinary History* 17 (Winter 1987): 509-536.

McCalman, Lain. "Females, Feminism, and Free Love in an Early Nineteenth Century Radical Movement." *Labour History* 38 (May 1980): 1-25.

McGovern, Constance M. "The Myths of Social Control and Custodial Oppression: Patterns of Psychiatric Medicine in Late Nineteenth-Century Institutions." *Journal of Social History* 20 (Fall 1986): 3-23.

McKinley, Blaine. "Free Love and Domesticity: Lizzie M. Holmes, *Hagar Lyndon* (1893), and the Anarchist-Feminist Imagination." *Journal of American Culture* 13 (Spring 1990): 55-62.

McMahon, Keith. "A Case for Confucian Sexuality: The Eighteenth-Century Novel, *Yesou Puyan*." *Late Imperial China* 9 (December 1988): 32-55.

Melching, Willem. "'A New Morality': Left-Wing Intellectuals on Sexuality in Weimar Germany." *Journal of Contemporary History* 25 (January 1990): 69-86.

Mullaney, Marie Marmo. "Sexual Politics in the Career and Legend of Louise Michel." *Signs* 15 (Winter 1990): 300-322.

Nead, Lynda. "The Female Nude: Pornography, Art and Sexuality." *Signs* 15 (Winter 1990): 323-335.

Nissenbaum, Stephen. "Sexual Radicalism and the Contested Norm." *Quaderno* 1 (1988).

Nugent, Georgia. "This Sex Which Is Not One: De-Constructing Ovid's Hermaphrodite." *Differences* 2 (Spring 1990): 160-185.

Oudshoorn, Nelly. "On Measuring Sex Hormones: The Role of Biological Assays in Sexualizing Chemical Substances." *Bulletin of the History of Medicine* 64 (Summer 1990): 243-261.

Padgug, Robert A. "Sexual Matters: On Conceptualizing Sexuality in History." *Radical History Review* 20 (Spring/Summer 1979): 3-24.

Pedersen, Susan. "Hannah More Meets Simple Simon: Tracts, Chapbooks, and Popular Culture in Late Eighteenth-Century England." *The Journal of British Studies* 25 (January 1986): 84-113.

Pellow, Deborah. "Sexuality in Africa." *Trends in History* 4, no. 4 (1990).

Perry, Lewis. "'Progress, Not Pleasure, Is Our Aim': The Sexual Advice of an Antebellum Radical." *Journal of Social History* 12 (Spring 1979): 354-366.

Peterson, M. Jeanne. "Dr. Acton's Enemy: Medicine, Sex, and Society in Victorian England." *Victorian Studies* 29 (Summer 1986): 569-590.

Rauch, Angelika. "The Trauerspiel of the Prostituted Body, or Woman as Allegory of Modernity." *Cultural Critique* no. 10 (Fall 1988): 77-88.

Rich, B. Ruby. "Maedchen in Uniform: From Repressive Tolerance to Erotic Liberation." *Radical America* 15 (November/December 1981): 17-38.

Riley, Philip F. "Michel Foucault, Lust, Women, and Sin in Louis XIV's Paris." *Church History* 59 (March 1990): 35-50.

Roetger, R. W. "The Transformation of Sexual Morality in 'Puritan' New England: Evidence From New Haven Court Records, 1639-1690." *Canadian Review of American Studies* 15 (Fall 1984): 243-258.

Roth, Guenther. "Divergent Histories of Sexual Science." *Telos* no. 82 (Winter 1989/90): 185-190.

Rupp, Leila J. "Feminism and the Sexual Revolution in the Early Twentieth Century: The Case of Doris Stevens." *Feminist Studies* 15 (Summer 1989): 289-309.

Schulenburg, Jane Tibbetts. "Sexism and the Celestial Gynaeceum--from 500 to 1200." *Journal of Medieval History* 4 (June 1978): 117-134.

Schwantes, Carlos A. "Free Love and Free Speech on the Pacific Northwest Frontier." *Oregon Historical Quarterly* 82 (Fall 1981): 271-293.

Sebire, Dawn. "'To Shield from Temptation': The Business Girl and the City."

*Urban History Review* 17 (February 1989): 203-208.

Seidman, S. "The Power of Desire and the Danger of Pleasure: Victorian Sexuality Reconsidered." *Journal of Social History* 24 (Autumn 1990): 47-68.

-----. "Sexual Attitudes of Victorian and Post-Victorian Women: Another Look at the Mosher Survey." *Journal of American Studies* 23 (April 1989): 68-72.

Shade, William G. "'A Mental Passion': Female Sexuality in Victorian America." *International Journal of Women's Studies (Canada)* 1 (1978): 13-29.

Simms, Norman. "Stone Age Sexuality." *Journal of Psychohistory* 18 (Summer 1990): 109-116.

Skaggs, Merrill. "Submission and Fidelity, Assertion and Surprise: Two 'Southern Woman' Films." *Southern Quarterly* 24 (Spring 1986): 5-13.

Slotkin, Wendy. "Maternity and Sexuality in the 1890s." *Woman's Art Journal* 1 (Spring/Summer 1980): 13-19.

Smart, Carol. "Law's Power, the Sexed Body, and Feminist Discourse." *Journal of Law and Society* 17 (Summer 1990): 194-210.

Snell, James G. "'The White Life for Two': The Defence of Marriage and Sexual Morality in Canada, 1890-1914." *Histoire sociale/Social History* 16 (May 1983): 111-128.

Solomon, Robert H. "The Prairie Mermaid, Love Tests of Pioneer Women." *Great Plains Quarterly* 4 (Summer 1984).

Spall, Richard Francis, Jr. "The Bedchamber Crisis and the Hastings Scandal: Morals, Politics, and the Press at the Beginning of Victoria's Reign." *Canadian Journal of History* 22 (April 1987): 19-40.

Spurlock, John. "The Free Love Network in America, 1850 to 1860." *Journal of Social History* 21 (Summer 1988): 765-780.

Stehle, Eva. "Sappho's Gaze: Fantasies of a Goddess and Young Man." *Differences* 2 (Spring 1990): 88-125.

Stevens, Carolyn. "The History of Sexuality in Britain and America, 1800-1975: Course Method and Bill of Rights." *Women's Studies Quarterly* 16 (Spring/Summer 1988): 87-96.

Tanger, Deborah. "Real Men Don't Eat Strong Women: The Virgin-Madonna-Whore Complex Updated." *Journal of Psychohistory* 12 (Spring 1985): 487-496.

Taves, Ann. "Spiritual Purity and Sexual Shame: Religious Themes in the Writings of Harriet Jacobs." *Church History* 56 (March 1987): 59-72.

Thomas, Samuel J. "Catholic Journalists and the Ideal Woman in Late Victorian America." *International Journal of Women's Studies* 4 (January/February 1981): 89-100.

Trennert, Robert A. "Victorian Morality and the Supervision of Indian Women Working in Phoenix, 1906-1930." *Journal of Social History* 22 (Fall 1988): 113-128.

Vaughan, Virginia Mason. "Daughters of the Game: Troilus and Cressida and the Sexual Discourse of 16th-Century England." *Women's Studies International Forum* 13, no. 3 (1990): 209-220.

Verduin, Kathleen. "'Our Cursed Natures': Sexuality and the Puritan Conscience."

*New England Quarterly* 56 (June 1983): 220-238.

Westphal-Wihl, Sarah. "The Ladies' Tournament: Marriage, Sex, and Honor in Thirteenth-Century Germany." *Signs* 14 (Winter 1989): 371-398.

White, Luise. "Separating the Men from the Boys: Constructions of Gender, Sexuality, and Terrorism in Central Kenya, 1939-1959." *International Journal of African Historical Studies* 23, no. 1 (1990): 1-26.

White, Sarah Melhado. "Sexual Language and Human Conflict in Old French Fabliaux." *Comparative Studies in Society and History* 24, no. 2 (1982): 185-210.

Williams, Carolyn. "The Changing Face of Change: Fe/male In/constancy." *British Journal for Eighteenth-Century Studies* 12 (Spring 1989): 12-28.

Wood, Charles T. "The Doctor's Dilemma: Sin, Salvation, and the Menstrual Cycle in Medieval Thought." *Speculum* 56 (1981): 710-727.

## Lesbianism (see also Lifestages and Lifestyles)

Allen, Paula Gunn. "Lesbians in American Indian Culture." *Conditions* 3 (Spring 1981): 67-87.

Berube, Allan, and John D'Emilio. "The Military and Lesbians During the McCarthy Years." *Signs* 9 (Summer 1984): 759-775.

Brown, Judith C. "Lesbian Sexuality in Renaissance Italy: The Case of Sister Benedetta Carline." *Signs* 9 (Summer 1984): 751-758.

Califia, Pat. "Feminism and Sadomasochism." *The CoEvolution Quarterly* (Spring 1982): 33-40.

Chauncey, George, Jr. "From Sexual Inversion to Homosexuality: Medicine and the Changing Conceptualization of Female Diseases." *Salmagundi* 58/59 (Fall/Winter 1983): 114-146.

Cook, Blanche. "The Historical Denial of Lesbianism." *Radical History Review* no. 20 (Summer 1979): 60-65.

Davis, Madeline, and Elizabeth Lapovsky Kennedy. "Oral History and the Study of Sexuality in the Lesbian Community: Buffalo, New York, 1940-1960." *Feminist Studies* 12 (Spring 1986): 7-26.

Duberman, Martin Bauml. "'I Am Not Contented': Female Masochism and Lesbianism in Early Twentieth-Century New England." *Signs* 5 (Spring 1980): 825-841.

Engelstein, Laura. "Lesbian Vignettes: A Russian Triptych from the 1890s." *Signs* 15 (Summer 1990): 813-831.

Erickson, Brigette, trans. "A Lesbian Execution in Germany, 1721. The Trial Records." *Journal of Homosexuality* 6 (Fall 1980/Winter 1981): 27-40.

Faderman, Lillian. "Lesbian Magazine Fiction in the Early Twentieth Century." *Journal of Popular Culture* (Spring 1978): 800-817.

Goldstein, Melvin. "Some Tolerant Attitudes Toward Female Homosexuality Throughout History." *Journal of Psychohistory* 9 (Spring 1982): 437-460.

Matter, E. Ann. "My Sister, My Spouse: Women-Identified Women in Medieval Christianity." *Journal of Feminist Studies in Religion* 2 (Fall 1986): 81-94.

O'Brien, Sharon. "'The Thing Not Named': Willa Cather as a Lesbian Writer." *Signs* 9 (Summer 1984): 576-599.

Padgug, Robert. "More Than the Story of a Virus: Gay History, Gay Communities and AIDS." *Radical America* 21 (March/April 1987): 35-42.

Rolley, Datrina. "Cutting a Dash: The Dress of Radclyffe Hall and Una Troubridge." *Feminist Review* no. 35 (Summer 1990): 54-66.

Roof, Judith A. "Freud Reads Lesbians: The Male Homosexual Imperative." *Arizona Quarterly* 46 (Spring 1990): 17-26.

Roscoe, Will. "Making History: The Challenge of Gay and Lesbian Studies." *Journal of Homosexuality* 15, no. 3/4 (1988): 1-40.

Ross, Becki. "The House That Jill Built: Lesbian Feminist Organizing in Toronto, 1976-1980." *Feminist Review* no. 35 (Summer 1990): 75-91.

Rupp, Leila J. "Imagine My Surprise': Women's Relationships in Historical Perspective." *Frontiers* 5 (Fall 1980): 61-70.

Sahli, Nancy. "Smashing: Women's Relationships Before the Fall." *Chrysalis* 8 (Summer 1979): 17-27.

Sankar, Andrea. "Sisters and Brothers, Lovers and Enemies: Marriage Resistance in Southern Kwantung [Hong Kong, 1865-1935]." *Journal of Homosexuality* 11 (Summer 1985): 69-81.

Sedgwick, Eve K. "Across Gender, across Sexuality: Willa Cather and Others." *South Atlantic Quarterly* 87 (Winter 1989): 53-72.

Smith, Elizabeth A. "Butches, Femmes, and Feminists: The Politics of Lesbian Sexuality." *NWSA Journal* 1 (Spring 1989): 398-421.

Whitlock, Gillian. "'Everything Is Out of Place': Radclyffe Hall and the Lesbian Literary Tradition." *Feminist Studies* 13 (Fall 1987): 555-582.

Wolverton, Terry, and Christine Wong. "An Oral Herstory of Lesbianism." *Frontiers* 4 (Fall 1979): 52-53.

## Practices

Abelove, Henry. "Some Speculations on the History of Sexual Intercourse During the Long Eighteenth Century in England." *Genders* no. 6 (November 1989): 125-130.

Adams, Kenneth Alan. "Love American Style II: 'Octopoid' Genitality and the Medusal Madonna." *Journal of Psychohistory* 10 (Spring 1983): 409-462.

Boswell, John. "Concepts, Experience, and Sexuality." *Differences* 2 (Spring 1990): 67-87.

Brown, Steven E. "Sexuality and the Slave Community." *Phylon* 42 (Spring 1981): 1-10.

Bullough, Vern L. "The Fielding H. Garrison Lecture: The Physician and Research into Human Sexual Behavior in Nineteenth-Century Germany." *Bulletin of the History of Medicine* 63 (Summer 1989): 247-267.

Burt, Eugene C. "Eroticism in Baluyia Body Arts." *African Arts* 15 (February 1982): 68-69, 88.

Chapman, Terry L. "Women, Sex and Marriage in Western Canada, 1890-1920."

*Alberta History* 33 (Autumn 1985): 1-12.

Duberman, Martin. "Male Impotence in Colonial Pennsylvania." *Signs* 4 (Winter 1978): 395-401.

Dunfey, Julie. "'Living the Principle' of Plural Marriage: Mormon Women, Utopia, and Female Sexuality in the Nineteenth Century." *Feminist Studies* 10 (Fall 1984): 523-536.

Engel, Barbara Alpern. "Peasant Morality and Pre-Marital Relations in Late 19th Century Russia." *Journal of Social History* 23 (Summer 1990): 695-714.

Fairchilds, Cissie. "Female Sexuality and the Rise of Illegitimacy: A Case Study." *Journal of Interdisciplinary History* 8 (Spring 1978): 627-667.

Freedman, Estelle. "Sexuality in Nineteenth-Century America: Behavior, Ideology, and Politics." *Reviews in American History* 10 (December 1982): 196-215.

Gillis, John R. "Servants, Sexual Relations, and the Risks of Illegitimacy in London, 1801-1900." *Feminist Studies* 5 (Spring 1979): 142-173.

Gladwin, Lee A. "Tobacco and Sex: Some Factors Affecting Non-Marital Sexual Behavior in Colonial Virginia." *Journal of Social History* 12 (Fall 1978): 57-75.

Harper, Donald. "The Sexual Arts of Ancient China as Described in a Manuscript of the Second Century B.C." *Harvard Journal of Asiatic Studies* 47, no. 2 (1987): 539-594.

Holmgren, J. "The Harem in Northern Wei Politics--398-498 A.D.: A Study of T'o-pa Attitudes towards the Institution of Empress, Empress-Dowager, and Regency Governments in the Chinese Dynastic System During Early Northern Wei." *Journal of the Economic and Social History of the Orient* 26 (February 1983): 71-96.

Hyam, R. "Empire and Sexual Opportunity." *The Journal of Imperial and Commonwealth History* 1, no. 2 (1986): 34-90.

Johnson, Susan L. "Sharing Bed and Board: Cohabitation and Cultural Difference in Central Arizona Mining Towns." *Frontiers* 7, no. 3 (1984): 36-42.

Kernaghan, Lois D. "A Man and His Mistress: J. F. W. DesBarres and Mary Cannon." *Acadiensis* 11 (Autumn 1981): 23-42.

Klassen, John. "The Development of the Conjugal Bond in Late Medieval Bohemia." *Journal of Medieval History* 13 (June 1987): 161-178.

Ling, P. "Sex and the Automobile in the Jazz-Age." *History Today* 39 (November 1989): 18-24.

Moore, Shelley. "An Historical Look at Male-Female Relationships in the Black Community." *Crisis* 93, no. 10 (1986): 20-23, 31.

Payer, Pierre J. "Early Medieval Regulations Concerning Marital Sexual Relations." *Journal of Medieval History* 6 (December 1980): 353-376.

Rogers, Nicholas. "Carnal Knowledge: Illegitimacy in Eighteenth-Century Westminster." *Journal of Social History* 23 (Winter 1989): 355-376.

Roodenburg, Herman W. "The Autobiography of Isabella DeMoerloose: Sex, Childrearing and Popular Belief in Seventeenth Century Holland." *Journal of Social History* 18 (Summer 1985): 517-540.

Rothman, Ellen K. "Sex and Self-Control: Middle-Class Courtship in America,

1770-1870." *Journal of Social History* 15 (Spring 1982): 409-426.

Treckel, Paula A. "Breast Feeding and Maternal Sexuality in Colonial America." *Journal of Interdisciplinary History* 20 (Summer 1989): 25-52.

Tual, Jacques. "Sexual Equality and Conjugal Harmony: The Way to Celestial Bliss. A View of Early Quaker Matrimony." *The Journal of the Friends' Historical Society* 55, no. 6 (1988): 161-174.

Warnicke, Retha M. "Sexual Heresy at the Court of Henry VIII." *The Historical Journal* 30 (June 1987): 247-268.

Weeks, Jeffrey. "Sexuality and the Working-Class Family in the Nineteenth Century." *Society for the Study of Labour History* 48 (Spring 1984): 15-16.

Weinberg, M. S., and C. J. Williams. "Sexual Embourgeoisment? Social Class and Sexual Activity: 1938-1970." *American Sociological Review* 45 (1980): 33-48.

## Sexually Transmitted Diseases

Buckley, Suzann, and Janice Dickin McGinnis. "Venereal Disease and Public Health Reform in Canada." *Canadian Historical Review* 63 (September 1982): 337-354.

Guy, Donna J. "White Slavery, Public Health, and the Socialist Position on Legalized Prostitution in Argentina, 1913-1936." *Latin American Research Review* 23, no. 3 (1988): 60-80.

Harsin, Jill. "Syphilis, Wives, and Physicians: Medical Ethics and the Family in Late Nineteenth-Century France." *French Historical Studies* 16 (Spring 1989): 72-95.

King, Donna. "'Prostitutes as Pariah in the Age of Aids': A Content Analysis of Coverage of Women Prostitutes in *The New York Times* and the *Washington Post* September 1985-April 1988." *Women & Health* 16, no. 3/4 (1990): 155-176.

Leja, Michael. "'Le Vieux Marcheur' and 'Les Deux Risques': Picasso, Prostitution, Venereal Disease, and Maternity, 1899-1907." *Art History* 8 (March 1985): 66-81.

Padgug, Robert. "More Than the Story of a Virus: Gay History, Gay Communities and AIDS." *Radical America* 21 (March/April 1987): 35-42.

Pierson, Ruth Roach. "The Double Bind of the Double Standard: VD Control and the CWAC in World War II." *Canadian Historical Review* 62 (March 1981): 31-58.

Savage, Gail. "'The Wilful Communication of a Loathsome Disease': Marital Conflict and Venereal Disease in Victorian England." *Victorian Studies* 34 (Autumn 1990): 35-54.

Smith, John H. "Abulia: Sexuality and Diseases of the Will in the Late Nineteenth Century." *Genders* no. 6 (November 1989): 102-124.

Sturma, Michael. "Public Health and Sexual Morality: Venereal Disease in World War II Australia." *Signs* 13 (Summer 1988): 725-740.

White, Suzanne. "Mom and Dad, (1944): Venereal Disease 'Exploitation.'"

*Bulletin of the History of Medicine* 62 (Summer 1988): 252-270.

## Virginity/Celibacy

Archer, Leonie. "Virgin and Harlot in the Writings of Formative Judaism."
    *History Workshop* 24 (Autumn 1987): 1-16.
Atkinson, Clarissa W. "Precious Balsam in a Fragile Glass: The Ideology of
    Virginity in the Later Middle Ages." *Journal of Family History* 8 (Summer
    1983): 131-143.
Burrus, Virginia. "Chastity as Autonomy: Women in the Stories of the Apocryphal
    Acts." *Semeia* 38 (1986): 101-117.
Castelli, Elizabeth. "Virginity and Its Meaning for Women's Sexuality in Early
    Christianity." *Journal of Feminist Studies in Religion* 2 (Spring 1986): 61-88.
Casteras, Susan P. "Virgin Vows: The Early Victorian Artists' Portrayal of Nuns
    and Novices." *Victorian Studies* 24 (Winter 1981): 157-184.
Corrington, Gail Peterson. "Salvation, Celibacy, and Power: 'Divine Women' in
    Late Antiquity." *Society of Biblical Literature: Seminar Papers* no. 24 (1985).
Crosthwaite, Jane F. "'A White and Seamless Robe': Celibacy and Equality in
    Shaker Art and Theory." *Colby Library Quarterly* 25 (September 1989):
    188-198.
Davis, Tracy C. "Does the Theatre Make for Good?: Actresses' Purity and
    Temptation in the Victorian Era." *Queen's Quarterly* 93 (Spring 1986): 33-49.
Elvin, Mark. "Female Virtue and the State in China." *Past and Present* no. 104
    (August 1984): 111-152.
Gillespie, Joanna Bowen. "Modesty Canonized: Female Saints in Antebellum
    Methodist Sunday School Literature." *Historical Reflections/Reflexions
    Historiques* 10 (Summer 1983): 195-220.
Hanna, Martha. "Iconology and Ideology: Images of Joan of Arc in the Idiom of
    the Action Francaise." *French Historical Studies* 14 (Fall 1985): 215-239.
Holmgren, Jennifer. "Widow Chastity in the Northern Dynasties: The Lieh-nu
    Biographies in the Wei-shu." *Papers on Far Eastern History* no. 23 (March
    1981): 165-186.
Langum, David J. "Californio Women and the Image of Virtue." *Southern
    California Quarterly* 59 (Fall 1977): 245-250.
Manheim, Daniel L. "Motives of His Own: Henry Adams and the Genealogy of
    the Virgin." *New England Quarterly* 63 (December 1990): 601-623.
Newton, Sarah Emily. "Wise and Foolish Virgins: 'Usable Fiction' and the Early
    American Conduct Tradition." *Early American Literature* 25, no. 2 (1990):
    139-167.
Rooke, Patricia, and R. L. Schnell. "Chastity as Power: Charlotte Whitton and the
    Ascetic Ideal." *American Review of Canadian Studies* 15 (Winter 1985):
    389-404.
Sturcken, H. T. "The Unconsummated Marriage of Jaime of Aragon and Leonor
    of Castile (Oct 1319)." *Journal of Medieval History* 5 (September 1979):
    185-202.

Worobec, Christine D. "Temptress or Virgin? The Precarious Sexual Position of Women in Postemancipation Ukranian Peasant Society." *Slavic Review* 49 (Summer 1990): 227-238.

Xiao, Zhou. "Virginity and Premarital Sex in Contemporary China." *Feminist Studies* 15 (Summer 1989): 279-289.

Ziegler, J. E. "The Medieval Virgin as Object: Art or Anthropology?" *Historical Reflections/Reflexions Historiques* 16 (Summer/Fall 1989): 251-264.

# SOCIAL REFORM/COMMUNITY ORGANIZING

## Biography

Ashlee, Laura R. "Ellen May Tower: Guardian Angel of the Michigan Volunteers." *Michigan History* 74 (January/February 1990): 46-47.

Barker-Benfield, G. "'Mother Emancipator': The Meaning of Jane Addams' Sickness and Cure." *Journal of Family History* 4 (Winter 1979): 395-420.

Berrol, Selma. "When Uptown Met Downtown: Julia Richman's Work in the Jewish Community of New York, 1880-1912." *American Jewish History* 70 (September 1980): 35-51.

Blend, Benay. "Mary Austin and the Western Conservation Movement: 1900-1927." *Journal of the Southwest* 30, no. 1 (1988): 12-34.

Brinker, Lea J. "The Charitable Impulse of Sarah Worthington King Peter." *Queen City Heritage* 42 (Winter 1984): 27-40.

Bulazik, Mary J. "The Bonds of Belonging: Leonora O'Reilly and Social Reform." *Labor History* 24 (Winter 1983): 60-83.

Carlisle, Lilian Baker. "Humanities' Needs Deserve Our Fortune: Mary Martha Fletcher and the Fletcher Family Benevolences." *Vermont History* 50 (Summer 1982): 133-142.

Carson, Mina J. "Agnes Hamilton of Fort Wayne: The Education of a Christian Settlement Worker." *Indiana Magazine of History* 80 (March 1984): 1-34.

Cloud, Barbara. "Laura Hall Peters: Pursuing the Myth of Equality." *Pacific Northwest Quarterly* 74 (January 1983): 28-36.

Crocker, Helen B. "Ida Tarbell Follows Lincoln's Kentucky Footsteps." *Filson Club History Quarterly* 61 (April 1987): 217-233.

Culley, Margaret. "Dorothy Dix: The Thirteenth Juror." *International Journal of Women's Studies* 2, no. 4 (1979): 349-357.

DeBlasio, Donna. "'The Greatest Woman in the Reserve': Betsy Mix Cowles, Feminist, Abolitionist, Educator." *Old Northwest* 13 (Fall/Winter 1987): 223-236.

Fraser Antonia. "Mary Ward, A Seventeenth Century Reformer." *History Today* 31 (May 1981): 14-18.

Geer, Emily Apt. "Lucy W. Hayes and the Woman's Home Missionary Society." *Hayes Historical Journal* 4 (Fall 1984): 5-14.

Greenstone, David J. "Dorothea Dix and Jane Addams: From Transcendentalism to Pragmatism in American Social Reform." *Social Service Review* 53, no. 4

(1979): 527-559.

Hanson, Mary Ellen, and Carl A. Hanson. "Wilma Loy Shelton: Library Leader in New Mexico, 1920-1950." *New Mexico Historical Review* 64 (January 1989): 51-76.

Hornbein, Marjorie. "Frances Jacobs: Denver's Mother of Charities." *Western States Jewish History* 15 (January 1983): 131-145.

Hunt, James B. "Jane Addams: The Presbyterian Connection." *American Presbyterians* 68 (Winter 1990): 231-244.

Japp, Phyllis M. "Esther or Isaiah?: The Abolitionist-Feminist Rhetoric of Angelina Grimke." *Quarterly Journal of Speech* 71 (August 1985): 335-348.

Kemp, Kathryn W. "Jean and Kate Gordon: New Orleans Social Reformers, 1898-1933." *Louisiana History* 24 (Fall 1983): 389-401.

Lapsansky, Emma Jones. "Feminism, Freedom, and Community: Charlotte Forten and Women Activists in Nineteenth Century Philadelphia." *Pennsylvania Magazine of History and Biography* 113 (January 1989): 3-20.

Mathes, Valerie Sherer. "Annie E. K. Bidwell: Chico's Benefactress." *California History* 68 (Spring/Summer 1989): 14-25.

------. "Helen Hunt Jackson: A Legacy of Indian Reform." *Essays and Monographs in Colorado History* no. 4 (1986): 25-58.

-----. "Helen Hunt Jackson and the Campaign for Ponca Restitution, 1880-1881." *South Dakota History* 17 (Spring 1987): 23-41.

-----. "Helen Hunt Jackson and the Ponca Controversy." *Montana* 39 (Winter 1989): 42-53.

-----. "Helen Hunt Jackson: Official Agent to the California Mission Indians." *Southern California Quarterly* 63 (Spring 1981): 63-82.

-----. "Indian Philanthropy in California: Annie Bidwell and the Mechoopda Indians." *Arizona and the West* 25 (Summer 1983): 153-166.

Murray, Anne H. "Eleanor Norcross: Artist, Collector and Social Reformer." *Woman's Art Journal* 2 (Fall 1981/Winter 1982): 14-19.

Pincetl, Stephanie S. "The Peculiar Legacy of Progressivism: Claire Dedrick's Encounter with Forest Practices Regulation in California." *Forest & Conservation History* 34 (January 1990): 26-34.

Querry, Susan. "The Jane Addams Papers." *Humanities* 10 (September/October 1989): 19-20.

Rabine, Leslie W. "Textual Practice/Social Practice: Flora Tristan and the Problem of the Woman Activist-Writer." *Western Society for French History* 11 (November 1983): 272.

Rooke, Patricia T. "Public Figure, Private Woman: Same-Sex Support Structures in the Life of Charlotte Whitton." *International Journal of Women's Studies* [Canada] 6 (November/December 1983): 412-428.

Rynder, Constance B. "Progressive into a New Dealer: Amy Maher and the Public Works Administration in Toledo." *Northwest Ohio Quarterly* 58 (Winter 1986): 3-19.

Schenken, Suzanne O'Dea. "The Immigrants' Advocate: Mary Treglia and the Sioux City Community House, 1921-1959." *Annals of Iowa* 50 (Fall

1989/Winter 1990): 181-213.

Sherrick, Rebecca. "Their Fathers' Daughters: The Autobiographies of Jane Addams and Florence Kelley." *American Studies* 27 (Spring 1986): 39-53.

Shofner, Jerrell H. "Mary Grace Quackenbos, a Visitor Florida Did Not Want." *Florida History Quarterly* 58 (January 1980): 273-290.

Smith, D. Anthony, and Arthur H. Keeney. "Linda Neville (1873-1961): Kentucky Pioneer Against Blindness." *Filson Club History Quarterly* 64 (July 1990): 360-376.

Stephens, Jane. "May Wright Sewall: An Indiana Reformer." *Indiana Magazine of History* 78 (December 1982): 273-295.

Swaim, Ginalie. "Cora Bussey Hillis: Woman of Vision." *Palimpsest* 60 (November/December 1979): 162-177.

Swain, Martha H. "'The Forgotten Woman': Ellen S. Woodward and Women's Relief in New Deal." *Prologue* 15 (Winter 1983): 201-213.

Taggart, Robert J. "Etta J. Wilson (1883-1971): A Delaware Reformer." *Delaware History* 24 (Spring/Summer 1990): 33-52.

Todd, Jan. "Bernard Macfadden: Reformer of Feminine Form." *Journal of Sports History* 14 (Spring 1987): 61-75.

Topping, Eva Catafygiotu. "Frances Wright: Petticoat Lecturer." *Cincinnati Historical Society Bulletin* 36 (Spring 1978): 43-56.

Towne, Marion K. "Charlotte Gilman in California." *Pacific Historian* 28 (Spring 1984): 1.

Turner, James C. "How the Other Half Lived: Jane Addams's Hull House." *Humanities* 10 (September/October 1989): 15-18.

Vertinsky, Patricia. "Sexual Equality and the Legacy of Catharine Beecher." *Journal of Sport History* 6 (Spring 1979): 38-49.

## Family Planning and Aid to Children

Abeele, Cynthia R. "'The Infant Soldier': The Great War and the Medical Campaign for Child Welfare." *Canadian Bulletin of Medical History/Bulletin canadien d'histoire de la medicine* 5 (Winter 1988): 99-119.

Abrams, Jeanne. "'For a Child's Sake': The Denver Sheltering Home for Jewish Children in the Progressive Era." *American Jewish History* 79 (Winter 1989/1990): 181-202.

Back, Kurt W. "Myth in the Lives of Leaders of Social Movements: The Case of the Family Planning Movement." *Biography* 11 (Spring 1988): 95-107.

Bullen, John. "J. J. Kelso and the 'New' Child-Savers: The Genesis of the Children's Aid Movement in Ontario." *Ontario History* 82 (June 1990): 107-128.

Dick, Kriste Lindenmeyer. "The Silent Charity: A History of the Cincinnati Maternity Society." *Queen City Heritage* 43 (Winter 1985): 29-33.

Dwork, Deborah. "The Milk Option: An Aspect of the History of the Infant Welfare Movement in England 1898-1908." *Medical History* 31 (January 1987): 51-69.

Hanley, Marla Martin. "The Children's Crusade of 1922: Katie O'Hare and the Campaign to Free Radical War Dissenters in the Era of America's First Red Scare." *Gateway Heritage* 10 (Summer 1989): 34-43.

Hunt, Marion. "Women and Childsaving: St. Louis Children's Hospital 1879-1979." *Bulletin of the Missouri Historical Society* 36 (January 1980): 65-79.

Jenkins, Gary C. "Almira S. Steele and the Steele Home for Needy Children." *Tennessee Historical Quarterly* 48 (Spring 1989): 29-36.

Levering, Patricia W., and Ralph B. Levering. "Women in Relief: The Carroll County Children's Aid Society in the Great Depression." *Maryland Historical Magazine* 72 (Winter 1977): 534-546.

Lothrop, Gloria Ricci. "Nurturing Society's Children." *California History* 65 (December 1986): 274-283, 313-314.

Rooke, Patricia T. and R. L. Schnell. "'Making the Way More Comfortable': Charlotte Whitton's Child Welfare Career, 1920-48." *Journal of Canadian Studies/Revue d'études canadiennes* 17 (Winter 1983): 33-45.

-----. "Charlotte Whitton Meets 'The Last Best West': The Politics of Child Welfare in Alberta, 1929-1949." *Prairie Forum* 6 (Fall 1981): 143-162.

-----. "The Rise and Decline of British North American Protestant Orphan's Homes as Woman's Domain, 1850-1930." *Atlantis* 7 (1982): 21-35.

-----. "Charlotte Whitton and the 'Babies for Export' Controversy, 1947-48." *Alberta History* 30 (Winter 1982): 11-16.

Rynder, Constance B. "Amy Grace Maher and Toledo's Crusade for Child Welfare Reform, 1916-1926." *Northwest Ohio Quarterly* 55 (Fall 1983): 105-125.

Schmeling, Kathleen. "'Every Child Is Worthy of Kindness and Care': The Founding and Early Development of the Children's Hospital of Michigan, 1886-1922." *Michigan History* 74 (January/February 1990): 24-31.

Seligman, Stanley A. "The Royal Maternity Charity, the First Hundred Years." *Medical History* 24 (October 1980): 403-418.

Shoemaker, Susan Turnbull. "The Philadelphia Pediatric Society and Its Milk Commission, 1896-1917: An Aspect of Urban Progressive Reform." *Pennsylvania History* 53 (October 1986): 273-288.

Stadum, Beverly A. "'Says There's Nothing Like Home': Family Casework with the Minneapolis Poor, 1900-1930." *Minnesota History* 51 (Summer 1988): 42-54.

Stehno, Sandra M. "Public Responsibility for Dependent Black Children: The Advocacy of Edith Abbott and Sophonisba Breckenridge." *Social Service Review* 62, no. 3 (1988): 485-503.

Thavenet, Dennis. "Tending Their Flock: Dirt, Hygiene, and Health for Nineteenth Century Reform Children." *Michigan Historical Review* 15 (Fall 1989): 23-46.

## Health Reform

Atwater, Edward C. "Of Grandes Dames, Surgeons, and Hospitals: Batavia, New York, 1900-1940." *Journal of the History of Medicine and Allied Sciences* 45 (July 1990): 414-451.

Buckley, Suzann, and Janice Dickin McGinnis. "Venereal Disease and Public Health Reform in Canada." *Canadian Historical Review* 63 (September 1982): 337-354.

Ferguson, Earline Rae. "The Woman's Improvement Club of Indianapolis: Black Women Pioneers in Tuberculosis Work, 1903-1938." *Indiana Magazine of History* 84, no. 3 (1988): 237-261.

Marks, Lara. "'Dear Old Mother Levy's': The Jewish Maternity Home and Sick Room Help Society 1895-1939." *Social History of Medicine* 3 (April 1990): 61-88.

## Industrial Reform

Brito, Patricia. "Protective Legislation in Ohio: The Inter-war Years." *Ohio History* 88 (Spring 1979): 173-197.

Harmon, Sandra D. "Florence Kelley in Illinois." *Journal of the Illinois State Historical Society* 74 (Autumn 1981): 162-178.

Howard, Irene. "The Mother's Council of Vancouver: Holding the Fort for the Unemployed, 1935-38." *B.C. Studies* 69/70 (Spring/Summer 1986): 249-287.

McDougall, Mary Lynn. "The Meaning of Reform: The Ban on Women's Night Work, 1892-1914." *Western Society for French History* 10 (October 1982): 404-417.

McTighe, Michael J. "'True Philanthropy' and the Limits of the Female Sphere: Poor Relief and Labor Organization in Ante-Bellum Cleveland." *Labor History* 27 (Spring 1986): 227-256.

Perry, Elizabeth Israels. "Industrial Reform in New York City: Belle Moskowitz and the Protocol of Peace, 1913-1916." *Labor History* 23 (Winter 1982): 5-31.

Strasser, Susan M. "Mistress and Maid, Employer and Employee: Domestic Service Reform in the United States, 1892-1920." *Marxist Perspectives* 1, no. 1 (1978): 52-67.

Walkley, Christina. "Charity and the Victorian Needlewoman." *Costume* 14 (1980): 136-143.

Weiner, Lynn. "'Our Sister's Keepers': The Minneapolis Woman's Christian Association and Housing for Working Women." *Minnesota History* 46 (Spring 1979): 189-200.

## Moral Reform

Beisel, Nicola. "Class, Culture, and Campaigns Against Vice in Three American Cities, 1872-1892." *American Sociological Review* 55 (February 1990): 44-62.

Gilfoyle, Timothy J. "Strumpets and Misogynists: Brothel 'Riots' and the Transformation of Prostitution in Antebellum New York City." *New York History* 68 (January 1987): 45-65.

Ginzberg, Lori D. "'Moral Suasion Is Moral Balderdash': Women, Politics, and Social Activism in the 1850s." *Journal of American History* 73 (December 1986): 601-622.

Jeffreys, Sheila. "'Free from All Uninvited Touch of Man': Women's Campaigns around Sexuality 1880-1914." *Women's Studies International Forum* 5, no. 6 (1982): 629-645.

Kaplan, Marion. "Prostitution, Morality Crusades and Feminism: German-Jewish Feminists and the Campaign Against White Slavery." *Women's Studies* 5, no. 6 (1982): 619-628.

Lansbury, Coral. "Gynaecology, Pornography, and the Antivivisection Movement." *Victorian Studies* 28 (Spring 1985): 413-438.

Levesque, A. "Turning Off the Red Light: Reformers and Prostitution in Montreal 1865-1925." *Urban History Review* 17 (February 1989): 191-202.

Morton, Marian J. "Fallen Women, Federated Charities, and Maternity Homes, 1913-1973." *Social Science Review* 62, no. 1 (1988): 61-82.

-----. "'Go and Sin No More': Maternity Homes in Cleveland, 1869-1936." *Ohio History* 93 (Summer/Autumn 1984): 117-146.

Petrik, Paula. "Strange Bedfellows: Prostitution, Politicians, and Moral Reform in Helena, Montanta, 1885-1887." *Montana* 35 (Summer 1985): 2-13.

Pivar, David J. "Cleansing the Nation: The War on Prostitution, 1917-1921." *Prologue* 12 (Spring 1980): 29-40.

Ryan, Mary P. "The Power of Women's Networks: A Case Study of Female Moral Reform in Antebellum America." *Feminist Studies* 5 (Spring 1979): 66-86.

Sims, Anastasia. "'The Sword of the Spirit': The WCTU and Moral Reform in North Carolina, 1883-1933." *North Carolina Historical Review* 64, no. 4 (1987): 395-415.

Tennant, Margaret. "'Magdalens and Moral Imbeciles': Women's Homes in Nineteenth-Century New Zealand." *Women's Studies* 9, no. 5/6 (1986): 491-502.

White, Luise. "Prostitutes, Reformers, and Historians." *Criminal Justice History* 6 (1985): 201-228.

## Social Movements/General

Anderson, M. Christine. "Home and Community for a Generation of Women: A Case Study of the Cincinnati Y.W.C.A. Residence, 1920-1940." *Queen City Heritage* 43 (Winter 1985): 34-41.

Andrews, Janice L. "Female Social Workers in the Second Generation." *Affilia* 5 (Summer 1990): 46-59.

Barrows, Robert G. "'The Homes of Indiana': Albion Fellows Bacon and Housing Reform Legislation, 1907-1917." *Indiana Magazine of History* 81 (December

1985): 309-350.

Benson, Susan Porter. "Business Heads and Sympathizing Hearts: The Women of the Providence Employment Society, 1837-1858." *Journal of Social History* 12 (Winter 1978): 302-312.

Blum, Carol J. "The Cincinnati Women's Christian Association: A Study of Innovation and Change, 1868-1880." *Queen City Heritage* 41 (Winter 1983): 56-64.

Brandt, Gail Cuthbert. "'Pigeon-Holed and Forgotten': The Work of the Subcommittee on the Post-War Problems of Women, 1943." *Histoire sociale/Social History* 15 (May 1982): 239-259.

Brown, Ira V. "'Am I Not a Woman and a Sister?': The Anti-Slavery Convention of American Women, 1837-1839." *Pennsylvania History* 50 (January 1983): 1-19.

------. "Cradle of Feminism: The Philadelphia Female Anti-Slavery Society, 1833-1840." *Pennsylvania Magazine of History and Biography* no. 102 (April 1978): 143-166.

Castle, Alfred L. "Harriet Castle and the Beginnings of Progressive Kindergarten Education in Hawai'i 1894-1900." *Hawaiian Journal of History* 23 (1989): 119-136.

Chambers, Clarke A. "Women in the Creation of the Profession of Social Work." *Social Service Review* 60 (March 1986): 1-33.

Clawson, Mary Ann. "Nineteenth-Century Women's Auxiliaries and Fraternal Orders." *Signs* 12 (Autumn 1986): 40-61.

Cumbler, John T. "The Politics of Charity: Gender and Class in Late 19th Century Charity Policy." *Journal of Social History* 14 (Fall 1980): 99-111.

Davis, C. Anne. "History of the Carver School of Church Social Work." *Review and Expositor* 85 (Spring 1988): 209-220.

Forbes, Geraldine H. "In Pursuit of Justice: Women's Organisations and Legal Reforms." *Samya Shakti* 1, no. 2 (1984): 33-54.

Forderhase, Nancy K. "Eve Returns to the Garden: Women Reformers in Appalachian Kentucky in the Early Twentieth Century." *Register of the Kentucky Historical Society* 85 (Summer 1987): 237-261.

Gifford, Carolyn DeSwarte. "Sisterhoods of Service and Reform: Organized Methodist Women in the Late Nineteenth Century: An Essay on the State of the Research." *Methodist History* 24 (October 1985): 15-30.

Gittell, Marilyn, and Theresa Shtob. "Changing Women's Roles in Political Volunteerism and Reform of the City." *Signs* 5 (Spring 1980): 567-578.

Gozemba, Patricia, and Marilyn Humphries. "Women in the Anti-Ku Klux Klan Movement, 1865-1985." *Women's Studies International Forum* 12, no. 1 (1989): 35-40.

Handen, Ella. "Social Service Stations: New Jersey Settlement Houses Founded in the Progressive Era." *New Jersey History* 108 (Spring/Summer 1990): 1-30.

Hanson, Cynthia A. "Catheryne Cooke Gilman and the Minneapolis Better Movie Movement." *Minnesota History* 51 (Summer 1989): 202-216.

Hefner, Loretta L. "The National Women's Relief Society and the U.S.

Sheppard-Towner Act." *Utah Historical Quarterly* 50 (Summer 1982): 255-267.

-----. "This Decade Was Different: Relief Society's Social Services Department, 1919-1929." *Dialogue* 15 (Autumn 1982): 64-73.

Horowitz, Helen Lefkowitz. "Hull House as Women's Space." *Chicago History* 12 (Winter 1983/84): 40-55.

Jensen, Richard L. "Forgotten Relief Societies, 1844-67." *Dialogue* 16 (Spring 1983): 105-125.

Kihlstrom, Mary F. "The Morristown Female Charitable Society." *Journal of Presbyterian History* 58 (Fall 1980): 255-272.

Kimble, J., and E. Unterhalter. "We Opened the Road for You, You Must Go Forward: ANC Women's Struggles 1912-1982." *Feminist Review* 12 (1982): 11-36.

Kunze, Bonnelyn Young. "'Poore and In Necessity': Margaret Fell and Quaker Female Philanthropy in Northwest England in the Late Seventeenth Century." *Albion* 21 (Winter 1989): 559-580.

Lissak, Rivka. "Myth and Reality: The Pattern of Relationship Between the Hull House Circle and the 'New Immigrants' on Chicago's West Side, 1890-1919." *Journal of American Ethnic History* 2 (Spring 1983): 21-50.

Mathes, Valerie Sherer. "Nineteenth Century Women and Reform: The Women's National Indian Association." *American Indian Quarterly* 14 (Winter 1990): 1-18.

Miller, Kathleen Atkinson. "The Ladies and the Lynchers: A Look at the Association of Southern Women for the Prevention of Lynching." *Southern Studies* (Fall 1978): 221-240.

Mitchinson, Wendy. "The YWCA and Reform in the Nineteenth Century." *Histoire sociale/Social History* 12 (1979): 368-384.

Pedersen, Joyce Senders. "Some Victorian Headmistresses: A Conservative Tradition of Social Reform." *Victorian Studies* 24 (Summer 1981): 463-488.

Roberts, D. "Dealing with the Poor in Victorian England." *Rice University Studies* 67 (1981): 57-74.

Rosenthal, Naomi, Meryl Fingrutd, Michele Ethier, Roberta Karant, and David McDonald. "Social Movements and Network Analysis: A Case Study of Nineteenth-Century Women's Reform in New York State." *American Journal of Sociology* 90 (March 1985): 1022-1054.

Rothschild, Mary Aickin. "White Women Volunteers in the Freedom Summers: Their Life and Work in a Movement for Social Change." *Feminist Studies* 5 (Fall 1979): 466-494.

Safa, Helen Icken. "Women's Social Movements in Latin America." *Gender & Society* 4 (September 1990): 354-369.

Scott, Anne Firor. "Most Invisible of All: Black Women's Voluntary Associations." *Journal of Southern History* 56 (February 1990): 3-22.

Sexton, Richard D. "The San Diego Woman's Home Association: A Volunteer Charity Organization." *Journal of San Diego History* 29 (Winter 1983).

Sheehan, Nancy M. "The Red Cross and Relief in Alberta, 1920s-1930s." *Prairie Forum* 12 (Fall 1987): 277-294.

Sklar, Kathryn Kish. "Hull House in the 1890s: A Community of Women Reformers." *Signs* 10 (Summer 1985): 658-677.

-----. "'Women Who Speak For an Entire Nation': American and British Women Compared at the World Anti-Slavery Convention, London, 1840." *Pacific Historical Review* 59 (November 1990): 453-500.

Sochen, June. "Jewish Women as Volunteer Activists." *American Jewish History* 70 (September 1980): 23-34.

-----. "Some Observations on the Role of American Jewish Women as Communal Volunteers." *American Jewish History* 70 (September 1980): 23-34.

Sumler-Lewis, Janice. "The Forten-Purvis Women of Philadelphia and the American Anti-Slavery Crusade." *Journal of Negro History* 66 (Winter 1981/82): 281-288.

Underwood, June. "Civilizing Kansas: Women's Organizations, 1880-1920." *Kansas History* 7 (Winter 1984/85): 291-306.

Van Broekhoven, Deborah Bingham. "'A Determination to Labor. . .': Female Antislavery Activity in Rhode Island." *Rhode Island History* 44 (May 1985): 35-46.

Wenger, Beth W. "Jewish Women and Voluntarism: Beyond the Myth of Enablers." *American Jewish History* 79 (Autumn 1989): 16-36.

Whites, LeeAnn. "The Charitable and the Poor: The Emergence of Domestic Politics in Augusta, Georgia, 1860-1880." *Journal of Social History* 17 (Summer 1984): 601-616.

Williamson, Erik Lather. "'Doing What Had to Be Done': Norwegian Lutheran Ladies Aid Societies of North Dakota." *North Dakota History* 57 (Spring 1990): 2-13.

Williams, Lillian. "And Still I Rise: Black Women and Reform, Buffalo, New York, 1900-1940." *Afro-Americans in New York Life and History* 14 (July 1990): 7-33.

## Temperance

Alduino, Frank. "Prohibition in Tampa." *Tampa Bay History* 9 (Spring/Summer 1987): 17-87.

Bader, Robert Smith. "Mrs. Nation." *Kansas History* 7 (Winter 1984/85): 246-262.

Blochowiak, Mary Ann. "'Woman with a Hatchet': Carry Nation Comes to Oklahoma Territory." *Chronicles of Oklahoma* 59 (Summer 1981): 132-151.

Blocker, Jack S., Jr., ed. "Annie Wittenmyer and the Women's Crusade." *Ohio History* 88 (Autumn 1979): 419-422.

-----. "Separate Paths: Suffragists and the Women's Temperance Crusade." *Signs* 10 (Spring 1985): 460-476.

Bordin, Ruth. "Marching For Temperance: The Woman's Crusade in Adrian." *Chronicle* 15, no. 4 (1980): 16-23.

Clifford, Deborah P. "The Women's War Against Rum." *Vermont History* 52 (Summer 1984): 141-160.

Dannenbaum, Jed. "The Origins of Temperance Activism and Militancy Among American Women." *Journal of Social History* 15 (Winter 1981): 235-252.

Davis, Jack E. "The Spirits of St. Petersburg: The Struggle for Local Prohibition, 1892-1919." *Tampa Bay History* 10 (Spring/Summer 1988): 19-33.

George, Paul S. "Bootleggers, Prohibitionists and Police: The Temperance Movement in Miami, 1896-1920." *Tequesta* no. 39 (1979): 34-41.

Hardesty, Nancy A. "'The Best Temperance Organization in the Land': Southern Methodists and the W.C.T.U. in Georgia." *Methodist History* 28 (April 1990): 187-194.

Harris, Katherine. "Feminism and Temperance Reform in the Boulder WCTU." *Frontiers* 4 (Summer 1979): 19-24.

-----. "A Study of Feminine and Class Identity in the Woman's Christian Temperance Union, 1920-1970: A Case Study." *Historicus* 2 (Fall/Winter 1980): 55-87.

Kerr, K. Austin. "Organizing for Reform: The Anti-Saloon League and Innovation in Politics." *American Quarterly* 32 (Spring 1980): 37-53.

Kraft, Susan Metzner. "Drusilla Wilson: A Friend of Temperance." *Heritage of the Great Plains* 13 (Fall 1980): 11-23.

McClary, Andrew. "The WCTU Discovers Science: The Women's Christian Temperance Union, Plus Teachers, Doctors and Scientific Temperance." *Michigan History* (January/February 1984): 16-23.

Mitchinson, Wendy. "The Woman's Christian Temperance Union: A Study in Organization." *International Journal of Women's Studies* 4 (March/April 1981): 143-156.

Morton, Marian J. "Temperance, Benevolence, and the City: The Cleveland Non-Partisan Woman's Christian Temperance Union, 1874-1900." *Ohio History* 91 (1982): 58-73.

Pauly, Philip J. "The Struggle for Ignorance about Alcohol: American Physiologists, Wilbur Olin Atwater, and the Woman's Christian Temperance Union." *Bulletin of the History of Medicine* 64 (Fall 1990): 366-392.

Pierard, Richard V. "The Church of the Brethren and the Temperance Movement." *Brethren Life and Thought* 26 (Winter 1981): 36-44.

Sheehan, Nancy M. "Temperance, Education and the WCTU in Alberta 1905-1930." *Journal of Educational Thought* 14 (August 1980): 108-124.

-----. "The WCTU and Educational Strategies on the Canadian Prairie." *History of Education Quarterly* 24 (Spring 1984): 101-120.

-----. "The WCTU on the Prairies, 1886-1930: An Alberta-Saskatchewan Comparison." *Prairie Forum* 6 (1981): 17-33.

-----. "'Women Helping Women': The WCTU and the Foreign Population in the West, 1905-1930." *International Journal of Women's Studies* 6 (November/December 1983): 395-411.

Shiman, Lilian Lewis. "The Blue Ribbon Army: Gospel Temperance in England." *Historical Magazine of the Protestant Episcopal Church* 50 (December 1981): 391-408.

Sims, Anastasia. "'The Sword of the Spirit': The WCTU and Moral Reform in

North Carolina, 1883-1933." *North Carolina Historical Review* 64, no. 4 (1987): 395-415.

Tyrell, Ian R. "Women and Temperance in Antebellum America, 1830-1860." *Civil War History* (June 1982): 128-152.

Williamson, Douglas J. "The Rise of the New England Methodist Temperance Movement, 1823-1836." *Methodist History* 21 (October 1982): 3-28.

## Women's Clubs

Allen, D. E. "The Women Members of the Botanical Society of London: 1836-1856." *British Journal for the History of Science* 13 (1980): 240-254.

Allen, Susan L. "Progressive Spirit: The Oklahoma and Indian Territory Federation of Women's Clubs." *Chronicles of Oklahoma* 66 (Spring 1988): 4-21.

Bland, Lucy. "Rational Sex or Spiritual Love?: The Men and Women's Club of the 1880s." *Women's Studies International Forum* 13, no. 1/2 (1990): 33-48.

Bowers, Ann M. "White-Gloved Feminists: An Analysis of Northwest Ohio Women's Clubs.'" *Hayes Historical Journal* 4 (Fall 1984): 38-47.

Boylan, Anne M. "Women in Groups: An Analysis of Women's Benevolent Organizations in New York and Boston, 1797-1840." *Journal of American History* 71 (December 1984): 497-523.

Brady, Marilyn Dell. "Kansas Federation of Colored Women's Clubs, 1900-1930." *Kansas History* 9 (Spring 1986): 19-30.

-----. "Organizing Afro-American Girls' Clubs in Kansas in the 1920's." *Frontiers* 9, no. 2 (1987): 69-72.

Crake, Mary Claire. "'In Unity There Is Strength': Women's Clubs in Tampa During the 1930s." *Tampa Bay History* 11 (Fall/Winter 1989): 5-21.

Ferguson, Earline Rae. "The Woman's Improvement Club of Indianapolis: Black Women Pioneers in Tuberculosis Work, 1903-1938." *Indiana Magazine of History* 84, no. 3 (1988): 237-261.

Flanagan, Maureen A. "Gender and Urban Political Reform: The City Club and the Woman's City Club of Chicago in the Progressive Era." *American Historical Review* 95 (October 1990): 1032-1050.

Forderhase, Nancy K. "'The Clear Call of Thoroughbred Women': The Kentucky Federation of Women's Clubs and the Crusade for Educational Reform, 1903-1909." *Register of the Kentucky Historical Society* 83 (Winter 1985): 19-35.

-----. "'Limited Only by Earth and Sky': The Louisville Woman's Club and Progessive Reform, 1900-1910." *Filson Club History Quarterly* 59 (July 1985): 327-343.

Hickey, Joseph V., and June O. Underwood. "In the Name of the Thurman Church: Women's Clubs and the Revitalization of a Flint Hills Neighborhood." *Locus* 1, no. 1 (1988): 65-83.

Howe, Barbara J. "West Virginia Women's Organizations, 1880s-1930 or 'Unsexed Termagants . . . Help the World Along.'" *West Virginia History* 49

(1990): 81-102.

Kornbluh, Andrea Tuttle. "Woman's City Club: A Pioneer in Race Relations." *Queen City Heritage* 44 (Summer 1986): 21-38.

Mohraz, Judy Jolley. "The Equity Club: Community Building Among Professional Women." *Journal of American Culture* 5 (Winter 1982): 34-39.

Moses, Wilson Jeremiah. "Domestic Feminism, Conservativism, Sex Roles, and Black Women's Clubs, 1893-1896." *Journal of Social and Behavioral Sciences* 24 (Fall 1987): 166-177.

Stanislow, Gail. "Domestic Feminism in Wilmington: The New Century Club, 1889-1917." *Delaware History* 22 (Spring/Summer 1987): 158-185.

Thatcher, Linda, and John R. Sillito. "'Sisterhood and Sociability': The Utah Women's Press Club, 1891-1928." *Utah Historical Quarterly* 53 (Spring 1985): 144-156.

Toll, William. "A Quiet Revolution: Jewish Women's Clubs and the Widening Female Sphere, 1870-1920." *American Jewish Archives* 41 (Spring/Summer 1989): 7-26.

Tubbs, Stephanie Ambrose. "Montana Women's Clubs at the Turn of the Century." *Montana* 36 (Winter 1986): 26-35.

Wenger, Beth S. "Jewish Women of the Club: The Changing Public Role of Atlanta's Jewish Women (1870-1930)." *American Jewish History* 76 (March 1987): 311-333.

## Women's Rights Movements

Aberg, I. "Revivalism, Philanthropy and Emancipation: Women's Liberation and Organization in the Early Nineteenth Century." *Scandinavian Journal of History* 13, no. 4 (1988).

Arendale, Marirose. "Tennessee and Women's Rights." *Tennessee History Quarterly* 39 (Spring 1980): 62-78.

Beahan, Charlotte. "The Women's Movement and Nationalism in the Chinese Women's Press, 1902-1911." *Modern China* 1 (October 1975): 379-416.

Benson, Peter. "'No Murmured Thanks': Women and Johnson Brigham's Midland Monthly." *American Studies* 21 (Spring 1980): 57-72.

Berkeley, Kathleen Christine. "'The Ladies Want to Bring about Reform in the Public Schools': Public Education and Women's Rights in the Post-Civil War South." *History of Education Quarterly* (Spring 1984): 45-58.

Blair, Karen J. "Pagentry for Women's Rights: The Career of Hazel Mackaye, 1913-1923." *Theatre Survey* 31 (May 1990): 23-46.

Boutelle, Ann Edwards. "Frances Brooke's Emily Montague (1769): Canada and Woman's Rights." *Women's Studies* 12, no. 1 (1986): 7-16.

Caine, Barbara. "Feminism, Suffrage and the Nineteenth-Century English Women's Movement." *Women's Studies International Forum* 5, no. 6 (1982): 537-550.

Clark, Elizabeth B. "Religion, Rights, and Difference in the Early Woman's Rights Movement." *Wisconsin Women's Law Journal* 3 (1987): 29-58.

Costain, Anne N., and W. Douglas Costain. "Movements and Gatekeepers: Congressional Response to Women's Movement Issues, 1900-1982." *Congress and the Presidents* 12 (Spring 1985): 21-42.

Friedlander, Alice G. "A Portland Girl on Women's Rights--1893." *Western States Jewish Historical Quarterly* 10 (January 1978): 146-150.

Gerhard, Ute. "A Hidden and Complex Heritage: Reflections on the History of Germany's Women's Movements." *Women's Studies* 5, no. 6 (1982): 561-568.

Guethlein, Carol. "Women in Louisville: Moving toward Equal Rights." *Filson Club History Quarterly* 55 (April 1981): 151-178.

Hewitt, Nancy A. "Feminist Friends: Agrarian Quakers and the Emergence of Woman's Rights in America." *Feminist Studies* 12 (Spring 1986): 27-50.

Hudson, Winthrop S. "Early Nineteenth-Century Evangelical Religion and Women's Liberation." *Foundations* 23 (April/June 1980): 181-185.

Katzenstein, Mary Fainsod. "Organizing Against Violence: Strategies of the Indian Women's Movement." *Pacific Affairs* 62 (Spring 1989): 53-71.

Kawan, Hildegard, and Barbara Weber. "Reflections on a Theme: The German Women's Movement, Then and Now." *Women's Studies* 4, no. 4 (1981): 421-434.

Kennon, Donald R. "'An Apple of Discord': The Woman Question at the World's Anti-Slavery Convention of 1840." *Slavery and Abolition* 5 (December 1984): 244-266.

Koehler, Lyle. "Women's Rights, Society, and the Schools: Feminist Activities in Cincinnati, Ohio, 1864-1880." *Queen City Heritage* 42 (Winter 1984): 3-17.

Larson, T. A. "Wyoming's Contribution to the Regional and National Women's Rights Movement." *Annals of Wyoming* 52 (Spring 1980): 2-15.

Masaud, Samar F. "The Development of Women's Movements in the Muslim World." *Hamdard Islamicus* 8 (Spring 1985): 81-86.

McBride, Genevieve G. "Theodora Winton Youmans and the Wisconsin Woman Movement." *Wisconsin Magazine of History* 71, no. 4 (1988): 243-275.

McMillan, James F. "Clericals, Anticlericals, and the Women's Movement in France under the Third Republic." *The Historical Journal* 24 (June 1981): 361-376.

Minault, Gail. "Sayyid Mumtaz Ali and 'Huquq un Niswan': An Advocate of Women's Rights in Islam in the Late Nineteenth Century." *Modern Asian Studies* 24, no. 1 (1990): 147-192.

Nienling, Liu. "The Vanguards of the Women's Liberation Movement--LuYin, Bingxin, and Ding Ling." *Chinese Studies in History* 23 (Winter 1989/90): 22-45.

Popkin, Annie. "An Early Moment in Women's Liberation: The Social Experience within Bread and Roses." *Radical America* 22 (January/February 1989): 199-234.

Pugh, Evelyn L. "Florence Nightingale and J. S. Mill Debate Women's Rights." *Journal of British Studies* (Spring 1982): 118-138.

Rosen, Andrew. "Emily Davies and the Women's Movement, 1862-1867." *The Journal of British Studies* 19 (Fall 1979): 101-121.

Ross, Frances Mitchell. "James Mitchell, Spokesman for Women's Equality in Nineteenth Century Arkansas." *Arkansas History Quarterly* 43 (Autumn 1984): 222-235.

Rutledge, Essie. "Black/White Relations in the Women's Movement." *Minority Voices* 6 (Fall 1989): 53-62.

Ryan, Barbara. "Ideological Purity and Feminism: The U.S. Women's Movement from 1966 to 1975." *Gender & Society* 3 (June 1989): 239-257.

Sauter-Bailliet, Theresia. "'Remember the Ladies': Emancipation Efforts of American Women from Independence to Seneca Falls." *European Contributions to American Studies* [Netherlands] 14 (1988): 271-279.

Shapcott, Jennifer. "The Red Chrysanthemum: Yamakawa Kikue and the Socialist Women's Movement in Pre-War Japan." *Papers on Far Eastern History* no. 35 (March 1987): 1-30.

Sigel, Roberta S., and John V. Reynolds. "Generational Differences and the Women's Movement." *Political Science Quarterly* 94 (Winter 1979): 635-648.

Smedley, Katherine. "Martha Schofield and the Rights of Women." *South Carolina Historical Magazine* 85 (July 1984): 195-210.

Takedo, Kiyoko. "Ichikawa Fusae: Pioneer for Women's Rights in Japan." *Japan Quarterly* 31 (October/December 1984): 410-415.

Taylor, Verta. "Social Movement Continuity: The Women's Movement in Abeyance." *American Sociological Review* 54 (October 1989): 761-775.

Tiesheng, Rong. "The Women's Movement in China Before and After the 1911 Revolution." *Chinese Studies in History* 16 (Spring/Summer 1983): 159-200.

Weir, Angela, and Elizabeth Wilson. "The British Women's Movement." *New Left Review* no. 158 (1984): 74-103.

Wellman, Judith. "The Seneca Falls Women's Rights Convention: A Study of Social Networks." *Journal of Women's History* 3 (Spring 1991): 9-37.

Yen-lin, Ku. "The Feminist Movement in Taiwan, 1972-87." *Bulletin of Concerned Asian Scholars* 21 (January/March 1989): 12-23.

## SOVIET UNION

Aleksandrov, V. A. "Typology of the Russian Peasant Family in the Feudal Period." *Soviet Studies in History* 21 (Fall 1982): 26-62.

Andreeva, I. S. "Sociophilosophical Problems of Sex, Marriage, and the Family." *Soviet Review* 22, no. 1 (1981/82): 20-43.

Bell, John. "Giving Birth to the New Soviet Man: Politics and Obstetrics in the USSR." *Slavic Review* 40 (Spring 1981): 1-16.

Ben-Barak, Shalvia. "Fertility Patterns Among Soviet Immigrants to Israel: The Role of Cultural Variables." *Journal of Family History* 15, no. 1 (1990): 87-100.

Black, J. L. "Educating Women in Eighteenth-Century Russia: Myths and Realities." *Canadian Slavic Papers* 20 (March 1978): 23-43.

Blackman, Charles F. "The Civil Sacrament: Law and Practice of Soviet Weddings." *American Journal of Comparative Law* 28 (1980): 555-576.

Burgin, Diana Lewis. "After the Ball is over: Sophia Parnok's Creative Relationship with Marina Tsvetaeva." *Russian Review* 47, no. 4 (1988): 425-444.

Clements, Barbara Evans. "Working-Class and Peasant Women in the Russian Revolution, 1917-1923." *Signs* 8 (Winter 1982): 215-235.

Cottam, K. Jean. "Soviet Women in Combat in World War II: The Ground Forces and the Navy." *International Journal of Women's Studies* 3 (July/August 1980): 345-357.

-----. "Soviet Women in Combat in World War II: The Rear Services, Resistance Behind Enemy Lines and Political Workers." *International Journal of Women's Studies* 5 (September/October 1982): 363-378.

DeMadariaga, Isabel. "The Foundation of the Russian Educational System by Catherine II." *Slavonic and East European Review* 57 (July 1979): 369-395.

Dewey, H. W., and A. M. Kleimola. "Muted Eulogy: Women Who Inspired Men in Medieval Rus'." *Russian History* 10, Part 2 (1983): 188-200.

Dudgeon, Ruth A. "The Forgotten Minority: Women Students in Imperial Russia, 1872-1917." *Russian History* 9, no. 1 (1982): 1-26.

Engel, Barbara Alpern. "Peasant Morality and Pre-Marital Relations in Late 19th Century Russia." *Journal of Social History* 23 (Summer 1990): 695-714.

-----. "St. Petersburg Prostitutes in the Late 19th-Century--A Personal and Social Profile." *Russian Review* 48 (January 1989): 21-44.

-----. "Women Medical Students in Russia, 1872-1882: Reformers or Rebels?" *Journal of Social History* 12 (Spring 1979): 394-414.

-----. "Women, Work and Family in the Factories of Rural Russia." *Russian History* 16, no. 2/4 (1989): 223-238.

Engelstein, Laura. "Gender and the Juridical Subject: Prostitution and Rape in Nineteenth-Century Russian Criminal Codes." *The Journal of Modern History* 60 (September 1988): 458-495.

-----. "Lesbian Vignettes: A Russian Triptych from the 1890s." *Signs* 15 (Summer 1990): 813-831.

Evans, Janet. "The Communist Party of the Soviet Union and the Women's Question: The Case of the 1936 Decree 'In Defence of Mother and Child.'" *Journal of Contemporary History* 16 (October 1981): 757-776.

Evans, N. E. "The Anglo-Russian Royal Marriage Negotiations of 1600-1603." *The Slavic & East European Review* 61 (July 1983): 363-387.

Farnsworth, Beatrice. "The Litigious Daughter-in-law: Family Relations in Rural Russia in the Second Half of the Nineteenth Century." *Slavic Review* 45 (Spring 1986): 49-64.

Fiesler, Beate. "The Making of Russian Female Social Democrats, 1890-1917." *International Review of Social History* 34, no. 2 (1989): 193-226.

Fitzpatrick, Sheila. "Sex and Revolution: An Examination of Literacy and Statistical Data on the Mores of Soviet Students in the 1920s." *Journal of Modern History* 50 (June 1978): 252-278.

Gray, Francine du Plessix. "The Russian Heroine: Gender, Sexuality and Freedom." *Michigan Quarterly Review* 28, no. 4 (1989): 699-718.

Griesse, Anne Eliot, and LCDR Margaret A. Harlow, U.S.N. "Soldiers of Happenstance: Women in Soviet Uniform." *Minerva: Quarterly Report on Women and the Military* 3 (Fall 1985): 127-151.

Halperin, Charles J. "Women in Medieval Russia." *Russian History* 10, Part 2 (1983): 139-140.

Hellie, Richard. "Women and Slavery in Muscovy." *Russian History* 10, Part 2 (1983): 213-229.

Hudson, Hugh D., Jr. "Urban Estate Engineering in Eighteenth-Century Russia: Catherine the Great and the Elusive Meschanstvo." *Canadian/American Slavic Studies/Revue canadienne-américaine d'études slaves* 18 (Winter 1984): 393-410.

Hughes, Lindsey. "Sofiya Alekseyevna and the Moscow Rebellion of 1682." *Slavonic & East European Review* 63 (October 1985): 518-539.

Johnson, Richard. "The Role of Women in the Russian Civil War, 1917-1921." *Conflict* 2, no. 2 (1980): 201-217.

Kaiser, Daniel H. "Soviet Studies on the History of the Family." *Soviet Studies in History* 21 (Fall 1982): v-xvi.

Kelly, Mary B. "Goddess Embroideries of Russia and the Ukraine." *Woman's Art Journal* 4 (Fall 1983/Winter 1984): 10-13.

Knight, Amy. "Female Terrorists in the Russian Socialist Revolutionary Party." *The Russian Review* 38 (April 1979): 139-159.

Kollman, Nancy Shields. "The Seclusion of Elite Muscovite Women." *Russian History* 10, Part 2 (1983): 170-187.

Lackow, Manya Prozanskaya. "In the Russian Gymnasia." *Lilith* 15 (Winter 1990): 15-20.

Lenhoff, Gail. "Hellenistic Erotica and the Kiev Cave Patericon 'Tale of Moses the Hungarian'." *Russian History* 10, no. 2 (1983): 141-153.

Levin, Eve. "Women and Property in Medieval Novgorod: Dependence and Independence." *Russian History* 10, Part 2 (1983): 154-169.

Levy, Sandry. "Women and the Control of Property in Sixteenth-Century Muscovy." *Russian History* 10, Part 2 (1983): 201-212.

Lubin, Nancy. "Women in Soviet Central Asia: Progress and Contradictions." *Soviet Studies* 33, no. 2 (1981): 182-203.

McGlashan, Zena Beth. "Women Witness the Russian Revolution: Analyzing Ways of Seeing." *Journalism History* 12 (Summer 1985): 54-61.

Nash, Carol S. "Educating New Mothers: Women and the Enlightenment in Russia." *History of Education Quarterly* 21 (Fall 1981): 301-316.

Norton, Barbara T. "The Making of Female Marxist: E. D. Kuskova's Conversion to Russian Social Democracy." *International Review of Social History* 34, no. 2 (1989): 227-247.

Pachmuss, Temira. "Women Writers in Russian Decadence." *Journal of Contemporary History* 17 (January 1982): 111-136.

Pushkareva, N. L., and E. Levin. "Women in Medieval Novgorod from the Eleventh to the Fifteenth Century." *Soviet Studies in History* 23 (Spring 1985): 71-90.

Rabinovich, M. G. "The Russian Urban Family at the Beginning of the Eighteenth Century." *Soviet Studies in History* 21 (Fall 1982): 63-87.

Ransel, David L. "Problems in Measuring Illegitimacy in Prerevolutionary Russia." *Journal of Social History* 16 (Winter 1982): 111-128.

Rasmussen, Karen. "Catherine II and the Image of Peter I." *Slavic Review* 37 (March 1978): 51-69.

Reeves, Connie L. "The Story of 'Yashika': Commander of the Russian Women's Battalion of Death." *Minerva: Quarterly Report on Women and the Military* 6 (Fall 1988): 67-73.

Sacks, Michael P. "Missing Female Occupational Categories in the Soviet Censuses." *Slavic Review* 40 (1981): 251-268.

Shelley, Louise. "Female Criminality in the 1920s: A Consequence of Inadvertent and Deliberate Change." *Russian History* 9, no. 2/3 (1982): 265-284.

Strighenova, Tatiana. "The Soviet Garment Industry in the 1930s." *The Journal of Decorative and Propaganda Arts* no. 5 (Summer 1987): 160-175.

Sverdlov, M. B. "Family and Commune in Ancient Russia." *Soviet Studies in History* 21 (Fall 1982): 1-25.

Thomas, Marie A. "Muscovite Convents in the Seventeenth Century." *Russian History* 10, Part 2 (1983): 230-242.

Waters, Elizabeth. "Restructuring the 'Woman Question': *Perestroika* and Prostitution." *Feminist Review* no. 33 (Autumn 1989): 3-19.

Zimmerman, Judith E. "Natalie Herzen and the Early Intelligentsia." *The Russian Review* 41 (July 1982): 249-272.

## SPORTS

Allen, E. John B. "Sierra 'Ladies' on Skis in Gold Rush California." *Journal of Sport History* 17 (Winter 1990): 347-353.

Beezley, William H., and Joseph P. Hobbs. "'Nice Girls Don't Sweat': Women in American Sport." *Journal of Popular Culture* 16 (Spring 1983): 42-53.

Bodnar, L. N. "Historical Role of Women in Sports." *American Journal of Sports Medicine* 8 (January/February 1980): 54-55.

Bulger, Margery A. "American Sportswomen in the 19th Century." *Journal of Popular Culture* 16 (Fall 1982): 1-16.

Crawford, S. "An Emancipation of Sports: Recreational and Sporting Opportunities for Women in Nineteenth Century Colonial New Zealand." *Canadian Journal of the History of Sport* 16, no. 1 (1985): 38-56.

Daughenbaugh, Leonard. "On Top of Her World--Anna Mills' Ascent of Mount Whitney." *California History* 64 (Winter 1985): 42-51.

Hall, M. A. "Women and the Lawrentian Wrestle." *Arena Review* 3 (May 1979): 25-32.

Hargreaves, Jennifer. "The Early History of Women's Sport." *Society for the Study of Labour History* 50 (Spring 1985): 5-6.

-----. "Playing like Gentlemen While Behaving like Ladies: Contradictory Features of the Formative Years of Women's Sport." *British Journal of Sports History*

2, no. 1 (1985): 40-52.

Jable, J. Thomas. "Eleanor Egg: Paterson's Track-and-Field Heroine." *New Jersey History* 102 (Fall/Winter 1984): 69-84.

Jennings, Susan E. "'As American as Hot Dogs, Apple Pie, and Chevrolet': The Desegregation of Little League Baseball." *Journal of American Culture* 4 (Winter 1981): 81-91.

Lansdell, Avril. "Costume for Oarswomen, 1919-1979." *Costume* 13 (1979): 73-79.

LeCompte, Mary Lou. "Home on the Range: Women in Professional Rodeo: 1929-1947." *Journal of Sport History* 17 (Winter 1990): 318-346.

Leigh, M. H., and T. M. Bonin. "The Pioneering Role of Madame Alice Milliat and FSFI in Establishing International Track and Field Competition for Women." *Journal of Sport History* 4 (Spring 1977): 72-83.

Lenskyi, Helen. "Femininity First: Sport and Physical Education for Ontario Girls, 1890-1930." *Canadian Journal of the History of Sport* 13 (December 1982): 4-17.

Lewis, Robert M. "American Sport History: A Bibliographical Guide." *American Studies International* 29 (April 1991): 35-59.

McCrone, Kathleen E. "Play Up! Play Up! And Play the Game! Sport at the Late Victorian Girls' Public School." *Journal of British Studies* 23 (Spring 1984): 106-134.

Morrow, Don. "Sweetheart Sport: Barbara Ann Scott and the Post War II Image of the Female Athlete in Canada." *Canadian Journal of the History of Sport* 8 (May 1987): 36-54.

Park, Roberta J. "'Embodied Selves': The Rise and Development of Concern for Physical Education, Active Games and Recreation for American Women, 1776-1865." *Journal of Sport History* 5 (Summer 1978): 5-41.

-----. "Sport, Gender and Society in a Transatlantic Perspective." *British Journal of Sports History* 2, no. 1 (1985): 5-28.

Pointon, M. "Factors Influencing the Participation of Women and Girls in Physical Education, Physical Recreation and Sport in Great Britain During the Period 1850-1920." *History of Education Bulletin* no. 24 (Autumn 1979): 46-56.

Ransom, Diane. "'The Saskatoon Lily': A Biography of Ethel Catherwood." *Saskatchewan History* 41 (Autumn 1988): 81-98.

Schrodt, B. "Canadian Women at the Commonwealth Games: 1930-1974." *CAHPER Journal* 44 (March/April 1978): 26-29.

Seltzer, Anne-Marie R. "Sporting Women Play the Field." *New Directions for Women* 19 (July/August 1990): 12-13.

Smith, Michael J. "Graceful Athleticism or Robust Womanhood: The Sporting Culture of Women in Victorian Nova Scotia, 1870-1914." *Journal of Canadian Studies* 23 (Spring/Summer 1988): 120-137.

Spears, Betty. "Mary, Mary Quite Contrary, Why Do Women Play." *Canadian Journal of the History of Sport* 18 (May 1987): 67-75.

Stiffler, Liz, and Tona Blake. "Fannie Sperry-Steele: Montana's Champion Bronc Rider." *Montana* 32 (Spring 1982): 44-57.

Struna, N. L. "Beyond Mapping Experience: The Need for Understanding in the History of American Sporting Women." *Journal of Sport History* 11, no. 1 (1984): 120-133.

Todd, Jan. "Bernard Macfadden: Reformer of Feminine Form." *Journal of Sports History* 14 (Spring 1987): 61-75.

Vertinsky, Patricia. "Exercise, Physical Capability, and Eternally Wounded Women in Late Nineteenth Century North America." *Journal of Sport History* 14 (Spring 1987): 7-27.

-----. "God, Science and the Market Place: The Bases for Exercise Prescriptions for Females in Nineteenth Century North America." *Canadian Journal of the History of Sport* 17, no. 1 (1986): 38-44.

-----. "Sexual Equality and the Legacy of Catharine Beecher." *Journal of Sport History* 6 (Spring 1979): 38-49.

Warner, Patricia Campbell. "Public and Private: Men's Influence on American Women's Dress for Sport and Physical Education." *Dress* 14 (1988): 48-55.

Yost, Nellie Snyder. "Nebraska's Scholarly Athlete: Louise Pound, 1872-1958." *Nebraska History* 64 (Winter 1983): 477-490.

## SUFFRAGE

## Anti-Suffrage

Apostol, Jane. "Why Women Should Not Have the Vote: Anti-Suffrage Views in the Southland in 1911." *Southern California Quarterly* 70 (Spring 1988): 29-42.

Chafetz, Janet Saltzman, and Gary Dworkin. "In the Face of Threat: Organized Antifeminism in Comparative Perspective." *Gender & Society* 1 (1987): 33-60.

Frenier, Mariam Darce. "American Anti-Feminist Women: Comparing the Rhetoric of Opponents of the Equal Rights Amendment with That of Opponents of Women's Suffrage." *Women's Studies International Forum* 7, no. 6 (1984): 455-465.

Green, Elna C. "Those Opposed: The Antisuffragists in North Carolina, 1900-1920." *North Carolina Historical Review* 67 (July 1990): 315-333.

Howard, Jeanne. "Our Own Worst Enemies: Women Opposed to Woman Suffrage." *Journal of Sociology and Social Welfare* 9 (1984): 463-474.

Mambretti, Catherine Cole. "The Battle Against the Ballot: Illinois Woman Antisuffragists." *Chicago History* 9 (Fall 1980): 168-177.

Marshall, Susan E. "In Defense of Separate Spheres: Class and Status Politics in the Antisuffrage Movement." *Social Forces* 65 (1986): 327-351.

-----. "Ladies Against Women: Mobilization Dilemmas of Antifeminist Movements." *Social Problems* 32, no. 4 (1985): 348-362.

Ryan, Thomas G. "Male Opponents and Supporters of Woman Suffrage: Iowa in 1916." *Annals of Iowa* 45, no. 7 (Winter 1981): 537-550.

Stevenson, Louise L. "Women Anti-Suffragists in the 1915 Massachusetts Campaign." *New England Quarterly* 52, no. 1 (March 1979): 80-93.

## International

Alberti, Johanna. "Inside out: Elizabeth Haldane as a Women's Suffrage Survivor in the 1920s and 1930s." *Women's Studies International Forum* 13, no. 1/2 (1990): 117-126.

Bacchi, Carol. "'First Wave' Feminism in Canada: The Ideas of the English-Canadian Suffragists, 1877-1918." *Women's Studies* 5, no. 6 (1982): 575-584.

Billington, R. "Ideology and Feminism: Why the Suffragettes Were 'Wild Women.'" *Women's Studies International Forum* 5 (1982): 663-674.

Bostick, T. "The Press and the Launching of the Women's Suffrage Movement, 1866-1867." *Victorian Periodicals Review* 13 (1980): 125-131.

Caine, Barbara. "Feminism, Suffrage and the Nineteenth-Century English Women's Movement." *Women's Studies International Forum* 5, no. 6 (1982): 537-550.

Campbell, Gail G. "Disfranchised but not Quiescent: Women Petitioners in New Brunswick in the Mid-19th Century." *Acadiensis* 18 (Spring 1989): 22-54.

Evans, Richard J. "German Social Democracy on Women's Suffrage 1891-1918." *Journal of Contemporary History* 15 (July 1980): 533-558.

Fowler, Rowena. "Why Did Suffragettes Attack Works of Art?" *Journal of Women's History* 2 (Winter 1991): 109-125.

Hahner, June E. "The Beginnings of the Women's Suffrage Movement in Brazil." *Signs* 5 (Fall 1979): 200-204.

-----. "Feminism, Women's Rights and the Suffrage Movement in Brazil, 1850-1932." *Latin American Research Review* 15, no. 1 (1980): 65-111.

Hause, Steven C. "Women Who Rallied to the Tricolor: The Effects of World War I on the French Women's Suffrage Movement." *Western Society for French History* 6 (November 1978): 371-377.

-----. "The Development of the Catholic Women's Suffrage Movement in France, 1896-1922." *Catholic Historical Review* 67 (January 1981): 11-30.

Hause, Steven C., and Anne R. Kenney. "The Limits of Suffragist Behavior: Legalism and Militancy in France, 1876-1922." *American Historical Review* 86 (October 1981): 781-806.

Hirshfield, Claire. "A Fractured Faith: Liberal Party Women and the Suffrage Issue in Britain, 1892-1914." *Gender & History* 2 (Summer 1990): 173-197.

Katzenstein, Mary. "Feminism and the Meaning of the Vote." *Signs* 10 (1984): 4-26.

Marcus, Jane. "Transatlantic Sisterhood: Labor and Suffrage Links in the Letters of Elizabeth Robbins and Emmeline Pankhurst." *Signs* 3 (Spring 1978): 744-755.

Mason, Francis M. "The Newer Eve: The Catholic Women's Suffrage Society in England, 1911-1923." *Catholic Historical Review* 72 (October 1986): 620-638.

Park, Jihang. "The British Suffrage Activists of 1913: An Analysis." *Past & Present* no. 120 (August 1988): 147-162.

Pearson, Gail. "Reserved Seats--Women and the Vote in Bombay." *Indian*

*Economic and Social History Review* [Delhi] 20, no.1 (1983): 47-66.

Trager, Hannah. "Votes for Women, with a Foreword by Yaffa Berlovitz." *Journal of Women's History* 2 (Spring 1990): 196-200.

Ward, Margaret. "'Suffrage First--Above All Else': An Account of the Irish Suffrage Movement." *Feminist Review* 10 (Spring 1982): 21-36.

## Suffrage and Other Issues

Alonso, Harriet Hyman. "Suffragists for Peace During the Interwar Years, 1919-1941." *Peace & Change* 14 (July 1989): 243-262.

Baum, Dale. "Woman Suffrage and the 'Chinese Question': The Limits of Radical Republicanism in Massachusetts, 1865-1876." *New England Quarterly* 56 (March 1983): 60-77.

Billington, Rosamund. "Ideology and Feminism: Why the Suffragettes Were 'Wild Women.'" *Women's Studies* 5, no. 6 (1982): 663-674.

Blocker, Jack S., Jr. "Separate Paths: Suffragists and the Women's Temperance Crusade." *Signs* 10 (Spring 1985): 460-476.

Bostick, Theodora P. "The Press and the Launching of the Women's Suffrage Movement, 1866-1867." *Victorian Periodicals Review* 13 (1980): 125-131.

-----. "Women's Suffrage, the Press, and the Reform Bill of 1867." *International Journal of Women's Studies* 3 (July/August 1980): 373-390.

Byles, J. M. "Women's Experience of World War One: Suffragists, Pacifists and Poets." *Women's Studies International Forum* 8 (1985): 473-487.

Cott, Nancy F. "Feminist Politics in the 1920s: The National Woman's Party." *Journal of Amercian History* 71 (June 1984): 43-68.

Fishburn, Janet Forsythe. "The Methodist Social Gospel and Woman Suffrage." *Drew Gateway* 54, no. 2/3 (1984): 85-104.

Iversen, Joan. "The Mormon-Suffrage Relationship: Personal and Political Quandaries." *Frontiers* 11, no. 2 & 3 (1990): 8-16.

Jeffreys, S. "'Free from All Uninvited Touch of Men': Women's Campaigns around Sexuality, 1880-1914." *Women's Studies International Forum* 5 (1982): 629-645.

McDonagh, Eileen Lorenzi. "The Significance of the Nineteenth Amendment: A New Look at Civil Rights, Social Welfare, and Woman Suffrage Alignments in the Progressive Era." *Women & Politics* 10, no. 2 (1990): 59-94.

Sheppard, Alice. "Suffrage Art and Feminism." *Hypatia* 5 (Summer 1990): 122-134.

Sloan, Kay. "Sexual Warfare in the Silent Cinema: Comedies and Melodramas of Woman Suffragism." *American Quarterly* 33 (Fall 1981): 412-436.

Strong, Karen Heetderks. "Ecclesiastical Suffrage: The First Women Participants at General Conference in the Antecedents of the United Methodist Church (1888-1946)." *Methodist History* 25 (October 1986): 29-33.

# United States

## *National*

Alpern, Sara, and Dale Baum. "Female Ballots: The Impact of the Nineteenth Amendment." *Journal of Interdisciplinary History* 16 (Summer 1985): 43-67.

Anderson, Kathryn. "Anne Martin and the Dream of Political Equality for Women." *Journal of the West* 27 (April 1988): 28-34.

Boles, Janet K. "Systematic Factors Underlying Legislative Responses to Woman Suffrage and the Equal Rights Amendment." *Women & Politics* 2, no. 1/2 (1982): 5-22.

Baker, Paula. "The Domestication of Politics: Women and American Political Society, 1780-1920." *American Historical Review* 89, no. 3 (1984): 620-647.

Buechler, Steven M. "Elizabeth Boynton Harbert and the Ideological Transformation of the Woman Suffrage Movement, 1870-1896." *Signs* 13 (Autumn 1987): 78-97.

DuBois, Ellen Carol. "Outgrowing the Compact of the Fathers: Equal Rights, Woman Suffrage, and the United States Constitution, 1820-1878." *Journal of American History* 74 (December 1987): 836-862.

Graham, Sally Hunter. "Woodrow Wilson, Alice Paul, and the Woman Suffrage Movement." *Political Science Quarterly* 98 (Winter 1983/84): 665-679.

Hurwitz, Edith. "Carrie C. Catt's 'Suffrage Militancy'." *Signs* 3, (Spring 1978): 739-743.

Klotter, James C. "Sex, Scandal, and Suffrage in the Gilded Age." *The Historian* 42 (February 1980): 225-243.

Lehman, Godfrey D. "Susan B. Anthony Cast Her Ballot for Ulysses S. Grant." *American Heritage* 37, no. 1 (1985): 24-31.

Lunardini, Christine A., and Thomas J. Knock. "Woodrow Wilson and Woman Suffrage: A New Look." *Political Science Quarterly* 95 (Winter 1980/81): 655-671.

Masel-Walters, Lynne. "To Hustle with the Rowdies: The Organization and Functions of the American Woman Suffrage Press." *Journal of American Culture* 3 (Spring 1980): 167-183.

McDonagh, Eileen L., and H. Douglas Price. "Woman Suffrage in the Progressive Era: Patterns of Opposition and Support in Referenda Voting, 1910-1918." *American Political Science Review* 79 (June 1985): 415-435.

Nutt, Rick. "Robert Lewis Dabney: Presbyterians and Women's Suffrage." *Journal of Presbyterian History* 62 (Winter 1984): 339-353.

O'Neill, William L. "Feminism in America, 1848-1986: The Fight for Suffrage." *Wilson Quarterly* 10 (Autumn 1986): 99-109.

Papachristou, Judith. "Woman's Suffrage Movement: New Research and New Perspectives." *OAH Newsletter* 14, no. 3 (1986): 6-8.

Rolley, Katrina. "Fashion, Femininity and the Fight For the Vote." *Art History* 13 (March 1990): 47-71.

Sauter-Bailliet, Theresia. "'Remember the Ladies': Emancipation Efforts of

American Women from Independence to Seneca Falls." *European Contributions to American Studies* (Netherlands) 14 (1988): 271-279.

Taylor, Caroline. "Women and the Vote in Eighteenth-Century America." *Humanities* 8 (July/August 1987): 16-17.

Walker, S. Jay. "Frederick Douglass and Woman Suffrage." *Black Scholar* 14, no. 5 (1983): 18-25.

## East

Bland, Sidney R. "'Never Quite as Committed as We'd Like': The Suffrage Militancy of Lucy Burns." *Journal of Long Island History* 17, no. 2 (1981): 4-23.

Clifford, Deborah P. "The Drive for Women's Municipal Suffrage in Vermont, 1883-1917." *Vermont History* 47 (Summer 1979): 173-190.

Daniels, Doris. "Building a Winning Coalition: The Suffrage Fight in New York State." *New York History* 60 (January 1979): 59-80.

DuBois, Ellen Carol. "Working Women, Class Relations, and Suffrage Militance: Harriot Stanton Blanch and the New York Woman Suffrage Movement, 1894-1909." *Journal of American History* 74 (June 1987): 34-58.

Gertzog, Irwin N. "Female Suffrage in New Jersey, 1790-1807." *Women & Politics* 10, no. 2 (1990): 47-58.

Gordon, Felice D. "After Winning: The New Jersey Suffragists in the Political Parties, 1920-1930." *New Jersey History* 101 (Fall/Winter 1983): 13-36.

Grandfield, Robert S. "The Massachusetts Suffrage Referendum of 1915." *Historical Journal of Massachusetts* 7, no. 1 (1979): 46-57.

Hoffecker, Carol E. "Delaware's Woman Suffrage Campaign." *Delaware History* 20 (Spring/Summer 1983): 149-167.

Leach, Roberta J. "Jennie Bradley Roessing and the Fight for Woman Suffrage in Pennsylvania." *Western Pennsylvania Historical Magazine* 67 (July 1984): 189-212.

Lerner, Elinor. "Jewish Involvement in the New York City Woman Suffrage Movement." *American Jewish History* 70 (June 1981): 442-461.

Monoson, S. Sara. "The Lady and the Tiger: Women's Electoral Activism in New York City Before Suffrage." *Journal of Women's History* 2 (Fall 1990): 100-135.

Nichols, Carole. "Votes and More for Women: Suffrage and after in Connecticut." *Women and History* no. 5 (1983): 1-86.

Stevenson, Louise L. "Women Anti-Suffragists in the 1915 Massachusetts Campaign." *New England Quarterly* 52 (March 1979): 80-93.

## Midwest

Fuller, Steven J., and Alsatia Mellecker. "Behind the Yellow Banner: Anna B. Lawther and the Winning of Suffage for Iowa Women." *Palimpset* 65 (May/June 1984): 106-116.

Grant, Marilyn. "The 1912 Suffrage Referendum: An Exercise in Political Action." *Wisconsin Magazine of History* 64 (Winter 1980/81): 107-118.

Grant, Philip A., Jr. "Kansas and the Woman Suffrage Amendment, 1917-1919." *Heritage of the Great Plains* 19 (Fall 1986): 1-8.

Harmon, Sandra A. "Altgeld the Suffragist." *Chicago History* 16 (Summer 1987):.

Noun, Louise. "Amelia Bloomer, a Biography: Part II: The Suffragist of Council Bluffs." *Annals of Iowa* 47 (Spring 1985): 575-621.

Potter, James E. "Barkley vs. Pool: Woman Suffrage and the Nebraska Referendum Law." *Nebraska History* 69 (Spring 1988): 11-18.

Ryan, Thomas G. "Male Opponents and Supporters of Woman Suffrage: Iowa in 1916." *Annals of Iowa* 45 (Winter 1981): 537-550.

Smith, Wilda M. "A Half Century of Struggle: Gaining Woman Suffrage in Kansas." *Kansas History* 4 (Summer 1981): 74-95.

Staley, Laura. "Suffrage Movement in St. Louis During the 1870s." *Gateway Heritage* 3 (Spring 1983): 34-41.

Wheeler, Adade Mitchell. "Conflict in the Illinois Woman Suffrage Movement of 1913." *Journal of the Illinois State Historical Society* 76, no. 2 (Summer 1983): 95-114.

Young, Dina M. "The Silent Search for a Voice: The St. Louis Equal Suffrage League and the Dilemma of Elite Reform, 1910-1920." *Gateway Heritage* 8 (Spring 1988): 2-19.

## South

Berkeley, Kathleen Christine. "Elizabeth Avery Meriwether, 'An Advocate for Her Sex': Feminism and Conservatism in the Post-Civil War South." *Tennessee Historical Quarterly* 43, no. 4 (1984): 390-407.

Bland, Sidney R. "Fighting the Odds: Militant Suffragists in South Carolina." *South Carolina Historical Magazine* 82 (January 1981): 32-43.

Carver, Joan S. "First League of Women Voters in Florida: Its Troubled History." *Florida Historical Quarterly* 63 (April 1985): 406-422.

Effland, Anne Wallace. "Exciting Battle and Dramatic Finish: The West Virginia Woman Suffrage Movement, Part I: 1867-1916." *West Virginia History* 46 (1985/1986): 137-158.

Gilley, B. H. "Kate Gordon and Louisiana Woman Suffrage." *Louisiana History* 24 (Summer 1983): 289-306.

Jemison, Marie Stokes. "Ladies Become Voters: Pattie Ruffner Jacobs and Women's Suffrage in Alabama." *Southern Exposure* 7, no. 1 (1979): 48-59.

Keeler, Rebecca T. "Alva Belmont: Exacting Benefactor for Women's Suffrage." *Alabama Review* 41 (April 1988): 132-145.

Kirkley, Evelyn A. "'This Work Is God's Cause': Religion in the Southern Woman Suffrage Movement, 1880-1920." *Church History* 59 (December 1990): 507-522.

Prince, Vinton M. "Will Women Turn the Tide? Mississippi Women and the 1922 United States Senate Race." *Journal of Mississippi History* 42 (August 1980):

212-220.

Shawhan, Dorothy. "Women behind the Woman Voter." *Journal of Mississippi History* 49 (May 1987): 115-128.

Smedley, Katherine. "Martha Schofield and the Rights of Women." *South Carolina Historical Magazine* 85, no. 3 (1984): 195-210.

Taylor, A. Elizabeth. "South Carolina and the Enfranchisment of Women: The Later Years." *South Carolina Historical Magazine* 80 (October 1979): 298-310.

-----. "Woman Suffrage Activities in Atlanta." *Atlanta History Journal* (Winter 1980): 45-54.

## West

Beeton, Beverly. "Woman Suffrage in Territorial Utah." *Utah Historical Quarterly* 46 (Spring 1978): 100-120.

Beeton, Beverly, and G. Thomas Edwards. "Susan B. Anthony's Woman Suffrage Crusade in the American West." *Journal of the West* 21 (April 1982): 5-15.

Belleranti, Shirley W. "An Educated State of Equality." *Westways* 77, no. 5 (1985): 42-45.

Bennion, Sherilyn Cox. "The *Pioneer*: The First Voice of Women's Suffrage in the West." *Pacific Historian* 25 (Winter 1981): 15-21.

-----. "Woman Suffrage Papers of the West, 1869-1914." *American Journalism* 3 (1986): 129-141.

Berman, David K. "Male Support for Woman Suffrage: An Analysis of Voting Patterns in the Mountain West." *Social Science History* 11 (Fall 1987): 281-294.

Cole, Judith K. "A Wide Field for Usefulness: Women's Civil Status and the Evolution of Women's Suffrage on the Montana Frontier, 1864-1914." *American Journal of Legal History* 34 (July 1990): 262-294.

Easton, Patricia O'Keefe. "Woman Suffrage in South Dakota: The Final Decade, 1911-1920." *South Dakota History* 13 (Fall 1983): 206-226.

Fleming, Sidney Howell. "Solving the Jigsaw Puzzle: One Suffrage Story at a Time." *Annals of Wyoming* 62 (Spring 1990): 23-72.

James, Louise Boyd. "The Woman Suffrage Issue in the Oklahoma Constitutional Convention (1906)." *Chronicles of Oklahoma* 56 (Winter 1979): 379-392.

Jensen, Joan M. "'Disfranchisement Is a Disgrace': Women and Politics in New Mexico, 1900-1940." *New Mexico Historical Review* 56 (January 1981): 5-36.

Kessler, Lauren. "The Ideas of Woman Suffrage and the Mainstream Press." *Oregon Historical Quarterly* 84 (Fall 1983): 257-276.

-----. "The Ideas of Women Suffragists and the Portland *Oregonian*." *Journalism Quarterly* 57, no. 4 (1980): 597-605.

-----. "A Siege of the Citadels: Search for a Public Forum for the Ideas of Oregon Woman Suffrage." *Oregon Historical Quarterly* 84 (Summer 1983): 116-149.

Kneeland, Marilyn. "The Modern Boston Tea Party: The San Diego Suffrage Campaign of 1911." *Journal of San Diego History* 23 (Fall 1977): 35-42.

Massie, Michael A. "Reform Is Where You Find It: The Roots of Woman

Suffrage in Wyoming." *Annals of Wyoming* 62 (Spring 1990): 2-22.

Norlin, Dennis A. "The Suffrage Movement and South Dakota Churches: Radicals and the Status Quo, 1890." *South Dakota History* 14 (Winter 1984): 308-334.

Scharff, Virginia. "The Case for Domestic Feminism: Woman Suffrage in Wyoming." *Annals of Wyoming* 56 (Fall 1984): 29-37.

Smith, Jean M. "The Voting Women of San Diego, 1920." *Journal of San Diego History* 26, no. 2 (1980): 133-154.

Thatcher, Linda, ed. "'I Care Nothing for Politics': Ruth May Fox, Forgotten Suffragist." *Utah Historical Quarterly* 49 (Summer 1981): 239-253.

Wheeler, Leslie. "Henry B. Blackwell, Woman Suffrage's Gray-Bearded Champion Comes to Montana, 1889." *Montana* 31 (July 1981): 2-13.

Wittmayer, Cecelia M. "The 1889-1890 Woman Suffrage Campaign: A Need to Organize." *South Dakota History* 11 (Summer 1981): 199-225.

Wygant, Larry J. "'A Municipal Broom': The Woman Suffrage Campaign in Galveston, Texas." *Houston Review* no. 3 (1984): 117-134.

## THEORY

## Construction/Deconstruction/Reconstruction

Alcoff, Linda. "Cultural Feminism versus Post-Structuralism: The Identity Crisis in Feminist Theory." *Signs* 13 (Spring 1988): 405-436.

Alexander, Sally. "Women, Class, and Sexual Difference." *History Workshop* 17 (Spring 1984): 125-149.

Banner, Lois W. "A Reply to 'Culture et Pouvoir' from the Perspective of United States Women's History." *Journal of Women's History* 1 (Spring 1989): 101-107.

Barrett, Michele. "Rethinking Women's Oppression: A Reply to Brenner and Ramas." *New Left Review* no. 146 (1984): 123-128.

Bennett, Judith M. "Comment on Tilly: Who Asks the Questions for Women's History?" *Social Science History* 13 (Winter 1989): 471-478.

Bock, Gisela. "Women's History and Gender History: Aspects of an International Debate." *Gender & History* 1 (Spring 1989): 7-30.

Boris, Eileen. "Looking at Women's Historians Looking at 'Difference.'" *Wisconsin Women's Law Journal* 3 (1987): 213-238.

Brenner, Johanna, and Maria Ramas. "Rethinking Women's Oppression." *New Left Review* no. 144 (1984): 33-71.

Cott, Nancy F. "What's in a Name? The Limits of "Social Feminism"; or, Expanding the Vocabulary of Women's History." *Journal of American History* 76 (December 1989): 809-829.

De Lauretis, Teresa. "The Essence of the Triangle or, Taking the Risk of Essentialism Seriously: Feminist Theory in Italy, the U.S., and Britain." *Differences* 1 (Summer 1989): 3-37.

Evans, Richard. "Modernization Theory and Women's History." *Archiv für Sozialgeschichte* 20 (1980): 492-514.

Friedman, Michelle. "The Social Construction of Gender: Historically Changing Meanings of (White) Femininity and Masculinity." *Critical Arts* 5, no. 2 (1989): 67-111.

Gordon, Linda. "Family Violence, Feminism, and Social Control." *Feminist Studies* 12 (Fall 1986): 453-478.

Gullickson, Gay L. "Comment on Tilly: Women's History, Social History, and Deconstruction." *Social Science History* 13 (Winter 1989): 463-470.

Irving, Katrina. "(Still) Hestitating on the Threshold: Feminist Theory and the Question of the Subject." *NWSA Journal* 1 (Summer 1989): 630-643.

Jarratt, Susan C. "The First Sophists and Feminism: Discourses of the 'Other.'" *Hypatia* 5 (Spring 1990): 27-41.

Kerber, Linda K. "Women and Individualism in American History." *Massachusetts Review* 30 (Winter 1989): 589-609.

Kessler-Harris, Alice. "Gender Ideology in Historical Reconstruction: A Case Study from the 1930s." *Gender & History* 1 (Spring 1989): 31-49.

Lerner, Gerda. "Reconceptualizing Differences Among Women." *Journal of Women's History* 1 (Winter 1990): 106-122.

Loesberg, Jonathon. "Deconstruction, Historicism, and Overdetermination: Dislocations of the Marriage Plot in *Robert Elsmere* and *Dombey and Son*." *Victorian Studies* 33 (Spring 1990): 441-464.

McCarthy, Bill, and John Hagan. "Gender, Delinquency, and the Great Depression: A Test of Power-Control Theory." *Canadian Review of Sociology and Anthropology/Revue canadienne de Sociologie et d'Anthropologie* 24 (May 1987): 153-177.

McKinnon, Catherine. "Feminism, Marxism, Method, and the State: An Agenda for Theory." *Signs* 7 (1982): 515-541.

Mirkin, Harris. "The Passive Female: The Theory of Patriarchy." *American Studies* 25 (Fall 1984): 39-59.

Motz, Marilyn Ferris. "Garden as Woman: Creation of Identity in a Turn-of-the-Century Ohio Town." *NWSA Journal* 2 (Winter 1990): 35-51.

Mullaney, Marie Marmo. "Gender and the Socialist Revolutionary Role, 1871-1921: A General Theory of the Female Revolutionary Personality." *Historical Reflections/Reflexions Historiques* 11 (Summer 1984): 99-152.

Newman, Louise. "Critical Theory and the History of Women: What's at Stake in Deconstructing Women's History." *Journal of Women's History* 2 (Winter 1991): 58-68.

Newton, Judith. "Family Fortunes: 'New History' and 'New Historicism.'" *Radical History Review* 43 (Winter 1989): 5-22.

-----. "A Feminist Scholarship You Can Bring Home to Dad?" *Journal of Women's History* 2 (Winter 1991): 102-108.

-----. "History as Usual? Feminism and the 'New Historicism.'" *Cultural Critique* no. 9 (Spring 1988): 87-122.

Offen, Karen. "Thoughts on 'Culture et Pouvoir des Femmes.'" *Journal of Women's History* 1 (Spring 1989): 89-91.

Ong, Aihwa. "Disassembling Gender in the Electronics Age." *Feminist Studies* 13

(Fall 1987): 609-626.

Painter, Nell Irvin. "French Theories in American Settings: Some Thoughts on Transferability." *Journal of Women's History* 1 (Spring 1989): 92-95.

Patel, Sujata. "Construction and Reconstruction of Women in Gandhi." *Economic and Political Weekly* 23 (February 20, 1988): 377-387.

Perrot, Michelle, et al. "Women's Culture and Women's Power: An Attempt at Historiography." *Journal of Women's History* 1 (Spring 1989): 63-88.

Puka, Bill. "The Liberation of Caring: A Different Voice for Gilligan's 'Different Voice.'" *Hypatia* 5 (Spring 1990): 58-82.

Rabine, Leslie Wahl. "Essentialism and Its Contexts: Saint-Simonian and Post-Structuralist Feminists." *Differences* 1 (Summer 1989): 105-124.

Rothenberg, Paula. "The Construction, Deconstruction, and Reconstruction of Difference." *Hypatia* 5 (Spring 1990): 42-57.

Scott, Joan Wallach. "Deconstructing Equality-versus-Difference: Or, the Uses of Poststructural Theory for Feminism." *Feminist Studies* 14 (Spring 1988): 37-48.

-----. "Gender: A Useful Category of Historical Analysis." *American Historical Review* 91 (December 1986): 1053-1075.

-----. "History and Difference." *Daedalus* 116 (Fall 1987): 93-118.

Sheldon, Amy. "Gender, Language, and Historical Interpretation." *Oral History Review* 17 (Fall 1989): 92-96.

Smith, Hilda L. "Are We Ready for a Comparative Historiography of Women?" *Journal of Women's History* 1 (Spring 1989): 96-100.

Stanley, Liz. "Recovering *Women* in History from Feminist Deconstructionism." *Women's Studies International Forum* 13, no. 1/2 (1990): 151-158.

Strathern, Marilyn. "Between a Melanesianist and a Deconstructive Feminist." *Australian Feminist Studies* no. 10 (Summer 1989): 49-70.

Stuard, Susan Mosher. "The Annales School and Feminist History: Opening Dialog with the American Stepchild." *Signs* 7 (Autumn 1981): 135-143.

Tilly, Louise A. "Gender, Women's History, and Social History." *Social Science History* 13 (Winter 1989): 439-462.

Vogel, Lise. "Telling Tales: Historians of Our Own Lives." *Journal of Women's History* 2 (Winter 1991): 89-101.

Walkowitz, Judith, Myra Jehlen, and Bell Chevigny. "Patrolling the Borders: Feminist Historiography and the New Historicism." *Radical History Review* 43 (Winter 1989): 23-44.

Williams, Joan. "Domesticity as the Dangerous Supplement of Liberalism." *Journal of Women's History* 2 (Winter 1991): 69-88.

Withorn, Ann. "Radicalizing History: Writing about Women's Lives and the State." *Radical America* 22 (March/June 1989): 45-51.

## Women's History/Feminist History

Alpern, Mildred. "The Impact of Women's History." *Network News Exchange* 7 (Spring 1982).

Aruup, Katherine. "Lesbian Feminist Theory." *Resources for Feminist Research*

[Canada] 12, no. 1 (1983): 53-55.

Beechey, Veronica. "On Patriarchy." *Feminist Review* 3 (1979): 66-82.

Bennett, Judith M. "Feminism and History." *Gender & History* 1 (Autumn 1989): 251-272.

Blake, Susan L. "A Woman's Trek: What Difference Does Gender Make? *Women's Studies International Forum* 4, no. 4 (1990): 347-356.

Cuevas, Maria. "The National Women's History Project." *Woman of Power* no. 16 (Spring 1990): 10-21.

de Lauretis, Teresa. "Eccentric Subjects: Feminist Theory and Historical Consciousness." *Feminist Studies* 16 (Spring 1990): 115-150.

Degler, Carl N. "On Rereading 'The Woman in America.'" *Daedalus* 116, no. 4 (1987): 199-210.

Diamond, Irene, and Lisa Kuppler. "Frontiers of the Imagination: Women, History, and Nature." *Journal of Women's History* 1 (Winter 1990): 160-180.

DuBois, Ellen, Mari Jo Buhle, Temma Kaplan, Gerda Lerner, and Carroll Smith Rosenberg. "Politics and Culture in Women's History: A Symposium." *Feminist Studies* 6 (Spring 1980): 26-64.

Etulain, Richard W. "Revisioning the Feminine Frontier." *American Quarterly* 39 (Summer 1987): 301-305.

Evans, Richard. "Women's History: The Limits of Reclamation." *Social History* 5 (1980): 273-281.

Evans, Sara M. "Toward a Usable Past: Feminism as History and Politics." *Minnesota History* 48 (Summer 1983): 230-235.

Fauré, Christine. "Absent from History." Translated by Lillian S. Robinson. *Signs* 7 (Autumn 1981): 71-80.

Foster, Thomas. "History, Critical Theory, and Women's Social Practices: 'Women's Time' and Housekeeping." *Signs* 14 (Autumn 1988): 73-99.

Fox-Genovese, Elizabeth. "The Personal Is Not Political Enough." *Marxist Perspectives* 2 (Winter 1979/80): 94-113.

-----. "Placing Women's History in History." *New Left Review* no. 133 (1982): 5-29.

-----. "Socialist-Feminist American Women's History." *Journal of Women's History* 1 (Winter 1990): 181-210.

Friedensohn, Doris, and Barbara Rubin. "Generation of Women: A Search for Female Forebears." *History Workshop* 18 (Autumn 1984): 160-169.

Godelier, Maurice. "The Origins of Male Domination." *New Left Review* 127 (1981): 3-7.

Harrison, Brian and James McMillan. "Some Feminist Betrayals of Women's History." *The Historical Journal* 26 (June 1983): 375-390.

Hewitt, Nancy A. "Beyond the Search for Sisterhood: American Women's History in the 1980s." *Social History* 10 (October 1985): 299-321.

Hewitt, Nancy A., Judith Bennett, Irene Silverblatt, and Lyndal Roper. "What Should Women's History Be Doing?" *CGWH Newsletter* 21 (November 1990): 14-27.

Hoerning, Erika M. "The Myth of Female Loyalty." *Journal of Psychohistory* 16

(Summer 1988): 19-46.

Jensen, Joan M. "Comment on Gender Issues and Historic Interpretation at the Kelley Farm." *Oral History Review* 17 (Fall 1989): 102-106.

Jensen, Joan M., and Darlis A. Miller. "The Gentle Tamers Revisited: New Approaches to the History of Women in the American West." *Pacific Historical Review* 49 (May 1980): 173-213.

Kelly-Gadol, Joan. "The Doubled Vision of Feminist History: A Postscript to the 'Woman and Power' Conference." *Feminist Studies* 5 (1979): 216-217.

Kerber, Linda K., Nancy Cott, Robert Gross, Lynn Hunt, Carroll Smith-Rosenberg, and Christine M. Stansell. "Beyond Roles, Beyond Spheres: Thinking About Gender in the Early Republic." *William and Mary Quarterly* 46 (July 1989): 565-585.

-----. "Separate Spheres, Female Worlds, Woman's Place: The Rhetoric of Women's History." *Journal of American History* 75 (June 1988): 9-39.

Lerner, Gerda. "Writing Women into History." *Woman of Power* no. 16 (Spring 1990): 6-14.

Mathews, Donald G. "Women's History: Everyone's History." *Quarterly Review: A Scholarly Journal for Reflection on Ministry* 1 (Winter 1981): 41-60.

Mathews, Jill. "Feminist History." *Labour History* 50 (May 1986): 147-153.

Moseley, Eva S. "One Half Our History." *Harvard Library Bulletin* 32 (Summer 1984).

Minsky, Rosalind. "'The Trouble Is It's Ahistorical': The Problem of the Unconscious in Modern Feminist Theory." *Feminist Review* no. 36 (Autumn 1990): 4-14.

Murphy, Marjorie. "What Women Have Wrought." *American Historical Review* 93 (June 1988): 653-663.

Newton, Judith. "Making--and Remaking--History: Another Look at 'Patriarchy.'" *Tulsa Studies in Women's Literature* 3 (Spring/Fall 1984): 125-141.

O'Brien, Mary. "Feminist Theory and Dialectical Logic." *Signs* 7 (Autumn 1981): 144-157.

Offen, Karen. "Defining Feminism: A Comparative Historical Approach." *Signs* 14 (Autumn.1988): 119-57.

-----. "Women's Memory, Women's History, Women's Political Action: The French Revolution in Retrospect, 1789-1889-1989." *Journal of Women's History* 1 (Winter 1990): 211-230.

Rendall, Jane. "Women's History: Beyond the Cage." *History* 75 (February 1990): 63-72.

Riley, Denise. "Does a Sex Have a History? 'Women' and Feminism." *New Formations* 1 (1987): 35.

Rossi, Alice S. "Equality Between the Sexes: An Immodest Proposal." *Daedalus* 117 (Summer 1988): 25-72.

Rupp, Leila J. "Reflections on Twentieth-Century American Women's History." *Reviews in American History* 9 (June 1981): 275-284.

Schaffer, Kay. "Postmodernism and History: A Reply to Marian Aveling." *Australian Feminist Studies* no. 11 (Autumn 1990): 91-94.

Schulyer, David. "Inventing a Feminine Past." *New England Quarterly* 51, no. 3 (September 1978): 291-308.

Scott, Anne Firor. "Are We the Women Our Grandmothers Were?" *Atlanta History Journal* (Fall 1981): 5-18.

-----. "On Seeing and Not Seeing: A Case of Historical Invisibility." *Journal of American History* (June 1984): 7-21.

-----. "Women in Plantation Culture: Or What I Wish I Knew About Southern Women." *South Atlantic Urban Studies* 2 (1978): 24-33.

Singleton, Carrie Jane. "Race and Gender in Feminist Theory." *Sage* 6 (Summer 1989): 12-17.

Sklar, Kathryn Kish. "A Call for Comparisons." *American Historical Review* 95 (October 1990): 1109-1114.

Stage, Sarah L. "Women." *American Quarterly* 35 (Spring/Summer 1983): 169-190.

Swindells, Julia. "Hanging Up on Mum or Questions of Everyday Life in the Writing of History." *Gender & History* 2 (Spring 1990): 68-78.

Todd, Barbara. "Separate Spheres: Woman's Place in Nineteenth-Century America." *Canadian Review of American Studies* 16 (Fall 1985): 329-337.

Tuchman, Gaye. "Some Thoughts on Public and Private Spheres." *Centerpoint* 3 (Fall/Spring 1980): 111-113.

Vogel, Lise. "Questions on the Woman Question." *Monthly Review* 31 (June 1979): 39-59.

## Women's History Methodology and Other Disciplines

Adreadis, A. Harriette. "The Woman's Commonwealth: A Study in Coalescence of Social Forms." *Frontiers* 7, no. 3 (1984): 79-86.

Anderson, Kathryn, Susan Armitage, Dana Jack, and Judith Wittner. "Beginning Where We Are: Feminist Methodology in Oral History." *Oral History Review* 15 (Spring 1987): 103-128.

Anglin, Mary K. "Working Women: The Intersection of Historical Anthropology and Social History." *Appalachian Journal* 16 (Winter 1989): 154-164.

Armitage, Susan. "Making the Personal Political: Women's History and Oral History." *Oral History Review* 17 (Fall 1989): 107-116.

Armstrong, Hugh, and Pat Armstrong. "Beyond Sexless Class and Classless Sex: Towards Feminist Marxism." *Studies in Political Economy* 10 (1983): 7-44.

-----. "Comments: More on Marxist Feminism." *Studies in Political Economy* 15 (1984): 179-184.

Banner, Lois W. "Women's Studies and Men's Studies: An Alternative Approach." *Women's Studies International Forum* 9, no. 2 (1986): 141-144.

Barber, Marilyn, May Yee, and Varpu Linstrom-Best. "Oral Testimony and Women's History." *Polyphony* 9 (Fall/Winter 1987): 83-89.

Barstow, Anne. "The Uses of Archaeology for Women's History: James Mellaarts' Work on the Neolithic Goddess at Catal Huyuk." *Feminist Studies* 4 (October 1978): 7-18.

Bate, Kerry William. "Family History: Some Answers, Many Questions." *Oral History Review* 16 (Spring 1988): 127-130.

Bergland, Betty. "Immigrant History and the Gendered Subject: A Review Essay." *Ethnic Forum* 8, no. 2 (1988): 24-39.

Blair, Karen J. "Women's History as Local History." *Ohio History* (Autumn 1978): 438-443.

Bohan, Janis S. "Contextual History: A Framework for Re-Placing Women in the History of Psychology." *Psychology of Women Quarterly* 14, no. 2 (1990): 213-228.

Bowles, Gloria. "'Feminist Scholarship' and 'Women's Studies': Implications for University Presses." *Scholarly Publishing* 19 (April 1988): 163-168.

Bowles, Paul. "Millar and Engels on the History of Women and the Family." *History of European Ideas* 12, no. 5 (1990): 595-610.

Bradbury, Bettina. "Women's History and Working-Class History." *Labour/Le Travail* 19 (Spring 1987): 23-43.

Brown, Sharon A. "Recovering the History of Western Military Women." *Minerva: Quarterly Report on Women and the Military* 2 (Spring 1984): 83-97.

Buckley, Cheryl. "Made in Patriarchy: Towards a Feminist Analysis of Women and Design." *Design Issues* 3 (Fall 1986): 3-14.

Carroll, Berenice A. "The Politics of 'Originality': Women and the Class System of the Intellect." *Journal of Women's History* 2 (Fall 1990): 136-164.

Catarella, Teresa. "Feminine Historicizing in the *romancero novelesco.*" *Bulletin of Hispanic Studies* 67 (October 1990): 331-344.

Chmaj, Betty E. "'Away with Your Man-Visions!' How Women's Studies Is Challenging American Studies." *Amerikastudien* 31, no. 2 (1986): 241-259.

Cohen, Patricia Cline. "The Early (and Soon Broken) Marriage of History and Statistics, Boston 1839." *Historical Methods* 23 (Spring 1990): 63-71.

Covert, Catherine L. "Journalism History and Women's Experience: A Problem in Conceptual Change." *Journalism History* 8 (Spring 1981): 2-6.

Dain, Phyllis. "Women's Studies in American Library History: Some Critical Reflections." *Journal of Library History* 18 (Fall 1983): 450-463.

Degler, Carl. "What the Woman's Movement Has Done to American History." *Soundings: An Interdisciplinary Journal* 64 (1981): 403-421.

Diamond, Irene, and Lisa Kuppler. "Frontiers of the Imagination: Women, History, and Nature." *Journal of Women's History* 1 (Winter 1990): 160-180.

Dodd, Kathryn. "Cultural Politics and Women's Historical Writing: The Case of Ray Strachey's *The Cause.*" *Women's Studies International Forum* 13, no. 1/2 (1990): 127-138.

Donovan, Josephine. "Animal Rights and Feminist Theory." *Signs* 15 (Winter 1990): 350-375.

Downs, Fane. "The Spaces Between the Leaves: An Essay on Women's History and Theology." *Austin Seminary Bulletin* 104 (October 1988): 17-23.

Edson, Evelyn. "Must Women's History Be Social History?" *Women's Studies Quarterly* 16 (Spring/Summer 1988): 33-36.

Endres, A. M., and Katrina Alford. "Discussion: A Twentieth Century Economic

Historian on Colonial Women's Employment: Comment on Alford. On Polemics and Patriarchy: A Rejoinder." *Labour History* 52 (May 1987): 88-95.

Faragher, John Mack. "History from the Inside-Out: Writing the History of Women in Rural America." *American Quarterly* 33 (Winter 1981): 537-557.

Fausto-Sterling, Anne. "Society Writes Biology/ Biology Constructs Gender." *Daedalus* 116 (Fall 1987): 61-76.

Feather, Betty L., and Lucy R. Sibley. "Overlooked Pages of North American Clothing History." *Dress* 5 (1979): 63-73.

Feinson, Majorie Chary. "Where Are Women in the History of Aging?" *Social Science History* 9 (Fall 1985): 429-452.

Fisk, Mitton. "Feminism, Socialism and Historical Materialism." *Praxis International* 2 (July 1982): 117-140.

Fox-Genovese, Elizabeth. "Property and Patriarchy in Classical Bourgeois Political Theory." *Radical History Review* 4 (1977): 36-59.

Geiger, Susan. "What's So Feminist About Doing Women's Oral History?" *Journal of Women's History* 2 (Spring 1990): 169-182.

Goldberg, Marianne. "Turning History Around: Linda Mussman's Chronicles." *Women & Performance* 4, no. 1 (1988/89): 150-156.

Gordon, Jean, and Jan McArthur. "American Women and Domestic Consumption, 1800-1920: Four Interpretive Themes." *Journal of American Culture* 8 (Fall 1985): 35-46.

Gordon, Linda. "What Should Women Historians Do: Politics, Social History, and Women's History." *Marxist Perspectives* 1 (Fall 1978): 128-137.

Hartmann, Heidi. "The Unhappy Marriage of Marxism and Feminism: Towards a More Progressive Union." *Capital and Class* 8 (1979): 1-33.

Hashimoto, Mitsuru. "Ie, the World Women Make: Toward an Interpretive Sociology." *Journal of Family History* 11, no. 4 (1986): 353-370.

Howe, Adrian. "Prologue to a History of Women's Imprisonment: In Search of a Feminist Perspective." *Social Justice* 17 (Summer 1990): 5-22.

Humez, Jean M., and Laurie Crumpacker. "Oral History in Teaching Women's Studies." *Oral History Review* (1979): 53-69.

Janks, Hilary. "Language, Myth and Disempowerment." *Critical Arts* 5, no. 2 (1989): 58-66.

Judt, Tony. "A Clown in Regal Purple: Social History and the Historians." *History Workshop* no. 7 (1979): 66-94.

Kessler-Harris, Alice. "Women's History, Women's Studies, American Studies: The Cultural Connection." *Amerikastudien* 31, no. 1 (1986): 215-227.

Levine, Susan. "Labors in the Field: Reviewing Women's Cultural History." *Radical History Review* 35 (1986): 49-56.

Lewis, Jane. "The Debate on Sex and Class." *New Left Review* no. 149 (1985): 108-120.

Lichthlau, Klaus. "Eros and Culture: Gender Theory in Simmel, Tonnies and Weber." *Telos* no. 82 (Winter 1989/90): 89-110.

Lipschultz, Sybil. "Social Feminism and Legal Discourse: 1908-1923" *Yale Journal of Law and Feminism* 2 (Fall 1989): 131-160.

Long, Elizabeth. "Women, Reading, and Cultural Authority: Some Implications of the Audience Perspective in Cultural Studies." *American Quarterly* 38 (Fall 1986): 591-612.

Lorber, Judith. "Minimalist and Maximalist Feminist Ideologies and Strategies for Change." *Quarterly Journal of Ideology* 5 (Fall 1981): 61-66.

Lutz, Catherine. "The Erasure of Women's Writing in Sociocultural Anthropology." *American Ethnologist* 17 (November 1990): 611-627.

Martin, Biddy. "Feminism, Criticism and Foucault." *New German Critique* 27 (1982): 3-30.

Mayo, Edith P. "Women's History and Public History: The Museum Connection." *Public Historian* 5 (Spring 1983): 63-74.

McAlister, Linda Lopez. "Some Remarks on Exploring the History of Women in Philosophy." *Hypatia* 4 (Spring 1989): 1-5.

McCarthy, Kathleen D. "The Feminization of American Intellectual History." *Newsletter Intellectual History Group* 6 (Spring 1984).

Miller, Elise. "The Feminization of American Realist Theory." *American Literary Realism* 23 (Fall 1990): 20-41.

Offen, Karen. "The Beginnings of 'Scientific' Women's History in France." *Western Society for French History* 11 (November 1983): 255-264.

Olson, Richard. "Historical Reflections on Feminist Critiques of Science: The Scientific Background to Modern Feminism." *History of Science* 28 (June 1990): 125-147.

Padel, Ruth. "Between Theory and Fiction: Reflections on Feminism and Classical Scholarship." *Gender & History* 2 (Summer 1990): 198-211.

Parr, Joy. "Nature and Hierarchy: Reflections on Writing the History of Women and Children." *Atlantis* 11 (Fall 1985): 39-44.

Pollock, Griselda. "Women, Art, and Ideology: Questions for Feminist Art Historians." *Woman's Art Journal* 4 (Spring/Summer 1983): 39-47.

Purvis, J. "Towards a History of Women's Education in Nineteenth Century Britain: A Sociological Analysis." *Westminster Studies in Education* 4 (1981): 45-79.

Rader, Rosemary. "Recovering Women's History: Early Christianity." *Horizons: The Journal of the College Theology Society* 11 (Spring 1984): 113-124.

Rafter, Nicole Hahn, and Elena M. Natalizia. "Marxist Feminism: Implications for Criminal Justice." *Crime and Delinquency* 27 (January 1981): 81-98.

Robinson, Lillian S. "Sometimes, Always, Never: Their Women's History and Ours." *New Literary History* 21 (Winter 1990): 377-394.

Rogers, Susan. "Woman's Place: A Critical Review of Anthropological Theory." *Comparative Studies in Society and History* 20, no. 1 (1983): 123-162.

Roth, Guenther. "Durkheim and the Principles of 1789: The Issue of Gender Equality." *Telos* no. 82 (Winter 1989/90): 71-88.

Shefer, Tammy. "Feminist Theories of the Role of the Body Within Women's Oppression." *Critical Arts* 5, no. 2 (1989): 37-54.

Slaughter, Jane. "Feminism and Socialism: Theoretical Debates in Historical Perspective." *Marxist Perspectives* 2 (Fall 1979): 32-49.

Slavin, Sarah. "Authenticity and Fiction in Law: Contemporary Case Studies Exploring Radical Legal Feminism." *Journal of Women's History* 1 (Winter 1990): 123-159.

Tilly, Louise A. "People's History and Social Science History." *Social Science History* 7 (Fall 1983): 457-474.

-----. "Women's History and Family History: Fruitful Collaboration or Missed Connection?" *Journal of Family History* 12, nos. 1/3 (1987): 303-318.

Tilly, Louise A., and Miriam Cohen. "Does the Family Have a History? A Review of Theory & Practice in Family History." *Social Science History* 6 (Spring 1982): 131-180.

Waither, Mary Ellen. "On Not Teaching the History of Philosophy." *Hypatia* 4 (Spring 1989): 132-138.

Wellman, Judith. "Some Thoughts on the Psycho-Historical Study of Women." *Psychohistory Review* 7 (Fall 1978).

West, Robin L. "The Difference in Women's Hedonic Lives: A Phenomenological Critique of Feminist Legal Theory." *Wisconsin Women's Law Journal* 3 (1987): 101-105.

White, E. Frances, and Ann Woodhull-McNeal. "Challenging the Scientific Myths of Gender and Race." *Radical America* 20, no. 4 (1986): 25-32.

Wikander, Ulla. "On Women's History and Economic History." *Scandinavian Economic History Review & Economy and History* 38, no. 2 (1990): 65-71.

Woods, Thomas A. "The Challenge of Public History." *Oral History Review* 17 (Fall 1989): 97-101.

## Cross-Cultural Theory and Women's History

Afary, Janet. "Some Reflections on Third World Feminist Historiography." *Journal of Women's History* 1 (Fall 1989): 147-152.

Al-Hibri, Azizah. "A Study of Islamic Herstory: Or How Did We Ever Get into This Mess?" *Women's Studies* 5, no. 2 (1982): 207-220.

Andrews, Margaret W. "Attitudes in Canadian Women's History, 1945-1975." *Journal of Canadian Studies* 12 (Summer 1977): 69-78.

Beard, Linda Susan. "Daughters of Clio and Calliope: Afro-American Women Writers as Reclamation and Revisionist Herstorians." *Psychohistory Review* 17 (Spring 1989): 301-343.

Bengelsdorf, Carollee. "On the Problem of Studying Women in Cuba." *Race and Class* 27 (Autumn 1985): 35-50.

Bernstein, Alison. "Outgrowing Pocahontas: Toward a New History of American Indian Women." *Minority Notes* 2 (Spring/Summer 1981).

Chakravarti, Uma, and Kumkum Roy. "In Search of Our Past: A Review of the Limitations and Possibilities of the Historiography of Women in Early India." *Economic and Political Weekly* 23 (April 30, 1988): WS-2--WS-10.

Cicioni, Mirna. "'Love and Respect, Together': The Theory and Practice of *Affidamento* in Italian Feminism." *Australian Feminist Studies* no. 10 (Summer 1989): 71-84.

Clendinnen, Inga. "Yucatec Mayan Women and the Spanish Conquest: Role and Ritual in Historical Reconstruction." *Journal of Social History* (Spring 1982): 427-442.

Davin, Anna. "London Feminist History." *History Workshop* 9 (Spring 1980): 192-195.

Dickson, Lynda F. "Toward a Broader Angle of Vision in Uncovering Women's History: Black Women's Clubs Revisited." *Frontiers* 9, no. 2 (1987): 62-68.

Dill, Bonnie Thornton. "Race, Class, and Gender: Prospects for an All-Inclusive Sisterhood (1900-40)." *Feminist Studies* (Spring 1983): 131-150.

-----. "The Dialectics of Black Womanhood." *Signs* 4 (Spring 1979): 543-555.

Fiol-Matta, Liza. "Naming Our World, Writing Our History: The Voices of Hispanic Feminist Poets." *Women's Studies Quarterly* 16 (Fall/Winter 1988): 68-80.

Garcia, Alma M. "The Development of Chicana Feminist Discourse, 1970-1980." *Gender & Society* 3 (1989): 217-238.

Hahner, June E. "Recent Research on Women in Brazil." *Latin American Research Review* 20, no. 3 (1985): 163-179.

-----. "Researching the History of Latin American Women: Past and Future Directions." *Revista Interamericana de Bibliografía* 33, no. 4 (1983): 545-552.

Hardwick, Lorna. "Ancient Amazons--Heroes, Outsiders or Women?" *Greece & Rome* 37 (April 1990): 14-35.

Hewitt, Nancy. "Sisterhood in International Perspective: Thoughts on Teaching Comparative Women's History." *Women's Studies Quarterly* 16 (Spring/Summer 1988): 22-32.

Higginbotham, Evelyn Brooks. "Beyond the Sound of Silence: Afro-American Women in History." *Gender and History* 1 (Spring 1989): 50-67.

Jameson, Elizabeth. "Toward a Multicultural History of Women in the Western United States." *Signs* 13 (Summer 1988): 761-791.

Johnson-Odim, Cheryl, and Margaret Strobel. "Conceptualizing the History of Women in Africa, Asia, Latin America and the Caribbean, and the Middle East." *Journal of Women's History* 1 (Spring 1989): 31-62.

Johnson, Linda L. "Transforming Lives: Women's Study Circles in Historical and Cross-Cultural Perspective." *Feminist Teacher* 4 (Spring 1989): 13-15.

Johnson, Tina. "The Impact of the Women's Consciousness on the History of the Present." *Social Justice* 17 (Summer 1990): 126-135.

Kelly, Joan. "Early Feminist Theory and the *Querelle des Femmes*, 1400-1789." *Signs* 8 (Autumn 1982): 4-28.

King, Deborah K. "Multiple Jeopardy, Multiple Consciousness: The Context of a Black Feminist Ideology." *Signs* 14 (Autumn 1988): 42-72.

Kuznesof, Elizabeth Anne, and Robert Oppenheimer. "The Family and Society in Nineteenth-Century Latin America: An Historiographical Introduction." *Journal of Family History* 10 (Autumn 1985): 215-234.

Lambertz, Jan. "Feminist History in Britain." *Radical History Review* 19 (1979): 137-142.

Lavrin, Asuncion. "Comments on Sharon Sievers' 'Six (or More) Feminists in

Search of a Historian.'" *Journal of Women's History* 1 (Fall 1989): 153-157.

-----. "Gender and Latin American History." *Cronicas* 29, no. 2 (1985): 213-225.

-----. "Women in Latin American History." *History Teacher* 14 (May 1981): 387-400.

Lee, Jid. "Words in Silence: An Exercise in Third World Feminist Criticism." *Frontiers* 11, no. 2 & 3 (1990): 66-71.

Macintyre, Martha. "Recent Australian Feminist History." *History Workshop* 5 (Spring 1978): 98-110.

Mallon, Florencia E. "Studying Women's Work in Latin America: Reflections on the Direction of Feminist Scholarship." *Latin American Perspectives* 14 (Spring 1987): 255-261.

McGlashan, Zena Beth. "Women Witness the Russian Revolution: Analyzing Ways of Seeing." *Journalism History* 12 (Summer 1985): 54-61.

Middleton-Keirn, Susan. "Magnolias and Microchips: Regional Sub-cultural Constructions of Femininity." *Sociological Spectrum* 6, no. 1 (1986): 83-107.

Minault, Gail. "Making Invisible Women Visible: Studying the History of Muslim Women in South Asia." *South Asia* 9 (June 1986): 1-14.

Mullin, Molly. "Representations of History, Irish Feminism, and the Politics of Difference." *Feminist Studies* 17 (Spring 1991): 29-50.

Offen, Karen. "Women's Memory, Women's History, Women's Political Action: The French Revolution in Retrospect, 1789-1889-1989." *Journal of Women's History* 1 (Winter 1990): 211-230.

Papanek, Hanna. "False Specialization and the Purdah of Scholarship--A Review Article." *Journal of Asian Studies* 44 (November 1984): 127-148.

Patel, Sujata. "Construction and Reconstruction of Women in Gandhi." *Economic and Political Weekly* 23 (February 20, 1988): 377-387.

Peters, Pauline. "Gender, Development Cycles and Historical Process: A Critique of Recent Research on Women in Botswana." *Journal of South African Studies* 10 (October 1983): 100-122.

Robertson, Claire. "Changing Perspectives in Studies of African Women, 1976-1985." *Feminist Studies* 13 (Spring 1987): 87-136.

-----. "Never Underestimate the Power of Women: The Transforming Vision of African Women's History." *Women's Studies International Forum* 11, no. 5 (1988): 439-454.

Rogers, Susan G. "Efforts toward Women's Development in Tanzania: Gender Rhetoric vs. Gender Realities." *Women and Politics* 2, no. 4 (1982): 23-41.

Rutter, Itala T. C. "Feminist Theory as Practice: Italian Feminism and the Work of Teresa de Lauretis and Dacia Maraini." *Women's Studies International Forum* 13, no. 6 (1990): 565-576.

Sanchez, Virginia Korrol. "In Search of Unconventional Women: Histories of Puerto Rican Women in Religious Vocations Before Mid-Century." *Oral History Review* 16 (Fall 1988): 47-64.

Scarpaci, J. Vincenza. "La Contadina: The Plaything of the Middle Class Woman Historian." *Journal of Ethnic Studies* 9 (Summer 1981): 21-38.

Sievers, Sharon. "Six (or More) Feminists in Search of a Historian." *Journal of*

*Women's History* 1 (Fall 1989): 134-146.

Silverman, Elaine Leslau. "Writing Canadian Women's History 1970-1982: An Historiographical Analysis." *Canadian Historical Review* 63 (December 1982): 513-533.

Sklevicky, Lydia. "More Horses Than Women: On the Difficulties of Founding Women's History in Yugoslavia." *Gender & History* 11 (Spring 1989): 68-75.

Smith, Bonnie G. "The History of Women's History in Nineteenth-Century France." *Western Society for French History* 11 (November 1983): 265-271.

Stanley, Liz. "British Feminist Histories: An Editorial Introduction." *Women's Studies International Forum* 13, no. 1/2 (1990): 3-8.

Stoner, K. Lynn. "Directions in Latin American Women's History, 1977-1985." *Latin American Research Review* 22 (Spring 1987): 101-134.

Strong-Boag, Veronica. "Mapping Women's Studies in Canada: Some Signposts." *Journal of Educational Thought* 17 (August 1983): 94-111.

Terborg-Penn, Rosalyn. "Teaching the History of Black Women." *History Teacher* 13 (February 1980): 245-250.

Tucker, Judith. "Problems in the Historiography of Women in the Middle East: The Case of Nineteenth Century Egypt." *International Journal of Middle East Studies* 15, no. 3 (1983): 321-336.

Walby, Sylvia. "From Private to Public Patriarchy: The Periodisation of British History." *Women's Studies International Forum* 13, no. 1/2 (1990): 91-104.

Wang, Yeujin. "Mixing Memory and Desire: *Red Sorghum*: A Chinese Version of Masculinity and Femininity." *Public Culture* 2 (Fall 1989): 31-53.

Watson, Betty C., Dionne Jones, and Willy Smith. "Sex, Race, and Class: An Alternative Paradigmatic Approach." *Minority Voices* 6 (Fall 1989): 3-12.

White, E. Frances. "Africa On My Mind: Gender, Counter Discourse and African-American Nationalism." *Journal of Women's History* 2 (Spring 1990): 73-97.

# Biography

Albert, Judith Strong. "The Debate in Women's Studies: Contradictory Role Models in the Nineteenth Century--Margaret Fuller and Elizabeth Peabody." *Women's Studies International Forum* 12, no. 4 (1989): 463-474.

Apthorp, Elaine Sargent. "Speaking of Silence: Willa Cather and the "Problem" of Feminist Biography." *Women's Studies* 18, no. 1 (1990): 1-12.

Barr, Marleen. "Deborah Norris Logan, Feminist Criticism, and Identity Theory: Interpreting a Woman's Diary without the Danger of Separatism." *Biography* 8 (Winter 1985): 12-24.

Barry, Kathleen. "Biography and the Search for Women's Subjectivity." *Women's Studies International Forum* 12, no. 6 (1989): 561-578.

-----. "The New Historical Synthesis: Women's Biography." *Journal of Women's History* 1 (Winter 1990): 75-105.

Bassett, Mark T. "Man-Made Tales: Deconstructing Biography as a Feminist Act." *Auto/Biography Studies* 3 (Fall 1987): 46-56.

Mullen, Shirley A. "Women's History and Hannah More." *Fides et Historia* 19 (February 1987): 5-21.

Reagon, Bernice Johnson. "My Black Mothers and Sisters, or On Beginning a Cultural Autobiography." *Feminist Studies* 8 (Spring 1982): 81-96.

Rooke, Patricia T., and R. L. Schnell. "The Making of a Feminist Biography: Reflections on a Miniature Passion." *Atlantis: A Women's Studies Journal* 15 (Fall 1989): 56-64.

Smith, Sidonie. "The Impact of Critical Theory on the Study of Autobiography: Marginality, Gender, and Autobiographical Practice." *Auto/Biography Studies* 3 (Fall 1987): 1-12.

-----. "Self, Subject, and Resistance: Marginalities and Twentieth-Century Autobiographical Practice." *Tulsa Studies in Women's Literature* 9 (Spring 1990): 11-24.

Stanley, Liz. "Moments of Writing: Is There a Feminist Auto/Biography?" *Gender & History* 2 (Spring 1990): 58-67.

Wolff, Cynthia Griffin. "Emily Dickinson, Elizabeth Cady Stanton, and the Task of Discovering a Usable Past." *Massachusetts Review* 30 (Winter 1989): 629-644.

## Women's History and Labor

Boris, Eileen. "Looking at Women's Historians Looking at 'Difference.'" *Wisconsin Women's Law Journal* 3 (1987): 213-238.

Druker, Jan. "Women's History and Trade Union Records." *Society for the Study of Labour History* 36 (Spring 1978): 28-35.

Endres, A. M., and Katrina Alford. "Discussion: A Twentieth Century Economic Historian on Colonial Women's Employment: Comment on Alford. On Polemics and Patriarchy: A Rejoinder." *Labour History* 52 (May 1987): 88-95.

Hall, Jacqueline Dowd, Sandi E. Cooper, Dr. Rosalind Rosenberg, and Alice Kessler-Harris. "Women's History Goes to Trial: EEOC v. Sears, Roebuck and Company." *Signs* 11 (Summer 1986): 751-779.

Haskell, Thomas, and Sanford Levinson. "Academic Freedom and Expert Witnessing: Historians and the *Sears* Case." *Texas Law Review* 66 (1988): 301-331.

Helmbold, Lois Rita. "Writing the History of Black and White Working Class Women." *Women's Studies* 17, no. 1/2 (1989): 37-48.

-----, and Ann Schofield. "Women's Labor History, 1790-1945." *Reviews in American History* 17 (December 1989): 501-518.

Hilden, Patricia. "Re-Writing the History of Socialism: Working Women and the Parti Ouvrier Français." *European History Quarterly* 17 (July 1987): 285-306.

Kay, Herma Hill. "Models of Equality." *University of Illinois Law Review* 1 (1985): 57-61.

Levine, Susan. "Labors in the Field: Reviewing Women's Cultural History." *Radical History Review* 35 (1986): 49-56.

Magarey, Susan. "Labour History's New Sub-Title: Social History in Australia in

1981." *Social History* 8 (May 1983): 211-228.

Melosh, Barbara. "Historians and the Servant Problem." *Reviews in American History* 11, no. 1 (1983): 55-58.

Milkman, Ruth. "Women's History and the Sears Case." *Feminist Studies* 12 (1986): 394-395.

Norman, Elizabeth M. "Who and Where Are Nursing's Historians." *Nursing Forum* 20, no. 2 (1981): 138-152.

Scott, Joan Wallach. "Deconstructing Equality-versus-Difference: Or, the Uses of Poststructural Theory for Feminism." *Feminist Studies* 14 (Spring 1988): 37-48.

## Historiography and Sources

Akers, Regina T. "Female Naval Reservists During World War II: A Historiographical Essay." *Minerva: Quarterly Report on Women and the Military* 8 (Summer 1990): 55-61

Barstow, Anne Llewellyn. "On Studying Witchcraft as Women's History: A Historiography of the European Witch Persecutions." *Journal of Feminist Studies in Religion* 4 (Fall 1988): 7-20.

Bloch, Ruth H. "Untangling the Roots of Modern Sex Roles: A Survey of Four Centuries of Change." *Signs* 4 (Winter 1978): 237-252.

Bracey, John H., Jr. "Afro-American Women: A Brief Guide to Writings from Historical and Feminist Perspectives." *Contributions in Black Studies* no. 8 (1986/87): 106-110.

Carley, Julia. "Tracing Your Matrilineal Ancestry." *History Workshop* 16 (Autumn 1983): 137-142.

Castillo-Speed, Lillian. "Chicana Studies: A Selected List of Materials Since 1980." *Frontiers* 11, no. 1 (1990): 66-84.

Chakravarti, Uma, and Kumkum Roy. "In Search of Our Past: A Review of the Limitations and Possibilities of the Historiography of Women in Early India." *Economic and Political Weekly* 23 (April 30, 1988): WS-2--WS-10.

Chepesuik, Ron. "The Winthrop College Archives and the Special Collections: Selected Resources for the Study of Women's History." *South Carolina History Magazine* 82 (April 1981): 143-172.

Christian, Donna. "Women's Studies Archives in Northwest Ohio: Part 4: Toledo-Lucas County Public Library." *Northwest Ohio Quarterly* 57 (Winter 1985): 30-36.

Copelman, D. M. "Liberal Ideology, Sexual Difference, and the Lives of Women: Recent Works in British History." *Journal of Modern History* 62 (June 1990): 315-345.

Cronon, William, Howard R. Lamar, Katherine G. Morrissey, and Jay Gidin. "Women and the West: Rethinking the Western History Survey Course." *Western History Quarterly* 17 (July 1986): 269-290.

Donovan, Mary S. "Women and Mission: Towards a More Inclusive Historiography." *Historical Magazine of the Protestant Episcopal Church* 53, 4 (December 1984): 297-306.

Eichler, Margit, and Carol Ann Nelson. "History and Historiography: The Treatment in American Histories of Significant Events concerning the Status of Women." *Historian* 40 (November 1977): 1-16.

Foner, Philip S. "A Pioneer Proposal for a Women's Library." *Journal of Library History* 13 (Spring 1978): 157-159.

Foote, Cheryl J. "The History of Women in New Mexico: A Selective Guide to Published Sources." *New Mexico Historical Review* 57 (October 1982): 387-394.

Haggis, Jane. "Gendering Colonialism or Colonising Gender?: Recent Women's Studies Approaches to White Women and the History of British Colonialism." *Women's Studies International Forum* 13, no. 1/2 (1990): 105-116.

Hahner, June E. "Recent Research on Women in Brazil." *Latin American Research Review* 20, no. 3 (1985): 163-179.

Jeffrey, Kirk, and Diane Cirksena. "Women's History in the High School Survey: An Integrationist Approach." *History Teacher* 11 (November 1977): 39-46.

Kolmer, Elizabeth. "Catholic Women Religious and Women's History: A Survey of the Literature." *American Quarterly* 30 (Winter 1978): 639-651.

Kuznesof, Elizabeth Anne, and Robert Oppenheimer. "The Family and Society in Nineteenth-Century Latin America: An Historiographical Introduction." *Journal of Family History* 10 (Autumn 1985): 215-234.

Lerner, Gerda. "Priorities and Challenges in Women's History Research." *Perspectives* 26, no. 4 (1988): 17-20.

Loeb, Catherine. "La Chicana: A Bibliographic Survey." *Frontiers* 5 (Summer 1980): 59-74.

Martz, David J., Jr., comp. "Women's Studies Archives in Northwest Ohio: Part 2: Ward M. Canaday Center, University of Toledo." *Northwest Ohio Quarterly* 56 (Summer 1984): 111-112.

Moseley, Eva S. "Sources for the 'New Women's History.'" *American Archivist* (Spring 1980): 180-190.

O'Hanlon, Rosalind. "Cultures of Rule, Communities of Resistance: Gender, Discourse and Traditions in Recent South Asian Historiographies." *Social Analysis* no. 25 (September 1989): 94-114.

Offen, Karen M. "'First Wave' Feminism in France: New Work and Resources." *Women's Studies International Forum* 5 (1982): 685-689.

-----. "The New Sexual Politics of French Revolutionary Historiography." *French Historical Studies* 16 (Fall 1990): 909-922.

Papanek, Hanna. "False Specialization and the Purdah of Scholarship--A Review Article." *Journal of Asian Studies* 44 (November 1984): 127-148.

Patterson, Tiffany R. "Toward a Black Feminist Analysis: Recent Works by Black Women Scholars." *Women Organizing* no. 11 (Summer 1983): 33-36.

Perrot, Michelle, et. al. "Women's Culture and Women's Power: An Attempt at Historiography." *Journal of Women's History* 1 (Spring 1989): 63-88.

Peters, Pauline. "Gender, Development Cycles and Historical Process: A Critique of Recent Research on Women in Botswana." *Journal of South African Studies* 10 (October 1983): 100-122.

Relph, Anne Kimbell. "The World Center for Women's Archives, 1935-1940." *Signs* 4 (Spring 1979): 597-603.

Robertson, Claire. "Changing Perspectives in Studies of African Women, 1976-1985." *Feminist Studies* 13 (Spring 1987): 87-136.

Roth, Darlene R. "Growing Like Topsy: Research Guides to Women's History." *Journal of American History* 70 (June 1983): 95-100.

Ruiz, Vicki L. "Texture, Text and Context: New Approaches in Chicano Historiography." *Mexican Studies/Estudios Mexicanos* 2 (Winter 1986): 145-152.

Saunders, Kay. "Recent Women's Studies Scholarship: I: History." *Hecate: An Interdisciplinary Journal of Women's Liberation* 16, no. 1/2 (1990): 171-183.

Scott, Patricia Lyn, and Maureen Ursenbach Beecher, comps. "Mormon Women: A Bibliography in Process, 1977-1985." *Journal of Mormon History* 12 (1985): 113-128.

Silverman, Elaine Leslau. "Writing Canadian Women's History 1970-1982: An Historiographical Analysis." *Canadian Historical Review* 63 (December 1982): 513-533.

Smith, Bonnie. "The Contribution of Women to Modern Historiography in Great Britain, France and the United States 1750-1940." *American Historical Review* 89 (June 1984): 709-732.

Tucker, Judith. "Problems in the Historiography of Women in the Middle East: The Case of Nineteenth Century Egypt." *International Journal of Middle East Studies* 15, no. 3 (1983): 321-336.

# U.S. SOUTHERN WOMEN

## Biography

Baker, Vaughan B. "*Cherchez les Femmes*: Some Glimpses of Women in Early Eighteenth-Century Louisiana." *Louisiana History* 31 (Winter 1990): 21-37.

Bashaw, Carolyn Terry. "'To Serve the People of the State of Kentucky': Sarah Gibson Blanding and the Development of Administrative Skill, 1923-1941." *Filson Club History Quarterly* 65 (April 1991): 281-301.

Braxton, Joanne M. "Hariet Jacobs' Incidents in the Life of a Slave Girl: The Re-definition of the Slave Girl Narrative." *Massachusetts Review* 27 (Summer 1986): 379-387.

Bryant, F. Russell. "Lady Curzon, The Marchioness from Decatur." *Alabama Historical Quarterly* 44 (Fall/Winter 1982): 213-260.

Campbell, Edward D., Jr., ed. "'Strangers and Pilgrims': The Diary of Margaret Tilloston Kemble Nours, 4 April - 11 November 1862." *Virginia Magazine of History and Biography* 91 (October 1983): 440-508.

Clinton, Catherine. "Fanny Kemble's Journal: A Woman Confronts Slavery on a Georgia Plantation." *Frontiers* 9, no. 3 (1987): 74-79.

Cochran, Robert B. "'All the Songs in the World': The Story of Emma Dusenburg." *Arkansas History Quarterly* 44 (Spring 1985): 3-15.

Coke, Fletch, Eleanor Graham, and Attie Gene Shriver. "First Ladies of Travellers' Rest." *Tennessee Historical Quarterly* 37 (Fall 1978): 321-328.

Cook, Bernard, ed. "Two Depression Era 'Life-Histories' from Marion County, Mississippi, October 1938." *Journal of Mississippi History* 47 (May 1985): 126-128.

Cook, Charles Orson, and James M. Poteet. "'Dem Was Black Times, Sure 'Nough': The Slave Narratives of Lydia Jefferson and Stephen Williams." *Louisiana History* 20 (Summer 1979): 281-292.

Cooke, J. W. "Portrait of a Murderess: Anna Cook(e) Beauchamp." *Filson Club History Quarterly* 65 (April 1991): 209-230.

Copp, Robin VH. "Of Her Time, Before Her Time: Anne King Gregorie, South Carolina's Singular Historian." *South Carolina Historical Magazine* 91 (October 1990): 231-246.

Crowe-Carraco, Carol. "'Perusin' the Pennyrile': Sadie Price, 19th-Century Botanist." *Filson Club History Quarterly* 65 (April 1991): 252-267.

Darkis, Fred R., Jr. "Madame Lalaurie of New Orleans." *Louisiana History* 23 (Fall 1982): 383-399.

Dawe, Louis Belote, and Sandra Gioia Treadway. "Hannah Lee Corbin: The Forgotten Lee." *Virginia Cavalcade* 29 (Autumn 1979): 70-77.

DeGrummond, Jane Lucas. "Cayetana Susana Bosque of Fanqui, 'A Notable Woman.'" *Louisiana History* 23 (Summer 1982): 277-294.

Dolensky, Suzanne T. "Varina Howell Davis (1826-1906), 1889 to 1906: The Years Alone." *Journal of Mississippi History* 47 (May 1985): 90-109.

Durham, Walter T. "Tennessee Countess." *Tennessee Historical Quarterly* 39 (Fall 1980): 323-340.

Gaston, Kay Baker. "The Remarkable Harriet Whiteside." *Tennessee Historical Quarterly* 40 (Winter 1981): 333-347.

Greene, J. Lee. "Anne Spencer of Lynchburg (1882-1975)." *Virginia Cavalcade* 27 (Spring 1978): 178-185.

Hoder-Salmon, Marilyn. "Myrtle Archer McDougal (1866-1965): Leader of Oklahoma's 'Timid Sisters.'" *Chronicles of Oklahoma* 60 (Fall 1982): 332-343.

Holditch, W. Kenneth. "'A Creature Set Apart': Pearl Rivers in the Piney Woods." Noel Polk, ed. *Mississippi's Piney Woods: A Human Perspective* (1986): 103-120.

McArthur, Judith N. "Myth, Reality, and Anomaly: The Complex World of Rebecca Hagerty." *East Texas Historical Journal* 24, no. 2 (1986): 18-32.

McBride, Mary G., and Ann M. McLaurin. "Sarah G. Humphreys: Antebellum Belle to Equal Rights Activist, 1830-1907." *Filson Club History Quarterly* 65 (April 1991): 231-251.

Peacock, Jane Bonner. "Nellie Peters Black (1851-1919): Turn of the Century 'Mover and Shaker.'" *Atlanta History Journal* (Winter 1980): 7-16.

Prioli, Carmine Andrew. "The Indian 'Princess' and the Architect: Origin of a North Carolina Legend." *North Carolina Historical Review* 60 (July 1983): 283-303.

Pyron, Darden Asbury. "Nell Battle Lewis (1893-1956) and the New Southern

Woman." *Perspectives on the American South* 3 (1985): 63-85.

Rawson, Donald M. "Caroline Dormon: A Renaissance Spirit of Twentieth-Century Louisiana." *Louisiana History* 24 (Spring 1983): 121-139.

Ribblett, David L. "From Cross Creek to Richmond: Marjorie Kinnan Rawlings Researches Ellen Glasgow." *Virginia Cavalcade* 36 (Summer 1986): 4-15.

Robertson, Mary D., ed. "Northern Rebel: The Journal of Nellie Kinzie Gordon, Savannah, 1862." *Georgia Historical Quarterly* 70 (Fall 1986): 477-517.

Rouse, Parke Jr. "Belle Huntington, Her Men and Her Muse." *Virginia Magazine of History and Biography* 88 (October 1980): 387-400.

Scura, Dorothy M. "Ellen Glasgow's Virginia: Her Heart's Field." *Virginia Magazine of History and Biography* 94 (January 1986): 40-59.

Stegeman, John F. "Lady of Belvoir: This Matter of Sally Fairfax." *Virginia Cavalcade* 34 (Summer 1984): 4-11.

Stephenson, William. "How Sallie Southall Cotten Brought North Carolina to the Chicago World's Fair of 1893." *North Carolina Historical Review* 58 (October 1981): 364-383.

Still, Judith Anne. "Carrie Still Shepperson: The Hollows of Her Footsteps." *Arkansas History Quarterly* 42 (Spring 1983): 37-46.

Thrasher, Sue, and Eliot Wigginton. "You Can't Be Neutral: An Interview with Ann Braden." *Southern Exposure* 12 (November/December 1984): 79-85.

Trautmann, Frederic. "South Carolina through a German's Eyes: The Travels of Clara Von Gerstner, 1839." *South Carolina Historical Magazine* 85 (July 1984): 220-232.

Willis, Vera Arnold. "The Arkansas Years: 1926-1929." *Arkansas Historical Quarterly* (Spring 1984): 3-54.

Wolfe, Margaret Ripley. "Reflections of an Appalachian Historian: A Personal Odyssey." *Register of the Kentucky Historical Society* 83 (Autumn 1985): 299-314.

-----. "The Southern Lady: Long Suffering Counterpart of the Good Ole' Boy." *Journal of Popular Culture* 11 (Summer 1977): 18-27.

## Theories and Issues

Ad Hoc Committee on the Status of Women in the SHA. "A Statistical Report on the Participation of Women in the Southern Historical Association, 1935-1985." *Journal of Southern History* 52 (May 1986): 282-350.

Amos, Harriet E. "'City Belles': Images and Realities of the Lives of White Women in Antebellum Mobile." *Alabama Review* 34 (January 1981): 3-19.

Atkinson, Maxine P., and Jacqueline Boles. "The Shaky Pedestal: Southern Ladies Yesterday and Today." *Southern Studies* 24 (Winter 1985): 398-406.

Babb, Ellen, and Milly St. Julien. "Public and Private Lives: Women in St. Petersburg at the Turn of the Century." *Tampa Bay History* 8 (Spring/Summer 1986): 4-27.

Boles, Jacqueline, and Maxine P. Atkinson. "Ladies: South by Northwest." *Sociology Spectrum* 6, no. 1 (1986): 63-81.

Bonner, Thomas, Jr. "Ladies of the Old South." *Mississippi Quarterly* 38 (Fall 1985): 447-480.

Brabant, Sarah. "Socialization for Change: The Cultural Heritage of the Southern Woman." *Sociology Spectrum* 6, no. 1 (1986): 51-61.

Brown, Rita Mae. "Oh Southern Men; Oh Southern Women." *Civil War Times Illustrated* 26 (Summer 1987): 49-52.

Clinton, Catherine. "Women and Southern History: Images and Reflections." *Perspectives on the American South* 3 (1985): 45-62.

Dains, Mary K. "Missouri Women in Historical Writing." *Missouri Historical Review* 83 (July 1989): 417-428.

Darden, Donna Kelleher. "Southern Women Writing about Southern Women: Jill McCorkle, Lisa Alther, Ellen Gilchrist, and Lee Smith." *Sociology Spectrum* 6, no. 1 (1986): 109-118.

Dillman, Caroline Matheny. "The Sparsity of Research and Publications on Southern Women: Definitional Complexities, Methodological Problems, and Other Impediments." *Sociology Spectrum* 6, no. 1 (1986): 7-29.

Elkins, Sandra. "'A Share of Honour.'" *History News* 40 (March 1985): 6-13.

Fox-Genovese, Elizabeth. "Scarlett O'Hara: The Southern Lady as New Woman." *American Quarterly* 33 (Fall 1981): 391-411.

Good, Cherry. "The Southern Lady, or the Art of Dissembling." *Journal of American Studies* 23 (April 1989): 72-77.

Hazzard-Gordon, Katrina. "The Interaction of Sexism and Racism in the Old South: The New Orleans Bals du Cordon Bleu." *Minority Voices* 6 (Fall 1989): 13-26.

Lebsock, Suzanne. "Complicity and Contention: Women in the Plantation South." *Georgia Historical Quarterly* 74 (Spring 1990): 59-83.

Leslie, Kent Anderson. "A Myth of the Southern Lady: Antebellum Proslavery Rhetoric and the Proper Place of Woman." *Sociology Spectrum* 6, no. 1 (1986): 31-49.

May, Robert E. "Southern Elite Women, Sectional Extremism, and the Male Political Sphere: The Case of John A. Quitman's Wife and Female Descendants, 1847-1931." *Journal of Mississippi History* 50, no. 4 (1988): 251-285.

Scott, Anne Firor. "How Women Have Changed Georgia--and Themselves." *Atlanta History* 34 (Summer 1990): 5-16.

-----. "Women in Plantation Culture: Or What I Wish I Knew About Southern Women." *South Atlantic Urban Studies* 2 (1978): 24-33.

Silber, Nina. "Intemperate Men, Spiteful Women, and Jefferson Davis: Northern Views of the Defeated South." *American Quarterly* 41 (December 1989): 614-635.

Swain, Martha H. "A New Deal for Mississippi Women, 1933-1943." *Journal of Mississippi History* (August 1984): 191-212.

Watson, Alan D. "Women in Colonial North Carolina: Overlooked and Underestimated." *North Carolina Historical Review* 58 (January 1981): 1-22.

Whisnant, David. "Second Level Appalachian History: Another Look at Some

Fotched-on Women." *Appalachian Journal* 9 (Winter/Spring, 1982): 115-123.
Whites, Lee Ann. "The DeGraflenvied Controversy: Class, Race, and Gender in the New South." *The Journal of Southern History* 54 (August 1988): 449-478.

## UTOPIAS/COMMUNAL SOCIETIES

Albinski, Nan B. "Utopia Reconsidered: Women Novelists and Nineteenth-Century Utopian Visions." *Signs* 13 (Summer 1988): 830-841.

Andreadis, A. Harriette. "A Woman's Commonwealth: The Study in the Coalescence of Social Forms." *Frontiers* 7, no. 3 (1984): 79-86.

Brewer, Priscilla J. "The Demographic Features of the Shaker Decline, 1787-1900." *Journal of Interdisciplinary History* 15 (Summer 1984): 31-52.

Brooks, Leonard. "Sister Aurelia Mace and Her Influence on the Ever-Growing Nature of Shakerism." *Shaker Quarterly* 16 (Summer 1988): 47-60.

Campbell, D'Ann. "Women's Life in Utopia: The Shaker Experiment in Sexual Equality Reappraised--1810 to 1860." *New England Quarterly* 51 (March 1978): 23-38.

Cohn, Josephine. "Communal Life of San Francisco: Jewish Women in 1908." *Western States Jewish History* 20 (October 1987): 15-36.

Conway, Jill K. "Utopian Dream or Dystopian Nightmare? Nineteenth-Century Feminist Ideas about Equality." *Proceedings of the American Antiquarian Society* 96 (October 1986): 285-294.

Crosthwaite, Jane F. "'A White and Seamless Robe': Celibacy and Equality in Shaker Art and Theory." *Colby Library Quarterly* 25 (September 1989): 188-198.

Dawkins, Mary. "Utopia at Oneida Lake." *Daughters of the American Revolution Magazine* 124 (March 1990): 172-177.

Desroches, Richard. "Primitivism and Feminism in Utopia." *Western Society for French History* 15 (November 1987): 142.

Dunfey, Julie. "'Living the Principle' of Plural Marriage: Mormon Women, Utopia, and Female Sexuality in the Nineteenth Century." *Feminist Studies* 10 (Fall 1984): 523-536.

Eckhardt, Celia. "Fanny Wright: Rebel & Communitarian Reformer." *Communal Societies* 4 (Fall 1984): 183-196.

Elliott, Josephine Mirabella. "Madame Marie Fretageot: Communitarian Educator." *Communal Societies* 4 (Fall 1984): 167-182.

Foster, Lawrence. "Free Love and Feminism: John Humphrey Noyes and the Oneida Community." *Journal of the Early Republic* 1 (Summer 1981): 165-183.

Freibert, Lucy M. "World Views in Utopian Novels by Women." *Journal of Popular Culture* 17 (Summer 1983): 49-60.

Gaston, Paul M. "Irony in Utopia: The Discovery of Nancy Lewis." *Virginia Quarterly Review* 60 (Summer 1984): 473-487.

Gordon, Beverly. "Dress in American Communal Societies." *Communal Societies* 5 (Fall 1985): 122-136.

Hayden, Dolores. "Two Utopian Feminists and Their Campaigns for Kitchenless Houses." *Signs* 4 (Winter 1978): 274-290.

Kern, Louis J. "Ideology and Reality: Sexuality and Women's Status in the Oneida Community." *Radical History Review* 20 (Spring/Summer 1979): 180-204.

Kitch, Sally L. "'As a Sign That All May Understand': Shaker Gift Drawings and Female Spiritual Power." *Winterthur Portfolio* 24 (Spring 1989): 1-28.

Lahutsky, Nadia M. "'So God Created Man in His Own Image--Male and Female He Created Them': Shaker Reflections on the Nature of God." *Encounter* 49 (Winter 1988): 1-18.

LaManna, Mary Ann, and Jayme Sokolow. "Women in Community: The Belton Woman's Commonwealth." *Texas Journal of Ideas, History, and Culture* 9 (Spring 1987).

Leach, William. "Looking Forward Together: Feminists and Edward Bellamy." *Democracy* 2 (January 1982): 120-134.

Marini, Stephen A. "A New View of Mother Ann Lee and the Rise of American Shakerism, Part II." *Shaker Quarterly* 18 (Fall 1990): 95-114.

Matthews, Fred. "The Utopia of Human Relations: The Conflict-Free Family in American Social Thought, 1930-1960." *Journal of the History of the Behavioral Sciences* 24, no. 4 (1988): 343-362.

McLaughlin, Mary Martin. "Creating and Recreating Communities of Women: The Case of Corpus Domini, Ferrara, 1406-1452." *Signs* 14 (Winter 1989): 293-320.

Mullaney, Marie Marmo. "Feminism, Utopianism and Domesticity: The Career of Rebecca Buffum Spring, 1811-1911." *New Jersey History* 104 (Fall/Winter 1986): 1-21.

Pohl, Frances K. "Historical Reality or Utopian Ideal? The Woman's Building at the World's Columbian Exposition, Chicago, 1893." *International Journal of Women's Studies* 5 (September/October 1982): 289-311.

Polasky, Janet L. "Utopia and Domesticity: Zoe Galti de Gamond." *Western Society for French History* 11 (November 1983): 273-281.

Ribeiro, Aileen. "Dress in Utopia." *Costume* 21 (1987): 26-33.

Rusinowa, Izabella. "European Utopians in America: The Diary of Kalikst Wolski." *Quaderno* 1 (1988).

Schulenburg, Jane Tibbets. "Women's Monastic Communities, 500-1100: Patterns of Expansion and Decline." *Signs* 14 (Winter 1989): 261-292.

Setta, Susan M. "The Mother-Father God and the Female Christ in Early Shaker Theology." *Journal of Religious Studies* [Ohio] 12 (1985): 56-64.

Sokolow, Jayme A., and Mary Ann Lamanna. "Women and Utopia: The Woman's Commonwealth of Belton, Texas." *Southwestern Historical Quarterly* 87 (April 1984): 371-392.

Stam, Deirdre C. "Melvil and Annie Dewey and the Communitarian Ideal." *Libraries & Culture* 24 (Spring 1989): 125-143.

Taylor, Barbara. "Lords of Creation: Marxism, Feminism, and 'Utopian' Socialism." *Radical America* 14 (July/August 1980): 41-46.

Tumminelli, Roberto. "Etienne Cabet: The Alternative Community in Urban and Rural Settings, or the Adaptation of Theory to Circumstance." *Quaderno* 1 (1988).

Watkins, Susan Cotts, and James McCarthy. "The Female Life Cycle in a Belgian Commune: La Hulpe, 1847-1866." *Journal of Family History* 5 (Summer 1980): 167-179.

Wayland-Smith, Ellen. "The Status and Self-Perception of Women in the Oneida Community." *Communal Societies* 8 (1988): 18-53.

## VIOLENCE

## Domestic Violence

Anderson, Nancy F. "The 'Marriage with a Deceased Wife's Sister Bill' Controversy: Incest Anxiety and the Defense of Family Purity in Victorian England." *The Journal of British Studies* 21 (Spring 1982): 67-86.

Backhouse, Constance. "The Tort of Seduction: Fathers and Daughters in Nineteenth Century Canada." *Dalhousie Law Journal* 10 (June 1986): 45-80.

Bauer, Carol, and Lawrence Ritt. "'A Husband Is a Beating Animal': Frances Power Cobbe Confronts the Wife-Abuse Problem in Victorian England." *International Journal of Women's Studies* 6 (March/April 1983): 99-118.

-----. "Wife-Abuse, Late Victorian English Feminists, and the Legacy of Frances Power Cobbe." *International Journal of Women's Studies* 6 (May/June 1983): 195-207.

Bedard, Marcia. "Domestic Violence: Feminist Responses." *NWSA Journal* 2 (Summer 1990): 464-475.

Bixler, Ray H. "Comment on the Incidence and Purpose of Royal Sibling Incest." *American Ethnologist* 9 (August 1982): 580-582.

Breines, Wini, and Linda Gordon. "The New Scholarship on Family Violence." *Signs* 8 (Spring 1983): 490-531.

Burnston, Sharon Ann. "Babies in the Well: An Underground Insight into Deviant Behavior in Eighteenth Century Philadelphia." *Pennsylvania Magazine of History and Biography* 106 (April 1982): 151-186.

Burton, June K. "Infanticide in Napoleonic France: The Law, the Medical Profession, and the Murdering Mother." *Western Society for French History* 14 (November 1986): 183.

Chapman, Terry L. "'Til Death Do Us Part,' Wife Beating in Alberta, 1905-1920." *Alberta History* 36 (Autumn 1988): 13-22.

Chegwidden, Paula, Lawrence F. Felt, and Anne Miller. "Battered Women: Myths, Realities and New Directions for Future Research." *Atlantis: A Women's Studies Journal* 6 (1981): 186-193.

Cox, Cheryl Anne. "Incest, Inheritance and the Political Forum in Fifth-Century Athens." *The Classical Journal* 85 (October/November 1989): 34-46.

Demause, Lloyd. "The History of Child Assault." *Journal of Psychohistory* 18 (Summer 1990): 1-29.

Foote, Cheryl J. "'My Husband Was a Madman and a Murderer': Josephine Clifford McCrackin, Army Wife, Writer, and Conservationist." *New Mexico Historical Review* 65 (April 1990): 199-224.

Forbes, Thomas R. "Deadly Parents: Child Homicide in Eighteenth and Nineteenth Century England." *Journal of the History of Medicine and Allied Sciences* 41 (April 1986): 175-199.

Fridkis, Ari Lloyd. "Desertion in the American Jewish Immigrant Family: The Work of the National Desertion Bureau in Cooperation with the Industrial Removal Office." *American Jewish History* 71 (December 1981): 285-299.

Friedman, Reena Sigman. "'Send Me My Husband Who Is in New York City': Husband Desertion in the American Jewish Immigrant Community, 1900-1926." *Jewish Social Studies* 44 (Winter 1982): 1-18.

Gilje, Paul A. "Infant Abandonment in Early Nineteenth-Century New York City." *Signs* 8 (Spring 1983): 580-590.

Glenn, Myra C. "Wife Beating: The Darker Side of Victorian Domesticity." *Canadian Review of American Studies* 15 (Spring 1984): 17-33.

Gordon, Linda. "Family Violence, Feminism, and Social Control." *Feminist Studies* 12 (Fall 1986): 453-478.

-----. "The Politics of Child Sexual Abuse: Notes From American History." *Feminist Review* no. 28 (Spring 1988): 56-64.

-----. "Single Mothers and Child Neglect, 1880-1920." *American Quarterly* 37 (Summer 1985): 173-192.

Graulich, Melody. "Violence Against Women in Literature of the Western Family." *Frontiers* 7, no. 3 (1984): 14-20.

Griswold, Robert L. "The Evolution of the Doctrine of Mental Cruelty in Victorian American Divorce, 1790-1900." *Journal of Social History* 20 (Fall 1986): 127-148.

-----. "Law, Sex Cruelty, and Divorce in Victorian America, 1840-1900." *American Quarterly* 38 (Winter 1986): 721-745.

-----. "Sexual Cruelty and the Case for Divorce in Victorian America." *Signs* 11 (Spring 1986): 529-541.

Hammerton, A. James. "Victorian Marriage and the Law of Matrimonial Cruelty." *Victorian Studies* 33 (Winter 1990): 269-292.

Hirschhorn, Norbert. "A Bandaged Secret: Emily Dickinson and Incest." *Journal of Psychohistory* 18 (Winter 1991): 251-282.

Masse, Michelle A. "Gothic Repetition: Husbands, Horrors, and Things that Go Bump in the Night." *Signs* 15 (Summer 1990): 679-709.

May, Martha. "The 'Problem of Duty': Family Desertion in the Progressive Era." *Social Science Review* 62, no. 1 (1988): 40-60.

Nadelhaft, Jerome. "Wife Torture: A Known Phenomenon in Nineteenth-Century America." *Journal of American Culture* 10 (Fall 1987): 39-60.

Potter, David. "Marriage and Cruelty Among the Protestant Nobility in Sixteenth-Century France: Diane de Barbancon and Jean de Rohan, 1561-7." *European History Quarterly* 20 (January 1990): 5-38.

Rajan, Rajeswari Sunder. "The Subject of Sati: Pain and Death in the

Contemporary Discourse on Sati." *Yale Journal of Criticism* 3 (Spring 1990): 1-28.

Rasche, Christine E. "Early Models for Contemporary Thought on Domestic Violence and Women Who Kill Their Mates: A Review of the Literature from 1895 to 1970." *Women & Criminal Justice* 1, no. 2 (1990): 31-54.

Reitsma-Street, Marge. "More Control Than Care: A Critique of Historical and Contemporary Laws for Delinquency and Neglect of Children in Ontario." *Canadian Journal of Women and the Law/Revue juridique 'La femme et le droit'* 3, no. 2 (1989-1990): 510-530.

Rooke, Patricia, and R. L. Schnell. "Charlotte Whitton and the 'Babies for Export' Controversy, 1947-48." *Alberta History* 30 (Winter 1982): 11-16.

Roth, Martha T. "'She Will Die by the Iron Dagger': Adultery and Neo-Babylonian Marriage." *Journal of the Economic and Social History of the Orient* 31 (June 1988): 186-206.

Sharpe, J. A. "Domestic Homicide in Early Modern England." *The Historical Journal* 24 (March 1981): 29-48.

Shulman, David. "The Murderous Bride: Tamil Versions of the Myth of the Devi and the Buffalo Demon." *History of Religions* 16 (November 1976): 120-147.

Smithson, Isaiah. "Great Mothers, Son Lovers and Patriarchy." *Journal of American Culture* 4 (Summer 1981): 23-36.

Snell, James. "Marital Cruelty: Women and the Nova Scotia Divorce Court, 1900-1939." *Acadiensis* 18 (Autumn 1988): 3-32.

Stein, Dorothy K. "Women to Burn: Suttee as a Normative Institution." *Signs* 4 (Winter 1978): 253-268.

Taylor, Karen. "Blessing the House: Moral Motherhood and the Suppression of Physical Punishment." *Journal of Psychohistory* 15 (Summer 1987): 431-454.

Wu, Yenna. "The Inversion of Marital Hierarchy: Shrewish Wives and Henpecked Husbands in Seventeenth Century Chinese Literature." *Harvard Journal of Asiatic Studies* 48, no. 2 (1988): 363-382.

Yang, Anand A. "Whose Sati? Widow Burning in Early 19th-Century India." *Journal of Women's History* 1 (Fall 1989): 8-33.

## Other

Brenner, Sue Woolf. "Dead Woman's Crossing: The Legacy of a Territorial Murder." *Chronicles of Oklahoma* 60 (Fall 1982): 280-293.

Bularzik, Mary. "Sexual Harassment at the Work Place: Historical Notes." *Radical America* 12 (July/August 1978): 25-44.

Burton, William L. "Murder, Booze, and Sex: Three Perspectives on the Roaring Twenties." *Midwest Quarterly* 31 (Spring 1990): 374-395.

Cohen, Patricia Cline. "The Helen Jewett Murder: Violence, Gender, and Sexual Licentiousness in Antebellum America." *NWSA Journal* 2 (Summer 1990): 374-389.

Decew, Judith Wagner. "Violent Pornography: Censorship, Morality and Social Alternatives." *Journal of Applied Philosophy* 1, no. 1 (1984): 79-94.

Fewell, Danna Nolan and David M. Gunn. "Controlling Perspectives: Women, Men, and the Authority of Violence in Judges 4 & 5." *Journal of the American Academy of Religion* 58 (Fall 1990): 389-412.

Huffman, James R., and Julie L. Huffman. "Sexism and Cultural Lag: The Rise of the Jailbait Songs, 1955-1985." *Journal of Popular Culture* 21, no. 2 (1987): 65-83.

Ingalls, Robert P. "Lynching and Establishment Violence in Tampa, 1858-1935." *Journal of Southern History* 53 (November 1987): 613-644.

Klein, Dorie. "Violence Against Women: Some Considerations Regarding Its Causes and Its Elimination." *Crime and Delinquency* 27 (January 1981): 64-80.

Klotter, James C. "Sex, Scandal, and Suffrage in the Gilded Age." *The Historian* 42 (February 1980): 225-243.

Lambertz, Jan. "Sexual Harassment in the Nineteenth Century English Cotton Industry." *History Workshop* 19 (Spring 1985): 29-61.

Lesse, Stanley. "The Status of Violence Against Women: Past, Present, and Future Factors." *American Journal of Psychotherapy* 33 (April 1979): 190-200.

Martin, Benjamin F. "Sex, Property, and Crime in the Third Republic: A Statistical Introduction." *Historical Reflections/Reflexions Historiques* 11 (Fall 1984): 323-350.

Norton, Mary Beth. "Gender and Defamation in Seventeenth-Century Maryland." *William and Mary Quarterly* 44 (January 1987): 3-39.

Pleck, Elizabeth. "Feminist Responses to 'Crimes against Women,' 1868-1896." *Signs* 8 (Spring 1983): 451-470.

Roper, Lyndal. "Will and Honor: Sex, Words and Power in Augsburg Criminal Trials." *Radical History Review* 43 (Winter 1989): 45-71.

Senelick, Laurence. "Ladykillers and Lady Killers: Recent Popular Victoriana." *Victorian Studies* 21 (Summer 1978): 493-526.

Tomes, Nancy. "A 'Torrent of Abuse': Crimes of Violence Between Working-Class Men and Women in London 1840-1875." *Journal of Social History* 11 (Spring 1978): 328-345.

Way, Peter. "Violent Times." *Canadian Review of American Studies* 18 (Fall 1987): 399-405.

## Sex Crimes

Anderson, Nancy F. "The 'Marriage with a Deceased Wife's Sister Bill' Controversy: Incest Anxiety and the Defense of Family Purity in Victorian England." *The Journal of British Studies* 21 (Spring 1982): 67-86.

Angueira, Katherine. "To Make the Personal Political: The Use of Testimony as a Consciousness-Raising Tool Against Sexual Aggression in Puerto Rico." *Oral History Review* 16 (Fall 1988): 65-94.

Backhouse, Constance. "The Tort of Seduction: Fathers and Daughters in Nineteenth Century Canada." *Dalhousie Law Journal* 10 (June 1986): 45-80.

Bixler, Ray H. "Comment on the Incidence and Purpose of Royal Sibling Incest." *American Ethnologist* 9 (August 1982): 580-582.

Cannon, Kenneth L. "'Mountain Common Law': The Extralegal Punishment of Seducers in Early Utah." *Utah Historical Quarterly* 51 (Fall 1983): 308-327.

Carter, John Marshall. "The Status of Rape in Thirteenth-Century England: 1218-1275." *International Journal of Women's Studies* 7 (May/June 1984): 248-259.

Chapman, Terry L. "Sex Crimes in the West, 1890-1920." *Alberta History* 35 (Autumn 1987): 6-21.

Conley, Caroline A. "Rape and Justice in Victorian England." *Victorian Studies* 29 (Summer 1986): 519-536.

Edwards, Susan. "Sex Crimes in the Nineteenth Century." *New Society* 49 (13 September 1979): 562-563.

Engelstein, Laura. "Gender and the Juridical Subject: Prostitution and Rape in Nineteenth-Century Russian Criminal Codes." *The Journal of Modern History* 60 (September 1988): 458-495.

Geis, Gilbert. "Lord Hale, Witches and Rape." *British Journal of Law and Society* 5 (1978): 26-44.

Getman, Karen A. "Sexual Control in the Slaveholding South: The Implementation and Maintenance of a Racial Caste System." *Harvard Women's Law Journal* 7 (Spring 1984): 115-152.

Hall, Jacquelyn Dowd. "The Mind That Burns in Each Body: Women, Rape, and Racial Violence." *Southern Exposure* (November/December): 61-71.

Jennings, Thelma. "'Us Colored Women Had to Go Through a Plenty': Sexual Exploitation of African-American Slave Women." *Journal of Women's History* 1 (Winter 1990): 45-74.

Krone, K. A. "In Search of Jack the Ripper." *Dark Lantern* 2 (1985): 13-31.

Lal, Brij V. "Veil of Dishonour: Sexual Jealousy and Suicide on Fiji Plantations." *Journal of Pacific History* 20 (July 1985): 135-155.

Leibman, Nina C. "Sexual Misdemeanor/Psychoanalytic Felony." *Cinema Journal* 26 (Winter 1987): 27-38.

Lewis, Jan. "The Republican Wife: Virtue and Seduction in the Early Republic." *William and Mary Quarterly* 44 (October 1987): 689-721.

Lincoln, Bruce. "The Rape of Persephone: A Greek Scenario of Women's Initiation." *Harvard Theological Review* 72 (July/October 1979): 223-235.

Lindemann, Barbara S. "'To Ravish and Carnally Know': Rape in Eighteenth-Century Massachusetts." *Signs* 10 (Autumn 1984): 63-82.

Lisak, David. "Sexual Aggression, Masculinity, and Fathers." *Signs* 16 (Winter 1991): 238-262.

Mitchinson, Wendy. "Gynecological Operations on Insane Women: London, Ontario, 1895-1901." *Journal of Social History* 15 (Spring 1982): 467-484.

-----. "Gynecological Operations on the Insane." *Archivaria* 10 (1980): 125-144.

-----. "A Medical Debate in Nineteenth Century English Canada: Ovariotomies." *Histoire sociale/Social History* 17 (May 1984): 133-147.

Morton, Marian J. "Seduced and Abandoned in an American City: Cleveland and Its Fallen Women, 1869-1936." *Journal of Urban History* 11 (August 1985): 443-469.

Nead, Lynda. "Seduction, Prostitution, Suicide: 'On the Brink' by Alfred Elmore." *Art History* 5 (September 1982): 310-322.

Ng, Vivian. "Ideology and Sexuality: Rape Laws in Qing China." *Journal of Asian Studies* 46 (February 1987): 57-71.

Philips, David. "Sex, Race, Violence and the Criminal Law in Victoria: Anatomy of a Rape Case in 1888." *Labour History* 52 (May 1987): 30-49.

Rizzo, Tracy. "Sexual Violence in the Enlightenment: The State, the Bourgeoisie, and the Cult of the Vicitimized Woman." *Western Society for French History* 15 (November 1987): 122-128.

Scafuro, Adele. "Discourse of Sexual Violation in Mythic Accounts and Dramatic Versions of 'The Girl's Tragedy.'" *Differences* 2 (Spring 1990): 126-159.

Schlossman, Stephen, and Stephanie Wallach. "The Crime of Precocious Sexuality: Female Juvenile Delinquency in the Progressive Era." *Harvard Educational Review* 48 (February 1978): 65-94.

Schnur, Susan. "Badges of Shame." *Lilith* 14 (Fall 1989): 14-16.

Schoenewolf, Gerald. "The Feminist Myth About Sexual Abuse." *Journal of Psychohistory* 18 (Winter 1991): 331-344.

Shorter, Edward. "On Writing the History of Rape." *Signs* 3 (Winter 1977): 471-482.

Taylor, Barbara. "'The Men Are as Bad as Their Masters . . .': Socialism, Feminism, and Sexual Antagonism in the London Tailoring Trade in the Early 1830s." *Feminist Studies* 5 (Spring 1979): 7-40.

van Zyl, Mikki. "Rape Mythology." *Critical Arts* 5, no. 2 (1989): 10-36.

Walker, Sue Sheridan. "Convicted Ravishers: Statutory Strictures and Actual Practice in Thirteenth- and Fourteenth-Century England." *Journal of Medieval History* 13 (September 1987): 237-250.

Wriggins, Jennifer. "Rape, Racism, and the Law." *Harvard Women's Law Journal* 6 (Spring 1983): 103-141.

# WOMEN ON THE U.S. WESTERN FRONTIER

## Biography

Ahlquist, Roberta, and Ivan B. Kolozsvari. "Fragments from the Past: A New Teacher in a Frontier Town." *California History* 67, no. 2 (1988): 108-117.

Airheart, Debra Reed. "Caroline Ingalls: A Gentle Pioneer Spirit." *Heritage of the Great Plains* 20 (Winter 1987): 15-20.

Allen, Marney. "Prairie Life: An Oral History of Greta Craig." *Atlantis* 7 (1982): 89-102.

Apostol, Jane. "Gold Rush Widow." *Pacific Historian* 28 (Summer 1984): 49-55.

-----. "Margaret Collier Graham: First Lady of the Foothills." *Southern California Quarterly* 63 (Winter 1981): 348-373.

Armitage, Katie H. "Elizabeth 'Bettie' Duncan: Diary of Daily Life, 1864." *Kansas History* 10 (Winter 1987/88): 275-289.

-----. "'This Far Off Land': The Overland Diary, June-October, 1867 and

California Diary, January-March 1868, of Elizabeth 'Bettie' Duncan." *Kansas History* 12 (Spring 1989): 13-27.

Armitage, Susan. "The Letters of Hester McClung: Another Lady's Life in the Rocky Mountains." *Essays and Monographs in Colorado History* 5 (1987): 79-138.

-----. "Western Women: Beginning to Come into Focus." *Montana* 32 (Summer 1982): 2-9.

Armstrong, Jeanne. "Deserts and Dreams: The Life of Gwyneth Harrington (1894-1978)." *Journal of the Southwest* 30 (Winter 1988): 522-534.

Armstrong, Ruth W. "Nettie Chase's World: The Life of a New Mexico Ranch Woman." *El Palacio* 87 (Summer 1981): 33-37.

Bannan, Helen M. "Newcomers to Navajoland: Transculturation in the Memoirs of Anglo Women, 1900-1945." *New Mexico Historical Review* 59 (April 1984): 165-186.

Barnes, Ruth A. "Autobiography and the Western Woman." *Turn-of-the-Century Woman* 1, no. 1 (1984): 9-21.

Buecker, Thomas R., ed. "Letters of Caroline Frey Winne from Sidney Barracks and Fort Mc Pherson, Nebraska, 1874-1878." *Nebraska History* 62 (Spring 1981): 1-46.

Cheney, Lynne. "The Countess of Flat Creek." *Annals of Wyoming* 55 (Fall 1983): 28-32.

Coen, Rena N. "Eliza Dillon Taliaferro: Portrait of a Frontier Wife." *Minnesota History* 52 (Winter 1990): 146-153.

Davis, Gayle R. "Women's Frontier Diaries: Writing for Good Reason." *Women's Studies* 14, no. 1 (1987): 5-14.

Donnell, Eileen Hickson, ed. "Rowe Creek, 1890-91: Mary L. Fitzmaurice Diary, Part I." *Oregon Historical Quarterly* 83 (Summer 1982): 171-194.

-----. "Rowe Creek, 1890-91: Mary L. Fitzmaurice Diary, Part II." *Oregon Historical Quarterly* 83 (Fall 1982): 288-310.

Edwards, Thomas S. "Strangers in a Strange Land: The Frontier Letters of John and Anna Graves." *Hayes Historical Journal* 6 (Summer 1987): 16-28.

Enstam, Elizabeth York. "Opportunity versus Propriety: The Life and Career of Frontier Matriarch Sarah Horton Cockrell." *Frontiers* 6 (Fall 1981): 106-114.

Gillespie, Anna. "Coxville, Nebraska, to Fay, Oklahoma by Wagon (1899): The Journal of Anna Gillespie." *Nebraska History* 65 (Fall 1984): 344-365.

Gregory, Sarah J. "Pioneer Housewife: The Autobiography of Sally Dodge Morris." *Gateway Heritage* 3 (Spring 1983): 24-33.

Harrell, Claydeen. "Kate Hunter: Palestine's Guardian Angel." *Texas Liberator* 47 (Fall 1986): 78-79.

Heston, Flora Moorman. "'I Think I Will Like Kansas': The Letters of Flora Moorman Heston, 1885-1886." *Kansas History* 6 (Summer 1983): 70-95.

Hoar, Jay S. "Susan Haines Clayton, American Lady, 1851-1948." *Oregon Historical Quarterly* 84 (Summer 1983): 206-210.

Howgill, Woodie. "Honeymoon across the Plains: The Ellen Bell Tootle Diary." *Heritage of the Great Plains* 16 (Summer 1983): 11-17.

Ingells, David T. "Miss Cora Dow." *Cincinnati Historical Society Bulletin* 40 (Fall 1982): 151-166.

Lale, Max S., ed. "Letters from a Bride in Indian Territory, 1889." *Red River Valley History Review* 6 (Winter 1981): 12-24.

Luthy, Dorothy Beckley. "Memoirs of Delia Beckley, 1888-1898." *Oregon Historical Quarterly* 83 (Spring 1982): 5-23.

MacPhail, Elizabeth C. "Lydia Knapp Horton: A 'Liberated' Woman in Early San Diego." *Journal of San Diego History* 27 (Winter 1981): 17-42.

Maddox, Lucy B. "Susan Fenimore Cooper and the Plain Daughters of America." *American Quarterly* 40 (June 1988): 131-146.

Maxwell, Margaret F. "Ida Genung of Peeples Valley: 'Woman of the West.'" *Journal of Arizona History* 25 (Winter 1984): 331-348.

McDaniel, Morning Elizabeth. "Memories of a Pioneer Girl." *Tampa Bay History* 5 (Fall/Winter 1983): 64-74.

McIntosh, Kenneth. "Geronimo's Friend: Angie Debo and the New History." *Chronicles of Oklahoma* 66, no. 2 (1988): 164-177.

Myers, Rex C., ed. "To the Dear Ones at Home: Elizabeth Fisk's Missouri River Trip, 1867." *Montana* 32 (Summer 1982): 40-49.

Myres, Sandra L. "An Arizona Camping Trip: May Banks Stacey's Account of an Outing to Mount Graham in 1879." *Arizona and the West* 23 (Spring 1981): 53-64.

-----. "A Woman's View of the Texas Frontier, 1874: The Diary of Emily K. Andrews." *Southwestern History Quarterly* 86 (July 1982): 49-80.

Peavy, Linda, and Ursula Smith. "Women in Waiting in the Westward Movement: Pamela Dillin Fergus and Emma Stratton Christie." *Montana* 35 (Spring 1985): 2-17.

Petrik, Paula. "Mothers and Daughters of Eldorado: The Fisk Family of Helena, Montana, 1867-1902." *Montana* 32 (Summer 1982): 50-63.

Pieroth, Doris H. "Homestead on Hold: Edna Tompkins's Peace River Letters, 1916." *Pacific Northwest Quarterly* 80 (October 1989): 147-153.

Propst, Nell Brown. "Willa Clanton: A Remarkable Link with Colorado's Past." *Colorado Magazine* 56 (Winter/Spring 1979): 45-55.

Riley, Glenda, ed. "Eighty-Six Years in Iowa: The Memoir of Ada Mae Brown Brinton." *Annals of Iowa* 45 (Winter 1981): 551-567.

-----. "Kansas Frontierswomen Viewed through Their Writings." *Kansas History* 9 (Spring 1986): 2-9.

-----. "Kansas Frontierswomen Viewed through Their Writings: The Diary of Chestina Bowker Allen." *Kansas History* 9 (Summer 1986): 83-95.

-----. "Kansas Frontierswomen Viewed through Their Writings: The Journal of Carrie Robbins." *Kansas History* 9 (Autumn 1986): 138-145.

-----. "Kansas Frontierswomen Viewed through their Writings: The Memoir of Georgiana Packard." *Kansas History* 9 (Winter 1986/87): 182-189.

-----. "Proving Up: The Memoir of 'Girl Homesteader' Martha Stoecher Norby." *South Dakota History* 16 (Spring 1986): 1-17.

Roberts, Virginia Culin. "Heroines on the Arizona Frontier: The First

Anglo-American Women." *Journal of Arizona History* 23 (Spring 1982): 11-34.

Ross, Danita. "The Indian Captivity of Clara Blinn: Who Was to Blame for Her Death?" *American West* 25, no. 3 (1988): 44-47.

Scharf, Lois. "'I Would Go Wherever Fortune Would Direct': Hannah Huntington and the Frontier of the Western Reserve." *Ohio History* 97 (Winter/Spring 1988): 5-28.

Schlissel, Lillian. "Women's Diaries on the Western Frontier." *American Studies* 18 (Spring 1977): 87-100.

Schreier, Jim, ed. "'For This I Had Left Civilization': Julia Davis at Camp McDowell, 1869-1870." *Journal of Arizona History* 29, no. 2 (1988): 185-198.

Simmons, Marc. "Women on the Santa Fe Trail: Diaries, Journals, Memoirs. An Annotated Bibliography." *New Mexico Historical Review* 61 (July 1986): 233-243.

Smith, Annick. "The Two Frontiers of Mary Ronan." *Montana* 39 (Winter 1989): 28-33.

Stiffler, Liz, and Tona Blake. "Fannie Sperry-Steele: Montana's Champion Bronc Rider." *Montana* 32 (Spring 1982): 44-57.

Swanson, Kimberly. "Eva Emery Dye and the Romance of Oregon History." *Pacific Historian* 29 (Winter 1985): 59-68.

Uhler, Margaret Anderson, ed. "Well and Strong and Fearless: Etta Anderson in Washington Territory, 1853-1856." *Montana* 32 (Summer 1982): 32-39.

Urza, Monique. "Catherine Etchart: A Montana Love Story." *Montana* 31 (January 1981): 2-17.

Van Ackeren, Ruth, ed. "Adabelle Cherry Marshall on the Ellison-White Chautauqua Circuit." *Nebraska History* 66 (Summer 1985): 164-183.

Waltz, Anna Langhorne. "West River Pioneer: A Woman's Story, 1911-1915, Part One." *South Dakota History* 17 (Spring 1987): 42-77.

-----. "West River Pioneer: A Woman's Story, 1911-1915, Part Two." *South Dakota History* 17 (Summer 1987): 140-169.

-----. "West River Pioneer: A Woman's Story, 1911-1915, Parts Three and Four." *South Dakota History* 17 (Fall/Winter 1987): 241-295.

Whitlow, Leonard A., and Catherine Copper Whitlow, eds. "My Life as a Homesteader: Fannie Adams Cooper." *Oregon Historical Quarterly* 82 (Spring 1981): 65-84.

## Life on the Frontier

Armitage, Shelley. "Western Heroines: Real and Fictional Cowgirls." *Heritage of Kansas* 12 (Spring 1979): 12-20.

Armitage, Susan. "Household Work and Childrearing on the Frontier: The Oral History Record." *Sociology and Social Research* 63 (April 1979): 467-474.

Atkins, Annette. "Women on the Farming Frontier: The View from Fiction." *Midwest Review* 3 (Spring 1981): 1-10.

Bean, Lee L., Geraldine P. Mineau, Douglas L. Anderton, and Yung-chang Hsueh. "The Fertility Effects of Marriage Patterns in a Frontier American

Population." *Historical Methods* 20 (Fall 1987): 161-171.

Bennion, Sherilyn Cox. "Ada Chase Merritt and the *Recorder*: Pioneer Idaho Editor and Her Newspaper." *Idaho Yesterdays* 25 (Winter 1982): 22-30.

-----. "A Working List of Women Editors of the 19th-Century West." *Journalism History* 7, no. 2 (1980): 60-65.

Birch, Brian P. "Possessed of a Restless Spirit: A Young Girl's Memories of the Southern Iowa Frontier." *Palimpsest* 66 (September/October 1985): 174-184.

Boney, F. N. "A British 'Grand Tour' of Crackerland: Basil and Margaret Hall View Frontier Georgia in 1828." *Georgia Historical Quarterly* 74 (Summer 1990): 277-292.

Brent, Elizabeth Reed. "Childhood on the Western Frontier." *Oregon Historical Quarterly* 83 (Summer 1982): 117-152.

Bush, Corlann Gee. "The Way We Weren't: Images of Women and Men in Cowboy Art." *Frontiers* 7, no. 3 (1984): 73-78.

Castaneda, Antonia I. "Gender, Race, and Culture: Spanish-Mexican Women in the Historiography of Frontier California." *Frontiers* 11, no. 1 (1990): 8-20.

Chaudhuri, Nupur. "Good Homemakers Make Good Neighbors." *Kansas Quarterly* 18 (Summer 1986): 53-63.

Comstock, David A. "Proper Women at the Mines: Life at Nevada City in the 1850s." *Pacific Historian* 28 (Fall 1984): 65-73.

Cordier, Mary Hurlbut. "Prairie Schoolwomen, Mid-1850s to 1920s, in Iowa, Kansas, and Nebraska." *Great Plains Quarterly* 8 (Spring 1988): 102-119.

Curran, Nathaniel B. "Anna Durkee Tauzin Young, 1753-1839: Connecticut Lady, Illinois Pioneer." *Journal of the Illinois State Historical Society* 77 (Summer 1984): 94-100.

deGraaf, Lawrence B. "Race, Sex, and Region: Black Women in the American West, 1850-1920." *Pacific Historical Review* 49 (May 1980): 285-313.

Downs, Fane. "'Tryels and Trubbles': Women in Early Nineteenth-Century Texas." *Southwestern Historical Quarterly* 90 (July 1986): 35-56.

Enstam, Elizabeth York. "The Frontier Woman as City Worker: Women's Occupations in Dallas, Texas, 1856-1880." *East Texas History Journal* (Spring 1980): 12-28.

Fairbanks, Carol. "Lives of Girls and Women on the Canadian and American Prairies." *International Journal of Women's Studies* 2 (September/October 1979): 452-472.

"The First Mission of the Sisters Faithful Companions of Jesus in the North-West Territories, 1883." *Saskatchewan History* 36 (Spring 1983): 70-77.

Fischer, Christiane. "Women in California in the Early 1850s." *Southern California Quarterly* 60 (Fall 1978): 231-253.

Foote, Cheryl J. "The History of Women in New Mexico: A Selective Guide to Published Sources." *New Mexico Historical Review* 57 (October 1982): 387-394.

Foster, Lawrence. "From Frontier Activism to Neo-Victorian Domesticity: Mormon Women in the Nineteenth and Twentieth Centuries." *Journal of Mormon History* 6 (1979): 3-22.

-----. "Polygamy and the Frontier: Mormon Women in Early Utah." *Utah Historical Quarterly* 50 (Summer 1982): 268-289.

Fry, Mildred Covey. "Women on the Ohio Frontier: The Marietta Area." *Ohio History* 90 (Winter 1981): 54-73.

Garcia, Mario T. "The Chicana in American History: The Mexican Women of El Paso, 1880-1920--A Case Study." *Pacific Historical Review* 49 (May 1980): 315-337.

Goetz, Henry Kilian. "Kate's Quarter Section: A Woman in the Cherokee Strip." *Chronicles of Oklahoma* 61 (Fall 1983): 246-267.

Goodwin, Katherine G. "'A Woman's Curosity': Martha Gaffney and Cotton Planting on the Texas Frontier." *East Texas History Journal* 24, no. 2 (1986): 4-17.

Gundersen, Joan R. "The Local Parish as a Female Institution: The Experience of All Saints Episcopal Church in Frontier Minnesota." *Church History* 55 (September 1986): 307-322.

Hampsten, Elizabeth. "A German-Russian Family in North Dakota." *Heritage of the Great Plains* 20 (Winter 1987): 15-20.

"'Home Remedies in Pioneering' From the Effie Laurie Storer Papers." *Saskatchewan History* 42 (Autumn 1989): 104-105.

Jameson, Elizabeth. "Women as Workers, Women as Civilizers: True Womanhood in the American West." *Frontiers* 7, no. 3 (1984): 1-8.

Jensen, Carol. "Cleofas M. Jaramillo on Marriage in Territorial Northern New Mexico." *New Mexico Historical Review* 58 (April 1983): 153-172.

Kay, Jeanne. "Review Article: Western Women's History." *Journal of Historical Geography* 15 (July 1989): 302-305.

Kloberdanz, Timothy J. "The Daughters of Shiphrah: Folk Healers and Midwives of the Great Plains." *Great Plains Quarterly* 9 (Winter 1989): 3-12.

Leaphart, Susan. "Frieda and Belle Fligelman: A Frontier-City Girlhood in the 1890's." *Montana* 32 (Summer 1982): 85-92.

Leonard, Carol, and Isidor Wallimann. "Prostitution and Changing Morality in the Frontier Cattle Towns of Kansas." *Kansas History* 2 (Spring 1979): 34-53.

Locke, Mary Lou. "Out of the Shadows and into the Western Sun: Working Women of the Late Nineteenth-Century Urban Far West." *Journal of Urban History* 16 (February 1990): 175-204.

Matsuda, Mari J. "The West and the Legal State of Women: Explanations of Frontier Feminism." *Journal of the West* 24 (January 1985): 47-56.

Melville, J. Keith. "The First Lady and the Cowgirl." *Pacific Historical Review* 57, no. 1 (1988): 73-76.

Miller, Darlis A. "Cross-Cultural Marriages in the Southwest: The New Mexico Experience, 1846-1900." *New Mexico Historical Review* 57 (October 1982): 335-360.

Morrow, Delores J. "Female Photographers on the Frontier: Montana's Lady Photographic Artists, 1866-1900." *Montana* 32 (Summer 1982): 76-84.

Murphy, Miriam B. "Women in the Utah Work Force from Statehood to World War II." *Utah Historical Quarterly* 50 (1982): 139-159.

Myres, Sandra L. "Army Women's Narratives as Documents of Social History: Some Examples from the Western Frontier, 1840-1900." *New Mexico Historical Review* 65 (April 1990): 175-198.

-----. "Romance and Reality on the American Frontier: View of Army Wives." *Western Historical Quarterly* 13 (October 1982): 409-428.

Nomura, Gail M. "Tsugiki, a Grafting: A History of a Japanese Pioneer Woman in Washington State." *Women's Studies* 14, no. 1 (1987): 15-37.

Norwood, Vera L. "Western Women and the Environment: A Review Essay." *New Mexico Historical Review* 65 (April 1990): 267-275.

Oxford, June. "Rain at the Drop of a Hatfield." *Californians* 6 (May/June 1988).

Paradis, Roger. "Henriette, *La capuche*: The Portrait of a Frontier Midwife." *Canadian Folklore* 3, no. 2 (1981): 10-26.

Peterson, Susan. "Religious Communities of Women in the West: The Presentation Sisters' Adaptation to the Northern Plains Frontier." *Journal of the West* 21 (April 1982): 65-70.

Petrik, Paula. "Capitalists with Rooms: Prostitution in Helena, Montana, 1865-1900." *Montana* 31 (April 1981): 28-41.

-----. "The Gentle Tamers in Transition: Women in the Trans-Mississippi West." *Feminist Studies* 11, no. 3 (1985): 677-694.

Pickle, Linda Schelbitzki. "Rural German-Speaking Women in Early Nebraska and Kansas: Ethnicity as a Factor in Frontier Adaptation." *Great Plains Quarterly* 9 (Autumn 1989): 239-251.

Richard, K. Keith. "Of 'Gingham,' 'Barn Doors,' and 'Exquisites': George H. Hines on Pioneer Fashion." *Oregon Historical Quarterly* 90 (Winter 1989): 385-393.

Ridgley, Ronald. "'History with a Heart'--A Frontier Historian Looks at the 'Little House' Books of Laura Ingalls Wilder." *Heritage of the Great Plains* 20 (Winter 1987): 21-27.

Riley, Glenda. "American Daughters: Black Women in the West." *Montana* 38 (Spring 1988): 14-27.

-----. "European Views of White Women in the American West." *Journal of the West* 21 (April 1982): 71-81.

-----. "The 'Female Frontier' in Illinois." *Mid-America* 67 (April/July 1985): 69-82.

-----. "'Not Gainfully Employed': Women on the Iowa Frontier, 1833-1870." *Pacific Historical Review* 49 (May 1980): 237-264.

-----. "Torn Asunder: Divorce in Early Oklahoma Territory." *Chronicles of Oklahoma* 77 (Winter 1989/90): 392-413.

-----. "Women in the West." *Journal of American Culture* 3 (Summer 1980): 311-329.

-----. "Women on the Great Plains: Recent Developments in Research." *Great Plains Quarterly* 5 (Spring 1985): 81-92.

-----. "Women's History from Women's Sources: Three Examples from Northern Dakota." *North Dakota History* 52 (Spring 1985): 2-9.

Rochlin, Harriet. "Riding High: Annie Oakley's Jewish Contemporaries--Was the

West Liberating for Jewish Women?" *Lilith* 14 (Fall/Winter 1985/86): 14-18.

Rogers, Mary Beth. "Texas Women: A Celebration of History." *Texas Liberator* 45 (Winter 1984): 129-133.

Schaedel, Grace Logan. "The Story of Ernest and Lizzie Logan--A Frontier Courtship." *Annals of Wyoming* 54 (Fall 1982): 48-61.

Schlereth, Thomas J. "Chautauqua: A Middle Landscape of the Middle Class." *Old Northwest* 12 (Fall 1986): 265-278.

Schrems, Suzanne H. "Teaching School on the Western Frontier: Acceptable Occupation for Nineteenth Century Women." *Montana* 37 (Summer 1987): 54-63.

Schwantes, Carlos A. "Free Love and Free Speech on the Pacific Northwest Frontier." *Oregon Historical Quarterly* 82 (Fall 1981): 271-293.

Shine, Carolyn R. "Scalping Knives and Silk Stockings: Clothing the Frontier, 1780-1795." *Dress* 14 (1988): 39-47.

Stern, Norton B. "The First Triplets Born in the West--1867." *Western States Jewish History* 19 (July 1987): 299-305.

Swagerty, William R. "Marriage and Settlement Patterns of Rocky Mountain Trappers and Traders." *Western Historical Quarterly* 11 (April 1980): 159-180.

Sylvester, Stephen G. "Avenues for Ladies Only: The Soiled Doves of East Grand Forks 1887-1915." *Minnesota History* 51 (Winter 1989): 290-300.

Taylor, Quintard. "The Emergence of Black Communities in the Pacific Northwest, 1864-1910." *Journal of Negro History* 64 (Fall 1979): 342-354.

Underwood, June. "Civilizing Kansas: Women's Organizations, 1880-1920." *Kansas History* 7 (Winter 1984/85): 291-306.

-----. "Plains Women, History and Literature: A Selected Bibliography." *Heritage of the Great Plains* 16 (Summer 1983): 41-46.

-----. "Western Women and True Womanhood: Culture and Symbol in History and Literature." *Great Plains Quarterly* 5 (Spring 1985): 93-106.

Underwood, Kathleen. "The Pace of Their Own Lives: Teacher Training and the Life Course of Western Women." *Pacific Historical Review* 55 (November 1986): 513-530.

Wagner, Sally Roesch. "The Pioneer Daughters Collection of the South Dakota Federation of Women's Clubs." *South Dakota History* 19 (Spring 1989): 95-109.

Wales, Martha Gray. "When I Was a Little Girl: Things I Remember from Living at Frontier Military Posts." Willard B. Pope, ed. *North Dakota History* 50 (Spring 1983): 12-22.

Wayski, Margaret. "Women and Mining in the Old West." *Journal of the West* 20, no. 2 (1981): 38-47.

Webb, Anne B. "Forgotten Persephones: Women Farmers on the Frontier." *Minnesota History* 50 (Winter 1986): 134-148.

West, Elliott. "Child's Play: Tradition and Adaptation on the Frontier." *Montana* 38 (Winter 1988): 2-15.

## Moving West and Homesteading

Bauman, Paula M. "Single Women Homesteaders in Wyoming, 1880-1930." *Annals of Wyoming* 58 (Spring 1986): 39-49.

Benson, Nancy C. "Pioneering Women of New Mexico." *El Palacio* 85 (Summer 1979): 8-13, 34-38.

Bledsoe, Lucy Jane. "Adventuresome Women on the Oregon Trail: 1840-1867." *Frontiers* 7, no. 3 (1984): 22-29.

Conlin, Joseph R. "Eating on the Run: Organizing Meals on the Overland Trail." *California History* 64 (Summer 1985): 218-225.

Davis, Rodney O., ed. "A Hoosier Family Moves West, 1868-1895: Part I." *Indiana Magazine of History* 86 (March 1990): 50-93.

-----. "A Hoosier Family Moves West, 1868-1895: Part II." *Indiana Magazine of History* 86 (June 1990): 131-177.

Fredriksson, Kristine. "Growing Up on the Road: The Children of Wild West Shows and Rodeos." *Journal of American Culture* 8 (Summer 1985): 19-24.

Fryer, Judith. "Recovering the Garden: Women's Fantasies and Experiences of the Western Frontier." *Old Northwest* 10 (Fall 1984): 339-361.

Harmon, Florence. "Reminiscence: Florence Harmon on Depression-Era Homesteading in Lincoln County." *Oregon Historical Quarterly* 89, no. 1 (1988): 46-69.

Harris, Katherine. "Sex Roles and Work Patterns Among Homesteading Families in Northeastern Colorado, 1873-1920." *Frontiers* 7, no. 3 (1984): 43-49.

Hernandez, Salome. "No Settlement Without Women: Three Spanish California Settlement Schemes, 1790-1800." *Southern California Quarterly* 72 (Fall 1990): 203-234.

Hiatt, Richard G. "Lady Troupers along the Oregon Trail." *Dutch Quarterly Review of Anglo-American Letters* 19, no. 2 (1989): 113-123.

Jeffrey, Julie Roy. "'There Is Some Splendid Scenery': Women's Responses to the Great Plains Landscape." *Great Plains Quarterly* 8 (Spring 1988).

Kohl, Seena B. "Memories of Homesteading and the Process of Retrospection." *Oral History Review* 17 (Fall 1989): 25-46.

Lindgren, H. Elaine. "Ethnic Women Homesteading on the Plains of North Dakota." *Great Plains Quarterly* 9 (Summer 1989): 157-173.

Mineau, Geraldine P., Lee L. Bean, and Douglas L. Anderson. "Migration and Fertility: Behavioral Change on the American Frontier." *Journal of Family History* 14, no. 1 (1989): 43-54.

Myres, Sandra L. "Mexican Americans and Westering Anglos: A Feminine Perspective." *New Mexico Historical Review* 57 (October 1982): 317-334.

----. "Women on the Santa Fe Trail." *Essays and Monographs in Colorado History* no. 6 (1987): 27-46.

Norwood, Vera L. "Heroines of Nature: Four Women Respond to the American Landscape." *Environmental Review* 8 (1984): 34-56.

Riley, Glenda. "The Frontier in Process: Iowa's Trail Women as a Paradigm."
    *Annals of Iowa* 46 (Winter 1982): 167-197.
-----. "Women's Responses to the Challenges of Plains Living." *Great Plains
    Quarterly* 9 (Summer 1989): 174-184.
Sunoo, Sonia S. "Korean Women Pioneers of the Pacific Northwest." *Oregon
    Historical Quarterly* 79 (Spring 1978): 51-64.
Thompson, Tommy R., ed. "Searching for the American Dream in Arkansas:
    Letters of a Pioneer Family." *Arkansas Historical Quarterly* 38 (Summer
    1979): 167-181.
Webb, Anne B. "Minnesota Women Homesteaders: 1863-1889." *Journal of Social
    History* 23, no. 1 (1989): 115-136.

## Native Americans

Abbott, Devon. "Ann Florence Wilson: Matriarch of the Cherokee Female
    Seminary." *Chronicles of Oklahoma* 67 (Winter 1989/90): 426-437.
-----. "'Commendable Progress': Acculturation at the Cherokee Female
    Seminary." *American Indian Quarterly* 11 (Summer 1987): 187-201.
-----. "Medicine for the Rosebuds: Health Care at the Cherokee Female Seminary,
    1876-1909." *American Indian Culture and Research Journal* 12 (1988): 59-71.
Ackerman, Lillian A. "The Effect of Missionary Ideals on Family Structure and
    Women's Roles in Plateau Indian Culture." *Idaho Yesterdays* 31
    (Spring/Summer 1987): 64-74.
Allen, Paula Gunn. "Lesbians in American Indian Culture." *Conditions* 3 (Spring
    1981): 67-87.
Allen, Susan L. "Progressive Spirit: The Oklahoma and Indian Territory
    Federation of Women's Clubs." *Chronicles of Oklahoma* 66 (Spring 1988):
    4-21.
Babcock, Barbara A. "At Home, No Women Are Storytellers: Potteries, Stories,
    and Politics in Cochiti Pueblo." *Journal of the Southwest* 30 (Autumn 1988):
    356-389.
Bahr, Donald, and Susan Fenger. "Indians and Missions: Homage to and Debate
    with Ruport Costo and Jeanette Henry." *Journal of the Southwest* 31 (Autumn
    1989): 300-321.
Banks, Anne. "Jessie Donaldson Schultz and Blackfeet Crafts." *Montana* 33
    (Autumn 1983): 18-35.
Bernstein, Alison. "A Mixed Record: The Political Enfranchisement of American
    Indian Women During the Indian New Deal." *Journal of the West* 23 (July
    1984): 13-20.
-----. "Outgrowing Pocahontas: Toward a New History of American Indian
    Women." *Minority Notes* 2 (Spring/Summer 1981).
Blackwood, Evelyn. "Sexuality and Gender in Certain Native American Tribes:
    The Case of Cross-Gender Females." *Signs* 10 (Autumn 1984): 27-42.
Bonvillain, Nancy. "Gender Relations in Native North America." *American Indian
    Culture and Research Journal* 13, no. 2 (1989): 1-28.

Brady, Victoria, Sarah Crome, and Lyn Reese. "Resist! Survival Tactics of Indian Women." *California History* 63 (Spring 1984): 140-151.

Braund, Kathryn E. Holland. "Guardians of Tradition and Handmaidens to Change: Women's Roles in Creek Economic and Social Life During the Eighteenth Century." *American Indian Quarterly* 14 (Summer 1990): 239-258.

Brodribb, Somer. "The Traditional Roles of Native Women in Canada and the Impact of Colonization." *Canadian Journal of Native Studies* 4, no. 1 (1984): 85-103.

Brown, Jennifer S. H. "Woman as Centre and Symbol in the Emergence of Metis Communities." *Canadian Journal of Native Studies* 3, no. 1 (1983): 39-46.

Buckley, Thomas. "Menstruation and the Power of Yurok Women: Methods in Cultural Reconstruction." *American Ethnologist* 9, no. 1 (1982): 47-60.

Buffalohead, Priscilla K. "Farmers, Warriors, Traders: A Fresh Look at Ojibway Women." *Minnesota History* 48 (Summer 1983): 236-244.

Castellano, Marlene Brant. "Women in Huron and Ojibwa Societies." *Canadian Woman Studies/Les cahiers de la femme* 10 (Summer/Fall 1989): 45-48.

Conte, Christine. "Ladies, Livestock, Land and Lucre: Women's Networks and Social Status on the Western Navajo Reservation." *American Indian Quarterly* 6 (Spring/Summer 1982): 105-124.

Ewers, John C. "Climate, Acculturation, and Costume: A History of Women's Clothing Among the Indians of the Southern Plains." *Plains Anthropologist* 25, no. 7 (1980): 63-82.

Frisbie, Charlotte J. "Traditional Navajo Women: Ethnographic and Life History Portrayals." *American Indian Quarterly* 6 (Spring/Summer 1982): 11-27.

Gray, John S. "The Story of Mrs. Picotte-Galpin, a Sioux Heroine: Eagle Woman Becomes a Trader and Counsels for Peace, 1868-1888." *Montana* 36 (Summer 1986): 2-21.

-----. "The Story of Mrs. Picotte-Galpin, a Sioux Heroine: Eagle Woman Learns about White Ways and Racial Conflict, 1820-1868." *Montana* 36 (Spring 1986): 2-21.

Green, Rayna. "Native American Women: A Review Essay." *Signs* 6 (Winter 1980): 248-267.

Griffen, Joyce. "Life Is Harder Here: The Case of Urban Navajo Woman." *American Indian Quarterly* 6 (Spring/Summer 1982): 90-104.

Hartmann, Susan M. "Women's Work Among the Plains Indians." *Gateway Heritage* 3 (Spring 1983): 2-9.

Harris, Betty J. "Ethnicity and Gender in the Global Periphery: A Comparison of Basotho and Navajo Women." *American Indian Culture and Research Journal* 14, no. 4 (1990): 15-38.

Herring, Rebecca. "Their Work Was Never Done: Women Missionaries on the Kiowa-Comanche Reservation." *Chronicles of Oklahoma* 64 (Spring 1986): 69-83.

Hoig, Stan. "Diana, Tiana or Talihana? The Myth and Mystery of Sam Horton's Cherokee Wife." *Chronicles of Oklahoma* 64 (Summer 1986): 53-59.

Hurtado, Albert L. "'Hardly a Farm House--A Kitchen without Them': Indian and

White Households on the California Borderland Frontier in 1860." *Western Historical Quarterly* 13 (July 1982): 245-270.

Johnson, David L., and Raymond Wilson. "Gertrude Simmons Bonnin, 1876-1938: 'Americanize the First Americans'." *American Indian Quarterly* 12 (Winter 1988): 27-40.

Kaplan, Sidney. "Historical Efforts to Encourage White-Indian Intermarriage in the United States and Canada." *International Social Sciences Review* 65 (Summer 1990): 126-132.

Kidwell, Clara Sue. "The Power of Women in Three American Indian Societies." *Journal of Ethnic Studies* 6 (Fall 1978): 113-122.

Kirk, Sylvia Van. "The Role of Native Women in the Fur Trade Society of Western Canada, 1670-1830." *Frontiers* 7, no. 3 (1984): 9-13.

Knack, M. C. "Philene T. Hall, Bureau-of-Indian-Affairs Matron: Planned Culture Change of Washakie Shoshone Women." *Prologue* 22 (Summer 1990): 151-168.

Koehler, Lyle. "Native Women of the Americas: A Bibliography." *Frontiers* 6 (Fall 1981): 73-101.

Koester, Susan H. "'By the Words of Thy Mouth Let Thee Be Judged': The Alaska Native Sisterhood Speaks." *Journal of the West* 27 (April 1988): 35-44.

LaFromboise, Teresa D., Anneliese M. Heyle, and Emily J. Ozer. "Changing and Diverse Roles of Women in American Indian Cultures." *Sex Roles* 22 (April 1990): 455-476.

Liberty, Margot. "Hell Came with Horses: Plains Indian Women in the Equestrian Era." *Montana* 32 (Summer 1982): 10-19.

Lyon, William H. "Gladys Reichard at the Frontiers of Navajo Culture." *American Indian Quarterly* 13 (Spring 1989): 137-164.

Mathes, Valerie Sherer. "American Indian Women and the Catholic Church." *North Dakota History* 47 (Fall 1980): 20-25.

-----. "Helen Hunt Jackson: A Legacy of Indian Reform." *Essays and Monographs in Colorado History* no. 4 (1986): 25-58.

-----. "Helen Hunt Jackson and the Campaign for Ponca Restitution, 1880-1881." *South Dakota History* 17 (Spring 1987): 23-41.

-----. "Helen Hunt Jackson and the Ponca Controversy." *Montana* 39 (Winter 1989): 42-53.

-----. "Helen Hunt Jackson: Official Agent to the California Mission Indians." *Southern California Quarterly* 63 (Spring 1981): 63-82.

-----. "Indian Philanthropy in California: Annie Bidwell and the Mechoopda Indians." *Arizona and the West* 25 (Summer 1983): 153-166.

-----. "Native American Women in Medicine and the Military." *Journal of the West* 21 (April 1982): 41-48.

-----. "Nineteenth Century Women and Reform: The Women's National Indian Association." *American Indian Quarterly* 14 (Winter 1990): 1-18.

-----. "Susan LaFlesche Picotte: Nebraska's Indian Physician, 1865-1915." *Nebraska History* 63 (Winter 1982): 502-530.

McDonnell, Janet A. "Sioux Women: A Photographic Essay." *South Dakota*

*History* 13 (Fall 1983): 227-244.

Medicine, Bea. "American Indian Family: Cultural Change and Adaptive Strategies." *Journal of Ethnic Studies* 8 (Winter 1981): 13-23.

Metcalf, Ann. "Navajo Women in the City: Lessons from a Quarter-Century of Relocation." *American Indian Quarterly* 6 (Spring/Summer 1982): 71-89.

Moore, John H. "The Dialectics of Cheyenne Kinship: Variability and Change." *Ethnology* 27, no. 3 (1988): 253-269.

Munroe, Mary Barr. "The Seminole Women of Florida." *Tequesta* no. 41 (1981): 23-32.

Ogden, Annegret. "A Lady Tours the Wigwams: The Voice of Idea Pfeiffer, Amateur Ethnologist and Globe Trotter from Austria." *Californians* 7 (March/April 1990): 14-16, 54-55.

Olsen, Karen. "Native Women and the Fur Industry." *Canadian Woman Studies/Les cahiers de la femme* 10 (Summer/Fall 1989): 55-57.

Oshana, Maryann. "Native American Women in Westerns: Reality and Myth." *Frontiers* 6 (Fall 1981): 46-50.

Perdue, Theda. "Cherokee Women and the Trail of Tears." *Journal of Women's History* 1 (Spring 1989): 14-30.

Peterson, Susan C. "Challenging the Stereotypes: The Adaptation of the Sisters of St. Francis to South Dakota Indian Missions, 1885-1910." *Upper Midwest History* 4 (1984): 1-10.

-----. "Doing 'Women's Work': The Grey Nuns at Fort Totten Indian Reservation, 1874-1900." *North Dakota History* 52 (Spring 1985): 18-25.

-----. "'Holy Women' and Housekeepers: Women Teachers on South Dakota Reservations, 1885-1910." *South Dakota History* 13 (Fall 1983): 245-260.

Pool, Carolyn Garrett. "Reservation Policy and the Economic Position of Wichita Women." *Great Plains Quarterly* 8 (Summer 1988): 158-171.

Powers, Marla N. "The Americanization of Indian Girls." *Society* 24, no. 2 (1987): 83-85.

Riley, Glenda. "Frontierswomen's Changing Views of Indians in the Trans-Mississippi West." *Montana* 34 (Winter 1984): 20-35.

-----. "Some European (Mis)Perceptions of American Indian Women." *New Mexico Historical Review* 59 (July 1984): 237-266.

Roberts, Charles. "A Choctaw Odyssey: The Life of Lesa Phillip Roberts." *American Indian Quarterly* 14 (Summer 1990): 277-288.

Russell, Scott C., and Mark B. McDonald. "The Economic Contributions of Women in a Rural Western Navajo Community." *American Indian Quarterly* 6 (Fall/Winter 1982): 262-282.

Schackel, Sandra K. "'The Tales Those Nurses Told!': Public Health Nurses Among the Pueblo and Navajo Indians." *New Mexico Historical Review* 65 (April 1990): 225-250.

Schily, Thomas, and Jodye Lynn Dickson Schily. "Amazons, Witches, and Country Wives: Plains Indian Women in Historical Perspective." *Annals of Wyoming* 59 (Spring 1987): 48-56.

Schroer, Blanche. "Boat-pusher or Bird Woman? Sacagawea or Sacajawea?"

*Annals of Wyoming* 52 (Spring 1980): 46-54.

Sheridan, Mary Ann E., and Daniel P. Sheridan. "Changing Woman and the Dis-ease of the Navajo: Psychological and Historical Perspective." *Anima* 6 (Spring 1980): 84-95.

Shoemaker, Nancy. "The Rise or Fall of Iroquois Women." *Journal of Women's History* 2 (Winter 1991): 39-57.

Smith, S. L. "A Window on Themselves--Perceptions of Indians by Military Officers and Their Wives." *New Mexico Historical Review* 64 (October 1989): 447-462.

Smits, David D. "'Abominable Mixture': Toward the Repudiation of Anglo-Indian Intermarriage in Seventeenth Century Virginia." *Virginia Magazine of History and Biography* 95 (April 1987): 157-192.

Topolinski, John Renken Kahai. "Nancy Sumner, Hawaiian Courtlady." *Hawaiian Journal of History* 15 (1981): 50-58.

Trennert, Robert A. "Educating Indian Girls at Nonreservation Boarding Schools, 1878-1920." *Western Historical Quarterly* 13 (July 1982): 271-290.

-----. "Victorian Morality and the Supervision of Indian Women Working in Phoenix, 1906-1930." *Journal of Social History* 22 (Fall 1988): 113-128.

Tsosie, Rebecca. "Changing Women: The Cross-Currents of American Indian Feminine Identity." *American Indian Culture and Research Journal* 12, no. 1 (1988): 1-37.

White, Richard. "Race Relations in the American West." *American Quarterly* 38, no. 3 (1986): 396-416.

Wilson, Terry P. "Osage Indian Women During a Century of Change, 1870-1980." *Prologue* 14 (Winter 1982): 185-201.

Wright, Mary C. "Economic Development and Native American Women in the Early Nineteenth Century." *American Quarterly* 33 (Winter 1981): 525-536.

Young, M. Jane. "Women, Reproduction, and Religion in Western Puebloan Society." *Journal of American Folklore* 100 (October/December 1987): 436-445.

Zulawski, Ann. "Social Differentiation, Gender and Ethnicity: Urban Indian Women in Colonial Bolivia, 1640-1725." *Latin American Research Review* 25, no. 2 (1990): 93-114.

# WORK

## Housework

Alpers, Edward A. "'Ordinary Household Chores': Ritual and Power in a 19th-Century Swahili Women's Spirit Possession Cult." *International Journal of African Historical Studies* 17, no. 4 (1984): 677-702.

Armitage, Susan. "Household Work and Childrearing on the Frontier: The Oral History Record." *Sociology and Social Research* 63 (April 1979): 467-474.

Arpad, Susan S. "'Pretty Much to Suit Ourselves': Midwestern Women Naming Experience through Domestic Arts." *Hayes Historical Journal* 4 (Fall 1984): 15-27.

Bennett, Mary. "Women at Home." *Palimpsest* 63 (March/April 1982): 34-38, 40-41.

Berch, Bettina. "The Development of Housework." *International Journal of Women's Studies* 1 (July/August 1978): 336-348.

-----. "Scientific Management in the Home: The Empress's New Clothes." *Journal of American Culture* 3 (Fall 1980): 440-445.

Blackwelder, Julia Kirk. "Mop and Typewriter: Women's Work in Early Twentieth-Century Atlanta." *Atlanta History Journal* (Fall 1983): 21-30.

Bland, Sue. "Henrietta the Homemaker and Rosie the Riveter: Images of Women in Advertising 1939-1950." *Atlantis* 8 (Spring 1983): 61-86.

Bose, Christine E., Philip L. Bereano, and Mary Malloy. "Household Technology and the Social Construction of Housework." *Technology and Culture* 25 (January 1984): 53-82.

-----. "Technology and Changes in the Division of Labor in the American Home." *Women's Studies* 2, no. 3 (1979): 295-304.

Bourke, Joanna. "'The Health Caravan': Domestic Education and Female Labor in Rural Ireland, 1890-1914." *Eire-Ireland* 24 (Winter 1989): 7-20.

Boydston, Jeanne. "To Earn Her Daily Bread: Housework and Antebellum Working-Class Subsistence." *Radical History Review* 35 (1986): 7-25.

Bruce, Janet. "Of Sugar and Salt and Things in the Cellar and Sun: Food Preservation in Jackson County in the 1850." *Missouri Historical Review* 75 (July 1981): 417-447.

Burchfield, Robert, and Linda K. Kerber, eds. "The Household: Conducted by Mrs. Nellie M. Rich." *Palimpsest* 61 (March/April 1980): 42-55.

Carrell, Kimberly W. "The Industrial Revolution Comes to the Home: Kitchen Design Reform and Middle-Class Women." *Journal of American Culture* (Fall 1979): 488-499.

Carroll, William K., and Rennie Warburton. "Feminism, Class Consciousness and Household-Work Linkages Among Registered Nurses in Victoria." *Labour/Le Travail* 24 (Fall 1989): 131-146.

Daniels, Arlene Kaplan. "Invisible Work." *Social Problems* 34 (December 1987): 403-415.

Douglas, Diane M. "The Machine in the Parlor: A Dialectical Analysis of the Sewing Machine." *Journal of American Culture* 5 (Spring 1982): 20-29.

Foster, Thomas. "History, Critical Theory, and Women's Social Practices: 'Women's Time' and Housekeeping." *Signs* 14 (Autumn 1988): 73-99.

Frank, Dana. "Housewives, Socialists, and the Politics of Food: The 1917 New York Cost-of-Living Protests." *Feminist Studies* 11 (Summer 1985): 255-286.

Gaitskell, Deborah. "Housewives, Maids or Mothers: Some Contradictions of Domesticity for Christian Women in Johannesburg, 1903-39." *Journal of African History* 24, no. 2 (1983): 241-256.

Glazer, Nona. "Servants to Capital: Unpaid Domestic Labor and Paid Work." *Review of Radical Political Economics* 16 (Spring 1984): 61-87.

Godfrey, Audrey M. "Housewives, Hussies, and Heroines, or the Women of

Johnston's Army." *Utah Historical Quarterly* 54 (Spring 1986): 157-178.

Gordon, Linda. "Domestic Revolution: History of a Good Idea." *Radical America* 15 (November/December 1981): 57-62.

Gregory, Sarah J. "Pioneer Housewife: The Autobiography of Sally Dodge Morris." *Gateway Heritage* 3 (Spring 1983): 24-33.

Hayden, Dolores. "Charlotte Perkins Gilman and the Kitchenless House." *Radical History Review* 21 (Fall 1979): 225-247.

-----. "Two Utopian Feminists and Their Campaigns for Kitchenless Houses." *Signs* 4 (Winter 1978): 274-290.

Husted, Margaret. "Mary Randolph's *The Virginia Housewife*: America's First Regional Cookbook." *Virginia Cavalcade* 30 (Autumn 1980): 76-87.

Hyman, Paula E. "Immigrant Women and Consumer Protest: The New York City Kosher Meat Boycott of 1902." *American Jewish History* 70 (September 1980): 91-105.

Jensen, Joan M. "Buttermaking and Economic Development in Mid-Atlantic America from 1750 to 1850." *Signs* 13 (Summer 1988): 813-829.

-----. "Cloth, Butter and Boarders: Women's Household Production for the Market." *The Review of Radical Political Economics* 12 (Summer 1980): 14-24.

Kelley, Mary. "At War with Herself: Harriet Beecher Stowe as Woman in Conflict within the Home." *American Studies* 19 (Fall 1978): 23-40.

Kerber, Linda K. "The Politicks of Housework." *Signs* 4 (Winter 1978): 402-406.

Lebsock, Suzanne. "'We Have Not Lived for Ourselves Alone': Women and Domesticity in Antebellum Petersburg." *Virginia Cavalcade* 33 (Autumn 1983): 53-63.

Mathews, Jill. "Education for Femininity: Domestic Arts Education in South Australia." *Labour History* 45 (November 1983): 30-53.

Mullaney, Marie Marmo. "Feminism, Utopianism and Domesticity: The Career of Rebecca Buffum Spring, 1811-1911." *New Jersey History* 104 (Fall/Winter 1986): 1-21.

Nolan, Mary. "'Housework Made Easy': The Taylorized Housewife in Weimar Germany's Rationalized Economy." *Feminist Studies* 16 (Fall 1990): 549-578.

Olien, Diana Davids. "Keeping House in a Tent: Women in the Early Permian Basin Oil Fields." *Permian History Annual* 22 (1982): 3-14.

"Practices: 'Women's Time' and Housekeeping." *Signs* 14 (Autumn 1988): 73-99.

Prochaska, F. K. "Female Philanthropy and Domestic Service in Victorian England." *Bulletin of the Institute of Historical Research* 54, no. 129 (1981): 78-85.

Riley, Glenda. "'Not Gainfully Employed': Women on the Iowa Frontier, 1833-1870." *Pacific Historical Review* 49 (May 1980): 237-264.

Roper, Lyndal. "Housework and Livelihood: Towards the *Alltagsgeschichte* of Women." *German History* no. 2 (Summer 1985): 3-9.

Stone, May N. "The Plumbing Paradox: American Attitudes toward Late Nineteenth-Century Domestic Sanitary Arrangements." *Winterthur Portfolio* 14 (Autumn 1979): 283-310.

Strasser, Susan M. "Mistress and Maid, Employer and Employee: Domestic

Service Reform in the United States, 1892-1920." *Marxist Perspectives* 1, no. 1 (1978): 52-67.

Strong-Boag, Veronica. "'Wages for Housework': Mothers' Allowances and the Beginnings of Social Security in Canada." *Journal of Canadian Studies/Revue d'études canadiennes* 14 (Spring 1979): 24-34.

Valadez, Joseph J., and Rémi Clignet. "Household Work as an Ordeal: Culture of Standards versus Standardization of Culture." *American Journal of Sociology* 89 (January 1984): 812-835.

Vinson, Michael. "From Housework to Office Clerk: Utah's Working Women, 1870-1900." *Utah Historical Quarterly* 53 (Fall 1985): 326-335.

Walton, Whitney. "Feminine Hospitality in the Bourgeois Home of Nineteenth-Century France." *Western Society for French History* 14 (November 1986): 197-203.

## Theory and Issues

Alexander, Sally, Anna Davin, and Eve Hostettler. "Labouring Women: A Autumn Reply to Eric Hobsbawm." *History Workshop* 7 (Autumn 1979): 174-182.

Andersen, Kristi, and Elizabeth A. Cook. "Women, Work, and Political Attitudes." *American Journal of Social Science* 29 (August 1985): 606-625.

Anglin, Mary K. "Working Women: The Intersection of Historical Anthropology and Social History." *Appalachian Journal* 16 (Winter 1989): 154-164.

Berger, Iris. "Gender and Working-Class History: South Africa in Comparative Perspective." *Journal of Women's History* 1 (Fall 1989): 117-133.

Bose, Christine E. "Household Resources and U.S. Women's Work: Factors Affecting Gainful Employment at the Turn of the Century." *American Sociological Review* 49 (August 1984): 474-490.

Bradbury, Bettina. "Women's History and Working-Class History." *Labour/Le Travail* 19 (Spring 1987): 23-43.

Bularzik, Mary. "Sexual Harassment at the Work Place: Historical Notes." *Radical America* 12 (July/August 1978): 25-44.

Cohen, Marjorie. "Changing Perceptions of the Impact of the Industrial Revolution on Female Labour." *International Journal of Women's Studies* 7 (September/October 1984): 291-305.

Conk, Marge A. "Accuracy, Efficiency and Bias: The Interpretation of Women's Work in the U.S. Census of Occupations, 1890-1940." *Historical Methods* 14 (Spring 1981): 65-72.

de Grazia, Victoria. "Women and Communism in Advanced Capitalist Societies: Readings and Resources." *Radical History Review* 23 (Spring 1980): 80-101.

Dennis, Carolyne. "Women in African Labour History." *Journal of Asian and African Studies* 23 (January/April 1988): 125-140.

Druker, Jan. "Women's History and Trade Union Records." *Society for the Study of Labour History* 36 (Spring 1978): 28-35.

Dublin, Thomas. "Women Workers and the Study of Social Mobility." *Journal of*

*Interdisciplinary History* 9 (Spring 1979): 647-665.

-----. "Working Women and the 'Women's Question.'" *Radical History Review* 22 (Winter 1979-80): 93-98.

Dubnoff, Steven. "Gender, the Family, and the Problem of Work Motivation in a Transition to Industrial Capitalism." *Journal of Family History* 4 (Summer 1979): 121-136.

DuBois, Ellen Carol. "Working Women, Class Relations, and Suffrage Militance: Harriot Stanton Blanch and the New York Woman Suffrage Movement, 1894-1909." *Journal of American History* 74 (June 1987): 34-58.

Endres, A. M., and Katrina Alford. "Discussion: A Twentieth Century Economic Historian on Colonial Women's Employment: Comment on Alford. On Polemics and Patriarchy: A Rejoinder." *Labour History* 52 (May 1987): 88-95.

Evans, Vella Neil. "Mormon Women and the Right to Wage Work." *Dialogue* 23 (Winter 1990): 45-63.

Gaudron, Mary. "Women in the Workforce and the Elimination of Discrimination--Whose Responsibility?" *Labour History* 42 (May 1982): 106-111.

Gilman, Amy. "'Cogs to the Wheels': The Ideology of Women's Work in Mid-Nineteenth-Century Fiction." *Science and Society* 47 (Summer 1983): 178-204.

Goldin, Claudia. "The Historical Evolution of Female Earnings Functions and Occupations." *Explorations in Economic History* 21 (January 1984): 1-27.

-----. "The Work and Wages of Single Women, 1870-1920." *Journal of Economic History* 40 (March 1980): 81-88.

Haine, W. Scott. "Privacy in Public: The Compartment of Working-Class Women in Late Nineteenth-Century Parisian Proletarian Cafes." *Western Society for French History* 14 (November 1986): 204-211.

Handl, Johann. "Educational Chances and Occupational Opportunities of Women: A Sociohistorical Analysis." *Journal of Social History* 17 (Spring 1984): 463-487.

Harzig, Christiane. "The Role of German Women in the German-American Working Class Movement in Late Nineteenth-Century New York." *Journal of American Ethnic History* 8 (Spring 1989): 108-126.

Helmbold, Lois Rita. "Writing the History of Black and White Working Class Women." *Women's Studies* 17, no. 1/2 (1989): 37-48.

Higgs, Edward. "Women, Occupations and Work in the Nineteenth Century Censuses." *History Workshop* 23 (Spring 1987): 59-80.

Hilden, Patricia. "Re-Writing the History of Socialism: Working Woman and the Parti Ouvrier Francais." *European History Quarterly* 17 (July 1987): 285-306.

Katz, Michael, and Mark Stern. "Fertility, Class, and Industrial Capitalism: Erie County, New York, 1855-1915." *American Quarterly* 33 (Spring 1981): 63-92.

Kessler-Harris, Alice. "The Just Price, the Free Market, and the Value of Women." *Feminist Studies* 14 (Summer 1988): 235-250.

King, M., and S. Ruggles. "American Immigration, Fertility and Race Suicide at the Turn of the Century." *Journal of Interdisciplinary History* 20 (Winter

1990): 347-370.

Laslett, Barbara. "Women's Work in Late-Nineteenth-Century Los Angeles: Class, Gender and the Culture of New Womanhood." *Continuity and Change* 5, no. 3 (1990): 417-442.

Linton, Derek S. "Between School and Marriage, Workshop and Household: Young Working Women as a Social Problem in Late Imperial Germany." *European History Quarterly* 18 (October 1988): 387-408.

Magarey, Susan. "Labour History's New Sub-title: Social History in Australia in 1981." *Social History* 8 (May 1983): 211-228.

Marcus, Jane. "Transatlantic Sisterhood: Labor and Suffrage Links in the Letters of Elizabeth Robbins and Emmeline Pankhurst." *Signs* 3 (Spring 1978): 744-755.

May, Elaine Tyler. "Expanding the Past: Recent Scholarship on Women in Politics and Work." *Reviews in American History* 10 (December 1982): 216-233.

Murphy, Marjorie. "The Aristocracy of Women's Labor in America." *History Workshop* 22 (Autumn 1986): 56-69.

Musselman, Barbara L. "The Shackles of Class and Gender: Cincinnati Working Women, 1890-1920." *Queen City Heritage* 41 (Winter 1983): 35-40.

O'Shane, Pat. "On the Treadmill: Women In and Out of Employment." *Labour History* 44 (May 1983): 99-106.

Ognibene, Elaine. "Moving Beyond 'True Woman' Myths: Women and Work." *Humboldt Journal of Social Relations* 10 (Spring/Summer 1983): 7-25.

Oppenheimer, Valerie Kincaide. "Structural Sources of Economic Pressure for Wives to Work: An Analytical Framework." *Journal of Family History* 4 (Summer 1979): 177-197.

Power, Marilyn. "From Home Production to Wage Labor: Women as a Reserve Army of Labor." *Review of Radical Political Economy* 15 (Spring 1983): 71-91.

Quataert, Jean H. "The Shaping of Women's Work in Manufacturing: Guilds, Households, and the State in Central Europe, 1648-1870." *American Historical Review* 90 (December 1985): 1122-1148.

Ramaswamy, V. "Aspects of Women and Work in Early South India." *Indian Economic and Social History Review* 26 (January/March 1989): 81-100.

Reagon, Bernice Johnson. "African Diaspora Women: The Making of Cultural Workers." *Feminist Studies* 12 (Spring 1986): 77-90.

Richardson, Ruth. "'In the Posture of a Whore'? A Reply to Eric Hobsbawm." *History Workshop* 14 (Autumn 1982): 132-137.

Richter, Linda. "The Ephemeral Female: Women in Urban Histories." *International Journal of Women's Studies* 5 (September/October 1982): 312-328.

Robinson, Gertrude. "The Media and Social Change: 30 Years of Magazine Coverage of Women and Work (1950-1977)." *Atlantis* 8 (Spring 1983): 87-112.

Rose, Sonya O. "'Gender at Work': Sex, Class, and Industrial Capitalism." *History Workshop* 21 (Spring 1986): 113-132.

-----. "Proto-Industry, Women's Work and the Household Economy in the

Transition to Industrial Capitalism." *Journal Family History* 13, no. 2 (1988): 181-194.

Sacks, Michael P. "Missing Female Occupational Categories in the Soviet Censuses." *Slavic Review* 40 (1981): 251-268.

Schneider, Jo Anne. "Patterns for Getting By: Polish Women's Employment in Delaware County, 1900-1930." *Pennsylvania Magazine of History and Biography* 114 (October 1990): 517-541.

Scott, Anne Firor. "On Seeing and Not Seeing: A Case of Historical Invisibility." *Journal of American History* (June 1984): 7-21.

Sharpless, John, and John Rury. "The Political Economy of Women's Work, 1900-1920." *Social Science History* 4 (Summer 1980): 317-346.

Smillie, Christine. "The Invisible Workforce: Women Workers in Saskatchewan from 1905 to World War II." *Saskatchewan History* 34 (Summer 1986): 62-78.

Smith, Eleanor. "Black American Women and Work: A Historical Review-- 1619-1920." *Women's Studies* 8, no. 4 (1985): 343-350.

Smith, Ruth L., and Deborah M. Valenze. "Mutuality and Marginality: Liberal Moral Theory and Working-Class Women in Nineteenth-Century England." *Signs* 13 (Winter 1988): 277-298.

Strom, Sharon Hartman. "Old Barriers and New Opportunities: Working Women in Rhode Island, 1900-1940." *Rhode Island History* 39 (May 1980): 43-56.

Tillotson, Shirley. "The Operators Along the Coast: A Case Study of the Link Between Gender, Skilled Labour and Social Power, 1900-1930." *Acadiensis* 20 (Autumn 1990): 72-88.

Tilly, Louise A. "Paths of Proletarianization: Organization of Production, Sexual Division of Labor, and Women's Collective Action." *Signs* 7 (Winter 1981): 400-417.

Towner, Margaret. "Monopoly Capitalism and Women's Work During the Porfiriato." *Latin American Perspectives* 2, no. 1/2 (1979): 90-105.

Willen, Diane. "Women in the Public Sphere in Early Modern England: The Case of the Urban Working Poor." *Sixteenth Century Journal* 19, no. 4 (1988): 559-575.

Williams, Walter L. "Women and Work in the Third World: Indonesian Women's Oral Histories." *Journal of Women's History* 2 (Spring 1990): 183-195.

## Crafts, Trades, and Home-Based Work

Abel, Trudi. "The Diary of a Poor Quaker Seamstress: Needles and Penury in Nineteenth Century London." *Quaker History* 75 (Fall 1986): 102-114.

Baron, Ava. "Questions of Gender: Deskilling and Demasculinization in the U.S. Printing Industry, 1830-1915." *Gender & History* 1 (Summer 1989): 178-199.

Bates, Christina. "Blue Monday: A Day in the Life of a Washerwoman, 1840." *Canadian Collector* (July/August 1985): 44-48.

Benhamou, Reed. "The Verdigris Industry in Eighteenth-Century Languedoc: Women's Work, Women's Art." *French Historical Studies* 16 (Spring 1990): 560-575.

Biggs, Mary. "Neither Printer's Wife nor Widow: American Women in Typesetting, 1830-1950." *Library Quarterly* 500, no. 4 (1980): 431-452.

Biola, Heather. "The Black Washerwoman in Southern Tradition." *Tennessee Folklore Society Bulletin* 45, no. 1 (1979): 17-27.

Blewett, Mary H. "I Am Doom to Disapointment: The Diaries of a Beverly, Massachusetts, Shoebinder, Sarah E. Trask, 1849-51." *Essex Institute Historical Collections* 117 (July 1981): 192-212.

-----. "The Union of Sex and Craft in the Haverhill Shoe Strike of 1895." *Labor History* 20 (Summer 1979): 352-375.

-----. "Women Shoeworkers and Domestic Ideology: Rural Outwork in Early Nineteenth-Century Essex County." *New England Quarterly* 60 (September 1987): 403-428.

-----. "Work, Gender, and the Artisan Tradition in New England Shoemaking, 1780-1860." *Journal of Social History* 17 (Winter 1983): 221-248.

Bloom, Florence Teicher. "Struggling and Surviving: The Life Style of European Immigrant Breadwinning Mothers in American Industrial Cities, 1900-1930." *Women's Studies* 8, no. 6 (1985): 609-620.

Boris, Eileen. "Homework and Women's Rights: The Case of the Vermont Knitters 1980-1985." *Signs* 13 (Autumn 1987): 98-120.

-----. "Regulating Industrial Homework: The Triumph of 'Sacred Motherhood'." *Journal of American History* 71 (March 1985): 745-763.

Campbell, Catherine. "H. Bessie Hall, Master Mariner." *Nova Scotia Historical Review* [Canada] 7, no. 2 (1987): 8-12.

Chauncey, George, Jr. "The Locus of Reproduction: Women's Labour in the Zambian Copperbelt, 1927-1953." *Journal of South African Studies* 7 (April 1981): 135-164.

Cho, Haejong. "Neither Dominance: A Study of a Female Divers' Village in Korea." *Korea Journal* 19, no. 6 (1979): 23-34.

Clark, Sallye. "Carrie Taylor, Kentucky Dressmaker." *Dress* 6 (1980): 13-23.

Cunningham, Patricia A. "Northwest Ohio Coverlet Weavers: An Update." *Northwest Ohio Quarterly* 58 (Winter 1986): 20-24.

-----. "The Woven Record: Nineteenth-Century Coverlets and Textile Industries in Northwest Ohio." *Northwest Ohio Quarterly* 56 (Spring 1984): 43-76.

Daily, Christie. "A Woman's Concern: Millinery in Century, Iowa, 1870-1880." *Journal of the West* 21 (April 1982): 20-32.

Davis, Natalie Zemon. "Women in the Crafts in Sixteenth-Century Lyon." *Feminist Studies* 8 (Spring 1982): 47-80.

Dreves, Vivien E. "The New Woman Goes Home: Myrtle Mae Borsodi Pits Home Production Against Industrialization, 1929-1940." *New York History* 71 (July 1990): 283-307.

Edelstein, T. J. "They Sang 'The Song of the Shirt': The Visual Iconology of the Seamstress." *Victorian Studies* 23 (Winter 1980): 183-210.

Eisenberg, Susan. "Shaping a New Decade: Women in the Building Trades." *Radical America* 23, no. 2-3 (1990): 29-38.

Grubitzsch, Helga. "Women's Projects and Co-operatives in France at the

Beginning of the 19th Century." *Women's Studies* 8, no. 4 (1985): 287-290.

Haiken, Elizabeth. "'The Lord Helps Those Who Help Themselves': Black Laundresses in Little Rock, Arkansas, 1917-1921." *Arkansas Historical Quarterly* 49 (Spring 1990): 20-50.

Hamblett, Barbara. "Lighthouse Keeping: A Womanly Art." *Michigan History* 65 (November/December 1981): 28-29.

Henry, Susan. "Work, Widowhood and War: Hannah Bunce Watson, Connecticut Printer." *Connecticut Historical Society Bulletin* 48 (Winter 1983): 25-39.

Hunt, Felicity. "The London Trade in the Printing and Binding of Books: An Experience in Exclusion, Dilution and De-skilling for Women Workers." *Women's Studies* 6, no. 5 (1983): 517-524.

Jerde, Judith. "Mary Molloy: St. Paul's Extraordinary Dressmaker." *Dress* 7 (1981): 82-89.

-----. "Mary Molloy: St. Paul's Extraordinary Dressmaker." *Minnesota History* 47 (Fall 1980): 93-99.

Kowaleski, Maryanne, and Judith M. Bennett. "Crafts, Guilds, and Women in the Middle Ages: Fifty Years after Marian K. Dale." *Signs* 14 (Winter 1989): 474-501.

Lipton, Eunice. "The Laundress in Late Nineteenth-Century French Culture: Imagery, Ideology and Edgar Degas." *Art History* 3 (September 1980): 295-313.

Malcolmson, Patricia E. "Laundresses and the Laundry Trade in Victorian England." *Victorian Studies* 24 (Summer 1981): 439-462.

Melder, Keith. "Women in the Shoe Industry: The Evidence from Lynn." *Essex Institute Historical Collections* 115 (October 1979): 270-287.

Mohanty, Gail Fowler. "From Craft to Industry: Textile Production in the United States." *Material History Bulletin* [Canada] 31 (Spring 1990): 23-31.

Nash, Michael. "Women and the Pennsylvania Railroad: The World War II Years." *Labor History* 30 (Autumn 1989): 608-621.

Osaki, Amy Boyce. "A 'Truly Feminine Employment': Sewing and the Early Nineteenth-Century Woman." *Winterthur Portfolio* 23 (Winter 1988): 225-242.

Porter, Marilyn. "'She Was Skipper of the Shore-Crew': Notes on the History of the Sexual Division of Labour in Newfoundland." *Labour/Le Travail* 15 (Spring 1985): 105-124.

Preston, Jo Anne. "'To Learn Me the Whole of the Trade': Conflict Between a Female Apprentice and a Merchant Tailor in Ante-Bellum New England." *Labor History* 24 (Spring 1983): 159-273.

Robertson, Claire. "Invisible Workers: African Women and the Problem of the Self-Employed in Labour History." *Journal of Asian and African Studies* 23 (January/April 1988): 180-198.

Ruddell, David-Thiery. "Domestic Textile Production in Colonial Quebec, 1608-1840." *Material History Bulletin* [Canada] 31 (Spring 1990): 39-49.

Ryan, Edna. "Proving a Dispute: Laundry Workers in Sydney in 1906." *Labour History* 40 (May 1981): 98-106.

Sanderson, Elizabeth. "The Edinburgh Milliners, 1720-1820." *Costume* 20 (1986): 18-28.

Seligmann, L. J. "To Be in Between: The Cholas as Market Women." *Comparative Studies in Society and History* 31 (October 1989): 694-721.

Stark, Suzanne J. "The Adventures of Two Women Whalers." *Amercian Neptune* 44 (Winter 1984): 22-24.

Stewart, Miller J. "Army Laundresses: Ladies of the 'Soap Suds Row'." *Nebraska History* 61 (Winter 1980): 421-436.

Taylor, Barbara. "'The Men Are as Bad as Their Masters . . .': Socialism, Feminism, and Sexual Antagonism in the London Tailoring Trade in the Early 1830s." *Feminist Studies* 5 (Spring 1979): 7-40.

Trautman, Pat. "Personal Clothiers: A Demographic Study of Dressmakers, Seamstresses, and Tailors." *Dress* 5 (1979): 74-83.

Walkley, Christina. "Charity and the Victorian Needlewoman." *Costume* 14 (1980): 136-143.

Walton, Whitney. "Working Women, Gender, and Industrialization in Nineteenth-Century France: The Case of Lorraine Embroidery Manufacturing." *Journal of Women's History* 2 (Fall 1990): 42-65.

Whyte, Ann W. "Helen Bagrie, Costumiere, 343 Union Street, Aberdeen." *Costume* 16 (1982): 71-85.

Willen, Diane. "Guildswomen in the City of York, 1560-1700." *The Historian* 46 (February 1984): 204-218.

## Domestics

Arru, Angiolina. "The Distinguishing Features of Domestic Service in Italy." *Journal of Family History* 15, no. 4 (1990): 547-566.

Barber, Marilyn J. "Below Stairs: The Domestic Servant." *Material History Bulletin* no. 19 (Spring 1984): 37-46.

-----. "The Women Ontario Welcomed: Immigrant Domestics for Ontario Homes, 1870-1930." *Ontario History* 72 (September 1980): 148-172.

Beasley, Maurine Hoffman. "Life as a Hired Girl in South Dakota, 1907-1908: A Woman Journalist Reflects." *South Dakota History* 12 (Summer/Fall 1982): 147-162.

Berch, Bettina. "'The Sphinx in the Household': A New Look at the History of Household Workers." *Review of Radical Political Economists* 16, no. 1 (1984): 105-120.

Brown, Gillian. "Getting in the Kitchen with Dinah: Domestic Politics in Uncle Tom's Cabin." *American Quarterly* 36 (Fall 1984): 503-523.

Da Molin, Giovanna. "Family Forms and Domestic Service in Southern Italy from the Seventeenth to the Nineteenth Centuries." *Journal of Family History* 15, no. 4 (1990): 503-528.

Dubofsky, Melvyn. "Neither Upstairs, Nor Downstairs: Domestic Service in Middle-Class American Homes." *Reviews in American History* 8, no. 1 (1980): 86-91.

Dudden, Faye E. "Experts and Servants: The National Council on Household Employment and the Decline of Domestic Service in the Twentieth Century." *Journal of Social History* 20 (Winter 1986): 269-289.

Fairchilds, Cissie. "Masters and Servants in Eighteenth Century Toulouse." *Journal of Social History* 12 (Spring 1979): 368-393.

Gaitskell, Deborah, Judy Kimble, Moira Maconachie, and Elaine Unterhalter. "Class, Race and Gender: Domestic Workers in South Africa." *Review of African Political Economy* 27/28 (1983): 86-108.

Gannage, Charlene. "Haven or Heartache: Immigrant Women Workers in the Household." *Anthropologica* 26, no. 2 (1984): 217-254.

Gibson, Dale. "A Scandal at Red River: The Judge and the Serving Girl." *Beaver* 70 (October/November 1990): 30-38.

Gillis, John R. "Servants, Sexual Relations, and the Risks of Illegitimacy in London, 1801-1900." *Feminist Studies* 5 (Spring 1979): 142-173.

Glazer, Nona. "Servants to Capital: Unpaid Domestic Labor and Paid Work." *Review of Radical Political Economics* 16 (Spring 1984): 61-87.

Glenn, Evelyn Nakano. "The Dialectics of Wage Work: Japanese-American Women and Domestic Service, 1905-1940." *Feminist Studies* 6 (Fall 1980): 432-471.

-----. "Occupational Ghettoization: Japanese-American Women and Domestic Service, 1905-1970." *Ethnicity* 8 (December 1981): 352-386.

Goldberg, P. J. P. "Marriage, Migration, Servanthood and Life-Cycle in Yorkshire Towns of the Later Middle Ages." *Continuity and Change* 1, no. 2 (1986): 141-168.

Grossman, Allyson Sherman. "Women in Domestic Work: Yesterday and Today." *Monthly Labor Review* 103, no. 8 (1980): 17-21.

Grubb, Farley. "Servant Auction Records and Immigration into the Delaware Valley, 1745-1831: The Proportion of Females Among Immigrant Servants." *Proceedings of the American Philosophical Society* 133 (June 1989): 154-169.

Hansen, Karen Tranberg. "Body Politics: Sexuality, Gender, and Domestic Service in Zambia." *Journal of Women's History* 2 (Spring 1990): 120-142.

Harper, C. W. "Black Aristocrats: Domestic Servants on the Antebellum Plantation." *Phylon* 46 (June 1985): 123-135.

Higgs, Edward. "Domestic Servants and Households in Victorian England." *Social History* 8 (May 1983): 201-210.

-----. "The Tabulation of Occupations in the Nineteenth-Century Census, with Special Reference to Domestic Servants." *Local Population Studies* 28 (1982): 58-66.

Hinde, P. R. A. "Household Structure, Marriage and the Institution of Service in Nineteenth Century Rural England." *Local Population Studies* no. 35 (Autumn 1985): 43-51.

Kent, D. A. "Ubiquitous but Invisible: Female Domestic Servants in Mid-Eighteenth Century London." *History Workshop* no. 28 (Autumn 1989): 111-128.

Kushner, Tony. "Politics and Race, Gender and Class: Refugees, Fascists and

Domestic Service in Britain, 1933-1940." *Immigrants & Minorities* 8 (March 1989): 49-60.

Lasser, Carol. "The Domestic Balance of Power: Relations Between Mistress and Maid in Nineteenth-Century New England." *Labor History* 28 (Winter 1987): 5-22.

-----. "A 'Pleasingly Oppressive' Burden: The Transformation of Domestic Service and Female Charity in Salem 1800-1840." *Essex Institute Historical Collections* 116 (July 1980): 156-175.

Leashore, Bogart R. "Black Female Workers: Live-in Domestics in Detroit, Michigan, 1860-1880." *Phylon* 45 (June 1984): 111-120.

Lenskyi, Helen. "A 'Servant Problem' or a 'Servant-Mistress Problem?' Domestic Service in Canada, 1890-1930." *Atlantis* 7 (1981): 3-11.

Levenstein, Harvey. "The 'Servant Problem' and American Cookery." *Revue française d'études américaines* no. 27/28 (1986): 127-135.

Lintelman, Joy K. "'America Is the Woman's Promised Land': Swedish Immigrant Women and American Domestic Service." *Journal of American Ethnic History* 8 (Spring 1989): 9-23.

McKinley, Blaine. "Troublesome Comforts: The Housekeeper-Servant Relationship in Antebellum Didactic Fiction." *Journal of American Culture* 5 (Summer 1982): 36-44.

Melosh, Barbara. "Historians and the Servant Problem." *Reviews in American History* 11, no. 1 (1983): 55-58.

Perkins, Elizabeth A. "The Forgotten Victorians: Louisville's Domestic Servants, 1880-1920." *Register of the Kentucky Historical Society* 85 (Spring 1987): 111-137.

Riley, Barbara. "Domestic Work: Oral History and Material Culture." *Canadian Oral History Association Journal* 8 (1985): 9-14.

Romero, Mary. "Domestic Service in the Transition from Rural to Urban Life: The Case of La Chicana." *Women's Studies* 13, no. 3 (1987): 199-222.

Salinger, Sharon V. "'Send No More Women': Female Servants in Eighteenth-Century Philadelphia." *Pennsylvania Magazine of History and Biography* 107 (January 1983): 29-48.

Sallquist, Sylvia Lea. "The Image of the Hired Girl in Literature: The Great Plains, 1860 to World War I." *Great Plains Quarterly* 4 (Summer 1984): 166-177.

Schlegel, Katharina. "Mistress and Servant in Nineteenth Century Hamburg." *History Workshop* 15 (Spring 1983): 60-77.

Souden, David. "'Rogues, Whores, and Vagabonds'? Indentured Servant Emigrants to North America, and the Case of Mid-Seventeenth-Century Bristol." *Social History* 3 (January 1978): 23-41.

Spence, Mary Lee. "They Also Serve Who Wait." *Western Historical Quarterly* 14 (January 1983): 5-28.

Tucker, Susan. "A Complex Bond: Southern Black Domestic Workers and Their White Employers." *Frontiers* 9, no. 3 (1987): 6-13.

Wierling, Dorothee. "Women Domestic Servants in Germany at the Turn of the

Century." *Oral History* no. 2 (Autumn 1982): 47-57.

Wilcox, Penelope. "Marriage, Mobility and Domestic Service in Victorian Cambridge." *Local Population Studies* no. 29 (Autumn 1982): 19-34.

Yancy, Dorothy Cowser. "Dorothy Bolden, Organizer of Domestic Workers: She Was Born Poor but She Would Not Bow Down." *Sage* 3, no. 1 (1986): 53-55.

## Factory

Aldrich, Mark. "State Reports on Women and Child Wage Earners, 1870-1906." *Labor History* 21, no. 1 (1980): 86-90.

Anderson, Harry H. "The Women Who Helped Make Milwaukee Breweries Famous." *Milwaukee History* 4 (Autumn/Winter 1981): 66-78.

Anderson, Karen T. "Last Hired, First Fired: Black Women Workers During World War II." *Journal of American History* 69 (June 1982): 86-97.

-----. "Teaching about Rosie the Riveter: The Role of Women During World War II." *OAH Magazine of History* 3 (Summer/Fall 1988): 35-37.

Berger, Iris. "Gender, Race, and Political Empowerment: South African Canning Workers, 1940-1960." *Gender & Society* 4 (September 1990): 398-420.

Bradbury, Bettina. "Women and Wage Labour in a Period of Transition: Montreal, 1861-1881." *Histoire sociale/Social History* 17 (May 1984): 115-131.

Brandt, Gail Cuthbert. "'Weaving It Together': Life Cycle and the Industrial Experience of Female Cotton Workers in Quebec, 1910-1950." *Labour/Le Travail* 7 (Spring 1981): 113-126.

-----. "Women in the Quebec Cotton Industry, 1890-1950." *Material History Bulletin* [Canada] 31 (Spring 1990): 99-105.

Brown, Judith C., and Jordan Goodman. "Women and Industry in Florence." *Journal of Economic History* 40 (March 1980): 73-80.

Bulbeck, Chilla. "Manning the Machines: Women in the Furniture Industry, 1920-1960." *Labour History* 51 (November 1986): 24-32.

Burns, Stewart. "Capacitors and Community: Women Workers at Sprague Electric, 1930-1980." *Public Historian* 11 (Fall 1989): 61-82.

Chai, Alice Yun. "Freed from the Elders but Locked into Labor: Korean Immigrant Women in Hawaii." *Women's Studies* 13, no. 3 (1987): 223-234.

Clive, Alan. "Women Workers in World War II: Michigan as a Test Case." *Labor History* 20 (Winter 1979): 44-72.

Corbett, Katherine T. "St. Louis Women Garment Workers." *Gateway Heritage* 2 (Summer 1981): 18-25.

Croucher, Richard. "Women and Militancy in the Munitions Industries 1935-45." *Society for the Study of Labour History* 38 (Spring 1979): 8-9.

Davis, Lynne. "Minding Children or Minding Machines...Women's Labour and Child Care During World War II." *Labour History* 53 (November 1987): 85-98.

Engel, Barbara Alpern. "Women, Work and Family in the Factories of Rural Russia." *Russian History* 16, no. 2/4 (1989): 223-238.

Erazo, Blanca Vazquez. "The Stories Our Mothers Tell: Projections-of-Self in the Stories of Puerto Rican Garment Workers." *Oral History Review* 16 (Fall 1988): 23-28.

Estomin, Lynn, and Andrea Kornbluh. "Cincinnati Industry: Women Were There." *Queen City Heritage* 41 (Winter 1983): 30-34.

Francis, Raelene. "'No More Amazons': Gender and Work Process in the Victorian Clothing Trades, 1890-1939." *Labour History* 50 (May 1986): 95-112.

Garrett, Eilidh M. "The Trials of Labour: Motherhood versus Employment in a Nineteenth-Century Textile Centre." *Continuity and Change* 5, no. 1 (1990): 121-154.

Gluck, Sherna Berger. "Interlude or Change: Women and the World War II Work Experience: A Feminist Oral History." *International Journal of Oral History* 3 (June 1982): 92-113.

Goldberg, Vicki. "Woman of Steel." *American Heritage of Invention & Technology* 2 (Spring 1987): 16-22.

Greene, Janet W. "Strategies for Survival: Women's Work in the Southern West Virginia Coal Camps." *West Virginia History* 49 (1990): 37-54.

Hammam, Mona. "Women and Industrial Work in Egypt: The Chubra El-Kheima Case." *Arab Studies Quarterly* 2, no. 1 (1980): 50-69.

Hensley, Frances S. "Women in the Industrial Work Force in West Virginia, 1880-1945." *West Virginia History* 49 (1990): 115-124.

Hewitt, Nancy A. "Women in Ybor City: An Interview with a Woman Cigar Worker." *Tampa Bay History* 7 (Fall/Winter 1985): 161-165.

Hilden, Patricia. "Class and Gender: Conflicting Components of Women's Behaviour in the Textile Mills of Lilli, Roubaix and Tourcoing, 1880-1914." *Historical Journal* [Great Britain] 27 (June 1984): 361-386.

Hirsch, Susan E. "Rethinking the Sexual Division of Labor: Pullman Repair Shops, 1900-1969." *Radical History Review* 35 (1986): 26-48.

Hirshfield, Deborah Scott. "Women Shipyard Workers in the Second World War." *International History Review* 11 (August 1989): 478-485.

Honey, Maureen. "Recruiting Women for War Work: OWI and the Magazine Industry During World War II." *Journal of American Culture* 3 (Spring 1980): 47-52.

Honig, Emily. "Burning Incense, Pledging Sisterhood: Communities of Women Workers in the Shanghai Cotton Mills, 1919-1949." *Signs* 10 (Summer 1985): 700-714.

-----. "The Contract Labor System and Women Workers: Pre-Liberation Cotton Mills of Shanghai." *Modern China* 9 (October 1983): 421-454.

Ilcan, Suzan M. "Women and Casual Work in the Nova Scotia Fish Processing Industry." *Atlantis* 11, no. 2 (1986): 23-34.

Jones, Beverly W. "Race, Sex, and Class: Black Female Tobacco Workers in Durham, North Carolina, 1920-1940, and the Development of Female Consciousness." *Feminist Studies* 10 (Fall 1984): 441-452.

Jordan, Ellen. "The Exclusion of Women from Industry in Nineteenth-Century

Britain." *Comparative Studies in Society and History* 31 (April 1989): 273-296.

Kessner, Thomas, and Betty Boyd Caroli. "New Immigrant Women at Work: Italians and Jews in New York City, 1880-1905." *Journal of Ethnic Studies* 5 (Winter 1978): 19-32.

Kumar, Radha. "Family and Factory: Women Workers in the Bombay Cotton Textile Industry, 1919-1939." *Indian Economic and Social History Review* 20 (March 1983): 81-110.

Lambertz, Jan. "Sexual Harassment in the Nineteenth Century English Cotton Industry." *History Workshop* 19 (Spring 1985): 29-61.

Lazerow, Jama. "Religion and the New England Mill Girl: A New Perspective on an Old Theme." *New England Quarterly* 60 (September 1987): 429-453.

Leighow, Susan R. "Joanna Furnace Women: 1881-1925." *Pennsylvania Heritage* 8 (Fall 1982): 13-16.

Lynch, Katherine A. "Marriage Age Among French Factory Workers: An Alsatian Example." *Journal of Interdisciplinary History* 16 (Winter 1986): 405-429.

Matthies, Susan A. "Families at Work: An Analysis By Sex of Child Workers in the Cotton Textile Industry." *Journal of Economic History* 42 (March 1982): 173-180.

May, Martha. "The Historical Problem of the Family Wage: The Ford Motor Company and the Five Dollar Day." *Feminist Studies* 8 (Summer 1982): 399-424.

McGaw, Judith A. "'A Good Place to Work,' Industrial Workers and Occupational Choice: The Case of Berkshire Women." *Journal of Interdisciplinary History* 10 (Autumn 1979): 227-248.

McGouldrick, Paul, and Michael Tannen. "The Increasing Pay Gap for Women in the Textile and Clothing Industries, 1910-1970." *Journal of Economic History* 40 (December 1980): 799-814.

Milkman, Ruth. "Female Factory Labor and Industrial Structure: Control and Conflict over 'Woman's Place' in Auto and Electrical Manufacturing." *Politics and Society* 12 (1983): 159-203.

-----. "Organizing the Sexual Division of Labor: Historical Perspectives on 'Women's Work' and the American Labor Movement." *Socialist Review* 10, no. 1 (1980): 95-150.

-----. "Redefining 'Women's Work': The Sexual Division of Labor in the Auto Industry During World War II." *Feminist Studies* 8 (Summer 1982): 337-372.

Mohanty, Gail Fowler. "Industrialization and Production of Textiles in the United States: A Bibliography." *Material History Bulletin* [Canada] 31 (Spring 1990): 33-38.

Nash, Gary B. "The Failure of Female Factory Labor in Colonial Boston." *Labor History* 20 (Spring 1979): 165-188.

Nisonoff, Laurie. "Bread and Roses: The Proletarianisation of Women Workers in New England Textile Mills, 1827-1848." *Historical Journal of Massachusetts* 9 (January 1981): 3-14.

Nordstrom, Byron. "Evelina Mansson and the Memoir of an Urban Labor

Migrant." *Swedish Pioneer Historical Quarterly* 31 (1980): 182-195.

Norkunas, Martha K. "Women, Work and Ethnic Identity: Personal Narratives and the Ethnic Enclaves in the Textile City of Lowell, Massachusetts." *Journal of Ethnic Studies* 15 (Fall 1987): 27-48.

Parr, Joy. "Rethinking Work and Kinship in a Canadian Hosiery Town, 1910-1950." *Feminist Studies* 13 (Spring 1987): 137-162.

Pena, Devon Gerardo. "Las Maquiladoras: Mexican Women and Class Struggle in the Border Industries." *Aztlan: International Journal of Chicano Studies Research* 11 (Fall 1980): 159-230.

Perry, Elizabeth Israels. "Industrial Reform in New York City: Belle Moskowitz and the Protocol of Peace, 1913-1916." *Labor History* 23 (Winter 1982): 5-31.

Quataert, Jean H. "A Source Analysis in German Women's History: Factory Inspectors' Reports and the Shaping of Working Class Lives, 1878-1914." *Central European History* 16 (June 1983): 99-121.

Riley, Denise. "The Free Mothers: Protonationalism and Working Class Mothers in Industry at the End of the Last War in Britain." *History Workshop* 11 (Spring 1981): 59-119.

Rios, Palmiran. "Export-Oriented Industrialization and the Demand for Female Labor: Puerto Rican Women in the Manufacturing Sector, 1952-1980." *Gender & Society* 4 (September 1990): 321-337.

Roberts, Richard. "Women's Work and Women's Property: Household Social Relations in the Maraka Textile Industry of the Nineteenth Century." *Comparative Studies in Society and History* [Great Britain] 26, no. 2 (1984): 48-69.

Rose, Sonya O. "Gender Segregation in the Transition to the Factory: The English Hosiery Industry, 1850-1910." *Feminist Studies* 13 (Spring 1987): 163-84.

Salt, Annette. "Women on the Northern Coalfields of NSW." *Labour History* 48 (May 1985): 44-53.

Schoen, Carol. "Anzia Yezierska: New Light on the 'Sweatshop Cinderella.'" *Melus* 7 (1980): 3-11.

Scott, Joan Wallach. "The Mechanization of Women's Work." *Scientific American* 247, no. 3 (1982): 167-187.

Simon, Rita, and Margo Deley. "The Work Experience of Undocumented Mexican Women Migrants in Los Angeles." *International Migration Review* 18, no. 4 (1984): 1212-1229.

Strighenova, Tatiana. "The Soviet Garment Industry in the 1930s." *The Journal of Decorative and Propaganda Arts* no. 5 (Summer 1987): 160-175.

Taylor, Paul S. "Mexican Women in Los Angeles Industry in 1928." *Aztlan: International Journal of Chicano Studies Research* 11 (Spring 1980): 99-132.

Thomas, Mary Martha. "Rosie the Alabama Riveter." *Alabama Review* 39 (July 1986): 196-212.

Thornton, Robert, and Thomas Hydak. "The Increasing Pay Gap for Women in the Textile and Clothing Industries, 1919-1970: An Alternative Explanation." *Journal of Economic History* 42 (1982): 427-439.

Treble, J. "The Seasonal Demand for Adult Labour in Glasgow, 1890-1914."
    *Social History* 3 (January 1978): 43-60.
Tsurumi, E. Patricia. "Serving in Japan's Industrial Army: Female Textile
    Workers, 1868-1930." *Canadian Journal of History* 20 (August 1988):
    155-176.
Vecchio, Diane C. "Italian Women in Industry: The Shoeworkers of Endicott,
    New York, 1914-1935." *Journal of American Ethnic History* 8 (Spring 1989):
    60-86.
Vogel, Lisa. "'Humorous Incidents and Sound Common Sense': More on the New
    England Mill Women." *Labor History* 19 (Spring 1978): 280-286.
Wayski, Margaret. "Women and Mining in the Old West." *Journal of the West*
    20, no. 2 (1981): 38-47.
Zavella, Patricia. "'Abnormal Intimacy': The Varying Networks of Chicana
    Cannery Workers." *Feminist Studies* 11 (Fall 1985): 541-557.
Zonderman, David A. "From Mill Village to Industrial City: Letters from
    Vermont Factory Operatives." *Labor History* 27 (Spring 1986): 265-285.

## Family

Abbott, Ruth K., and R. A. Young. "Cynical and Deliberate Manipulation? Child
    Care and the Reserve Army of Female Labour in Canada." *Journal of
    Canadian Studies* 24 (Summer 1989): 22-38.
Carter, Susan B., and Mark Prus. "The Labor Market and the American High
    School Girl, 1890-1928." *Journal of Economic History* 42 (March 1982):
    163-172.
Costa, Janeen Arnold. "A Struggle for Survival and Identity: Families in the
    Aftermath of the Castle Gate Mine Disaster." *Utah Historical Quarterly* 56
    (Summer 1988): 279-292.
Crafts, N. F. R. "Duration of Marriage, Fertility and Women's Employment
    Opportunities in England and Wales in 1911." *Population Studies* 43 (1989):
    325-335.
Fraundorf, Martha Norby. "The Labor Force Participation of Turn-of-the-Century
    Married Women." *Journal of Economic History* 39, no. 2 (1979): 401-418.
Gough, Austin. "French Workers and Their Wives in the Mid-Nineteenth
    Century." *Labour History* 42 (May 1982): 74-82.
Greenwald, Maurine Weiner. "Working-Class Feminism and the Family Wage
    Ideal: The Seattle Debate on Married Women's Right to Work, 1914-1920."
    *Journal of American History* 76 (June 1989): 118-149.
Guy, Donna J. "Lower-Class Families, Women, and the Law in
    Nineteenth-Century Argentina." *Journal of Family History* 10 (Fall 1985):
    318-330.
Harley, Sharon. "For the Good of Family and Race: Gender, Work and Domestic
    Roles in the Black Community, 1880-1930." *Signs* 15 (Winter 1990): 336-349.
Helmbold, Lois Rita. "Beyond the Family Economy: Black and White Working

Class Women During the Great Depression." *Feminist Studies* 13 (Fall 1987): 629-656.

Humphries, Jane. "Working, Family Structure and Paid Labour: Historic Patterns." *Society for the Study of Labour History* 48 (Spring 1984): 14-15.

Kain, Edward L., and Niall Bolger. "Social Change and Women's Work and Family Experience in Ireland and the United States." *Social Science History* 10 (Summer 1986): 171-194.

Kamerman, Sheila B. "Work and Family in Industrialized Societies." *Signs* 4 (Summer 1979): 632-650.

Li, Peter S. "Immigration Laws and Family Patterns: Some Demographic Changes Among Chinese Families in Canada, 1885-1971." *Canadian Ethnic Studies/Etudes Ethniques Au Canada* 12, no. 1 (1980): 58-73.

McLaren, Angus. "'What Has This To Do with Working Class Women': Birth Control and the Canadian Left, 1900-1939." *Histoire sociale/Social History* 14 (November 1981): 435-454.

Millard, Peggy. "Company Wife." *The Beaver* 315 (Spring 1985): 30-39.

Mitchell, Margaret. "The Effects of Unemployment on the Social Condition of Women and Children in the 1930s." *History Workshop* 19 (Spring 1985): 105-127.

Mosk, Carl. "Fertility and Occupation: Mining Districts in Prewar Japan." *Social Science History* 5 (Summer 1981): 293-316.

Neuman, R. "Working Class Birth Control in Wilhelmine Germany." *Comparative Studies in Society and History* 20 (1978): 408-428.

Parr, Joy. "The Skilled Emigrant and Her Kin: Gender, Culture, and Labour Recruitment." *Canadian Historical Review* 68 (December 1987): 529-551.

Plutzer, Eric. "Work Life, Family Life and Women's Support of Feminism." *American Sociological Review* 53 (1988): 640-649.

Quester, Aline O., and William H. Green. "The Labor Market Experience of Black and White Wives in the Sixties and Seventies." *Social Science Quarterly* 66 (December 1985): 854-866.

Ray, Dorothy Jean. "Sinrock Mary: From Eskimo Wife to Reindeer Queen." *Pacific Northwest Quarterly* 75 (July 1984): 98-107.

Reynolds, Sian. "Who Wanted the Creches? Working Mothers and the Birth-Rate in France 1900-1950." *Continuity and Change* 5, no. 2 (1990): 173-198.

Rosenfeld, Mark. "'It Was a Hard Life': Class and Gender in the Work and Family Rhythms of a Railway Town 1920-1950." *Historical Papers/Communications Historique* (1988): 237-279.

Safa, Helen. "Female Employment and the Social Reproduction of the Puerto Rican Working Class." *International Migration Review* 18, no. 4 (1984): 1168-1187.

Seccombe, Wally. "Starting to Stop: Working-Class Fertility Decline in Britain." *Past & Present* no. 126 (February 1990): 151-188.

Seider, Reinhard. "'Vata, derf i aufstehn?': Childhood Experiences in Viennese Working-Class Families Around 1900." *Continuity and Change* 1, no. 1

(1986): 53-88.

Smith, Joan. "Transforming Households: Working-Class Women and Economic Crisis." *Social Problems* 34 (December 1987): 416-436.

Strumingher, Laura S. " 'A Bas Les Pretres! A Bas Les Couvents!': The Church and the Workers in 19th Century Lyon." *Journal of Social History* 11 (Summer 1978): 546-552.

Turbin, Carole. "Beyond Dichotomies: Interdependence in Mid-Nineteenth Century Working Class Families in the United States." *Gender & History* 1 (Autumn 1989): 293-308.

Vincent, David. "Love and Death and the Nineteenth-Century Working Class." *Social History* 5 (May 1980): 223-247.

Wegs, J. Robert. "Working Class Respectability: The Viennese Experience." *Journal of Social History* 15 (Summer 1982): 621-636.

Weiner, Lynn. "'Our Sister's Keepers': The Minneapolis Woman's Christian Association and Housing for Working Women." *Minnesota History* 46 (Spring 1979): 189-200.

## Pre-Industrial

Alford, Katrina. "Colonial Women's Employment as Seen by Nineteenth-Century Statisticians and Twentieth-Century Economists." *Labour History* 51 (November 1986): 1-10.

Blom, Ida. "Changing Gender Identities in an Industrializing Society: The Case of Norway c. 1870-c. 1914." *Gender & History* 2 (Summer 1990): 131-147.

Earle, Peter. "The Female Labour Market in London in the Late Seventeenth and Early Eighteenth Centuries." *The Economic History Review* 42 (August 1989): 328-353.

Goldin, Claudia, and Kenneth Sokoloff. "Women, Children, and Industrialization in the Early Republic: Evidence from the Manufacturing Censuses." *Journal of Economic History* 42 (December 1982): 741-774.

Guy, Donna J. "Women, Peonage, and Industrialization: Argentina, 1810-1914." *Latin American Research Review* 16, no. 3 (1981): 65-89.

Hilton, Rodney. "Women Traders in Medieval England." *Women's Studies* 11, no. 1/2 (1984): 139-156.

Kinsman, Margaret. "'Beasts of Burden': The Subordination of Southern Tswana Women, ca. 1800-1840." *Journal of South African Studies* 10 (October 1983): 39-54.

Kirk, Sylvia Van. "The Role of Native Women in the Fur Trade Society of Western Canada, 1670-1830." *Frontiers* 7, no. 3 (1984): 9-13.

Mbilinyi, Marjorie. "'Women in Development' Ideology: The Promotion of Competition and Exploitation." *The African Review* 2, no. 1 (1984): 14-33.

McDougall, Mary Lynn. "Women's Work in Industrializing Britain and France." *Atlantis* 4 (Spring 1979): 143-151.

Olsen, Karen. "Native Women and the Fur Industry." *Canadian Woman Studies/Les cahiers de la femme* 10 (Summer/Fall 1989): 55-57.

Penn, Simon A. C. "Female Wage-Earners in Late Fourteenth-Century England."
    *Agricultural History Review* 35, no. 1 (1987): 1-14.
Schmidt, E. "Farmers, Hunters, and Gold-Washers: A Reevaluation of Women's
    Roles in Precolonial and Colonial Zimbabwe." *African Economic History* no.
    17 (1988): 45-80.
Stansell, Christine. "Women of the Laboring Poor in Early National New York."
    *Quaderno* 1 (1988).
Strong-Boag, Veronica. "Working Women and the State: The Case of Canada,
    1889-1945." *Atlantis* 6 (Spring 1981): 1-10.
Truant, Cynthia M. "The Guildswomen of Paris: Gender, Power and Sociability
    in the Old Regime." *Western Society for French History* 15 (November 1987):
    130-138.
Ulrich, Laurel Thatcher. "'A Friendly Neighbor': Social Dimensions of Daily
    Work in Northern Colonial New England." *Feminist Studies* 6 (Summer 1980):
    392-405.

## Sexual Division of Labor

Afonja, Simi. "Changing Modes of Production and the Sexual Division of Labor
    Among the Yoruba." *Signs* 7, no. 2 (1981): 299-313.
Albelda, Randy. "A Job of One's Own: The Sexual Division of Paid Labor."
    *Socialist Review* 86 (March/April 1986): 131-144.
Bernstein, Deborah. "The Plough Woman Who Cried into the Pots: The Position
    of Women in the Labor Force in Pre-State Israeli Society." *Jewish Social
    Studies* 45 (Winter 1983): 43-56.
Bielby, William, and James Baron. "Men and Women at Work: Sex Segregation
    and Statistical Discrimination." *American Journal of Sociology* 91 (1986):
    759-799.
Brown, Barbara B. "The Impact of Male Labour Migration on Women in
    Botswana." *African Affairs* no. 328 (1983): 367-388.
Burris, Val, and Amy Wharton. "Sex Segregation in the U.S. Labor Force."
    *Review of Radical Political Economics* 14 (Fall 1982): 43-56.
Carruthers, Susan L. "'Manning the Factories': Propaganda and Policy on the
    Employment of Women, 1939-1947." *History* 75 (June 1990): 232-256.
Faber, Fokje. "Gender and Occupational Prestige. Some Observations about
    'Sullerot's Law.'" *Netherlands' Journal of Social Sciences* 26 (April 1990):
    51-66.
Flanagan, Thomas. "Equal Pay for Work of Equal Value: An Historical Note."
    *Journal of Canadian Studies/Revue d'études canadiennes* 22 (Fall 1987): 5-19.
Fox, Bonnie J., and John Fox. "Occupational Gender Segregation in the Canadian
    Labour Force, 1931-1981." *Canadian Review of Sociology and
    Anthropology/Revue canadienne de Sociologie et d'Anthropologie* 24 (August
    1987): 374-397.
Hatem, Mervat. "Egypt's Middle Class in Crisis: the Sexual Division of Labor."
    *Middle East Journal* 42 (Summer 1988): 407-422.

Helmbold, Lois Rita. "Downward Occupational Mobility During the Great Depression: Urban Black and White Working Class Women." *Labor History* 29, no. 2 (1988): 135-172.

Humphries, Jane. "'...The Most Free from Objection...': The Sexual Division of Labor and Women's Work in Nineteenth-Century England." *Journal of Economic History* 47 (December 1987): 929-950.

Johansson, Ella. "Beautiful Men, Fine Women and Good Workpeople: Gender and Skill in Northern Sweden, 1850-1950." *Gender & History* 1 (Summer 1989): 200-212.

Keremitsis, Dawn. "Latin American Women Workers in Transition, Sexual Division of the Labor Force in Mexico and Colombia in the Textile Industry." *The Americas* 40 (April 1984): 491-504.

Lyson, Thomas A. "Industrial Change and the Sexual Division of Labor in New York and Georgia: 1910-1920." *Social Science Quarterly* 70 (June 1989): 356-374.

McCallum, Margaret E. "Separate Spheres: The Organization of Work in a Confectionery Factory: Ganong Bros., St. Stephen, New Brunswick." *Labour/Le Travail* 24 (Fall 1989): 69-90.

McLanahan, Sara S., Annemette Sorensen, and Dorothy Watson. "Sex Differences in Poverty, 1950-1980." *Signs* 15 (Autumn 1989): 102-122.

Mindiola, Tatcho. "The Cost of Being a Mexican Female Worker in the 1970 Houston Labor Market." *Aztlan: International Journal of Chicano Studies Research* 11 (Fall 1980): 231-248.

Montgomerie, Deborah. "Men's Jobs and Women's Work: The New Zealand Women's Land Service in World War II." *Agricultural History* 63 (Summer 1989): 1-14.

Murphy, Mary. "Women's Work in a Man's World." *Speculator* 1 (Winter 1984): 18-25.

Niemi, Albert W., Jr. "The Male-Female Earnings Differential: A Historical Overview of the Clerical Occupations from the 1880s to the 1970s." *Social Science History* 7 (Winter 1983): 97-108.

Parr, Joy. "Disaggregating the Sexual Division of Labour: A Transatlantic Case Study." *Comparative Studies in Society and History* [Great Britain] 30, no. 3 (1988): 511-533.

Philips, Peter. "Gender-Based Wage Differentials in Pennsylvania and New Jersey Manufacturing, 1900-1950." *Journal of Economic History* 42 (March 1982): 181-186.

Ramphele, Mamphela. "The Dynamics of Gender Politics in the Hostels of Cape Town: Another Legacy of the South African Migrant Labour System." *Journal of South African Studies* 15 (April 1989): 393-414.

Rose, Nancy E. "Discrimination Against Women in New Deal Work Programs." *Affilia* 5 (Summer 1990): 25-45.

Segura, Denise. "Labor Market Stratification: The Chicana Experience." *Berkeley Journal of Sociology* 29 (1984): 57-91.

Thornton, Robert, and Thomas Hydak. "The Increasing Pay Gap for Women in the Textile and Clothing Industries, 1919-1970: An Alternative Explanation." *Journal of Economic History* 42 (1982): 427-439.

White, W. Thomas. "Race, Ethnicity, and Gender in the Railroad Work Force: The Case of the Far Northwest, 1883-1918." *Western Historical Quarterly* 16 (July 1985): 265-284.

Whitehead, Ann. "Gender Divisions and Working Class Culture." *Society for the Study of Labour History* 48 (Spring 1984): 9-10.

Wiesner, Merry E. "Guilds, Male Bonding and Women's Work in Early Modern Germany." *Gender & History* 1 (Summer 1989): 125-137.

# Unions

Amsterdam, S. "National Women's Trade Union League." *Social Service Review* 56 (1982): 259-272.

Asher, Martha Stone. "Recollections of the Passaic Textile Strike of 1926." *Labor's Heritage* 2 (April 1990): 4-23.

Aulette, Judy, and Trudy Mills. "Something Old, Something New: Auxiliary Work in the 1983-1986 Copper Strike." *Feminist Studies* 14 (Summer 1988): 251-268.

Baden, Macaomi. "Developing an Agenda: Expanding the Role of Women in Unions." *Labor Studies Journal* 11 (1986): 229-249.

Baron, Ava. "Women and the Making of the American Working Class: A Study of the Proletarianization of Printers." *Review of Radical Political Economics* 14 (Fall 1982): 23-42.

Beattie, M. "The Representation of Women in Unions." *Signs* 12 (1986): 118-129.

Bemmels, Brian. "The Effect of Grievants' Gender and Arbitrator Characteristics on Arbitration Decisions." *Labor Studies Journal* 15 (Summer 1990): 48-61.

Bennett, Laura. "Job Classification and Women Workers: Institutional Practices, Technological Change and the Conciliation and Arbitration System, 1907-72." *Labour History* 51 (November 1986): 11-23.

Bernstein, Deborah. "The Women Workers' Movement in Pre-State Israel, 1919-1939." *Signs* 12 (Spring 1987): 454-470.

Bohlander, George, and Suzanne Caser. "Women Unionists: Attitudes towards Local Union Policies." *Labor Studies Journal* 7 (1982): 142-157.

Boston, Sarah. "The Rego Strike." *Society for the Study of Labour History* 38 (Spring 1979): 9-10.

Brooks, Raymond. "The Melbourne Tailoresses' Strike 1882-1883: An Assessment." *Labour History* 44 (May 1983): 27-38.

Candela, Joseph L., Jr. "The Struggle to Limit the Hours and Raise the Wages of Working Women in Illinois, 1893-1917." *Social Service Review* 53, no. 1 (1979): 15-34.

Catlett, Judith. "After the Goodbyes: A Long-Term Look at the Southern School for Union Women." *Labor Journal* 10 (1986): 300-311.

Cobble, Dorothy Sue. "Rethinking Troubled Relations Between Women and Unions: Craft Unionism and Female Activism." *Feminist Studies* 16 (Fall

1990): 510-548.

Collette, Christine. "Socialism and Scandal: The Sexual Politics of the Early Labour Movement." *History Workshop* 23 (Spring 1987): 102-111.

Conn, Sandra. "Three Talents: Robins, Nestor, and Anderson of the Chicago Women's Trade Union League." *Chicago History* 9, no. 4 (1981): 234-247.

Conner, Valerie J. "'The Mothers of the Race' in World War I: The National War Labor Board and Women in Industry." *Labor History* 21, no. 1 (1980): 31-54.

Corcoran, Theresa. "Vida Scudder and the Lawrence Textile Strike." *Essex Institute Historical Collections* 115, no. 3 (1979): 183-195.

Dodyk, Delight, and Steven Golin. "The Paterson Silk Strike: Primary Materials for Studying About Immigrants, Women, and Labor." *Social Studies* 78, no. 5 (1987): 206-209.

Duron, Clementina. "Mexican Women and Labor Conflict in Los Angeles: The ILGWU Dressmakers' Strike of 1933." *Aztlan: International Journal of Chicano Studies Research* (Spring 1984): 145-161.

Dye, Nancy Schrom. "The Louisville Woolen Mills Strike of 1887: A Case Study of Working Women, the Knights of Labor, and Union Organization in the New South." *Register of the Kentucky Historical Society* 82 (Spring 1984): 136-150.

Faue, Elizabeth. "The Dynamo of Change: Gender and Solidarity in the American Labour Movement of the 1930s." *Gender & History* 1 (Summer 1989): 138-158.

Feldberg, Roslyn L. "'Union Fever': Organizing Among Clerical Workers, 1900-1930." *Radical America* 14, no. 3 (1980): 53-70.

Ferland, Jacques. "'In Search of the Unbound Prometheia': A Comparative View of Women's Activism in Two Quebec Industries, 1869-1908." *Labour/Le Travail* 24 (Fall 1989): 11-44.

Gabin, Nancy. "'They Have Placed a Penalty on Womanhood': The Protest Actions of Women Auto Workers in Detroit-area UAW Locals, 1945-1947." *Feminist Studies* 8 (Summer 1982): 373-398.

-----. "Women Workers and the UAW in the Post-World War II Period: 1945-1954." *Labor History* 21 (Winter 1979/80): 5-30.

Hall, Jacquelyn Dowd. "Disorderly Women: Gender and Labor Militancy [1929] in the Appalachian South." *Journal of American History* 73 (September 1986): 354-382.

Hansen, Karen V. "The Women's Unions and the Search for a Political Identity." *Socialist Review* 86 (March/April 1986): 67-95.

Hield, Melissa. "'Union-Minded': Women in the Texas ILGWU, 1933-1950." *Frontiers* 4 (Summer 1979): 59-70.

Hilden, Patricia J. "Women and the Labour Movement in France, 1869-1914." *Historical Journal* [Great Britain] 29 (December 1986): 809-832.

Horodyski, Mary. "Women and the Winnipeg General Strike of 1919." *Manitoba History* 11 (Spring 1986): 28-37.

Howard, Irene. "The Mother's Council of Vancouver: Holding the Fort for the Unemployed, 1935-38." *B.C. Studies* 69/70 (Spring/Summer 1986): 249-287.

Jonas, Raymond A. "Equality in Difference? Patterns of Feminine Labor

Militancy in Nineteenth-Century France." *Western Society for French History* 15 (November 1987): 291-298.

Kates, Carol. "Working Class Feminism and Feminist Unions: Title VII, the UAW and NOW." *Labor Studies Journal* 14 (Summer 1989): 28-45.

Katz, Sherry. "Francis Nocke Noel & 'Sister Movements': Socialism, Feminism, & Trade Unionism in Los Angeles, 1909-1916." *California History* 67 (September 1988): 180-190.

Kennedy, Susan Estabrook. "'The Want It Satisfied Demonstrates the Need of It': A Study of Life and Labor of the Women's Trade Union League." *International Journal of Women's Studies* 3 (July/August 1980): 391-406.

Kirkby, Diane. "'The Wage Earning Woman and the State': The National Women's Trade Union League and Protective Legislation, 1903-1923." *Labor History* 28 (Winter 1987): 54-74.

Ladd-Taylor, Molly. "Women Workers and the Yale Strike." *Feminist Studies* 11 (Fall 1985): 465-490.

Lavrin, Asuncion. "Women, Labor, and the Left: Argentina and Chile, 1890-1925." *Journal of Women's History* 1 (Fall 1989): 88-116.

Levine, Susan. "'Honor Each Noble Maid': Women Workers and the Yonkers Carpet Weavers' Strike of 1885." *New York History* 62 (April 1981): 153-176.

-----. "Labor's True Woman: Domesticity and Equal Rights in the Knights of Labor." *Journal of American History* 70 (September 1983): 323-339.

Maggard, Sally Ward. "Women's Participation in the Brookside Coal Strike: Militance, Class, and Gender in Appalachia." *Frontiers* 9, no. 3 (1987): 16-21.

McTighe, Michael J. "'True Philanthropy' and the Limits of the Female Sphere: Poor Relief and Labor Organization in Ante-Bellum Cleveland." *Labor History* 27 (Spring 1986): 227-256.

Milkman, Ruth. "Organizing the Sexual Division of Labor: Historical Perspectives on 'Women's Work' and the American Labor Movement." *Socialist Review* 10, no. 1 (1980): 95-150.

Miller, Sally M. "From Sweatshop Worker to Labor Leader: Theresa Malkiel, a Case Study." *American Jewish History* 68 (December 1978): 189-205.

Murphy, Marjorie. "'Work, Protest, and Culture': New York on Working Women's History." *Feminist Studies* 13 (Fall 1987): 657-667.

Muszynski, Alicja. "The Organization of Women and Ethnic Minorities in a Resource Industry: A Case Study of the Unionization of Shoreworkers in the B.C. Fishing Industry 1937-1949." *Journal of Canadian Studies/Revue d'études canadiennes* 19 (Spring 1984): 89-107.

Nelson, Anne H. "A Union Woman's Influence." *Labor Studies Journal* 10 (1986): 312-324.

Nicol, W. "Women and the Trade Union Movement in New South Wales: 1890-1900." *Labour History* 36 (May 1979): 18-30.

O'Connell, Lucille. "The Lawrence Textile Strike of 1912: The Testimony of Two Polish Women." *Polish American Studies* 36, no. 2 (1979): 44-62.

Reekie, Gail. "Industrial Action by Women Workers in Western Australia During World War II." *Labour History* 49 (November 1985): 75-82.

Reitano, Joanne. "Working Girls Unite." *American Quarterly* 36 (Spring 1984): 112-134.

Rock, Howard B., ed. "A Woman's Place in Jeffersonian New York: The View from the *Independent Mechanic*." *New York History* 63 (October 1982): 434-459.

Rose, Margaret. "'From the Fields to the Picket Line: Huelga Women and the Boycott,' 1965-1975." *Labor History* 31 (Summer 1990): 271-293.

-----. "Traditional and Nontraditional Patterns of Female Activism in the United Farm Workers of America, 1962 to 1980." *Frontiers* 11, no. 1 (1990): 26-32.

Rosenthal, Star. "Union Maids: Organized Women Workers in Vancouver, 1900-1915." *B.C. Studies* 41 (1979): 36-55.

Rothbart, Ron. "'Homes Are What Any Strike Is About': Immigrant Labor and the Family Wage." *Journal of Social History* 23 (Winter 1989): 267-284.

Sangster, Joan. "The 1907 Bell Telephone Strike: Organizing Women Workers." *Labour* 3 (1978): 109-129.

-----. "Women and Unions in Canada: A Review of Historical Research." *Resources For Feminist Research* 10 (July 1981): 2-6.

Satre, Lowell I. "After the Match Girls' Strike: Bryant and May in the 1890s." *Victorian Studies* 26 (Autumn 1982): 7-32.

Schofield, Ann. "Mother Jones in Kansas: An Archival Note." *Labor History* 27 (Summer 1986): 431-442.

-----. "Rebel Girls and Union Maids: The Woman Question in the Journals of the AFL and IWW, 1905-1920." *Feminist Studies* 9 (Summer 1983): 335-358.

-----. "The Women's March: Miners, Family, and Community in Pittsburg, Kansas, 1921-1922." *Kansas History* 7 (Summer 1984): 159-168.

Scholten, Pat Creech. "The Old Mother and Her Army: The Agitative Strategies of Mary Harris Jones." *West Virginia History* 40 (Summer 1979): 365-374.

Schrode, Georg. "Mary Zuk and the Detroit Meat Strike of 1935." *Polish American Studies* 48 (Autumn 1986): 5-39.

Shelton, Brenda K. "Organized Mother Love: The Buffalo Women's Educational and Industrial Union, 1885-1915." *New York History* 67 (April 1986): 155-176.

Smith, Harold. "Sex vs. Class: British Feminists and the Labour Movement, 1919-1929." *The Historian* 47 (November 1984): 19-37.

Snyder, Robert E. "Women, Wobblies, and Workers' Rights: The 1912 Textile Strike in Little Falls, New York." *New York History* 60, no. 1 (1979): 29-57.

Stranaban, Patricia. "Labor Heroines of Yan'an." *Modern China* 9 (April 1983): 228-252.

Strom, Sharon Hartman. "Challenging 'Woman's Place': Feminism, the Left and the Industrial Unionism in the 1930s." *Feminist Studies* 9 (Summer 1983): 359-386.

Tamplin, John C. "Mary Heaton Vorse, Journalist: Victim of Strike Violence?" *Labor History* 28 (Winter 1987): 84-88.

Tax, Meredith. "The United Front of Women." *Monthly Review* 32 (October 1980): 30-48.

Tsurumi, Patricia. "Female Textile Workers and the Failure of Early Trade

Unionism in Japan." *History Workshop* 18 (Autumn 1984): 3-27.

Turbin, Carole. "Reconceptualizing Family, Work and Labor Organizing: Working Women in Troy, 1860-1890." *Review of Radical Political Economics* 16 (Spring 1984): 1-16.

White, Kate. "May Holman: 'Australian Labor's Pioneer Woman Parliamentarian.'" *Labour History* 41 (November 1981): 110-117.

Windschuttle, Elizabeth. "Discipline, Domestic Training and Social Control: The Female School of Industry, Sydney, 1826-1847." *Labour History* 39 (November 1980): 1-14.

Yancy, Dorothy Cowser. "Dorothy Bolden, Organizer of Domestic Workers: She Was Born Poor but She Would Not Bow Down." *Sage* 3, no. 1 (1986): 53-55.

## General

Andors, Phyllis. "Women and Work in Shenzhen." *Bulletin of Concerned Asian Scholars* 20 (July/September 1988): 22-42.

Badran, Margot. "Women and Production in the Middle East." *Trends in History* 2, no. 3 (1982): 59-88.

Bahr, Howard M. "The Declining Distinctiveness of Utah's Working Women." *Brigham Young University Studies* 19 (Summer 1979): 525-543.

Bird, Patricia. "Hamilton Working Women in the Period of the Great Depression." *Atlantis* 8 (Spring 1983): 125-136.

Blackwelder, Julia Kirk. "Women in the Work Force: Atlanta, New Orleans, and San Antonio, 1930 to 1940." *Journal of Urban History* (May 1978): 331-358.

Bravo, Anna. "Solidarity and Loneliness: Piedmontese Peasant Women at the Turn of the Century." *International Journal of Oral History* 3 (June 1982): 76-91.

Bromberg, Nicolette. "Kansas Women in the Workplace." *Journal of the West* 28 (January 1989): 51-58.

Cookingham, Mary E. "Working after Childbearing in Modern America." *Journal of Interdisciplinary History* 14 (Spring 1984): 773-792.

Dunnigan, Kate, Helen Kebabian, Laura B. Roberts, and Maureen Taylor. "Working Women at Work in Rhode Island, 1880-1925." *Rhode Island History* 38 (February 1979): 3-23.

Enstam, Elizabeth Yark. "The Frontier Woman as City Worker: Women's Occupations in Dallas, Texas, 1856-1880." *East Texas History Journal* (Spring 1980): 12-28.

Farley, Mary Allison. "Iowa Women in the Workplace." *Palimpsest* 67 (January/February 1986): 2-27.

Forestell, Nancy M. "Times Were Hard: The Pattern of Women's Paid Labour in St. John's Between the Two World Wars." *Labour/Le Travail* 24 (Fall 1989): 147-166.

Kanipe, Esther S. "Working Class Women and the Social Question in Late 19th-Century France." *Western Society for French History* 6 (November 1978): 298-306.

Kenny, Donna S. "Women at Work: Views and Visions from the Pioneer Valley,

1870-1945." *Historical Journal of Massachusetts* 13 (January 1985): 30-41.

Krupnik, Dorothy Vogel. "Women Go to Work!" *Pennsylvania Heritage* 11 (Winter 1985).

Locke, Mary Lou. "Out of the Shadows and into the Western Sun: Working Women of the Late Nineteenth-Century Urban Far West." *Journal of Urban History* 16 (February 1990): 175-204.

Miller, Sally M. "Different Accents of Labor." *Labor's Heritage* 2 (July 1990): 62-75.

Moch, Leslie Page. "Women on the Move: Migration and Urban Work for Women in the Late Nineteenth Century." *Western Society for French History* 8 (October 1980): 281-282.

Moseley, Eva. "Labor Holdings at the Schlesinger Library, Radcliffe College." *Labor History* 31 (Winter/Spring 1990): 16-24.

Murphy, Miriam B. "Women in the Utah Work Force from Statehood to World War II." *Utah Historical Quarterly* 50 (1982): 139-159.

Pudup, Mary Beth. "Women's Work in the West Virginia Economy." *West Virginia History* 49 (1990): 7-20.

Saltvig, Robert. "The Tragic Legend of Laura Law." *Pacific Northwest Quarterly* 78 (July 1987): 91-99.

Sibisi, Harriet. "How Women Cope with Migrant Labor in South Africa." *Signs* 3 (Autumn 1977): 167-177.

Strong-Boag, Veronica. "The Girl of the New Day: Canadian Working Women in the 1920s." *Labour/Le Travail* 4 (1979): 131-164.

Wright, Kathryn Stephen. "Hobo Heresy: Three Women on an Unconventional Tour of the American West in 1922." *Montana* 39 (Summer 1989): 16-29.

# JOURNALS LIST

Acadiensis
Adventist Heritage
Africa [Great Britain]
African Affairs
African Economic History
African Languages and Cultures
African Studies Review
Afro-Americans in New York Life
and History
Agricultural History
Agricultural History Review
Alabama Historical Quarterly
Alabama Review
Alaska Journal
Albanian Catholic Bulletin
Alberta History
Alberta Law Review
Albion
Amerasia
Amerasia Journal
American Archivist
American Art Journal
American Baptist Quarterly
American Ethnologist
American Heritage
American Heritage of Invention &
Technology
American Historical Review
American History Illustrated
American Indian Culture and
Research Journal
American Indian Quarterly
American Jewish Archives
American Jewish History
American Journal of Ancient History
American Journal of Archaeology
American Journal of Comparative
Law
American Journal of Legal History
American Journal of Political
Science
American Journal of Social Science
American Journal of Sociology

American Journal of Sports
Medicine
American Journalism
American Literary History
American Literature
American Neptune
American Organist
American Political Science Review
American Presbyterians
American Quarterly
American Review of Canadian
Studies
American Scholar
American Sociological Review
American Sociologist
American Studies
American Studies in Scandinavia
American Vision
American West
Americas
Amerikastudien
Ancient World
Anglican and Episcopal History
Annals of Iowa
Annals of the New York Academy
of Sciences
Annals of Wyoming
Anthropologica
Antioch Review
Appalachian Journal
Arab Studies Quarterly
Arabian Studies
Archiv für Reformationsgeschichte
Archiv für Sozialgeschichte
Archivaria
Arena Review
Arizona and the West
Arizona Quarterly
Arkansas Historical Quarterly
Armed Forces & Society
Art & Antiques
Art History
Art Quarterly

Artibus et Historiae
Arts Magazine
Asbury Theological Journal
Asia
Asian and African Studies
Asian Culture Quarterly [Taipei]
Asian Folklore Studies
Asian Journal of Theology
Asian Studies [Quezon City]
Asian Survey
Atlanta History
Atlantis: A Women's Studies Journal
Austin Seminary Bulletin
Australian Feminist Studies
Australian Historical Studies
Auto/Biography Studies
Aztlan: International Journal of
    Chicano Studies Research
B.C. Studies
Baptist History and Heritage
Baptist Quarterly
Beaver
Bengal Past and Present
Berkeley Journal of Sociology
Berkeley Women's Law Journal
Bibliotheca Sacra
Biography
Black American Literature Forum
Black Scholar
Black Women's Writing
Books and Religion
Botswana Review
British Journal for Eighteenth-
    Century Studies
British Journal of Law and Society
British Journal of Sport History
British Medical Journal
British Museum Society Bulletin
British Studies Monitor
Buddhist Christian Studies
Bulletin of Bibliography
Bulletin of Concerned Asian
    Scholars
Bulletin of Hispanic Studies
Bulletin of Research in the
    Humanities

Bulletin of the History of Medicine
Bulletin of the Institute of Historical
    Research
Bulletin of the Missouri Historical
    Society
Caduceus
CAHPER Journal
California History
Californians
Canadian Bulletin of Medical
    History/Bulletin canadienne
    d'histoire de la medicine
Canadian Collector
Canadian Ethnic Studies/Etudes
    ethniques au Canada
Canadian Folklore
Canadian Historical Review
Canadian Horticultural History
Canadian Housing/Habitation
    canadienne
Canadian Journal of African Studies
Canadian Journal of History
Canadian Journal of History of Sport
Canadian Journal of Law and
    Society
Canadian Journal of Native Studies
Canadian Journal of Sociology
Canadian Journal of Women and the
    Law/Revue juridique La femme
    et le droit
Canadian Literature
Canadian Methodist Historical
    Society Papers
Canadian Oral History Association
    Journal
Canadian Review of American
    Studies
Canadian Review of Sociology and
    Anthropology/Revue canadienne
    de Sociologie et d'Anthropologie
Canadian Slavic Papers
Canadian Society of Church History
    Papers
Canadian Society of Presbyterian
    History Papers
Canadian Woman Studies/Les

cahiers de la femme
Canadian-American Slavic
   Studies/Revue canadienne-
   américaine d'études slaves
Caribbean Review
Catholic Biblical Quarterly
Catholic Historical Review
Central European History
Chicago History
China Notes
Chinese Studies in History
Chronicles of Oklahoma
Chrysalis
Church History
Cincinnati Historical Society Bulletin
Cinema Journal
Civil War History
Civil War Times
Civil War Times Illustrated
Clarion, America's Folk Art
   Magazine
Classical Antiquity
Classical Journal
CoEvolution Quarterly
Colby Library Quarterly
Colby Quarterly
Colorado Heritage
Colorado Magazine
Communal Societies
Comparative Political Studies
Comparative Studies in Society and
   History [Great Britain]
Concordia Historical Institute
   Quarterly
Conditions
Conflict
Congress and the Presidents
Connecticut Historical Society
   Bulletin
Connecticut Review
Conservative Judaism
Contemporary Marriage
Continuity and Change
Continuity, A Journal of History
Contributions in Black Studies
Costume

Crime and Delinquency
Criminal Justice History
Crisis
Critical Arts
Cronicas
Cultural Correspondence
Cultural Critique
Culture & History
Cultures
Czechoslovak and Central European
   Journal
Daedalus
Dalhousie Law Journal
Dalhousie Review
Dartmouth College Library Bulletin
Daughters of Sarah
Daughters of the American
   Revolution Magazine
Delaware History
Democracy
Demography
Design Issues
Diachronica: International Journal of
   Historical Linguistics
Diacritics
Diakonia
Dialogue
Differences
Doctrine and Life
Downside Review
Dress
Drew Gateway
Dublin Seminar for New England
   Folklife
Dutch Quarterly Review of
   Anglo-American Letters
Early American Literature
East European Politics and Societies
East Tennessee Historical Society
   Publication
East Texas History Journal
Economic History Review
Educational Theory
Eighteenth Century [Lubbock]
Eighteenth-Century Life
Eighteenth-Century Studies

Eire-Ireland
El Palacio
ELH
Encounter
English Historical Review
English Studies in Africa
Essays and Monographs in Colorado
    History
Essays in Economic and Business
    History
Essex Institute Historical Collections
Ethnic Forum
Ethnicity
Ethnohistory
Ethnology
Etudes inuit/Inuit Studies
Europe and America: Criss-Crossing
    Perspectives, 1788-1848
European History Quarterly
European Studies Review
Explorations in Economic History
Faith and Freedom
Feminisms
Feminist Art Journal
Feminist Issues
Feminist Review
Feminist Studies
Feminist Teacher
Fides et Historia
Filson Club History Quarterly
Florida Historical Quarterly
Folklore
Food & Foodways
Forest & Conservation History
Forum
Foundations
French Historical Studies
Frontiers
Furrow
Gallerie: Women's Art
Gateway Heritage
Gender & History
Gender & Society
Genders
George Washington Law Review
Georgetown Law Journal

Georgia Historical Quarterly
German History
German Quarterly
German Studies Review
Gesnerus
Great Plains Journal
Great Plains Quarterly
Greece & Rome
Hamdard Islamicus
Harvard Divinity Bulletin
Harvard Educational Review
Harvard Journal of Asiatic Studies
Harvard Library Bulletin
Harvard Library Journal
Harvard Theological Review
Harvard Women's Law Journal
Hawaiian Journal of History
Hayes Historical Journal
Hecate: An Interdisciplinary Journal
    of Women's Liberation
Hemisphere [Australia]
Heresies
Heritage of the Great Plains
Hesperia
Hispanic American Historical
    Review
Histoire sociale/Social History
Historian
Historic Kingston
Historical Archaeology
Historical Journal [Great Britain]
Historical Journal of Massachusetts
Historical Methods
Historical   Papers/Communications
    Historiques
Historical Reflections/Reflexions
    Historiques
Historical Research
History
History and Theory
History Magazine of the Protestant
    Episcopal Church
History News
History of Education
History of Education Bulletin
History of Education Quarterly

History of Education Review
[Australia]
History of European Ideas
History of Nursing
History of Religions
History of Science
History Teacher
History Today
History Workshop
Holocaust and Genocide Studies
[Great Britain]
Houston Review
Humanities
Humboldt Journal of Social
Relations
Humor
Huntington Library Quarterly
Hypatia
Idaho Yesterdays
Illinois Historical Journal
Image
Immigrants & Minorities
In Britain
Indian Church History Review
Indian Economic and Social History
Review [Delhi]
Indiana Magazine of History
Indiana Medical History Quarterly
Indonesia
Inland Seas
International History Review
International Journal of African
Historical Studies
International Journal of Middle East
Studies
International Journal of Oral History
International Journal of Women's
Studies [Canada]
International Migration Review
International Review of History
International Review of Social
History
International Social Science Review
Inventing the West
Irish Historical Studies
Isis

Issues in Ego Psychology
Japan Quarterly
Jewish Social Studies
Journal for the Study of Religion
Journal of Advanced Nursing
Journal of African History
Journal of American Culture
Journal of American Ethnic History
Journal of American Folklore
Journal of American History
Journal of American Studies
Journal of Applied Philosophy
Journal of Arizona History
Journal of Asian and African Studies
Journal of Asian History
Journal of Asian Studies
Journal of Black Studies
Journal of British Studies
Journal of Canadian Studies/Revue
d'études canadiennes
Journal of Church and State
Journal of Contemporary History
Journal of Cultural Geography
Journal of Decorative and
Propaganda Arts
Journal of Ecclesiastical History
Journal of Economic History
Journal of Educational Thought
Journal of Eritrean Studies
Journal of Ethnic Studies
Journal of European Studies
Journal of Family History
Journal of Feminist Studies in
Religion
Journal of Historical Geography
[Great Britain]
Journal of Historical Sociology
Journal of History of the Behavioral
Sciences
Journal of Homosexuality
Journal of Illinois State Historical
Society
Journal of Imperial and
Commonwealth History
Journal of Interdisciplinary History
Journal of Japanese Studies

Journal of Jewish Studies
Journal of Latin American Studies
Journal of Library History
Journal of Long Island History
Journal of Marriage and Family
Journal of Medieval and Renaissance
  Studies
Journal of Medieval History
Journal of Mennonite Studies
Journal of Military History
Journal of Mississippi History
Journal of Modern History
Journal of Mormon History
Journal of Negro Education
Journal of Negro History
Journal of Pacific History
Journal of Peasant Studies
Journal of Policy History
Journal of Political Economics
Journal of Politics
Journal of Popular Culture
Journal of Presbyterian History
Journal of Professional Nursing
Journal of Psychohistory
Journal of Religion
Journal of Religious History
Journal of Religious Thought
Journal of Research in Crime and
  Delinquency
Journal of Rutgers University
  Library
Journal of San Diego History
Journal of Social History
Journal of South African Studies
Journal of Southern History
Journal of Southwest Georgia
  History
Journal of Sport History
Journal of the American Academy of
  Religion
Journal of the American Dental
  Association
Journal of the American Oriental
  Society
Journal of the Ancient Near Eastern
  Society

Journal of the Canadian Church
  Historical Society
Journal of the Early Republic
Journal of the Economic and Social
  History of the Orient
Journal of the Friends' Historical
  Society
Journal of the History of Behavioral
  Sciences
Journal of the History of Ideas
Journal of the History of Medicine
Journal of the History of Medicine
  and Allied Sciences
Journal of the History of Sexuality
Journal of the History of Sociology
Journal of the Illinois State
  Historical Society
Journal of the Lancaster County
  Historical Society
Journal of the Moscow Patriarchate
Journal of the Society of
  Architectural Historians
Journal of the Southwest
Journal of the West
Journal of Third World Studies
Journal of Unconventional History
Journal of Urban History
Journal of Women's History
Journal of World History
Journalism History
Journalism Quarterly
Jurnal Undang-Undang/Journal of
  Malaysian and Comparative Law
  [Kuala Lumpur]
Kansas History
Kansas Quarterly
Korea Journal [Seoul]
Labor History
Labor Studies Journal
Labor's Heritage
Labour History
Labour History Review
Labour/Le travail
Late Imperial China
Latin American Perspectives
Latin American Research Review

Law and History Review
Legacy
Liberian Studies Journal
Libraries & Culture
Library
Library Quarterly
Lilith
Lion and the Unicorn
Literature and History
Local Population Studies
Locus
Lokayan Bulletin [New Delhi]
Louisiana History
Luso-Brazilian Review
Lutheran Historical Conference
Manitoba History
Manuscripts
Marxist Perspectives
Maryland Historian
Maryland Historical Magazine
Massachusetts Review
Material History Bulletin [Canada]
McGill Law Journal
Medical History
Melus
Mennonite Quarterly Review
Methodist History
Michigan Historical Review
Michigan History
Michigan Law Review
Michigan Quarterly Review
Mid-America
Middle East Journal
Midwest Quarterly
Midwest Review
Military Affairs
Milwaukee History
Minerva: Quarterly Report on
    Women and the Military
Minneapolis Institute of Arts Bulletin
Minnesota History
Minority Voices
Mississippi History
Mississippi Quarterly
Mississippi's Piney Woods: A
    Human Perspective

Missouri Historical Review
Missouri Historical Society Bulletin
Modern Age
Modern Asian Studies
Modern China
Modern Churchman
Montana
Monthly Labor Review
Mosaic
Museum News
Names
National Genealogical Society
    Quarterly
Nebraska History
Negro History Bulletin
Netherlands' Journal of Social
    Sciences
Network News Exchange
Nevada Historical Society Quarterly
New Community
New England Historical and
    Genealogical Register
New England Quarterly
New German Critique
New Jersey History
New Left Review
New Literary History
New Mexico Historical Review
New Political Science
New Society
New Theatre Quarterly
New York Historical Society
    Quarterly
New York History
New York University Review of
    Law and Social Change
Newsletter Intellectual History
    Group
Nineteenth-Century Contexts
North American Culture
North Carolina Historical Review
North Dakota History
North Dakota Quarterly
North Louisiana Historical
    Association Journal
Northwest Ohio Quarterly

Norwegian-American Studies
Nova Scotia Historical Review
Nursing Forum
NWSA Journal
OAH Magazine of History
Ohio Dentistry Journal
Ohio History
Old Fort News
Old Northwest
Ontario History
Oral History
Oral History Review
Oregon Historical Quarterly
Oxford Art Journal
Pacific Affairs
Pacific Historian
Pacific Historical Review
Pacific History Review
Pacific Northwest Quarterly
Palimpsest
Panhandle-Plains History Review
Papers on Far Eastern History
Parameters
Past & Present
Peace & Change
Pennsylvania Heritage
Pennsylvania History
Pennsylvania Magazine of History
  and Biography
Performing Arts Resources
Permian Historical Annual
Perspectives
Perspectives in Religious Studies
Perspectives on the American South
Pharmacy in History
Phylon
Pittsburgh History
Plains Anthropologist
Polish American Studies
Political Science Quarterly
Political Studies
Politics and Society
Polyphony
Population Studies
Prairie Forum
Present Tense

Presidential Studies Quarterly
Proceedings of the Academy of
  Political Science
Proceedings of the American
  Antiquarian Society
Proceedings of the American
  Philosophical Society
Proceedings of the Annual Meeting
  of the French Colonial Historical
  Society
Proceedings of the Massachusetts
  Historical Society
Proceedings of the Southeastern
  American Studies Association
Proceedings of the Unitarian
  Universalist Historical Society
Prologue
Prose Studies: History, Theory,
  Criticism
Prospects
Psychohistory Review
Psychology of Women Quarterly
Public Culture
Public Historian
Publishing History
Quaderno
Quaker History
Quarterly Journal of Speech
Quarterly Journal of the Library of
  Congress
Quarterly Review of Historical
  Studies [Calcutta]
Queen City Heritage
Queen's Quarterly
Quest
Race and Class
Radical America
Radical History Review
Railroad History
Records of the Columbia Historical
  Society of Washington, D.C.
Recusant History
Red River Valley Historical Review
Register of the Kentucky Historical
  Society
Religion

Religion and American Culture
Religion and Public Education
Religious Studies and Theology
Renaissance Quarterly
Renaissance Studies
Renditions
Representations
RES
Resources for Feminist Research
  [Canada]
Restoration and 18th Century
  Theatre Research
Retrospection
Review and Expositor
Review of African Political
  Economy
Review of English Studies
Review of Radical Political
  Economics
Reviews in American History
Revista Interamericana de
  Bibliografia
Revue de l'Université d'Ottawa
Revue française d'études américaines
Revue internationale d'histoire
  militaire
Rhode Island History
Rotunda
Russian History
Russian Review
Sage
Salmagundi
San Diego History
Saskatchewan History
Scandinavian Economic History
  Review & Economy and History
Scandinavian Journal of History
Scandinavian Studies
Scarlet Women
Scholarly Publishing
Science & Society
Scientific American
Scottish Historical Review
Semeia
Shaker Quarterly
Signs

Sindhological Studies [Hyderabad,
  Pakistan]
Sixteenth Century Journal
Slavery and Abolition
Slavic & East European Review
Slavic Review
Slavonic & East European Review
Social Analysis
Social History
Social History of Medicine
Social Justice
Social Problems
Social Science History
Social Science Medicine
Social Science Quarterly
Social Science Research
Social Science Review
Social Service Review
Social Studies
Social Text
Social Theory and Practice
Socialist Review
Societas
Society
Society for the Study of Labour
  History
Sociology and Social Research
Sociology Spectrum
South African Journal of Cultural
  History
South Atlantic Quarterly
South Atlantic Urban Studies
South Carolina Historical Magazine
South Dakota History
Southern Atlantic Quarterly
Southern California Historical
  Quarterly
Southern California Quarterly
Southern Exposure
Southern Friend
Southern Historian
Southern Quarterly
Southern Studies
Southwest Review
Southwestern Historical Quarterly
Soviet Review

Soviet Studies
Soviet Studies in History
Speculum
St. Mark's Review
State University of New York at
  Buffalo Studies in History
Studia Theologica: Scandinavian
  Journal of Theology
Studies in History and Politics
Studies in Latin American Popular
  Culture
Studies in the American Renaissance
Swedish Pioneer Historical Quarterly
Swedish-American Historical
  Quarterly
Tampa Bay History
Technology and Culture
Telos
Tennessee Historical Quarterly
Tequesta
Texas Journal of Ideas, History, and
  Culture
Texas Liberator
Theatre History in Canada
Theatre Journal
Theatre Notebook
Theatre Survey
Theodore Roosevelt Association
  Journal
Theological Studies
Theory and Society
Tiger Lily
Timeline
Toronto Journal of Theology
Trans. Gaelic Society Inverness
Trends in History
Trinity Journal
Tulsa Studies in Women's Literature
Turn-of-the-Century Woman
U.S. Catholic Historian
UCLA Historical Journal
Ufahamu
Union Seminary Quarterly Review
University of Dayton Review
University of Pittsburgh Law
  Review

Upper Midwest History
Urban History Review
Urbanism Past and Present
Utah Historical Quarterly
Vermont History
Vermont History News
Victorian Studies
Vintage Fashions
Virginia Cavalcade
Virginia Magazine of History and
  Biography
Virginia Quarterly Review
Vox Benedictina
West Georgia College Studies in the
  Social Sciences
West Tennessee Historical Society
  Papers
West Virginia History
Western Folklore
Western Historical Quarterly
Western Journal of Black Studies
Western Pennsylvania Historical
  Magazine
Western Political Quarterly
Western Society for French History
Western States Jewish History
Westminster Studies in Education
Westminster Theological Journal
William and Mary Quarterly
Wilson Quarterly
Windsor Yearbook of Access to
  Justice
Winterthur Portfolio
Wisconsin Magazine of History
Wisconsin Women's Law Journal
Woman of Power
Woman's Art Journal
Women & Criminal Justice
Women & Health
Women & Performance
Women & Politics
Women and History
Women's Studies
Women's Studies International
  Forum

Women's Studies International  
   Quarterly  
Women's Studies Quarterly

World Marxist Review  
Yale Journal of Criticism  
Yale Review

# CONTRIBUTORS

**Gayle V. Fischer** earned her M.A. in Women's History at Sarah Lawrence College. She is currently a Ph.D. candidate in the History Department at Indiana University, Bloomington.

**Christie Farnham** is founder and co-editor of the *Journal of Women's History*. Formerly Director of Women's Studies and faculty member in the Afro-American Studies Department at Indiana University, Bloomington, she is currently Associate Professor of History at Iowa State University. She edited *The Impact of Feminist Research In the Academy* and has published articles on African Americans in the nineteenth-century South.

**Joan Hoff** is a Professor of History at Indiana University, Bloomington, former Executive Secretary of the Organization of American History, and co-editor of the *Journal of Women's History*. Her most recent publication is *Law, Gender & Injustice: A Legal History of U.S. Women.*